PRINCIPLES OF MANAGEMENT

GEORGE R. TERRY, Ph.D.

College of Business, Ball State University

PRINCIPLES OF MANAGEMENT

1977   *Seventh Edition*

RICHARD D. IRWIN, INC.   Homewood, Illinois   60430
Irwin-Dorsey Limited   Georgetown, Ontario   L7G 4B3

Seventh Edition

3 4 5 6 7 8 9 0 MP 5 4 3 2 1 0 9 8

ISBN 0-256-01876-6
Library of Congress Catalog Card No. 76–13077

Printed in the United States of America

LEARNING SYSTEMS COMPANY—
a division of Richard D. Irwin, Inc.—has developed a
PROGRAMMED LEARNING AID
to accompany texts in this subject area.
Copies can be purchased through your bookstore
or by writing PLAIDS,
1818 Ridge Road, Homewood, Illinois 60430.

Preface

Management continues to change in response to the development of new ideas and frames of reference, the strong urge to improve, and the current demands placed upon managers by economic, social, technological, and political forces. This dynamic quality suggests the need for *Principles of Management*, Seventh Edition.

Even with all the changes, the purpose of management remains the same—to accomplish desired results. Likewise, the purpose of this book remains the same—namely to help in (1) acquiring management knowledge and (2) developing management skills so that the use of effective management is encouraged with the resultant human and material benefits enjoyed by all. This purpose has not changed since the book's first appearance in 1953.

This book is structured around the modified management process approach which expedites presenting the totality of current managerial concepts and activities in an orderly, easy-to-follow, and inclusive manner. In essence, a panorama of management built around a familiar central core is offered. The emphasis is upon a realistic and comprehensive presentation of total management—the big picture. Subsequent study can proceed along any of the several and important management specialties now available. Experience shows that the modified process approach is an effective nucleus about which beginning study can take place. And, quite importantly, the modified process is readily understood.

Principles of Management, Seventh Edition, is written primarily for basic study by the beginning student. It is also intended to help the active manager, and to provide an up-to-date review for the experienced manager.

The outstanding feature of this seventh edition is the addition of five new chapters. The first is entitled Selected Current Management Practices and includes coverage of participation, results management, job enrichment, productivity priority, contingency management, and conflict utilization. A new chapter on human behavior and management presents current behavioral knowledge vital to present day management practice. A new chapter on comparative management describes the managements existing in foreign countries. New Chapter 19 is on leading, and new Chapter 20 deals with communicating.

Additional features include more discussion on values and philosophy as they pertain to management; entitlements and their influence upon current management; and a greatly expanded coverage of social considerations and responsibilities as seen from the management viewpoint. Attention is given to contingency management and an entirely new section on strategic planning is now included also. The need for ethics and creativity in management planning is also highlighted. In addition, the material on organizing has been completely reworked and rearranged. New views about organizing, the behavior of individuals and groups within the organizational structure and environment, the effect of interactions among members and also upon the organization, and the task of organization development are discussed in some detail. Materials on the management grid, Parkinson's Law, and the Peter Principle, have been added.

The coverage on management actuating is expanded including updated treatments of motivation, behavioral concepts in dealing with people, individual behavior, group dynamics, managerial attention to the attitudes, needs, and expectations of employees, and the use of transactional analysis and flexible working hours. The latest developments in controlling such as anticipatory controlling, environmental conditioned controlling, and motivational controlling, are also included. A current management annotated bibliography continues to be a feature of this book.

With all these features and new coverage, the length of the book remains the same. The writing has been tightened, nonessentials deleted, and outdated material discarded. The total number of chapters is 27, including 5 new chapters, 12 chapters which were given a major rewrite, and 10 chapters which were given a minor rewrite.

Following each chapter are thought-provoking questions and case problems. Over one half of the nearly 400 questions are new. The number of cases is increased to 59, and two thirds of them have never before appeared in print. Selection was based not only on the experience of adopters of the book, but also on my own experience in the classroom. Much of the material was developed during the past several years from my consulting assignments and those of close professional associates.

A number of practitioners, educators, and students helped me directly and indirectly to formulate thoughts concerning this revision. Exchanging ideas with faculty members and students, discussing significant changes with practitioners in many different enterprises, and talking over certain managerial concepts with experts of various disciplines affecting management, all have supplied encouragement and support for preparing this revision. To acknowledge help by individual names would require a list far too long for inclusion here, but I hereby do express my sincere appreciation to all for their help and contributions. I simply must single out John F. Mee, Dean, Division of General and Technical Studies, and Mead Johnson Professor of Management, Indiana University, who by his incisive insight, personal encouragement, and contagious enthusiasm, in addition to his scholarly and extremely helpful suggestions, gave much assistance. Also Alfred H. Bornemann, James L. Fattore, and Bonnie D. Slager supplied helpful reviews and detailed suggestions which proved valuable in improving the book's coverage and content.

December 1976   GEORGE R. TERRY

Contents

Participation. Results management. The "top-down" or the "bottom-up" approach in results management. Motivational aspects of results management. Is anything missing in results management? Job enrichment: *Means for achieving job enrichment. The focus of job enrichment. Job enrichment and the organization. Limits to job enrichment.* Productivity priority: *What is productivity? Improving productivity.* Contingency management. Conflict utilization. The pattern of conflict. Dealing with conflict. Conflict location.

Definition and importance of objective. Type and classification of objectives. Writing an effective objective. Measurement of objectives. Hierarchy of objectives. Harmonizing objectives. Profits and objectives. Research of objectives. Guidelines for objectives.

Common problem areas for managers. Problem analysis. Problem solution and the management process. Management problems and controlling. Approaches to problem solution. Potential-problem analysis. Case study.

The meaning of decision making. Decision making and alternatives. Observations on selection of alternatives. Judgment and decision making. Nonquantitative bases for decision making: *Intuition. Facts. Experience. Considered opinions.* Who should make decisions: *Decision making by individual. Decisions by group.* Implementing the decision. Types of decisions. Decision making guidelines.

Operations research. Linear programming: *Linear programming— matrix algebra examples. VAM method for linear programming. Linear programming—graphic example. Linear programming—algebra example.* Simulation. Probability and decision making. Decision tree. Monte Carlo. Queueing. Gaming.

Meaning of planning. Examples of plans. Schedule planning. Profit planning. Product planning. Strategic planning: *Format of strategic*

sponsibility. Types of authority and organizational relationships: *Line authority. Staff authority. Line and staff organization. Line-staff relations. Advisory staff authority. Service staff authority. Control staff authority. Functional staff authority. The "assistant to" manager. The assistant manager. The general staff.* Organization charts. Titles.

20. Communicating   **430**

Communicating and management. Classification of managerial communication. The process of communicating. Human behavior and
communication. Language and communicating. Blueprint drawings. Improving communicating. Transactional analysis. Popular formal communication media. Communication—meetings, directives, and designs.

21. Appraising, developing, and compensating   **452**

Appraising managers: *Criteria used.* The appraisal conference. Performance appraisal in perspective. Developing managers: *Current concepts
on management development. Basic developmental considerations.
Major sources for identifying development needs. Participative media
for management development. Nonparticipative media for management
development.* Compensating: *Base pay. Bonus, commission, and profit
sharing. Deferred compensation. Financial incentives. Nonfinancial incentives. Fringe benefits.*

**PART VI
Controlling**   **479**

22. Management controlling   **481**

Controlling defined. Controlling and the management process. The control process. Influence of policies, procedures, and statistical techniques
upon controlling. Measuring the performance. Comparing performance
with the standard. Correcting deviation by means of remedial action.
Obtaining data on actual performance: *Oral reports. Written reports.*
Anticipatory controlling. Results management and controlling. Controlling and the human element. Major guides to effective controlling.

23. Overall managerial controls and audits   **501**

Controlling overall performance. Overall control reports. Key ratios of
total activities. Evaluation of ratio usage. Comparable companies ratios.
Fixed and variable costs analysis: *Algebraic solution.* Graphic solution.
Utilizing break-even point analysis. Return on machine investments.
Limited areas for overall controlling. Accounting audits. The manage-
ment audit. Identifying areas for an audit. Attributes used in auditing.

24. Quantity and quality controlling   **529**

Controlling quantity. Sales and quantity controlling. Quantity controlling of sales. Basis of sales control: *Sales control unit. Sales potential.
Characteristics of sales outlets.* Measuring sales performance: *Activities
of competitors. Comparing sales performance with standard. Correcting the sales deviation.* Controlling quality: *Inspection control. Statistical quality control. The basis of statistical quality control.* Control
charts. Suggestions for making quality controlling effective.

PART I
Basic background
for management

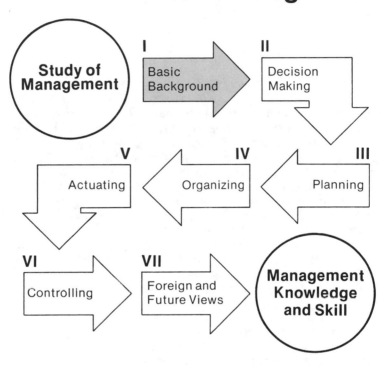

Chapter makeup for Part I:

1. Beginning our study of management.
2. Development of management thought and practice.
3. Management philosophy, values, and contemporary environment.
4. Selected current management practices.
5. Objectives.

Our study of management begins with presenting basic concepts which provide a practical reference framework within which management is normally conducted. In essence, an "attitudinal fix" toward management is provided so that its study is enhanced and made enjoyable and profitable.

Emphasis is placed on the meaning of management, its historical development, the influence of a manager's philosophy and values, and the effect of both internal and external environmental factors. Popular current management practices are reviewed and the importance of accomplishment in modern management is clearly set forth.

Throughout this orientation the central core is developed of studying management from the viewpoint of what a manager does. These activities make up a distinct process–a management process–parts of which may be modified by different approaches or schools of management considered especially helpful in the individual situation to which the management is being applied. More precisely what might be termed an eclectic-process school of management is the pattern around which management is presented. Hence, reality to both the theory and the study of management is offered as well as a coverage which is adequate, representative of management, and thoroughly modern. Avoided are the oversimplified general theory and the fractional theory focusing on a particular segment of total management.

Chapter 1

Beginning our study of management

Whatever is unknown is magnified.
Calgacus

Management is a most important subject because it deals with establishing and achieving objectives. Our main means, not only for identifying, analyzing, and deciding goals to be accomplished, but also for assembling effectively the talents of people and utilizing material resources, is management. Found in almost every human activity, management exists to some degree in the factory, office, school, bank, store, labor union, motel, church, armed forces, hospital, or home. In fact, there is a universality of management among enterprises. The hurdles to be overcome in achieving stated goals and the tasks management members perform have definite similarities even though present in widely different types of enterprises.

In many cases, the major objectives are provided by others, but when this is so, the objectives usually are stated in very broad terms and require elaboration and refinement to be understood by management members. More often than not, managers set forth their objectives, as illustrated by precise statements of the problems to be solved or hurdles to be overcome in outlining the work to be done. From the practical and operating viewpoint, a manager is expected to spell out objectives, giving adequate regard for the various constraints within which the goals must be achieved.

To achieve an objective there is inevitably the bringing together of available basic resources including men and women, materials, machines, methods, money, and markets. Referred to by some as the six Ms of management, these resources are brought together and related harmoniously so that the sought end result may be accomplished, all within the predetermined constraints of time, effort, and cost.

MANAGEMENT DEFINED

Management is defined in various ways depending upon the viewpoints, beliefs, and comprehension of the definer. To illustrate, some define management as "the force that runs an enterprise and is responsible for its success or failure." Others claim, "management is the performance of conceiving and achieving desired results by means of group efforts consisting of utilizing human talent and resources." Still others state that management is simply "getting things done through people," while others claim that it can be summarized as "planning and implementing." An additional definition is "management is the satisfying of economic and social needs by being productive for the human being, for the economy, and for society." Some state, "management is a resource used by everybody to achieve goals." All these definitions have merit; they highlight important aspects of management. However, for purposes of this book the following definition is used. *Management is a distinct process consisting of planning, organizing, actuating, and controlling, performed to determine and accomplish stated objectives by the use of human beings and other resources.* In other words there are distinguishing activities which make up a management process. Further, these activities are performed to accomplish stated objectives and they are performed by people with the help of other resources.

Figure 1–1 shows a graphic representation of this preferred definition of management. The basic resources are subjected to the funda-

FIGURE 1–1: The meaning of management

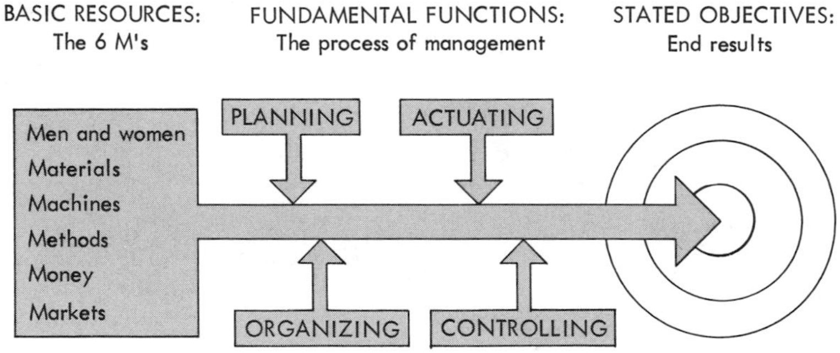

mental functions of management—planning, organizing, actuating, and controlling in order that the stated objectives are achieved. This approach to management study is developed fully in Chapter 2. Discussion is delayed to this chapter so that important considerations affecting management, no matter how it is defined, can be clarified so the full significance and use of management can be better appreciated.

It is helpful to remember that management is an activity; those who perform this activity are managers or management members. In a very real sense, management is an abstraction designed to convert disorganized resources into useful and effective goal accomplishments. This is achieved by utilizing nonhuman resources effectively and by working with people and motivating them in order to bring out their full capabilities and give reality to their dreams of having a richer, fuller life. Management is the most comprehensive, most demanding, most crucial, and most subtle of all human activities.

PIRO AND MANAGEMENT

It is also helpful to note the concept of PIRO (People, Ideas, Resources, and Objectives). These basically are what a manager works with, but not what one does, which, as stated above, are the fundamental functions of planning, organizing, actuating, and controlling.

People are by far the most important resource available to a manager. In the final analysis management is by, through, and for people. Its raison d'être is people. A manager knows that to achieve a stated objective, people need to be communicated with, persuaded, inspired, and they require leadership and the ability to perform work tasks that are satisfactory and satisfying. Ideas are among the most precious possessions of a manager for they represent the fundamental notions and conceptual thinking required of a manager. Questions such as what objectives to seek, what resources to allocate, what priorities, sequences, and timing to follow, and what problems to analyze are answered by the use of ideas and mental efforts of the manager. Resources, other than people, are essential to the manager's success. The manager must define liaison lines to facilitate coordination of resources and establish proper and up-to-date relationships among them. Objectives give purpose to the manager's use of people, ideas, and resources. There is a goal to reach, a mission to fulfill. A manager is goal-oriented.

WHY STUDY MANAGEMENT?

Management touches and influences the life of nearly every human being. Management makes us aware of our potentials, shows the way toward better accomplishment, reduces obstacles, and causes us to achieve goals that we probably would not otherwise attain. Common sense suggests that for our self-interest we know something about management. And certainly it is to be reckoned with in most actions that affect us as well as in actions we propose to affect others.

Few enterprises, business or nonbusiness, can long be successful that do not utilize effective management. To a great extent the establishment and the accomplishment of many economic, social, and political goals rest upon the competency of the manager. The task of making a better economic life possible, improving social standards, or achieving more efficient government is the challenge to modern managerial ability.

Management provides effectiveness to human efforts. It helps achieve better equipment, plants, offices, products, services, and human relations. It keeps abreast of changing conditions, and it supplies foresight and imagination. Improvement and progress are its constant watchwords.

Management brings order to endeavors. By means of management, apparently isolated events or factual information or beliefs are brought together and significant relationships discerned. These relationships bear on the immediate problem, point out future hurdles to be overcome, and assist in determining a solution to the problem.

Furthermore, it is being more widely recognized that management is the critical ingredient in a nation's growth. An underdeveloped nation, for example, usually lacks adequate management know-how. National development is not solely one of transferring capital, technology, and education to citizens of an undeveloped nation. It is also supplying or developing management which provides the generation and direction of effective human energies. Management know-how utilizes the available resources effectively toward achievement of basic needs.

In addition, there is no substitute for management. To determine worthwhile goals, carefully select and utilize resources efficiently by means of applying planning, organizing, actuating, and controlling require a high degree of judgment and the exercise of great courage. From time to time, gadgets and aids are offered to replace management, but actually at best they assist and do not represent management. Serious consideration of such devices usually points out the need for more managerial judgment and courage to be used. Nothing takes the place of management.

MANAGEMENT SCIENCE

There is a science of management. It may be incomplete in the eyes of many, but we do have a body of knowledge about management. This knowledge is objective, it is free from prejudice, and represents what is believed to be the best thinking on the subject of management. Management science is a body of systematized knowledge accumulated and accepted with reference to the understanding of general truths concerning management.

The science of management is neither as comprehensive nor as accurate as a so-called physical science, such as chemistry or physics. In these areas, accurate prediction is possible so that once certain actions are started, they cannot be regulated or duly influenced by human beings. In other words, a physical science deals with physical, material, nonhuman entities. In contrast, management deals with not only nonhuman but human entities as well. It is the inclusion and the effect of the human being in managerial knowledge that raises questions in some minds about management qualifying as a science. As yet it cannot be stated as a finality that a person will think, act, or react in a definite manner under certain given circumstances. Although great advances are being made in the science of management, it seems reasonable to state that management will approach, but probably never fully qualify as a pure science in the same sense as the well-known physical sciences. Perhaps the appropriate term "pseudoscience" or the generic term "social science" should be used to identify management. Such an identity more accurately represents the true context of management and demonstrates understanding of what management is all about.

MANAGEMENT ART

There is also the art of management. *The meaning of art is a personal creative power plus skill in performance.* The former emerges from contemplation of problems, events, and possibilities. The latter, or skill in performance, from experience, observation, and study. In other words, management art includes being able to envision the totality of many disparate parts and to create a representation of that vision, thus imposing order from chaos. In addition, management art includes the ability to communicate the vision with effective skills or craft. This involves choosing the correct form, media, and technique.

An important source of good management is management art—the imagination to create practical visions and to make them evident with a high degree of craft. Management is one of the most creative of all arts. It is the art of arts because it is the organizer and utilizer of human talent.

INTERRELATEDNESS OF MANAGEMENT SCIENCE AND ART

A manager is a scientist and an artist. For a given situation, science can reduce the amount of management art required, but it never eliminates it. The art of management is always present. In general, an increase in science brings about an increase in art, at least to the degree that the science increase is applied. Managers confront problems from time to time for which there is relatively little management science. In such cases the manager must rely greatly upon art— hunches, beliefs, creativity, and the skillful application of them.

Reduced to simplest terms, a science teaches one "to know," and an art, "to do." For example, astronomy is the science, while navigation is the art. Science and art are complementary fields of endeavor; they are not mutually exclusive. The medical doctor acquires the knowledge or science of chemistry, biology, and anatomy. But excellence in absorbing these funds of knowledge does not make one an excellent physician. One has to apply this wealth of knowledge expertly, and skill in perceiving how and when to use knowledge is essential to success as a practicing physician.

And the same is true of the manager. Both science and art are needed. There is knowledge about management, and it should be obtained and digested. Likewise, there is art, and excellent accomplishment in this area is to be sought. As the science of management increases, so should the art of management. A balance between the two is needed. Science should not be outweighed or art slighted. And it is equally shortsighted to emphasize art at the expense of science. The fact is that to be useful, knowledge or science must be applied; that is, art must be present. The real need in this respect appears to be greater emphasis given the art of management so that the science and the art of management advance together.

There is an old saying that "knowledge is power." This is only partially true. Knowledge can be power, but to state that it is ignores the importance of art. To be correct the saying should be "applied knowledge is power." Everyday observations reveal that many people have abundant knowledge but actually use little of it. They have never developed the needed art to apply what they know.

Some believe that art is superior to science because art starts from the beginning whereas science usually builds on its predecessors. The person who built the first automobile was a genius, but now many engineers can build one. Also, the person who writes a great play or applies knowledge of management to effectively bring about a service which people want is making a unique art of creation and is often hindered, rather than helped, by the past.

In a certain sense it can be said that the art of management begins where the science of management stops. Facts are first used, "knowns" are given preference, and data on tangibles initially considered. These scientific aids are pursued to their limits, but often, in any given case, they may seem inadequate. It is then that the manager must turn to artistic managerial ability to perform a job. Deciding to move ahead at one time rather than another time, to act even though all desirable data are lacking, or even to take action are illustrative of involvement of the art of management.

TECHNICAL, HUMAN, AND CONCEPTUAL
REQUIREMENTS

In the opinion of many practitioners, success in management is greatly conditioned by the knowledge and the skill in these three areas (1) technical, (2) human, and (3) conceptual.[1] As indicated in Figure 1-2, managerial jobs at the top organizational level usually necessitate relatively more human and conceptual knowledge and skill than technical knowledge and skill, but at the lower organizational level the need is for more technical and human and less conceptual knowledge and skill.

Technical knowledge and skill include understanding and proficiency in using a specific activity involving a process, procedure, or technique. It usually consists of a specialized knowledge and ability to perform within that specialty. Technical skill enables its possessor to accomplish the mechanics demanded in performing a particular job.

Human knowledge and skill, as the name suggests, includes the ability to work with others and to win cooperation from those in the

FIGURE 1-2

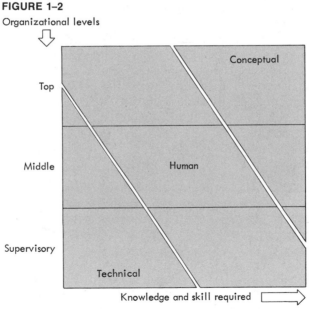

Knowledge and skill required for management varies with the organizational level.

---

[1] This discussion is based on the ideas advanced by Robert L. Katz in his excellent and still applicable article, "Skills of an Effective Administrator," *Harvard Business Review*, January–February 1955, pp. 33–42.

work group. It includes, for example, knowing what to do and being able to communicate ideas and beliefs to others, and to understand what thoughts others are trying to convey to you. In addition, the manager with human knowledge and skill understands and recognizes what views one brings to situations and in turn what adjustments or changes in these views might be made as a result of working with associates.

Conceptual knowledge and skill includes knowing the way and having the ability to visualize the enterprise as a whole, to see the "big picture," to envision all the various functions involved in a given situation or circumstance. It is this conceptual requirement that enables an executive to recognize the interrelationships and relative values of the various factors intertwined in a managerial problem. To conceptualize requires imagination, broad knowledge, and the mental capacity to conceive abstract ideas.

GUIDELINES FOR MANAGERIAL SUCCESS

Current managerial literature abounds in providing short lists of what it takes to succeed in management. While such lists are necessarily limited and frequently resemble platitudes, they nevertheless are of interest to the beginning student of management. Four such lists are included here in order to show the general nature of this material and hopefully to increase the student's interest in studying management.

The first list gives four simple suggestions: (1) know the company's goals, (2) select effective subordinates, (3) delegate by letting subordinates decide issues within their respective spheres of operation, and (4) check up to insure that results being obtained are satisfactory.

Another list includes (1) select your group members carefully, (2) motivate them, (3) develop good communication, (4) strive to attain effective interpersonal relationships, and (5) minimize conflicts among the group members.

Going into more depth and probably of greater assistance is the third list which includes (1) strengthen human relations skill, (2) learn to speak and to listen effectively, (3) set high standards or proposed levels of achievement, (4) see situations from the other person's viewpoint, (5) become effective in decision making, (6) adopt a questioning attitude to discover and to use new ideas, (7) be a leader by getting involved in the action, (8) view management as the opportunity to influence other people favorably, and (9) evaluate what's achieved carefully and, if necessary, take remedial action.

Last, list four points out that for most favorable results, the manager should (1) spend time on matters that are really important, (2) plan and follow through on programs, (3) express personal feelings and understand the feelings of others, (4) look for the best in others—not the worst, (5) make sure each group member is assigned the work best suited for that person, (6) encourage members to assume responsibility, (7) appraise his or her own self and performance honestly, (8) evaluate the group members consistently, (9) keep cost expenditures at a minimum compatible with the service required, and (10) increase personal overall knowledge.

PRINCIPLES OF MANAGEMENT

Another basic concept in management is that there are principles of management. Some prefer to call them propositions. A principle can be defined as *a fundamental statement or truth providing a guide to thought or action*. The fundamental statement signifies what results to expect when the principle is applied. Hence, by means of principles of management, a manager can avoid fundamental mistakes in his or her many efforts. Principles of management are to the manager as a table of strengths of materials is to a civil engineer. The table represents to a civil engineer fundamental truths, expressed as data, based on years of experience and testing. The engineer can predetermine the safe allowable load for a steel girder of a building simply by using the table and analyzing the design drawings and specifications.

From experiences and accomplishments come principles. Actually, the discovery and statements of principles are a product of any well-developed science. In the study and comprehension of any body of knowledge, particular bits of knowledge are relatively nothing; they are rapidly aging facts. Principles are enduring. In fact, every field of learning has its principles which represent the distillation of basic truths in that area as we know and understand them. There are basic principles of management that are reasonably well established, accepted, and used. These principles cover many facets of management.

It can be stated that the principles of management represent the current development of management. As more and more reliable knowledge is gained about it, new principles will emerge and at the same time, other management principles will be modified, and some discarded as not being truly representative of management knowledge.

APPLYING PRINCIPLES OF MANAGEMENT

Principles are basic; yet they are not absolute. They are neither laws, nor dogmas, and they should not be considered too rigid. Principles are working hypotheses. Principles should be (1) practical, which means they can be put to use no matter how remote or distant in time the applications are, (2) relevant to a basic and broad precept, thus providing an inclusive perspective, and (3) consistent in that for identical sets of circumstances similar results will occur.

The application of principles requires judgment and interpretation of the available facts in a given situation. This means that management principles have some flexibility in that their application should take into account the particular, special, or changing conditions. For example, consider the statement: "For maximum managerial efficiency, total costs should be kept to a minimum." Perhaps this is valid for most cases, but should it still be used as a guide in cases of emergency or in the efforts of defending our country against an invader?

The use of management principles is intended to simplify management work. Keys to what actions should be taken *are suggested* by principles of management. They provide the basic bench marks from which a comprehensive mastery of a subject area may be started and can be viewed as capsules of what is believed to be major considerations in effective current management thought.

MANAGEMENT AND MULTI-DISCIPLINES

To enrich its utility and adaptability, management is drawing and using more and more from various disciplines. Initially, in the development of management the emphasis was upon the economic aspects of the goals and the problems. Attention was directed to cost, efficiency, and measured accomplishments. With time, however, other viewpoints have been added until today disciplines contributing to management include psychology, sociology, anthropology, ecology, mathematics, political science, biology, and geography. Some of these have developed to the point where they are referred to as separate schools of management thought or theory.[2]

Although management draws from and uses these disciplines, management is not inclusive of all these disciplines. If it were inclusive, such a subject area would truly stagger the imagination. It would be beyond the capacity of the human mind to comprehend since it would represent nearly the totality of knowledge. No doubt management of the future will continue to seek knowledge and ideas from whatever disciplines appear feasible. In utilizing these various disciplines, management will tend to integrate them and as a result, management possibly will be viewed more and more as the important medium serving as the integrator and the applicator of total knowledge. This brings us back, so to speak, to the validity of the truism that all knowledge is interrelated. Since management is broad and universal in its concept, it appears that drawing from and utilizing many disciplines is proper and such practice will help bring the best knowledge known to answer a managerial problem.

Actually, managers need all the help they can get. The problems are seldom of any one given field of study. For example, a business corpo-

---

[2] This is discussed fully in Chapter 2.

ration is not simply an economic entity, but a social institution as well. And while great advances have been made in engineering and industrial technology, we have not as yet made similar headway in human relations. It takes a long while for the habits and attitudes of people to catch up with their technology. Further, the task of motivating employees so that they gain a sense of accomplishment from their work and apply themselves with gusto to the task at hand remains an important problem faced by many management members.

CHARACTERISTICS GIVING KEY TO UNDERSTANDING MANAGEMENT

Management is unique and a review of the following listing will be beneficial to the beginning student of management. Although portions of the following are implied in the above discussion, this orderly listing commonly proves helpful.

1. *Management is purposeful.* Management deals with the achievement of something specific, expressed as an objective. Commonly, managerial success is measured by the extent to which the objectives are achieved. Management exists because it is an effective means of getting needed work accomplished. The fact that some executives have a number of subordinates reporting to them does not ipso facto, make them managers.

2. *Management makes things happen.* Managers focus their attention and efforts on bringing about successful action. They know where to start, what to do to keep things moving, and how to follow through. Successful managers have an urge for accomplishment.

Management is acceptable because by its means things are accomplished that people know should be done and that they want done, but they realize probably won't be done if management is absent. This means that in some cases the person practicing management may find she or he is not "winning a popularity contest," but members of the group respect the manager. The management member gets along with people by not only liking them, but also by being firm, helpful, and expectant of the best. The people, in turn, are glad that they have the management member they do because they are getting somewhere.

3. *Management is an activity, not a person or group of persons.* The word "managing" is a more precise and descriptive term than management. Popular usage, however, has made management the widely accepted term. Management is not people, it is an activity like walking, reading, swimming, or running. People who perform management can be designated as managers, members of management, or executive leaders. In addition, management is a distinct activity. It can be studied, knowledge about it obtained, and skill in its application acquired.

4. Management is accomplished by, with, and through the efforts of others.   To participate in management necessitates relinquishing the normal tendency to perform all things yourself and get tasks accomplished by, with, and through the efforts of the group members. This is far more difficult than it sounds. Normally a person acquires ability in a specialized type of work and wins promotions by acquiring increasing knowledge and skill in this given field of specialization. However, the time comes when further promotion requires shifting from the role of a specialist to that of a management member. The prime measure of success now becomes setting or securing agreement on the proper goals and getting others to accomplish these specific goals. How successfully this deliberate shift is made determines the potentialities of the new manager. This characteristic merits recognition by the ambitious specialist. All too frequently the salesperson promoted to district sales manager remains a salesperson, because of failure to comprehend the managerial difference between getting salespeople to sell and knowing how to sell. Likewise, the employee training expert advanced to assistant personnel manager may continue to be a training expert, thus not succeeding in the new managerial post.

5. Management is usually associated with efforts of a group.   The management-group association is the common viewpoint. However, management is applicable to an individual's efforts. For example, a person manages his or her personal affairs. The group emphasis stems from the fact that an enterprise comes into existence to attain most goals and these are achieved more readily by a group than by one person alone. People become members of an enterprise in order to satisfy their needs and because they feel their gains will outweigh their losses or burdens as members of a group.

6. Management is intangible.   It has been called the unseen force—its presence evidenced by the results of its efforts—orderliness, enthusiastic employees, buoyant spirit, and adequate work output. Strange as it may seem, in some instances the identity of management is brought in bold relief by its absence or by the presence of its direct opposite, *mis*management. The results of mismanagement are quickly noticed; and thus, the identity of management is brought into clear focus.

7. Management is aided, not replaced by the computer.   The computer is an extremely powerful tool of management. It can widen a manager's vision and sharpen insight by supplying information for key decisions. The computer has enabled the manager to conduct analyses far beyond the normal human being's analytical capacities. It has forced managers to reexamine their analytical and judgmental processes in view of the almost unbelievable data processing and feedback facilities of the modern computer.

However, a manager must supply judgment and imagination as well as interpret and evaluate what the data mean in a specific individual case. It is doubtful that Gen. George Washington would have crossed the Delaware River had he relied on a computer to help him decide. The data of using leaky boats, at night, during a snow storm, to face a numerically superior enemy would have indicated a low probability of success. However—despite such rationale—General Washington believed he could succeed, seized the initiative, assumed the large risk, and won his objective.

8. *Management is an outstanding means for exerting real impact upon human life.*   A manager can do much to improve the work environment, to stimulate people to better things, and to make favorable actions take place. Frustrations and disappointments need not be accepted at face value and passively viewed as inevitable. A manager can achieve progress, can bring hope, and can help group members achieve the better things in life.

MANAGEMENT AND YOU

Management offers abundant opportunities. The choice of careers is broadening steadily and covers a wide range of talent and ability. Every major activity in every enterprise involves management personnel. Women, as well as men, and members of minority groups are occupying positions of managerial importance.

Just what are the chances of getting into management? Very good. Management ability will be in increasing demand. With the growth in the U.S. economy, improvement in government and social order, the development of a nationwide health care program, and the maintenance of a strong national defense, the need for people with management knowledge and skill will be tremendous. Of all the people gainfully employed in the United States, approximately 10 percent are classified as managerial. Hence, assuming a total national work force of 100 million, there are roughly 10 million management jobs in the United States. This means that during next year, about 250,000 management jobs will have to be filled, assuming an average working span of 40 years.

MANAGEMENT AND CHANGE

Change constantly challenges the manager. Some of this change is evolutionary, some revolutionary, some recognizable, some nonrecognizable. Both forces within an enterprise as well as forces outside the enterprise cause managers to act and react in initiating changes in their immediate working environment.

Change is inevitable; the challenge is to seize the opportunity that change presents and shape it for human progress. It appears quite likely that we are just beginning to see the real effects of change in our society; the pace probably will accelerate in ways that few really understand or know what to do about. Both technology and social changes have overtaken the fiction writers and it is a bit jolting to realize that 95 percent of all the professors, engineers, and scientists in existence since the beginning of history are alive and working today. The volume of their work is overwhelming and seems to ensure that change will continue at an even greater rate in the future.

Change always poses certain problems, but the most disturbing feature of present day change is the speed with which it is occurring. Some enterprises have been subjected to change so traumatic that certain employees have experienced shock and have been unable to cope with the new situation. Further, most enterprises themselves spawn change and each new development tends to compound the problem and the task of the manager.

Managers must cope with change. If an enterprise is not adapted to changing times, decay is in process. External forces demand change; internal forces press for it. Successful managers sense change and encompass it into their efforts. To do this, two apparently incompatible actions are taken: (1) order is promoted and the status quo is maintained—a sort of "satisfying the orderly majority"—and at the same time (2) the innovators seeking change are protected and places for their contributions are provided.

The human resource is the most flexible of all the resources which a manager employs. And it is by means of people that managers most successfully deal with change. Knowledge gives people insight into change and the consequences of change. Hence, the manager alert to change strives to attract compeers who are as flexible as the events of the times, are open-minded, and are not those devoted completely to a particular discipline of thinking, or "hung up" on a specific conclusion to a specific problem.

It is worth noting that people do not resist change as such. What they do resist is change that threatens their security, adds to their workloads without any rewards, or seriously disturbs their work or its environment to which they have grown accustomed. On the other hand, compared with the past, significant changes have taken place in the human resource. Today's employees have more education, are younger, dislike boring work, have limited work experience, possess new and challenging attitudes, and are guided by economic and social standards unheard of several decades ago.

Furthermore, numerous changes are taking place in the implementation of management itself. New concepts are being developed, new ideas being evaluated, and the manner of carrying out the management function is being radically altered. To illustrate, some believe that management should be viewed as the important resource for all achievement and recommend abandonment of its traditional, "you tell 'em—authoritative hierarchy" concept. In other words, management is a resource to nearly all achievement and every member of an enterprise performs the management functions to accomplish goals. This view is rapidly gaining followers. It is in contrast to the traditional viewpoint of management being viewed basically as a system of authority. Also, participation in managerial decision making and also job enrichment, whereby the number and variety of tasks making up the job are increased, are now widely advocated and practiced by many managers. Inclusion of these and other newer managerial concepts are featured in this book.

When more managers can adapt to the changing nature of our present day requirements, many pertinent questions raised today will be answered. At that time, we will have found the right method for the attainment of fair profits, the supplying of good service consistently, the alleviation of poverty and hunger, the provision of jobs for all who seek employment, and work environments where people can find their dignity and satisfaction.

QUESTIONS

1. Define management.
2. What are several important reasons for your studying management?
3. What is your understanding of the statement, "Management is a resource"?
4. Using the given lists of what it takes to succeed in management and your own experience and thoughts, compile your own list of six suggestions. Substantiate the selections you have made.
5. Identify each of the following fully: (*a*) management science, (*b*) the concept of PIRO, and (*c*) conceptual knowledge and skill.
6. Name the three characteristics helping to understand management that you believe are most important. Substantiate your answer.
7. As you see it, what is meant by a "principle of management"? Does it have practical value? Discuss.
8. Explain Figure 1–2 in your own words.
9. Do you favor the trend of managers using multi-disciplines in their work? Why?
10. Discuss the subject of "management art," including what it is, its importance, and how to acquire it.
11. Discuss the subject, "management and change."
12. If a student memorizes all the available principles of management, does this accomplishment mean this student is a potentially competent manager? Discuss.
13. Discuss the opportunities available in management.
14. From your experience or reading, relate a major change that took place and what management did to bring about or to cope with that change.

CASE 1–1. GEORGE MANCHESTER

A native of the southeastern United States, George Manchester attended a state university of Florida and earned his B.S. degree in marketing. He was the son of Henry Manchester, who was the sole owner of a small hardware wholesale company in Savannah, Georgia. The business provided Henry Manchester a medium income. There were good years and bad years. Henry never seemed able to build any surplus. George worked his way through college doing part-time jobs. Upon graduation, George received a job offer with a national retailing corporation. In talking over the offer with his father, it was decided that George should accept the offer and after several years return to his hometown and join his father's business. George believed that the advancement opportunities to him would be greater this way, and although he dreamed many times of working with his father, he wanted to "make it" on his own. Besides, he did not feel his father's business was large enough to support both of them.

Four years later George has made excellent progress with his employer. Competent and very well liked, he has received three promotions and is currently receiving a pay check almost double his starting wage. His future is bright indeed, and he is happily married and has a two-year-old son.

While visiting his parents in Savannah recently, he learned that his father had developed a serious physical ailment. The doctor has stated that Henry must quit working. None of the six employees of the business are qualified to take his place in the business, and without Henry the survival of the company is questionable. George's mother said she hoped George would come back and help out now that he is needed. She added that he could make a comfortable living by taking over the business.

George likes Savannah and would enjoy living there. He is doing so well with his present employer, however, that he can't make up his mind what to do. He talked it over with his wife, who counseled, "I like it here, but would probably like Savannah, too. So whatever you decide to do, George, I'll go along with it."

Questions

1. What major considerations do you feel George Manchester should take into account? Discuss.
2. What action should George take? Why?

Chapter 2

Development of management thought and practice

He who hath a good harvest may be content with some thistles.

John Ray

With the tremendous changes in all aspects of life, discussed in Chapter 1, have come new challenges and efforts to improve management. Also, the progress in acquiring knowledge, the use of multi-disciplines, and the availability of the computer, opened up numerous opportunities for improvement of the managerial mind. As a result, a number of different beliefs and viewpoints about management, commonly referred to as schools of management, have come into existence. To provide a helpful perspective, let us briefly note these managerial beliefs and views.

DEVELOPMENT OF MANAGEMENT THOUGHT

Early civilizations west of Mesopotamia and the writings of the Egyptians extending back to around 1200 B.C. indicate knowledge and use of management for guiding political affairs. Likewise, the history of ancient Greece and that of the Roman Empire gives much evidence of managerial knowledge, especially in the area of courts, operation of government practices, army organization, unity of group efforts, and establishing authority. In addition, throughout the history of Western civilization the church has contributed to the knowledge of management by means of developing a worldwide organization structure and by the use of authority in managerial work.

Until about the middle of the 18th century, the people of western Europe used basically the same methods and implements of production that had been used for nearly 20 centuries. Then, within a few decades a series of inventions was discovered, and the whole picture of industrial activity was enormously altered. This new period, commonly referred to as the Industrial Revolution, brought about the greater utilization of machines, the centralization of production activities, the establishment of new employer-employee relationships, and the separation of consumers from producers. Under these new conditions, the customary means of establishing and achieving objectives proved unsatisfactory and gave rise to new management means.

A number of people contributed to this movement. For example, Charles Babbage, a professor of mathematics at Cambridge University in England, advocated as early as the first half of the 19th century that accurate data obtained from rigid investigation be utilized in the managing of an enterprise. He wanted work measurement, cost determination, and wage incentives.

Frederick W. Taylor (1856–1915) contributed enormously to the development of management thought. He conducted extensive studies of specific production components—the lathe department, or the work produced on a certain lathe—by observing, measuring, and relating the contributions of the given components. He employed precise, analytical means to verify or to reject definite hypotheses or assumptions, a method known as the scientific method and which developed into a school of management known as the scientific management school. It will be discussed several pages later in this chapter.

In Taylor's opinion, four principles or guidelines of management were vital. They include (1) the development of the best work method, (2) the selection and development of workers, (3) the relating and bringing together of the best work method and the selected and trained worker, and (4) the close cooperation of managers and nonmanagers, which cooperation includes the division of work and the manager's responsibility for planning the work. Taylor also pointed out that managers and nonmanagers must have complete understanding about the quantity and quality of work to be accomplished within a given period. He indicated that the answer to this question was needed: *What constitutes an honest day's work?* By answering this question equitably, a basis for mutual understanding would be provided and a focal point around which to build better management would be available. Many believe this question is as valid today as it was several decades ago when Taylor suggested it.

Henri Fayol, a French contemporary of Taylor, also made valuable contributions to management thought and development. A successful industrialist, Fayol headed a steel and coal combine. He was a management pioneer in that he made universal generalizations about management based on his keen insight and practical management experience. Unlike Taylor, Fayol's efforts dealt with "classical administration" in that the focus was upon the enterprise as a whole, not upon a single segment of it. He was the pioneer of the conept of viewing management as being made up of functions, and his work supplied a comprehensive framework about which management thought could be studied and developed. Fayol emphasized rationalism and logical consistency. Although his book, written in French, first appeared in 1916, his contributions were somewhat beclouded until 1949, when the English translation became widely available.

Subsequently, other approaches to management thought came into being. During the early 1930s, for example, increasing emphasis was being given to the idea that people are the important consideration in management, that objectives are established and achieved with and through people. Hence, an important concept in the study of management should be human beings, their work environment, and interpersonal relations. These considerations were stressed in the famous Hawthorne studies in the Hawthorne plant of Western Electric and are generally considered the classical initiation of a new development in management thought.

About 1950, another approach to management started to win favor. It is the use of quantitative methods of analysis employing mathematical models and relationships as well as statistics. To illustrate, algebraic equations are employed to represent basic relationships of factors bearing on a problem. By substituting tentative numerical values in the equation, the result these values bring about can be determined. From statistics, the theory of probability also can be used advantageously in reaching certain managerial decisions.

Other developments have come into the limelight during the past several decades. They include concentration on decision making whereby how the decision is made, who makes it, the environment affecting it, and its implementation are believed of prime importance. Another is to study management by means of the systems approach. In essence the belief here is that for a given entity, all activities are interrelated and can be identified as interdependent systems forming a pattern or network of related activities. By use of these networks, the true overall meaning and the directing of the various work activities are best comprehended and utilized.

From these various developments of management study have evolved different thought patterns about management. A number of schools of management thought exist today. For purposes of this book the following are included: (1) management by custom school, (2) scientific management school, (3) behavior school, (4) social school, (5) systems management school, (6) decisional management school, (7) quantitative measurement school, (8) management process school and (9) contingency management school. To some degree the names are self-explanatory. Some are relatively broad in their scope; others tend to relatively specialized areas. Some are closely related; others have little relationship among them. Some tend to elaborate or extend further the developments of previously held concepts; others take basic portions of different schools and, along with new core ideas, weave a composite new approach, while still others strike out in new directions, employing entirely different concepts and tools. However, each school emphasizes what its advocates view management to be. The perception or shortcoming might be in the concept of total management.

MANAGEMENT BY CUSTOM SCHOOL

Some believe that current managerial tasks should basically be thought of and performed in a manner similar to those of the recent past, that is, by custom or tradition. "How would my predecessor have solved such a problem?" is a typical approach used in the custom school. It is also exemplified by observing what leading managers are doing in circumstances similar to yours and then following this example by applying the same techniques and actions in your managerial work. Sometimes this school is called the empirical school because it contributes generalizations and masses of practical management descriptive information. Included are the biographies of outstanding managers and the studies of the management of phenomenal companies. Answers to what objectives were sought, what practices did the managers follow, and what results were achieved are made and these serve to build a fund of knowledge for the practicing manager to apply.

Favorable results are obtained by following the custom school. It is simple, gives a feeling of assurance, and keeps a manager informed on activities outside the enterprise. Detailed information on progress in other firms can be of considerable help in solving managerial problems. It maintains the status quo and, in the mind of the custom manager, is the safest and surest key to managerial stability and success. On the other hand, little effort is made to blaze new trails. What others or the majority practice cannot always be evaluated as best for an individual concern. What fits one enterprise might not fit another at all, and comparing past management issues with those of the present and future can be questionable. Yet few will deny that disseminations by "old pros" of how they handled difficult managerial problems can be extremely helpful.

SCIENTIFIC MANAGEMENT SCHOOL

As mentioned above, this school uses the scientific method which verifies or rejects assumptions by means of controlled experimentation. In other words, experiments or tests are conducted under specific conditions in order to discover *causal* relationships, if any, between the assumption, or originally posed proposition, and the results obtained from the tests. Causal relationship means that the presence of certain things or their taking place are accompanied causally by other things which are present or will take place. This is not to be confused with what is the cause and what is the effect. The scientific manager does not identify the cause and the effect, but shows what conditions or factors are related and exist together. Definite steps followed in a prescribed sequence constitute the scientific method. These are shown in Figure 2–1.

FIGURE 2–1:   The steps of the scientific method

1. *Identify proposition.* This defines the objective and points the entire investigation to a specific goal.

2. *Acquire preliminary observations about proposition.* This is exploratory, supplies acquaintance with existent knowledge, and provides helpful background material.

3. *State tentative solution to proposition.* The hypothesis, so stated, will be confirmed or disproved by controlled experimentation. All factors affecting the proposition will be kept constant throughout the test, except one factor which, permitted to vary, will reveal its relationship to the proposition. Considerable creativity is required to formulate the tentative solution by thinking beyond what is presently available. Also, history reveals that many major discoveries result from seeking the answer to one proposition and winding up with an unexpected answer to another proposition.

4. *Investigate proposition thoroughly, using both current knowledge and controlled experiments.* The degree of relationship, or total lack of it, between the data and the tentative solution is sought. Used are both analysis and synthesis. Analysis means to break down the entity into its components and examine each component by itself and also in relation to its remaining components. Synthesis means to combine, build up, or put together the various entities being considered. In addition, controlled experiments are set up to provide data on the specific proposition under discussion. Sufficient tests must be run to establish consistency of results.

5. *Classify data obtained.* Classification expedites the handling of data. The classes selected depend upon the proposition and its tentative answer. For example, data on published books can be classified by publisher, size, or subject. For a manufacturer of bookcases, the size of book would be the most meaningful, whereas for a library, the subject would be selected.

6. *State tentative answer to proposition.* This is accomplished by careful interpretation of the classified data. For this purpose, two types of reasoning are used: (a) inductive reasoning and (b) deductive reasoning. The former is reasoning from the results of a relatively few but adequate parts, in this case tests, to the probable results of many tests concerning the same phenomenon. In contrast, deductive reasoning is reasoning from the truth of an entirety, revealed by many tests, to a portion or segment of that entity.

7. *Adjust and state answer to proposition.* To help insure validity and completeness, the tentative answer is tried out under the prescribed conditions and the results are noted. If needed, the answer is adjusted and then clearly stated, care being taken to relate it to the originally stated proposition of step No. 1.

The scientific management school has contributes tremendous management knowledge to us. Its essence is the development of an inquiring mind with the resultant intelligent searching for more knowledge, more facts, more relationships. Historically, it is associated with economic considerations such as cost, time-use, and efficiency, but the method it employs is basic in research of other areas such as chemistry, physics, psychology, and sociology. Hence, the scientific method is found in other than the scientific management school. Advocates of scientific management firmly believe better management is possible and seek to find it by using the scientific method. Yet they realize the best of management is never permanently attained because the continuous new knowledge paves the way for constant improvement. Scientific management enjoys wide usage, but is by no means universal.

Principle of scientific management

The use of thorough investigation, controlled experimentation, and careful interpretation of the resultant data provides a reliable basis for the determination and evaluation of new facts used by managers.

Principle of analysis and synthesis

Segregating a problem into its components and, in contrast, combining various entities under consideration assist in identifying and in establishing the relative importance of each factor of that problem.

BEHAVIOR SCHOOL

As viewed by the follower of this school the important and focal point of managerial action is the behavior of the human being and human beings. What is achieved, how it is achieved, and why it is achieved is viewed in relation to its impact and influence upon people who, it is believed, are the really important entity of management. Followers of this school say, "Management does not do; it gets others to do." Voluminous writings of this school show the need for the manager to use the best human relations practices. Among the more common topics are human relations, motivation, leadership, training, and communication.

This school is a development from the application of the behavioral sciences, especially psychology and social psychology, to management. The individual is viewed as a sociopsychological being, and the question facing the manager ranges from understanding and securing the best efforts from an employee by satisfying psychological needs, to comprehending the whole gamut of psychological behavior of groups as representing the totality of management.

Figure 2–2 illustrates the pragmatic concepts of psychology widely used in the behavior school. Both clinical and experimental ap-

FIGURE 2–2

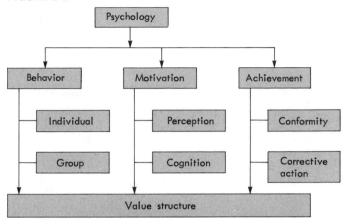

proaches are used in order to discover new avenues of learning, motivating, adjusting, and achieving.

Outstanding and significant contributions by this school have been made. For example, the emphasis upon the use of participation, and the ways to handle conflict arising from strong differences of opinion and of conduct within an organization. Also this school recognizes the vital influence of the environment and constraints affecting behavior. This had led to fruitful discoveries regarding the needs and motivations of people at work, the use of authority, the importance of irrationality in people's behavior, and the informal relationships existing within a work environment. The behavior school is popular; it has many followers. Few question the importance of people and their behavior as vital in the study of management. On the other hand, one might ask whether the field of human behavior is inclusive to or covers the entire area of management. Perhaps, in addition to insight into human behavior, knowledge of things exemplified by technology, machines, and buildings is helpful in determining and achieving objectives beneficial to us.

SOCIAL SCHOOL

This approach views management as a social system or, what is more specific, as a system of cultural interrelationships. This school is sociologically oriented and deals with identifying the various social groups as well as their cultural relationships and, in addition, integrating these groups into a complete social system. Both the social school and the behavior school stem from the development of behavioral sciences applied to management.

Fundamental to most of the social school's belief is the need to solve through cooperation the various limitations which humans and their environs may have. Commonly used is a social unit which ideally is one in which people communicate effectively with each other and willingly contribute toward achievement of a common goal. In many cases, constraints are those of a single enterprise and hence the name, organization-behavior, to designate this approach has come into common use. Sometimes the unit considered is the entire social entity. When this is done, the school is ecologically influenced and is concerned with the relationships among (1) the organization, (2) the internal and external environment, and (3) forces bringing about change and adjustments. Some students of management believe there is an ecological school of management thought. It begins with basic units—customers, students, soldiers—and then adds the elements of operations required to accomplish the goals. Such a school has interesting possibilities but as yet is not prominent.

Ordinarily a social group develops conflicts, cohesions, and interactions among its members. There are social feelings, perceptions, and identifications as well as culturally patterned responses, all of which makes for problems of power control and reconciliation of interests. These forces are neither confined to formal leadership, organization relationships, and group reactions, nor to forces within the particular system. But they are conditioned by informal organization—the leadership and group relationships coming into being as a result of social forces which can help or hinder the official or formal purposes. In addition, activities within a social group are affected by social forces outside that group, for example, by members of a community that are not employees of the enterprise, such as trade unions and government agencies. Furthermore, consideration for ethics, or what is morally

FIGURE 2–3

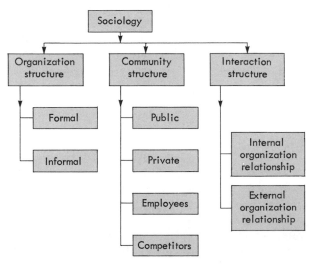

right, is brought to light by the social school, since a relationship to a social group or groups is involved.

In essence, the social school stresses the interaction and cooperation of people making up a social entity. It utilizes nonrational as well as rational organization behavior and the development of understanding based on empirical investigations. Figure 2–3 shows the integrated concepts of sociology as currently applied to management.

SYSTEMS MANAGEMENT SCHOOL

As suggested by its name, systems are the essentials of this school of management. A system can be thought of as an organized whole made up of parts connected in some fashion and directed to some purpose. Systems are basic to most activities. Analysis reveals that an activity is in reality the result of many other subactivities, and in turn, these subactivities of many sub-subactivities. To illustrate, the activities of the human body can be considered a system and a result of many subsystems, including the digestive system, the circulatory system, and the nervous system.

Each system has an input, a process, and an output, and is a self-contained unit, but it is also related to a system of a wider and higher order as well as to its own subsystems that represent the integration of several systems of the lower order. Thinking in terms of systems simplifies, to some degree, the conception of the multitudinous activities with which a manager must work, and it also enables the manager to see better the nature of the complex problems to be solved. An enterprise is looked upon as an artificial system, the internal parts of which work together to achieve established goals, the external parts to achieve interplay with its environment, including customers, the general public, suppliers, and government. The manager integrates available facilities toward goal achievement by means of systems which relate needed activities required for the end result. The systems serve as the media through which the manager operates. For example, using a physical distribution system for managing materials usage and movement from the time raw materials are received until they are delivered to the customer affords an integrated arrangement aiding a manager to take effective action in handling problems dealing with materials.

Figure 2–4 suggests a possible systems management organization. The president has an executive committee which, upon advice and information from product, market, personnel, and finance research, decides what products or services the enterprise will provide. With this established, the system to produce and sell the output is designed by the systems design unit which takes into account the constraints, policies, and practices to be followed. Next, the allocation of resources

FIGURE 2–4: Systems management organization chart

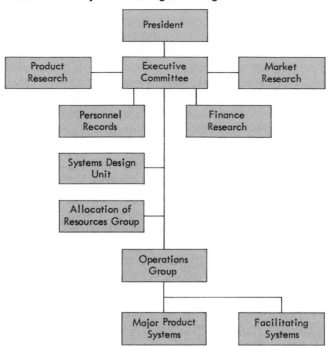

is worked out, by the group with the same name, as required by the major systems to be followed. It is then turned over to the operations group and assigned to either the major product systems or facilitating systems subgroups. The latter includes those organized to produce a service or an assistance necessary in carrying out the major system.

The computer is a great aid in the implementation of systems management. Masses of data can be processed to help determine the relationships among various parts and the change brought about in one part due to a change in another. Systems management enables a manager to use broad concepts; to envision wide, sweeping areas; and to push back the constraints. The "big picture" is emphasized. In turn, this emits more meaningful and inclusive relationships, revealing more precisely how the various parts act and react to bring out designated actions. Further, this interrelationship characteristic makes systems a very effective vehicle of thought.

DECISIONAL MANAGEMENT SCHOOL

Focus here is upon the managerial decisions. This, claim the followers of this school, is the real job of the manager. The decision of what to achieve and how to achieve it are the vital characteristics and challenges of the manager. The decision maker is the manager. The approach is sometimes limited to the economic rationale of the marginal utility and economic behaviors under uncertainties. In other instances, the area of consideration is broadened to include any event that takes place within the enterprise or any impact from the outside which in some direct or indirect way might influence the decision reached. The problem, risks, and predicted outcome of each alternative are customarily followed.

Almost all human activity is now considered legitimate for a decision-making study. To illustrate, decisional adherents have grappled with decisions pertaining to the diagnosis and the resulting prescriptions for improving communication, incentives, and the reactions of the individual to a group. The trend of this school is toward more of an examination of the entire enterprise via the decisional making approach than a concentration on decision making itself.

There can be no question that decision making is vital in every school management. However, contemporary decision conceptualization is neither confined to a limited area nor is it determined by a simple exercise in common sense. The query can be made whether decision making alone is the proper and best medium for the understanding and application of management. In a given case, what decision-making basis includes all the important aspects of the issue to be decided? Furthermore, does the decision finalize the sought action or does it commence the action? If the latter, the means for implementation must be determined. Many believe that a managerial decision includes not only what to do but how and when to do it as well.

QUANTITATIVE MEASUREMENT SCHOOL

This school includes those who see management as a logical entity, the actions of which can be expressed in terms of mathematical symbols, relationships, and measurable data. It is important to state that this school is primarily concerned with decision making. The techniques followed are ultimately for this purpose.

Two characteristics feature the quantitative school: (1) optimizing or minimizing input-output, and (2) the use of mathematical models. Optimizing or minimizing means that which is most desirable for a selected factor, is chosen from an entirety such as an entire organization, department, or work group, and any alternative would be less desirable. Optimizing is usually associated with sales, gross margin, machine utilization, service, or productivity. In contrast, minimizing (to seek a minimum amount) is typical of cost and time taken.

Suppose our objective is to maximize production profits. To achieve this we consider the common portions of most enterprises to be (1) input, (2) process, and (3) output. Also, we optimize production, assuming all we can produce will be sold at a satisfactory market price. Since the totality—production—is to be optimized, its components of input, process, and output are optimized, as each relates to the totality. Common parlance for this is to suboptimize the components. Step No. 1: Input, or raw materials being received, are suboptimized. This will depend upon forecast demand, inventory carrying cost, and order processing cost. Likewise, Step No. 2: Process, or materials processed, are suboptimized by adequate consideration to production capacity, machine setup cost, and processing cost for each product. Last, Step No. 3: Suboptimization of output or products finished is obtained by considering product demand and transportation cost.

Use of a mathematical model makes the optimizing or minimizing work feasible. A mathematical model is an abstract presentation of symbolic character showing all pertinent factors quantitatively and reflecting the relative influence of each factor upon the entire situation represented and the impact of a change in any one, or group, of the factors upon the remaining factors and upon the total. The mathematical model can be a single equation or a series of equations, depending upon the complexity and number of factors involved.

By inserting numerical values in the mathematical model equations, different outcomes from different values used can be determined. The maximum or minimum result value is found by the use of calculus. Calculus deals with the rate of change of one mathematical variable, called a dependent variable, with another mathematical variable, called an independent variable. The point at which this rate of change is zero represents either an optimization or a minimization in the relationships of the two variables for the following reason. If the rate of change is a positive amount, the relationship is increasing at that point; if negative, the opposite is true. When the change is neither positive nor negative, i.e., is zero, the rate of change has ceased at that point; so it must represent either a optimum or a minimum in the relationship between the dependent variable and the independent variable.

Illustration of optimizing using a mathematical model

A simple illustration will prove helpful. Assume we have created the mathematical model in the form of a single equation:

$$Y = 15X - \tfrac{3}{2}X^2 \tag{1}$$

where Y is gross profits and X is the number of different products handled. This equation says that the gross profits, Y, are equal to 15 times the number of products handled, $15X$, less $\tfrac{3}{2}$ times the number of products handled squared (or multiplied by itself, i.e., X times X equals X^2) making the total expression, $\tfrac{3}{2}X^2$. Gross profits, Y, are dependent upon number of products handled, X, and this relationship is represented by Equation (1) above.

At what number of products, X, will profits, Y, be a maximum? Referring again to our mathematical model

$$Y = 15X - \tfrac{3}{2}X^2 \tag{1}$$

The rate of change of Y with respect to X, expressed as dY/dX, is

$$dY/dX = 15 - 3X \tag{2}$$

Equating this rate of change to zero for optimization, the equation becomes

$$0 = 15 - 3X \tag{3}$$

or

$$X = 5$$

FIGURE 2–5: Some general, helpful rules for determining derivatives as used in calculus

1. The derivative of one variable is equal to its exponent times the variable to the exponent of one less than the initial exponent.

    Example 1: $Y = X^2$
    $dY/dX = 2$ times X^1
    $= 2X$

    Example 2: $Y = X$
    $dY/dX = 1$ times X^0
    $= 1$ (Any variable with the exponent of 0 is equal to 1.)

2. The derivative of a sum of variables is the sum of its derivatives.

    Example 3: $Y = X^4 + X^3 - X^2$
    $dY/dX = 4X^3 + 3X^2 - 2X^1$

3. The derivative of any constant is zero.

    Example 4: $Y = X^2 + 2$
    $dY/dX = 2X^1 + 0$
    $= 2X$

4. The derivative of a variable dependent upon several independent variables is the derivative of the dependent variable to the first independent variable, and the derivative of the dependent variable to the second independent variable, etc., considering, for each derivative, all independent variables as constants except the one being derived.

    Example 5: $Y = 3X^3 + 2R + 4$
    $dY/dX = 9X^2 + 0 = 0$
    $= 9X^2$
    $dX/dR = 0 + 2 + 0$
    $= 2$

In other words, when the number of products, X, equals 5, maximum profits, Y, are realized.

The transition from Equation (1) to Equation (2) above represents the use of calculus. It is not our purpose here to present all the details of calculus, but inclusion of several general rules to aid in understanding are given in Figure 2–5 (p. 31).

In addition to mathematical models used in management, there are also graphs, charts, special formats such as rows and columns of matrix algebra, and physical models. These means are not new in management. They have been used for centuries. But refinements in their use along with mathematical models have given wide usage of the quantitative measurement school.

The follower of this school must define precisely the objectives, problems, and problem areas. In addition, orderly thinking, logical methodology, and recognition of definite constraints are encouraged. There is no doubt that the quantitative measurement school supplies a powerful tool for solving complex problems and has influenced the rearrangement of information sources to provide more meaningful quantitative data. The approach is especially effective when applied to the measurable physical problems of management—such as inventory, material, and production control—rather than to problems where measurement is difficult such as for human behavior. It is important to know what is being measured. The derived alternatives or tentative answers are predetermined and evaluated without actually employing the combination of real factors on a trial-and-error basis. Observe that risk is not eliminated by use of this approach, but assistance is provided to enable the manager to assume the correct risk.

MANAGEMENT PROCESS SCHOOL

Followers of the management process school view management as an activity made up of certain subactivities or basic management functions that constitute a unique process—the management process. This process is considered the essential core of management and is widely viewed as an effective format for study by the beginning student of management. This school provides the framework for the structuring of this book. Hence, it will be discussed here in more detail than the other schools of management.

FUNDAMENTAL FUNCTIONS OF MANAGEMENT

For a manager and a group of employees, one of the important things to be decided or identified is what objectives are to be accomplished. The next step is to accomplish them. This raises the issue of what work needs to be done, when and how it will be done, what the necessary work components should be, the contributions of each such component, and the manner of accomplishing them. In essence, a plan or a predetermined integrated pattern of future activities is drawn up. This requires an ability to foresee, to visualize, to look ahead purposefully. In short, *planning* is necessary. This is a fundamental function of management.

The direction and makeup of future action having been determined, the next step, in order to accomplish the work, is to distribute or allocate the necessary component work activities among the members of the group, and to enlist the help of each member of the group. This work distribution is guided by consideration for such things as the nature of the component activities, the people of the group, and the physical facilities available. These component activities are grouped and assigned so that accomplishment with minimum expenditure or maximum employee work satisfaction is attained, or in accordance with some similar worthwhile endeavor. Should the group be deficient in either number or quality of necessary management members, such members are secured. Each member assigned to a component activity is faced with the situation of his or her relation to the group and that of the member's group to other groups of the enterprise. Typical are the questions of who decides what issues and when? This work of task-allocating and relationship-establishing and relationship-maintaining by the manager is known as *organizing*. It may be thought of as making the plan, created by the manager, meaningful to each member of the group. Organizing is a fundamental function of management.

To carry out physically the activities resulting from the planning and organizing steps, it is necessary for the manager to take measures that will start and continue actions as long as they are needed in order to accomplish the task by the members of the group. The measures selected will depend upon the particular members of the group, the component activity to be done, and the manager's judgment. Among the more common measures utilized by the manager to put the group into action will be leading, developing managers, instructing, helping members to improve themselves and their work through their own creativity, and compensating. This work is referred to as *actuating*. It is a fundamental function of management. The word actuate means literally "move to action," and its use is thus appropriate for this managerial function that deals with either the supplying of stimulative power to the group members or maintaining a work environment within which the members want to perform their best.

Managers have always found it desirable to check up or follow up what is being done in order to make sure that the work of others is progressing satisfactorily toward the predetermined objective. The establishing of a sound plan, the allotting of component activities required by this plan, and the successful actuating of each member do not assure that the undertaking will be a success. Discrepancies, imponderables, misunderstandings, and unexpected hindrances may arise and must be communicated quickly to the manager so that corrective action may be taken. Answers are sought to the questions: How well should the work be done? How well is it being done? This function by the manager constitutes *controlling*. It is a fundamental function of management.

THE PROCESS OF MANAGEMENT

These four fundamental functions of management—planning, organizing, actuating, and controlling—constitute the process of management. They are the means by which a manager manages. They are the distinguishing marks between a manager and a nonmanager. A summary statement of these fundamental functions of management is (1) *planning*, to determine the objectives and the courses of action to be followed, (2) *organizing*, to distribute the work among the group and to establish and recognize needed relationships, (3) *actuating* the members of the group to carry out their prescribed tasks willingly and enthusiastically, and (4) *controlling* the activities to conform with the plans. A graphic representation of the management process is shown by Figure 2–6.

These concepts become more meaningful with the study of Figure 2–7. Here are listed the more important activities for each fundamental

FIGURE 2–6

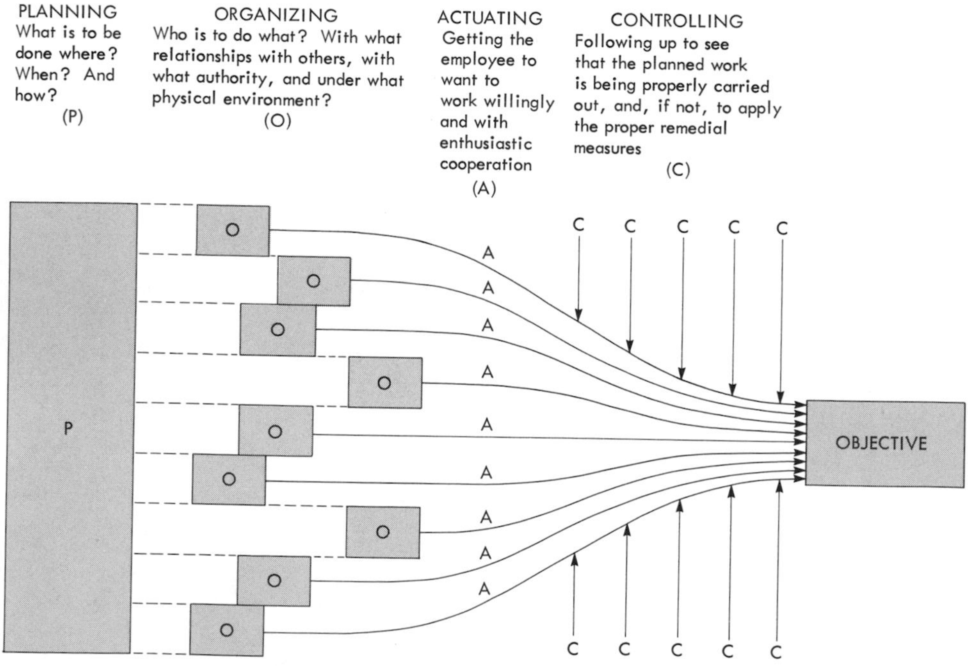

PLANNING
What is to be done where? When? And how?
(P)

ORGANIZING
Who is to do what? With what relationships with others, with what authority, and under what physical environment?
(O)

ACTUATING
Getting the employee to want to work willingly and with enthusiastic cooperation
(A)

CONTROLLING
Following up to see that the planned work is being properly carried out, and, if not, to apply the proper remedial measures
(C)

The vital process of management consists of planning, organizing, actuating, and controlling.

FIGURE 2–7: Important activities of each fundamental function of management

The work of the manager

Planning	Organizing	Actuating	Controlling
1. Clarify, amplify, and determine objectives.	1. Break down work into operative duties.	1. Practice participation by all affected by the decision or act.	1. Compare results with plans in general.
2. Forecast.	2. Group operative duties into operative positions.	2. Lead and challenge others to do their best.	2. Appraise results against performance standards.
3. Establish the conditions and assumptions under which the work will be done.	3. Assemble operative positions into manageable and related units.	3. Motivate members.	3. Devise effective media for measuring operations.
4. Select and state tasks to accomplish objectives.	4. Clarify position requirements.	4. Communicate effectively.	4. Make known the measuring media.
5. Establish an overall plan of accomplishment, emphasizing creativity to find new and better means for accomplishing the work.	5. Select and place individual on proper job.	5. Develop members to realize full potentials.	5. Transfer detailed data into form showing comparisons and variances.
6. Establish policies, procedures, standards, and methods of accomplishment.	6. Utilize and agree upon proper authority for each management member.	6. Reward by recognition and pay for work well done.	6. Suggest corrective actions, if needed.
7. Anticipate possible future problems.	7. Provide personnel facilities and other resources.	7. Satisfy needs of employees through their work efforts.	7. Inform responsible members of interpretations.
8. Modify plans in light of control results.	8. Adjust the organization in light of control results.	8. Revise actuation efforts in light of control results.	8. Adjust controlling in light of control results.

function of management. Some of the terms shown in this figure have not yet been defined in this book, but the illustration is included here because it shows effectively an overall and inclusive view of management. The terms are completely discussed in the following chapters.

For convenience, we now repeat the definition of management using the process of management approach just described as first stated in the beginning of Chapter 1: *Management is a distinct process consisting of planning, organizing, actuating, and controlling, performed to determine and accomplish stated objectives by the use of human beings and other resources.*

INTERRELATIONSHIP AMONG FUNCTIONS

In actual practice, these four fundamental functions of management are inextricably interwoven and interrelated; the performance of one function does not cease entirely before the next is started. And they normally are not carried out in a particular sequence but as the situation being considered seems to require. In establishing a new enterprise, the order of the functions probably will be as outlined in this discussion, but for a going concern a manager may perform, for example, controlling at a given time and follow this by actuating, then by planning.

The sequence should be suited to the specific objective. Typically, a manager is involved with many goals, and may be at different stages in the process with each one. To the nonmanager this may give the impression of inefficiency or a lack of order, whereas actually the manager may be acting quite purposefully and forcefully. In the long run, greater emphasis is usually placed on certain functions than on others, depending upon the individual situation. Also, it should be noted that some functions must be performed before others can be put into action. Effective actuating, for example, requires that persons either have been assigned activities or have determined their own in keeping with overall plans and objectives. Likewise, controlling cannot be exercised in a vacuum; there must be something to control.

As a matter of fact, there is planning involved in the work of organizing, of actuating, and of controlling. Likewise, the elements of organizing are employed in effective planning, actuating, and controlling. Each fundamental function of management affects the others, and they are all intimately interrelated to form the management process.

UNIVERSALITY OF THE MANAGEMENT PROCESS

The management process has universal application; this is significant. It means that the fundamental functions of planning, organizing, actuating, and controlling are basic and are performed by the manager, regardless of the type of enterprise, the major activity, or the level at which the manager works. The management process represents the common fabric of similarity among managers and serves to expedite the study of management. It is universally found whereever people work together to achieve common objectives. It is, for example, used successfully by the executive in the United States, the business leader in Japan, the government official in Turkey, and the military officer in France. To be sure, familiarity with the background, technology, and environment of the new enterprise probably helps the new manager to arrive at more effective decisions than otherwise might be made.[1] However, the important observation is that what a manager does— planning, organizing, actuating, and controlling—is basic and consists of the same type of activities no matter what is managed. To illustrate, a successful manager of an electronics manufacturing company switched to a company constructing houses and enjoyed outstanding success. Many managers in industry are called to serve in government posts, and it is worth noting that they are called, not because of their intimate knowledge of government, but because they can apply effectively the fundamental management functions. And the same is true for management members in the educational field going into business enterprises and public utility managers leaving their chosen field and admirably serving charitable enterprises.

Erroneously, and all too frequently, management is thought of as existing only in the top-managerial level and not in all levels down to the supervisory level of management. The fact is however, that when acting in their respective managerial capacities, not only the company president but also the office supervisor perform the fundamental functions of management. The difference lies in such things as the breadth of the objectives, the actions which comprise the plans, the magnitude of the decisions made, the organization relationships affected, and the amount of leadership required.

ADDITIONAL CONSIDERATIONS OF THE MANAGEMENT PROCESS

It is possible to extend the number of functions making up the management process beyond these four. The additions are many, and over a period, suggestions to add any of the following have been made:

---

[1] Under technology it is helpful to distinguish between technical background and technical skill. The former means possession of a general understanding or of training in the use of technology. It is helpful to the manager operating in a technical area. The latter, or technical skill, normally implies proficiency in operative work of a technical nature and usually is not a requirement of a manager.

advocating, authorizing, changing, choosing, confirming, coordinating, counseling, directing, evaluating, improving, integrating, leading, measuring, modernizing, motivating, recommending, representing, specifying, and staffing. A manager does these, but the addition of any of these terms seems unnecessary and undesirable. Of course, any or all of these could be added, but such action would make the process approach somewhat unwieldly and difficult to handle. Also, some of the suggested additions are simply different terms for the four designated as making up the process. For example, measuring in the sense of measuring results is similar to controlling. The stated four functions adequately identify the management process and limit discussion of the management process to an acceptable length. The outstanding advantages offered by the management process school are given in Figure 2–8.

FIGURE 2–8:   Advantages of using the management process school

1. *An inclusive, easy-to-understand, conceptual framework of management is offered.* This school fosters the idea that management is a distinct activity that can be identified, taught, and practiced.

2. *A foundation for the study of management is provided.* It supplies helpful guidance for management education, development, and progress. It promotes understanding of what management really is.

3. *Contributions by other schools of management are feasible.* A simple and convenient framework is provided to which the best contributions of other schools can be added so that the best contemporary thought concerning the particular managerial activity can be employed.

4. *Flexibility is provided, innovation and progress are encouraged.* While constant and rigorous, it is neither too broad nor too precise. Applicable to a variety of situations, its user is given the needed leeway to suit a particular set of circumstances.

5. *The knowledge and the art of management are recognized.* How best to utilize them in a practical situation is encouraged.

6. *Genuine assistance to practitioners of management is supplied.* The process pattern enables a manager to ferret out and to understand the problem. Is it primarily one of planning, organizing, actuating, or controlling? Or is it a combination of several or all of these? The straight-forward and practical approach helps the manager put his or her knowledge and skill to use and determine objectives and the means to their attainment.

7. *Management principles are derived, refined, and used.* These principles serve as needed bench marks for useful management research, give increased meaning to management, and assist in management application.

8. *The development of a purposeful philosophy of management is encouraged and expedited.* The process school is not mechanistic. Each phase of its application requires drawing from the manager's values, beliefs, and understanding of the goals, resources, and environments with which she or he is working.

Modified management process school

Since the activities of a manager—planning, organizing, actuating, and controlling—are basic, the process school provides an excellent framework not only for the study of management using this fundamental approach, but also from the viewpoint of utilizing valuable contributions offered by the other schools of management. The recommendation here is to follow such an approach which can be termed *the eclectic-process school of management,* featuring the basic framework of the process approach modified by certain theories from other appropriate schools of management thought. Eclectic means "consisting of what is selected" and this term has been interpreted to indicate taking the best from what is available in management thought and working it into a single theory molded around the process framework as the central core.

FIGURE 2–9: Modified management process school

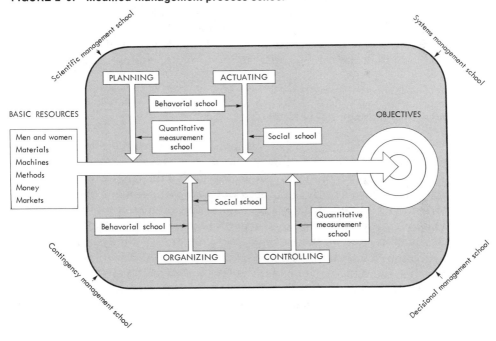

Figure 2–9 shows a graphical interpretation of this modified process approach. The basic resources consisting of the six *M*'s are subjected to the four fundamental functions of management in order to achieve the objective. Contributing to planning efforts is the quantitative measurement school which offers for some situations excellent techniques,

such as precision forecasting and revealing possible outcomes for different tentative plans. Likewise, both organizing and actuating efforts utilize outstanding and pertinent contributions of the behavior school and the social school as indicated in the sketch. Further, controlling is improved by modifications of the quantitative measurement school which add desirable precision and accuracy to these efforts. In addition, the entire process is affected by the scientific systems, decisional, and contingency management schools.[2]

The modified management process school is probably the most effective and inclusive thought pattern of management yet devised. It is believed that this modified process school extracts the best of current management thinking and synthesizes it into an effective unity. Furthermore, following the modified approach means that this book is not simply a process management book or a principles book, but a composite of the best of current basic management thinking brought together in a single volume, which is believed most appropriate for the beginning study of management. Minimized are the chances of the management scholar getting trapped within one set of assumptions or another, and thus needlessly constraining the scholar's whole management outlook. In the final analysis, the ultimate criterion is the degree to which the school assists in attaining the stated management goal.

Contingency management school

One of the relatively recent schools to emerge is the contingency management school. Its followers emphasize the relevancy of managerial actions to the particular characteristics of the situation in which the actions take place. It is pointed out that management must fit its environment. Whatever the managerial action such as communicating or leading, it is conditioned by the particular variables or factors of the total situation, that is, the various characteristics of the manager and the situation in which the managerial work is carried out. In practice, it means that the effective manager shapes the actions taken to fit in with or conform to the total given situation. Recognition is given to the complexity of modern management—seldom will one way of communicating or one way of leading give equal results in every situation. By its very nature, success in the art of management depends on actions taken in a probabilistic environmental situation.

Knowledge of a relationship between A and B is insufficient. Also required is knowledge of the conditions under which this relationship is valid. What brings about what under what conditions are the important considerations. Sought is the relationship between a certain man-

---

[2] Discussion of contingency management school immediately follows.

agerial action taken and the specific environmental factors under which that action is taken. The basic premise is that a managerial action is valid only under certain conditions.

The word *contingent* means conditioned or liable but not certain to occur. In contingency management it means the conditions or environment within which the management is taking place. The term is common in the military which has contingent plans drawn up for various assumed conditions that may take place. Illustrative is that under certain of these conditions, such and such a plan will be followed, if different conditions exist, then a different plan will be used.

The idea of taking into account the variables of the environment affecting management is not new. This concept has been stressed in what is referred to as "situational management," and in a paper published in 1919, Mary Parker Follett used the phrase, "law of the situation" to express the same general idea.[3] Actually, most practicing managers consider the individual situation in carrying out their managerial duties, but perhaps neglect some situational factors. As more knowledge is gained as to which factors should be taken into account in what situations, the caliber of management will improve and the manager will be able to manage with more certainty than at present. With increasing knowledge about the various psychological, sociological, and technical circumstances of various situations, the contingency school will offer much to our theory and practice of management.

Some believe that the development of the contingency approach with its situational emphasis and integration of environment into management theory and practice will encourage a manager to use the various schools of management in his or her work. In other words, the greater consideration for the environmental and situational aspects of a given problem will suggest the greater use of the different schools of management in solving that problem. The result will be an eclectic format which utilizes the most useful contributions of the various schools. This leads to the use of the modified management process approach recommended above—an approach that utilizes the popular and familiar process format as well as pertinent contributions of various management schools, thus providing an inclusive, modern, and practical approach to management study and practice.

---

[3] See for example, Mary Parker Follett, "Community Is a Process," New York: *Philosophical Review*, vol. 28, November 1919, pp. 576–88; Henry C. Metcalf and L. Urwick, *Dynamic Administration: The Collected Papers of Mary Parker Follett* (New York: Harper and Brothers, 1940), pp. 27–8; John K. Hemphill, *Situational Factors in Leadership* (Columbus: The Ohio State University, 1949); Harlow H. Curtice, *The Development and Growth of General Motors*, Statement before the Subcommittee on Antitrust and Monopoly on the U.S. Senate Committee on the Judiciary, December 1955, p. 13; *Staff Officers' Field Manual FM 101-5*, War Department (U.S. Government Printing Office, 1960), p. 142: Elliot M. Fox, *Mary Parker Follett: The Enduring Contribution*, Washington D.C.: American Society for Public Administration, *Public Administration Review*, vol. 28 No. 6, November–December 1968, pp. 17–26.

QUESTIONS

1. As an advocate of the behavior school of management, how would you justify your favoring this approach?

2. Identify each of the following fully: (a) optimization, (b) scientific management, (c) mathematical model, and (d) hypothesis of scientific method.

3. Discuss briefly the two characteristics that feature the quantitative measurement school.

4. Do you feel that Taylor's question, "What constitutes an honest day's work?" is valid today? Why?

5. George Munson, now 52 years of age, has followed custom management in his job as production manager for a long time. He states that he is not against any of the other and more recent approaches but clings to custom management because he is achieving his objectives very satisfactorily by its use. Do you feel that George Munson should change to any other school of management? Why?

6. Assume you have just been appointed general manager of a motel. How would you apply systems management to your new job? Repeat the question using scientific management.

7. A follower of the process school of management states that its most outstanding advantages are: (a) an effective and practical framework for management study is provided, (b) flexibility is offered, and (c) the art of management is recognized and promoted. Do you feel these are advantages and, if so, are they outstanding? Substantiate your answer.

8. Dolores Duncan believes that two additional functions, improving and representing, should be added to the four fundamental functions stated in this chapter. What is your reaction to her suggestion? Justify your answer.

9. Comment fully on each of the following definitions of management, stating for each one whether you agree or disagree, and why: (a) management is the balancing of what workers want with what is best for the company; (b) management is a process used by managers to coordinate activities, influence the direction of efforts by others, and achieve their goals by getting things done through others; (c) management is the planning, direction, control, and development of activities and more importantly, people; (d) management is leadership—it is the organization, motivation, and control of a group of individuals to accomplish certain tasks; (e) management consists of decision makers who guide an organization to its objectives.

10. What is the modified management process approach to management?

11. The process of management is cited to supply excellent assistance in finding and understanding the problem to be solved. In your opinion would the behavior school and the quantitative measurement school be equally effective in this respect? Why?

12. Based on your personal experience and reading, do you feel that any one of the fundamental functions of management is of greatest importance? Elaborate on your answer.

13. Refer to Figure 2–9 and, in your own words, explain the meaning of this illustration.
14. Visit the manager of a well-known enterprise located near your home. Find out what school of management this manager follows and the reasons for doing so. What conclusions do you draw from your interview?

CASE 2–1. PROFESSORS TRIER AND ADAIR

Professor Trier: With all the developing new approaches to management, you must agree that change and adjustment have been outstanding characteristics of modern management.

Professor Adair: Well, I'd say yes and no.

Trier: What do you mean, yes and no?

Adair: Change takes place, yes. But management tends to deceive itself during periods of change.

Trier: Really?

Adair: For example, many managers rely on myths such as saying they welcome change, whereas actually managers do not. Managers resist change as much as anybody else; they are simply more clever at not revealing any change in their work behavior.

Trier: If that's so, how do you account for all the different management theories?

Adair: There are a few, of course, relatively very few, who pioneer and stick their heads out, but not many. Most keep plodding along, doing what they have always done, staying with the tried and true.

Trier: But they are always looking for new ideas. It is one of their big problems.

Adair: No, you're wrong. That is one of the myths I was referring to. Typically, management has more ideas than it can put into effect. Everywhere I go I'm told the challenge or the problem is to implement the ideas they already have. The big deal is to make something work, to put it to use. They've got the idea.

Additional phonies are that we are good at change, we thrive on it, that is, managers do. Competition forces change. Also, the bit about guaranteeing a job with good wages assures acceptance of change just isn't true.

Trier: I always have thought so. I remember when . . .

Adair: No, not at all. A person wants more than pay from a job today. Employees want recognition, status, and influence. They resent changes disturbing their established routines.

Trier: Yes, that's probably right. But they want pay too.

Adair: I . . . a . . . a . . . I don't believe it is the main consideration.

Questions

1. With whom are you inclined to agree, Professor Trier or Professor Adair? Discuss. Justify your answer.

2. As you see it, what are the major reasons for the number of approaches used in management?

3. Do you feel the spawning of management approaches will continue or decline in the future? Justify your viewpoint.

CASE 2–2. LAHODY COMPANY

Six weeks ago, Joseph West was transferred from the company's New York plant to its Cleveland plant and promoted to Administrative Assistant to the General Manager. Top officials were not pleased with the Cleveland operation, which is one of the company's three plants manufacturing small components and assemblies for vending machines. Since his arrival at the Cleveland plant, Mr. West has busied himself studying various reports on the Cleveland operation, interviewed many management and nonmanagement members of the plant, and observed a number of operators.

From the information collected, he has formulated the following:

1. Management team. Not much enthusiasm and little will to achieve. Heads of receiving, stamping, quality control, packaging, shipping, accounting, engineering, purchasing, and personnel seem satisfactory, but not outstanding. They follow authoritative management for the most part, yet are reluctant to exercise authority. Plant is loosely run. All department heads state they feel the general manager, Mr. Gene Royce is all right, but none believe he is outstanding in his work performance.

2. Cost trend. Upward for the past four years. Prior to this, costs, although not given much attention, seemed in general to be in line. There is no cost control department. Some talk of this, but Mr. Royce said it is being delayed pending decision on having some quantitative management people come to the plant and work out a purchasing-inventory control and a material allocation setup. I was not informed about this when leaving New York. Materials management now leaves much to be desired. Plant runs out of raw stock, and inventory on certain popular items appears very low.

3. Machines and equipment. Some very old machines are in use, but appear to be trouble free up to now. No complaints from employees about them. Have no data on newer machine productivity compared to what we are accomplishing.

4. Supervisors and staff members. All but 2 of the 11 total supervisors came up from the ranks. They know the technical aspects of the work. Impression gained is that they are mediocre in performance, are reluctant to discuss any supervisory problem they have. Seem to have a fear that they might lose their jobs. Staff members talk as though they know what they are doing. So far haven't been able to get any information on their competency. They send few reports to Mr. Royce's office.

5. Personnel.   Mixed ethnically and about 20 percent of work force from minority groups. Turnover is high in certain departments. Of the total 264 employees on payroll, one fourth, or 66 employees have been with the company less than one year. Personnel appears to keep busy most of the day—little loafing on the job.

6. Overall coordination.   I get the feeling that the plant is operating as a number of separate departments, each going its own independent way. Little consideration is given to the fact that production hang-ups, for example in spot welding, can seriously affect assembly, or delays in receiving interrupt the stamping department's output. Looks like something is needed to pull the plant together. Systems approach, maybe?

7. Productivity.   Appears low. Some work standards have been the same for the past ten years. Current production level is 91.6 percent of what is expected, but no strong effort to raise it to required 100 percent is in evidence.

8. Community relations.   Company rated neutral as a place to work. Little participation in civic affairs by the company. Mr. Royce supports the corporate citizen idea but feels getting his management team members active in civic affairs is "pretty much a waste of time."

Questions

1. What is the problem faced by Lahody Company?
2. What contribution do you feel the systems management school and the quantitative measurement school can make to the company? Discuss.
3. Based on information compiled by Joseph West, what recommended plan of action should be made? Why?
4. What major difficulties do you envision in putting your recommended action into use? Discuss.

Chapter 3

Management philosophy, values, and contemporary environment

*Great Spirit, grant that I may not criticize my neighbor until
I have walked a mile in his moccasins.*

Old Indian prayer

Managers as well as nonmanagers today differ from those of pre-ceeding generations in life style, values, and environment. Currently, people have a broader education, are better informed, are more so-cially aware, and expect more from their work efforts. Likewise, values of people have undergone significant changes during the last several decades. The present patterns of beliefs that people hold on important aspects of life—about work, pay, profits, loyalty, and government are modifying management and its implementation. Further, the growth of government, the generation of tremendous amounts of knowledge, and the development of almost unbelievable technology, are exerting strong pressures on the environment in which people work and espe-cially on how managers manage.

Actually the diversity and the newness of these developments are so great that they are literally rocking our society. The challenge and the need are to recognize them in our managerial efforts in order that the attainment for a better and more equitable way of life in the future is a realistic possibility. To discuss satisfactorily these new patterns of thought affecting management brings up the subject of the philosophy of management and its subsequent values as well as the environment in which present-day management operates.

PHILOSOPHY OF MANAGEMENT

A philosophy of management can be viewed as a way of management thinking. It consists of the attitudes, beliefs, and concepts of an individual or a group about management. No one can manage without having a philosophy of management either implied or implicit. A person cannot manage without some basic concepts that are believed and to which reference can be made and used. In other words, a manager cannot operate in a vacuum. There is some system of thought that prevails in a person's management efforts. A manager is required to exercise thinking, make decisions, and take actions. As a result, the manager builds a pattern of judgments, measures, tests, and uses criteria which reveal true motives, the real objectives sought, the psychological and social relations deemed appropriate, and the general economic atmosphere that is preferred. To ignore management philosophy is to deny that character, emotions, and values are related to a manager's ideas, and that a person's mental and physical processes influence managerial behavior.

USE OF MANAGEMENT PHILOSOPHY

Three major advantages accrue to a manager in having and using a philosophy of management. First, *it helps win effective support and followers.* People know what a manager stands for and what overall actions that manager is most likely to take. They know why the manager acts a certain way, and they have confidence in what is being done. Second, *it provides bench marks and a foundation for managerial thinking.* Where scientific and social conditions are changing rapidly, the importance of a body of basic knowledge and beliefs constituting a philosophy is apparent. New management challenges to which there are no tailor-made solutions must be met. Here a management philosophy is especially useful. Third, *it supplies a framework within which a manager can commence thinking.* Normally this will not only orient but will also stimulate the thinking process to effective and satisfactory solutions.

Over the decades, various philosophies of management have developed, flourished, and given way to new philosophies or have been modified by the contemporary thought of a particular era. No exhaustive treatment of these philosophies will be attempted here, but several will be mentioned in order to indicate briefly the nature of their respective makeups.

Some managers give considerable weight to the importance of the individual—trust each employee by employing minimum rules and controls, make certain the work for each person is not only meaningful but also rewarding, and fix responsibility with each employee. Other managers modify this by emphasizing rugged individualism. Immense self-reliance, sanctity of decision unity, and outstanding personal abilities appear necessary for this particular philosophy to be used. The strong-willed and powerful industrialists at the turn and beginning of the 20th century are examples of advocates of this particular philosophy. More specifically, Henry Ford and his gospel of production may be cited.

During recent years, however, management followers giving emphasis to the group have increased tremendously. Here a fundamental belief is to consider the group in all managerial decisions and actions. This has resulted in such activities as planning by groups, decision making by groups, extensive use of committees, and consideration for a mutuality of interests between management and nonmanagement members. Likewise, social constraints, behavior, and influence have been given greater recognition.

Further, the influence of technological and environmental changes—especially fuller utilization of the computer, automatic devices, government climate, and the U.S. historical perspective in which management concepts have developed, are other important ingredients that have helped shape other systems of thought for accomplishing desired results and resolving problems. As both these ingredients change as well as our viewpoints toward them, certain philosophies flourish while others shrivel. The entire setting and background is one of dynamics.

SIGNIFICANT CHANGES IN MANAGEMENT PHILOSOPHY

It will be helpful to include what was a prevailing philosophy until about 1965, and contrast it with what is now developing. The former approach can be characterized as being based on command systems. The modus operandi of the manager was the power-over-people position. The manager "ran the whole show." Who decides what issues and enforces the decision was viewed as a key consideration. The total concept was activities-oriented—stress was given to what was done. The manager prescribed the organization structure, set the tasks of the nonmanagement people, delegated decision making power, determined the best way to perform the work, and exercised tight controls. These concepts are depicted by the top illustration of Figure 3–1.

In contrast, the emerging management philosophy is much broader than that of its predecessor and is more relevant to the present day cultural understanding and the changing environment as well as to the current technological changes and opportunities. Emphasis upon the decision making power of the manager is being reduced and the emerging philosophy is oriented around the *results desired.* In other words, *results-oriented,* not activities-oriented is the coming theme. See bottom illustration of Figure 3–1.

Management is viewed as a resource providing power through people's participation. By utilizing the full resources of its people, an enterprise shapes its future and its destiny. Goal setting and creativity

FIGURE 3–1:   (Top) Prevailing management philosophy during the middle portion of the 20th century; (Bottom) New emerging management philosophy during last portion of the 20th century

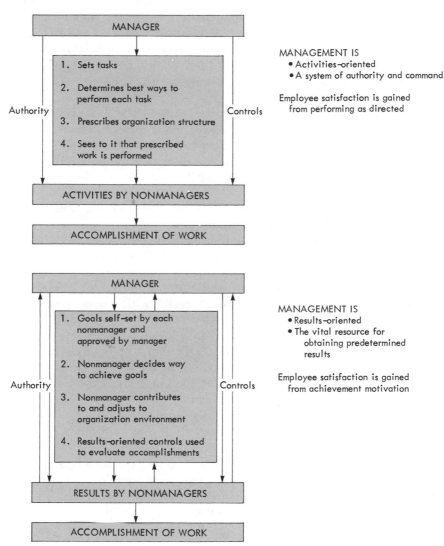

and assistance to achieve that goal are given much attention. The decision-making right stems from the objective; personnel work for objectives—not simply to achieve certain activities; managers develop self-commitment and self-direction for results; personnel have a part in determining the methods of work; and control is evaluated by results rather than by activities.[1]

It should be observed that a given enterprise is neither wholly activities oriented nor wholly results oriented, but the enterprise tends to be predominantly one or the other. What determines the characteristic is the type of managers and employees. For example, if there is a lack of self-commitment and self-direction for results among employees, this must be corrected if success is to be experienced with a results-oriented theme. On the other hand, if these personal characteristics exist among the managers and the members, the results-oriented approach should be used; i.e., results are highlighted and management as a resource for helping to achieve results is emphasized.

Another change worth noting is the shift to the managerial goal sought and a softening of the means of management. That is, more emphasis is being placed on what and why, and less on how and when. More and more the overall managerial evaluation is in terms of whether the goals sought are worthwhile, and less on the means of achieving them.

This view follows not only because pushing back the horizons of knowledge used in management entails concepts of reasons why, relative worth, and the human being and the better life, but also because the present know-how of management is at such a peak that we have the means to solve almost any problem we make up our minds to solve. Modern management has tremendous ability to accomplish stated goals including having a human walk on the moon. Many experts say that with the support of science and technology, managers today have the knowledge and ability to achieve virtually any desired result. Some feel we have a surplus of management means. The challenge is to use these means for worthwhile endeavors. Specifically, what goals should managers seek and are these goals the ones most desired when they are achieved? Answers to such questions are highly influenced by the philosophy of management followed.

Additional illustrations of changes bringing about shifts in management philosophy can be cited. Since about 1950 the general belief has grown that managers should learn to reject outmoded traditions and past practices and not simply ignore them as used to be considered the proper viewpoint to take. Or consider that in the past, training and developing the individual was a primary managerial goal. Now the

---

[1] Results management is discussed fully in Chapter 4, pp. 68–73.

goal is considered to be that of developing the organization, its culture and environment, and to provide the necessary tools for human effectiveness within the sound organizational culture created. And not too many years ago the purpose of human development was to gain harmony with mutual good feelings. Now it is strongly flavored with using and resolving conflict among employees to enhance problem solving.

VALUE AND VALUE SYSTEMS

A value entails some evaluation of moral or social good expressed as a concept not merely of the desired, but also of the desirable. It is commonly thought of as a "concept of the desirable," which has many connotations. For purposes here, we can say that the value of a manager is the relative esteem, estimated worth, or excellence attributed to a belief or a preference. Values are assimilated to the extent that they appear to satisfy our needs. We learn them from personal interaction of various groups in which we are a part, such as the home, the school, the church, and the place of work. Values are not only important to managerial life but also to private life.

Values stem from personal choice based on beliefs, opinions, prejudices, and standards. They are dynamic; people seek values, test them, and change them. However, the process is slow, for it is a human tendency to repeat and continue ways of life as long as it is possible to do so. It has been stated many times that values are tested by every generation. By critically analyzing our values and value positions, we deepen our understanding of situations and our own reactions and behaviors. Examining one's values is one of the best ways to keep mentally alive, alert, and flexible.

By way of explanation, let us state that culture can be viewed as a way of life. In the broad sense, culture refers to learned behavior or predominant patterns of life. In the more concentrated sense, culture can be thought of as a system of values and sanctions of society. Culture determines what is desirable and defines what is possible by means of its institutions. An institution is an establishment of public character affecting a community, i.e., marriage is an institution, competition is an institution in some economies. Both culture and institutions can and do vary among people, communities, and nations. Actually an institution serves as a cultural unit by means of which influence is applied upon an individual or, of special interest here, upon a manager. An institution serves as an equilibrating mechanism between the value structure and the environment. It is both a determining and a determined medium and as such, merits consideration in managerial activities.

Values are the basis for a management philosophy. That is, the acceptance of various different values by a manager helps formulate that person's management philosophy. Values reveal what is really important to a manager, what is truly personally meaningful, and what will temper the managerial thrusts taken.

Values and management

What a manager believes in and stands for is the result of what is acquired in the course of that person's development, what is reflected by the influence, the mores, and the values of the culture of which that person is a part. A manager may, for example, believe strongly in the Protestant ethic, which can be summarized as the bourgeois virtues of hard work, perseverance, frugality, pride of workmanship, obedience to constituted authority, and loyalty to employer. These concepts represent strong basic values. An elaboration of the basic beliefs of the work ethic is shown by Figure 3–2.

FIGURE 3–2: Basics of the work ethic

> 1. Almost all members of society must work in order for society to survive.
> 2. Work behavior is learned from work experience in the home, school, and community, plus the individual's evaluation of these experiences.
> 3. Work enables a person to support his or her style of life and to meet successfully psychological and emotional needs.
> 4. Adequate and proper work values help in adjusting to rapid changes within our institutions.
> 5. The role of work in our lives is as important and valid today as it has been during the past.

In marked contrast, some people, including managers, believe in the Mediterranean ethic, which in essence states that a human being should expend only enough energy to earn what is needed to enjoy the good life and such worldly pleasures as may be personally appealing. Proponents of this philosophy point out that applauding the work ethic was never anything more than a literary fashion. The plain truth is that people work because they have to work; if they could afford not to work, they would not. Evidence of this, so claim the proponents, was demonstrated in the 1960s when many, especially the young, could afford not to work or could work poorly and get terminated, because finding another job was easy.

Figure 3–3 lists two columns of values headed A and B. They represent extreme opposits in values or bipolar values. For example, a certain manager's values may be best represented by those listed in column A, another by those listed in column B. Many managers would be classified as intermediary to *A* and *B*. To characterize by a particular set of values is to generalize and such characterization would neither apply uniformly to all cultures nor to the institutions within any culture. Rather the evaluation should be considered as representative of somewhat enduring regularities in feelings and values. There appears to be, however, for the typical person, an increasing heterogeneity of values.

FIGURE 3–3:   Example of bipolar values

Column A	Column B
1. Conservative, traditional, against innovation.	1. Liberal, progressive, revolutionary.
2. Repression and restraint.	2. Spontaneity and exhibition stressed.
3. Law and justice emphasized.	3. Mercy and compassion stressed.
4. Emphasis on duty, discipline, conscience.	4. Emphasis on zest for life, not guilt stressed.
5. Sacrifice, fear of pleasure.	5. Leisure welcomed.
6. Distrust of research and inquiry.	6. Encourage creativity and inquiry.
7. Build, produce, save.	7. Enjoy, appreciate, consume.
8. Competition stressed.	8. Cooperation stressed.
9. Sex differences maximized, especially in dress.	9. Sex differences minimized, especially in dress.
10. Rational, abstract, cause and effect relationships.	10. Emotion, intuition, and instinct.

With further reference to Figure 3–3, the current trend of American management and society is toward values of column *B*. Since the Great Depression days of the early thirties, column *B* has been increasingly more popular. We can see this in everyday events. Historically the trend can be substantiated by evidence of the "great society," Medicare, increasing fringe benefits, civil rights, antipoverty, and equal opportunity legislation.

Additional examples of values concern the effect of increasing corporate size, the responsibility of an American manager in a foreign country, and the relationship between government and business. Specifically with expansion, mergers, and acquisitions taking place, are some business enterprises becoming so large and powerful that there is no effective control over their activities? What social values are in order regarding this concentration of power? Regarding the American manager in a foreign country, what should be the relationship of profit to national interests? What should the manager do in terms of what values? Furthermore, what values are pertinent in the relationship between government and business? What role, if any, should government play? In brief, what values should be used?

The work place and values

Managers require not only understanding and accepting themselves, but also understanding and accepting others. In these respects, values are the key. Whether a managerial desire or action will be effective is conditioned by the value system of the persons involved. For example, what happens if a management member believing strongly in job security and well-defined rules is managing a person whose values give top priority to free wheeling and a constant searching for new opportunities? Will an employee with strong sociocentric values gain maximum satisfaction under a results oriented type of management? Is the communication style being used in keeping with employees' values? Or do we need different styles or possibly a multi-value communication so that managers do not find themselves talking to and about themselves instead of really getting through and reaching employees.

Value patterns for managing

From what has been stated, it follows that value systems are complex. What is vital to one manager may be given little consideration by another manager. The accomplishments of most enterprises stem ultimately from the different values which the various management personnel bring to the enterprise. Usually several values must be accepted simultaneously, and this may cause conflict. To avoid such conflict, a manager usually recognizes a scale, or rank, of values. That is, of all the values, a person will choose one as dominant, with all other values subordinate. Self-interest, for example, may be viewed above all others, and sacrifice of respect for excellence or of efficiency would be made in order to satisfy the self-interest value.

Much of our present difficulties in managing the human resource is a direct result of rapidly changing values, especially those expressed by younger employees and members of minority groups. The need is for the manager to see exactly what value lies beneath the traditional way of doing things. Some present managerial tools used are not inclusive of values. To illustrate, in the typical employment application form and interview there is little concern for the value system of the applicant. And in current job evaluation efforts (determining the relative ratings and salary ranges) there is almost a total lack of the job's requirements in terms of what human values are best suited for the particular job.

There is today a goodly number of people who want to come and go as they desire, to decide for themselves, to say exactly what they think, to do unconventional things, and to criticize persons in positions of authority. They tend to dislike and cannot or do not adapt to a structured, disciplined life. However, these people are a part of society, a part of the human resources affecting and being affected by management. The challenge is to understand their behavior, to obtain their contributions to desirable mutual goals, and to help in bringing about satisfaction of their needs.

In any employee population, there exists a number of different value systems. Various research studies have identified these systems.[2] The important point here for management is that the means for accomplishing goals should be adapted to the value systems of the employees performing the work. In Figure 3–4, the manager, in order

FIGURE 3–4

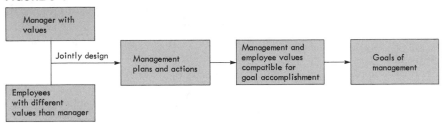

Values of both manager and employees should be considered in formulating plans and actions for goal accomplishment.

to accomplish the desired goal, develops plans and actions jointly with employees who have different values than the manager. The resultant manager-group conditioned plans and actions are then implemented to accomplish the goal.

At one time in management history, conformity to a prescribed set of values was expected (meaning the manager's), but this can no longer be expected. Further, the successful manager today avoids the error of presupposing that all persons of a work group have values close to those the manager holds. If the values do coincide, it is quite by accident. Likewise, distortion concerning value usage comes about by believing all people have uniquely different values from those of the manager, such as believing all young people are not dependable, all Chicanos cannot be trusted, and all females are not career-minded. Such beliefs, of course, simply are not true.

---

[2] See V. Flowers, C. Hughes, M. Scott, and S. Scott, "Managerial Values for Working" (New York: American Management Association, 1975). This is an excellent discussion of values and management. In this source, seven major types of people are identified according to their values as revealed by their predominant characteristics.

CONTEMPORARY ENVIRONMENT OF MANAGEMENT

What is outside an organism—neither governing it directly nor governed by it directly—is technically known as environment. In management there is environment surrounding and affecting the individual worker's efforts. Likewise, there is environment surrounding an enterprise. That is, management is not performed solely as an internal activity within an enterprise. External factors, making up the external environment in which the enterprise operates, must also be taken into account in the practice of management. A manager of a Chicago electronics plant transferred to another plant may initially be less efficient. The manager has not changed, but the environment has. Or suppose the manager transferred to a government executive job. Again the manager remains the same, but the environment within which the manager operates has changed.

The crucial external factors which directly influence the internal management of an enterprise are many. In this discussion we will include five such factors, generally believed most important. They are (1) social, (2) governmental, (3) economical, (4) technological, and (5) educational. The setting of these factors in relation to the total framework of attaining results is shown by Figure 3–5. Beginning at

FIGURE 3–5:   The management process in its total framework of attaining results

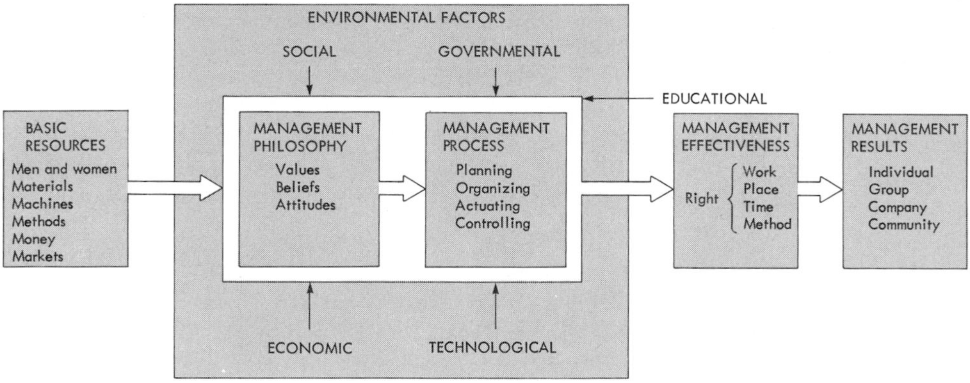

the left, a manager draws upon the basic resources and subjects them first to the management philosophy followed and then to the management process. However, both the manager's philosophy and the application of the management process are infected by environmental factors which condition, constrain, and influence managerial decisions and actions. This leads to management effectiveness of attaining the right work, at the right place, at the right time, and with the right method. From this, management results bringing benefits and satisfactions to the individual, group, company, and community, are obtained.

The environmental factors included here are complex and to comprehend them thoroughly requires much study. However, our interest here is confined to that portion of the factor that influences management effectiveness directly. This simplifies our task and helps to gain some practical insight into the environmental effect upon management. Each of the five factors will now be discussed.

Social environment considerations

We are witnessing more and more concern for social environmental questions, especially those dealing with the social responsibility of management. In business, for example, we have gone from a profit-maximizing phase to an equitable-balancing phase—a fair shake for everyone, to the present phase of quality of life social responsibility. Most people agree that economic abundance with declining physical and social environment does not make sense.

The issues are clear and familiar. Putting a stop to the poisoning of our environment and squandering of natural resources, implementing the betterment of cultures, and improving race relationships rank high on the list of social desires. Business must have more direct concern for that part of society which exists beyond its plant doors. The social environment of management is changing because the expectations of society are changing. No management can be effective if it differs significantly from the beliefs and processes in which it is operating.

The social problems are so great that, left unsolved, they will bring down the entire structure of business and of society as we know them today. Pockets of poverty, defacement of landscape, employee safety at work, product reliability, and health care availability rank high on the list of social ills that require solutions and that challenge modern management. Many people are turning to managers, especially business managers, to help solve these social ills because these managers have the technical know-how, the skill, and the power to solve them. The need is to cultivate and interact with dynamic self-generative interdisciplinary programs with relevance to problems of tomorrow.

Whether motivated by intelligent self-interest or humanitarian beliefs, the vast majority of business managers do not embrace the narrow concept that their social obligation is fulfilled simply by supplying needed goods and services, providing employment, and realizing profits. The real difficulty appears to be to what extent a manager can deploy personal energies so that the good corporate citizenship status is attained in the opinion of the various publics and at the same time fulfills obligations in maintaining a healthy operation of the business enterprise. Further, the problems in and among our social interactions involve traditions, philosophies, and values that are quite different from those encountered in the business area. In many cases, to solve social problems pulls the business manager away from familiar territory.

Yet, participation in social programs by business managers has become common. The activities include such diverse programs as employment counseling to minorities, finding jobs for "unemployables," remedial language instruction, senior citizen assistance, prisoner readjustment, alcoholic and drug guidance, educational grants, scholarships, medical research funding, and gifts to hospitals, libraries, and universities. In addition, changes in manufacturing processes to minimize pollution of the air and rivers, installation of various pollution control devices, and relocation of plants, can be cited.

A major difficulty is determining appropriate targets and guidelines in meeting social responsibilities. What and how far should the business manager go with the community as a whole, with customers, with competitors, with employees? When does the manager overexpend the stockholders' dollars or abrogate decisions that belong to elected public officials? And what guidelines can be followed? Keith Davis suggests several pertinent social responsibility propositions that are briefed in Figure 3–6.

FIGURE 3–6: Five basic propositions for social responsibility

1. *Social responsibility arises from social power.* Decisions by businesspersons have social consequences and unless the responsibility for these consequences is assumed by the decision makers, they will lose in the long run the power that goes with this decision making.

2. *Open disclosure of operations and open receipt of inputs from society are essential.* To have social responsibility requires letting the public know what you are doing and having a sensitivity to social actions, needs, and wants—to know what is going on in society.

3. *Social costs as well as technical feasibility and economic profitability should be taken into account in deciding what to proceed with in any given activity, product, or service.* A cost/benefit analysis including sufficient weight to social costs is suggested.

4. *Social costs should be included in the ultimate price of the product or service.* In general, the consumer should pay for his or her consumption including social costs.

5. *Managers and nonmanagers have responsibilities for social involvement in their areas of competence.* Since all members of a society benefit from an improvement of that society, they should all contribute their talents to help solve social problems.

Source: Adapted from the excellent article by Keith Davis, "Five Propositions for Social Responsibility," *Business Horizons,* June 1975 pp. 19–24.

Governmental influence and entitlements

Any discussion of major factors affecting the environment in which a manager operates must include the activities of government. Statutes, protective measures, and governmental services constitute a wide range of influence and in some manner as well as degree affect just about everything a manager does. The U.S. government is founded on the premise that each citizen has the inalienable right to life which in turn implies the right to defend and sustain that life, a condition which government assists in making possible. In the case of business managers, government in its regulatory efforts has sought the goals of business competition, the prevention of monopolies or any business pursuits that restrain trade, and the provision of ample facilities to ensure healthy business activities, i.e., regulation of banks and rates charged by public carriers, assistance in road building, pollution controls, and the like. Governmental activities are mostly in the realm of what cannot be done rather than what can be done. This affords the individual much choice in the selection of action, i.e., freedom.

But total freedom to the individual is a mirage. Freedom is always based on self-determination which has an important limitation, namely, one person's freedom stops where the other person's freedom begins. When an infringement penetrates another's rights, rationalization and apologies follow. Freedom necessitates responsibility which, in turn, requires mutual respect.

The trend is toward more and more governmental activities. This deepening penetration has come about through an almost continuous series of regulations, each one appearing quite plausible at the time of its adoption. With this growth, government cost has skyrocketed. The fastest growing segment is transfer payments—money spent by the government for social security and welfare payments. Around 1950 only 0.5 percent of the federal budget was spent on these income-maintenance payments. Today the figure is nearly 25 percent.

With this development has come a rising tide in the demands for entitlements—claims that the government put into effect many expanded social rights. Historically this stems from the government's guarantee of equality of opportunity for each citizen. This equality, however, has now become broadened to include many political, social, and economic demands which are defined as rights. In effect, government is expected to fulfill not only public needs, but private wants as well. This makes for a broad new setting from the business manager's viewpoint. And the restraints on the body politic are far different from those on a privately owned enterprise. The task of balancing public responsibility and private offerings will not be easy, but no matter how the result is obtained, the fact remains that government will continue to play an important role in shaping the environment under which management will be conducted.

Modern economic forces

This major area influencing the functioning of management includes the basic economic system—whether private or public ownership prevails—the fiscal policy of government expenditures, the organization of capital markets, the size of the market, and total purchasing power of the population. Also of interest are the controls over commercial banks' operations, credit, discounting, availability of power, water, and transportation as well as labor skills and productivity.

Economics has always been a significant influence upon the development of management thinking and the manner in which it is practiced. Like management, economics deals with decision making involving the use of resources devoted to different goals. Modern economics gives emphasis to questions of international trade, taxation, and governmental regulations—all areas of major contemporary importance. World-wide economic issues are moving toward the center stage of much management practice. Representative are the maintenance of a market in a world economy, frictions arising from the growth of multi-national corporations, international monetary systems, and world-wide inflation. Likewise, taxation is a major consideration in managerial decision making. The amount of taxes, how paid, by whom, and for what purpose, are fundamental and influence what a manager does or does not do. And every manager today finds time must be spent in grappling with the constantly increasing and entwining coils of government. Minimum wage laws set the wages that must be paid to the unskilled. The decision to hire or fire is regulated by equal-opportunity laws. The desire of a large business corporation to smash a competitor is suppressed as a result of enforced antitrust regulations.

In addition, economic forces direct attention to costs and revenues which are vital in the management of an enterprise. Analysis of costs, incomes, and the use of formulas and mathematical techniques for assessing dollar expenditures and receipts, are highly influential in the behavior and decisions of the manager.

Influence of technology

The general environment in which a manager operates is greatly conditioned by technology. Among the most dynamic of all influences, it can change the entire manufacturing process or activities of an enterprise. It is a major consideration that merits much thought in most organizations for the simple reason that it brings about numerous changes in its quest for improvements and progress.

Included under technological influences are the ways, especially the application of new ways, to transfer resources into a product or service by means of the discovery and the use of new materials, new methods, and new machines. As used here, it is inclusive of new knowledge which because of its extreme importance, some prefer to designate as a separate factor and use the term "a knowledge society" to indicate that portion of the total labor force accomplishing work based on knowledge rather than on manual skill. Automation and the widespread use of computers are also important facets of the technological factor.

Technology has solved many of our problems, but all too frequently it is blamed for them. Actually the solution to many of society's problems lie in creative and intelligent application of technology. The chief criticisms center around the growth of population and of industrial output. These growths will inevitably collide with finite physical limits of mineral resources, farm land, and the environment's ability to absorb pollutants. The ultimate result, so say the critics, will be total collapse.

On the other hand, history shows that the human race has demonstrated outstanding ingenuity and adaptability to survive and to progress. It is not solely a question of what raw materials are available or of a favorable climate. Our ability to cope with our problems is the important part of the answer, and in these efforts technology plays a dominant role. To illustrate, agricultural technology has made it possible to feed more people. With genetic advances in hybrid grains, improved livestock, chemical fertilization, extensive farm mechanization, and pest control, one agricultural worker in 1975 can produce over 12 times as much food as a farm worker in 1930. Further, technology has given rise to many new products. In 1925, aluminum was rare, now it is a contemporary, important material. And the same is true for another creation of technology—plastics—which had limited use several decades ago. The national supply of raw materials is indeed finite, but improved means of exploration, industrial processing, and recycling have contributed toward solving the problem of scarcity.

Management will be influenced by, and in turn will influence, technology in that the implementation and the course followed with new scientific developments will be determined by human beings. The uses made of technology will determine its good or its harm. The past goals of more and better products and services at lowest cost are being modified by emphasis given resource conservation and protection of the human environment. Technology will be used to help in achieving these new goals. Technology can be our greatest servant in the future. The challenge is to make good use of it in attaining worthy goals. And that is mainly the responsibility of the manager who believes in the promise of technology.

Educational considerations

This factor is made up of the general attitude toward education, the literacy level, and the practicality of education offered. Further, the number and types of persons obtaining higher education as well as the availability of specialized vocational and technical training are included.

Mention has already been made of the increasing trend toward more and more formal education for the typical employee-to-be and the employee in the United States. With this growth has come more knowledge and awareness, a desire to participate in decisions affecting oneself, the need for challenging work, and a decline in the practice of authoritarian management. Further changes are inevitable. For example, it is estimated that by the year 2000, only 15 percent of the U.S. labor force will be utilized in the production of products while 85 percent will be composed of people providing services.

To most people, education is the guiding and influential force giving that direction that is taken in life. In fact, the direction a society takes is dependent in great measure upon the educational opportunities afforded its people. The current greater educational activities widens the horizons of human capabilities and makes management more and more challenging.

People's beliefs, fears, and prejudices are determined largely by tendencies and predispositions acquired through learning. In fact, all behavior is influenced by learning. To live and grow in awareness is dependent upon an ability to learn from personal experiences and the experiences of others. As this awareness grows in both managers and nonmanagers, the positive contribution of the educational influence will contribute toward better understanding and cooperation as well as improved management practices in the years to come.

QUESTIONS

1. What is meant by environment and of what importance is it in the study of management? Justify your answer.
2. Explain the meaning of each of the following: (*a*) culture of society; (*b*) a value that a person has; (*c*) governmental entitlements; and (*d*) Protestant ethic.
3. Name four basics of the work ethic.
4. Are you of the opinion that many of our current difficulties in managing the human resource are the direct result of rapidly changing values? Discuss, using an example.

5. Discuss Figure 3–1, pointing out what is conveyed and its importance to management study.

6. Of what importance are the values of a manager and of a nonmanager in management?

7. From your reading and observation, how sensitive or aware do you feel management is to social environmental considerations? Justify your viewpoint.

8. Give some examples of values that a manager might have and point out the influence, if any, that they might have upon his or her managerial efforts.

9. As you see it, is internal or external environment of greater importance to the manager of today? Why?

10. What are some significant and contemporary changes in management philosophy? Discuss.

11. Discuss fully the influence of technology upon the environment in which a manager works.

12. Discuss the importance and role of "philosophy of management" in the study of management.

13. In your opinion, what will be some major factors in the philosophy of a manager in the year 2000? Elaborate on your answer.

14. Enumerate and discuss briefly three common economic forces that affect management environment.

CASE 3–1. MATTHEWS CORPORATION

After an extensive research, Nelson Forbusch was hired to head the quality control department. Mr. Forbusch, a recent engineering honor graduate, has no supervisory experience, but his knowledge of quality control, sincerity, and industriousness convinced the general manager that Forbusch deserved a chance and would make good. The department has been inefficient and troublesome. Employment of its former head was terminated after much bickering and squabbling.

Mr. Forbusch was given no details of past difficulties in the department. He was assured by top management that he could do the job and was given a free hand to manage the department as he felt it ought to be. He was told the main task is to make certain that quality standards are maintained.

After four months, the general manager cited quality control as one of the best run and most efficient departments in the entire company. However, during the past week a senior level employee of this department requested a transfer, and another stated to the personnel manager that she has decided to retire even though she is only 56 years old. Several days following the citation for department excellence, two more employees put in requests for transfer "to any department." In confidential interviews with the personnel manager, each of these four employees revealed that the department isn't like it used to be, that they are permitted to make few, if any work decisions, and that Mr. Forbusch is selfish, has no interest in their personal welfare or future, is all work- and production-minded, and will use any employee he can in order to achieve gains for himself.

Questions

1. Is there a problem here requiring managerial attention? Discuss.
2. Of what importance are management philosophy, values, and environment in this case? Elaborate on your answer.
3. As the general manager of Matthews Company, would you take any action? Why?

CASE 3–2. PRESIDENT HERMAN D. KAYLOR

Interviewer Myron Rist: Mr. Kaylor, as president of the Zigler Products Company and a man who has been quite outspoken on current controversial issues, it is a pleasure to have this opportunity to interview you.

Kaylor: It is my pleasure to be here.

Rist: You have stated that broad and profound developments have been and will continue to transform our entire society. These changes also affect management. Would you care to comment?

Kaylor: Yes. In my opinion, we are having sort of a revolution of affluence—a higher standard of living, plenty of goods and services available, large diversity and choice. I believe this has come about largely because business has satisfied public demand. Now we in the managing of business are being blamed for many of society's ills and as managers of business are being asked to solve these problems.

Rist: You don't believe managers should be asked?

Kaylor: Yes, they should be asked, but I'm not at all certain that they have the answer.

Rist: What makes you feel that way?

Kaylor: What makes me feel that way? Well, first of all, managers of business firms are not familiar with the scope and the background of many of these social ills. They are public issues and they involve politics. Most business leaders are not politicians and many of them don't understand politics. If they did, they would have gone into politics. Also, I believe business today has become so complicated that top management success of the future will demand almost complete absorption of a person's time and energy. To include, on top of this, the solving of social and governmental problems will spread the manager's efforts far too thin for effectiveness. Third, . . .

Rist (interrupting): May I inject a thought?

Kaylor: Certainly.

Rist: In order to control our future and not let it overwhelm us, it seems to me that we should shape it to our needs. In fact, we must invent it. And that's what and where you managers have expertise.

Kaylor: Well, that's true up to a point. I was going to say, third, a manager cannot be all things to all people. There is no simple, all-inclusive solution to society's problems. I feel we all have responsibility in this.

Rist: Yes, but managers have more power than the person on the street to grapple with and solve these troublesome issues.

Kaylor: People complain of dirty cities and then throw debris into the streets. Government regulates and forces restrictions on manufacturers. Many people think in terms of a quick dollar, not in the quality of their work. I'm tired of listening to people who accept no responsibility themselves.

Rist: Well, people are taking a keen interest in current problems, aren't they? What about consumerism, for example?

Kaylor: Consumerism is part of the much deeper doubts all about us, along with the cry for a better quality of life, fear of loss of individuality, and the demands of minority groups. That's my point.

Rist: I see. Well, thank you very much Mr. Kaylor.

Kaylor: Not at all. Thank you.

Questions

1. What do you think of Mr. Kaylor's views? Why?
2. What basic values do you feel Mr. Kaylor has? Discuss.
3. If you were interviewing Mr. Kaylor, what questions other than those of Mr. Rist, would you ask? Why?

Chapter 4

Selected current management practices

In this world there are only two tragedies.
One is not getting what one wants,
And the other is getting it.

Oscar Wilde

With all the tremendous changes in philosophy, values, environment, norms, situations, and goals taking place as described in the previous chapters, it should come as no surprise to state that management, in order to cope and to be viable in these new settings, has likewise changed. Not only have these dynamics come about to satisfy modern economic demands, but also and, probably more important, to satisfy changes in individual and social behavior. The changing value system, the challenging attitude, especially among younger people, improvements in material standards of living, and disillusionment with strict authoritarian organizational structures have been major contributors in emphasizing important new expectations which modern management is expected to fulfill.

From this state of change and development has emerged management practices molded and shaped to meet modern demands. These practices include new theories and new techniques that have been spawned, developed, modified, and disseminated to aid in management's search for improvement. Included here for discussion are management practices of (1) participation, (2) results management, (3) job enrichment, (4) productivity priority, (5) contingency management, and (6) conflict utilization.

It should be noted that all these practices are utilized within and against the background of the modified management process including planning, organizing, actuating, and controlling. When emphasis is given to participation or to results management, it might be assumed that only actuating needs attention. Seldom, however, is this true. Participation works best when the essential management process is sound—when planning, organizing, actuating, and controlling are sound. No single management practice, old or new, will bring about its peak potential unless the management process is adequate or is made adequate through the gains derived from the practice followed.

PARTICIPATION

Participation, commonly referred to as participative management, can be thought of as an overall management view that encourages all employees to have a part in or share in decision making, especially as it affects goal setting and problem solving. Participation can be formally defined as *both mental and emotional involvement of a person to make contributions to the decision making process, especially on matters in which personal involvement of the person exists, and assuming his or her share of the responsibility for them.* It is believed the manager's full and sympathetic hearing of ideas and reactions of employees is satisfying to them and makes for improvement in conditions under which the work is done. Participation is based on the psychological principle that one is more motivated toward goals that one helped establish compared with those set for one by others, and one assumes a personal interest in decisions and solutions to problems that one has helped establish.

A number of means can be followed to encourage participation. The oportunity to express ideas via the suggestion system is one. While rather formal, it can be effective, but is relatively somewhat removed from the day to day interactions of the manager and the subordinate. Organized plans can also be followed and give a foundation for habitual consultations. Employee councils or organizations can also be used. They are effective for discussing policies for the whole organization or for matters where group discussion is paramount. However, probably the superior means is the informal day to day relationship between the manager and the subordinate. It is more personal, permits more flexibility, and can be quite informal, yet effective.

In general, participation has much deeper implications than the limited idea of interpersonal considerations. Research in this area points to participative decision making being preferable when most of the following conditions exist. First, the decision is not routine and need not be reached within a short period. Second, the information required for the decision can neither be concentrated in one person or in a computer. Also, the participant must feel that her or his activity is legitimate and worth while. One must believe the employee's views are wanted and will be considered. Fourth, the participant should feel a need for independent thought and action—close supervision is not essential. Finally, the subordinate must have the knowledge to make meaningful contributions. This means that subordinates neither take over the decision making process nor do they participate in all decisions. Participation is restricted to those subjects about which they have relevant knowledge ans sufficient time to think about the particular question at hand.

The payoff from following participation can be quite high. Figure 4–1 shows results commonly obtained. However, participation should not be used indiscriminately. Effective planning and sound personnel relations appear necessary. While results cannot be predicted, it appears that important influences include the nature of the work groups, the organization background, present organizational relationships, and the technologies used. Participation does not have the same degree of validity in all circumstances.

FIGURE 4–1:   Results from participation

From the manager's viewpoint	From the nonmanager's viewpoint
1. Acceptance of change is enhanced.	1. Knowledge and understanding of management's problems are gained.
2. Improved quantity and quality of product or service.	2. Goals of manager and nonmanager are brought closer together.
3. More effective decisions are reached.	3. Improved attitude and more satisfaction are gained from performing work.
4. Work of manager is more difficult, but it is also more challenging and satisfying.	4. More satisfaction makes it less desirable to jeopardize job by absenteeism.

RESULTS MANAGEMENT

Results management gives emphasis to results or the achievement of objectives and to human behavior through the fulfillment of needs from the work efforts. Present is unremitting attention to results instead of activities. Management is purposeful; it is performed to attain accomplishment. Therefore why not place emphasis upon the results, key all managerial efforts to results, and while attaining the results make better use of the human resource and contribute to the employee's satisfaction. In many instances, objective accomplishment falls short of its intended mark because the objective is not clearly known to all affected by it, the scope within which a member is permitted to exercise decision making is too narrow, or the major problem areas are not given preferred attention. To correct these shortcomings, participation in formulating an objective by the users of that objective

can be followed. This leads to a current practice in management sometimes referred to as management by objectives, management by mission, or as we prefer to call it, results management, because results are
the core of attention. Results are the focus of and the criteria that
determines the success of the management member.

What is results management? It is a system made up of definite
components whereby each employee participates in the determining
of personal objectives as well as the means by which one hopes to
achieve these objectives. Developed within the overall boundaries set
forth by a superior, subsequently the objectives and plans for attaining
them are discussed by the initiator and the superior, altered if necessary, and finally adopted, if mutually agreed upon. The specific expected results serve as the guides for directing the operations, and also
as the standards of performance against which the subordinate is appraised. Following results management tends to make each employee
a manager of his or her own particular work. It diminishes the authoritarian practice of deciding and telling subordinates exactly what to do.
The individual has a greater part in one's own work decisions and
purposes. Results management is a way of managing. It applies to
managers in any kind and size of organization at all levels and in all
functional areas.

Figure 4–2 shows the three basic components of results management. Under component No. 1, key areas refer to those activities believed critical to the success of the organization and include productivity, profitability, social responsibility, personnel development, and
market position. The goals set must be within reasonable limits. Illustrative of No. 1.b. "Determine the measurement unit," is hours of
machine operation, units completed per day, or market share as shown
by the amount of dollar sales. Faulty measurement units are a common
cause of results management failure.

Component No. 2 must be given adequate attention if results management is to reach its zenith. How well the development of action
plans is performed can make or break the entire approach. It is not
simply recognizing and establishing the objectives that counts, but
also the practical determination of how these objectives will be accomplished. Objectives themselves help in the planning for their
achievement, but the necessary unity of purpose and of actions to
follow are supplied by well-thought-out plans. Inflexible policies and
communication can wreck a results management program.

The last component zeros in on the important consideration of results. Periodic reviews are essential so that excessive variations from
the expectancy are known before they get too bad or continue for too
long. A yearly autoposy is totally inadequate. Reviews should be made
when the manager believes they are appropriate. A company operating under a project concept should conduct appraisal reviews at the

FIGURE 4–2:   The components of results management

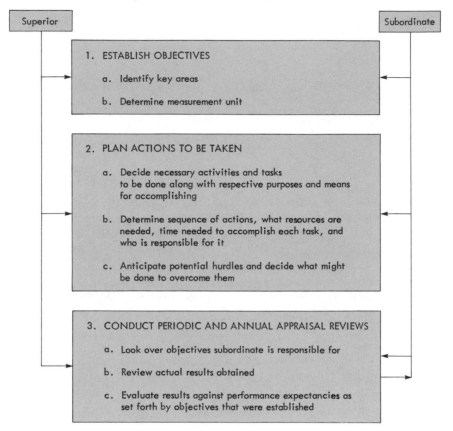

completion of each project. Annual reviews provide a good starting point for preparing for the next year.

THE "TOP-DOWN" OR THE "BOTTOM-UP" APPROACH IN RESULTS MANAGEMENT

Either the "top-down" or the "bottom-up" approach can be used in results management. The former is exemplified by the practice of a president of a company who near the end of each year writes all vice presidents asking:

1. What were your outstanding accomplishments during the past twelve months?
2. What major accomplishments do you contemplate during the coming new year?

3. Are these accomplishments measurable? If so, explain how you will measure them.

Similar requests are sent by each vice president to his or her key people, who in turn do the same, and so on down to the bottom level. The replies form the basis for establishing the objectives. Each superior reviews the replies of subordinates and working together with them sets pertinent goals with the knowledge, understanding, and acceptance of both superior and subordinates. In turn, each superior consults with the next higher level superior and goals are established for this next higher level. The process is repeated for successively higher levels up to the president.

In contrast, the bottom-up approach starts with individuals stating their objectives and submitting them for modification and mutual approval with their respective superior. In turn, each superior consolidates and drafts objectives and then submits them to the next higher superior for discussion, modification, and mutual .approval. The process is continued until the chief executive decides, in counsel with chief associates, the top or company objectives. Then, these objectives are given to departmental managers who determine their respective departmental objectives that must be achieved to accomplish the overall goal. After approval by the chief executive, the departmental goals become the required objectives of these respective units and the stated accomplishment against which the departmental manager will be measured. In like manner, objectives are established for members at each level throughout the entire enterprise. In establishing the objectives the superior's evaluation of them is quite important. For example, the future period must be specific; the task required to meet the objective must be practical, sufficient, and obtainable; the method of measuring accomplishment must be clearly stated, i.e., in dollars, hours paid, or labor efficiency; and the objectives must be compatible with the overall enterprise plans for the period.

MOTIVATIONAL ASPECTS OF RESULTS MANAGEMENT

Let us look closely at the built-in high motivational elements of results management. The employee starts with self-appraisal of performances, abilities, and potential. From this, the employee begins to know better personal strengths and weaknesses, to gain self-confidence, to receive feedback on accomplishments, to know why the actions being taken are performed, and to be a self-directed and self-improved member. By participating in establishing their own goals, employees are encouraged to think about the work, to capitalize on experiences, and to believe in the objectives. In addition, results management motivates from within, the individual has a closer feeling of what the end results should and can be, senses that he or she is an important part of getting the work achieved, and feels a vital part of the team effort. All these qualities contribute to making management effective.

Results management helps satisfy the human need of achievement. Most people desire to get results—to achieve—as a result of their work efforts. The viewpoint is taken in results management that involvement leads to commitment and most people are eager to assume responsibility if they have some say about their work content and environment. Further, when given the opportunity, they exercise self-control in performing their jobs because it provides psychological needs satisfaction to them.

Results management supplies a special framework for participation. Decisions and actions that affect a person's job are determined jointly by the superior and the subordinate. And the participation is closely tied to results so that they are supportive of one another. This combination makes for a highly motivational effort.

In addition, results management tends to shift controlling from people to operations. The evaluation is not a radar of the person's traits and characteristic behavior, but is centered on what is achieved. The subordinate exercises self-control. Dependence upon others for inputs required for control is lessened.

Further, the superior-subordinate relationship is improved. The subordinate has greater freedom, a more supportive role, and communication about the organization becomes more open. All of this leads to personal development for both the superior and the subordinate. Opportunities to increase knowledge and skill are opened up and performance can be more effective and satisfying.

IS ANYTHING MISSING IN RESULTS MANAGEMENT?

Criticism has been leveled against results management claiming that it is really an illusion and actually increases pressure on the subordinate. One of the main targets is the lack of defining the necessary interaction between the superior and the subordinate, especially with regards to the superior's role in helping the subordinare reach set goals. It is not simply a task behavior question, so state the critics, but also a relationship behavior. To achieve goals, most subordinates need interpersonal relationships as well as communication with and emotional support from the superior. Further, it is contended that the typical job in an organization is interdependent upon other jobs in that organization. What a person achieves depends on what other employees do. Group goal setting might be a more appropriate and meaningful practice. Also, in many cases the person really has a very limited choice of objectives from which to choose. Personal objectives may, for example, be entirely lacking.[1]

Without question, some of the criticism of results management has arisen due to its improper installation. Adequate preparation and explanation were not made. In and of itself, the practice was considered erroneously to be the panacea for all managerial ills and valid in all circumstances—assumptions unwarranted and never claimed for results management. As already pointed out, results management is more than establishing objectives cooperatively and appraising results periodically. Careful planning of the means by which goals will be achieved, time tables, facilities needed, and changes required are essential to the success of every results management program. Then, too, adequate time for results management to take hold is required. Instant success is quite unlikely, especially if the concept and mode of operation is new to the members of the organization.

We must also remember that employees differ and the human resource is vital in all management practices. For results management to be successful, at least some of the employees must have a sense of achievement and sufficient background and experience to formulate and implement objectives intelligently. The higher educational level of people today and their deep desire to be "a part of the action" help make results management feasible. Another factor, however, must be noted. It is the "Zeigarnik effect" which is a compulsion in some individuals to complete a task or accomplish a given result. A psychologist, B. Zeigarnik, reported her research in 1927 and found that some people have a high Zeigarnik effect, others have a low one.

This is important in results management for it means that the setting of an objective does not result in its achievement unless the person or persons involved have a sufficient compulsion for closure of actions to attain the goal. We require members with a need for achievement and at the start of activities will push the tasks to completion. That is, our demands are for personnel motivated by the Zeigarnik effect; they realize great personal satisfaction from accomplishment of completed tasks. In fact, accomplishments preoccupy them. In contrast, others have weak or very little compulsion to finish work assignments. Activities preoccupy them. Without a sufficient number of persons having a high Zeigarnik effect, the use of results management will prove disappointing. Unless a company has hired or developed members with high Zeigarnik effects, results management should not be adopted.

---

[1] For thought-provoking evaluations of results management, see Paul Hersey and Kennth H. Blanchard, "What's missing in M.B.O.?" *Management Review*, October 1974, pp. 25–32, and Harry Levinson, "Management by Whose Objectives?" *Harvard Business Review*, July–August 1970, pp. 125–34.

JOB ENRICHMENT

Those favoring job enrichment claim that excessive task simplification, close control over the employee's actions, and the repetitive minimal-cycle scope of work places the employee in the role of a machine designed to perform small tasks in accordance with precise quantity and quality specifications. Under these conditions the employee is thought to be incapable of dealing with variables in the production flow and to be motivated primarily by economic means—pay, security, and shorter work hours. These work conditions are a cause of employee dissatisfaction and discontentment with performing work. Proponents of job enrichment claim a restructuring of the work to make it meaningful and fulfilling is required. By utilizing job enrichment the work becomes more challenging to the person doing it, becomes more in keeping with the employee's capabilities, and the employee is given a voice in the needed job restructuring.

Job enrichment is the redesign of jobs to improve task efficiency and human satisfaction by increasing either or both the scope and the depth of the required work and providing more autonomy, authority, and responsibility for the employee. It is intended to make the work more challenging and provide more opportunity for recognition, growth, and advancement. More specifically the goals are to (1) supply the most fulfilling and interesting work possible for an employee, and (2) utilize to the maximum the competence and skill of the employee. Sometimes job enrichment is referred to as job enlargement or job expansion.

It should be noted that job enrichment does not discard the imperatives of technology. Most adherents of job enrichment recognize machines and natural science processes as being of utmost importance in job design. A punch press, for example, determines what and where certain tasks will be done and how the work is arranged. Yet, the scope and the relationship of the employee to this work can be varied in keeping with the requirements of the employee's human qualities.

Means for achieving job enrichment

Jobs can be enriched either by (1) horizontal loading, (2) vertical loading, or (3) closure. The first typically involves giving an employee additional work at his or her particular organizational level. To illustrate, a file clerk is given the job of not only removing requested material from the file, but also of replacing removed file material back into the files. The job has changed, but the work level remains the same. This is actually a question of comparing the job content with the work actions of the employee. In contrast, No. 2, vertical loading, deals with changing the level of responsibility required by the job holder and/or a change in the employee's ability as indicated by authority or decision making practice, the capacity and potential of the employee. To our file clerk's job may be added responsibility of maintaining confidential material from general viewers, a condition requiring the file clerk to decide which people can see specified filed material. Vertical loading, while a fruitful source of job enrichment, is also the most threatening. A management member may fear losing control or may fear that a subordinate is taking over the manager's work.

Figure 4–3 shows graphically the concepts of horizontal loading and

FIGURE 4–3

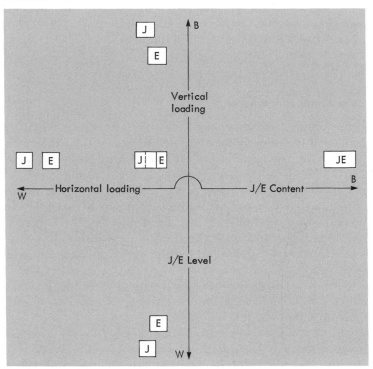

J = Job
E = Employee
B = Best condition
W = Worst condition
Job enrichment can be carried out either by horizontal loading (job content) or by vertical loading (job level).

vertical loading. At the extreme left of the figure the job content is not matched at all with the employee work actions. By horizontal loading—move to extreme right of figure—the matching of job content and employee work action is improved. Similarly, at the bottom of the figure, the employee level of responsibility, authority, and potential is above that required by the job. However, through vertical loading the *J* and *E* qualities can be brought to the same level or continued until the job level or requirements are above that of the employee. The best overall loading would be the condition indicated by the arrangement marked by *B* and *B* on the chart where, for content, there is a perfect match between job and employee, and for level, the job is above the employee. Likewise, the worst condition is indicated by *W* and *W* on the chart.

The third means for job enrichment, closure, means the extent to which a job provides to the employee a sense of contribution to and completion of something meaningful. In the case of the file clerk's job, for example, changing the job to include determining who should get what filed material, what material in the files should be discarded, and deciding the overall filing system to be followed, would give closure to that job.

The focus of job enrichment

Job enrichment is not confined to the job. From what has been stated, it also includes the employee and more than this, a group of employees. We are actually talking about a three-fold improvement made up of job development, employee development, and group development. Current managerial practice tends to emphasize employee development, but these efforts untied to the realities of job demands and co-employee relationships can be unhealthy. An integrated and reasonable balance among the three areas is desirable. Job enrichment helps to bring about this needed equilibrium and should be viewed in this light.

Furthermore, job enrichment concerns a working group and the individual's relations to the group. The initial concept of job enrichment encompassed the job and its ramifications as the source of bringing about what was the real problem, namely, the relationship of the employee to that job. Now, it is realized that job enrichment's relationship to the group is vital. The interaction of group members is an important reinforcing element to any employee performing a job. If, for example, these interactions are reduced by job enrichment, much of the benefit from job enrichment is simultaneously reduced.

Also, the superior of any work group is affected by job enrichment. When jobs and work relationships are restructured as well as the employee performing more tasks, deciding certain issues, and assuming more responsibility, the superior becomes definitely involved and reacts to these changes in many different ways. Commonly, the superior views job enrichment as a threat to his or her job. Certainly this is understandable. It suggests what is often neglected, namely to explain the whole effort to the superior, point out that she or he will become more of a planner and counselor, and that the superior will definitely be needed and actually increase in importance. In the case of a superior encased in a rigid authoritarian hierarchy, the adjustment is most difficult. In some cases the superior's job is formally upgraded so that its holder can adjust to the new relationship.

Job enrichment and the organization

This brings up the subject of coming to grips in job enrichment with the employee-organization relationships. Actually the modification of one job can cause repercussions throughout an entire organization. This means that job enrichment includes not only employee-work, and employee-employee relationships, but also the total work environment of the organization. From this viewpoint, perhaps the term, employment enrichment, would be preferred over that of job enrichment. While the job is a key means of interface, it is only a part of the employee's total relationship with the organization.

Also helpful is an organization analysis to identify possible interrelationships that will be affected by a contemplated job change. Usually such information helps spot the constraints under which any job enrichment program will be operating. Further, information on each employee's present and potential skills should be available. Essentially, we are interested in knowing which employees are ready and willing to accept change in their jobs. Normally not all are willing. Research shows that generally the employee nonresistant to job enrichment is youthful, has more education, and probably works in a department where similar tasks are performed.[2]

With such a background, the work of evolving what jobs will be enriched can proceed. Both management and nonmanagement members should participate. An atmosphere free from restraint of the consideration for policy, cost, participation, and shortcomings, helps get suggestions and ideas for job enrichment out in front of the group. Depending upon the makeup of the group, either members are selected and assigned areas of the jobs with the request to develop ways to redesign them by means of open discussion, or a group is asked to prepare a list showing major job problems and what to do about them. Subsequently, the jobs for enrichment are selected, plans for implementation drawn up, and eventually put into effect. This whole process requires much time; it cannot and should not be hurried.

The important point here is that job enrichment is not simply giving

---

[2] See the interesting article by Donald C. Collins and Robert R. Raubolt, "A Study of Employee Resistance to Job Enrichment," *Personnel Journal*, April 1975, pp. 232–35.

an employee more tasks to do nor adding decision making and problem solving to the job. It also includes providing the employee with the skills required to do these added ingredients of the enriched job. If these skills are not supplied, the employee likely will become frustrated and the whole program will prove to be a costly waste of time.

Limits to job enrichment

Like other recent practices of management, job enrichment is not a cure-all for any management difficulty. And it requires careful preparation before adopting. Most any job can be enriched and its environment improved, but it may entail dramatic changes and be fraught with serious difficulties for some employees. Usually the situation where employees are performing a variety of tasks is not considered the most ideal from whence to start a job enrichment program. Above all, never initiate job enrichment in a unit where strong resistance to it exists. Commitment and enthusiasm are prerequisites for its success. A disenchanted employee or group can destroy the best of efforts.

It should also be observed that a particular job can have different meanings to different people. To some, it may be routine and boring, but to others this is not so. A person's job expectations and wanted social satisfaction from a job are not the same for everybody. It is not unusual to find some members of a work group who prefer to perform unenlarged familiar jobs.[3] If a manager decides to enrich a job because he or she thinks it is monotonous and nonchallenging, it doesn't necessarily follow that the person performing that job thinks the same about it. In such a situation, for the manager to force enrichment may lead to unanticipated and needless problems.

PRODUCTIVITY PRIORITY

The U.S. economy is highly productive but it is not productive enough for what U.S. citizens ask of it. Ever-increasing social benefits are wanted, labor expects annual wage increments, and business owners would like more equitable profit margins in view of the risks assumed and competition faced from challengers in the world markets. To meet these various demands, an increase in the total output is necessary and the only way to do this is to increase productivity. This is the key factor and it is being given priority by the leaders of the U.S. economy.

To achieve these needed increases pose difficult problems. The

---

[3] C. Argyris, "Personality and organization revisited," *Administrative Science Quarterly*, 1973, vol. 18, pp. 141–67.

U.S. productivity gains since 1970 have been the lowest in the modern industrial world. Our investment in research and development is at the bottom and, right after Great Britain, the United States has the lowest investment in fixed assets. Germany and Japan have not only far outgained us in productivity gains during recent years, but they have passed us in some areas. Serious economic deterioration in U.S. international economic leadership is also indicated by the dollar weakness in international markets, formal devaluation, and the balance of payments status in our foreign trade.

What is productivity?

One of the difficulties in efforts to give productivity priority and improvement is the lack of a clean-cut definition of what it is. Without precise identity, measurement is open to question. Economists commonly define productivity as "the ratio of physical output to physical input" and customarily with reference to total industries or sectors of the economy. Further, the measurements are quantitative. In contrast, managers and business practitioners view productivity in terms of output with reference to overall efficiency and performance of the individual organization and where both quantitative and qualitative considerations are included. The effectiveness of the organization, absence of disruption and difficulty, and customer satisfaction are normally included.

The inclusion of quality in productivity changes is merited. The physical improvement in a new automobile, for example, is certainly a gain. Likewise, inputs by brains, attitudes, and efforts certainly make some difference in productivity. Presumably, confining input to that by material, labor, land, and capital is incomplete. In addition, the greater nonphysical outputs such as that produced by the university professor and the dentist certainly add to productivity but commonly are ignored. All of this means that productivity is a many-splendored thing with myriad ways of calculating it. Utilizing simple ratios such as "output per work-hour" to indicate productivity is without doubt inadequate and nonapplicable for most organizations.

Improving productivity

Yet there is some general consensus on the identity of productivity because there exists interest and effort to improve productivity. For the most part these cluster around selected factors believed to affect productivity the most in a given organization, or are conditions that probably can be improved by means of chosen managerial techniques.

Based on productivity research, the view is widespread that the burden of productivity improvement rests on management.[4] Managers must show the way, develop the understanding and make the required investment in personnel, time, and money. There is no question that managers favor increasing productivity. By supplying the needed leadership, managers will show where to begin and how to go about achieving productivity gains.

Productivity being the result of a combination of many factors, there is no simple formula to follow. Whatever is done should be designed to meet the unique conditions in each organization. A start is to identify the critical productivity elements in the particular organization, devise a measurement for each element so that orientation as well as progress in productivity can be determined, devise a program to achieve specific productivity improvements, and apply sound management practices in efforts to achieve these gains.

While technology, materials utilization, and methods improvements are important, it appears that improvement in the human resource usage, especially at the managerial levels, is vital to any genuine productivity gain. Management techniques, in and of themselves, do not magically get the work achieved. In the final analysis, success depends on the people who use the techniques.

Figure 4–4 shows ten suggestions for increasing productivity. These are suggestive, not inclusive, of all the actions that might be taken. By adopting these guides at a high level in the organization and following them throughout the entire organization, it is reasonably certain that gains in productivity will be won.

CONTINGENCY MANAGEMENT

Considerable attention is being given in modern management to the contingency aspects affecting management decisions in a given situation. This "it all depends" type of attribute was stated in Chapter 2, but its importance warrants further discussion at this time. To reiterate, managerial action should be appropriate for the particular conditions that exist in a given situation. The manager's choice of what to do is influenced tremendously by what the environment factors are. The same problem but in different settings may call for different managerial actions. Contingency management aids in getting away from excessive generalizations. It promotes more precision in management by tailoring the action to fit the individual environment. And it is also helpful in solving management problems where probability is of major concern. If a decision has a 60 percent probability of bringing about a

---

[4] See Mildred E. Katzell, "Productivity: The Measure and the Myth," *American Management Association Survey Report*, 1975, and Herman S. Jacobs and Katherine E. Jillson, "Executive Productivity," *American Management Association Survey Report*, 1974.

FIGURE 4–4: Suggestions to increase productivity

1. Realize that the employee must find his or her performance recognized, rewarded, and satisfactory.

2. Personal goals and values of the employee must articulate and be compatible with the organization's goals. This contributes to the employee's sense of involvement in the organization.

3. Employees should have a reasonable amount of influence and control of their jobs along with broad opportunities to become involved in the work action that interests them most. Improved work attitude and lower turnover probably will result and will indirectly favorably influence productivity.

4. Strive constantly to improve communication and to make it more effective.

5. Tie compensation to performance and share in quantitative and qualitative gains achieved.

6. Avoid having too many programs with little productivity. They tend collectively to have little impact and commonly give transitory results. Adopt modest goals that necessitate some change and place a respected value on productivity increase.

7. Consider using two categories: (a) labor productivity, and (b) capital productivity. In the former are teamwork, self-actualization, humanizing work, and improving the work environment; in the latter are capital investment, return on investment, and cost.

8. Improve planning so that all necessary details are spelled out as to who does what, when, with what resources, and toward what goals.

9. Use new technology, modern machines, and equipment.

10. Devise and adopt the best available work methods. Consider every method tentative and a candidate for improvement.

certain result, certain factors or conditions within the environment are related to this probability and are primarily responsible for this result. Further, some changes take place among these or additional environmental relationships when the probability becomes only 40 percent. In other words, where different degrees of uncertainty exist about the projected outcome, contingency management can assist in revealing what environmental relationships tend to increase and what ones tend to decrease the uncertainty. Assessment of the contingency variables in many of the common areas of management are as yet incomplete, but progress is being made and a considerable amount of knowledge in this area is available.

Let us consider several illustrations starting with examples from communication. What constitutes the best communication? It depends or is contingent upon the problem involved, time available, media restrictions, complexity of subject, and the people involved. The degree of importance and the relationships existing among these variables will influence the answer to what communication is best. We might give the solution which is valid for the great majority of cases, but it would not be valid for all cases.

Consider written reports. Contingency school followers feel one type of report should differ from another. When a manager is handling a financial report, the situation commonly calls for secrecy, consideration for inflation, and interest rates, while none of these need be taken into account for production reports. Circumstances make it realistic to believe that communicating will differ not only for different tasks, but also for different situations. What is communicated, and how, is contingent upon the individual situation as the manager perceives it.

Returning for a moment to the subject of job enrichment, experience shows there may be difficulty in applying programs designed to enrich jobs. To overcome the difficulty, research indicates some of the important guidelines to follow are included in answers to questions such as:

1.   Are the employees discontent with their present jobs? If things are running smoothly, perhaps it is best to let the work as it is. On the other hand, excessive absenteeism, poor quality, sabotage, or indifferent attitudes may indicate work dissatisfaction. Such a circumstance offers the opportunity to correct these conditions, possibly by means of job enrichment.

2.   Is it feasible to give the employee control over his or her task? Highly structured jobs may be required due to the degree of technology followed.

3.   Is recognition or reward possible to the employee assuming increased responsibility? A sense of accomplishment upon completion of the task should exist as well as sufficient flexibility to permit the employee to practice high workmanship and reflect his or her personality in the work effort.

4.   Can the employee be informed fully on individual work accomplishments? Feedback to the employee tends to help work performance.

5.   Does the enriched work require the interaction of several compatible employees? Such individuals commonly attain more consistent and higher productivity in task accomplishment than do incompatible employees.

The answers to these questions will vary both in content and degree among different organizations and among departments within these organizations. There is no one set of guidelines that apply equally to all situations. In each case the contingencies qualify what considerations to abide by and help guide the determination of what action the manager should take based on the individual characteristics of the specific case.

The pattern of relationships rather than the causal links are stressed in the contingency theory. Multivariate models are required. As pointed out above, usually a number of influential factors are present and must be dealt with. An excellent example is a well known leadership theory which states that leadership depends mainly upon three factors: (1) leader-member relations—the leader enjoys the confidence of group members, (2) task structure—the goal is clear and a decision by the leader can be verified "from above," and (3) position power—the leader has the influence to direct, decide, and secure cooperation.[5] That is, various combinations of these three situational factors condition the managerial leadership actions.

All told there are eight possible combinations of these three factors. See Figure 4–5. When the leader-member relations are good, the task

FIGURE 4–5: Eight possible combinations of three leadership factors determining leadership effectiveness

Leader-member relations	Task structure	Position power
Good	Structured	Strong
Good	Structured	Weak
Good	Unstructured	Strong
Good	Unstructured	Weak
Poor	Structured	Strong
Poor	Structured	Weak
Poor	Unstructured	Strong
Poor	Unstructured	Weak

Source: Adapted from Fred E. Fiedler, "The Effects of Leadership Training and Experience: A Contingency Model Interpretation," *Administrative Science Quarterly*, December 1972, pp. 453–70.

structured, and the position power is strong, the most effective leadership is characterized as being controlling, active, and structuring (line 1 of Figure 4–5). In contrast, when the three factors are respectively good, unstructured, and weak (line 4 of Figure 4–5), the leadership is permissive, passive, and considerate. In other words, the leadership effectiveness and style depends or is contingent upon the qualities of the three leadership factors and the leadership style varies with the combinations of the three leadership factors present in the particular environment being considered. No one leadership style is appropriate for all conditions. It depends. The factors in each case govern. This is the essence of the contingency approach.

CONFLICT UTILIZATION

Conflict is the existence of opposition or dispute between persons, groups, or organizations. With all the developments and changes taking place in management, it is rational to expect differences of opinion, beliefs, and ideas to exist. Further, whenever people are closely as-

[5] See also discussion of Fred E. Fiedler's theory of leadership in chapter 19.

sociated and particularly when in pursuit of common goals, it is reasonable to assume that given sufficient time, differences will occur among them. It has always been so. Perhaps the term, conflict, is a bit too sharp and too strong, but it is the common terminology and hence will be used here.

Since conflict is inevitable, a helpful approach for the manager is to try and utilize it so that an appropriate and effective means for achieving goals can be followed. Such an approach requires acceptance of the view that the perfect organization is not free from conflict and that conflict is helpful in bringing about needed changes. Several decades ago conflict was considered harmful and something to be avoided. Now, the trend is to recognize that some anxiety and conflict are needed for us to behave most effectively. Rather than suppress or try to avoid conflict, it should be managed so it contributes to an organization's success.

In other words, approach conflict as a normal part of behavior which can be exploited as a means of promoting and achieving change. Realize that in performing work today, we subject ourselves to the dynamics of our job makeup, our relationships with others, and our work environment. Further, we ourselves change. However, the rates of change are not uniform so that there are constantly new conditions which provide fertile soil for the emergence of conflict. And it should be noted that the resolving of conflict can bring about needed redefining of goals, reallocating of resources, and changing of procedures.

THE PATTERN OF CONFLICT

Conflict usually follows a rather well defined pattern which consists of four steps. *First, a crisis emerges.* Some potential danger and harm are present. They threaten the harmonious operation and perhaps the very existence of the organization. Serious disagreements are present. *Second, escalation of the disagreement takes place.* The conflict is brought to the attention of a management member, if she or he is not already a part of it. Corrective action is demanded, but actually not expected at this step. *Third, confrontation occupies the center of attention.* This amounts to a showdown with managers hopefully at a higher level than those in step No. 2. Usually some arrangement to investigate the charges is promised and a tentative plan of how to proceed is drawn up. *Fourth, further crisis is resorted to* in that the legitimacy of the initial charges will be investigated, the handling of the proposed procedures are challenged and ultimately rejected. Subsequently, other possible means of reaching an agreement are tried to which the same crisis-rejection answer pattern is used. Finally the conflict is resolved and the required adjustments, if any, are designed and implemented.

DEALING WITH CONFLICT

In dealing with conflict it is advisable first to recognize its existence and to identify the persons involved. Check out the others' thoughts to make certain you know what they are—don't assume you know. By all means avoid using personal labels such as calling another person a narrow-minded clown. Stick to the controversy involved and stay with the present—what is believed and being done now are major considerations.

Figure 4–6 shows a conflict continuum. One can assume a win or

FIGURE 4–6: A conflict continuum

Win or lose	In between	Compromise
Take firm stand	Structure organization change	Encourage interaction pattern
Emphasize own goals	Utilize interdependency of jobs	Seek solution, not putting pressure on other
Blame others for failure or difficulty	Practice avoidance	Take broad view of situation and problem
Strive to gain advantage solely for yourself	Change work makeup and content	Trust the other party
Threaten and vent hostilities on others	Employ interpersonal skill training	Don't take initial position

lose, a compromise, or an in between profile as noted by column headings. What is assumed will depend mainly upon (1) the personality of the focal person and (2) the characteristics of the interpersonal relationships. For example, under win or lose, line 1, "Take firm stand" includes using punishment or threat of it, demanding certain actions be taken, or stating you can't see the issue any other way but your own and turning in your resignation, if necessary. For the second column, line 3, "Practice avoidance," one might ignore answering memos or letters, be out of town when meeting is held, or excuse oneself with the reason, "not sufficient time to study the problem."

CONFLICT LOCATION

As stated above, conflict exists between individuals, groups, and organizations. When two individuals hold diametrically opposed viewpoints, never compromise, jump to conclusions, and are inclined to be intolerant of ambiguities, conflict will sooner or later occur. The common pattern is as follows: A's perception of B's behavior toward A conditions A's response (plans and intentions) toward B. In turn, these are interpreted by B in accordance with B's plans and intentions toward A, and conditions B's response. In other words, perceptions play an important part in forming and maintaining conflict positions. To deal with a situation of this sort, inject intelligence that shows characteristics and behavior similar to both parties. Such information provides a cognitive consonance or an assurance that a person's beliefs do not contain contradictory elements, and as such may lead to diminishing the hostility and well established prejudices.

Group conflict is common and perhaps is of greater importance in management. Such conflict usually arises under any of these conditions: (1) new values are adopted by certain group members, (2) a new difficulty or problem is encountered by the group with members perceiving it differently, and (3) a member's role outside the group clashes with that member's role within the group. Sometimes the conflict is so strong that the original group is split into two competing groups. And, commonly, aims of the conflicting groups are such that one group attains its aims at the expense of the other. An interesting effect of group conflict is the tendency to increase morale within each group. The astute manager deals with group conflict by disseminating favorable information about one group to the other group (get to know them better), exchanging members from one to the other group (know what the other group is thinking about and doing), and pointing out a common enemy that threatens survival of both groups (unless you get together you will perish).

Last, there is conflict between organizations. It is not uncommon and includes both inter- and intra-organizational conflict. Representative of the former is conflict between company A and company B, or company C and a governmental agency such as the Department of Agriculture. For the latter, production control versus personnel, and supervisor versus shop stewards can be cited. In many cases the same general means suggested for dealing with group conflict can be used with organization conflict.

QUESTIONS

1. Of the five current management practices discussed in this chapter, what similarities exist among them? What dissimilarities? Which practice most appeals to you? Why?

2. Under what general conditions is participative decision making preferable?

3. Explain Figure 4–3 in your own words.

4. Discuss common results from the nonmanager's viewpoint when participative management is followed.

5. What is meant by each of the following: (*a*) "bottom-up" approach in results management, (*b*) job enrichment, (*c*) results management, (*d*) Zeigarnik effect?

6. Briefly relate some major criticisms that have been leveled against results management. Are you inclined to agree with them? Why?

7. Is job enrichment confined to job redesign? Discuss fully and give reasons for your answer.

8. With reference to Figure 4–2, elaborate and discuss fully the meaning of component No. 2 (i.e.) Plan actions to be taken.

9. Enumerate six ways to increase productivity and discuss one of these ways in depth.

10. In your opinion does the use of results management or of job enrichment have the higher motivational value? Justify your answer.

11. Of what importance is it to a manager to note that a given job can have different meanings to different people? Elaborate on your answer.

12. What is conflict in management and when does it usually arise in a group?

13. With reference to productivity, (*a*) what is it? (*b*) why should it be improved? (*c*) who is responsible for improving it?

14. You have been asked to talk to your class on the subject, "Conflict and modern management." Outline the major topics that you would cover and justify the inclusion of the topics you select.

CASE 4–1: ELLIOTT CORPORATION

This item appeared on the business page of the local newspaper:

Elliott Corporation announced today purchase of Dolin Products, Inc. This is the third acquisition completed by Elliott during the past 14 months. Dolin Products, Inc., one of the largest poultry processors in the south, will increase Elliott's annual sales to nearly $400 million. Terms of the transaction were not disclosed.

A management team from Elliott Corporation consisting of Ray Conklin, general manager, Harry Petroski, personnel manager, and Ellen Hutton, vice president of finance, visited the Dolin Products plant to discuss possible future management activities and changes to be made as a result of the acquisition. The official spokesperson of Dolin Products was Mr. Victor Wade, general manager. The company had been owned by a family, none of whom took an active part in its management. Mr. Wade has managed the company almost entirely by himself. Resourceful and ambitious, he has shown good profits to its owners, who have respected his wishes and have never interfered with his efforts. He receives a good salary plus a percentage of the net profits of the company. He has a reputation for being firm and running "a tight ship," but he is also fair and assumes full responsibility for the plant with little or no "buck-passing."

During the visit, members of the Elliott management team stated that in all their plants, results management was used. Excellent achievements were being won. They stated their intention was to use a similar approach here at Dolin Products. A number of committees and meetings was also utilized.

Wade: It won't work here, but of course, you fellows own the plant now and can do what you like.

Petroski: Why won't it work here, Mr. Wade?

Wade: It just won't, that's all. You can't turn the management of a plant like this over to them. They just can't handle it. They don't have the know-how and they don't have the experience. And I doubt if they have the interest. I've been in this business for over 16 years and I know what I'm talking about.

Hutton: You have an excellent profits record, Mr. Wade. You must be doing many things correctly.

Wade: Well, the former owners were always pleased.

Petroski: I am interested in how much participation you permit others to have in your organization.

Wade: Suppose it looks like we must work overtime. They are not just told—you're working overtime tonight. We talk it over. If they want to OK; if they don't, that's all right too. I'd say every employee in this plant is told everything necessary to do the job they were hired to do. Employees don't need to know everything that's going on. That's not what they were hired for.

Conklin: Do you have work expectancies or what you expect each employee to accomplish?

Wade: Yes, sir. Yes, sir. We have very fair work standards. You can ask anyone out on the floor and they'll tell you the same thing. We expect them to meet standard; if they don't they are not with us very long. We pay top wages in the community. I get very few gripes. Every employee knows where he or she stands. Every employee knows what is expected and that is the way to run a business. At least, that's what my granddaddy used to say. Once in awhile we get a troublemaker who isn't satisfied with anything you do. We either set him straight or ask him to leave.

Conklin: Do you have many like that?

Wade: No, when we do it is usually a new employee who doesn't like the work or doesn't want to work. We get maybe six or eight like that a year.

Hutton: Your outstanding record of profits intrigues me, Mr. Wade.

Wade: Well, thank you. I can continue to show good profits. This is a good business, and we have good employees.

Questions

1. What major decisions does the management of Elliott Corporation face? Discuss.
2. Of what management school of thought would you say Mr. Wade is a member? Why?

3. What objectives should Elliott Corporation adopt for its newly acquired company?

4. What specific actions do you recommend the management team of Elliott Corporation take? Justify your answer.

CASE 4–2: SCHRAMM MANUFACTURING COMPANY

Rick McDonald, factory manager, believes that the necessary help for production line 27, making an airplane component, can be secured from production line 21, making small hydraulic components. Line 21 was well established but due to design changes was being phased out. In contrast, line 27 was a new growing line and currently is estimated to be some nine weeks behind schedule. Further, quality maintenance is a problem on line 27. Production employees of the company work under a group wage incentive plan. Most have been with the company for the last six years.

It is believed by Mr. McDonald that line 27 can use all the surplus employees from line 21. And he favors doing this. He also feels job enrichment might well be used on line 27 as a means for performance improvement, better quality, and higher morale.

In discussing the matter with Myron Bishop, chief of the Industrial Engineering Department, Mr. McDonald was cautioned about making any change in manufacturing operations. "Those airplane parts are tricky to make and must meet precise specifications. We have experimented with a number of different arrangements and in my opinion have just about determined the best one. I would not disturb it for some new fad that you don't know whether it will work out or not. And it would mean we'd have to start from the very beginning again."

The personnel manager, Ms. Sara Spellman, likes the idea of job enrichment and has been trying to get the company to adopt it during the past several years. "We've got excellent people and should give them more of a voice in how we do things," is the way she puts it. She advocated improved communication, especially that of giving the employee more feedback on how the manufacturing employee is doing. Ms. Spellman feels this is particularly important in view of the present incentive plan of compensation. Based on questions she is asked, she claims employees want to know more about what is going on and want more participation in company affairs that concern them. "Satisfactory answers are not always forthcoming," Ms. Spellman adds. She has long advocated suggestion boxes along the production lines where manufacturing employees could drop ideas, criticisms, and views which would subsequently be reviewed and responded to by a peer committee meeting weekly. To date nothing like this has been done.

Mr. McDonald feels there might be a problem with the supervisors if something like job enrichment is followed. They may feel insecure of their positions and roles. He is not sure how to handle this. His uncertainty was increased in talking with Elmer Gensetti, head of Quality Control, who stated, "I tell you, Rick, I've been to several of these meetings where they talk about job enrichment, job improvement, have the blue-collar people have more say and all that. Maybe all that stuff is good, maybe not. I don't know. But I can tell you that letting the employees do what they want, make the decisions on quality, change their job designs and all that . . . well, your quality is going to go out the window. I know what I am talking about. I've been working like a horse to improve quality on 27. It is one of the toughest problems we have. And it is not going to go away as we step up production."

Questions

1. What do you think of the suggestions and reactions of Mr. Bishop? Why? Of Ms. Spellman? Why?
2. What is the problem Mr. McDonald faces? Discuss.
3. What action, if any, do you feel Mr. McDonald should take? Why?

Chapter 5

Objectives

"Would you tell me, please, which way I ought to go from here?"
"That depends a good deal on where you want to go to," said the Cat.
"I don't much care where," said Alice.
"Then it doesn't matter which way you go, said the Cat."

Lewis Carroll
Alice in Wonderland

The essence of management is to achieve a stated goal. If there is no purpose or end result sought, there is no justification for management. Centuries ago Seneca stated, "If a man doesn't know to what port he is steering, no wind is favorable to him." Having purpose, management revolves around objectives. And management is effective to the extent that its actions result in desired accomplishments.

One can reason, "certainly, every manager knows what she or he is trying to achieve—that's fundamental." Fundamental, of course, but from the practical viewpoint, objectives tend to get lost in the shuffle of managerial activity, their identities become obscured, activity is mistaken for accomplishment, and emphasis on what to do completely overshadows what is to be accomplished. Always good questions in management are: "What is the manager trying to accomplish? Why?"

DEFINITION AND IMPORTANCE OF OBJECTIVE

A managerial objective is the intended goal which prescribes definite scope and suggests direction to efforts of a manager. Note that this definition includes four concepts: (1) goal, (2) scope, (3) definiteness, and (4) direction. From the manager's viewpoint, the target to be attained is identified in clear and precise terms. A goal should not be confused with a general area of desired activities, for to do so places emphasis on the means, not the target. The scope of the intended goal is included by stating the prescribed boundaries or constraints to be observed. Also, an objective connotes definiteness. Purposes stated in

91

vague and double-meaning terms have minimum managerial value because they are subject to various interpretations and frequently result in confusion and turmoil. Finally, direction is indicated by the objective in that it shows the results to be sought and segregates these sought-for results from the mass of possible targets that might otherwise be utilized.

The importance of objectives is widely accepted; most managers agree that they are vital. Inappropriate and inadequate objectives can retard the management and suffocate the operations of any organization. A profitable suggestion to any manager is to sit back periodically and reiterate the objectives sought and then determine whether action taken is actually working toward these goals. Such a practice helps to minimize the difficulty by many management members in knowing what their *current* objectives are, in identifying them both to themselves and to their associates, in updating them, and in using them effectively in their management work.

Part of the outstanding success of Sears, Roebuck and Company is due to the company's ability to update its objectives. Starting as a small catalog merchant, it has grown into a giant distributor serving the public with a broad range of goods and services. Today it operates mail-order plants, retail stores, a life insurance business, an auto, fire, and casualty insurance business, an acceptance corporation, and a motor club. Throughout the company's history, its managers have continuously updated and refined their objectives as well as lived by them.

It should be observed that objectives have inherent power within themselves to stimulate action. When known or defined, they help identify what is to be done and minimize forgetfulness and misunderstanding. Too often, efforts are wasted because energies are expended on a mass of uncertain directives and interpersonal conflicts. A primary need of most enterprises is a single target or several major ones toward which the efforts of all members, and particularly the leaders, are drawn with the greatest force.

TYPE AND CLASSIFICATION OF OBJECTIVES

Existing, facilities, technological skills, public requirements of a situation, demands of the people, financial capacity, and market conditions prescribe many objectives of an organization. The subjects covered by the more common objectives include (1) to provide good products and services, (2) to stay ahead of competition, (3) to provide for the welfare of employees, (4) to grow, (5) to be efficient, (6) to make our streets free from crime, (7) to eliminate the pollution of air and rivers, (8) to clean up our highways and streets and keep them clean, (9) to disseminate new knowledge, and (10) to develop international trade.

In turn, these may suggest specific key areas for which subobjectives can be derived and the extent of their accomplishment evaluated. For example, the managers of the General Electric Company identify eight areas which are believed vital in maintaining and advancing the leadership, strength, and competitive ability of that company. These key result areas are:

1.	Profitability	5.	Personnel development
2.	Market position	6.	Employee attitudes
3.	Productivity	7.	Public responsibility
4.	Product leadership	8.	Balance between short-range and long-range plans

Establishing goals for each of these areas, implementing them, and evaluating the results achieved, constitute an important part of the company's management efforts.

It is traditional to think in terms of short-run, intermediate, and long-run objectives. While some differences exist, short-run goals usually extend for a period of less than one year—three to six months is common. Intermediate usually covers one to five years, and long-run objectives are those extending beyond five years. The time division of goals is one of the oldest and most widely used classifications.

For convenience and to assist management study, objectives can also be classified as (1) primary, (2) secondary, (3) individual, and (4) social. Providing salable goods and services for the market illustrates primary objectives which are normally thought of as being related to a company, not an individual. By providing such goods and services, consumers are offered what they want, and rewards can be given to participating members of the company. The primary goal of a mattress manufacturer is to provide a line of mattresses which are deemed desirable on the market; the primary goal of a department of this manufacturer is to produce a certain mattress part. Primary goals can be traced, in this manner, to the level of the work assignment performed by the individual member.

Secondary objectives assist in attaining primary objectives and identify targets for efforts designed to increase efficiency and economy in the work performance. Goals dealing with analysis, advice, and interpretation are illustrative. Their contribution is indirect in that they provide supportive efforts to those directed by the primary objectives. Secondary objectives, like primary objectives, are impersonal in nature.

Individual objectives, as implied by its name, are those of the individual members of an organization. Depending upon the viewpoint taken, they are attained by subordinating them to the primary or secondary objectives or by having such objectives realistically fostering the achievement of individual objectives. Most individual objectives are either economic—money, material needs goals, or psychologic—status, recognition, or nonfinancial rewards, desired in return for the use of their personal resources. The specific nature of the needs an individual attempts to satisfy by working within an organization and the relationships between inducements by an organization and individual contributions are interdependent and quite complex.[1]

Simple illustrations of individual objectives of top managers are shown by the goal to achieve bigness and by the goal to maintain their managerial positions. In the first case, the year-to-year profits might be bypassed in order to increase the long-run capital value of the enterprise. The manager secures considerable satisfaction and is completely contented to see the enterprise acquire great stature. In the second case, dealing with maintenance of their positions, moderate degrees of risks are not assumed, conservative plans are followed, and most actions follow a well-beaten path which by only the remotest chance will disturb the present security of the managers. This "management maintenance" objective, sometimes referred to as "satisfying," may be found where present operations are considered satisfactory by the owners, where the additional gains mean little to the managers, or where the failure of a new project might jeopardize the manager's position. Such an objective usually is not publicized yet underlies most managerial action, especially at the top level.

Social objectives deal with the goals of an organization toward society. Included are obligations to abide by requirements established by the community, such as those pertaining to health, safety, labor practices, and price regulation. Further, they include goals intended to further social and physical improvement of the community and to contribute to desirable civic activities. It should be noted that most business companies in achieving their primary goals also contribute to their respective communities by creating needed economic wealth, employment and financial support to the community.

WRITING AN EFFECTIVE OBJECTIVE

From what has been stated, it follows that writing an objective is difficult. Let's consider the following objective of a university:

The basic objective of Victory University is to provide opportunities in higher education in the fields of liberal and applied arts, teaching, business, and preprofessional study.

And the following for a manufacturer:

The purpose of this business enterprise is to produce through mass production low-unit-cost air conditioners and distribute them through company-

---

[1] See Chapter 18, Managerial motivation.

owned outlets in selected areas at highly competitive retail prices in order for the company to realize a reasonable return.

At first, both these statements appear reasonable, but after study, raise some suspect as to their quality and suitability for managerial purposes. The statement for the university is almost certain to bring up debatable issues regarding the scope and definiteness of activities in keeping with the basic objective. Are the opportunities limited to certain people, i.e., those who pass an examination? What study areas are included in preprofessional? Likewise, while the business enterprise statement gives basic information, it raises controversial questions: What is meant by selected areas for distribution? What is a reasonable return? Can products other than air conditioners be manufactured?

All of which means that *every managerial objective is subjected to interpretation*. The exact meaning will depend respectively upon the manager's and the nonmanager's personal value systems. The test of clarity and understanding is the recipient's perception and comprehension of the goal statement. But, it should not be excessively detailed so that the recipient is unable to use personal creativity and initiative. In addition, the institutional values dealing with the relationship of the individual to the community and to the work environment can have considerable influence.

Further, *derivative goals* are linked by members of an organization to the stated goal or goals of an enterprise. For the most part, these are logical linkages as viewed by each member, yet, in reality, they are conditioned by the personal values held by the particular person. For example, referring to the university objective given above, from the phrase "to provide opportunities in higher education in business" will certainly emerge a myriad of derivative goals which the holder believes are implied in the written major objective and are required to provide a complete meaning of that objective. The presence of interpretation and the addition of derivative goals make writing an objective anything but an easy task.

MEASUREMENT OF OBJECTIVES

During the past decade or so, considerable attention has been directed to measurable or verifiable expressions for objectives. A statement such as "make as many as you can" has minimum managerial value because its meaning differs with different people. Far better to use a measurable expression such as "make 200 units by 5 o'clock tonight." This gives definiteness and expedites mutual understanding. Figure 5–1 shows some typical examples of measurable objectives.

The determination of what should be measured and how it should be measured pose difficulties in the measuring of goals in areas where the goal is somewhat abstract, for example, for employee loyalty, em-

FIGURE 5-1:   Examples of measurable objectives

Objective subject	Current objective	Accomplishment last month
Sales............................	$275,000 per month	$257,940
Production cost	$ 77,850 per month	$ 80,722
Labor stability	One quit for employees with three years or more service	Three quits for employees with three years or more service
Orders completed on schedule	98%	91%

ployment development, or social responsibility. However, in such areas, approximations can be used and reasonably satisfactory results can be gained.

Generally speaking, business organization managers are better able to measure their goals than are the managers of nonbusiness organizations such as hospitals, governmental agencies, and universities. To illustrate, business has many information systems giving measurements on accomplishments for various factors throughout the entire organization. Typical are measures of physical and financial means to acquire and handle sufficient resources along with rate-of-return ratios, turnover, and debt-to-equity ratios. Also production measures including machine utilization and labor productivity are common as well as marketing measures dealing with sales penetration and advertising effectiveness. In contrast, the hospital administrator has difficulty measuring what the hospital provides—hospital care for a patient. However, contributing factors to hospital care are measured and include such measurements as room cost per day, number of service calls, patient-days per type of illness, and the like. While not precise, the approach can be used to give helpful measurable expression for hospital care.

HIERARCHY OF OBJECTIVES

For every enterprise there exists a hierarchy of objectives. This can encompass objectives dealing with enterprises in general, such as those concerning customers' aims, as well as those of the public or society as a whole. However, it more commonly connotes only objectives within the enterprise, and includes these at the different organizational levels of the enterprise. This concept will be followed in this discussion.

At the top organizational level and providing the goal for the entire effort is the major objective, or objectives, as the case might be. Subordinate to, but definitely related to, the major objectives are objectives including departmental objectives that set forth the goal of particular segments or organizational units of the enterprise. These department objectives, in turn, have subordinate group objectives, which in a similar manner are subsequently broken down into unit objectives and finally into individual objectives.

Figure 5–2 shows the various levels of objectives in diagrammatic form. As illustrated, the major objective is to "beat Z Company in production and sales." To the production department this means achieving a high volume of output interpreted in terms of the department objective to "manufacture 100,000 complete units A-6243 by

FIGURE 5–2:   Illustrating a hierarchy of objectives

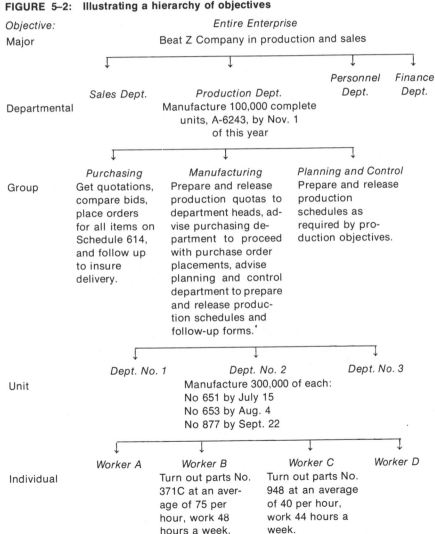

Objective:	Entire Enterprise
Major	Beat Z Company in production and sales

Sales Dept. — *Production Dept.* — *Personnel Dept.* — *Finance Dept.*

Departmental — Production Dept.: Manufacture 100,000 complete units, A-6243, by Nov. 1 of this year

Group

Purchasing — Get quotations, compare bids, place orders for all items on Schedule 614, and follow up to insure delivery.

Manufacturing — Prepare and release production quotas to department heads, advise purchasing department to proceed with purchase order placements, advise planning and control department to prepare and release production schedules and follow-up forms.´

Planning and Control — Prepare and release production schedules as required by production objectives.

Unit

Dept. No. 1 — *Dept. No. 2* — *Dept. No. 3*

Dept. No. 2: Manufacture 300,000 of each:
No 651 by July 15
No 653 by Aug. 4
No 877 by Sept. 22

Individual

Worker A — *Worker B* — *Worker C* — *Worker D*

Worker B: Turn out parts No. 371C at an average of 75 per hour, work 48 hours a week.

Worker C: Turn out parts No. 948 at an average of 40 per hour, work 44 hours a week.

November 1 of this year." This departmental objective can be stated at
the group level; for example, purchasing, as "get quotations, compare
bids, place orders for all items on Schedule 614, and follow up to
insure delivery." Figure 5–2 indicates other group objectives along
with unit and also individual objectives.

The accomplishment of each subsidiary objective should contribute
to the achievement of its respective immediate superior objective,
thus providing a thoroughly integrated and harmonious pattern of objectives to all members of the enterprise. For maximum effectiveness,
an objective must be meaningful and timely to the individual. To tell
an individual operating a lathe that the objective of the company is to
"beat Z Company in production and sales" means little until that
objective is translated into meaningful terms in that immediate task.

HARMONIZING OBJECTIVES

The fact that different types of objectives exist and also that within
every enterprise there is a hierarchy of objectives suggests that harmony should exist among objectives if a unity of effort is to be won.
Particularly is this true of so-called internal objectives—those within a
given enterprise. However, these internal objectives must also be
compatible with external objectives—those dealing with factors outside a given enterprise in order for the enterprise to function smoothly
in the external environment within which it exists.

Harmony among the goals of managers within an enterprise is vital;
they should not be at cross-purposes. Each manager's goal should supplement and assist the goals of colleagues. There is nothing wrong
with having the same objective for more than one manager of a given
enterprise. Some overlap of objectives usually exists; it is a normal
state of affairs.

Likewise, the objectives of individuals or nonmanagement members should be harmonized with those of the manager. When this is
accomplished, genuine teamwork is enjoyed, and human relations are
aided materially. For example, if the aim of one manager is to contribute a needed service and this corresponds to one's subordinate's goal,
the needed foundation is present for getting things accomplished effectively by this subordinate in this enterprise. The integration of
managers' and individuals' goals aids in achieving greater work satisfaction at all levels. Reconciling a manager's objectives and an individual's goals, however, is no easy task. Helpful suggestions include
getting the individual to:

1. Visualize in the work of the enterprise an opportunity to satisfy
   personal work interests, to use personal capacities, and progress
   toward personal career goals.

2. Develop an overall understanding of the enterprise's activities in order to anticipate improvements for accomplishing work and to meet the requirements of the enterprise.
3. Analyze work assignments and promotional opportunities with reference to reasonable expectancy of personal goals.
4. Determine periodically personal changing interests and abilities in light of the plans and changes taking place within the enterprise.

Likewise the manager should:

1. Recognize the capacity of the employee to contribute toward realization of managerial goals.
2. Encourage self-development of the employee for exceeding ordinary job performance.
3. Relate the employee's work contributions to that of other members of the enterprise and to the end product or service supplied.
4. Demonstrate that an employee advances only to the extent that one contributes directly and ultimately to the accomplishment of stated goals.

It is claimed by some management students that a key consideration in harmonizing objectives is to get important members of a group to place team goals before their personal goals. We know that most individual goals will be surrendered if group goals, or those established by the manager, are a sufficiently rewarding substitute for the individual goals. Where the managerial goals are strong enough to persuade the individuals to abandon or modify individual goals, wonders can be accomplished.

PROFITS AND OBJECTIVES

Because many feel that the major management objective applicable to *all* enterprises is to realize a financial profit, a discussion of this subject is warranted. Not *all* enterprises are interested in making a profit. For example, churches, hospitals, schools, charitable institutions, and government agencies are not concerned basically with the acquisition of profits. The nonprofit enterprises customarily rely on gifts, endowments, receipts from money-raising projects, certain charges, assessments, or taxes which are needed "to keep the enterprise going." The basic managerial objective in such enterprises is the providing of a service that is useful and socially desirable. However, the kind of service these enterprises render and how well they render it are important factors in determining the amount of financial support they win.

Whether a business manager is profit seeking will depend greatly upon the manager's personal goals and values as well as those of the manager's enterprise. Profits are residual in nature and come into existence as the result of other endeavors. A profit seeking manager cannot go out and directly secure profits; one must do something else one hopes will result in a realization of profits. In this sense profits can be thought of as an indirect goal, a possible and desired by-product of other direct efforts. Profits lie at the final link of a long chain of interrelated events. If the manager is profit seeking, profits can be looked upon as the outcome of successful pursuits of objectives that included the realization of profits.

Profits are important to the business manager. Under the competitive system and for the long term, a business enterprise must show a profit to survive in order to pay a reasonable return to its owners for risks assumed and, by custom, to fulfill the means for assessing the overall results of a business manager's efforts. Many feel that profit seeking is required to continue offering a product or service, to contribute to the community, and to pay for the cost of government. However, emphasis upon profits alone can misguide the manager. For instance, promoting only products with high margins, ignoring research, and failing to provide working conditions satisfactory to employees, may in the ultimate bring about the demise of an enterprise.

RESEARCH OF OBJECTIVES

Organizational goals and their relative importance to managers have been subjected to research. A well-written article by Professor George W. England in the *Academy of Management Journal* gives the results from a survey of over 1,000 U.S. managers of business organizations regarding their evaluation of the goals they consider important.[2] The results found, listed in order of their importance, are condensed here for convenience. They include goals pertaining to:

1. Organizational efficiency, high productivity, and profit maximization.
2. Organizational growth, industrial leadership, and organizational stability.
3. Employee welfare considerations.
4. Social and community interests.

For the most part these results concur with those found from previous studies having similar areas of investigation. Customer satisfaction with general efficiency and profitability is the dominant, but not the only objective of successful business firms. This should come as no surprise, for the broad purpose of business is to make available goods

---

[2] George W. England, "Organizational Goals and Expected Behavior of American Managers," *Academy of Management Journal*, June 1967, pp. 107–17.

and services and, in a competitive private enterprise system, managers of such enterprises strive for efficiency in their operations with the hope that, as a result, a profit will be realized.

It should also be noted that the above four types of goals are not mutually exclusive. A decision to influence the "general efficiency," for example, is commonly checked to see what the probable effect is on the organizational growth and stability as well as on social and community interests. Also, observe that over the long term the objective as well as the means for achieving the end results are altered as public demands change. Illustrative are the demands for social responsibility by business and the demands by government, representing the public, in enforcing regulatory measures such as equal employment opportunity and safety and health laws.

GUIDELINES FOR OBJECTIVES

Management objectives should be set with great care. They serve best and stand a better chance of being fulfilled when the following guidelines are taken into account:

1. Objectives should be the result of participation by those responsible for carrying them out.   Those near the situation probably know best what is achievable. Persons helping to formulate objectives have a strong commitment to achieve them. In addition, they gain a feeling of belonging and of importance. Top management members must participate in the setting of objectives and seldom, if ever, should accept proposals or objectives from their subordinates with no review or question. Recommended is the arrangement whereby the subordinate supplies information to the superior on what the objectives should be. These suggestions are then jointly discussed, altered if believed necessary, and the final objectives determined. When a serious crisis is faced, objectives may be imposed by top managers, but the reason for this approach should be explained and the opportunity for the subordinate to assist in determining the stated objective should be followed.

2. All objectives within an enterprise should support the overall enterprise objectives.   In other words, objectives should be mutually consistent throughout an organization. The sales department, for example, should not have a variety of products as its objective while the production department has two or three products as its goal. The test of goal consistency helps attain unity of efforts and compatibility of goals. To follow this guideline, emphasize the targets themselves, not how to achieve them.

3. Objectives should have some "reach."   Most people are more satisfied and they work better when there is a reasonable challenge. People want to exert themselves and to enjoy a feeling of accomplishment. Proper objectives can help in these efforts.

4. Objectives should be realistic.   The goal must not only be reasonable to the person responsible for its attainment, but it must also be realistic in view of both the internal and the external environmental constraints present in a given case. It is well to guard against trying to attain too much in too short a time. And remember that a simply stated objective usually can be remembered, whereas a long, detailed description is quickly forgotten.

5. Objectives should be contemporary as well as innovative.   The successful manager keeps objectives up-to-date, reviews them periodically, and makes revisions when it is believed advantageous to do so. In a number of cases the decision will be to continue with the same objective. However, in these times of rapid change, no updating or the lack of any innovation in objective setting may be a possible danger signal for present management.

6. Objectives established for each management member should be limited in number.   Too many cause confusion and neglect; too few permit waste and inefficiency. Four or five objectives per management member is maximum. If there are more objectives, they should be consolidated in some way. Too many objectives diminish the relative importance of the really major ones and emphasize unduly those of minor status.

7. Objectives should be ranked according to their relative importance.   This places the needed emphasis upon major objectives. Establishing goal priorities and giving every management member a percentage value for each objective that concerns him or her helps to allocate efforts effectively. Thus, the entire management effort is improved. Also, note that it is human nature to delay the accomplishment of the more difficult objectives and to gain satisfaction from completing other objectives even though they are minor ones.

8. Objectives should be in balance within a given enterprise.   The various objectives should not collectively point to an excess of any one condition. For example, the objective for customer service may be overstressed to the detriment of the objective for realizing adequate earnings. Likewise, the objective of management development should be in balance with the growth objective of the overall organization.

QUESTIONS

1. Discuss the importance of objectives in management.
2. Assume you are the owner and manager of a grocery store located in a middle-income neighborhood in a city of 100,000 population. What would be your major objectives? Discuss.
3. What is your reaction to the following statement: 'Since most managers agree that objectives are essential in management, it is academic to discuss objectives in the typical management course."? Why?

4. Distinguish carefully between the two concepts in each of the following pairs: (*a*) satisfying objective and "reach of an objective"; (*b*) individual objectives and social objectives; and (*c*) a primary objective and a secondary objective.

5. From your own observations or experience, relate an example of an enterprise showing an ability to update its objectives.

6. Briefly discuss the subject of the hierarchy of objectives and its importance in management.

7. Other than profit, discuss some major objectives that a manager of a business enterprise might establish.

8. In your own words, tell what is meant by the statement that profits are residual in nature.

9. Relate the importance you attach to the harmonizing of objectives in acquiring effective management.

10. Talk with a friend and seek to discover what individual goals are held by this person. Do your friend's goals differ from your own? As a result of this project, do you feel it might be well for you to change any of your goals? Discuss.

11. What is your understanding of derivative goals? Of what importance are they in management?

12. Select three widely separate enterprises, such as a hospital, manufacturing company, sales agency, hotel, government agency, club, and school, and for each one find out the major managerial objective by communicating with a member of that enterprise. What conclusions do you draw from this experience and also from the information obtained? Discuss.

13. Name and discuss briefly two guidelines for objectives that you feel are important.

14. Give several major goals that might well be used in the management of a motel? Repeat using a local nursing home for senior citizens.

CASE 5–1: STRADLING COMPANY

Elevator parts and maintenance service are offered by this company on a nearly nation-wide coverage. The company's reputation is outstanding for prompt service and quality parts. Data on the four major sales territories of this company are:

| Territory | Last year | | This year | |
	Sales	Net profits	Sales	Net profits
Northeast	$6,370,161	$158,980	$5,451,245	$ 63,714
Midwest	4,289,034	265,381	4,470,632	277,286
South	2,553,417	107,250	2,831,870	138,760
West coast	5,682,729	153,514	6,011,694	171,772

It is the opinion of the top managers that sales in the northeast territory represent a problem and some corrective action must be taken. Currently, the northeast headquarters is located in Boston with three branch offices in Buffalo, Newark, and Philadelphia. Each branch carries a complete stock of replacement parts and offers full maintenance service. It is believed that the sales and service coverage now made in this area should be continued. The belief is strong that some effective solution for the northeast area is mandatory.

Questions

1. Is there a problem in the northeast territory? Justify your answer.
2. Does the company appear to have a sales problem? Discuss.
3. What objectives do you feel should be established by the company? Defend your suggestions.

CASE 5–2: KOVELL PRODUCTS COMPANY

The executive committee of Kovell Products Company is considering the acquisition of Ralos, Inc. ("solar" spelled backwards), a firm owning some interesting and promising patents in the area of solar energy. At a recent meeting the following conservation took place.

Roger Haber (president of Kovell): It is our pleasure to have with us today the president of a young and aggressive company engaged in developing, producing, and marketing of solar energy equipment. Meet Dr. Connie Siefert. Our group has some questions for you. However, first will you say a few words about solar energy, its technology, economic feasibility and the like.

Siefert: Certainly. It is always a plasure to talk about my favorite subject and especially so when the audience is a prospective buyer of my business. The total power output of the sun is estimated to be several thousand-trillion times the power requirements of humans on earth. When the sun is directly overhead, one square yard of earth receives the equivalent of about 1.4 kilowatts of solar power which is reduced about 30 percent when passing through the atmosphere. Solar energy is measured in Langley units. One such unit is the amount of energy required to supply one calorie of heat energy to one centimeter of area directly below the sun's rays.

The amount of energy generated by the sun varies with the climatic conditions of the particular geographic area. In Miami, Florida, for example, some 600 Langleys of solar energy are received daily, whereas in December in western Canada the figure is around 75 Langleys. Solar energy in summer is probably economical north of a certain latitude. In contrast, application of solar energy may be economically feasible south of that latitude during the entire year.

Haber: Since solar energy is available only during the day, it requires storage of energy. Right?

Siefert: Correct. Actually, the storage is the biggest cost of solar energy. It is the opinion of our engineers that the technologic conversion by which sunlight is directly converted into electricity will prove to be the most popular.

Frey (production manager): Why is that?

Siefert: Because the cost is lower and it produces energy in the conventional electrical form. The direct conversion using alternate layers of semiconducting material that form a continuous, light-sensitive junction appears to be superior as of now.

Haber: There are other means being used?

Siefert: Yes, for example, converting the solar energy directly into heat is feasible. When sunlight hits a black surface, its energy is converted into heat. This thermal method is inexpensive, requires materials readily available, and is convenient for applications such as space heating and water heating. Storage is by means of insulated hot water tanks. However, it takes a very high temperature of water to convert the thermal heat into other forms of energy.

Haber: Is solar energy being used now—is it practical?

Siefert: Oh my, yes. Very much so. Several large home builders have included solar energy in their building designs to reduce house heating requirements. The Energy Research and Development Administration (ERDA) will have some 4,000 buildings as a demonstration project to show heating and cooling by means of solar energy. A number of remote installations are now in existence including many by the Department of Defense. In one government installation, for example, a 5,000 sq. ft. solar collector provides about 75 percent of the heat and hot water requirements for some 50 housing units.

Haber: Very interesting. Very interesting.

Siefert: There is also the idea of orbiting the world with a satellite that would collect solar energy which would be converted to microwave energy and then to ordinary electric power.

Haber: Despite all these developments, solar energy is still in its formative stages. Don't you agree?

Siefert: Yes, I believe that is true.

Haber: I favor our buying Dr. Siefert's firm. It has basic patents in the solar processes that appear to be practical. Our goal should be to stay out ahead and progress with technology.

Singer (vice president of finance): But Roger, you can sink a lot of money in trying to be first in technology. Dr. Siefert will confirm that.

Siefert: Yes, that's true. But you have to manage your expenditures just like any other activity.

Singer: Yes, I understand. Profits are really our end goal. Our financial resources have limitations. I think it might be better to wait and see how this solar energy concept progresses.

Haber: We might lose by waiting. Siefert's outfit has gone through the costly development stage. Their products are ready to go.

Singer: Seems to me our business is electronic devices. That's what we know, that's where we should stay. Electronic devices have helped us build a satisfactory business. Maybe we should develop improvements for electronic devices and not get into what is a new field for us.

Haber: You may be right. Dr. Siefert would stay with us several years and help in establishing the solar energy business.

Questions

1. What do you believe is the future of solar energy? Discuss.
2. What would be some advantages to Kovell Products Co. in buying Ralos, Inc.? Disadvantages?
3. What should be the objectives of Kovell Products Co.? Explain.
4. What action should Mr. Haber now take? Why?

PART II
Decision making

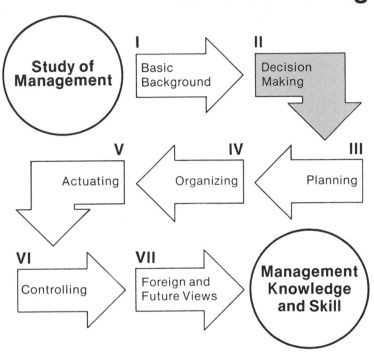

Chapter makeup for Part II:

6. *Managerial problems and decision making.*
7. *Decision making-nonquantitative means.*
8. *Decision making-quantitative means.*

To make the modified process of management feasible, problems or obstacles in the way of the process must be identified and eliminated or at least minimized. Further, decisions must be made in connection with the fundamental functions of planning, organizing, actuating, and controlling. Actually, many consider problem identifying and solving and the making of decisions a part of the management process itself. We segregate them here to point out and clarify their essentiality in management.

Problem identification and minimization as well as decision making are fundamental in the facilitation of management. They merit discussion, in some detail, because their conditioning of planning, organizing, actuating, and controlling is so great.

Chapter 6

Managerial problems and decision making

A trouble either can be remedied, or it cannot. If it can be, set about it; if it cannot be, dismiss it from your consciousness.

Lillian Whiting

Typically a manager encounters difficulties in striving to accomplish the desired results. Employees don't show up for work, machines break down, incorrect materials are received from suppliers, sales decline, cost increases, product quality becomes unacceptable, and a million and one other problems take place. All managers must deal with problems or hurdles preventing managerial planning, organizing, actuating, and controlling from taking place as designed. A formal definition of a problem is as follows: *A problem is a deviation from some standard or desired level of dimension, important enough to be solved, and to which a person is committed to find a solution.*

Problems exist because most goals we want to achieve will just not be achieved unless we strive to make them a reality. Further, attempts to win improvements over what is currently being done raises problems. Typical managers look for problems if they are not brought to them. The urge is constant to produce a better product or service, to improve product design, reduce selling price, serve more people, and finance more economically. In a very real sense, a manager is oriented around problems.

Some view problems as opportunities to make improvements. We progress by solving pertinent problems, by seizing the opportunity to correct errors and making the total effort the best we possibly can. This necessity to overcome obstacles to goal achievement is a favorable circumstance because most progress is stimulated by opposition. The field of medicine, for example, has advanced by combatting disease, education by combatting ignorance, and law enforcement by combatting crime. In similar manner, management has gone forward by combatting problems. Problems are the diet upon which a manager thrives. By successfully resolving problems, the manager not only serves the enterprise but also achieves personal growth and advancement.

COMMON PROBLEM AREAS FOR MANAGERS

Among the broad problem areas faced from time to time by many managers are the following: the development and improvement of long- and short-term objectives for the entire enterprise and for each major part of it; the improvement of resources, including personnel, facilities, and finance, and better allocation and evaluation of their respective adequacies; the clarification of managerial ethics which prevails in the enterprise's relationships with outsiders; and the effectiveness of presently used communication means and how improvement in the media may be obtained.

More specifically, common managerial problem areas, arranged alphabetically, include the following:

1. *Costs:* Utilization of standard cost plan, distribution of cost data, better use of cost information.
2. *Decision making:* Adequacy of present techniques, use of latest techniques, developing skill in ascertaining alternative actions.
3. *Employee training:* Sufficiency of present efforts, utilizing advanced techniques, advisability of changing supervisory training.
4. *Financing:* Securing short-term loans on better terms, increasing the working capital, planning future money needs.
5. *Information distribution:* Providing adequate and complete oral and written information to all personnel so that they are fully informed and can do their respective jobs better.
6. *Inventory records:* Improvements to reduce inventory losses, correlation with sales and manufacturing data, simplification needed.
7. *Markets:* Efforts to find out what buyers want, determining market potentials, finding areas of greatest sales opportunities.
8. *Morale:* Determining what employees think of their company, areas in which morale can be improved, possible improvements that can be started.
9. *Plant location:* Utilization of centralized or decentralized arrangement, build or rent, reduction of maintenance costs.
10. *Pricing:* Appraisal of present prices, probable effect on volume due to price change, competitive pricing.
11. *Production planning:* Determination and achievement of economic runs; maintenance of proper inventories of raw, in-process, and finished goods; increasing machine and equipment utilization.

12. *Products and services:* Development that meets favorably the requirements of the market and of the enterprise.
13. *Quality control:* Economical maintenance of higher quality standards, training personnel for this work, availability of qualified people.
14. *Recruitment and selection:* Finding and attracting the best prospective employees, effectiveness of interviews and tests.
15. *Reports:* Improvement in format and writing style, distribution and evaluation of reports, and data supplied.
16. *Sales effectiveness:* Reducing time required for processing a sales order, establishing sales quotas, improving sales reports.
17. *Social responsibility:* Contributing managerial talent to projects designed to improve social relationships, better understanding among people, and satisfactory environmental conditions.
18. *Supervising:* Guiding and directing efforts of employees and other resources to accomplish stated work outputs.
19. *Wage and salary administration:* Improving equitableness of present plan, winning greater acceptance for it, adequacy of plan in the future.
20. *Waste elimination:* Employee awareness of waste, data on extent of waste material, means of reducing waste, effectiveness of waste campaigns.

PROBLEM ANALYSIS

To eliminate a problem requires problem analysis which consists of two parts: (1) problem identification and (2) problem solution. Before a problem can be solved, it must be identified. Problem identification is vital for problem solution. Analysis and decision making regarding the wrong problem can be fatal. We seek effectiveness with efficiency. A manager should perform the right things right. Importance of problem identification is also given by an old truism, "A problem well stated is half solved." Problem identification is one of the most difficult tasks that a manager faces. It is helped by the manager's acquisition of knowledge, improvement of skill, and experience.

Refrain from identifying the problem as "we need better managers," or "our problem is lack of sales." These are too general and represent a superficial identification of the real problem. Usually evidence can be found to support such a statement and the investigation ends prematurely.

Observe also the important contribution of results management to the problem identification. A person with no objective has no problem. A problem is what is keeping a person from achieving an objective. When results are stressed, as in results management, the problem preventing the results achievement is highlighted. Remove this obstacle and the sought objective will be won.

Problem solution is the end result of problem analysis. It follows problem identification. It is mandatory to know what the problem is, or even if you have one, before you can begin to draw up a solution for it. Like problem identification, the superior solution is aided greatly by the manager's adequate knowledge, skill, and thinking.

PROBLEM SOLUTION AND THE MANAGEMENT PROCESS

To enable managers to understand their current problems and to assist in providing a course of action to follow, the framework provided by the management process is extremely helpful. It is sufficiently flexible to be used in a variety of situations, is relatively simple to apply, and provides the needed overall viewpoint.

The obtaining of data on all aspects of the enterprise's operations over a period and analyzing these data by applying measures of efficiency, reveal trouble spots, if any, throughout the enterprise. The problem analyst, however, should avoid classifying the data by departments. This relates problems to isolated units of the entire enterprise and leads to the fallacious conclusion that the problem and its solution lies within the realm of that particular unit. In some cases this assumption may be reasonably correct, but in many others, it will not be true. Problems have a way of cutting across departmental boundaries and commonly are not properly identified or solved by a "department-by-department" approach. The problems simply do not fit departmental categories and will not be completely solved by tackling them one by one.

Use of the process management approach provides the needed perspective. Departmental activities are interrelated and an impact on the enterprise is quite likely to produce ripples of reaction in various departments and many of the trouble spots within these departments are probably interrelated to one another. These trouble spots, such as rising production cost, declining sales, and slow collection payments, are in essence symptoms rather than the problem to be solved. They have come into being as the result of some higher, more fundamental weakness. The challenge is to find out the cause or the problem permitting these symptoms to emerge. The process of management provides an adequate way to generalize and bring together these underlying symptoms. It offers a comprehensive diagnostic approach which is logical and frequently suggests additional analyses overlooked during the initial stages of examining the basic data.

In addition the major problems are expressed in terms of management when the process approach is used. This suggests what managerial action may be taken to solve the problem. Figure 6–1 includes suggestions under each major function of management. The subheadings will be discussed in the subsequent chapters of this book.

FIGURE 6–1: Possible managerial actions to solve management problems arranged by fundamental functions of the management process

  I. Planning
    1. Objectives of individuals.
    2. Objectives of the enterprise.
    3. Policies covering authority, prices, attitude toward competition.
    4. Procedures—specific means of handling paper and products.
    5. Internal programs.
 II. Organizing
    1. Span of authority.
    2. Delegation of authority.
    3. Use of staff and service groups.
    4. Informal groups.
    5. Integration of structural activities.
III. Actuating
    1. Leading.
    2. Developing and evaluating employees.
    3. Fulfilling personal needs through work satisfaction.
    4. Job enrichment and enlargement.
    5. Supervising.
 IV. Controlling
    1. Establishing standards of performance.
    2. Measuring work performance.
    3. Improving rate of return on investment.
    4. Developing adequate budgeting.
    5. Employing better cost and quality controls.

Specifically, does the problem appear to be one primarily in planning? In organizing? In actuating? In controlling? Studying the trouble spots in light of these fundamental functions of management reveals suggestions to solve the problem.

Assume the area of the problem is believed to be planning. As will be discussed in future chapters of this book (Chapters 9–12 inclusive), the management process school contributes much to planning and assists in solving problems in planning. The size of the market for a given product or service, the cost, and the return on the investment required, are illustrative of contributions by the process school. Likewise, if the problem under planning is essentially one of policies or procedures, the management process school is very helpful. Also, as already indicated in Chapter 2 (page 29), the quantitative measurement school can be of significant help in planning. On the other hand, if actuating appears to be the major problem area, the process school will assist in the subareas such as supervising, developing, and evaluating employees. Additional and excellent assistance is provided by use of the behavioral and social school especially for the sub-areas of job enrichment and leading.

Problem solving by the manager must be free of bias; possible causes must not be supported with arguments prompted by the manager's subjective feelings. It is also well to include the ideas and suggestions of others. Excellent solutions emerge from groups working constructively as a team. Figure 6–2 shows helpful guides for problem solving.

MANAGEMENT PROBLEMS AND CONTROLLING

Although all the fundamental functions of management are important in problem identification and problem solution, controlling is especially so. A management problem can be thought of as the deviation between what should be and what actually is. In other words, the amount by which we are off the planned target represents the problem. This represents the imbalance which the manager needs first to identify and then decide what action to take to correct.

In addition, controlling identifies and locates precisely the deviation or deviations. With such information, rationality, represented by analysis and synthesis, can then be followed to find the possible cause or causes of such deviations and hence of the problem. The cause is a change or an action from the plan being followed that has taken place to produce the unwanted effect. Every problem has a cause. There are always one or more things that have brought about the cause, as distinguished from that thing or things that have not brought about the cause. Care should be taken to avoid the common tendency to jump to conclusions by accepting the first deviating thing and justifying it, at least tentatively, as the sole responsible one.

APPROACHES TO PROBLEM SOLUTION

There are five major approaches to management problem solutions. As shown on Figure 6–3, they include (1) routine, (2) scientific, (3) decisional, (4) creative, and (5) quantitative approaches. Referring to this figure, we start at the top with a desired result. As clearly indicated in this chapter, as soon as a manager begins efforts to accomplish a desired result, management problems will appear to impede actions. By what means can the manager solve these problems?

First, employ the routine approach. This includes solving the problem via traditional means, or doing what has always been done when a problem of this type is confronted. Reference is simply made to habit or history and the same answer used before is used now. It is also possible to use standard operating procedures (SOP), which are writ-

FIGURE 6–2: Guides to improve your problem solving

1. *Review quickly all the elements of the problem so that a composite entity of the entire problem is obtained.* This focuses attention upon the "big picture" and avoids seeing the problem as a mosaic of numerous individual considerations. Also, pertinent relationships are more easily disclosed, the memory is relieved, and the mental capacity is enlarged.

2. *Try a change in the manner in which the problem is expressed.* Switching from verbal terms to a mathematical model, graph, or numbers to represent the problem may shed new and wanted light on the task. If dealing with nonverbal terms, try stating the problem in simple action terms.

3. *Consider the work environment and try rearranging the space and time characteristics of the problem.* This can help in revealing known and common patterns that originally are hidden by an unfamiliar arrangement. Stating the identical relationships in a different and perhaps more normal manner can contribute to the solution.

4. *Evaluate your own ideas and those of others constructively.* Guard against complacency in accepting your own ideas. They may be brilliant, but also consider the insights of others wrestling with the same or similar problems.

5. *Discuss problem with others.* This practice forces you to restate all the aspects of the problem and in so doing brings out considerations requiring further attention not considered in the tentative solution. It also requires a relating of the fundamentals so that the listener knows what is being considered. By such communication, obscure and inconsistent points are uncovered; and furthermore, the listener, by asking questions, reveals gaps which appear inconsistent and inadequate, thus pointing out areas for bettering the problem solution.

ten forms telling the manager what to do under certain described conditions. Usually SOPs are in the format of a manual. Another means under the routine approach is to abide by superior's order. Here the manager has actually no choice at all, but follows the edict of the superior.

The scientific approach is a widespread means of solving problems. As pointed out in Chapter 2 (see pages 22–24), the scientific method consists of a controlled experimentation to prove or disprove an assumed answer, or hypothesis. The steps taken, in sequence, are indicated on Figure 6–3.

FIGURE 6–3:   Approaches to management problem solving

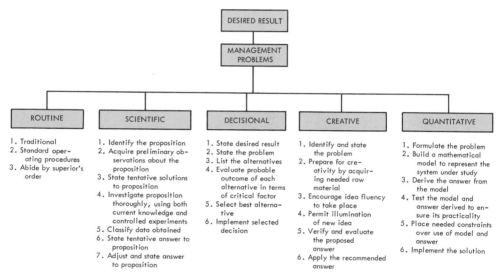

The third approach is decisional, one of the most common and popular of all the approaches. To gain the desired result, a decision is made. Hopefully this decision will solve the management problem which is the barrier to obtain the desired result. For clarity, it is essential that the desired result be stated first and then the problem. Confusion is common in this portion of the decisional approach. For example, suppose you are fullback on a football offense team. The play called is for you to carry the ball through the line between your left tackle and left guard. What is the problem? If you answer, "to get through the line," that is wrong. That's the end result. The problem or barrier is the opposing team's defense—all 11 players. They are trying to keep you from gaining yardage. Eliminate or neutralize the defense and you will achieve the end result.

For any given situation, several decisions leading to alternative actions are possible. Any of these alternatives are possible to resolve the problem. The alternatives, resulting from a situation requiring a decision, are identified and one of them is selected as being the best, based on the probable predicted outcome of that alternative. Usually the evaluation is on the basis of what is the least costly, conforms with legal requirements, is the quickest, the best quality, or the best quantity. The basis used is referred to as the critical factor. It is not the same in every case, but will vary depending upon the individual requirements. The final step is to implement the selected decision.

Some managers feel that decision making should not be viewed as a logical action, that is, the problem need not be defined and strictly rational steps need not be taken to decide what to do. They point out that stated objectives need not exist. The decision maker studies the information, people, and facilities involved and concentrates on the interactions and the possible outputs from these resources. Creativity hopefully will assist in these efforts. In part, this viewpoint is justified on the basis that the decision maker is able to see more and know better what to do, as he or she progresses in efforts and reaches "the top of the next hill." They contend it is impractical to reach final decisions when many unknowns lie ahead in the future. This "decide as you go" approach emphasizes the human behavior factor in decision making, gives freedom in decision making to managers, minimizes misunderstanding about stable and defined end goals, and recognizes decision making as quasi and temporary rather than a complete and final resolution of a conflict.

The creative approach is the fourth method of problem solving to be discussed. This method utilizes the ability to evolve new workable ideas and to implement them. A positive attitude, imagination, and the ability to put together new relationships along heretofore unconventional lines are basic requirements for applying this method. The gist is to create and apply new ideas—those never used before or known. It represents a brand new way of achieving the desired result and is not determined judicially, that is, by making logical analysis or rational comparisons. As indicated in Figure 6–3, the sequence to follow for the creative method is: (1) identify and state the problem, (2) prepare for creativity by acquiring needed raw materials, (3) encourage idea fluency to take place, (4) permit illumination of new idea, (5) verify and evaluate the proposed answer, and (6) apply the recommended answer.[1]

The last method to be discussed is the quantitative approach. As stated in Chapter 2, the emphasis here is on the mathematical modeling of systems. Comparison of various feasible actions such as cost reduction, revenues, and rates of return on investment are expressed by measurable values. The relationship of the factors for any given

---

[1]See also Chapter 11 for a discussion of creating and innovating ideas.

action is stated in mathematical form, i.e., by a formula or an equation. By substituting different mathematical values for the variables of the equation, different results are obtained and evaluated in keeping with the requirements of the stated problem. The computer is of great assistance in using this method, especially where the mathematical model is complex or the volume of the calculations is large. Shown in Figure 6–3 are the six steps to follow.

POTENTIAL-PROBLEM ANALYSIS

Actions to minimize or possibly to prevent the effects of potential problems are among the most rewarding that a manager can take. The first step is to list all the major potential problems that you think might arise from the proposed action. Sources for such problems include situations where there is no outstanding desired alternative action, responsibility is difficult to fix, a given sequence must be followed, the action is new or unfamiliar, or the scheduling is tight. Next, describe each potential problem. This helps to identify accurately each problem, revealing precisely the what, where, and when of it. Following this, the classification of potential problems by their degree of risk is suggested. Further, for each high-risk problem identify its possible causes. In this way a priority of problems is determined and concentration on those most threatening to the management plan can be followed. The setting forth of possible causes of these major problems shows what the manager may have to cope with. One doesn't know for sure since one is dealing with possibilities only. The small-risk problem will be accepted and the chance is taken that it will not occur. Next, assess the probability of occurrence to the causes of each major potential problem. In essence, for each major problem this points to the major causes which merit the most watching. And logically, efforts are then taken to minimize the effects of these major causes. Efforts in widely different areas may have to be taken since causes commonly are from multiple sources. And finally, decide how to handle the most serious potential problems. This supplies contingency actions to adopt at once should any of the potential problems become a reality. Such actions are rewarding when the potential problem could bring about chaotic conditions and the removal of its causes or reduction of its probability appear slim.

This list of steps is so logical that one wonders why managers do not follow it as a routine practice. The reasons are several and are mentioned here so that if any of them is observed in an actual situation, they will serve as signals to adopt the potential-problem analysis just described. First, the managers are more concerned with correcting present-day problems than with minimizing or preventing tomorrow's problems. Praise and recognition are rarely, if ever, bestowed on managers for things that do not happen. Also there is a tendency by the employees to believe they fully understand all the implications of a proposed plan because they agree with the intent of the plan. The potential problem remains invisible until the planned activities take form and content. At that time the opportunity for prevention is passed; the problem exists and must be solved. In addition, the critical consequences of a managerial action is not adequately analyzed. The possibility for failure are simply ignored perhaps because "such thinking is negative" or the analysis of such consequences are unsavory and disagreeable to face. Last, a persistent conviction exists among management members that plans they suggest are nearly infallible; otherwise they would not recommend them. They reason that "there is little use in looking for trouble." But experience demonstrates that actions do go wrong, troubles do arise. Hence, it is wise to probe for possible errors and to evaluate their effects.

CASE STUDY

Case studies are commonly used to study managerial problem identification and solution. A case study is a description of a situation involving problems to be solved. The problem solver is forced to face up to the uncertainties of the practical world and to develop skill in applying the knowledge possessed. The case study provides a strong educational means for arousing the student's interest because it makes the student an active, not a passive, participant.

A major task of working with case studies is problem identification. Frequently, it requires deep and concentrated thought. A common criticism by the nonprofessional is that the case does not include all the facts. This is true; few case studies do include all the facts. But managers seldom have all the facts, a concept itself subject to wide interpretation by the case solver. So while not perfect, case studies do have a definite sense of reality. Attempting to determine a solution without full knowledge may be frustrating, but actually it is part of the essence of managerial problem solving.

The four fundamental functions of management plus the five approaches to management problem solving should be used in studying management cases. Different problem solving approaches can be used for different problems. That is, for a particular case perhaps the superior solution is found via the creative approach that recommends an entirely new set of actions be taken to solve the problem. Or in another case, the social approach may supply what appears to be the best answer.

In most instances, the usual suggestion is to view the case study as requiring the development of an orderly analysis. When this view-point is followed, certain prescribed steps should be followed as shown in Figure 6–4.

FIGURE 6–4:   Steps to follow in analyzing a management case

1. *Identify the central issues.*   Focus on what seems to be the key problems. Separate superficial issues from the key problems. The superficial issues are usually just symptoms of deeper, ingrained problems. Use the planning, organizing, actuating, and controlling framework to assist in identifying what the central issues are. Also decide on the management problem solving approach to follow.

2. *Organize the pertinent facts.*   Utilize the central issues as centers around which substantiating and relevant facts are organized. Put the facts in a different format if this will assist understanding of them. Use of charts and matrix forms, for example, are helpful.

3. *Determine the alternatives.*   There is always more than one possible answer. Think and imagine until at least three or four possibilities are evolved. In some case studies the alternatives are quite clear while in others some deep thinking and probing are required.

4. *Evaluate the alternatives.*   Basically this is a matter of relating certain important facts in support of a certain alternative, and repeating for each alternative. Some facts will support a given alternative, others will indicate preference for a different alternative. Also some facts will suggest the consequences of choosing one alternative over another. Judgment and experience will also assist in evaluating the alternatives.

5. *Select the alternative recommended.*   All things considered, what appears to be the strongest, most appropriate, and most feasible alternative is selected and recommended. This selection is a natural outgrowth of step No. 4 above. By this means the case solver is aware of the strengths as well as the limitations of a choice.

QUESTIONS

1. Discuss problem identification as a part of a manager solving a problem.
2. Should the problem be stated first, then the end results sought, or should the end results be stated first and then the problem? Substantiate your answer and include an example to demonstrate your answer.
3. Define each of the following: (a) problem, (b) seeing the "big picture" in solving a management problem, and (c) case study.
4. List six specific problems of managers and discuss two of them in some detail.
5. Explain Figure 6–3 in your own words.
6. What is the relationship between management problems and controlling?
7. Give an example from your own observation of progress being stimulated by opposition.

8. What are potential problems? Do you feel they can be eliminated by potential problem analysis? Justify your answer.

9. Enumerate the five approaches to management problem solving. Which one are you inclined to favor? Why?

10. What approach for solving a management problem would you say would be used by each of the following: (*a*) the manager of an auto-design unit trying to complete the work for a new instrument panel; (*b*) a surgeon in the operating room of a hospital discovering that the diagnosis of the patient before him is incomplete; (*c*) an air force officer, leading a squadron in flight, receiving word of an impending crisis in making a forthcoming landing within the next seven minutes? Justify your answer in each case.

11. How do you explain the lack of potential-problem analysis in today's management?

12. Do you agree with this statement: "Case studies are extensively used in management study, but they are not totally satisfactory. One reason is that they provide all the information in a neat package to the problem solver—a condition that is totally unreal in practicing management. The manager of an enterprise must dig up the facts." Explain why you have answered this question as you have.

13. Enumerate and discuss the suggested five steps for analyzing a management case.

14. List the symptoms and their related problems for three situations you have experienced or read about. Suggest, for one of these situations, how the process of management would assist in problem identification and solution.

CASE 6–1: LIDS, INC.

In January of a recent year a U.S. senator asked if the Federal Trade Commission would investigate the home canning equipment business, particularly canning lids used on glass jars by home canners for fruit and vegetables. Consumer complaints about lids being unavailable in retail stores were numerous and frequent. Restraint of trade and restriction of competition were frequently voiced. Consumer groups turned to their public officials to do something to alleviate the shortage.

Although simple in appearance, a modern canning lid combines a considerable amount of engineering and technical skill. A rubber composition is affixed to a formed metal disc or lid. When the lid is forced onto the top of the glass jar, an adhesive or fastening action takes place. The cooling of the contents, i.e., canned tomatoes, cherries, or peaches, creates a suction on the lid, causing it to depress slightly in the center portion and form an air-tight covering over the jar.

Canning lids are packed one dozen to a box and retail for around 40 cents. Lids, Inc. is one of eight major glass companies manufacturing home canning lids. It's canning products are well known and the corporation enjoys an excellent reputation throughout the entire industry. At one time a large number of manufacturers were in the canning lids business; but beginning back about 1950, the business began to decline—people preferred to buy canned and frozen fruit and vegetables in the store rather than follow home canning practices. For awhile the demand for home canning equipment remained fairly constant at a relatively low level. Then growth in the demand took place with average annual increases of 15–20 percent taking place for a period of about six years as shown by the following Exhibit 1.

EXHIBIT 1: Production of canning lids by Lids, Inc.

	Millions of packages (one dozen lids per package)
9 years ago	33.653
8 years ago	39.705
7 years ago	44.910
6 years ago	55.429
5 years ago	59.172
4 years ago	64.531
3 years ago	62.452
2 years ago	90.864
1 year ago	120.017
Recent year	250.131

Three years ago, Lids, Inc. were taking back jars and lids from the wholesalers because the bad weather on the east coast wiped out most of the home gardens. Two years ago, the sales of seeds and the effect of inflation on food prices indicated a strong demand for home canning equipment probably would take place. It did. Sales of Lids, Inc. shot up 50 percent. A common rule of thumb followed by the industry until that time was that one third of the American families bought home canning equipment. Important factors generally considered affecting demand of 2 years ago were shortages in two raw materials: one in glass, one in the metal for lids. The glass shortage had its roots in the shut down of synthetic soda ash manufacturers, commonly attributed to the influence of EPA (Environmental Protection Agency) banning phosphates from detergents with the result that increasing demand for natural soda ash by the soap companies followed. At the same time, metal stock for lids became in short supply. These shortages remained in the minds of the manufacturers and also the consumers of canning lids with the result that purchases started early during the period one year ago, and sky-rocketed during the recent year. As can be observed from the table, the quantity of home canning lids by Lids, Inc. during this year were over four times the amount of three years ago.

Currently Lids, Inc. cannot satisfy the demand or the fancied demand for lids of the American public. It is operating its equipment 24 hours a day, 7 days a week. The corporation has a major supporting plant in Birmingham, Alabama that is producing lids to its capacity. During the winter and spring periods of this year, new machines to increase the production of lids were installed and full operation by mid-September was achieved.

The finding of the Federal Trade Commission with reference to the investigation requested as noted above, was to the effect that the current shortage was "the result of temporary and unanticipated economic phenomena." No trust violations were evident. The question has been raised many times regarding how the lids produced are allocated or distributed to customers. Lids, Inc. determined a distributing quota based on previous purchases from Lids, Inc. during the periods one year ago and two years ago. That is, if wholesaler ABC in Memphis got 1.05 percent of Lids, Inc. production during the year-ago and two-years-ago periods, they got 1.05 percent of Lids, Inc. production during the recent year. Lids, Inc. believes this is a fair plan to follow.

Questions

1. As you see it, why is there a shortage of canning lids in retail stores at the present time? Discuss.
2. What is your opinion regarding the decisions made by the top managers of Lids, Inc.? Justify your answer.
3. What decisions do you feel the top managers of Lids, Inc. should have taken? What decisions by consumers? Elaborate on your answers.

CASE 6–2: CONWAY COMPANY

Mr. Alfred M. Rice, president, recognized the need for improving his company executive group and personal performance. Associates of Mr. Rice shared his belief and concurred in his decision to call in Mr. James Lee, a management consultant for professional help. Within several weeks, Mr. Lee arrived at Conway Company and during the first day had a long interview with Mr. Rice, who answered a number of questions posed by Mr. Lee. They were primarily designed to give him background information about the company.

Subsequently, Mr. Lee talked with all the company's top and middle managers. He was interested in finding out what they believed the problems were that the company faced, their ideas of what actions should be taken, and the probable hurdles in implementing the suggested actions. From this Mr. Lee senses that all the management members needed a greater perspective, to see their jobs and their departmental effort in relationship to the total company effort. Further, they needed to be informed about the company's plans for all phases of the business.

Accordingly, Mr. Lee recommended interaction among the top managers and among top and middle managers by means of a series of scheduled meetings at which appropriate top managers discussed the plans and problems of the company as they saw them. At each meeting, a question and answer session was featured. From these meetings, individual study, and observation, Mr. Lee suggested that each department manager hold for her or his group "roadblock meetings," the purpose of which was: (1) to identify roadblocks preventing the manager from doing the most effective job possible, and (2) to suggest practical ways that these roadblocks could be eliminated. The recommendation was approved and in the meetings that followed some 850 roadblocks were identified. There was of course some duplication in these, but the range varied from "improving our managerial leadership" to "making every Conway employee cost conscious and reduce present overall cost by 5 percent."

In the opinion of Mr. Lee the situation was now ripe for problem-solving conferences. Again Mr. Rice agreed. Three-day conferences were scheduled. They featured sessions conducted by specialists in developing effective human relations with emphasis upon implementing change and maintaining motivation. Also, unstructured sessions for developing plans to eliminate selected roadblocks from the departmental meetings discussed above were held. A separate meeting for each selected roadblock took place concurrently and the manager was free to choose which to attend.

Armed with the problem identification and suggestions for its solution, each manager was encouraged to dispel roadblocks in her or his area of operation. To assist in these efforts, a task force was appointed consisting of two outside specialists and three key company executives. Care was taken that the operating manager remained the manager of her unit and continued to decide what corrective action would be taken.

After being in operation for three months, a total of 307 roadblocks had been reviewed, of which 123 were acted upon. Mr. Lee cautioned that it would require time to realize full benefits from the program. In his words, "The important thing is to keep it alive and continue to work together in identifying and solving problems that keep you from achieving your goals. How this is done is just as important as what is done."

Questions

1. What is your reaction to the help supplied by Mr. Lee? Discuss.
2. Would you say the program followed has elements of a results management-modified process management approach? Elaborate on your answer.
3. Are you of the opinion that a program such as Conway Company followed could be applied successfully in most enterprises today? Why?

Chapter 7

Decision making—nonquantitative means

Hide not your talents
They for use were made.
What's a sundial in the shade?
Benjamin Franklin

Managers are paid to make decisions and act on them. From the popular point of view, the manager is the one who decides what is to be done. In the process school of management, for example, decisions are mandatory for planning, organizing, actuating, and controlling to have significance. Decision making permeates every aspect of management, exists in every part of an organization, and deals with every possible subject.

THE MEANING OF DECISION MAKING

Decision making is always related to a problem or a difficulty. By means of a decision and its implementation it is hoped that an answer to the problem or a resolution of the conflict will be gained. Literally, decision making means "to cut off" or, in practical content, to come to a conclusion. As stated in Webster's, it is "the act of determining in one's own mind upon an opinion or course of action." Stated formally, decision making can be defined as *the selection based on some criteria of one behavior alternative from two or more possible alternatives.*

Making decisions means making choices from several possibilities or alternatives. And what choice is made is important because it determines the action or inaction, and further makes a person a participant rather than a passive observer. Many so-called decision making situations really do not require decisions, but simply additional infor-

125

mation, and in some instances, prediction. Secure the needed information and/or make the prediction, and you secure the answer. There is no resolution of conflict to be made, no choice to be followed.

DECISION MAKING AND ALTERNATIVES

It follows then that for decision making to exist, there must be two or more alternatives present. If no choice or one choice, there is no decision to be made. Consider for example the situation stated publically that the Social Security system under present arrangements will probably go into a cash flow deficit by 1977 and will be unable to pay benefits as now scheduled in the year 2000. The problem is how to remove the barrier that will prevent social security from functioning adequately. What are the alternatives? There must be two or more for a decision to be required. We offer three: (1) reduce the scheduled benefits, (2) make up the deficit by general tax revenue, or (3) increase employer and employee taxes. There are more alternatives and as is true in all decision making, as many alternatives as possible should be determined so that the best decision will be made.

Figure 7–1 shows a situation for which there are five possible behav-

FIGURE 7–1

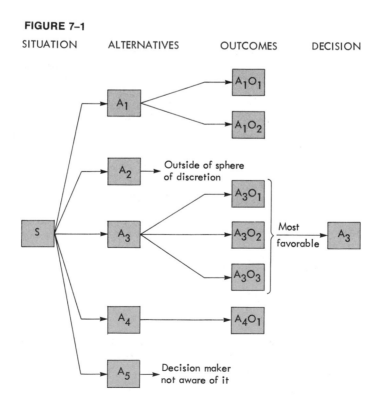

ior alternatives, A_1, A_2, A_3, A_4 and A_5. Moving to the right on the figure, of these five alternatives, three are available for choice. A_2, for example, is outside the sphere of discretion and hence is eliminated; the decision maker is unaware of A_5. The possible outcomes for each available alternative are predicted, followed by an evaluation of each outcome in terms of relative desirability. To illustrate, for A_3, the outcomes are A_3O_1, A_3O_2, and A_3O_3. Comparing the outcomes of the various available alternatives, A_3O_1, A_3O_2, and A_3O_3 are considered most favorable, and hence A_3 is the decision followed. The decision is based on the criterion or basis believed important in the particular situation and represents a choice, from a group of alternatives, or what one manager feels is the best action to be taken for the particular state of affairs as one sees them.

OBSERVATIONS ON SELECTION OF ALTERNATIVES

It is a simple matter to state that alternatives are evaluated in terms of their respective probable outcomes, but to determine the relative merits usually poses real difficulties. The requirement is to make comparisons based on values, be they economic, psychological, social, or political. And conflict among these values is quite likely. There are normally both desirable and undesirable aspects in every alternative, but these conflicting values must be reconciled in some manner satisfactory to the manager.

Many problems requiring a decision are not solved by a simple "Yes" or "No." There is a little "Yes" and a little "No" in most decisions. In other words, decision making is not a matter of black or white, but mostly in-between, or gray. It is appropriate to visualize a strip one-mile wide labeled "black" and another strip one-mile wide labeled "white." Between these strips is another strip 1,000-miles wide of "gray" and it is within this wide gray band with all the degrees and combinations of black and white that most decisions exist.

Commonly attention is given to the probability of each outcome taking place. The decision making is guided by the reality of what seems to fit best the practical consideration of what can be implemented and will be accepted by all concerned with the decision. Thus, impossible, pie-in-the-sky decisions are avoided.

Help in decision making is gained by concentrating on the really important facets of the problem. This is a common mark of most successful managers. It also helps to eliminate the least attractive alternatives as well as those which are impractical for the manager to follow with available resources. Also to be observed is that in any given case none of the alternatives may be entirely satisfactory, but they are the best in that given case.

Furthermore, the alternatives selected by the manager may prove to be inadequate, owing to inability to see the future without error. In decision making the manager is dealing with future values which for the most part are unknown. Efforts are made to reduce the element of chance due to futurity, but it can never be reduced to zero.

In most cases there are limitations of the decision maker's knowledge which condition the alternative selected. A manager's ability to decide is bounded by the scope of comprehension and understanding of the area for which the decision is being made. A decision can only be as good as the decider's values permit one to see the problem and to conceive what might possibly be done about it. Generally speaking, in most decision making, some alternatives are ignored simply because the decision-maker's knowledge does not permit one to be aware of them. This condition was included in Figure 7–1.

In contrast, it should be noted that normally the alternatives must be within certain stated constraints. The financial position of an enterprise may eliminate consideration of a decision necessitating large capital expenditures. And all managerial decisions are constrained by the abilities of employees to carry out the decisions. Furthermore, it is common for trade unions, through collective bargaining, to establish various constraints which the manager recognizes in decision-making. Likewise, governments through their various regulatory measures place constraints upon much managerial decision making. There are also constraints placed upon decision making by factors external to the enterprise, including the public, technology, other enterprises, and world affairs.

Frequently, aid in evaluating alternatives is gained from answers to specific and pertinent questions. A production control manager, for example, might ask questions such as these: Is special handling of the production order necessary? Are regular work-hours and machine-hours available for this activity? Will overtime be used? Can other production orders be delayed?

Last, it should be noted that the selection of the alternative can be strongly influenced by following the practice of a leader. In such instances, the managers of a well-known company set the precedent and others calmly follow. Also, in many instances, and, especially at the top management levels, the decision has already been tacitly accepted when the formal investigation for formulating a decision is launched. That is, by the time a formal study is launched about a problem, the fundamental decision has unwittingly been reached; determining the means of implementation is the main issue. When this condition exists, the decision-making process is reduced to a corroboratory ex post facto analysis. Influences such as these—follow-the-leader and acceptance prior to determination—tend to make for "patterned" decisions.

JUDGMENT AND DECISION MAKING

Important in decision making is judgment. When values are clear, information is adequate, and risks are reasonably predictive, the decision making may appear to be void of judgment. But such is not the case because, in selecting the alternative, comparison of values and relations of things must be mentally formulated and asserted. Consider, in contrast, the situation where value comparisons are difficult, information spotty, and risks are mostly unknown. Here the presence and need for judgment is more evident. In fact, under such conditions, judgment becomes the medium by which conflicting values are resolved, risks assessed, and alternatives evaluated.

Figure 7–2 shows these concepts in which might be termed "the

FIGURE 7–2: The spectrum of decisions

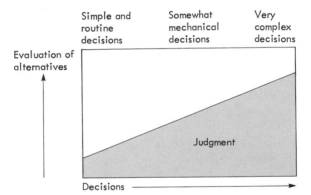

spectrum of decisions." Evaluation of alternatives is represented by the vertical scale; decisions are represented on the horizontal scale. On the left or lower end of the spectrum are the simple, routine decisions—those requiring easy comparison of alternatives; toward the middle are the more complex decisions; at the right or upper end are the extremely complex decisions. Judgment is present throughout the entire spectrum but at the lower left end is relatively small. In moving to the right, or going up the spectrum, more and more judgment is injected into the decision making.

NONQUANTITATIVE BASES FOR DECISION MAKING

Many different bases for decision making are used. The span of technique extends from guesses on one end to complex mathematical analyses on the opposite end. At this point, we are concerned with

nonquantitative bases only; in the following chapter quantitative
bases are discussed. From the practical viewpoint, there is neither one
best technique or combination that should be used under all circumstances. The selection is individual and usually is predicated upon the
manager's background, knowledge, and the resources available.

The nonquantitative means are helpful not only for problems dealing with objectives, but also for problems dealing with the means to
accomplish the objectives. In application the nonquantitative bases are
highly personal in nature, are widely known, and are considered by
many as the natural way to make a decision. Selected for discussion here
are (1) intuition, (2) facts, (3) experience, and (4) considered opinions.

Intuition

Decision making based on intuition is characterized by the use of
hunches, inner feelings, or the "gut feeling".of the person reaching the
decision. Suggestions, influences, preferences, and the psychological
makeup of the deciding individual play an important part; the subjective element is vital. It is believed by many that the intuitive decider
has more "precognitive" ability and is better able to anticipate the
future in instances where reliable data are lacking.

Quite probably the intuitive decision maker is influenced *unconsciously* by past knowledge, training, and background. But these influences are not habitually utilized. The common explanation by the
decider is usually "It's just the way I feel about it." No set pattern of
decisions is usually made by a person using intuition as a basis. Each
problem is apparently handled and given an individual decision.
However, some consistency in the type of decisions reached can usually be observed.

The intuitive decision maker is usually an activist, moves fast, in-
cisely questions about situations, and finds unique solutions to difficult
problems. Such a person leans heavily upon instincts, on personal feel
for a situation, but tempers all actions taken with realism. An ability to
sense opportunities and, by sheer conviction of belief, push forward
major decisions are common characteristics. Perhaps never fully aware
of the exact how or why for any particular action taken, this person
while not rational in the usual meaning of that word, does bring to the
work place each day a form of thought process conditioned by values
and experiences.

At one time, intuition was considered a precious mental faculty
which provided a direct line to the essence of truth. With the advances
in the use of other decision-making bases, intuition is sometimes
scorned as having little or no validity. This is unfortunate because
intuition is an indispensable asset in decision making. In most management problems there are incommensurables consisting of in-

tertwining tangles of human values, needs, and emotions. Even though most people view themselves as logical, no-nonsense decision makers, the truth is that many decisions are not the result of true thought but of instinct and intuition.

Managers wishing to improve their intuition might try (1) becoming more casually involved by filling their minds with facts and experiences in the areas where their future decisions will be made, (2) practicing intuitive decision making and keeping a score on how well such decision turned out, and (3) developing an awareness that hunches can help in the decision making.

As a basis of decision making, intuition has advantages. Decisions so reached usually require a relatively short period of time. Also, decisions on problems having limited influence is supplied. In addition, decision making ability is utilized. On the other hand, there are shortcomings including the decision may prove bad, that is, the hunch was incorrect. Further, the means for substantiating the decision to compeers of the decider are unavailable. And finally, other bases for reaching decisions may be unduly minimized.

Facts

Facts are popularly regarded as constituting an excellent basis upon which decisions can be made. The statement that "a decision should be based on adequate facts" is widely accepted. When facts are employed, the decision has its roots, so to speak, in the factual data; and this implies that the premises upon which the decision is based are sound, solid, and intensely applicable to the particular situation.

The steadily increasing number of computers being installed adds greater and greater emphasis to the use of facts in decision making. Information as a management tool has already acquired high status, and the activities in this area are well-defined and employ the use of highly sophisticated techniques and equipment.

"Adequate facts," however, are not always available. To secure them may cost too much, present too difficult a task, or require too much time. Complete factual information is an ideal to be sought, but perhaps seldom achieved. A manager frequently is forced to make a decision without as many facts as one might deem adequate. And there must be a willingness to follow the facts even thought they lead to a disagreeable conclusion. Furthermore, in arriving at a decision, facts must be carefully diagnosed, classified, and interpreted. The process of relating facts in their correct perspective, in applying proper weights, and in extracting the essential information induces the subjective element of the decision maker and requires an ability, training, and skill wholly apart from that simply of collecting all facts that are available. Further, every fact should be tested for its truth.

In reality, facts alone are seldom sufficient to reach a decision. Imagination, experience, and beliefs are usually required to interpret the facts in their proper perspective and to utilize them advantageously. Facts should give the decision maker confidence and courage to go ahead when the person's imagination and experience suggest a certain decision is the thing to do. There is always the element of the unknown, no matter what decision-making technique is followed. Facts might reduce, but they never eliminate the unknown. And this is good because it makes the job of the manager exciting.

Costs, an important type of facts, are employed by many managers as a basis for decision making. Cost is so widespread in decision making that some believe "all management decisions are cost decisions." But the manager also faces decision making situations in which it is difficult to utilize cost data. Which of three candidates to select for a new management job is an example. Facts help assure consistency. Factual data on progress reports, sales and service accomplishments, and selected operations assist in arriving at helpful decisions. Evaluation of accomplishment suggests whether any new decision needs to be made, but the facts seldom tell in detail what the new decision should be. That remains the task of a human being.

Experience

When a decision must be reached, it is common practice to draw assistance from past events. Having participated in or witnessed a situation similar to the one being decided provides an intimacy and understanding of the issue and suggests possible actions which might be taken. A person sees and understands things in terms of concepts with which one is familiar. One forgoes and in some cases resists approaches which are foreign to one's individual experience.

Experience furnishes guides for decision making. It helps answer the question of what to do in particular types of situations. Perhaps the chief value of experience in decision making is developing an ability to discriminate and to generalize past situations. Thus, similar situations along with their decisions, as well as unlike situations and their decisions, can be recognized and evaluated.

Experience may tend to emphasize excessive conservatism in decision making, but this need not follow. "Nothing succeeds like success," but in a rapidly changing economy, past success in decision making does not insure future success, nor by the same reasoning does it necessarily mean failure will result. Decisions based on experience utilize practical knowledge. Presumably the best portions of the decision-maker's background are used. Also, the decision includes "tried-and-true" ingredients and enjoys acceptance by others. In contrast, decisions based on experience may be predicated on events which are outmoded. The time element is important. The dictates of the experience of last year might be inappropriate today. In addition, the experiences of the decision maker may be somewhat limited, and hence the decision is derived from too narrow a background. It is also possible to overemphasize the traditional and maintain too rigidly the status quo, with the result that progress and improvement are unduly retarded. A manager should use experience, but need not be blindly bound by it.

Considered opinions

Many managers rely upon considered opinions in their decision making. This particular basis is distinguished by the use of logic behind the decision—logic which is made explicit and derived from careful analysis of the situation. Furthermore, quantification of the tentative decision is employed. To do this, varying amounts of statistics are collected and related to the decision. For the most part the statistics substantiation is technically valid and acceptable, but there are instances when inappropriate statistical techniques are followed in collecting the data or a very small and sometimes nonrepresentative portion of the data collected is actually utilized.

Considered opinions have won acceptance as managers have given more attention to the group and its acceptance of decisions. Also some managers frequently seek some logical analyses of their decision-making problems. They want some rational process, even though it be small, in their decision making. A simple example will illustrate to what extent rationalization may enter into a considered opionions decision.

Suppose a company general sales manager has decided to reduce sales cost by eliminating the selling to one of two marginal customers. During the past eight years, such a customer, A, has purchased $40,000, while another such customer, B, over the last five years has purchased $25,000. The data are shown by Figure 7–3.

FIGURE 7–3: Sales two to marginal customers for selected years

Sales	Customer A	Customer B
Last year	$ 3,500	$ 9,300
2 years ago	5,600	7,200
3 years ago	6,400	4,000
4 years ago	5,900	3,000
5 years ago	7,200	1,500
6 years ago	5,400	—
7 years ago	3,000	—
8 years ago	3,000	—
Total	$40,000	$25,000
Average per year	$ 5,000	$ 5,000

These data help sharpen up the difference between the customers. Eliminating either customer would not represent an average loss of $5,000. Customer A would probably cost the least, customer B, the most. Also the purchasing trend of customer B is increasing while that of customer A is decreasing. Other considerations, especially opinions of the sales manager's colleagues would also be taken into account, but the decision here could well be to retain customer B and eliminate customer A.

WHO SHOULD MAKE DECISIONS

For any given situation, the decision is the result of efforts by one person or of a group. The individual approach is common when the decision is fairly easy to reach. This approach recognizes that decision making is essentially a lonely task. Also, when the group has little knowledge or background in the subject area or the issue is of an emergency nature, the individual approach is probably superior. In contrast, group decision making helps develop the members of the group and gives them a chance to voice their opinions concerning matters that affect their work. Participation in management usually means participation in decision making, or decisions by the group. Figure 7–4 is a comparison chart spelling out what group decision is and what it is not.

In the interest of clarity, it is appropriate to state that decision making consists basically of several steps including: (1) define the problem, (2) analyze the problem, (3) determine alternatives, (4) evaluate each alternative, (5) select the alternative which becomes the decision, and (6) put into action. When the individual approach is followed, the

FIGURE 7–4

Group decision	
is	*is not*
Being fair to all members of the group.	Giving each individual what she or he wants.
A means of getting together different attitudes.	Manipulating group members.
Letting a member tell what he or she thinks should be done to solve a problem.	Selling the ideas of the superior manager to the members of the group.
Group discipline through social pressure.	Throwing discipline to the winds.
Problem solving cooperatively.	Seeking mere advice through consultative supervision.

individual decision maker performs all the steps and the process is called *individual determinative* decision making. Likewise, when the group performs all the steps, it is called *group determinative* decision making. However, under the group approach, additional steps may be injected between the evaluating and selecting of the alternative. For example, added might be "suggesting to an individual manager, who, in turn, selects the alternative." This arrangement is called *group advisory* decision making. Under this approach, the individual manager can modify or even reject the group's recommendation. In some cases the individual manager's selection of the group's recommendation may be almost routine; this is especially true if the group predominantly favors one alternative that is entirely agreeable to the individual manager. Various combinations of steps are possible in group decision making. Let us now look more closely at decision making by the individual and also by a group.

Decision making by individual

The one-manager decision making setup is in keeping with the popular concept of a manager. This arrangement stems from the one owner beginning of many business enterprises. One person made all the decisions, or at least all the major ones. As the enterprise grew, the tendency was for this individual to continue to handle most of the decision making because that person believed secretly that others in the enterprise were perhaps less competent, that decisions by others might prove costly, or that to permit others to make decisions might mean a loss of prestige or power by him or her. Many managers want to be the ones that decide, at least in the ultimate or upon important issues.

The decision to meet an emergency is typically of the individual manager type. In an emergency there isn't time to talk it over, seek advice, or resolve many different ideas of what might be done. The decision must be made without delay. However, before implementing the decision, or at least in its very early stages of implementation, the manager should communicate with those to be affected by the decision in order to help them understand the decision and know the circumstances that caused such action to be taken. See Figure 7–5.

In many respects crisis decisions test the true measure of a manager's ability. There are always emergencies, but there is cause for real concern if emergency decision making is the order rather than the exception. Whether to make or defer an emergency decision is a question depending mainly on the consequences of not acting. There can be no uniform set of rules to cover emergency decision making; yet reason cannot be abandoned. History is rich with stories of people who have risen to the challenge requiring emergency decisions. Julius

FIGURE 7–5:   **What a manager's subordinates should be told about a crisis decision**

The manager should:

1. Tell why the decision was made without giving them prior notice.
2. Relate expectancies in the execution of the decision.
3. Discuss the extent to which particular activities or interests were considered before the decision was made.
4. Tell them the flexibility they have in carrying out the decision.
5. Be sure they understand that (*a*) an emergency came up, (*b*) a decision had to be made quickly, and (*c*) their cooperation is needed to make the decision effective.

Caesar, Cleopatra, the Duke of Wellington, General Robert E. Lee, General Dwight D. Eisenhower, and Admiral Nimitz are a few from the long list of such decision makers. These were people who interpreted facts imaginatively, recognized opportunity, and understood decision making.

Decisions by group

Many favor group decision making, believing it gives those who will be affected by a decision a chance to participate in its formulation and helps to develop the members of the group. A person who had some part in shaping a decision is more inclined to follow it enthusiastically. And group decisions help satisfy individual needs, such as a sense of feeling wanted, of being important, and being "in the know." Also, at its best, decision making should involve vigorous discussion of the various alternatives, a condition fulfilled by the group decision approach.

Further, the group advocates state that in this age of technological change, government influence, and social responsibility, the issues to be decided have grown beyond the expertise of the top manager in many companies. The input of many people is called for, each unique in knowledge and experience. This sharing of decision-making responsibilities establishes interdependence among the parties. Thus, group cooperation is enhanced and the old individual authoritarian concept of decision making is reduced.

There is also strong belief among many that, in decision making, assistance can and should be obtained from others, but the task of selecting the alternative should remain basically an individual task for these reasons. The manager must accept and retain the decision making task in order to retain managerial status. The real purpose of seeking suggestions from others is to gain a better understanding of the issue to be decided, not to abdicate managerial responsibility. Further, the decision maker can evaluate best the suggestions and opinions offered in terms of their real meaning and consequence to the particular group or the enterprise.

In actual practice group decision making is of itself subjected to a great many limitations. Some members will contribute far more than others, and both the status and power of some members will exceed that of other members. Furthermore, it will be found that certain members seldom differ with the opinions expressed by other group members, and when they do differ, they can exercise little influence upon what is finally decided.

Committees, the membership of which may vary widely, commonly make up the group to do the deciding. While a committee is satisfactory, its decisions evolve as a result of compromise and are based not on the best but on the average on which the committee members can agree. There can be an element of procrastination in their decisions in that they omit controversial elements, which subsequently appear for debate. Furthermore, from the very nature of a committee it follows that there is some lack of fixed responsibility for specific contributions. A committee may accept this responsibility, but inherently it is divided among its members.[1]

There is also the question of the degree of freedom which the manager permits. If one is subordinate-centered, one will define fairly broad limits and expect the group members to make their decision within these limits. Then one follows the decision usually with very minor, if any, adjustments. Various degrees of decisional freedom can be followed as indicated by Figure 7–6. At the top is the subordinate-centered, great freedom arrangement. In contrast, the bottom or the situation where the manager makes the decision and tells the group members what it is, represents the area of no freedom and symbolizes one type of the individual manager approach to decision making.

In addition, the manager frequently finds that after talking it over he or she still must make the decision; it does not evolve from the group discussion. Approval of many proposed ideas may have been won and a number of excellent suggestions received, but in the final analysis the decision must be made and the manager is expected to make it. In some instances, a new course emerges which course is neither a compromise nor simply a fusion of the material submitted.

IMPLEMENTING THE DECISION

The successful manager not only knows how to make good decisions but also to construct an effective plan for carrying out the decision. Some executives have trouble getting their decisions implemented, thus to a degree voiding the goodness of the decision formulated. Effective implementation of a decision necessitates a questioning at-

---

[1] Committees are discussed in detail in Chapter 13, pp. 283–87.

FIGURE 7–6: Relative degrees of decision making

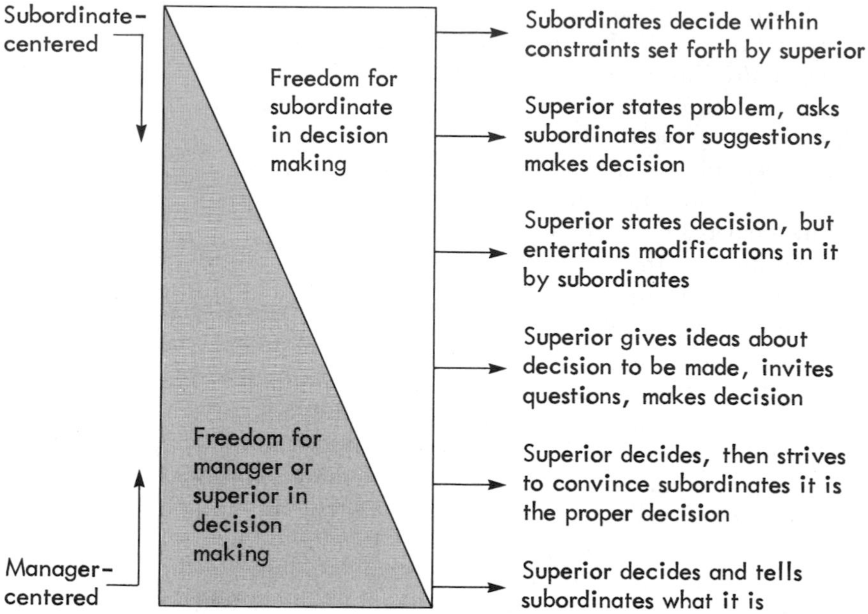

Subordinate-
centered

Freedom for
subordinate
in decision
making

Freedom for
manager or
superior in
decision
making

Manager-
centered

Subordinates decide within
constraints set forth by superior

Superior states problem, asks
subordinates for suggestions,
makes decision

Superior states decision, but
entertains modifications in it
by subordinates

Superior gives ideas about
decision to be made, invites
questions, makes decision

Superior decides, then strives
to convince subordinates it is
the proper decision

Superior decides and tells
subordinates what it is

titude toward every detail of the decision and toward the steps required to carry it out. The sequence of the steps, the responsibilities of the individuals involved, and the controls to be practiced must be spelled out. It is helpful to pinpoint in advance difficulties likely to be encountered and to make provisions for handling these difficulties.

Further, the decision and how it is to be implemented must be communicated to those who will be involved or affected by the decision. The reason for the decision, the action called for, what adjustments are required, each individual's role, and what results are expected are among the major types of information that should be communicated.

The task of adequate communication is lightened when employee participation in decision making is followed for in such cases, the employees have some familiarity with what is decided and why, as well as the hoped-for gains to be made by implementing the decision. In many cases the participants' most helpful contributions are in determining how to implement the decision. Their intimate knowledge of both the work and other memebers of the work force make this so.

TYPES OF DECISIONS

Decisions can be classified into any number of types. For purposes of this book, three major classifications will be used. Included are decisions by (1) major organizational activity, (2) degree of certainty, and (3) entity to which applied. The first type encompasses *production decisions* relating to plant layout, production methods, and inventories; *sales decisions* pertaining to product packaging, marketing channels, and price. In addition, *finance decisions* relating to capital structure, credit terms, and the securing of new funds are typical. Also, included are *personnel decisions* on matters of finding and selecting new employees, extent and kind of training, and safety promotion.

Decisions viewed by their degree of certainty is especially helpful. Usually decisions of a high certainty, or low risk, are made at the lower organization levels and decisions involving great uncertainty, or high risk, are made at the higher levels. See Figure 7–7. The higher the certainty, the more simple, routine, and repetitive the decision making. Decisions of this type can be standardized by establishing prescribed means for performing certain work and normally reliable quantity and quality measurements are involved. Such decisions feature reasonable predictability of involved activities.[2]

The types of entity to which applied include those directed by managers to the seeking of opportunities for improvement and the general progress of the enterprise. Called, *administrative decisions,* they are concentrated in the top management group. A second type under this classification are those dealing with resource allocation, or *resource decisions.* Commonly the request for resources must be bal-

FIGURE 7–7: Classification of decisions by the extent of certainty involved

	Risk	*Characteristics*
1. High certainty	Low	Repeated sufficiently to reduce uncertainty to a minimum. Decisions are of a routine nature, usually affect a small group only, and are easy to apply. Prediction of decision outcome is nearly perfect.
2. Fair amount of certainty	Medium	Reasonable estimates of uncertainty are possible. Decisions affect two or three departments at maximum.
3. Considerable uncertainty . . .	Above average	Little surety of hoped-for results from decisions. Includes large areas of activity.
4. Great uncertainty	High	Situations cover very broad areas and many nonpredictable factors.

[2] See discussion on probability and decision making, Chapter 8, pp. 158–60.

anced among different activities and the basis for this allocation and its justification must be taken into account. There are also decisions dealing with *benefits to the total organization*. Such decision types could be called team building decisions. They represent decisions of a negotiating characteristic, are of a positive nature, and are intended to benefit the entire organization rather than concentrate on individual self-aggrandizement. Last, the fourth type, or *disturbance decisions*, as the name implies, deal with disturbances, whether possible loss of a unit's resources, conflicts among subordinates, or strong differences of opinion and behavior between groups. Disturbance decisions are commonly of an unannounced crisis nature. Effectiveness in handling such decisions is a common mark of most successful managers.

DECISION MAKING GUIDELINES

Figure 7–8 shows a helpful list of suggestions for becoming an effective decision maker. By making these suggestions a part of your thinking, you will gradually acquire proficiency in decision making.

In addition and in keeping with what has already been stated in this chapter, it is well to keep in mind that every decision should contribute toward goal achievement. Make the decision productive. Also, recognize that a decision will bring change by means of a chain of actions. Commonly the actions will extend beyond the boundaries of the initial intended boundaries. Project results from the decision. What things can go wrong—and if they do, how serious would each one be? In addition, for better decisions, tap your creativity and imagination—more than cold logic is required for the superior decision. Include practical compromises. Consider a sample or trial run to

FIGURE 7–8: Steps to be a good decision maker

1. Be alert to signs indicating the need for a decision.
2. Make quiet uninterrupted time for thinking and reflecting about things to be decided.
3. Set priorities for different decisions.
4. Separate yourself from the problem and answer, "How would another person decide the issue?"
5. Ask whether the contemplated decision seems honorable and right.
6. Ask whether you will think well of yourself when you review what has resulted from your decision.
7. Have a backup decision, just in case.
8. Take adequate time to reach a decision—mulling over the subject serves as a defense against impulsive decisions. In contrast, don't delve into so many aspects that confusion presides and no definitive action is taken.

see how the decision will work out. This approach will reveal not only portions for change and possible weak points, but also avoid full commitment at the start without retrieval. Furthermore, institute follow-up to each decision in order to see that it is carried out and to appraise the results. Some decisions will prove poor and when this occurs, correct as quickly as possible. Remember if you make no mistakes, you make no progress. Finally, recognize that few, if any, decisions please everybody. There is usually someone who feels a different decision would have been better. After you have decided, the challenge is to explain the decision and to win the enthusiastic cooperation of the entire group.

QUESTIONS

1. As you see it, which is better: a decision reached by an individual or by a group? Discuss.

2. Suppose you could use only one nonquantitative decision-making base. Which one would you use? Why?

3. Explain what each of the following means: (*a*) group advisory decision making, (*b*) uncertainty of decision, (*c*) patterned decision.

4. Are you of the opinion that limitations of the decision maker's knowledge affect the alternatives selected? Justify your viewpoint by relating several examples from your own experience.

5. Discuss considered opinions as a base for managerial decision making.

6. What suggestions can you give a person wanting to improve his or her intuition for use in decision making?

7. As a member of a group, such as of a school, business, church, or community, what amount of freedom or relative degree of decision making (see Figure 7–6) does the formal manager of this group practice? Why in your opinion does she or he follow this practice? Elaborate on your answer.

8. For each of the following problems state whether it is one of information, prediction, or decision, along with the reasons for your answers: (*a*) Should Mr. Kay, the assistant controller, be promoted to controller? (*b*) What paper forms are used in company M for controlling production? (*c*) Will the 3:15 P.M. flight get Miss Smidt to New Orleans in time for her meeting? (*d*) Which manufacturing process is better for order R M 365?

9. Discuss group decision making pointing out the advantages and the disadvantages of this practice.

10. Discuss some of the different and common types of decisions found in management.

11. Rodney Faber, a manager, faces a very difficult situation about which to make a decision. He does not know what to do. Consulting with his immediate subordinates, he finds that they do not know what to decide any more than he does. Rodney decides to not decide, hoping that with time the situation will either ease or will suggest what decision to make. Is this action of Rodney Faber's good or bad? Why?

12. Discuss briefly three ways in which decisions can be made more effective.

13. Relate an experience in which you reached a decision by intuition. How did it work out? Do you feel another base would have been better? Discuss.

14. In view of the fact that effective decision making requires sufficient time, are crisis decisions usually effective? Justify your answer, using an example to illustrate your viewpoint.

CASE 7–1.   HAVOC CHEMICAL COMPANY

The manager of production must finish an important report for a meeting scheduled to begin at 2:00 P.M. It is now 1:20 P.M. Several rush jobs are not yet finished, and the manager of production is concerned about them. A tow truck has just moved into a busy work area to take a quantity of finished molded-plastic parts to shipping. The truck is emitting much smoke which has an extremely foul odor. Within a few minutes, several employees complain to the truck driver, who states, "Aw, you get used to it. I'll be out of here before long." One employee then goes to the supervisor who advises that the parts have to be taken to shipping immediately. The supervisor offers the employee an aspirin tablet, but it is refused. About five minutes later another employee talks with the supervisor and complains about the odor. The supervisor states, "It will soon be over. Let's don't make mountains out of mole hills."

A little later, another employee talking with the trucker exclaims, "That exhaust is poisonous. It's making me sick." The trucker grins and says, "It's sort of smelly, but it won't hurt you. It isn't dangerous. It hasn't hurt me."

Some ten minutes later, eight employees as a group go to the supervisor, announcing that they are going home "because of the terrible gas from the truck." Their leader says, "If we stick around here we'll all get sick." All of them go home. Right after they leave, the manager of production stops by the supervisor's office to inquire about a production delay that is to be discussed at the 2 P.M. meeting. He observes a number of employees absent from their work places even though it is not time for a break. He also becomes aware of the foul odor in the area and says, "What an odor! What's causing it?" The supervisor replies, "It is from a tow truck picking up those parts Sullivan is waiting for."

Questions

1. Did the supervisor handle the situation correctly and make the proper decision regarding the handling of the tow truck emitting the odor? Discuss.

2. Should the manager of production get involved in the odor problem of the department? Why?
3. Who should decide when a working condition is unsafe?
4. What decision should be made about the employees leaving their jobs? Justify your answer.

CASE 7–2. EAST BEND HEAT TREATERS, INC.

The service rendered by this company consists of heat treating machined metal parts and foundry castings in order to give them required hardness or desired internal structure, in keeping with the use to which they would be applied. Over the years, Mr. Orwell Busch built the business to its present level, which consists of annual sales of about $500,000; number of employees, 37; average profits after taxes, $32,000 (last three years); and number of "regular" customers, 207. The selling and interviews with customers were handled personally by Mr. Busch. The shop was managed by Mr. Charles Bertnicki, a competent shop man who came up through the ranks at the plant, as did also his five supervisors. Mr. Bertnicki works closely with Mr. Busch, who makes all the major decisions and is the real head of the corporation.

A month ago Mr. Busch suffered a fatal heart attack. He was 55 years old. His will specified his 57 percent ownership of the corporation be given to his wife, Amelia, age 52, who never had been active in the business and knows very little about it. Her lawyer suggested that she get someone to manage the corporation and stated that perhaps some present member of the corporation should be selected. Mrs. Busch talked with Mr. Bertnicki, who said he did not feel he knew enough about the sales end of the business, he didn't like selling, and he would not be interested in assuming the responsibility of managing the corporation.

Mr. Henry M. Dellwood, an officer of a real estate company and owner of 40 percent of the stock of East Bend Heat Treaters, Inc., advised Mrs. Busch to find a new manager from outside the corporation. He stated he would like to retain his interest in the corporation but admitted he did not consider himself capable to assume its management.

In conversation with Mr. Timothy O'Leary, a local banker, Mrs. Busch was advised to sell the business. Mrs. Busch countered that she needed the business income and doubted that the return on her proceeds from sale of the business invested in securities would supply her with ample income. It is Mr. O'Leary's opinion that a total net amount from the sale of the business for her would be in the $125- to $150-thousand range. He believes the business might be merged into another corporation, but if such could be arranged, Mrs. Busch would be better off getting her money out of it now, rather than own a portion of a merged corporation. He strongly urges Mrs. Busch not to try to manage the business herself, as she knows nothing about the business and could detract rather than add to the attractiveness of the corporation to an interested buyer. However, Mrs. Busch stated that in times of necessity one can do things formerly believed impossible and since the business means a great deal to her, she feels with time she could learn to manage it reasonably well. Mr. O'Leary as well as Mr. Dellwood stated to Mrs. Busch that the final decision was up to her. They were simply offering suggestions.

Questions

1. What is your general opinion of Mr. O'Leary?
2. In your opinion, how did the corporation get into the situation giving rise to this problem?
3. In addition to the possible decisions suggested, what other possibilities are open to Mrs. Busch?
4. What decision do you believe Mrs. Busch should make? Why?

Chapter 8

Decision making—quantitative means

Complacency is the enemy of progress.
David Stutman

Many decisions in management are determined by quantitative means which represent an important part of modern management study. A myriad of different means involving measurements are available. While measurements have been used in management since its earliest use, the development and application of quantitative techniques spurted beginning during the middle 1940s. This growth was due mainly to improvements in measurements, availability of the computer, increase in the interest of applied mathematics, and the desire for more logical approaches to current managerial problems.

For the most part when quantitative means are used for decision making, the emphasis is upon the means or how best to reach the stated goal. The end result or goal is usually given, for example, as: Minimize total cost for all activities or maximize total return to the company. Employing a quantitative base is relatively personal in selecting or creating the mathematical representation to be used, but the processing of the quantitative data is impersonal yet cannot be followed in a mechanical way. The quantitative means usually involve problem conception, hypothesis, definition, experiment, and a trading-off among alternatives. The assumptions made are of special importance and usually are carefully defined. The processing toward the answer is rational, orderly patterns of behavior are assumed, and logical explanations and predictions are utilized. Management skill is enhanced because the quantitative techniques seek to support this skill by bringing maximum rationality to it. Our discussion here will include the following quantitative means: (1) operations research, (2) linear programming, (3) simulation, (4) Monte Carlo, (5) queueing, and

FIGURE 8–1: Different quantitative bases of decision making related to selected schools of management thought

	Schools of management thought								
Quantitative bases	*Custom*	*Scientific*	*Behavioral*	*Social*	*Systems*	*Decisional*	*Quantitative measurement*	*Process*	*Contingency*
Operations research						x	x		x
Linear programming						x	x		x
Simulation		x			x	x	x		x
Monte Carlo		x			x	x	x		
Queueing						x	x		
Gaming			x	x		x	x	x	

(6) gaming. These bases related to selected schools of management are shown in Figure 8–1.

OPERATIONS RESEARCH

The term operations research has grown to mean different things to different people. Some consider it as one technique; others use it to designate most of the quantitative techniques. It originated during World War II, when persons of special competence were assigned the problem of how to get the most out of Great Britain's limited air power during the early years of the war. Later such problems as determining the best pattern for a convoy of ships and the optimum rapidity for operating certain weapons were solved using this technique. The name "operational research" in Great Britain became operations research in the United States, probably because it applied to many operations.

Operations research consists of bringing together available data on a specific problem, processing these data, and from them resolving quantitative reports on the relative merits of various potential courses of action. The concepts of optimization, input-output, and mathematical model are utilized. The model is frequently a series of complex equations of highly involved relationships and applies to a problem that could not be worked by other quantitative techniques. Specifically the steps of operations include (1) precise statement of the problem, (2) collection of relevant data, (3) creation of a valid mathematical model for the pertinent forces or values involved, (4) substitution of data in the model and calculation of results under varying circumstances, (5) selection of the optimum course of action, and (6) follow-up on the model validity with availability of new data.

Problems best suited for operations research are those involving recurring decisions. Generally the problem concerns time, cost, or amount of profits which are to be optimized. Consider the problem of inventory. Operations research can determine the lowest amount of materials to satisfy production requirements, when and what to order, and the manner in which to dispose of an inventory most profitably. In the area of shipping, the elimination of backlogs and the location of production centers for minimum shipping costs are illustrative of operations research application. The evaluation of the economic value of new plant investment, of adding or subtracting products, and of cash flow and cash requirements are further examples.

By means of operations research every important variable, and reasonable outcome for a given decision or set of decisions can be determined before the action is adopted. Operations research not only points out the significant relationships of activities taking place as they do but also predicts events when certain actions are taken. Usually the basic problem is to improve present operations by using the available facilities, but operations research will reveal what, if any, equipment can be improved for better results. These advantages are appealing; yet on the other hand, the amount of data required can be tremendous and the interpretation of these data into a mathematical form commonly is an extremely difficult and time-consuming task. Use of a computer is normally required to make the technique feasible.

LINEAR PROGRAMMING

For linear programming to be applicable, the following conditions must be satisfied. First, an objective is to be optimized—either a maximum or a minimum value is sought and is expressed in terms of money—profits or cost, time, or quantity. Second, the variables or forces affecting the outcome have linear or straight-line relationship, meaning if one unit requires 5 minutes to produce, then ten units will require 50 minutes. Mathematically, this is defined as the condition where none of the independent variables have exponents greater than 1; i.e., there are no second or third powers, such as X^2 or X^3, in the equation. Third, obstacles or restrictions on the relationships of the variables exist. Without the restriction, linear programming would be unnecessary, since the objective could be obtained unencumbered. The computation is by means of "iteration," a method by which a mechanical rule determines, at the end of each step, what the next step should be. Hence, the value from each step leads on closer and closer to the correct answer. Usually either matrix algebra or linear mathematical equations are used in this technique. Examples of each follow.

Linear programming—matrix algebra examples

Assume a corporation has three factories and five warehouses. Costs of shipping differ among the 15 different routes from the factories to the warehouses. Monthly capacities of the factories are 300, 375, and 450 units, respectively. The warehouses, located near large market centers, have the following monthly requirements: 150, 180, 210, 240, and 270 units, respectively. Each warehouse must be supplied with the units required; yet *total shipping costs* should be kept at a minimum. The problem is: How should production be distributed to the warehouses?

The arrangement of the given data, as shown in Figure 8–2, is known as a distribution matrix. Actually it is a type of model. The

FIGURE 8–2: Distribution matrix showing data for transportation problem

Factories	Warehouses						Capacities in units	
	A	B	C	D	E	Slack		
X	37	27	28	34	31	0	300	Row
Y	29	31	32	27	29	0	375	Row
Z	33	26	35	30	30	0	450	Row
Requirements in units	150	180	210	240	270	75	1125	
	Column	Column	Column	Column	Column	Column		

shipping costs per unit for each of the 15 routes between three factories, X, Y, and Z, and five warehouses, A, B, C, D, and E are shown in the figure by the number in the lower right box of each cell. The shipping cost from factory X to warehouse A, for example, is 37 cents per unit; from factory Z to warehouse D, the cost is 30 cents per unit. Row refers to data horizontally or across the matrix, column to data vertically or down the matrix. The factory capacities are shown at the extreme right of each horizontal row; the warehouse requirements are shown at the bottom of each column.

Observe that the total warehouse requirement, 1,050 units, is less than the factory capacities, 1,125 units, meaning that a capacity of 75 units (1,125 less 1,050) will not be used. To show this condition and to have a balanced matrix, we add a "slack" column with zero cost from each factory since these slack sales requirements will not be produced and hence not transported.

To start, we will use the "northwest corner" approach, which means beginning with the northwest, or upper left, corner of the matrix, AX, work down the column, completely meeting the requirements of warehouse A; then shift to the next column representing warehouse B and complete its requirements, always being alert to, and keeping within, the corresponding factory capacities for each row. We continue this process until we finish in the southeast corner, EZ. Such a distribution, which we will term "first distribution," is shown in Figure 8–3.

Each row and each column must have at least one value in it to meet the requirements of the problem. Also for the answer to be valid, the number of entries cannot exceed the quantity equal to 1 less than the sum of the rows and the columns. Sometimes a solution with less than this number of entries is obtained. In Figure 8–3, there are 8

FIGURE 8–3: First distribution or tentative solution to transportation problem

Factories	Warehouses						Capacities in units	
	A	B	C	D	E	Slack		
X	150 37	150 27	28	34	31	0	300	Row
Y	29	30 31	210 32	135 27	29	0	375	Row
Z	33	26	35	105 30	270 30	75 0	450	Row
Requirements in units	150	180	210	240	270	75	1125	
	Column	Column	Column	Column	Column	Column		

entries; the sum of the rows and the columns, or 3 plus 6, equals 9. This amount less 1, or (9 less 1), equals 8, or in this example equals the number of entries. This shows that the problem can be solved by this approach.

Referring to Figure 8–3, the question is: Can this distribution be improved? That is, can entries be shifted so as to reduce the total cost? Note the qualification "total" cost. What we seek is the combination or pattern of shipments giving the lowest cost within the constraints enumerated. The solution is therefore not a matter of simply picking out the lowest cost shipping routes. We can find out if this northwest corner, or first distribution, is the best by a number of ways, but one simple and effective way is to evaluate each of the blank cells to determine if cost reduction would result by assigning an entry to any one of them. We must maintain the overall balance which this first distribution shows in order to keep within the specifications of the problem. Considering blank cell XC, if we add one unit to it, we must subtract one unit out of YC to maintain the condition of column C. In turn, this will mean adding one unit to YB to maintain the condition of row Y and this, in turn, subtracting one unit from cell XB. By these moves the overall balance is maintained, but what happens to cost? One unit added to XC will increase cost 28 cents; subtracted from YC will decrease cost 32 cents; added to YB will increase cost 31 cents; subtracted from XB will decrease cost 27 cents. The net change in cost, therefore, is zero ($\$0.28 - 0.32 + 0.31 - 0.27$); so there is no cost advantage in making an entry in XC.

This procedure is repeated for each blank cell of the first distribution of Figure 8–3. In doing this, the shortest loop from the unfilled cell back to the unfilled cell is used. Also, in this loop only right angle turns are permitted and such turns must be made only at filled cells. Any filled cells can be skipped over to form the required loop. Again, these conditions are required in order to maintain the balance required and to stay within the confines of the stated problem. The calculated data, in cents, for all blank cells are shown in Figure 8–4.

FIGURE 8–4

XC	XD	XE	X slack	YA	YE	Y slack	ZA	ZB	ZC
+28	+34	+31	+ 0	+29	+29	+ 0	+33	+26	+35
−32	−27	−30	− 0	−37	−30	− 0	−37	−31	−32
+31	+31	+30	+30	+27	+30	+30	+27	+27	+27
−27	−27	−27	−27	−31	−27	−27	−31	−30	−30
0	+11	+31 / −27	+31 / −27	−12	+ 2	+ 3	+27 / −30	− 8	0
		+ 8	+ 7				−11		

The deduction from these data is that the unfilled cell YA offers highest cost reduction opportunity. For each unit put in YA, total costs are reduced 12 cents. How many units can we transfer to cell YA? The answer is 30 units as revealed by analysis of the loop utilized to get units in cell YA from the first distribution. The total number of moves is therefore YB to YA, 30 units; XA to XB, 30 units making the new total 120 units in XA and 180 units in XB; the new total of YB is zero since the 30 units were moved to YA. This transferring or moving units into cell YA results in a second distribution, the remaining cells of the matrix staying the same as in the first distribution.

The process of evaluating each unfilled cell of the second distribution is now performed. It will be found that cell XC offers the greatest opportunity to reduce total costs. The data, in cents, are shown in Figure 8–5. By the same reasoning as above, the maximum number of units that can be transferred to this cell are carried out and the resultant third distribution is evolved and analyzed for cost reduction

FIGURE 8–5

XC	XD	XE	X slack	YB	YE	Y slack	ZA	ZB	ZC
+28	+34	+31	+ 0	+31	+29	+ 0	+33	+26	+35
−32	−27	−30	− 0	−29	−30	− 0	−29	−27	−32
+29	+29	+30	+30	+37	+30	+30	+27	+37	+27
−37	−37	−27	−27	−27	−27	−27	−30	−29	−30
−12	− 1	+29	+29	+12	+ 2	+ 3	+ 1	+27	0
		−37	−37					−30	
		− 4	− 5					+ 4	

opportunity in any of its blank cells. The process is repeated until a distribution is reached that has no blank cells offering cost reduction opportunity. For the example under discussion this is shown in Figure 8–6. This answer to our problem is precise and it represents the best

FIGURE 8–6: Final solution to transportation problem

Factories	Warehouses						Capacities in units	
	A	B	C	D	E	Slack		
X	37	15	27 210	28	34	31 75	300	Row
		15	27 210	28	34	31 75 0		
Y	150 29	31	32	225 27	29	0	375	Row
Z	33	165 26	35	15 30	270 30	0	450	Row
Requirements in units	150	180	210	240	270	75	1125	
	Column	Column	Column	Column	Column	Column		

arrangement to obtain total minimum distribution costs. No other arrangement will result in a lower total cost. The total cost can be calculated as follows:

Units	Cost per unit	Total cost
150 ×	$0.29	$ 43.50
15 ×	.27	4.05
165 ×	.26	42.90
210 ×	.28	58.80
225 ×	.27	60.75
15 ×	.30	4.50
270 ×	.30	81.00
	Total......................	$295.50

VAM method for linear programming

The above method is acceptable, but less time-consuming approaches are available, among which the VAM (Vogel Approximation Method) merits inclusion in this discussion. The steps taken in this method include:

1. For each row and each column, find and post differences between the two lowest cell costs. Include and consider slack the same as any other cost.
2. Choose the largest difference of a row or column.
3. Assign maximum possible quantity to available lowest cost cell in the selected row or column.
4. If row or column is satisfied, eliminate the difference and consider all other unfilled cell costs in that row or column as no longer available by filling them in with a zero.
5. After each assignment, calculate new differences for effective rows and columns.

An example will clarify how this is done. For simplicity let us consider the same problem as above. Figure 8–7 shows the data. For cycle No. 1, the differences between the two lowest cell costs for each row and column are indicated under cycle 1 on the figure. For row X, the difference is 27 (27 − 0); likewise for row Y, it is 27. We will select the first, or row X, indicated by the circled 27, but either row X or row Y could be used. For row X we assign the maximum quantity possible in the cell of the lowest cost. This is X *Slack* and this entry eliminates the *Slack* column from further consideration in the problem. Next, the differences for cycle 2 are calculated and these are entered under cycle 2 in the figure. For this cycle, the difference of 4 for column A, indicated by the circled 4, is selected and in cell YA, the lowest cost cell of that column, are assigned 150 units, the most that can be assigned. The procedure is continued until all assignments have been made.

In this case the identical result is obtained with that of the initial method discussed above. This may or may not happen in similar problems of this type. VAM gives an approximate solution, which should always be checked by means of the blank cell evaluation method as described above in order to ensure that the VAM result is the lowest total cost answer. We did this in the previous method; so there is no need to check out VAM results in this particular illustration.

Linear programming—graphic example

Some problems suitable for linear programming analysis can best be solved by use of the graphic method. Consider a radio manufacturer

FIGURE 8–7: VAM method for determining initial solution to transportation problem

Factories	A	B	C	D	E	Slack	Capacities in units		Cycle 1	2	3	4	5	6	7
X	0 | 37	15 | 27	210 | 28	0 | 34	0 | 31	75 | 0	300	Row	(27)	1	1	(4)	—	—	—
Y	150 | 29	0 | 31	0 | 32	225 | 27	0 | 29	0 | 0	375	Row	27	2	2	2	2	2	—
Z	0 | 33	165 | 26	0 | 35	15 | 30	270 | 30	0 | 0	450	Row	26	4	4	4	4	0	0
Requirements in units	150	180	210	240	270	75	1125								

Cycle	A	B	C	D	E	Slack
	Column	Column	Column	Column	Column	Column
1	4	1	4	3	1	0
2	(4)	1	4	3	1	—
3	—	1	(4)	3	1	—
4	—	1	—	3	1	—
5	—	(5)	—	3	1	—
6	—	—	—	(3)	1	—
7	—	—	—	—	—	—

producing two different product models, A and B. The data, shown per unit, are as follows:

		Production time in hours per unit		
Model	Revenue	Subassembly	Final assembly	Trim
A	$20	1.0	0.7	0.5
B	30	1.3	2.0	None

The following maximum hours are available for the production of these products:

Subassembly .... 1300 hours
Final assembly .... 1400 hours
Trim .... 500 hours

We want to find the combination of models A and B that will produce the maximum revenue.

First, let us show graphically the constraints within which the products must be produced. Referring to Figure 8–8, units of A will be shown on the vertical axis and those of B on the horizontal axis. For product A, the subassembly time per unit is 1.0 hours. If we subassemble no B products and devoted all our available subassembly time to product A, we could produce 1,300 units of product A (1,300 divided by 1.0). Contrariwise, if we subassemble no A products and used all our subassembly time for B products, we could produce 1,000 units of product B (1,300 divided by 1.3 hours). The line representing the relationship between A and B is indicated by line (1) in Figure 8–8. It is a straight line because the constraints are linear; it intercepts the A-axis at 1,300 and the B-axis at 1,000. In a like manner we can determine line (2) on Figure 8–8 for the final-assembly work. And line (3) represents the trim work. It is a straight horizontal line with an intercept of 1,000 units on the A-axis because trim time does not affect B. It is all applied to A; so the maximum A production, due to this constraint, is 1,000 units (500 divided by 0.5).

The solution to our problem has now been reduced to knowledge that it lies somewhere within the area bounded by the vertical axis, the line ARR'B. Calculating the revenue for production combinations represented by points A, R, R', and B, we get the results shown in Figure 8–9.

The maximum total revenue occurs at point R'. Points to either side of R'. on line ARR'B will show less revenue than the amount at point R'. The answer to our problem is, therefore, to produce 715 units of A and 450 units of B.

FIGURE 8–8:   Linear programming graphic solution

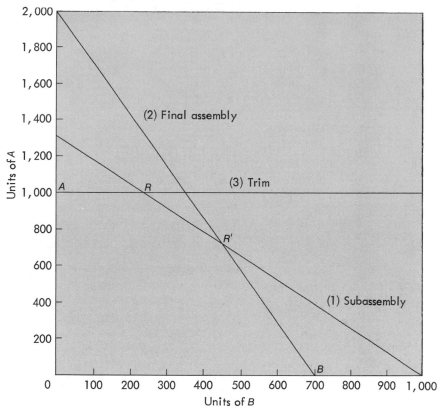

FIGURE 8–9

| | Product A | | Product B | | |
Point	No. of units	Revenue per unit	No. of units	Revenue per unit	Total revenue
A	1,000	$20	0	$ 0	$20,000
R	1,000	20	230	30	26,900
R′	715	20	450	30	27,800
B	0	0	700	30	21,000

Linear programming—algebra example

The above graphic solution is actually a problem in product mix, which is a common type of problem for which linear programming is suited. Blending of gasoline is a similar and common example of this type application. Actually; product mix is a part of a larger category of problems under the heading of allocation. These problems involve assigning resources such as men and women, machines, materials, and money in a way that will result in maximum efficiency within the constraints of the particular case. Characteristically, alternate uses of the facilities are restricted. There is not enough of each one, and the best way to use the existing facilities is the problem. Stated differently, there is a given or fixed amount of work to be accomplished for which several resources are required. What is the best combination of quantity mix of these required resources?

Let us consider a simple problem involving product mix which illustrates the allocation aspect. In this illustration, the linear programming—algebra means will be utilized. A manufacturer processes peanuts and cashews, packages them in one-pound bags, and employs two different mixes. The one mix is .5 peanuts and .5 cashews; the other mix is .7 peanuts and .3 cashews. From the former a profit is realized of 5 cents a bag; from the latter, 4 cents a bag. The manufacturer's facilities limit daily capacity to 200 pounds of peanuts and 100 pounds of cashews, and he must supply some of each mix to satisfy the market demands.

First set up these data in a matrix-type form to visualize the facts easily. Figure 8–10 shows such a matrix. From these data we can state,

FIGURE 8–10

Item	Mix A	Mix B	Restrictions
Peanuts	.5 pound	.7 pound	200 pounds
Cashews..........................	.5 pound	.3 pound	100 pounds
Profit (per pound bag)	$0.05	$0.04	

reading across the peanut row, that .5 pound of mix A plus .7 pound of mix B equals, and cannot be more than, 200 pounds, the peanut capacity. Likewise, reading across the cashew row, .5 pound of mix A plus .3 pound of mix B equals, and cannot be more than, 100 pounds, the cashew capacity. Expressed algebraically:

$$.5A + .7B = 200 \tag{1}$$

and

$$.5A + .3B = 100 \tag{2}$$

Here we have two equations with two unknowns. To solve, we subtract one from the other to eliminate one of the unknowns, and then calculate the value of the remaining unknown as follows:

$$.5A + .7B = 200 \qquad (1)$$
$$\text{less } \underline{.5A + .3B = 100} \qquad (2)$$
$$\text{remainder} \quad 0 + .4B = 100$$
$$B = 250$$

Substituting this value for B in one of the equations, say equation (1),

$$.5A + .7 \times 250 = 200$$
$$.5A = 25$$
$$A = 50$$

This means the manufacturer should process 250 one-pound bags of mix B, for which profit per bag is 4 cents and 50 one-pound bags of mix A, for which profit per bag is 5 cents. For this product mix which is best in keeping with the problem restraints, the total profit realized is $12.50 (250 × $0.04 plus 50 × $0.05).

SIMULATION

Another quantitative means for decision making is simulation. By its use, helpful decisions to certain types of problems are obtained. The idea of simulation is to make a dry run of the problem at hand by carrying through the experiment or process completely to observe the effect of variables upon the finished result. A model based on empirical data is set up and then subjected to the same influences as it is in actual practice. In simulation these influences are measured quantities, and their occurrence is determined by the use of random number tables which synthesize the happenings on a strictly chance basis. In other words, the approach is to duplicate systematically what happens in reality by setting up a model and putting it through the same paces or influences that affect it in real life.

It should be noted that simulation models are empirical; they are not mathematical in the same concept that models of operations research are mathematical formulae into which values are substituted to calculate the answer. The model in simulation is a quantitative representation of the behavioral characteristics, interactions, and intangible and nonlogical attributes of the entity under study. Further, in simulation it is possible to trace from the model the activities as relationships and variables change, that is, as the characteristic activities take place. This is not true in the case of solving equations for an optimization objective. In fact, the simulation model is not used for optimization. It serves basically for the systematic trial-and-error approach to complex problems.

Chance behaves in an unexpected manner. Machines break down, bottlenecks pop up in key operations, and important suppliers fail in critical shipments. Chance events take place in the best of managed enterprises. This is because there are several variables interacting and thus affecting the outcome. Some of these usually involve probability which is discussed below. Such variables are not constant through time or space. They are called *stochastic*.

In simulation we construct distributions empirically from actual or logically assumed data and then at random generate an artificial sequence of events against which the behavior of the distribution can be evaluated. Many random sequence generations, taken from the probability distribution applicable to the process being studied, tend to disclose the behavior of the process. Mathematics is not used in simulation to represent a general solution; rather an approximate solution is determined by systematically running the simulated process a large number of times with the alternatives under test.

Hence, it is also feasible to test changes in relationships of important variables of a problem before actual installation of the assumed set of forces or conditions. With such comparisons, the accomplishment of goals; the determination of how much "off-target"; and the change in the pattern of actions and results, or what is sometimes called the change in the "configuration of the totality," being considered can be quickly assessed. If required, simulation can be broad in scope; it can encompass a maze of different activities. This provides insight into the total, or multicomponent, concept of an extensive area.

PROBABILITY AND DECISION MAKING

It is appropriate to inject at this point a discussion of probability and its relation to decision making. As mentioned in Chapter 7, most management decisions involve uncertainty in various degrees, but normally not total ignorance. Managers have long sought to minimize the uncertainty in the outcome of their decisions and to this end, they have utilized various means such as insurance, analysis of past performances, various statistical techniques, and application of the probability theory wherever possible. The use of probability has grown in importance as certain quantitative decision making means have become more widely applied, especially in the use of simulation, Monte Carlo, and queueing.

Probability can be viewed as a way of dealing systematically with uncertainty by evaluating mathematically data believed to be representative of the phenomenon being considered. Probability is what you make it. If you feel from carefully weighing your experience, knowledge, and emotion that the likelihood of an event happening or of a certain outcome taking place, it is possible to rate the probability of that event taking place. When a sales manager states there is a 70 percent probability of achieving $200,000 in sales in the New England states next year, he is saying that from his background and experience in acquiring sales, his knowledge of the product and the market, plus his desire to sell in this area, and his judgment, that there is a very good chance that the $200,000 sales amount can be accomplished. He is estimating that the chances are 70 out of 100, a highly favorable odd, that his prediction will prove correct. Certainty is 100 percent or unity. The 70 percent is pure estimate; it may turn out to be 68 percent or 72 percent, either of which would be excellent.

Probability denotes the extent of an individual's belief in the truth of a declared statement. Basically it consists of figuring the odds. An "80 percent chance of snow in Chicago by November 15" amounts to a 4-to-1 odds that it will snow. However, the source is not certain of this statement, but the probability of it being true is 80 percent.

Also, it should be pointed out that probability is basically long run. A person may state that the probability for general taxes to increase is 100 percent. Given sufficient time, this will probably happen so the 100 percent probability is correct. On the other hand, the statement may be that the probability for general taxes to increase within the next two years is 65 percent, and this too may prove to be correct.

If an event is repeated sufficiently, a pattern of outcomes is usually established so that if we can measure what causes seem to bring about or are related to identifiable results, it is within reason to determine what the odds are that a particular result will occur. The safety analyst, for example, doesn't say 10 accidents will happen this month, but rather that the chances for 10 accidents are 90 percent probability which means there is some possibility that they will not occur, but the overwhelming odds are that they will occur.

In one sense, probability means the relative frequency with which a specific event occurs when an action is repeated many times. For example, the probability of drawing the ace of spades from a deck of cards is 1/52, or 1 time in 52 on the average. This is the common concept that mathematicians use in applying the theory of probability.

In connection with decisions and probability, the mathematical theorem developed by Thomas Bayes of the 18th century is helpful. In effect this theorem states that the knowledge of a certain probability of an event occurring can be modified should additional evidence which seems to differ from the first be obtained. An adjusted, or new probability, is derived by means of the Bayesian formula which is written mathematically as:

$$P\left(\frac{E_1}{E_0}\right) = \frac{PE_1 \times P\left(\dfrac{E_0}{E_1}\right)}{PE_1 \times P\left(\dfrac{E_0}{E_1}\right) + PE_2 \times P\left(\dfrac{E_0}{E_2}\right)}$$

where

$$P\left(\frac{E_1}{E_0}\right) = \text{the adjusted probability due to additional knowledge}$$

PE_1 = the initial probability of the first operation or by the first party

$$P\left(\frac{E_0}{E_1}\right) = \text{the probability of the second operation or by the second party}$$

PE_2 = the coefficient of the initial probability of the first operation made by the first party. Mathematical value is $(1 - PE_1)$

$$P\left(\frac{E_0}{E_2}\right) = \text{the probability of the second operation or by the second party being, or is, erroneous.}$$

An example will clarify how this theorem is used. Assume a business leader wants to expand manufacturing facilities and estimates the price for the major product will not increase. Based on knowledge of market conditions, experience, and talks with friends, the leader feels about 65 percent certain of price stability, but wants to be at least 80 percent sure before going ahead with the expansion. The business leader engages the help of a management consultant who utilizes all relevant information and analyses to the product under discussion to determine the probability of price not increasing. The consultant concludes that price will not increase and further estimates that his conclusion has a 75 percent probability of being correct, and that if there is an increase, the probability is 25 percent that the consultant would be in error; that is, it would be very unlikely for a rise in price to take place. Substituting appropriate values in the formula above gives:

$$P\left(\frac{E_1}{E_0}\right) = \frac{0.65 \times 0.75}{0.65 \times 0.75 + 0.35 \times 0.25}$$

$$= \frac{0.4875}{0.5750}$$

$$= 84.8\%$$

In other words, the business leader can be 84.8 percent sure that the price of the product will not increase.

The use of probability in management decision making is increasing. To calculate the likelihood of certain events and to supply an estimate of the gain or loss from a decision assists the manager in selecting the best decision for a given set of circumstances. In addition, knowledge of probability helps shape effective conclusions from evidence that appears at first to be insufficient or inadequate. This involves sampling and the use of small amounts of data to represent their totality.

DECISION TREE

Related to probability and helpful in decision making is the decision tree. It is a representation in diagram form of a number of possible future events that may effect a decision. Relative values for the predicted outcomes of each decision are evaluated and taken into account. The outcome having the highest desirable end value indicates the course to follow since it is most likely to produce the best return. From a decision point the decision tree approach links a number of possible actions and possible events by means of straight lines so that the total effect resembles a tree lying on its side. See Figure 8–11.

FIGURE 8–11: A decision tree

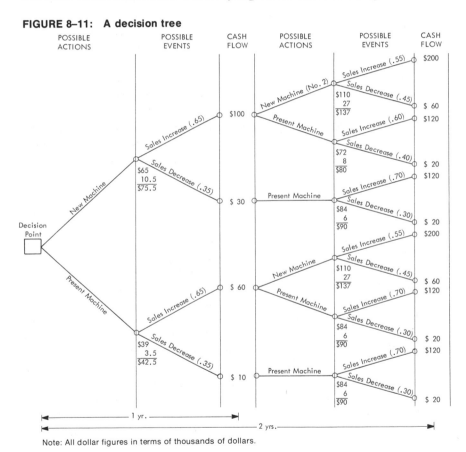

Note: All dollar figures in terms of thousands of dollars.

In this illustration a manufacturer has the alternatives of acquiring a new machine or keeping the present machine. These two possible actions are shown emerging from the decision point at the left of the drawing. We can assume that sales of material parts made on this machine may increase or decrease with respective probabilities of

0.65 and 0.35 as indicated on the diagram. For simplicity of analysis, we will use estimated net cash flows which will result for the several outcomes. To illustrate, the estimated net cash flow for a new machine and a sales increase is $100,000, for a new machine and for sales decrease the amount is $30,000. In contrast, by the manufacturer running the present machine and sales increasing (lower left of Fig. 8–11), the net cash flow is estimated at $60,000, whereas, for sales decreasing the amount is $10,000. These data are for one year's operations.

Multiplying the probabilities by the net cash flow and summing them gives the total expected value the manufacturer can expect from any possible action. In Figure 8–11, this is $75,500 for the new machine (0.65 × $100,000 plus 0.35 × $30,000) and $42,500 for the present machine (0.65 × $60,000 plus 0.35 × $10,000). The better decision is to use the new machine as the expected value from it is greater than that from the present machine by $33,000 ($75,500–$42,500). The decision tree approach enables the decision maker to evaluate alternatives in terms of the best estimates of future results.

Extending the analysis we continue the diagram as shown by the right portion of Figure 8–11. For example, at the decision point of the new machine-sales increase (top of illustration) at the beginning of the second year the manufacturer has the alternative of buying another new machine (machine number 2) to replace the one acquired last year or continue with the then present one. For a sales decrease forecast it is assumed continuation of the then present machine will be followed. For the new machine (number 2) the probabilities for sales increase and for sales decrease are shown under the possible events column to the right. Likewise, alternatives and subsequent probability values are shown for all other points included in the diagram. Again, working from right to left, and using the estimated net cash flow data for the end of the second year, the total expected value for new machine (number 2) and sales increase is $110,000 (0.55 × $200,000), for sales decrease $27,000 (0.45 × $60,000), or a total of $137,000. Comparable data are shown on the diagram. From these data we would decide to (1) buy the new machine at the beginning of the first year and again buy a new machine at the beginning of the second year. This would probably give us a two-year total expected value of $137,000. Based on the data used in this illustration we would get this same result ($137,000) by using the old machine at the beginning of the first year and using a new machine at the beginning of the second year. Actually this would be the more economical decision as it would entail less expenditure since only one new machine is acquired.

Analysis for the third year might result in a changed pattern for the manufacturer. Decision trees are helpful not only in decision making, but also in planning. However, the technique becomes rather cumbersome for periods exceeding three years and also estimates of probabilities and of net cash flows are quite speculative for too distant periods.

MONTE CARLO

Let us return now to quantitative means for decision making. Monte Carlo is a somewhat narrow form of simulation, but it also includes probability factors. The simulation is guided by random sampling to take into account the probability of the event happening. In other words, random sampling is employed to simulate the natural events in order to determine the nature of the probability of events under study. A table of random numbers is employed to obtain the random sample. Monte Carlo is a trial and error means to see what would take place when certain occurrences, normal and abnormal, as you select, were to occur. The approach is predictive and tells what will probably happen in actual events without analyzing comparable existing events. The possible applications are numerous. The technique is easy to comprehend and to use. Figure 8–12 shows the basic pattern followed.

Monte Carlo can be employed to answer problems having these typical questions: What are the chances of an event, or combinations of events, occurring in a given process? Based on this frequency and time of occurrence, what decision in relation to possible alternatives should be followed? What is the current chance of a breakdown of a given machine?

Applications of Monte Carlo include the determination of the quantity to produce of a special material for a given order so as to minimize excess. Determining the factors that affect the excess and then calculating the probability of these factors occurring in the proper proportions to get just the quantity desired is the essence of one suitable approach. In addition, Monte Carlo can be used to determine the amount of stock most feasible to produce for a good, repeat customer in order to get satisfactory production runs. Surplus from one production run is stored, but the approximate certainty of the time and quantity of its future sale to the good customer can be calculated. Likewise, and in the same vein, Monte Carlo is helpful in determining the optimum personnel level that will balance overtime cost with excess human resource costs. Another application is the calculating of the optimum period between maintenance inspections for certain equipment, and the sequence of orders to minimize time in process.

To more fully understand the Monte Carlo means, assume a manufacturing company buys ten machines. They will receive unequal usage so each will last a different length of time before having to be replaced. It is desired to have ten machines of this type operable at all times. To achieve this goal, how many replacement machines is the company likely to buy during the next ten years? From past experi-

FIGURE 8–12: Basic pattern of Monte Carlo technique

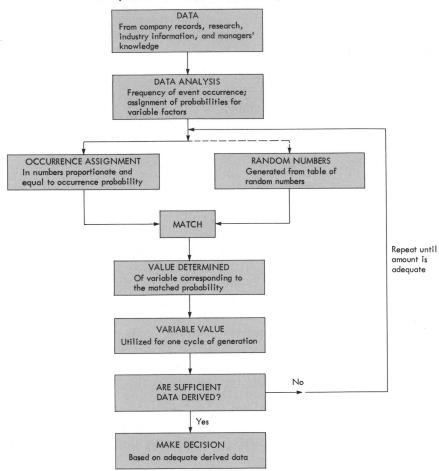

ence, educated guesses, information from the machine manufacturer and sundry sources, the lives of the machines are assumed to be as shown in the top portion of Figure 8–13. That is, 5 percent of the machines will wear out in 21 months, another 5 percent within 24 months, etc. Note that these estimated percentages total 100, or unity, i.e., all ten machines.

The answer to replacements for the machines is determined by Monte Carlo means. To do this, we are going to determine by random selection from the data of our estimated machine lives, how long each machine probably will last. To carry this out, 20 tabs are used each representing 5 percent of the initial total machines. Since 5 percent of the total represents a machine life of 21 months, we mark one tab with a "21." Likewise, we mark another tab with a "24," three (15 divided

FIGURE 8–13

Estimated percentage which will wear out	Estimated life of machine (in months)
5	21
5	24
15	27
25	30
35	33
10	36
5	39
100	

Machine	No. 1 drawing	No. 2 drawing	Cumulative Nos. 1 and 2	No. 3 drawing	Cumulative Nos. 1, 2, and 3	No. 4 drawing	Cumulative Nos. 1, 2, 3, and 4
1	30	30	60	36	96	27	123
2	33	21	54	27	81	33	114 ←
3	30	39	69	33	102	30	132
4	30	30	60	36	96	30	126
5	36	30	66	30	96	27	123
6	33	33	66	36	102	33	135
7	27	33	60	21	81	33	114 ←
8	33	33	66	33	99	30	129
9	30	39	69	30	99	36	135
10	33	27	60	33	93	24	117 ←

by 5) tabs with a "27" and so forth. We now have a sample of the different lives of the machines. Drawing randomly from these 20 tabs will give us a pattern of the lives of the machines as best we can estimate. When this is done, the data at the bottom portion of Figure 8–13 are obtained. The first tab drawn had a "30" marked on it so the entry 30 was made opposite machine 1 under column No. 1. This tab was returned to the pile thus keeping the total drawn from always equal to 20, and again a drawing was made. A tab with a "33" was drawn and entered opposite machine 2. The process is continued for all ten machines, then repeated by the second round of drawing. At the finish of this drawing, it is found that in no case is the estimated cumulative life per machine ten years. The third round of drawing values are shown in the illustration along with the cumulative drawing values for each respective machine. The process is continued through the fourth round of drawing, after which it is found all but three machines, No. 2, No. 7 and No. 10, will last beyond the ten-year period (120 months).

This means that to have ten machines operable at all times for ten years, the company will have to buy replacements 3 times, and buy 3 more machines, making a total of 33 replacement machines required. To reiterate, this answer is a sophisticated approximation. No one really knows how long a group of machines in use will last. However, if the initial data being used, i.e., the estimated percentage of time to wear out and the respective lives of the machines are quite correct, the answer to the replacement machines question will likewise be quite correct.

QUEUEING

Problems occur in management that arise due to (1) employees, machines, or materials made to wait because of insufficient facilities to handle them immediately or (2) less than maximum facilities utilization is taking place because of the arrival sequence of resources using the facilities. There is lost time, unused labor, and excessive cost caused by waiting lines, or queues. To minimize these losses is the objective of queueing. Representative is the situation at a check-out counter in a supermarket, material waiting for machining (line balancing), airplanes circling an airport waiting for landing directions, and ramp design and toll gate provisions for expressways. Queueing is concerned with flow and, in addition to the above examples, includes flow of communication and of materials. Hence, it includes reconsideration of paper-work processes and of material handlings.

Normally this technique involves a balancing of expenditures of existing queues with the cost of providing additional facilities. The Monte Carlo approach is commonly used to ascertain the arrival rates at facilities and thus reveal the expected delays. This is especially useful where the queue is not constant. Computer mathematical analysis is resorted to, and it is common for complex equations or models to be required.

Under given conditions, queueing has shown that for 29 patrons arriving randomly each hour at a post office stamp window, each patron taking 2 minutes to transact business, there will be an average waiting line of 28 patrons and an average wait of 58 minutes. If an additional stamp window is opened, the average waiting line is reduced to less than one patron. The 26 patron-hours saved $(28 - 1) \times 58/60$, are won at the additional cost of just one additional window attendant, truly a worthwhile gain.

GAMING

To give reality to the situation, gaming can be utilized. Actually this is a type of simulation. The theory of games was developed by scientists Von Neumann and Morgenstern. Advocates of gaming state that it is helpful when the problem is concerned fundamentally with the actions of competitors. That is, if company A alters its plans and manufactures a product in greater quantities, how will the competitors to company *A* meet this new condition? The theory of games implies use of the strategy of least regret. In other words, the course that will cause company *A* the minimum amount of trouble is determined and can be followed if and when its competitors do the smartest action possible for them to do. In this manner, the planning of company *A* can be made the most beneficial to company *A*.

One approach in using "business games" is to begin with each decision maker in an identical position as shown by a balance sheet revealing the current condition of an enterprise. Auxiliary information to supply a needed background is provided. Decisions are made which affect the balance sheet. For example, it is decided to invest so much money in research, so many units will be manufactured, and the selling price is adjusted. Periodically subsequent decisions are determined, keeping in mind the results derived from the previous decision and also the effect of the decisions of competitors.

Although commonly thought of as a management-training device, business games can also be considered a type of quantitative decision-making technique. Although the mathematics is relatively simple since basic ratios, projections, and statistics are employed, the data are used in every phase of the game. The decisions are expressed in quantitative terms, such as a certain number of sales obtained, units purchased, or inventory added. "Playing the game" provides the manager with practice, insight, and the opportunity to improve managerial actions as well as to decide courses of action from typical situations that are experienced in everyday managerial activity.

QUESTIONS

1. Referring to Figure 8–3, what is the total shipping costs under this northwest corner solution? How does your answer compare with that for the solution given in Figure 8–6? Discuss.

2. How do you account for the development and wide usage of the quantitative techniques in managerial decision making? As you see it, will their usage increase or decrease in the future? Why?

3. Do you feel that quantitative means for decision making can be employed advantageously for managerial problems of a social type, i.e., for problems of urban development, pollution of air and water, and providing adequate school facilities? Discuss fully.

4. Discuss probability. How is it used in decision making?

5. For what purpose can the Bayesian formula be used? Discuss.

6. Identify each of the following fully: (*a*) linear equation; (*b*) configuration of the totality; (*c*) matrix distribution; and (*d*) stochastic variables.

7. Describe Figure 8–7 in your own words, explaining how this arrangement of data was obtained by VAM.

8. With reference to operations research, what are (*a*) the steps taken in applying it, and (*b*) the advantages in using it?

9. Referring to Figure 8–8, suppose an operation required on model B only is added to the problem. This operation requires on model B only is added to the problem. This operation requires 2 hours and there is a maximum of 600 hours available for this work. What combination of models A and B will now provide the maximum revenue? Explain how you derive your answer.

10. What is simulation? Is it similar to the technique of operations research? Discuss.

11. Explain how the data in the lower portion of Figure 8–13 were obtained. What use can be made of these data? Discuss.

12. In your own words relate what a decision tree is and of what use it is in decision making.

13. In general, what types of problems would you say are best suited for the technique of simulation? Linear programming? Gaming?

14. Compare Monte Carlo with queueing, noting the similarities as well as the differences, and relate for what types of problems each may be used.

CASE 8–1. BAYS COMPANY

Business has been good, and to fulfill purchase orders received, the company must increase its production. Two alternatives are available: (*a*) buy a new unit of equipment or (*b*) work overtime. In either case, sales can increase or decrease. In the case of buying new equipment, it is estimated that the net cash flow or conditional value would be $50,000 in the case of a sales increase, $30,000 in case of a sales decrease. Should the overtime alternative be followed, the estimates are $25,000 for a sales increase and $10,000 for a sales decline. For each alternative (buy equipment or work overtime), the probability for a sales rise is 60 percent, for a sales drop 40 percent.

For the new equipment, sales *rise* approach, subsequent alternatives are (*a*) buy another new unit of equipment which it is believed will result in either high sales increase (50 percent probability) or moderate sales increase (50 percent probability) giving net cash flow of $80,000 and $60,000 respectively. Or to the new equipment sales rise approach, a subsequent alternative is (*b*) use overtime resulting in either high sales increase (50 percent probability) or moderate sales increase (50 percent probability) with net cash flow of $60,000, and $40,000 respectively.

For the new equipment, sales *decrease* approach, the subsequent alternatives are (*a*) high sales increase (80 percent probability) net cash flow $50,000 or moderate sales increase (20 percent probability) net cash flow $40,000.

If initially the company decided to work overtime followed by a sales rise or a sales drop, the results from the sales rise are estimated as follows:

Alternatives and results	Net cash flow	Probability (percent)
Buy 2 units of equipment		
High sales	$100,000	50
Moderate sales		
increase	80,000	50
Buy 2 units of equipment plus overtime		
High sales	110,000	50
Moderate sales		
increase	90,000	50

The results from a sales drop are:

Alternative and results	Net cash flow	Probability (percent)
Overtime		
High sales	$40,000	80
Moderate sales increase	25,000	20

Questions

1. Draw the decision tree based on the above data.
2. What decision should be made by the managers of Bays Company?
3. What other important considerations, not included in the above analysis should also be taken into account by the managers? Discuss.

CASE 8–2. ALEXANDER PRODUCTS COMPANY

This company has three warehouses, W_1, W_2, and W_3, with capacities respectively of 70 tons, 85 tons, and 105 tons to handle the outputs of four factories, F_1, F_2, F_3, and F_4, with capacities respectively of 25 tons, 80 tons, 100 tons, and 60 tons. The management wants to know what factories should ship to which warehouses in order to obtain a minimum of total freight costs.

Freight rates are as follows:

From	To	Cost per ton	From	To	Cost per ton
F_1	W_1	$100	F_3	W_1	$25
	W_2	40		W_2	30
	W_3	55		W_3	65
F_2	W_1	40	F_4	W_1	70
	W_2	30		W_2	20
	W_3	25		W_3	75

Questions

1. Arrange the data in matrix form.
2. Using the VAM method, determine the cost pattern required showing what factory should ship what quantities to which warehouses.

CASE 8–3. McKEE DAIRY

A popular item of McKee Dairy is chocolate milk made by mixing chocolate and milk. Two brands, Supreme and Regular, of this drink are made by the McKee Dairy. The former brand consists of 85 percent milk and 15 percent chocolate for each gallon of chocolate milk. The latter, Regular, is made of 95 percent milk and 5 percent chocolate for each gallon of chocolate milk. The diary has facilities to handle daily 500 gallons of milk and 30 gallons of chocolate. From each gallon of Supreme, the dairy realizes a profit of 27 cents; from Regular, 16 cents. To satisfy the market, at least 30 gallons of each brand must be made daily. The dairy can sell all the chocolate milk it can produce.

Questions

1. How many gallons of Supreme and of Regular brands of chocolate milk do you recommend the company make? Justify your answer.
2. For your recommendation in answer to question No. 1 above, what will be the dairy's weekly profit (6 days)?
3. Suppose the dairy could make milk and chocolate in any combination of Supreme and Regular brands that it wished. Could the dairy realize a greater total profit than that in answer to question No. 2? Why?

PART III
Planning

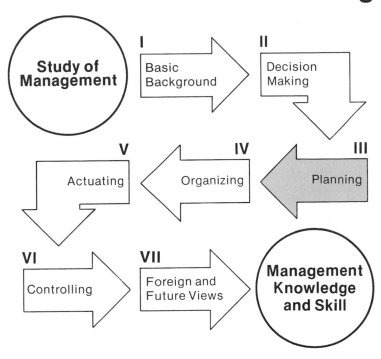

Chapter makeup for Part III:

The first fundamental function of management to be discussed in detail is planning. It provides the blueprints of actions to be followed in order to achieve goals.

Discussed in Part III are the important and interesting major topics of the strategies used in planning, the need and contribution of policies, implementation of planned actions, the consideration of managerial ethics, the need for creativity, and the types of plans in use.

Chapter 9

Planning—strategies and policies

They copied all they could follow
But they couldn't copy my mind
And I left them sweatin' and stealin'
A year and a half behind.

Kipling

As pointed out in Chapter 1, planning is a fundamental function of management. For any enterprise to survive, grow, or enjoy a healthy mode of operations, necessitates planning. It affords the practical means to bring together all the resources of an enterprise into an effective unity and to think about the future and what actions should be taken.

Planning is vital in management because it is basic to the other fundamental management functions. Without the activities determined by planning, there would be nothing to organize, no one to actuate, and no need to control. And planning is required in each of the other fundamental functions, i.e., in organizing, actuating, and controlling. Planning must be done at all management levels. The president, vice president, the department head, the section head must plan in order to manage effectively.

MEANING OF PLANNING

Planning is the selecting and relating of facts and the making and using of assumptions regarding the future in the visualization and formulation of proposed activities believed necessary to achieve desired results. It is the determining in advance what is to be done and how it is to be done. One can look upon planning as being made up of a bundle of decisions, planning being considered as preparing for the future by making decisions now. Planning is oriented to and requires a

173

feeling for the future. It represents expenditure of thought and time now for an investment in the future. Some have expressed it as uncovering things today so that we may have a future tomorrow.

It is true that some goals are achieved with relatively little planning, but in this modern age where many tasks have become quite complex, more technology is involved, more people want to be informed and participate in what's going to be done, and with the ever increasing diversity of products and services, planning has become a necessity. In fact, it is difficult to understand why planning is sometimes neglected. It is probably an intense desire to act immediately, the objective is wanted now or it may not be achieved if immediate action is not taken, or the situation is such that the potential of immediate mistakes is so great that efforts must be directed toward their correction.

EXAMPLES OF PLANS

As might well be expected, there are multitudinous plans in management. Every segment, nook, and corner of about every type of enterprise and environmental factor has been subjected to planning to some degree. However, one common ingredient of all planning is time, and plans with respect to time can be coveniently expressed as (1) short-range (SR), covering a period of 1 year and less, (2) intermediate-range (IR), over 1 but less than 5 years, and (3) long-range (LR), over 5 years. These are arbitrary definitions. The length of the planning period is partly a function of the particular enterprise's production cycle, sales fluctuation, stability of service pattern, and the desires of top managers. Also important is the belief of what time period is needed to make effective future actions designed to make things happen that otherwise probably would not occur. Figure 9–1 shows for each of these three types, several representative examples of

FIGURE 9–1: Major types of planning with subtypes under each heading

Planning for		
Short range (1 year or less)	Intermediate range (over 1 year but less than 5 years)	Long range (5 years and over)
Schedule* Use of resources	Profit* Growth	Product* Goal adjustments and changes Strategies*

* Discussed briefly in this book.

plans. These are indicative only and are not intended to be complete. For each major heading, one type has been selected and will now be discussed briefly.

SCHEDULE PLANNING

Much short-range planning concerns scheduling which is affixing time values to each needed activity and to the total project. Scheduling gives vitality and a practical meaning to a plan. Consider the illustration shown by Figure 9–2. This scheduling plan emphasizes work-

FIGURE 9–2:   A chart used for scheduling

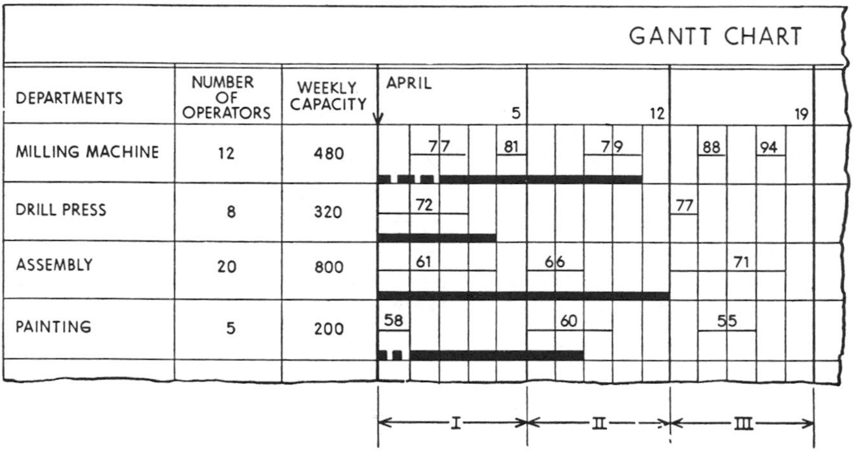

time relationships. It is known as a Gantt chart, having been devised by Henry L. Gantt, a prominent management scholar and practitioner around the beginning of the 20th century. Departments are listed on the left, along with the number of operators and their weekly capacity. Each main column of the chart, identified by I, II, and III for clarity, represents one week; and the small numbers at the right of each column indicate the week ending as of that date. To illustrate, column I represents the week ending April 5. Opposite each department heading are two lines, a light line and a heavy line. The position and length of the light line in a column represents the starting and ending times for work (by shop order number) in the respective department. For example, in the milling machine department, during the week ending April 5, order No. 77 is scheduled to start Tuesday morning and to be finished Wednesday night; order No. 81 is to be run all day Friday. For the week ending April 12, it is planned to run order No. 79 from Wednesday morning to Thursday night. The heavy line opposite each department represents the cumulative time scheduled for the respective department. Hence, for the milling department, the heavy line is seven days long, representing the total times scheduled for order Nos. 77, 81, 79, 88, and 94, as shown by the light lines opposite the milling machine department. The dotted heavy line indicates work scheduled but not yet completed. It amounts to two days' work for the milling machine department. The V mark at the top of the chart indicates the effective date of the chart. In the illustration, this is the end of March 31, and the data shown are effective as of that time. Subsequent changes can be drawn on the chart; it is unnecessary to redraw the entire chart. Note that values per day differ for departments. One day in milling machine represents 96 hours of work, while one day in the drill press represents 64 hours. The chart quickly reveals the amount and the "limits" of time available. by departments. For example, an additional order requiring 480 hours of assembly work, or three days (480 divided by 160), could be scheduled for one day, Friday, during the week ending April 5 and two days, Wednesday and Thursday, during the week ending April 12. The earliest date this assembly order could be completed would therefore be April 11, assuming previously scheduled orders as shown by the chart are not changed to give priority to this new order.

Many adaptations of the Gantt chart idea are in use today. They may not be identified as Gantt charts, but they all emphasize the importance of scheduling and of time values in planning. Observe that the determining of the particular activities and their sequence are normally included in the meaning of planning, but not of scheduling. The former has the broader connotation.

PROFIT PLANNING

While different opinions exist in different enterprises, profit planning is usually considered an intermediate range type of planning. As its name suggests, this planning focuses on improving the profit, especially from a particular product over a period of 1 or more years. As discussed here, it is not the same as corporate planning or a cost reduction program.

Profit planning involves streamlining activities in order to get employees profit minded and to secure maximum benefit from minimum effort and expenditure. Best results seem to be obtained by assigning a profit planner to investigate all the factors affecting the profit obtained from a single product. The planner is given the right to probe the economics, organization, mode of operations, pricing, marketing, or any other facet of making and selling the product that it is believed affects profit accruing from that product. The concentration of profit efforts upon one product and the right of the planner to cross traditional functional boundaries of the enterprise to translate needs from one group to another and to obtain concerted profit-building efforts among those who can effect profits are the fundamental factors that contribute to the success of profit planning.

A big portion of the planner's job is to make management members aware of the untapped profit potential in the given product. Qualifications include a local business and corporate background, a capacity to analyze problems, and the ability to innovate to improve the profit picture. Also helpful is the knack of working with specialists and recommending improvements without telling the specialists how to do their work.

In a number of business enterprises today, profit planning is given casual treatment. Some managers remain unconvinced of the power of planning to realize a profit. They concede profit planning is logical and is an exciting concept, but feel strongly that it just does not apply in certain businesses. Profit planning can assist any business enterprise. To think otherwise is erroneous and commonly arises from two major misconceptions. First, the belief that profit planning is a job for staff experts only. Profit planning is pointless unless the direct operative managers play a principal role in the planning and are active in implementinting the planning. Second, the feeling that profit planning need not really concern the nonmanagement members. Such members with their detailed knowledge of operating conditions are highly qualified to translate the profit goals of top management into specific goals, plans, and accomplishments. In fact, by their participation in the profit planning, they will become truly committed to achieving the profit goals.

PRODUCT PLANNING

Typical of long-range planning is product planning which provides good discussional material because products are familiar objects, they have wide interest, and they illustrate many excellent examples of planning techniques. Figure 9–3 shows a useful product long-range planning approach. Referring to the figure, for each present product an estimate of the desired future sales is made. To do so, estimates of the following are made: (1) sales requirements for the desired future sales of this product, (2) the technological recommendations for improved design and manufacturing cost reduction, and (3) the profit and loss statement (projected) for the improved product. From this information the decision is made whether to continue or terminate the sales of the product. In the case of future products, an estimate of sales is made for each one. Then the financial requirements are determineed for the combined improved present products to be continued and the new products. This is achieved by means of profit and loss statements. Based upon the financial requirements projected, the program is estab-

FIGURE 9–3:   An approach to long-range planning for a product

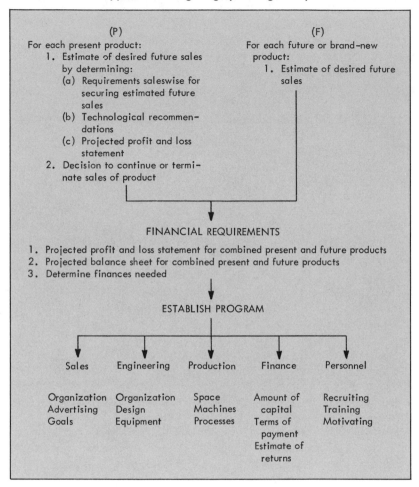

lished with the required activities being divided among sales, engineering, production, finance, and personnel departments.

Short-range planning is tied to the above format by developing a monthly, a six months', and a yearly sales forecast by products. Similar periodic statements are drawn up for activities in the other major areas of the enterprise. These forecasts serve as the intermediate goals and guide efforts along a course designed to achieve the long-range program.

STRATEGIC PLANNING

Recent interest has focused on the use of strategy as it applies to planning. Since it is broad of scope, of interest to the student of management, and important in today's management, it will be discussed in some detail. As the counterpart of strategic planning—tactical planning will be included. Further, policies, a type of plan supportive to strategic planning and essential to making strategic planning viable, will be discussed.

Strategic planning does not predict the future, but for a manager it can (1) assist in coping effectively with future contingencies, (2) provide an early opportunity to correct inevitable mistakes, (3) help in making decisions about the right things at the right time, and (4) focus on what actions to take in order to shape the future as desired.

Strategic planning begins by asking questions regarding the purpose and the operations to which an enterprise is presently devoted. To illustrate: What service are we trying to provide? What is our competition? Should we be doing everything we now are? Do we need more or fewer lines of products or services? What is the environmental dominance under which we operate? What's happening technologically, socially, politically that could have impact? To what degree? How will this effect us? What can we offer? What is unique about what we can do? Can this uniqueness, if any, be exploited by us?

Answers to questions such as these help managers of an enterprise turn the radar upon themselves and their activities, take a critical view of what is being done, decide what should be retained, what added, and put these thoughts and ideas into their plans. In brief, it is a thorough self-examination regarding the goals and means of their accomplishment so that both direction and cohesion are given the enterprise. For a business company, it is how its managers define its business, its competition, and its concept of itself.

Format of strategic planning

Stated succinctly, strategic planning consists normally of four distinct parts (1) strategic dimensions of environment affecting the enterprise, (2) resource audit of enterprise, (3) strategic alternatives and (4) strategic choice. Before we can start with part No. 1, it is necessary to gather and analyze pertinent information. Hence we will discuss this first, then proceed with the parts of the format.

INFORMATION GATHERING AND ANALYSIS

Today more information is available than can be used. The computer can yield reams and reams of data relating to products, services, costs, and prices. Libraries are a fruitful source. Trade associations offer industry statistics, and from the government are numerous studies, reports, and booklets on a variety of subjects. Don't forget vendors; they are an important source of current information. Volume alone is not satisfactory. The key consideration is to acquire information that is useful to decision making and problem solving. Nonessentials must be eliminated. One criterion is to seek information that will help answer the question, What is needed to improve what is being done or to make decisions about the future?

It is a good idea to obtain information by interview or questionnaire regarding the style and ambition of the company management team. They will condition any future strategic plans formulated and will be responsible for their implementation. A plan will not succeed if those charged with its implementation are not genuinely and highly satisfied with it.

Of considerable importance is the determination of significant trends in key areas: sales, services, costs, inventory, quality, employee turnover, and cash. Knowledge of seasonal patterns by product, market, or geography is helpful. All such data should be displayed graphically on a sheet of 8½ × 11-inch paper. This makes possible quick and broad appraisals.

STRATEGIC DIMENSIONS OF ENVIRONMENT

An enterprise's total external environment includes the influence of many factors. Typically, competition, technological, sociological, and political influences are considered. Competition, especially important for business enterprises, includes identification of the company's opponents, their number, and their characteristics. Comparison of achievement, the general behavior, and the importance of competitors are given top priority. Size, for example, is not necessarily governing. Zenith, for instance, is smaller than RCA, yet is quite successful in the television business. A technique usually effective is to write the names of competitors across the top of a sheet of paper and down the left-hand side put such factors as production cost, product quality, rank in sales, general strengths, general weaknesses, quality of management, competitive price, and growth. Fill in the information for this matrix, study it, and evolve an answer to what strategy might best be followed to face up to competition.

Attention to potential disasters should also be included. Questions regarding events that might happen and take the enterprise by surprise are, What should be done in case our important vendors cannot supply us? What if we lose our top manager in an air disaster? What if a big merger takes place involving our competitors?

Technological changes are becoming increasingly important in managerial planning. To cope with these changes poses tremendous tasks. It is important to know the major directions of technologic change and the approximate scope of these activities. Also, knowledge of natural resources is helpful. In addition, keeping up to date on technical processes and evaluating new concepts in this area are basic requirements.

It appears that the formulation for effective technological forecasts rests upon three bases: (1) strong research efforts and effective research policies, (2) a periodic evaluation of technology competition to know what others are doing, and (3) appraisals of radical technological developments with estimates of what these developments might mean to your particular company. Technological forecasts are not precise, the field is too dynamic, but the direction and probable range can be estimated.

Sociological factors are likewise of importance. The distribution of present and future populations with respect to size, age, sex, location, and ethnic structure are significant in assessing the environmental dimension. The emphasis that different members of society or of a community place upon personal needs, entertainment, home, and community can have an important bearing upon the makeup of the plan.

Further, the availability of skilled labor, extent of trade unionism, and types of fringe benefits should be taken into account. Likewise, in education, the number of college graduates, professional people, and scientists and their views toward foreign affairs, their research work, and their level of living should be included.

Political action represents a cardinal consideration in the environmental dimension. Government services, international affairs, protective measures, and regulations are so extensive and affect so many different activities of an enterprise that it is essential to keep in mind the effects of legislation in any strategic planning. The degree and direction of governmental influence differ widely among various types of enterprise. For example, certain laws encourage competition while others give noncompeting efforts a nod of approval. Some legal measures aid and others regulate the efforts of the group. Governmental regulations for protecting public health and safety imposed upon a food manufacturer may be far different and more numerous than those applicable to a manufacturer of metal stampings.

Also the areas of foreign markets, tariffs, international monetary stability, and foreign aid programs can be cited as having influence on the environment within which an enterprise must operate. Governmental fiscal actions merit special mention. Government is a dominant figure in income distribution and investment activities. Taxes represent a sizable amount of expenditure to many enterprises and consumers and cannot be ignored in planning. Governmental fiscal action regulating credit availability exerts tremendous influence upon general business activity.

RESOURCE AUDIT OF ENTERPRISE

Strategic environmental dimensions were discussed before the resource audit of enterprise because *resources are relative.* Strengths and weaknesses of an enterprise are meaningful in relation to the external environment in which that enterprise operates. And this applies not only to current but also to future external conditions. The exclusive advantages to a manufacturer of wrought iron stoves, for example, became a liability when the market, an external factor, shifted to a lighter portable designed stove.

What is the unique competence of a given company? It exists in most companies yet is usually difficult to identify simply because it has been taken for granted or because no probing in this area has ever been undertaken. Frequently, it is mundane, such as "successfully introduce new products faster," or "develop modified services at lower cost than anyone else," or "ship an order on same day it is received." Unique competence is vital in strategic planning because such competence should be used and protected.

The management of an enterprise is perhaps the greatest strategic asset and also constraint, and certainly one of the most important resources. The abilities and potentials of managers are difficult to assess, yet strong efforts must be made in this area for the resource audit to be meaningful. Judgment and decision making ability play a significant role in the calibre of strategic planning performed. And the addition or subtraction of a key executive may represent the presence or absence of a critical member of the management team.

Answers to the question, What are the major requirements for success in this enterprise? supply pertinent information for identifying and evaluating the resource of an enterprise. How competent must sales personnel be? What amount of advertising is required? Are research personnel able to keep abreast of technological advances? Is manufacturing capable of achieving the goals of growth sought? Can the enterprise compete favorably in manufacturing and selling in the international market? What about its financial resources—are they adequate to handle the capital requirements? How much cash is generated and how is it related to the company's financial needs? In short, how much growth or change can be financed internally. Guided by financial data, would transferring of financial resources from one segment of the enterprise to another segment be desirable? Can extensive mechanization, if needed, be handled financially by the company?

STRATEGIC ALTERNATIVES

From all the information collected and analyzed, the key strategic issues facing the enterprise are identified. Usually this work requires considerable time and a list showing the key issues and implications evolves slowly. Innovation within the well-defined framework evolved from the above environmental and resource audit work steps will be required. At first blush, many new ideas will be thought of as a bit impractical and silly, but persistence in finding a better way should be followed. When appealing strategic options constitute threats to existing strategies, the decision to strike out in new directions and manners is a most uncomfortable decision to make. But this does not mean that existing strategies must be discarded or that they have a limited life. In fact, the ultimate in many instances is that the existing strategies followed are the most appropriate.

Commonly the various alternatives will reduce to those under these classifications: (1) size of enterprise, (2) earnings, and (3) adding or subtracting certain activities. The "right size" for a company is open to many different viewpoints. Recommendation for either horizontal or vertical integration will be voiced while at the same time adherents for reducing the present size of the enterprise or its operations will be made. An adjustment in earnings is another common area. To illustrate, improvements in cost ratios for selling and administrative cost are common or a return on investment rather than on sales may be advocated. Finally, the deletion of some products or services, even liquidating certain present areas of endeavor, usually appear in the list of alternatives. Liquidation, however, is a painful verdict and normally is deferred as long as it is possible to do so. In the adding or subtracting of activities will frequently appear alternatives for diversification as well as for specialization. And whether to go into the international market is likewise a popular alternative.

STRATEGIC CHOICE

This last step of the strategic planning format is probably the most difficult of the entire format. The selection is not entirely rational but is also influenced by emotion, judgment, and tradeoffs among the numerous influences considered. Making commitments in an area of imperfect analyses and of uncertainty is highly flavored by the personal beliefs and values of the decider. In short, the strategic choice is a personal choice.

In selecting a strategic choice, willingness to assume risk is paramount and timing is critical. An eager risk taker, for example, in order to maximize opportunities will willingly expose itself to many external threats. The potential gains are worth the potential chances for failure, or nothing ventured nothing gained viewpoints are followed. In contrast, unwillingness to assume risk leads to a protected, sheltered, and conservative strategic choice. Commonly some compromise is followed—a combination of the most opportunities with the least threats. Early action, high risk, and high payoff usually go together. To delay action by following a wait and see attitude results in a reduction of risk and minimal payoffs.

The selection of strategy is also influenced by how a tentative choice compares with that of competitors. Does the tentative choice meet competition head on or does it avoid it. All things considered, is the tentative choice superior, the same as, or inferior to the strategy followed by competitors? Answers to such questions aid in selecting what is believed a good strategic choice for the enterprise.

PERSONNEL FOR STRATEGIC PLANNING

Commonly the doers are the planners in strategic planning. Professional outside planners and those within the enterprise spending full time on planning can lead the efforts, can provide data and analyses, and can give enthusiastic support. But for best results, the planning dimensions should be by those who will be responsible for eventual implementation. To the managers of an enterprise this makes strategic planning *their* planning, not somebody else's planning.

Group or team effort is therefore followed in strategic planning. It will include those doers of major activities from all over the enterprise. Functions in one area of an enterprise influence functions in other areas of that enterprise. In developing a strategic marketing plan, for example, not only would the sales manager, the sales promotion manager, the advertising manager, and the physical distribution manager be included, but also the chief executive officer, the company's general legal counsel, and possibly, the director of purchasing. Why these latter three executives? Because the marketing plan is vital to the very existence of the company—it will have important legal implications and since some of the company's products are purchased outside for resale by the company, the purchasing director's input can be valuable.

A group of doers for strategic planning needs a leader and this person *should not* be a ranking group member. From the viewpoint of objectivity and political reality, the leader should be selected from outside the group, but it should be a person who understands the group working process, wants to see a practical plan evolve, and is not directly involved with the success of the plan once it is implemented. The role of the leader is to guide and stimulate the group to create the best strategic plan possible. Full participation is invited. The leader is a facilitator. The leader's concentration is with the process followed, not on contributing to the content. Further, the leader selected should understand that if the group members do not feel the leader is helpful or for any similar reason do not want that person to continue in the leadership role, dismissal is automatic. However, the leader is expected at all times to be extremely candid with all group members including those of highest ranking in the company's hierarchy. Such candidness is not adequate cause for dismissal of the leader. In Chapter 10, further discussion of who performs planning and under what conditions are included.

STRATEGIES IN PLANNING

An interesting list of common strategies used in planning will now be given.[1] This list is illustrative, not inclusive, and is intended to show the variety of strategies that may be included in management planning. Which one, if any, is used depends upon the individual situation.

1. *Camel's head in the tent.* This stresses an infiltration approach. An entire plan may be quickly rejected; but by offering only a small portion of the plan, acceptance may be won for this portion. Subsequently other portions of the plan can be offered and accepted until the entire original plan is in operation.

2. *Sowing seed on fertile ground.* Some members of a group are normally more receptive to the provisions of a tentative plan than are others. To offer the plan outright may run the risk of its rejection by the group. However, by selecting those favorable to the plan, thoroughly indoctrinating them in the merits and desirability of the plan, answering their questions about the plan, and stimulating their enthusiasm for its adoption, a group favoring the plan is developed, and its attitude is spread and shared with others of the group. Eventually, a sufficient number are favorable to the tentative plan and will accept it when presented.

3. *Mass-concentrated offensive.* This strategy is to take in one lump sum the total action believed necessary and get the proposed plan into operation as rapidly as possible. Rather than an infiltration type, mass-concentrated offensive can be termed as "earthquake" approach. When this strategy is used, the belief is that it is better to get it over with, eliminate uncertaincy, and get started in the activities to be retained or inaugurated.

4. *Confuse the issue.* A deliberate effort is made to divert the attention of the group by bringing in questions or stressing approaches that have no direct bearing on the real issue on hand. This may be employed when concentration is desired upon favorable issues and soft-pedaling is believed essential concerning controversial issues.

5. *Use strong tactics only when necessary.* Basically it is well to use no more energy or motivation than is necessary to accomplish the stated result. Strong tactics and pressures can be held in reserve and used only in those situations where their extra push is required. The revolutionary way of achieving the objective or the use of a top key executive is applied for special events where their presence and impression will carry great weight.

---

[1] Professor L. C. Sorrell of the University of Chicago has prepared an extensive outline dealing with strategics. The listing included here has been adapted from this outline.

6. Pass the buck.   The transferring of blame or responsibility to someone else is provided by this strategy. The adopted plan makes it possible to pass unpleasant tasks willingly to others. Frequently the maneuver is handled in such a way that censure is made of the other party.

7. Time is a great healer.   Often the planning includes the strategy that with time many actions will take care of themselves. For some problems, time helps bring about the answer. The strategy is basically that it is a mistake to hurry or to insist that certain action take place, for by waiting the need for some of the actions will have been eliminated and many of the remaining actions will have been performed to some degree of satisfaction. This strategy is part of the same thinking expressed in the familiar "Everything comes to those who wait." Time and timing are very important elements in many planning strategies.

8. Strike while the iron is hot.   In other words, get on promptly with the application of the plan when acceptance to it is prevalent. Full advantage is thus taken of a favorable situation. Tomorrow may bring opposition or difficulties; so act today and avoid possible trouble. Act while the time for action is favorable is the essence of this strategy. Thus a sales manager established immediately a sales analysis unit following the suggestion made by the executive committee that such a unit might prove helpful. Had the sales manager waited until the time was more propitious for her, the committee may have changed its mind and approval of the unit may not have been won.

9. Two heads are better than one.   This emphasizes the obtaining of allies and applying joint action. One executive of an organization who wishes to adopt a plan regarding quality control may find that playing a lone hand is extremely difficult. However, should other executives be induced to join in adopting the plan, the resultant joint action may be highly effective.

10. Divide and rule.   An old strategy is for an individual to keep members of a group separated into different factions so that overall rule can be maintained by that individual. This strategy is well-known in politics, and to a somewhat lesser degree in other fields. Its use can be highly effective, although it has its drawbacks, such as dynamic leadership being curbed and cooperative efforts among the members being stifled.

TACTICAL PLANNING

It is helpful to view strategic planning as answering the question, Where should we be going? In contrast, tactical planning answers, How will we get there? Figure 9–4 is included to clarify the distinction between strategic planning and tactical planning. The parts making up

FIGURE 9–4: The planning cycle for strategic and tactical planning

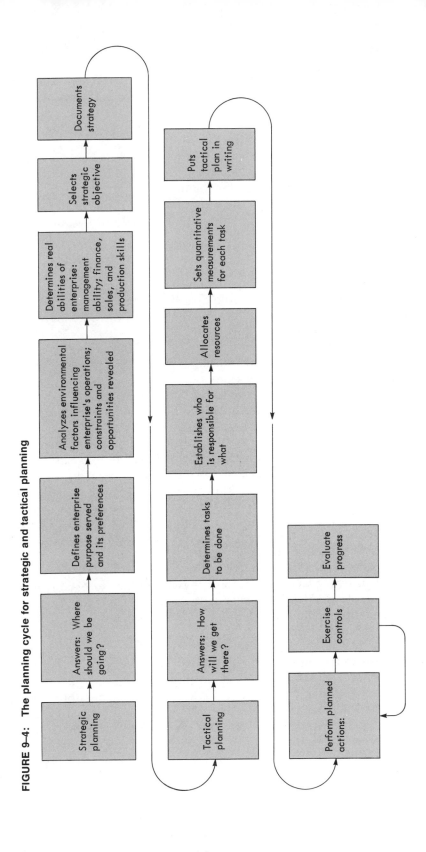

strategic planning are shown across the top line. When completed, tactical planning takes place. The components are shown across the second line. When completed, the planned actions are performed, with controls exercised in order to evaluate the progress being made as shown by the bottom line of the figure.

The purpose of tactical planning is to identify the major tasks required to achieve strategic objectives. Tactical planning is thus supportive to strategic planning. For tactical planning to exist, it must have the directions given by strategic planning. If one of the strategic choices were "to attain production equal to $20 million annually by the next four years," major tasks to achieve this goal would be evaluated and clarified by tactical planning. The possible tasks might include: (1) acquire a suitable competitor, (2) construct an addition to our present plants, (3) rearrange machines and equipment in present plants and in space made available install new production equipment, and (4) expand our buying of components from outside sources and convert our plants into assembly plants.

After the tasks for each strategic choice have been developed, a list is compiled of the various tasks by major unit of the company's organization. Usually it becomes obvious that to perform the needed tasks, certain units will have far more to do than other units. The resultant necessary adjustments in the shifting, adding, and subtracting of employees must be decided.

Likewise, the allocation of financial funds and time will be made. A healthy cash position or strength to borrow at favorable rates will alleviate the finance problem and permit management to act within reasonable flexibility. Capital allocation is a tactical consideration. Time is usually of a lesser amount than that considered ideal. So it too usually must be allocated similar to that of financial funds. The time constraints may limit the number of tasks planned for during the first quarter or half-year of the tactical plan.

Some acceptable means of measuring accomplishments must be included in every tactical plan and it is important to establish such measurements in advance. Devices to measure will vary depending upon the nature of the action being measured. All, however, should be quantitative and accurate.

Tactical planning supporting strategic planning provides a charter as it relates to the future of the enterprise. From practical experience it is reasonable to state that not everything will go as planned. But by means of strategic and tactical planning, it is possible for employees to have an understanding of the various activities of the company and of why these activities will be performed. However, another type of planning, policy, is helpful in making effective the strategic and tactical planning. Policies will now be reviewed.

POLICY

Policies reveal the manager's intentions for future time periods and are decided prior to the need for knowledge of such intentions. They are broad, comprehensive, elastic, dynamic guides and require interpretation in their use. A policy defines the area in which decisions are to be made, but it does not give the decision. Policies spell out the sanctioned, general direction and areas to be followed. By keeping within these predetermined boundaries, but with freedom to decide within the stated areas, the manager performs one's work in keeping with the overall planning of the enterprise of which one is a part. *A policy is a verbal, written, or implied overall guide setting up boundaries that supply the general limits and direction in which managerial action will take place.*

Policy formulation

A well-formulated policy requires time to develop and it is well to consider all contingencies in formulating a policy. Hastily conceived policies usually prove unsatisfactory. Several pointers in policy formulation should be kept in mind. First, good policies tend to be broad; they leave room for judgment, but do not require complex interpretation. Within an enterprise, policies should be consistent; no company should have two policies that say opposite things. Another consideration is to establish a sufficient number of policies to cover the areas deemed important. At the start, a company normally has enough to serve as needed bench marks in various areas. With time, more are added, and they should neither overlap existing policies nor leave any neglected gaps. In addition, sound policies will reflect and develop the unique personality or image of an enterprise. Effective policies possess individuality. They assist in giving an enterprise individual differences that distinguish it from others. Lastly, good policies are current. As conditions change for a company, policies need to be changed to fit the new condition. Selected management considerations in policy formulation are shown in Figure 9–5.

Why managers use policies

Policies assist managers in answering what to do. At all organizational levels better understanding of what is to be accomplished, as well as the means of accomplishment, is fostered by the use of sound policies. Confidence of the manager is enhanced, since a manager operating within a policy gains assurance that one's actions are in keeping with the wishes of, and will be backed up by, one's superiors.

FIGURE 9–5: Important considerations in policy formulation

1. The use of a policy should help in achieving the objective, and a policy should be built from facts, not personal reflections or opportunistic decisions.
2. A policy should permit interpretation; it should not prescribe detailed procedure.
3. The formulator's thoughts and ideas of the content of the policy should be conditioned by the suggestions and reactions of those who will be affected by the policy.
4. Wherever necessary to cover anticipated conditions, policies should be established, but care must be exercised to avoid having policies that are seldom, if ever, used.
5. Every policy should be expressed in definite and precise wording that is fully understood by every member of the enterprise.
6. All policies must conform to external factors such as laws and measures in the public interest.

Furthermore, the policies of an enterprise give meaning to the objective. The goal might be expressed in rather general terms which have small significance to the members of the enterprise. However, the policies translate the goal into terms which are comprehensible, individual, and intimate to the employees. And from a practical viewpoint, it is much less difficult to find out the policies than the objectives of an enterprise. In many instances, the first concrete evidence of a change in objective is revision of the present policies and the addition of new policies.

Policies implement the utilization of authority so that effective group action can be attained. By the presence of good policies, those having authority are encouraged to use it. This follows because, in effect, a policy informs (regarding what is to be attained) by making known the general areas within which activities are to take place.

Policies also encourage management development because *policies develop those who apply them.* Policies require interpretation and make it feasible for a manager to think *for*, not *by*, oneself. Policies encourage the development of sound judgment and the exercise of managerial activities in keeping within prescribed limits. Policies force positive, wanted action. They are not confined to the prevention of bad action.

Types of policies and examples

While there are many kinds or types of policies, a helpful classification is that based on the source of the policy, that is (1) external, (2) internal, and (3) appealed. The first group, external policies, include those policies arising to meet the various controls and requests of forces outside the enterprise, such as government, trade associations, and trade unions. The second group, internal policies, includes those started by the managers at any level of management in order to have needed guides established for their own and their subordinates' use in managing the enterprise. The third, appealed policies, come into being from the appeal of an exceptional case by a manager to his or her superior regarding how to handle the case. As such cases are decided, precedents develop and constitute additional policies or important modifications to existent policies. When many policies are being made by appeal, it may indicate an insufficient number of existent policies.

Another classification of policies is that based on the organizational levels of managers. That is to say, there are policies which are used primarily by top managers, other policies by the middle managers, and still other policies which are applicable chiefly to supervisors and group leaders. Various nomenclatures have been used to designate policies of different levels, but the terms *basic, general,* and *departmental* are satisfactory.

Another common classification of policies is by major functions of an enterprise: production policies, sales policies, financial policies, and personnel policies. A manufacturing company sets forth its personnel policy regarding promotions and transfers of employees in these words:

It is our policy to "promote from within" whenever qualified employees are available for vacancies in our organization. Diligent application to their present assignments, special preparation for positions immediately ahead, and length of service are considered in the selection of those for promotion. Employees on their present jobs a reasonable length of time may request transfers to other assignments in the company if they feel that different work will be better suited to their qualifications.

Observe that this policy statement provides the overall guides to be followed. It does not give a precise means of how "to promote from within," or of handling transfers. Such work is the duty of the individual charged with the particular activity, but guides or areas within which to operate are provided by the policy.

Policies—written and unwritten

Preferably policies should be in writing. Some managers feel that a policy actually does not exist unless it is written. Although many companies do not put all their policies in writing, the tendency to do so is increasing. Verbal policies are frequently too nebulous and lead to excessive misunderstanding for satisfactory use.

Written policies are especially desirable for (1) subjects of a highly controversial nature; (2) situations where the distance between top and lower levels of management is quite deep, thus making personal and informal association and communication difficult and infrequent; and (3) preciseness of the policy statement so that an adequate and a complete understanding is conveyed. The writing should feature a matter-of-fact style and convey the feeling of wanting to share information and to be of genuine assistance. Figure 9–6 lists the out-

FIGURE 9–6

Advantages of written policies are:

1. Managers are required to think through the policy's meaning, content, and intended use.
2. The policy is explicit and misunderstandings are reduced to a minimum.
3. Equitable and consistent treatment of problems is most likely to be obtained.
4. Unalterable transmission of policies is insured.
5. Authorization of policy, helpful in many cases, is provided.
6. A convenient and authoritative reference of policies can be supplied to all concerned with their use.

Disadvantages of written policies are:

1. Policies become too widely distributed and frequently are placed in the hands of persons who are not concerned with their use.
2. It is difficult to write a policy accurately and adequately—there may be uncertainty as to what the policy should be, and there is the constant danger of misinterpretation of certain words and phrases.
3. Flexibility in the use of the policy may become hampered—too rigid a course for practical management is defined.
4. Changes in policies to cope with changing conditions may be difficult to establish.
5. If confidential material is involved, nonwritten policies may be preferred for reasons of security and secrecy.

standing advantages as well as the disadvantages of putting policies in writing. In the great majority of cases the advantages outweigh the disadvantages.

Some policies are not expressed either in written or verbal form. They exist by inference or by means of consistent managerial behavior in certain subject areas. They may have little, if any, official approval, but they are operative. Such policies are termed *implied policies* and may be favorable or unfavorable to the enterprise. They result from tacit agreement or from the lack of any vigorous formal policy formulation efforts. Usually secrecy, difficulty of expressing, or reluctance to limit freedom of the manager's action are the chief reasons for the existence of implied policies.

Evaluating policies

Policies become antiquated, and to maintain their effectiveness they should be periodically reappraised, realigned, and restated in line with current opportunities and conditions. However, some managers feel that frequent requests for modification in a policy indicate its failure either in content or in usage. This may be true; yet it is difficult to attribute disagreement, conflict, and waste solely to poor policy, but policy can be a major contributing cause. The entire management process should be reviewed and studied for possible improvement.

The ultimate proof of a policy's correctness is in the desirable results which it helps the manager bring about in actual performance. Conducting interviews with managers and nonmanagers to ascertain the relationship between practices and policies is one effective approach. Another is to determine how useful the policy actually is by finding out how frequently it is used and what confidence the managers have in it. Policies not used regularly or not believed in suggest corrective action, such as elimination or restatement, possibly as a part of a more important policy. A simple check of current policies against objectives often reveals whether the policies are helping, or hindering, in the efforts to reach the objectives. Also, the "trial approach" can be employed. Here, a proposed revised policy can be applied to past problems to determine how it might have worked out. As an alternate, but similar, approach, hypothetical situations requiring the use of the present and the revised policy can be assumed and comparisons made between the probable assistance supplied by the two policies.

From the overall viewpoint, it is well to get opinions and facts both for and against an existent policy in order to uncover, for example, whether the stated policies and what is actually being done are compatible or in conflict. Furthermore, a review will reveal whether the ultimate aims are clearly known, whether activities are pointing to the established objectives, and whether all policies are integrated making, in effect, a unit or a whole from all the constituent or separate policies.

Who performs policy planning

Although as stated above, discussion of who performs planning is deferred to Chapter 10, it will be helpful to state at this point that in many enterprises, the members of the board of directors and top management members establish the basic policies. Sometimes an executive committee assumes this task and submits its recommendations to the board or top manager. However, at the immediate and lower organizational levels, policies are commonly formulated by managers in the respective areas with the aid of their nonmanagement members.

This participative approach is especially common when results management is followed. This is because the goals which nonmanagers help define and for which they are responsible to attain, are greatly influenced by the policies to be followed. Participation by nonmanagement members in policy formulation is recommended. Employees are consulted regarding their ideas and beliefs on a policy that is to be either established, modified, or abolished. In many cases the action taken is best described as a simultaneous working-down from the top managers, revealing what they perceive are the policy needs, and a working-up from the employees of the areas which will be affected by the policy.

QUESTIONS

1. Why perform planning if nobody, not even a manager, can be certain of events in the future? Elaborate on your answer.
2. Generally speaking, should a manager strive to plan for a relatively short- or a long-time period? Substantiate your answer.
3. What is profit planning and how is it conducted within an enterprise?
4. Distinguish between the two concepts in each of the following pairs: (*a*) policy and tactical plan, (*b*) strategic planning and tactical planning, and (*c*) the strategy of "confuse the issue" and that of "camel's head in the tent."
5. Discuss tactical planning and in your answer include what it is, why it is performed, and who normally performs it.
6. Based on either your experience or events about which you have heard or read, relate a strategy of planning that was or is being used. In your opinion could a better strategy be used? Explain.
7. Enumerate the parts making up the format of strategic planning. Which part do you feel is probably most difficult to perform? Why?
8. What are some common strategic alternatives arising from strategic planning by managers of a business enterprise?
9. Discuss several important reasons why managers use policies.
10. In your opinion are managerial policies motivational to those who use them? Justify your answer.
11. Relate an experience in either school or employment where you successfully applied the strategy of "time is a great healer."
12. Describe an example of tactical planning being used in your school, place of employment, or community enterprise.

13. Discuss four major considerations to take into account in formulating policies.

14. List some of the important policies of your university, business, or club. Classify them according to basic, general, and departmental groups. In your opinion, which policies are most effective? Why?

CASE 9-1. TANNER COMPANY

After considerable research and discussion, the decision was reached by the executive committee for new product planning to add a new product line to the Tanner line of household appliances. Members of this committee included the production manager, the sales manager, the purchasing agent, the director of research, and the advertising manager. The company has two new product lines that could be introduced to the market next year. However, due to the limitations of sales personnel and financial resources, only one product line can be added next year. Company personnel have devoted much effort to estimate sales potentials, production costs, administrative problems, and profits. Important data are shown in Exhibit 1.

EXHIBIT 1

	Economic prosperity		Economic recession	
	Expected profit	Expected loss	Expected profit	Expected loss
Product line No. 1	$275,000	—	—	$150,000
Product line No. 2	100,000	—	$300,000	—

Recent published economic reports state there is a 30–35 percent chance of a recession during the next year. The president of Tanner Company is anxious to secure as many pertinent facts upon which to plan the launching of the new product line as are necessary. Yet she strongly believes that the marketing campaign in launching the new product and the aggressiveness of promoting it are the essential and critical issues in the degree of the new product line's success or failure. On the other hand, the director of research suggests that there is no virtue in taking unnecessary chances. The company should not gamble—losses are too difficult to recoup. The best plan includes expectancy of the worst combined with the selection of the product line which can hurt the company the minimum amount.

Questions

1. What other criteria than that mentioned in the case might the manager use in planning for the new product line? Discuss.

2.   Which new product line do you recommend be adopted? Why?
3.   Is the company using strategic planning? Justify your answer.

CASE 9–2. MERRIAM PRODUCTS, INC.

Bruce Harcourt (employee): I'm going, that's all there is to it. I'm going. I've been here nearly 12 years and I'm taking my vacation in the fall and go deer hunting. I am entitled to take my vacation when I want to and that's when I want to.

Elias Pruis (personnel manager): But you can't go then, Bruce. I told you over a month ago you are scheduled for two weeks vacation during the middle of August. Now that's when you go. Any other time is not authorized.

Harcourt: That's no good. I don't see what difference it makes. And I don't understand why John Beecher over in electronics gets three weeks vacation. I have been here longer than John has.

Pruis: You'll have to talk with Zeke (the supervisor) to find the answer to that. The list comes through to me and it authorizes three weeks, two weeks, one week, or no vacation at all.

Harcourt: Oh, you don't decide it?

Pruis: No, not at all. I'm on the operations committee and vacation time has come up for discussion. I have expressed the view that each employee should have some say in his or her choice of vacation time. But the idea doesn't seem to be too popular. Mark (the works manager) claims no vacation plan is going to please everybody and never will. Maybe he's right. And he also contends that there really isn't anything wrong with the company telling the employee when the vacation starts. After all, it is a gift of the company.

Harcourt: Well I think I earn it. Most every company gives vacations, don't they?

Pruis: Yes, I would say they do, but it is not mandatory.

Harcourt: The company would get into real trouble if vacations were not given.

Pruis: There is another problem. Right now employees are required to work regularly scheduled workdays before and after the vacation period to receive vacation pay. For example, if the vacation is July 12–23, eligibility requirements call for working Friday, July 9, and Monday, July 26. Otherwise some will try to stretch the authorized two-week period. In addition, there is another consideration, which is the handling of holidays. For example, suppose Independence Day is included in the two-week period. Do we pay holiday pay for this day or give the preceding Friday or the following Monday in exchange for the holiday? I guess what I am trying to say is, do we give ten full working days as the prescribed vacation period?

Questions

1. What is the problem?
2. What's your general reactions to comments of Bruce Harcourt? Of Elias Pruis? Discuss.
3. What actions and plans of implementation do you recommend the company take? Justify your answer.

Chapter 10

Implementing management planning

It doesn't take great men to do things, but it is doing things that makes men great.

Arnold Glasow

The manner in which management planning is performed along with the activities allied in this effort will now be discussed. There are proven guides in this work; they are helpful and are included in this discussion. Answers to questions such as the following will be given: What are the specific steps taken in planning? Who should do the planning work? Why do plans go wrong?

At the outset it is well to note that how a management plan is to be put into action should be a part of every plan. To ignore this vital segment of a plan is to court delay, possible misuse of the plan, and ultimate disaster. Many feel that the means of implementation are equally important, if not more so, than the making up of the plan itself.

MAJOR STEPS IN PLANNING

In the previous chapter, it was indicated that planning is influenced greatly by the particular conditions external to the enterprise which affect its operation, pertinent characteristics of the enterprise, and the wishes of the members of an enterprise. The strategic planning and the tactical planning supply the foundation upon which all other plans of an enterprise are built. It is with these other plans, the many different plans typical in an enterprise and their implementation, that we are concerned with in this chapter. Most of this planning work is characterized by certain basic steps, which are enumerated and discussed as follows:

1. Clarify the problem. Visualize the problem clearly. State it concisely. See vividly the present condition that requires improvement and for which the planning is being undertaken. Do not attempt to formulate a plan until this step is completely mastered. The following questions will help in this step:

  a. What is the aim of the plan to be formulated?
  b. Does this aim require a new plan, modification of an existent plan, or the elimination of any present plan?
  c. What will the accomplishment of this aim mean to the enterprise?

2. Obtain complete information about the activities involved. Knowledge of the activities to be planned is essential, and their effect upon other activities both internal and external to the enterprise is necessary for intelligent planning. Experience, past solutions to problems, practices of other enterprises, observation, looking over records, and data secured from research and experiments constitute popular sources of usable information. To assist in this step, the following questions may be asked:

  a. Have all pertinent data been collected and are they sufficiently broad to cover all activities involved?
  b. Have operating personnel been solicited for suggestions?

3. Analyze and classify the information. Each component of information is examined separately and also in relation to the whole of the information. Causal relationships are revealed, and pertinent data to the planning at hand are discovered and evaluated. Information pertaining to similar subjects is classified so that like data are together. As a guide in this step, ask:

  a. Are apparent relationships among data real and confirmed by key operating personnel?
  b. Has information been tabulated or charted to facilitate analysis?

4. Establish planning premises and constraints. From the data pertinent to the problem as well as beliefs deemed important in the determination of the plan, certain assumptions upon which the planning will be predicted are now made. These premises and constraints will point out the background assumed to exist or take place to validate the plan. They are the backdrops on the stage of planning and should be carefully noted so that the plan can be thoroughly understood.[1] Helpful in this step are the following questions:

  a. What important assumptions regarding the future are being made in order to evolve the plan?

---

[1] "Premises of planning" are fully discussed in Chapter 11.

b. Are the premises inclusive, and do they cover all important contingencies?

c. What assumptions must be carefully watched in order to detect changes which might bring about a serious effect upon any plan based upon these assumptions?

5. Determine alternate plans. Usually several alternate plans exist to achieve the work to be done, and the various possibilities are evolved in this step. Ingenuity and creativeness frequently are required to arrive at several possible plans. The following questions may be considered:

a. For each plan, what adjustment, if any, will be needed in the event it is adopted?

b. Are cost, speed, and quality requirements satisfied?

c. Will mechanization expedite the work?

6. Choose proposed plan. The decision is now reached regarding which plan to adopt. The plan's expediency, adaptability, and cost are important. Considerations contributing to the proper selection include:

a. Does the plan possess flexibility to adjust to varying conditions?

b. Is the plan acceptable to the operating personnel?

c. What new equipment, space, personnel, training, and supervising will be needed?

7. Arrange detailed sequence and timing for the proposed plan. The translation of the plan and its relation to all activities affected by it are now worked out. The details of where the planned action should be done, by whom, and when are put in proper order for the intended purpose. The approach and the timing of the application are vital. These questions might be asked:

a. Is the proposed installation, both in content and timing, in keeping with maximum acceptance by those affected by the plan?

b. Are detailed instructions written to cover the plan?

c. Are the required paper forms and supplies available?

8. Provide progress checkup to proposed plan. Success of the plan is measured by the results obtained. Therefore provision for adequate follow-up to determine compliance and results should be included in the planning work. Normally, of course, this is included in the fundamental function of controlling. For this step, ask:

a. Will sufficient reports and records over a reasonable period be collected to inform proper management members and to measure the results?

b. Within what limits or range will results be considered satisfactory?

c. What remedial action is proposed if results indicate weakness?

BASIC QUESTIONS FOR PLANNING

Asking pertinent questions is a favorite means of stimulating thinking and obtaining the information needed for adequate planning. The
answers to such questions disclose not only material to incorporate
into the plan, but also areas for further study to make the plan complete. A number of helpful lists of such questions are available, but
most of them resolve ultimately to the basic questions commonly referred to as the "Five W's and the How" questions. Effective planning
involves the answering of these questions, and in turn these answers
provide the basic ingredients of planning. For existent plans, these
basic questions include:

1. *Why* must it be done?
2. *What* action is necessary?
3. *Where* will it take place?
4. *When* will it take place?
5. *Who* will do it?
6. *How* will it be done?[2]

To reiterate, this sequence of questions is for existent plans. For
initial planning, the *what* question should be asked first, followed by
the *why* question. In any event, the three questions, *where, when,* and
who follow with the *how* question always asked last. The inex-
perienced planner frequently asks the *how* question first and gets
confused with the manner of doing the required work instead of
determining first why the work must be done.

In performing planning step number one, "Clarify the problem,"
the answers to basic questions, *why* must it be done, and, if justifiable, *what* action is necessary, are essential. The tie-in between
the other planning steps, listed above, and these basic questions can
be readily ascertained. In fact, by answering the basic questions the
planner's thinking is directed into the proper area for satisfying planning efforts. The types of information revealed from these questions
will now be stated briefly.

Why must it be done alerts the planner to the need for the work and
encourages one to include only necessary activities. Those not needed
are excluded. The effective plan represents the best combination of
simple, well-combined, necessary activities.

The answer to the second question, *what* action is necessary, indicates the types of activities and their sequence necessary to achieve
the desired result. Also included are descriptions of the facilities and
equipment which will be required to carry out the proposed activities.

Number three, *where* will it take place, designates the specific
physical location for the performance of each activity of the plan. All

202 *Principles of management*

facilities must be available at the proper time in order for the planning to be meaningful.

The answer to *when* will it take place emphasizes the timing considerations. A definite beginning and ending time should be determined, not only for the entire course of action but also for each separate activity included in the plan. Maximum overlapping of required activities is usually recommended because such an arrangement requires the minimum time for completing the contemplated course of action.

Who will do it establishes assigned duties and responsibilities for the members of the group. Assignment of activities should be guided and usually made on the basis of matching the skills required with those respectively of the members.

Last, *how* will it be done brings out the manner of getting the work accomplished and serves as a review regarding the thoroughness in answering the above five questions. This last question actually checks the entire plan for completion and for direction toward the desired goal.

THE PLANNING PROCESS CHARTED

Figure 10–1 gives an overall view of the total planning process and relates planning to the total management process. Beginning at the top of the figure, planning is termed a systematic thought process which leads to strategic planning and tactical planning. Important considerations contributing to each of these planning efforts are indicated on the chart. These efforts were discussed in Chapter 9. With strategic and tactical planning as a background, the planning to develop a specific plan takes place. This work is conditioned and guided by policies and the use of creativity as shown in the figure. To develop the improved specific plan, the what, why, where, and etc. questions are asked.

The evolved plan then becomes included in the management process as shown by the line leading to organize, then to actuate, and to control. And then on to subsequent information and forecasts, to revaluation of the objectives and ultimately to a revision of the specific plan. This is followed by the analyzing of alternative actions by means of the familiar "5 W's and the How" questions and leading back to organize. This loop from organize to organize is the corrective action and is so marked on the chart.

WHO PERFORMS PLANNING?

All managers perform planning. Some plan more than others because of the requirements of their respective positions. In some instances the management member does all his or her own planning

FIGURE 10–1: Overall view of planning and its relationship to the management process.

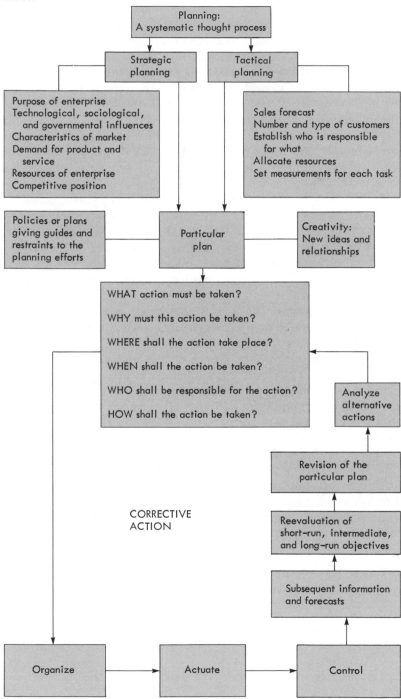

work; in other cases, it is shared with managerial subordinates, or it can also be delegated to specific personnel. A manager can follow any of a number of possibilities.

The first possibility is that a manager does all one's own planning. This requires a considerable amount of the managers' time, but it keeps *doing and planning* closely related. Usually planning under such conditions is highly practical; it provides flexibility, plans can be changed quickly; it permits closeness to immediate problems; and it develops capable managers. However, it is employed in relatively few enterprises today.

The second possibility, and probably most popular, is the manager plans but qualifies such planning by utilizing suggestions from associates. Many managers feel that since they know the goals and have the facts at hand they are in an advantageous position to plan effectively. But they encourage contribution of ideas by associates. These contributions can be either (1) before the formulation of the plan by the manager or (2) after the formulation, indicating its good and bad points as the subordinates see them. With this approach, acceptance of a plan by subordinates is high, but the planning work of the manager is slowed down. Participation in planning is fully discussed immediately below.

Also, a manager can supply a broad outline of plans to subordinates, who fill in the details. This arrangement conserves the manager's time and is helpful where the planning requires special or technical knowledge for full comprehension. However, this approach tends to be time consuming, and it removes the manager from the planning work.

Fourth, subordinates do planning and submit plans to manager for approval. This relieves the manager of most planning efforts and assists in developing subordinates. But there is risk that the plans will lack complete reality and feasibility. Also, the manager's personal contributions and importance are quite likely to be lessened.

No one of these approaches need be followed consistently. It is possible to use one approach in planning for one goal and another approach in planning for another goal. Individual circumstances and the personal wishes and abilities of the manager will determine the practice in any specific case.

PARTICIPATION IN PLANNING

The planner of today usually consults with others, thereby gaining sought-for advice, facts from many sources, opinions on different ideas of what might be done, and approval of all or of portions of a tentative plan. The result is not only improved plans but also more acceptable plans than those conceived entirely by a "master mind" and distributed as the blueprints of action. Participation helps win hearty endorsement and enthusiasm for the plan by all members of a group. This might well result in a mediocre plan bringing excellent results. Likewise, a well-conceived plan accepted halfheartedly by the work force will, at best, probably bring only average results.

The zenith of planning participation takes place where results management modifies the process of management approach. As pointed out in Chapter 4, under results management, with final approval by one's superior, an individual manager designates those things to be accomplished, plans for them, and implements one's own plans. The manager's performance is appraised on the results achieved. Obviously, this practice makes planning intimate and highly meaningful to the individual manager.[3]

While committees used for various assignments have been subjected to a great deal of criticism, they are employed for planning with reasonable success. The committee provides a means for gaining ideas from different parts and organizational levels of an enterprise. Ideas can be presented, suggestions discovered, and full information can be disseminated regarding current as well as tentative plans. Committee members are likely to feel a personal obligation to make the plan a success. Also, they become more interested in planning as a major function of the enterprise and in qualifying themselves to participate in the activity of planning. However, the possible tendency of a committee to spend its time discussing the information, but not evolving a plan from it should be noted.[4]

Many companies have a basic planning committee consisting of the chairperson of the board, president, and vice presidents of the company. The duties of the members of this committee include the establishing and clarifying of major goals and plans and the refining and integrating of recommendations submitted by subplanning committees called project teams. Each project team is composed of one member from the planning committee plus other management members who represent areas of activities pertinent to the work of the project team. Representation is from across functional lines so diversified backgrounds, ideas, and opinions are considered. Responsibilities of a project team include studying basic questions suggested or inferred by the planning committee, gathering information on the pertinent subject areas, and recommending courses of actions along with alternatives and an evaluation of each.

This use of a basic planning committee supplemented by project teams emphasizes major roles by top and middle managers in planning work. They, in turn, encourage other managers to participate in planning. The specialists, technicians, and managers of facilitating,

---

[3] See Chapter 4, pp. 68–73.
[4] See Chapter 13, pp. 283–86.

but not directly operating, functions should also play a part in the planning, but their efforts are mainly to provide help to the operating executives. Planning performed without involving operating managers usually winds up a waste of time and money.

PLANNING AND OPERATING

However, there are two distinct schools of thought regarding the answer to the question, Should the performance of planning be separate from that of operating? Some feel it is impractical to delimit the assignment of these functions. They contend that planning and doing are so closely related, especially at top-management levels, that the same executive can best perform both functions and, as a consequence, achieve the most satisfactory results. It is further argued that performance of planning and operating by the same individual is beneficial because it provides quick and needed flexibility in plans, permits closeness to immediate problems, furnishes complete familiarity with available facilities, and develops capable, well-balanced executives.

In contrast, many hold the opinion that planning should be performed by one person and operated by another. Members of this school believe the most effective planning evolves when the planner is free of current operating problems and can devote all thinking to the vital function of planning. When planning and operating are combined in one person, both suffer. In other words, planning is a speciality function and should be treated as such. A planner is an anticipator of problems and should be free to organize the probable consequences of many present or contemplated actions. This requires meditative thought, imagination, creativeness, and vision unperturbed by pressing operating problems which can probably best be solved by others. In addition, such things as consultations, keeping abreast of developments, reading literature on new techniques, and measuring results and performance in terms of objectives are important in turning out good planning work; and these activities frequently must be passed over if the planner's time is occupied with operating problems.

For various jobs in planning, a leading auto manufacturer employs people with extensive firsthand experience in other parts of its business. After a few years in planning, these employees move on to other operations. Specially trained, or so-called professional, planners are not used. The emphasis is placed on product planning. The manufacturer's executives claim this practice concerning planning keeps their program in line with developments in technology, marketing, and operating methods. Product planning becomes an integral part of their total operations, is highly practical, and is enthusiastically accepted by the nonplanning employees.

The length of time covered by the plan is an important consideration in the question Who performs the planning? Generally speaking, plans pertaining to relatively long periods are made by top managers; those of current or short-run duration are commonly handled by managers at the lower organizational levels.

A DEPARTMENT OF MANAGERIAL PLANNING

A number of enterprises have a department of managerial planning in their organization structure. Commonly this department is established because top managers feel that the importance of planning warrants such a department; or the developments in this activity require such a department; or the general belief that the amount and caliber of planning that should be done will not be done unless a planning department exists. Also in some companies problems arising out of rapid growth and diversity of operations have suggested the establishment of a planning department. In other cases, the planning department is set up and its work limited to one class of work, for example, financial planning or facilities planning. Many companies engaged heavily in defense work have adopted his arrangement.

Generally speaking, planning departments do not mastermind the whole enterprise. They do not represent the centralization of all planning efforts. Their real job is to get others within the enterprise to plan. They achieve this purpose by suggesting what should be planned, by supplying information, by demonstrating how specific planning could be performed, and by telling others the chief executive officer wants them (others) to do planning and the planning department stands ready to offer assistance and guidance. In some respects, the members of the planning department are viewed as idea people. With this arrangement the planning department does not have the power to decide the *what* or *how* of a plan. Usually a planning department helps give a stable and orderly quality to planning.

However, the exact status of a planning department is not always clear-cut. In extreme cases after the department has been established, it must hunt for work to do. There is no problem in most enterprises of finding planning work that ought to be done. But this approach is erroneous. The real question is, What kinds of work are appropriate for a planning department? Should it be a vehicle for gathering information; a clearinghouse for dispensing information; the recipient of specific assignments from top managers; the planner for acquisitions, new plant layouts, cost reduction opportunities; or what?

Figure 10–2 shows a portion of a memorandum on the planning function in a large university. Observe that the statement spells out the need for planning and details who handles the planning work and the practices to be followed in this respect.

FIGURE 10–2:   The planning function in a large university

The estàblishing of University needs and the accomplishing of them accord-ing to immediate and long-range goals requires planning. Planning is an impera-tive of any dynamic organization but in institutions of higher education planning is particularly necessary. As the responsibilities of the University continue to increase in diversity and magnitude, it is of utmost importance that the University consciously determine the directions it should take rather than react without design to forces directing change either inside or outside the institution.

There are many areas of planning. The most important is the determination of educational objectives and the means of attaining them. Other areas of planning in which the

Planning is centralized in the roles of the Department of Planning and two committees: the Faculty Planning Committee and the Administrative Planning and Policies Committee, both of which report to and through the Dean of Faculties.

The Faculty Planning Committee is responsible for initiating studies, review-ing plans and recommendations made by the respective schools and subcom-mittees, and making recommendations concerning long-range educational plans for the University. The Trustees, the President, or the Vice Presidents may make requests of or refer problems to the Committee for consideration and recommendations.

The reports and recommendations of the Faculty Planning Committee are submitted through the Educational Policies Committee (the senior faculty policy committee) to the Vice President and Dean of Faculties, who refers them or such parts as are pertinent to the deans of the various schools, department chairper-sons, the Dean of Students, Director of Admissions, Registrar, University Libra-rian, or other appropriate persons, committees, and agencies for discussion and comment. These comments may then be referred back to the Faculty Planning Committee for further review and comment. They are then forwarded to the Administrative Planning and Policies Committee.

The last-named Committee is responsible for ultimate review, staff approval, and forwarding, with recommendations, to the President. On review, if he ap-proves, they are then forwarded to the Board of Trustees for final approval.

CHARACTERISTICS OF THE PERFORMANCE OF PLANNING

Planning can be described as a tentative process. Initially certain concepts are visualized, but they are tentative and await the develop-ment of other components of the planning efforts. As these other com-ponents are selected or formulated, they are coordinated with the ini-tial concepts. As a result, some of the initial concepts may be changed or eliminated, or they might remain intact. Additional concepts and refinements are added until the complete plan is created. The process consists of a "back-and-forth," tentative adding and subtracting, of concepts to form the plan. It is something like putting together a jigsaw puzzle. A start is made in one area and extended as far as possible; then efforts are shifted and concentrated to another area of the puzzle. Eventually the various separate areas are consolidated, but this may require modification, discarding and reworking certain parts in order to present the final integrated picture.

Since the performance of planning is greatly influenced by the people who perform it, the suggestion is made that in every enterprise a working climate conducive to planning should be maintained. The prevalent attitude should be one of believing in the value of planning and recognizing the need for it. The entire force should be planning-conscious; continuous training in planning practices should be provided; and persons who plan should accept their responsibility for it and allocate an ample amount of time to planning so that it can be properly performed. In essence, planning must be planned—it does not just happen.

Also, while writing of people and plans, it is well to note that the degree of success of any plan is greatly influenced by the manner in which employees do their jobs. It is of significant importance, therefore, for the planner to take into consideration the skills and limitations of the people who will carry out the plan. If they lack the required skills, adequate training or an acceptable arrangement of transferring must be worked out.

The performance of planning is both an art and a science. The carrying out of the major steps in planning are not mechanistic. There is considerable skill in performing each step. Effective planning requires practice, creative thinking, insight, and a feel for the particular activity being planned. Being essentially a mental process, it is difficult to tell, for example, how plan X was determined. But plan X is available—the fruit of a manager's planning. Some have said that planning is like "shooting from the hip," or "portraying a character in a play," or "composing a hit tune"—some can do it effectively, others cannot, even though knowledge of what is supposed to be done can be enumerated logically and clearly. The details of what to do to plan can be memorized yet not performed effectively. The reason is that an essential ingredient of planning lies in the skill, the expertness, and the individualism with which it is personally performed.

ADDITIONAL CONSIDERATIONS IN PERFORMANCE OF PLANNING

It is also helpful to recognize the tangible from the intangible factors involved in planning work. Preferably the two types of factors should not be mixed. Normally the tangible factors can be expressed in common measurable units, such as dollars, and comparisons and summaries made of such factors to expedite the planning. In contrast, the intangible factors can be classified as well as possible and evaluated in terms of judgment and experience or in relation to data representing specific tangible factors. For example, a company planning to offer a new product on the market can express tangible costs like shipping costs, billing expenses, and advertising expenditures in dollars, and summary figures can be used; but the intangible factors— acceptance and willingness of the public to purchase the product, propensity for repeat sales, and so forth—must be appraised by judgment and experience.

Some managers in performing planning find it helpful to work backward from the objective. This approach helps insure that the planning work is directed to the needs of the enterprise and is properly synchronized with other plans. Also difficulties to overcome will be brought out in clear relief and will not be minimized. In addition, progress in the planning can be easily gauged when this approach is followed.

It is helpful to concentrate attention upon the variable issues and disregard those that are constant in the alternate courses being considered. Actually it is the variables that make the differences among the alternates; the constants are really irrelevant insofar as the selection of the makeup of the plan is concerned. For instance, in making the plan for the work of a given manufacturing department, assume that the floor space allotted and its cost to the department remains constant; hence the factor of floor space can be ignored in the considerations of planning the department's work. Instead planning efforts can concentrate upon variables such as accomplishing the work by manual means versus automation.

All other things being equal, it is better to start planning with the major issues. These will exert the greatest influence upon the design of the plan and should be resolved so that the broader structure of the plan is determined in the beginning stages of the planning. This approach is illustrated by the college professor planning a new course. Normally the plan of a list of assignments and the type of examinations constitute relatively minor issues and can be deferred in the initial stages of planning. Major issues, like what is to be achieved by this course, its content, and planning the presentation of the material, should be given prior considerations.

Planning is expedited by giving emphasis to the present and the future. Commitments made from which there is no turning back and past errors in actions which cannot be retrieved are valuable for the experience and knowledge that they provide. However, to brood over past unfortunate results and to wish that such and such had not been included in the plan is nonproductive and interferes with the application of clear thinking to present and future planning. A planner should learn from past mistakes and not repeat them. The goal of planning is to determine what action should be taken now and in the future. Foresight is the prime requisite, not hindsight.

WHY PLANS GO WRONG

What are major reasons why some plans do not work out successfully? The following represent the type of planning action to avoid.

First, having unrealistic and too many goals can prove fatal. Planning to double sales within 12 months will in most cases prove a flop—it simply is physically not possible no matter what is planned. Too many goals can likewise wind up in dismal failure. Restricting the goals to basic measurable targets will tend to keep the planning orderly and effective.

Second, failing to develop up-to-date strategic and tactical plans will negate the applicability and practical relatedness of a plan to a particular enterprise. The proper setting and constraints for the planning must be known if the plan evolved is to have value.

Next, ignoring the use of plans in everyday activities will contribute to the demise of plans. Neglect by managers to use the results of planning is foolhardy in this modern management age.

Also, forgetting about creativity in developing plans reduces planning to a routine activity of economic analysis and data gathering. Rethinking objectives, generating new ideas, and relating resources in better and more effective ways is the heart of good management planning.

Fifth, utilizing a standardized plan for individual needs and purposes is being unreal and like trying to fit a square into a round hole. The plans followed within an enterprise should be so tailored as to fit that enterprise's individual size, complexity, organization structure, and management style. Standardized plans meet only some of the total individual needs.

Last, concentrating on immediate short-range problems and short-range planning can prove disastrous. Putting out fires delays any overall efforts to establish a management mode of operation that minimizes the birth of troubles rather than permitting them to arise, multiply, and cause an endless chain of difficulties.

DYNAMIC PROGRAMMING

Many problems encountered by enterprises today are of a multistage type; i.e., there are a series of sequential phases or steps making up the entire problem. Referring to Figure 10–3 and reading from the top down the problem starts at S. The first stage is either to decide on course No. 1 or No. 2. Suppose the decision is to take No. 2 and

FIGURE 10–3: Dynamic programming permits reevaluation of plan at each stage before decision for subsequent stage of plan is finalized

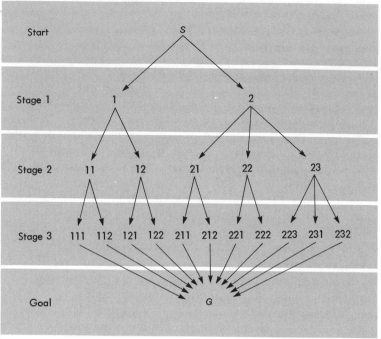

subsequently No. 22 at stage 2, No. 221 at stage 3 leading to our goal, G, shown at the bottom of the figure. To solve our problem, we plan to follow S–2–22–221–G. We have assumed that this plan is superior because it utilizes the optimum decision at every stage or phase. However, in actual practice this may not prove to be so; it depends upon the outcome or accomplishment at each phase. For example, at the accomplishment or results of 22 we may determine that 221 is not the best subsequent decision to make; it should be 222. In such an event we would be modifying our plan from its initial format. We do not know the best onward decision to stage 3 from stage 2 until activities are completed, or nearly so, at stage 2. Then the decision for stage 3 as predetermined, or a better one, can be determined in view of the unfolded current circumstances.

Dynamic Programming (DP) is intended to achieve utilization of the optimum decision at every stage of a multistage problem. This will provide the superior plan. DP takes into account the effect of each decision at each stage of the overall problem. The cumulative effect of the path of decisions is the concern of DP which permits reevaluation of the decisions as advancement along the prescribed pathway takes place. DP has been made feasible by the modern computer.

Representative of the type of problem suited for DP is that of investing in, replacing, and maintaining machines where the governing decisions are made periodically, for instance annually. The problem is basically to determine whether to buy a new machine or continue with the present one. Calculated are comparative expenditures of operating the new and the old machine respectively. Labor and amortized costs are included. A new machine is usually indicated when, on a year's basis, current labor, maintenance, and depreciation costs for the old machine exceed the minimum cost for the new machine.

QUESTIONS

1. Give the "Five W's and the How" questions in their prescribed sequence for evaluating existent plans.
2. Discuss the meaning of Figure 10–1 in your own words.
3. In general, which approach of a manager performing planning—do it all, none, or share it in any of several degrees—do you favor? Why?
4. Enumerate the eight steps recommended in performing planning.
5. Do you favor the use of a committee to perform planning work? Justify your views.
6. What are some questions to ask in order to gain help in the planning step of "determine alternate plans"?
7. Generally speaking, do you favor having the planning and the doing phases of a manager's job within that job, separated between two jobs, or some other arrangement? Substantiate your answer.
8. Elaborate on the statement, Planning is a tentative process. Illustrate your answer with an example.
9. What advantage is there to a planner to identify and keep separate in one's own thinking the tangible and intangible factors involved in one's planning efforts? Give an illustration to substantiate your viewpoint.
10. As a top-management member, assume your choice for improving current planning in your corporation in establishing and using either a basic planning committee or a department of managerial planning. What decision would you make? Why?
11. How would you justify the statement that the performance of planning is both an art and a science?
12. For an enterprise with which you are familiar, or of which you have been an employee, relate an example of planning that was performed. In your opinion how effectively was this planning conducted? Discuss.
13. Name and briefly discuss four reasons why plans go wrong.
14. What is dynamic programming and for what purpose and under what conditions do you recommend its use?

CASE 10–1. DONNAVAN BICYCLE COMPANY

Dear Mr. Douglas:

Your visit with me last week was indeed a pleasant occasion and I am highly impressed with your qualifications for our new position, Director of Planning. Several of my colleagues with whom you spoke likewise have a favorable opinion of you.

As I indicated, this is a new position for us and we want to make sure we select the right person. You have been selected as one of the three finalists from whom the selection will be made. We are inviting each finalist to meet with the members of our Executive Committee and Board of Directors to explore areas of special interest including answers to questions such as:

1. What objectives for the planning department do you feel essential and how might these relate to the authority and responsibility of other top members of our executive team?
2. What major economic and social problems do you envision will confront the Donnavan Bicycle Company during the next decade?
3. As you see it, what should be the priorities established concerning these major problems?
4. How would you describe the future of the Donnavan Bicycle Company and what thoughts serve as the basis for your prognostications?

Quite frankly we don't expect definitive answers, but we do feel the type of thinking required to answer these questions is the type which the directorship we are talking about will require.

I am looking forward to seeing you again at 2 P.M. next Thursday in the Conference Room of Donnavan Bicycle Company. If you have any questions, please call me. I shall be glad to help in any way that I can.

Sincerely,
Joseph M. Donnavan, Jr.
President

JDjr/ks

Question

1. Making whatever assumptions you feel necessary, answer each of the four questions stated in the president's letter. Discuss each fully.

CASE 10–2. THE HODGES BUILDING

The building manager of the Hodges Building, a well-known office building, is faced with the problem of how to improve its elevator service. The building is ten floors in height, was constructed in 1926, and has been maintained in a good state of repair. The location is on a main street of Oakland, California. Complaints regarding poor elevator service have been registered by several tenants. The building manager has delayed taking any action because she believes that whatever improvement can be made should be included in the planning of the elevator service for the new five-story addition to be constructed adjacent to the present building.

Currently, two elevators serve the building; each has a capacity of 20 persons. The speed of each elevator is approximately as follows:

10 seconds per floor going up if stop is made at each floor.

50 seconds for travel from ground to 11th floor (the ground floor is considered the first floor) with no intermediate stops.

9 seconds per floor going down if stop is made at each floor.

40 seconds for travel from 11th floor to ground floor with no intermediate stops.

The manager conducted a survey of elevator traffic in the building, and typical data are shown in Exhibit 1.

EXHIBIT 1

Time	Total traffic (no. of persons)	Destination to floor										Service required is mainly
		2	3	4	5	6	7	8	9	10	11	
7:30 A.M.– 8:30 A.M.	Average = 81	7	4	13	9	5	8	9	5	9	12	Up
8:30 A.M.– 8:45 A.M.	291	17	95	12	33	8	11	21	37	16	41	Up
8:45 A.M.– 9:00 A.M.	194	50	8	3	42	1	83	1	2	1	3	Up
9:00 A.M.– 9:15 A.M.	176	2	1	90	1	3	2	5	22	45	5	Up
9:15 A.M.– 9:30 A.M.	142	10	7	2	2	81	1	30	3	2	4	Up
9:30 A.M.–11:30 A.M.	Average = 94	3	2	14	2	16	8	3	10	29	7	Up and down
11:30 A.M.–12:30 P.M.	Same as 8:30 A.M.– 9:30 A.M. traffic											Down
12:30 P.M.– 1:30 P.M.	" " "											Up
1:30 P.M.– 4:30 P.M.	Average = 75	1	7	9	10	3	12	12	2	6	13	Up and down
4:30 P.M.– 4:45 P.M.	205	36	6	7	51	4	77	10	7	5	2	Down
4:45 P.M.– 5:00 P.M.	201	5	3	86	7	4	4	20	19	37	16	Down
5:00 P.M.– 5:15 P.M.	163	15	68	7	12	6	5	9	13	14	14	Down
5:15 P.M.– 5:30 P.M.	87	4	1	14	4	13	5	5	11	17	13	Down

In other words, during the time period 7:30 A.M.–8:30 A.M., the average traffic load is 81 persons for each 15-minute period, distributed among the various floors as indicated by the above data, namely 7 for the second floor, 4 for the third floor, and so forth. Traffic builds up rapidly at 8:30 A.M., and during the 15-minute period 8:30 A.M.–8:45 A.M., the total elevator traffic load is 291 persons, of which 17 are passengers for the second floor, 95 for the third floor, and so forth. The total load for each 15-minute period is almost evenly distributed over its 15-minute period. There is also interfloor traffic at all times, but the building manager feels this is relatively minor in volume and has received no complaints on such service.

It is anticipated that elevator traffic resulting from the proposed five-story addition will be as follows:

Time	Total persons
8:30 A.M.–8:45 A.M.	150
8:45 A.M.–9:00 A.M.	130
9:00 A.M.–9:15 A.M.	100
9:15 A.M.–9:30 A.M.	100

This pattern will be repeated between 11:30 A.M.—12:30 P.M., between 12:30 P.M.—1:30 P.M., and between 4:30 P.M.—5:30 P.M. For 15-minute periods during the day for other than times indicated, the load is assumed to be a maximum of approximately 60 persons with an average of 40 persons or less. Again the traffic load for each of these 15-minutes periods is almost evenly distributed over its 15-minute period. The lobby of the proposed addition will join onto the present building lobby so that the present elevators could be used for tenants in the addition.

Questions

1. Is there reasonable justification for the complaints regarding the elevator service at the present time? Substantiate your viewpoint.
2. Will the present elevators take care of the additional traffic predicted for the new five-story addition?
3. Based on information supplied in this case, what decision do you feel the building manager should make? Why?

Chapter 11

Planning—additional considerations and relationships to ethics and to creativity

What man can imagine, man can do.
John F. Mee

There are important considerations regarding planning that have not yet been discussed. In this chapter coverage of these items will be made including, such subjects as patterns of planning, premises, advantages and disadvantages, ethics, and creativity—all with reference to their influence upon planning. The student of management will find them not only interesting, but also helpful in fulfilling planning assigments in the future.

PATTERNS OF PLANNING

A study of planning among many enterprises will reveal that the patterns of planning differ widely. Some enterprises, for example, stress strong and persistent growth, while others include little intention to change future events. One enterprise may conduct elaborate planning with the aim of increasing its share of the market, entering new fields or markets, or making major organizational changes. Its planning calls for active product development and adoption of new manufacturing techniques. In contrast, in another enterprise, the planning is simply to maintain the present position of the company. Here "survival today" is emphasized, the reasoning being that an enterprise must survive today if it is to survive in the future.

Generally speaking, there are three divergent and current patterns in planning practice which include (1) satisficing, (2) optimizing, and

(3) adaptivizing.[1] *Satisficing* emphasizes the status quo; seldom are breaks with the past produced. Obvious deficiencies are corrected, but the customary and current way of conducting affairs is preserved. Survival is of major importance; growth and development are secondary and frequently ignored.

The pattern of *optimizing* stresses doing as well as possible. Truly optimum plans are not always attained, but close approximations of them are. Furthermore, in these efforts, valuable by-products of the behavior of important forces are gained, and this knowledge is helpful in further study and research.

Adaptivizing describes the planning pattern whereby operations can be adapted to short-run and also to major future changes. Basically sought is a reduction in the variations of the expected behavior of essential forces affecting the plan. For example, a company with a product line having a highly seasonal demand cannot effectively employ its personnel and its manufacturing facilities. To improve the situation, the company sought another line of products having a seasonal demand opposite to that of its present line. By this means wide variation in annual sales would be reduced to a fraction of their former amount. By adaptivizing or adjusting production requirements and outputs, the planning is simplified from the overall viewpoint.

Planning and time

Time is the omnipotent, omnipresent ingredient of all planning efforts. Recognition of its importance in planning has given rise to basic concepts of which a few will be mentioned here. First, planning should precede the actual physical doing of an action. That is, it is better to formulate a definite plan of what you are going to do before you start to do it. Too frequently in actual situations, physical efforts are expended before the proposed action is adequately planned, the justification being there isn't time for planning, or action must be taken immediately.

Principle of planning

To accomplish a goal most effectively, adequate planning, or mental effort, should take place before the doing, or physical effort.

Second, there is also a proper time for most actions. This usually depends upon the relative importance of the particular objective being sought, the internal and external environmental conditions and whether they are favorable or not to the sought goal, and the general attitude of the employees toward the plan. Help in recognizing the

---

[1] From an excellent article by Russell L. Ackoff, "The Meaning of Strategic Planning," *McKinsey Quarterly*, Summer 1966, pp. 4–7.

proper time is provided by preparing one's mind to look ahead so that possible changes can be anticipated and scheduled for future periods. Planning aids in these efforts and further helps to uncover opportunities of the present and future.

Third, there is the time element in the concept of phasing which is a part of many plans. Phases identify the successive time periods for activities, as set forth by the plan, to take place. By using phasing, a complex plan can be reduced to a simple series of actions, each one of which is easily understood and effectively handled. Also, in many cases phasing helps insure acceptance of the plan by all who will be affected by it.

Fourth, the length of time covered by a plan should be sufficiently long to cover the involved managerial commitments. Another way to express this is to speak of "recovery costs." How long will it take to get back the investment in equipment, sales promotions, and training of personnel required by the plan? This question is best answered by planning, which should include a sufficient time period to provide a complete answer. A manager is interested in using a period sufficient to justify the dollar expenditure involved

Principle of commitment

The time period covered by planning should preferably include sufficient time to fulfill the managerial commitments involved.

Following the commitment idea in determining the length of planning period is sound economically, but it means that an arbitrary universal length of time for a planning period is not feasible. The periods of commitment vary considerably among enterprises. In some cases the period may be only eight weeks, whereas in another, such as in a mine, many commitments are of a long-term single-use variety. In this latter case, the planning can be definite, but it is of a do-or-die type of commitment. Furthermore, in some instances the commitment is adjusted to conform with standard practices, such as quarterly or yearly accounting periods, or to certain tax years or periods. Also observe that a plan really becomes a working plan when definite commitments for executing it are made. True, some plans are canceled and commitments renegotiated or accepted at a loss, but such happenings are in the minority.

Planning premises

Although reference to planning premises has already been made, additional comments here are in order. What are premises? Formally stated: *Premises are assumptions providing a background against which estimated events affecting the planning will take place.* The selection of planning premises and their use depend upon the skill, perception, and experience of the planner. Some premises seem more appropriate than others, but for any given case final judgment must await the results obtained. The difficulty usually faced by the planner is twofold: (1) selecting what premise to use and (2) evaluating the essential assistance obtained from the use of the premise. If the assumption is one for which statistical or quantitative data are available, that is, gross national product, dollar sales, or costs of financing, a corollary to the second difficulty mentioned above is how to manipulate or make use of the data so that the derivations from them are meaningful to the planning efforts and are statistically correct.

Use of premises help to reduce the uncertainty inherent in the future, to have an identifiable foundation upon which to form a structure upon which planning can be based, and to give the planning reality and acceptance. Since planning deals with the future, a manager in order to manage, assumes that certain entities will act in certain ways, that certain forces will be present to known degrees, or that specific conditions will be absent during the future period under consideration.

By using premises a manager is able to plan; and further, by their use boundaries are established within which the planning efforts are to be performed. Premises tend to confine planning within areas considered appropriate and feasible by the planner.

Within any one enterprise, agreement regarding the planning premises is vital in order to achieve proper coordination and integration among the various plans. Obviously, one manager of a company using the premise of retrenchment over the next several years and another manager basing plans on an expansion of the company's facilities could result in confused and extremely costly operations. However, different premises can be used. In some instances this approach serves as a check upon past plans, or more commonly it is helpful to draw up different plans for consideration.

The makeup of planning premises changes, and it is sometimes difficult to keep a set of premises up to date. This is the result of both the actions of the future and the importance of a premise upon the plan. In addition, every major plan adopted by an enterprise tends to become a planning premise. This stems from the interrelatedness of plans and their dependence upon each other. If a company adopts a plan to market a new line of products, that plan will become an important premise in the determination of other plans where the presence of this new product line is significant.

Facts and planning

Emphasis should be placed on the importance of the use of facts in the establishing of premises and the formulating of the plan. Too many times what is accepted without question as fact turns out to be opinions, hopes, or estimates of the planner. A fact is an occurrence, quality, or relation that is manifestly real or actual. It represents a thing done or existing. Obviously not all information is made up of facts.

A person may be hasty in concluding that there are no facts available about a certain area of activity and proceed to a plan based on judgment, intuition, past experience, or some cultural pattern when facts are available. This is poor planning. Facts should be found and will be found if a diligent and consistent search is made for them. In some cases, the facts may be unpleasant and difficult to believe and accept. Nevertheless they should be included in the planning work if practical and effective plans are to be evolved.

Principle of facts and planning

To design an effective plan, it is necessary to obtain all the available pertinent facts, face the facts, and in the plan include the action that the facts dictate.

RANGE OF COURSES OF ACTION

It is well to keep in mind that planning for a range, not a single course, of action makes it possible for the manager to select the plan deemed best fitted to achieve the result, with due consideration given the conditions under which it must be applied. Planning is frequently done amid highly dynamic conditions, and ample allowances for needed modifications and changes in keeping with events and circumstances as they develop are mandatory. Having a range from which to select helps not only to determine the most suitable alternative, but also provides for the unexpected. After all, the "best" alternative is only best under a certain set of circumstances. Furthermore, alternatives make it possible to take advantage of opportunities.

By way of illustration, plan A may be the preferred plan because of the equipment and the time required for its execution. However, when the occasion arises for application of plan A, the conditions and setting to which the plan will be applied are so different from the premises used that plan A must be abandoned. In its place plan B, prepared originally in keeping with the new conditions, is substituted. A range, not just one course of action, is to be sought.

ADVANTAGES OF PLANNING

A listing of the advantages of planning expedite review and quick comprehension of the benefit of planning. Included are:

1. Makes for purposeful and orderly activities. All efforts are pointed toward desired results and an effective sequence of efforts is accomplished. Unproductive work is minimized. Usefulness of the achievement is stressed. As far as effort is concerned, a person running in circles can be working as hard as a one running down the street. The difference is in the usefulness of the achievements. Planning distinguishes between action and accomplishment.

2. Points out need for future change.　Planning helps to visualize future possibilities and to appraise new key future fields for possible participation. It enables the manager to avoid entropy or the tendency to let things "run down," to awaken to opportunities, to see things as they might be, not as they are.

3. Answers "what if" questions.　Such answers permit a planner to see through a complexity of variables that affect what action one decides to take. Typical questions are, What would happen to our employees if we automated production line No. 27? What would happen to our sales if we limited orders to $50 and over? What would happen to our budget if we called in the bonds and issued more preferred stock? Models can be built and computers used to process answers to such questions. Or intuition, judgment, and various contingency approaches or "studies of the situation" can be employed.

4. Provides a basis for control.　The twin of planning is controlling which is performed to make sure the planning is bringing about the results sought. Quite a number of new techniques combine the planning-controlling functions, as illustrated by budgeting. By means of planning, deadlines are determined for the starting and completing of each activity, and the setting of standards of performance is promoted. These serve as bases for controlling. A plan must establish such help for controlling.

5. Encourages achievement.　The act of putting thoughts down on paper and evolving a plan provides the planner with guidance and a drive to achieve. Spelling out desired results and how to achieve them are of themselves positive forces toward good management. Planning reduces random activity, needless overlapping efforts, and irrelevant actions.

6. Compels visualization of entirety.　This overall comprehension is valuable, for it enables the manager to see important relationships, gain a fuller understanding of each activity, and appreciate the basis upon which managerial actions are supported. Isolation and confusion are reduced. Through planning, a constructive identification with the problems and the potentialities of the enterprise as a whole is gained.

7. Increases and balances utilization of facilities.　Many managers point out that planning provides for a greater utilization of available facilities of an enterprise. For any given period of time the best use is made of what is available. Also, activities are balanced both in amount and in timing, thus ensuring needed support among them. The result is that the best possible use is made of available facilities.

8. Assists manager in gaining status. Proper planning helps a manager to provide confident and aggressive leadership. It enables a manager to have all essential affairs at hand rather than allow the affairs to dilute and negate his or her efforts. Thinking out things ahead of time provides long-term, stable guides to future activities.

DISADVANTAGES OF PLANNING

On the other hand, there are disadvantages or limitations to the use of planning. Again a listing will be used to show these disadvantages. We start with

1. Planning is limited by the accuracy of information and future facts. The usefulness of a plan is affected by both the current and the subsequent correctness of the premises used. No manager can predict completely and accurately the events of the future. If conditions under which the plan was formulated or must be implemented change significantly from those assumed by the planner, much of the value of the plan may be lost.

2. Planning costs too much. Some argue that the cost of planning work is in excess of its actual contribution. They believe that the money could better be spent in actually performing the physical work to be done. Planning expenditures can be high, but like all functions, planning must justify its existence; and the amount and extent of planning activities must be in keeping with the individual circumstances.

3. Planning has psychological barriers. A prevalent barrier is that people have more regard for the present than for the future. The present is more desirable and has certainty. The future means change and adjustments to new situations and conditions. Oddly and erroneously, some feel that if planning is soft-pedaled, the changes and the possible dangers of the future will in some way or other be minimized. Planning, they believe, tends to accelerate change and unrest.

4. Planning stifles initiative. Some feel that planning forces managers into a rigid mode of executing their work. It is contended these rigidities may tend to make the managerial work more difficult than it need be. Instead of helping, they actually hinder. There are elements of truth in these arguments, but as already implied, the most effective plans provide some degree of elasticity and interpretation in their application. Where every last detail is carefully planned and spelled out, the situation may be such that minute planning was deemed necessary, as for example in the case of performing a major surgical operation.

5. Planning delays actions. Emergencies and sudden uprisings of unusual situations demand on-the-spot decisions. Spending valuable time thinking over the situation and designing a plan cannot be followed. However in all events at least a modicum of planning is desirable for, as stated above, activity does not necessarily mean useful accomplishments. To start a course of action without giving some attention to what the desired results are appears nonsensical.

6. *Planning is overdone by planners.* Some critics state that those performing planning tend to overdo their contribution. This is evidenced by the preparation of elaborate reports and instructions beyond any practical need and the refusal to take risks mandatory for managerial work, attempting instead, through planning, to make risks minimal. Excessive time and money are spent on securing information and seemingly endless follow-ups of results are practiced.

7. *Planning has limited practical value.* Some contend planning is not only too theoretical, but other means are more practical. For example, they believe effective results are obtained by a muddling-through type of operation in which each situation is tackled when and if it appears pertinent to the immediate problem. In this way, opportunism can be utilized to full advantage.

ETHICS AND OBJECTIVES

A suitable definition of ethics is: *Ethics deals with personal conduct and moral duty and concerns human relations with respect to right and wrong.* Ethics concerns morals and philosophy. It deals with the behavior of individuals and the standards governing the interrelationships between individuals.

Violation of civil law tends to encourage the violation of moral law. Statutes which in effect encourage lying, cheating, and irresponsibility promote these vices as a way of life and encourage the pragmatic idea that anything an individual can get away with is right. The result is crime, corruption in public life, disrespect for authority, and disregard of properties. The true test of right is based on moral principles which are the product of social forces and human experiences over thousands of years.

Planning is influenced by the planner's ethics. What one believes "is right" and the correct action morally to take in a given circumstance shapes one's planning in important ways. Ethics is related to an individual. The ethical standards followed by the individual manager help determine the ethics of one's enterprise or of one's industry. A manager's code of conduct influences what degree of ethical behavior or unethical behavior is followed. But it is difficult to answer such questions as: When does business aggressiveness become bad ethics? What is the boundary between honorable self-interest and moral or legal dishonesty?

It is the belief of some that the character of an action can be evaluated by two major means: (1) the intention or subjective means and (2) the result or objective means. In some instances these two differ tremendously; in others, they do not. Suppose a manager with the good intention of giving a reward for a job well done presents a $500 bonus to a salesperson with the result that the salesperson decides to lay off several weeks to spend the bonus, thus causing inconvenience and loss of sales to the employer. Was this action by the manager ethically satisfactory in that it was generous and thoughtful, or was it wrong because it resulted in inconvenience and loss? Consider an opposite case in which an employment manager, wishing to get rid of an undesirable employee, wrote a letter of praise recommending this employee to a prospective employer. Subsequently, the employee is offered and accepts the new job and proves to be an entirely proficient, satisfactory, and valuable worker. Was the employment manager's action ethical because the results were beneficial, or was the action bad because the manager had purposely misstated facts as he knew them?

Also, ethical issues arise dealing with conflict of interest. This condition arises when a manager is simultaneously a member of several groups that have conflicting goals. Consider the case of a manager of one company having a financial interest in a second company that purchases from the first company. Should the manager demand the best for the employing company even though such demands reduce the profits of the second or supplying company? Or should one grant special favors to the supplying company? We can also include acceptance of special favors in the form of gifts and gratuities from the second company. It is "right" for the manager to do so? Is one obligated by acceptance of such favors, does one violate one's duties to one's employer by such actions, and to what extent is there a conflict of interest in such practices?

ETHICS—INTERNAL AND EXTERNAL

It is also helpful to discuss ethics in planning from the viewpoints of (1) internal ethics, or those within an enterprise, and (2) external ethics, or those with the enterprise and other enterprises, consumers, suppliers, and government agencies. With reference to the former, a manager must be honest with oneself, since one's greatest asset is one's character. And one should be honest and straight-forward with others, treating them in the same manner in which one wishes to be treated. Fairness in dealings with compeers and subordinates is mandatory; one should never discriminate by dispensing special favors as privileges, whether for remuneration or not. Information coming to one confidentially should neither be revealed nor used to the disadvantage of any of co-workers. One should ensure one's employees' right to privacy.

With reference to external ethics, the same suggestions stated above can be followed. Sincere efforts must be made, especially in planning, not to injure any outsider's rights, treat the person unjustly, or injure one's person or property. Corruption wherever discovered should be exposed. Determining what is right in external ethics poses some difficulties. To illustrate, consider the task of a businessperson proving superiority of one's product or service over that of a competitor. Upon what ethical basis can differences between competitive products be accurately measured, by what authority, and for what wanted purposes? Exaggerated claims, misleading comparisons, and tricky statements harshly asserted in print, radio, and television suggest possible violations of ethical conduct. Such practices create problems of good taste and raise the question of who benefits from such actions and why. Specifically, is a manager ethically justified in including such actions in one's planning and in promoting them?

Principle of ethics

Proper ethics in management requires a manager to be honest with self and with society, and to deal honorably with others just as one would like to be dealt with.

An important source of the ethical issue is the assumption by managers that as long as they behave in a way that is above reproach, they have discharged their moral obligation. This is erroneous. Every group must protect its good name and reputation with a measure of collective self-discipline. Ethical people doing nothing is the best way for moral decay to take over. And it is clear that in this day and age if managers make little effort to discipline themselves, the government will step in and exercise discipline over their behavior.

Assistance in improving the ethics of business is provided by the Better Business Bureaus, organized in 1914. They are nonprofit, independent corporations established and maintained by businesspersons to construct and promote programs of self-regulation in business transactions. There is no affiliation with any government agency. Located in nearly 100 cities throughout the entire United States, these bureaus provide assistance in writing needed codes to cope with local unethical trade practices, promoting honesty and dependability in advertising, providing control over certain types of peddling, the supplying of talks and information to schools on the subject of better business practices, sponsoring programs for consumer education on the operation of the competitive system, and the recording of all complaints and their disposition in a file which is convenient for reference regarding the record of a specific individual or company.

CREATIVITY AND PLANNING

Planning requires hundreds of applied ideas to be highly successful. The margin of success and in some instances survival itself depend upon the ability of the planner to evolve and use new ideas. Creativity deals with the generation of ideas, innovating with the application of ideas. From the managerial viewpoint, creativity alone is insufficient, the idea must be implemented too and this entails utilizing ideas in managerial plans.

WHO PERFORMS CREATING AND INNOVATING?

Every manager, as well as nonmanager, is born with creative potential. Certain managers do not have a monopoly on it. The challenge is to keep from inhibiting creativity. The capacity of most managers and nonmanagers to think up new ideas and to implement them can be doubled within a short period if they develop attitudes freeing their minds from the mental chains of pattern, conformity, and culture. The four main blocks of impediment include (1) lack of self-confidence, (2) fear of criticism and failure, (3) desire to conform, and (4) inability to concentrate. Overcome these hurdles and you release the ability to create and use ideas. We are all habit-prone. Certain time-tested methods of performing certain tasks become ritual.

It is also possible to encourage creativity of a person by counseling and coaching. In certain situations, these means are very effective. Generally speaking, however, group interactions produce more and better ideas because the members stimulate each other. Questions and suggestions focus each participant's attention on the process of creativity and make one aware that ideas exist, that they must be sought, and that many are not the result of genius, but of long, hard work.

Typically the creative person looks at things in divergent ways. One may feel some dissatisfaction with things as they are or believe strongly that present ways of doing things can be improved. Characteristically one (1) observes situations and problems that have previously escaped attention, (2) relates ideas and experience encountered from many different sources, (3) tends to have many alternatives on any given subject, (4) defies precedent and is not constrained by custom, (5) utilizes and draws readily from emotional, mental, and preconscious forces, and (6) maintains a high degree of flexibility in thoughts and actions.

TYPES OF THINKING

Most ideas start with thinking of which there are several major types. Some of these types are more productive than others. For purposes here, the following five will be considered: (1) creative, (2) causative, (3) inductive, (4) deductive, and (5) problem-solving. The first, or creative thinking, deals with deeply impressing a problem upon one's mind, clearly visualizing it, contemplating it, all toward the formulation of an idea or concept along new or different lines. Facts are used, but some of the facts are recognized as missing. In other words, creative thinking is performed with the understanding that only a partial knowledge of the situation is available and is utilized. Elimination of some and combination of other available facts help to clarify the idea that is new. Insight thus gained feeds the imagination with the sought new idea. It is imagination, not logic, that is the source of the new idea. Many competing hunches are evaluated and related in order to arrive at the best idea, but the thinking process is creative.

Causative thinking emphasizes the shaping of future events and achievements instead of waiting for destiny to decide them. The future reality is conceived and made the cause of each action event. The imagined future situation is viewed as a series of related events which will bring about the desired future situation. The imagined future effect becomes a causative factor in the series of events which are then planned and carried out. Hence, causative thinking is characterized by thinking in reverse, so to speak, in that results are derived by converting nonproductive present actions into related events leading to the desired future situation.

Inductive thinking is reasoning based on various particulars to a general principle or conclusion. It is reasoning from parts to a whole or from the individual to the universal. In the process, synthesis is used. The components are put together to form a whole.

Deductive thinking is the direct opposite of inductive thinking. From general conclusions to particular ideas, or from the whole to the part, typifies deductive thinking. For this type of thinking, the breaking down of the entirety into its components, or analysis, is employed. Deductive thinking provides explicit knowledge, not implicit or general knowledge. It is logical and is used extensively.

Problem-solving thinking as suggested by its name, is a judicial type of thinking. It is concerned with securing facts about a situation, ascertaining the problem, analyzing and evaluating the facts logically to determine meaningful relationships among them, and finally evolving the decision to the problem. It is greatly influenced by powers of judgment, past experience, and tradition.

THE CREATIVITY PROCESS

The generation of ideas normally follows a process which is made up of closely related, yet distinct steps. They are six in number. The first is:

1. Develop favorable attitude toward ideation.   For one to realize maximum creative potential, it is necessary to have a positive attitude toward freedom of ideas, regardless of any initial unfavorable reactions that one may receive. Many ideas will seem impractical at first, but the creative thinker must not permit this predisposition to influence one and give up in despair. Premature judgment, mental laziness, and cultural blocks can choke the seed of a new idea. These are self-explanatory with the exception of cultural blocks which include those elements in our cultural environment which are not conducive to ideation. They can include past experience, education, friends, and companies from which patterns of habit are developed. Normally, anything that violates the pattern of habit is either condemned or ignored. To illustrate, an architect showed a friend a picture of a proposed circular exhibition hall utilizing new materials and new building concepts. The friend exclaimed that it did not look like an exhibition hall. When asked why, he explained, "Because it does not have walls and vertical columns." The architect explained that it didn't need them. The friend replied that could be, but it should have walls and vertical columns to look right. The cultural pattern is set; this retards creative thinking.

2. Exhibit problem sensitivity. This is the ability to recognize that a problem exists or, what is the hurdle that keeps you from designing a better plan? The creative thinker determines first what she or he wants to accomplish—this is the focal point. A carefully worded statement of the objective sets the right stage for the creative efforts. Creativity can be effective when the reason or need for ideas is recognized. Merely looking for new ideas is a hopeless task. The idea must be tied in with a specific goal or planning effort.

Problem sensitivity also helps to acquire concentration which is an essential of the creative process. Efforts should be centered on relatively small areas; otherwise the creative thinker is spread too thin and is seriously retarding creativity. It is an excellent practice to devote some 20–25 minutes each day to complete concentration on a specific problem. This period should be free of interruptions.

3. Prepare for creativity by acquiring needed raw materials. Ideas are created from raw materials which include primarily knowledge, other ideas, and experiences. These materials are obtained from personal observations, talks with informed people, reading, radio and television, and travel. The search for facts should cover a broad field and deal with every facet of the problem. This broad fund of information forms the foundation upon which the mind can evolve ideas. In brief, ideas are not created out of a vacuum.

This step in the creative process is not easy. It requires much time, effort, self-discipline, and tenacity of purpose. Some material is difficult to obtain; much is incomplete; but it is well to remember that, if all the facts were known, the need for the creativity would be nil. In addition, the raw materials should be classified so that future reference and use of them are expedited.

4. Apply idea fluency.   Idea fluency means an ability to pile up a quantity of ideas about a given problem. The value of this is that the more ideas available, the greater the chance for disclosing a usable one.

In other words, idea volume is what is wanted. Also, a deadline for these ideas stimulates creativity. The human tendency is to procrastinate. Don't evaluate the ideas until later. Idea evaluation tends to stop the creating of new ideas; hence it is better to evaluate them after there is a quantity of ideas on which to work. We will come back to idea fluency after completing the list of the creative process.

This step of generating ideas should continue until a feeling of frustration, of complete exhaustion that any more ideas will be forthcoming.

Principle of creativity

Strive for a quantity of ideas within a given time and abstain from evaluating them during the idea-getting step of the creativity process.

5. Allow incubation or unconscious brain action to take place.   When frustration appears after laboring diligently over the development of a plan, the best thing to do is get away from it. Rest the conscious mind. However, the conscious mind is but a small part of the total mental power of a human being. There are many, many memory cells holding an infinite number of facts and associations, and this unconscious mind is now given a chance to help find a solution to the planning problem. This incubation period is commonly referred to as "sleeping on the problem." Actually there is little that one can contribute to this step directly. Rest, diversion, or thinking about other things are the alternatives to follow.

6. Permit illumination of new idea.   The beginning of this last step is determined by the individual circumstances. In some instances it may follow the previous step in a matter of minutes, hours, or perhaps days, or it may not (heaven forbid) come until years later. It appears that the thinker cannot force ideas to emerge, but being receptive, opportunistic, and alert helps the creative step to take place. The shutting out of distracting influences may be helpful. Many creative people feel that in the creative step some power outside themselves is trying to find expression through them.

A most difficult question to answer is: When does the idea or the creative material begin to flow? The illumination frequently takes place when least expected. The right idea may come while one is walking, looking out an airplane window, watching flames in an open fireplace, listening to music (without words), attending concerts, sitting in church, or sailing. Usually with little or no warning the creative person "starts clicking," and the ideas and creative suggestions begin appearing.

PRACTICAL SUGGESTIONS TO ATTAIN IDEA FLUENCY

Personal mental habits control idea fluency and they can be improved or developed in nearly every individual. A number of specific devices and aids are available. The more effective are the following ten:

1. *Make notes.* The use of notebooks, or "idea traps" as they are called, is a common practice for jotting down ideas as they occur. Small 3 × 5 cards can also be used. An idea is the most fleeting thing in the world; it comes and goes within a fraction of a second. Don't expect to bring back an idea and examine it carefully at your discretion. What is perfectly clear today may be a complete blank tomorrow. The best time to capture an idea is when it occurs. Hence, it is well to write down ideas or fragments of ideas as they appear. Tests have established that for information of average interest, either read or heard, about 25 percent is forgotten within the first 24 hours and 85 percent within a week. If the idea appears to have no particular use at the time, it can be filed in an "idea file" for future reference.

2. *Pick a time to be creative.* This time will vary with individuals; some will find early morning most productive, and others produce best late at night. The point is to find out which period is most productive and reserve it for the specific task of creative thinking. There is also usually a special location which seems superior for ideating. If so, effort should be made to utilize both the best time and location.

3. *Employ curiosity and questioning ability.* Ask questions such as: Why is this done this way? Is this really necessary? Why won't this work? This means is one of "challenging the obvious." A checklist made up of operational questions that challenge the obvious aspects of a problem is especially helpful.

4. *Utilize relationship of ideas.* Most ideas are related to other ideas. The power of association is especially consequential in the creating of ideas. The manager who aspires to create can start with known facts and build, step by step, upon them until the resemblance and relation of things suggest a new concept which is the signal for a new idea. Centuries ago this relationship of ideas was observed by Aristotle, who suggested to "hunt for the next in the series, starting our train of thought from what is now present or from something else, and from something similar or contrary or contiguous to it."

Among the best ideas are those which represent improvements over other ideas. The history of the development of a current idea might well reveal that idea as the last of a chain or series which has been thought about for a long time. Most inventions are in this category. They evolve slowly over a period and are improved step by step.

5. *Change existent form.* The clue for an idea might be found by changing the existent form. There are a number of ways in which this can be accomplished, including (a) *rearrange*—will it work inside out, backwards, upside down. A golfer's ball rolled into a paper bag on the fairway. To remove the ball from the bag would cost her a penalty; so she rearranged her thinking, deciding to remove the bag from the ball by burning the bag (b) *substitute*—what happens if a different process is used, a different sequence, women rather than men employees, a new material in place of the traditional metal, glue for nails; (c) *add*—duplicate the training program in the branch plants; make the product bigger; add more units to a package; (d) *subtract*—make fewer units to the package; reduce the car height; offer a smaller desk; leave something out, and (e) *switch*—turn the present arrangement around by having the employee offer suggestions instead of the managers; have the employees rate their supervisor; let the retailer call on customers at their homes. Figure 11–1 offers suggestions for design changes in materials.

FIGURE 11–1: Checklist for improving design changes in materials

Can you	
Change	size, shape, weight?
Reduce	weight, scrap, loose parts?
Eliminate	waste, frills, backtracking?
Improve	quality, delivery, packaging?
Substitute	new, stronger, or cheaper material?
Simplify	by using pallets or letting supplier do it?
Standardize	parts, routes, size, weight, finish?
Utilize	scrap, rejected parts?

6. *Obtain help from attribute listing.* Here the characteristics or parts of a concept or object are listed. For example, for desk, the list would include top, drawer, pedestal, wood, steel, file space, size, and so forth. Now association between these attributes is made, such as top and file space, pedestal and size, in the hope that a new idea helpful in desk use or manufacture can be created. A modification of this technique can also be followed. This consists of forcing or bringing together two objects or ideas never previously associated in order to evolve an idea from this new relationship. Commonly a list of objects or ideas that may have possible relationships is compiled, then one item is related to every other item on the list to find the idea.

7. Use brainstorming or free-association technique. This approach emphasizes the use of thinking that is ungoverned, visionary, erratic, or wild. It utilizes any thoughts which happen to come to mind on a problem or a plan. The mind is purposely permitted to "free wheel" and come up with all possible ideas, some of which will seem impractical and downright silly. In brainstorming, a group of about fifteen is given a subject and each member is encouraged to contribute ideas. Emphasis is on quantity of ideas. It is usually desirable to have the group with a wide diversity of backgrounds and to include some persons with little experience in the subject area. The intent of brainstorming is to supply leads and possible ideas for satisfactory solution. Evaluation of the ideas is done after the brainstorming session. However, this technique can be used in various ways; for example, a large group can be divided into smaller brainstorming groups, each one of which thinks up a quantity of ideas, then evaluates them and offers their No. 1 selection as the best idea from that group. Or reverse brain storming can be used in which all the possible shortcomings of a product or service are evolved. A manager can also practice solo brainstorming with oneself. Actually many managers do this to meet at least certain requirements of their work.

8. Read between lines. A lucrative source of practical ideas is reading between the lines of letters and reports. Various tips on what will help improve the product, achieve goals, contribute to better understanding, and build public relations can be acquired from this source. To illustrate, Figure 11–2 shows the report of a department

FIGURE 11–2: Report of department head to the merchandising manager of a large retail store

> In my opinion, the biggest problem in the paint department is teaching the clerks how to sell paint properly. The specific service for which the paint will be used is frequently not considered. A customer is allowed to buy cheap paint for outside use when we know that it isn't going to last. Only a few of our clerks know that the surface must be properly prepared so that it is clean, smooth, and free from all loose old paint.
> And we don't tell the customers how to take care of a painted surface because we do not know what to tell them. I doubt that any of our clerks know what the basic ingredients of paint are or how to explain to the customer why one quality costs more or less than another.

head to the merchandising manager of a large retail store. After reading this report the manager might note from the first paragraph, "Our paint clerks need education and training," and from the second paragraph, "How does one give proper care to painted surfaces." "What is paint?" "Explain different paint grades." Interpreting reports in terms of sales opportunities is simple, but it requires open-mindedness and the use of ideas.

9. *Reverse positions.* An excellent source of ideas is simply put yourself in the other person's place. Think creatively of what you would do if you had the various goals, problems, and wherewithal to accomplish the end results that the other person possesses. There is an old adage that it is well to know your competitor and never discount his or her intelligence.

10. *Make use of accidental events.* The clue to the sought idea might be an accidental event. An unusual happening or a sudden surprise has been known to start the creative process toward productive directions. Such events appear to give a new twist or angle to a person's thinking and afford the outlet to the sought solution.

THE INNOVATIVE PROCESS

As in the case of creativity, the adoption of a formal approach is recommended for satisfactory progress in applying the ideas. No matter how good the idea, it does not implement itself. Ideas have to be put out in the open and used if they are going to be helpful. Hoarding ideas seldom brings about any needed improvement. One does not run out of ideas by using them. Ideas multiply if you let them grow and put them to work. It can well be that a certain idea cannot be used immediately, but the chances are strong especially in planning work that something can be done with it.

Innovation is frequently a slow and tedious process. A single basic idea, for example, used in a plan may necessitate exhaustive study, thorough investigation, and complete examination. Furthermore, to apply a basic new idea usually requires many additional little ideas in order to achieve ultimate success. People of various degrees of capacities, interests, and attributes must be directed, assisted, and encouraged in many ways before the new idea is adopted. To assist in chieving acceptance of an idea, these points will be helpful:

1. Have the new idea worked out in detail. Make sure it is complete.
2. List the potential benefits to be received from the use of the new idea in the proposed plan and indicate who will receive what benefits. Help in terms of improved service, lower cost, or reduction in waste are usually most acceptable.
3. Make the new idea easy to understand. Avoid unusual and trick words in communicating it. Keep the plan simple even though it utilizes a new idea.
4. Talk about the new idea with several people to disclose possible weaknesses that need correction; then adjust the idea and the plan, if necessary.

5. Present the reworked plan at an appropriate time—when the need for it is great or when it will be given adequate consideration.

Meetings similar to those suggested above for encouraging the creativity of ideas are effective and should be followed, but in addition, other means should be considered. If the idea offers a possible solution to an acute problem or planning difficulty, its chances for implementation are excellent. But usually the idea must be brought through existing constraints. This suggests the practice of requiring each manager, say twice a year, to submit a written report to one's immediate superior. This report should detail (1) the operational effectiveness of one's unit's operation and (2) recommend changes that will lead to better realization of the unit's objectives. In essence this opens the door for idea implementation by targeting possible areas of application for new ideas.

However, a better practice is to route the improvement reports either through the respective supervisor, or to a committee whose expertise is in the same area as the type of recommendations being made. This committee serves as a clearing house for what ideas probably can most readily be used. Inappropriate ideas are weeded out, potential benefits are estimated, and technical feasibility is judged. In addition, opinions of the managers and of the supervisors are given the committee.

Next, those ideas passing the review tests are tried out on an experimental or limited basis under the guidance of the committee or a designated manager. The point here is to ascertain the soundness of the idea—whether better results are obtained, the idea's practicality, skills required, and cost. Also measured is the effect of varibles external to the new idea. In a larger enterprise, personnel proficient in experiments, data collection, and analysis can be used.

If tests show successful results, the next step is to implement the idea. This work entails acquiring raw materials and equipment; hiring, transferring, and training personnel; and establishing work patterns along with the necessary controls.

Last, is evaluating the results. Here the effort is to determine the gain by using the idea. An estimate of the idea's payoff is made available to the person who originated it. This serves as an incentive to continue creative thinking. Pay increases, promotions, and other recognitions will take place as a consequence of the favorable results from ideas that prove effective in the working environment.

QUESTIONS

1. Relate your understanding of the suggestion, "Plan for a range of courses of action."

2. What is the meaning and importance of each of the following: (*a*) phasing in planning, (*b*) causative thinking, (*c*) the planning pattern of adaptivizing.

3. As a practicing manager, discuss the importance you would attach to "what is right" in your work.

4. Discuss the importance and effect of time upon planning.

5. Give four advantages and four disadvantages of managerial planning. Discuss one of each in detail.

6. Discuss ways by which creativity is encouraged among both management and nonmangement members.

7. If innovating ideas is highly beneficial, how do you account for so many ideas being opposed and never put to use?

8. What is ethics? In what way or ways is it important in management?

9. Relate an experience wherein you encountered rejection of your idea. As you now see it, what should you have done to have your idea accepted?

10. Enumerate six aids to develop your idea fluency. Discuss one of these in detail.

11. For each of the following three situations, point out as many possible consequences as you can: (*a*) In making his rounds in a chemical plant, an elderly night watchman discovers a fire. Rushing to turn in an alarm, he observes that the connecting wire of the telephone has been severed. (*b*) While remodeling an apartment in Chicago, a carpenter finds a stamped but unmailed letter on the shelf of an old closet. On his way home that night, he mails the letter, (*c*) Alexander Parave, a research chemist, claims to have found a new chemical that when taken daily in the form of a pill (costing 13 cents a piece) will enable a person to get all the sleep needed by sleeping only two hours a day.

12. In your opinion, what problems in your community are in need of creativity being applied to them? Discuss.

13. Give as many reasons as you can for each of the following statements which are assumed to be true: (*a*) Women of today go to beauty shops 15 percent more often than did their grandmothers. (*b*) There are proportionately more houses painted white in San Francisco than in San Antonio. (*c*) The women of Minnesota have more perfect vision than the women in any other state of the United States.

14. Suppose as a result of circumstances you find yourself with no employment and stranded in a city of 25,000 population with a suitcase of clothes and $250 in cash. You are not to see or write any friend or relative. You are to achieve "success" by the end of four years. Explain what you would do and why.

CASE 11–1. KUEHN RESEARCH SERVICE

Barry Kuehn is proud of his company's broadcast media buying service developed for advertising agencies and advertisers who buy time for television and/or radio spot advertisements. Broadcast media, says Mr. Kuehn, is a highly perishable commodity. A spot at 7:30

tonight ceases to exist at 7:31. The spot planner wants maximum coverage for potential buyers of the planner's product or service. This is not necessarily the largest viewing or listening audience, but the maximum number conditioned by wanting the product or service and having the buying power, per advertising dollar expended.

The Kuehn Research Service (KRS) takes into account that each market has its own distinctive variations both in media supply and demand and also from one month to another. In addition, there is a cyclical characteristic with respect to supply and demand curves that makes it feasible to predict discernible repetitive patterns. Information for products and services by major classifications have been programmed for computer use by KRS. By this means, it is possible to predict *real* (economic) costs, for every continental U.S. market, and for any target audience. Further, the service will provide forecasts of actual going rates or costs for any start date up to three years into the future.

Mr. Kuehn explains that a client brings to his company a proposal to buy let us say a 70-market spot TV advertisement. Kuehn Research Service will budget it, provide detail costs (1) by 1,000 viewers with demand for the product or service, (2) by daytime exposure, (3) by nighttime exposure, (4) by TV market location, and (5) buying power per capita. In brief, KRS gives the advertiser the exposure needed to achieve the lowest cost effective spot sellers acceptable at any given time.

Questions

1. Explain as best you can with the limited information how KRS assists the media planner of TV or radio spot advertising.

2. Kuehn Research Service claims, "You don't pay for spots you don't need." Is this really true? Justify your answer.

3. As you see it, could Kuehn Research Service tell whether plan A consisting of TV spots on Tuesdays and Fridays for a given month would be more effective than spots on Mondays, Tuesdays, Thursdays, and Fridays for one half of that given month? Explain. For spots at 7:30 every morning rather than spots at 5:30 P.M.? Explain.

CASE 11–2. DESHLER CHEMICAL COMPANY

Nine years ago, after considerable negotiating, the city of Conroyville, Tennessee, succeeded in getting a new manufacturing company, the Deshler Chemical Company, to locate near Conroyville. The site is some two miles northwest of the city limits. The top managers of Deshler Chemical Company believed the city's packaged offer was attractive. In return for a guarantee of year-round employment for at least 50 persons, the city (1) sold the land to the company for $18,000, which, it was mutually agreed, was an attractive price, (2) constructed a plant to Deshler's specifications with the company repaying the building cost in equal monthly payments over a 12-year period with annual interest being charged at 6.5 percent on the unpaid balance, and (3) agreed to collect no property taxes for a 10-year period.

The city has grown westward during the last several years, and recent plans for civic developments include a general area which involves the Deshler Chemical Company's manufacturing operations. The city wants to develop a new park featuring boating and picnic facilities centering around Hickory Creek, but waste from the chemical plant contaminates the water. Hickory Creek adjoins the plant and was a big reason for locating the plant where it is. The creek empties into Beard River about three miles west of Conroyville's center of town. Beard River flows westward after winding through the western part of Conroyville.

The city government requests the company to install special chemical equipment to neutralize the waste materials now emptied by it into Hickory Creek. Company engineers estimate the cost of waste treatment at $750,000 for equipment and $50,000 for annual operating costs. The company contends it cannot afford such expenditures, the president stating that insistence for such an outlay by the company will result in the company abandoning the Conroyville plant and locating elsewhere.

The president further points out that the company has fulfilled every requirement of the initial agreement reached when the decision was made to locate in Conroyville. For example, the company has met all required payments, and since opening the plant has never employed fewer than 57 persons. The current employment is 63; this accounts for wage payments of approximately $550,000 per year, an amount representing nearly 20 percent of the total payrolls of the greater city area. The president also points out that the building is specially designed and built for this company's particular type of chemical manufacturing. It is not an all-purpose building and can be utilized economically only by a firm such as this. Last year's publicly available data on the company showed total sales of $3,817,632.91 and profits after taxes of $268.956.17.

The city takes the view that the initial packaged deal was offered to give the company assistance in getting established. With nominal land costs, favorably financed building costs, and availability of admittedly high productivity labor of the area, the company should be competitive or recognize that it must prepare itself to be so. The company is a part of the community and therefore should assume its obligations as such. Pouring waste into a public stream is harmful and simply cannot continue. Any long-range view by the company's managers must concur with the correctness of the city's position. Also, in the opinion of the city officials, the threat of the company abandoning its Conroyville plant is pure bluff. A suitable building at today's prices will cost more than twice what the one in Conroyville did, efficient labor will be lost, and moving itself is costly.

Questions

1. Point out the relationship of this problem to modern management planning.
2. What suggestions can you offer to solve the impasse between the company and the city?
3. Do you feel the package deal given by the city to the company was attractive? Discuss.
4. What action do you recommend the company take? Why?

CASE 11–3. NEWSON ADVERTISING AGENCY

Lewis Moore: As I stated, we have an opening for an account executive and you favorably impress me. There are a couple more questions I'd like to ask before I take you over to our Mr. Fairfax, who I already told you has the final approval in our hiring of an account executive.

Peter Wescott: Go ahead, shoot.

Moore: In the personal data you gave me, you give your age as 62. Is that your correct age, 62?

Wescott: Yes, sir. I was 62 last December.

Moore: You are certain—your age is 62.

Wescott: Yes, sir.

Moore: Well, Mr. Wescott, from a reliable source, your present employer, I am informed that you are 64 years old. Before you say anything, let me tell you that we will make adequate investigation. Our insurance company, for example, must have correct ages of employees because it affects our pension plan premiums. Now, how old *are* you?

Wescott: I am 62. When I was hired for my present job I told them I was two years older than I really was at that time because I found out it would help me get the job. Their records show me to be 64, but I am 62.

Moore: I see. I want also to ask you why you want to leave your present employer. Mysterom and Betz is an excellent agency.

Wescott: Yes, it has a good reputation. I am going to be transferred to another account with whom I don't want to work. We're losing the Belmont account effective in about . . . a . . . 'er . . . seven weeks. It will be announced in about a month.

Moore: Why is Belmont leaving you?

Wescott: I don't know for sure. They have a new sales manager, Bill

Boyce, who insists on changes in the present advertising campaigns they are running.

Moore: Bill Boyce. He's new at Belmont, isn't he?

Wescott: Yes, they got him from Portlands in Cincinnati. Portlands, you know, is quite an aggressive competitor of Belmont. From what I hear, he is difficult to work with and is trying to make a name for himself.

Moore: I see. Mr. Wescott, I believe Mr. Fairfax is waiting for us. I'll take you over to his office.

Wescott: Thank you very much, Mr. Moore.

Belmont is a major account that Newson Advertising Agency would like to get. Mr. Moore reported the possibility of the Belmont account to his superiors. It was news to them and they intend to aggressively seek this business. The following day Mr. Moore wrote a letter to Mr. Wescott telling him Newson Advertising Agency was very interested in him and Mr. Fairfax was favorably impressed. In the near future, Moore indicated he would get in touch with Wescott and advise if he were to join the Newson Agency. Following this, Mr. Moore informed his superiors that he intends to reject applicant Wescott on the grounds that he cannot be trusted with confidential information. None of the superiors disagree with Moore's decision and stated reason.

Questions

1. What ethical constraints are present in this case?
2. In this case are any persons unethical? Substantiate your answer. Elaborate.
3. Evaluate the personnel selection efforts of Mr. Moore.
4. What action, if any, do you feel the Newson Advertising Agency should take? Justify your recommendations.

Chapter 12

Major types of management plans

It is always with the best intentions that the worst work is done.

Oscar Wilde

A number of different types of management plans exist. Some are used over and over again, others are used but once and discarded. Some apply to physical features such as spatial plans. Some pertain to a single activity, a department, or to the entirety of an enterprise. The list is almost endless.

For the purpose of this chapter, certain types of plans have been selected. We discussed policy, a major type of plan, in Chapter 9, so it is excluded here, other than as a reference for other types of plans. Six types will now be discussed, including (1) procedure, (2) method, (3) standard, (4) budget, (5) program, and (6) techno-factor.

To clarify the meaning of these plans, Figures 12–1 and 12–2 are shown. In the former, the large circle represents the sphere of planning. The large rectangle within the circle designates a program. It encompasses the objective, is inclusive, and takes into account a relatively large undertaking. Standards, budgets, and techno-factors are also included within the circle of planning and, in the figure, provide respectively satisfactory levels and a desired balance of activities for the program to attain. Actually standards, budgets, and techno-factors can and are utilized in connection with plans other than programs. Policies are represented by the four vertical lines. As previously pointed out, they serve as guides for specific areas. The arrowheads on the ends of these vertical lines designate the boundaries or prescribed limits within which all activities are to take place. The horizontal line labeled "procedure" marks the specific fixed course of action to reach the objective. The procedure is made up of a series of tasks shown by marks X_1, X_2, X_3, etc., representing chronologically the various tasks to

FIGURE 12–1:   The meaning and relationship of selected categories of plans

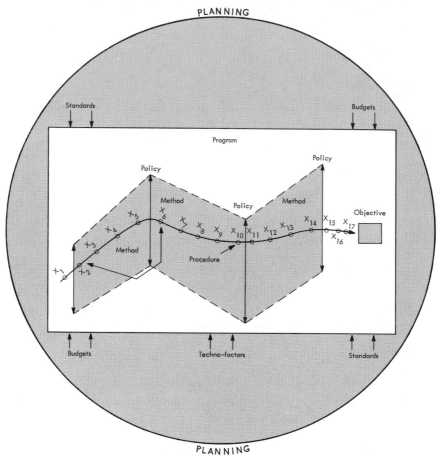

PLANNING

PLANNING

be performed. The procedure stays within the area limits established by the policies but cuts across these areas in establishing the path to the objective. The manner of performing each specific task of the procedure, such as X_1, X_2, or X_3, represents the respective methods.

Figure 12–2 shows tabulated key information about these types of plans. To illustrate, for a procedure the distinguishing attribute is that it defines a chronological series of tasks, its chief characteristic is that it is tailor-made to achieve specific work, its use requires compliance with slight interpretations, and once established it tends to remain. It should be noted that the identification of different plans as given here are not always employed. However, they are in common usage and serve to help clarify what plans result from typical planning efforts in the average company.

FIGURE 12–2:   Comparable information concerning selected categories of plans

Kind of plan	Distinguishing attribute	Chief characteristics	Required for use	Common erroneous situation
Policy	Sets up the over-all boundaries for activities	Broad, general, comprehensive	Interpretation, judgment	Improper identi-fication for every mana-gerial decision
Procedure	Defines chrono-logical series of tasks	Tailor-made to achieve spe-cific work	Compliance with slight interpretation required	Once established tends to remain
Method	Prescribes course of action to ac-complish a task	Specific and detailed in how a task is to be done	Compliance	Ignored or insufficient planning directed to it
Standard	Gives level of expected achievement	Tailor-made for specific work	Compliance	Not brought up to date in line with current operations
Budget	For a given period, con-solidates many operational expectancies into a concise format	Tailor-made for specific work	Compliance with slight interpretation required	Difficult to modify as situations require
Program	Integrates di-verse but related activi-ties into a unity	Comprehensive, covers rela-tively large scope of facili-ties and activities	Interpretation, judgment, and managerial competency	Used to identify any type of plan
Techno-factor . . .	Assists in visualizing probable effect of selected factor	Comprehensive for selected factor	Interpretation	Believed to be rigid plan

PROCEDURE

A procedure is specific and tailor-made to achieve certain work. Procedures exist in every part of an enterprise; they are a highly im-portant category of plans. They have received considerable attention in the fields of office management, production, and sales engineering. Formally defined: *A procedure is a series of related tasks that make up the chronological sequence and the established way of performing the work to be accomplished.* The chronological sequence of tasks is a distinguishing mark of any procedure.

A procedure includes how each of its tasks will take place, when it will take place, and by whom it is to be performed. The best way from the viewpoint of time, effort, and money expenditures is usually represented by the procedure. However, this is not always the case. In some instances, the influence of certain environmental factors, such as competition, taxes, or the equipment available, may alter the procedure somewhat from the theoretically most efficient way of handling the work.

Normally time limits are placed on each step of a procedure to insure that each task as well as the end result will be accomplished when desired. Procedures are usually thought of as applying to repetitive work, and in the typical enterprise, much work is of this type. Once the procedure for handling such work is established, the procedure can be used over and over again, thus sparing the manager the problems of deciding the course of action to be followed for much of the work.

A purchasing procedure is shown graphically by Figure 12–3. In this illustration two main categories of purchases are recognized (1) stock orders and (2) special orders. For each group, the procedure starts with three steps—recognition of need for the material, description of the material needed, and transmission of purchasing requisition for the material. Stock orders are handled on stock replacement purchases by means of blanket purchase orders. In contrast, special orders are handled on individually placed purchase orders. All requisitions are sent to the purchasing department for negotiation of supplier. For stock orders, the approved sources and their immediate past performances are checked, and if found OK, the order is written and placed. In the case of special orders, bids are requested, proposals received and analyzed, sources selected, the purchase order written and placed. As indicated in Figure 12–3, seven copies of the purchase order are made. Copies 1 and 2 are sent to supplier who returns copy 2 which goes to the Expediting Department. Copies 3, 4, and 5 go to the Expediting Department, copy 6 to Receiving Department, and copy 7 to Requisitioner which lets him know the material has been ordered. Copies 3 and 4 are used to expedite the order with the supplier. When order is received, the Receiving Department sends its copy to Expediting which matches copies 5 and 6, sending them to the Auditing Department, which checks the records, writes the invoice, and sends copy 5 to Purchasing for its closed order file and copy 6 to Accounting authorizing payment to vendor. In addition, as shown in the illustration, the records of Auditing are reviewed by the Purchasing Manager to reveal the status of purchasing efforts.

FIGURE 12–3: A purchasing procedure

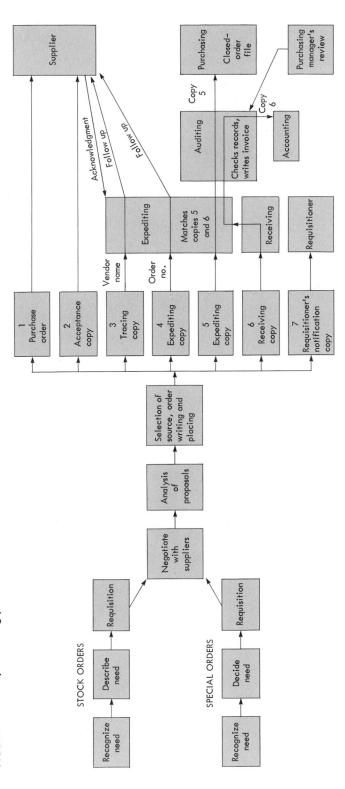

DESIRABLE CHARACTERISTICS OF PROCEDURES

Procedures should be based on adequate facts with proper consideration given to the objectives, physical facilities, the personnel, and the type of work. A procedure that is best for a given enterprise may not be best for another simply because significant differences among the factors affecting the procedure may be present. The end result governs what steps are taken and is of prime consideration. The steps should be complementary and lead cumulatively to the accomplishment of the desired goal. Each step should fulfill a definite need, and be in proper relationship to the remaining steps of the procedure.

A procedure should possess stability in that it provides a steadfastness of the established course, with changes made only when fundamental modifications in the objective or in the factors affecting the operation of the procedure occur. On the other hand, flexibility of procedures is desirable in order to cope with a crisis or emergency, special demands, or adjustment to a temporary condition. However, emergencies may become too commonplace, and the benefits from the use of stable procedures are lost. The problem is essentially one of maintaining a proper balance between the stability and the flexibility of the procedure.

Also there is a tendency for procedures to remain once they are started in an enterprise. New procedures are commonly added to the existent ones instead of reworking and modifying existing procedures, or eliminating those no longer needed as a result of change and in view of current requirements. The results are that some procedures that are useless continue and much costly duplication of efforts is permitted to exist. Again, the solution is to review periodically all procedures within an enterprise and to ascertain if they are needed under present operating conditions. If not, they should either be eliminated or modified as the facts in the case indicate.

METHOD

Fundamental to every action is a method which can be defined as *a prescribed manner for performing a given task with adequate consideration to the objective, facilities available, and total expenditures of time, money, and effort.* A method deals with a task comprising one step of a procedure and specifies how this one step is to be performed. It normally is confined within one department and frequently to the efforts of one employee while engaged in the specified work. A method is more limited in scope than a procedure. Referring again to Figure 12–3, the manner of writing seven copies, for example, constitutes a method. In it would be prescribed such things as the arrangement of the work area and the work, the operation of the machine, the necessary details to observe, and the use of certain printed paper forms.

METHODS IMPROVEMENT

The determination of the method to be employed in any given case depends mainly upon the manager's experience, knowledge, and creativeness. Historically, Frank B. Gilbreth and Lillian M. Gilbreth, American management pioneers, stressed the importance of methods in management. The Gilbreths developed what is today known as "motion study," which is conducted to find a better way of performing work. Analysis of methods shows that the greatest output is achieved when the task is carefully defined, performed in a definite manner, and within a definite period of time. Methods have been a focal point for improvement and for quite logical reasons. In the first place, of all planning efforts, methods are probably the easiest to comprehend. Second, methods are tangible to a greater degree than other plans, and third, they are more intimately associated with the employee who is normally most interested in her or his own work and improvements in it.

WORK SIMPLIFICATION—METHODS

Efforts to improve the planned method of work performance are commonly termed work simplification. As its name implies, work simplification deals with the simplifying of work. *Work simplification is applying common sense for finding the most economical use of human efforts, materials, machines, time, and space so that easier and better ways of doing work can be employed.*

In the interest of clarity and brevity, work simplification can be said to consist of five major steps, which are:

1. Select the work to which work simplification will be applied. This includes bottleneck tasks or those which represent a relatively expensive or time-consuming task.

2. Analyze the work selected, carefully and in detail. Each component is identified and carefully examined. Various charts are commonly used to depict pertinent facts about the present work method.

3. Utilize the questioning attitude for each component. Used are the basic questions of why is this component performed, what is performed, where, when, by whom, and how. Answers to these questions suggest possible means for improvement.

4. Seek improvements. These are gained by (*a*) eliminating, (*b*) combining, (*c*) rearranging, or (*d*) simplifying the present components. Also, can mechanical means replace present manual means? Can the current machine method be improved? What is the best way to reduce the operator's physical effort and fatigue?

5. *Put improved course of action into effect.* Implementing the improved method is the final'and a very important step.

Observe that work simplification determines what components are essential and results in work performance that includes only those essential components carried out in the most economical manner. That is, work simplification results in performing only the necessary components in an efficient manner. It is economic by nature. Efficiency and low cost are emphasized. Psychological and social considerations, while included, are not the prime issues. It should be pointed out that *work simplification is not speedup.* Speedup is the hurrying of the work performance and includes the essential and nonessential operations, it implies no analytical study to determine how time, space, or human effort can be better utilized.

The key to successful work simplification is participation by those performing the work being simplified. Give the employee help and encouragement in applying the five work simplification steps listed above. Let each employee improve the job being performed as that person sees fit to improve it. Work simplification is as much an attitude of mind as it is a science. Fundamental to its success is the belief that *there is always a better way.* Amazing results have been credited to the use of work simplification. Savings in effort and time frequently reach 40–50 percent, and in certain instances they are as high as 80–85 percent of the initial work performance requirements.

Principle of work simplification

Waste in performing work can be eliminated by diligent application of work simplification, which stresses making every component of the work productive by the application of common sense aided primarily by participation with know-how of and by employees.

WORK SIMPLIFICATION—PROCEDURES

Work simplification is not confined to methods; it applies to other plans, for example, to procedures. Which should be simplified first—the method or the procedure? Answer: improve the plan of the broader scope first, i.e., the procedures and then the methods. To reverse this order might mean that method plans are improved only to find later that these methods are unnecessary after improving the procedure plans.

An important principle to follow in improving procedures is to arrange and perform the series of tasks in a shingling, or overlapping, pattern. Figure 12–4 shows an arrangement A for assembling product P by performing four consecutive tasks—Nos. 1, 2, 3, and 4. None of the products completed by task No. 1 are subjected to task No. 2 until all No. 1's are completed, and so on down through task No. 4. Total

FIGURE 12–4: Overlapping consecutive tasks permit shorter overall completion time

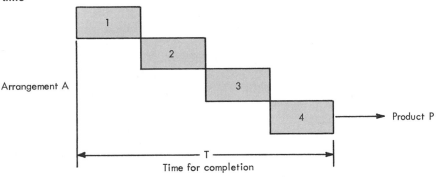

Arrangement A

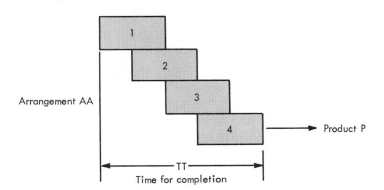

Arrangement AA

time for completion is T. In contrast, with an overlapping pattern for the consecutive tasks, arrangement AA, task No. 2 is started on completed products of task No. 1 before all No. 1's are completed and so forth through task No. 4. With this arrangement the total time for completion is TT. Ideally a successive task should start at a time which will permit its completion once it has started; that is, it need not be temporarily stopped due to the rate of output of the preceding task.

Principle of overlap

The minimum overall time required to perform a group of successive tasks on one product is obtained by performing the tasks arranged with a maximum overlapping.

STANDARD

A standard is a type of plan. It is *a unit of measurement established to serve as a criterion or level of reference*. For example, a standard cost of $5.00 for one item of A is a measurement of expenditure and represents the amount of cost to which the cost of other items of A can be referred or of other items comparable to A. Standards are essential in planning schedules, determining requirements, and achieving proper balance and relationship among the basic resources of an enterprise. To illustrate, it is difficult to plan the work of eight employees unless the standard of what should reasonably be expected of one employee is known. In addition, a standard forms the basis of controlling. What is accomplished, in terms of the standard is a fundamental step in controlling.[1]

Standards assist measurement in that they record the number of times a unit is used or taken in a given application. Further, they provide an expression of a level of performance which is usually termed normal. Standards apply to all resources that a manager utilizes. Uniformity of products is also an important purpose of standards. This makes not only for manufacturing efficiency, but also expedites inspection and desirable practices in product design. In addition, standards are helpful in describing and identifying products, processes, and activities, the pertinent characteristics being set forth in terms, tests, and measurements as set forth by standards. Especially is this important in production and sales. Finally, standards assist in settling disputes because they serve as base or reference levels and thus help to clarify the issue and suggest investigative courses to pursue.

THE ESTABLISHMENT OF STANDARDS

A standard is usually established by using one of the following sources: (1) past experience, (2) appraisal, or (3) scientific method. In establishing standards by past experience, a manager uses past records, memory, and knowledge acquired from one's intimate work with the particular factor or with one the manager believes is similar to it.

Standards set by appraisal are arrived at through guesses or estimates of what the standard probably should be. This means is resorted to when available time is short, the work is temporary, or the cost of determining more accurate standards is prohibitive.

The scientific method, widely used for the setting of standards, is to be preferred because it utilizes factual data in a carefully prescribed and proved manner.[2] Common means for determining time standards include stop-watch studies whereby the work is divided into elements, each of which are timed and adjusted for selected factors such

---

[1] This is discussed in Chapter 2, p. 35. A complete treatment of controlling is contained in Chapter 22.

[2] The scientific method is discussed in Chapter 2.

as effort and consistency of the employee. Time allowances are added for personal needs of the employee. Also synthetic studies arrived at by detailed study and interpolation of data from a number of stop-watch studies are quite popular. In addition, the use of Methods Time Measurement (MTM) and Work Factor (Wofac) approaches are used. As mentioned above, standards of materials and machines expedite adequate product inspection, statistical quality control, and production classifications and capacities. Some common media to express standards are shown in Figure 12–5.

FIGURE 12–5: Common media for expressing standards

1. *Written description* giving in detail the complete specifications covering all pertinent requirements stated precisely and accurately.
2. *Verbal statement* including a representation by spoken words of the impor-tant factors making up the standard.
3. *Legal regulations,* usually enforced by a recognized authority, stating a range or area within which the standard must conform.
4. *Typical sample* providing and exact reprsentation of the particular item or unit; in some cases a scaled model is used.
5. *Customary procedure,* either written or verbal, setting forth the generally accepted or habitual practice followed.

Nearly all companies carry on some work involving the setting of standards and develop standards strictly for their own use. Many standards, in fact, are of this sort. However, in the interests of communication, trade, and general welfare, it is desirable to have uniform standards, at least for many common items and activities. To this end, technical societies, trade associations, and government agencies have served as a clearinghouse or a group approach to a common standard problem. In this work, the American Standards Association (ASA) has been very active. The ASA is a federation of technical societies, trade associations, and several agencies of the federal government.

FLEXIBILITY OF STANDARDS

Standards tend to stabilize plans; yet they contain some element of flexibility necessary to adjust them to the needs of current managerial efforts and changing conditions. This does not mean that standards should be changed to meet current whims or altered within relatively short periods of time. Quite the contrary, stability must be maintained, but this does not mean that a rigid, never-changing practice must be followed. The needed flexibility is assumed by making provisions for finding out how satisfactory the established standards are and reviewing periodically technological and economic changes which might affect the standard. Normally some deviation from the standard is permissible in view of practical considerations. This deviation is referred to as tolerance.

Within a given enterprise, standards are interdependent. That is, for a company the standard for a material is definitely related to the standard for its inspection; and in the same manner, the design standards are related to the manufacturing standards and, in turn, to the sales standards. This means that, within an enterprise, a change in one standard frequently requires a compatible change in another standard or standards. A manager should review all standards, within meaningful limits, when any one standard is changed. It should also be noted that usually the standard employed represents what is believed best for the intended purpose at a given time. It does not necessarily represent a level of perfection.

BUDGET

A budget is a plan for income or outgo, or both, of money, personnel, purchased items, sales items, or any other entity about which the manager believes the determining of the future course of action will assist in the managerial efforts. Budgets are comprehensive in that they include an entire enterprise or they can be drawn up for any segment of it. At the same time they establish goals for each activity, so they are relatively detailed. Budgets always apply to a certain time period, and again, the data making up the budget are normally segregated by small time periods, such as hours or days in a monthly budget or weeks and months in a yearly budget.

The initial creating of a budget for a specific unit may pose difficulties. However, the continuing of a budget is relatively simple, since past budgets serve as excellent guides. But the budget, like all plans, is forward looking; nothing can be done about the past; and what you are doing in budgeting is planning for things that are to happen. The best budget makers profit from experience. It usually requires much time to develop skill in budget preparation for a specific area of operations.

Budgets are plans, but their use for controlling is so great that many think of them as control media. The term, budgeting, designates controlling based on a budget. The budget comes first; just as in any planning-controlling endeavor, the planning precedes the controlling. Comparison of actual to planned expenditures by items represents the common format of budgetary control. In addition, a budget can be used to authorize expenditures in that a department head can spend the amount budgeted for each item without asking permission. In this sense, budgetary controlling is being practiced. Budgets are so closely, and in most instances so completely, identified with controlling that further discussion of them has been included in Part VI of this book.[3]

PROGRAM

A program is a plan frequently encompassing a relatively large undertaking, although not all of them can be so classified. The term itself is used in many different ways, and this unfortunately leads to misunderstanding. *A program can be defined as a comprehensive plan that includes future use of different resources in an integrated pattern and establishes a sequence of required actions and time schedules for each in order to achieve stated objectives.* The makeup of a program can include objectives, policies, procedures, methods, standards, and budgets, but it does not necessarily have to include all these categories of plans. Programs outline the actions to be taken, by whom, when, and where. The assumptions, commitments, and areas to be affected are also set forth. Most programs are not continuing phenomena.

Consider the work of a telephone company to provide plant expansion, service modernization, and operations improvement. These objectives necessitate effective utilization of different resources, such as buildings, carrier systems, dial switchboards, cable, trucks, and sundry tools. To perform this work on a time basis, communication designs must be created, checked, and rechecked. Materials must be acquired from the proper sources and delivered to the proper places when needed. Personnel must be trained, assigned, and dispersed. All the components must be kept in balance and scheduled to take place in accordance with a master timetable. This requires managerial efficiency, and the first step is to draw all these future actions into a comprehensive plan which we can designate as a program.

The increasing practice of considering large segments of an enterprise for management analysis instead of isolated components has stressed the use of programs. A production program, for example, can include the designation of materials, the processes to be followed, the machines to be used, the skills to be utilized, the production schedules to be met, and the warehouses to which shipments are to be made. This entire gamut of materials acquisition to completed shipments as a single entity represents a program in modern management.

TECHNO-FACTOR

Utilizing a technical approach to a selected factor such as time, cost, or material flow, techno-factor represents a relatively new type of plan. A number of such plans are already being used and it seems quite

---

[3] Budgetary controlling is discussed in Chapter 25.

likely that more will be seen in the future. They provide assistance to the manager that no other type of plan supplies. The first to be discussed is PERT (Program Evaluation Review Technique).

Introduced in 1958, PERT was originated to achieve a reduction in the time span projected for the Polaris Ballistic Missile Project of the U.S. Navy. PERT includes not only planning but also controlling. Justification for including it under planning in this book is that it starts with the formulating, with respect to time, of the interrelated activities making up the overall program. From this planning effort, changes or adjustments as required can be made in order to ensure that the plan is carried out. This latter effort is the controlling aspect of PERT.

The basic analytical device of PERT is a network consisting of a pictorial description of the necessary work. This network is made up of activities and events that comprise a project. Figure 12–6 illustrates a

FIGURE 12–6: A PERT network

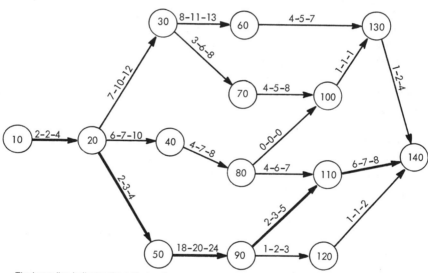

The heavy line indicates the critical path.

PERT network. An activity is shown by an arrow; an event, by a circle. The former represents work required to accomplish an event. Estimates of time to complete each activity are indicated on the network. For example, the activity from event 30 to event 60 is estimated at 8–11–13, which means, respectively, the optimistic, most likely, and the pessimistic times for completion of this activity. Only activities consume time, events cannot.

To accomplish the project objective represented by event 140 in Figure 12–6 it is necessary to start with event 10 and accomplish a series of events related in a pattern as indicated by the network. All networks start with one event and end with one event. An event is accomplished when all activities leading to it are completed, and no activity can begin until all preceding activities have been accomplished.

A network path is a series of related events and activities from the beginning to the end event of the network. We are interested in the network path that requires the *longest* time because this path time-controls the project; that is, any delay or lengthening of the time along this network path will delay completion of the entire project. This path is called the critical path. There are also semicritical paths and slack paths requiring successively shorter time periods for completion than the critical path. By means of a trade-off of time to one of these paths from the critical path, the elapsed time of the latter may be reduced and thus shorten the time required to complete the total project. However, in the calculation of the data and in determining trade-offs, the basic elements of production control are present and must be understood. The sequence of events must not be disturbed and the required work must be finished at each required event before the actual work proceeds to the next event.[4]

There are different formats for calculating pertinent data of a network. Commonly, an average value is determined for the estimated times for each activity. This is termed the expected time. Subsequently, the earliest expected time to achieve the activity from the entire network viewpoint is calculated. This value is the sum of the expected times along the longest path from the start of the network to the event in question. Finally, the latest allowable time is determined. This is the time by which an event must be accomplished to meet the scheduled completion date for the entire project. It is the value found by subtracting from the scheduled length of the project the length of the longest path backward from the finish of the project to the event in question.

When these calculations are made for the network shown in Figure 12–6, the critical path is found to be that indicated by the heavy line, that is, 10–20–50–90–110–140. All the other activities take less time so there is nothing to be gained by shifting or trading off among the activities. Either manual or computer calculating methods can be followed. The former is practical up to about 100 events. In some of the large governmental projects over 20,000 events have been involved and performing the needed calculations would not have been practical without operations research and the computer.

PERT is advantageous for nonrepetitive, nonroutine projects. It is being used in research and development projects, the conducting of new-product developments, the preparation of building bids and proposals, periodic maintenance shutdowns, pilot plant runs, and the construction of buildings, bridges, and power stations. PERT helps (1) to

---

[4] See Chapter 24 for further discussion of how controlling efforts are applied.

focus attention on potential problems in projects, (2) to reasonably predict the attainment of project objectives, (3) to evaluate progress toward this attainment, and (4) to indicate feasible adjustments in related activities to improve overall project accomplishment.

Another techno-factor plan is PERT–COST which is similar to PERT but with the data referring to cost rather than time. Cost expenditure is normally contingent upon more variable factors than time expenditure, and hence, cost results are more difficult to plan for. In PERT–COST, the planning and controlling efforts are directed toward expenditures of money and provide an effective management tool for the modern manager. PERT–COST seems destined to increase in importance, although its predecessor, PERT, is currently much better known and more widely used.

RAMP (Review Analysis of Multiple Projects) is another example of a techno-factor plan. It refers to multiple related projects rather than to a single project as does PERT. With respect to time constraint, it helps guide the activities of several projects simultaneously. To illustrate, a contractor building several buildings can use RAMP for the several buildings and know the critical areas and activities to watch carefully from the viewpoint of all the buildings considered as a unit, not each building considered separately.

Rhochrematics is still another techno-factor worthy of mention. It deals with the management of material flow and includes the concept of integrating the management of all material flow from its original source through production facilities to final consumers. It is very helpful in automation studies. The traditional concept of considering autonomous, but related, units in accomplishing material flow is abandoned. Rhochrematics includes an efficient system of interactions among information, personnel, money, and materials. Its proponents claim better customer service at lower costs, better integration of the production process, and better use of working capital. The development of rhochrematics depends upon improved accounting data and mathematical techniques for computer use. It can be considered a specialized application of the systems concept of management discussed in Chapter 2.

QUESTIONS

1. Contrast the distinguishing attributes of a method, a program, and a techno-factor.
2. Figure 12–3 shows a purchasing procedure. What might be some policies to go with this procedure? Discuss.
3. Enumerate and discuss briefly the five major steps of work simplification.
4. What is the meaning of each of the following: (*a*) critical path of PERT, (*b*) synthetic standard, (*c*) work simplification, and (*d*) rhochrematics?

5. Is there any significant effect upon policy, procedure, method, or standard when the approach of results management conditions the planning efforts? Elaborate on your answer.

6. Explain Figure 12–4 in your own words.

7. Discuss the subject of "flexibility of standards in management."

8. Comment on this statement: "The only way to lower the time required to accomplish a specific amount of work is to perform it faster. Other suggested ways are pure phonies." Discuss.

9. As a manager, what importance do you attach to the statement, "procedures have a tendency to remain once they are started in an enterprise"?

10. In your opinion, should budgets be considered a plan, a medium of control, or what? Justify your answer.

11. Carefully distinguish between the two concepts in each of the following pairs: (*a*) a budget and a procedure, (*b*) a procedure and a method, (*c*) a practice and a policy, and (*d*) a techno-factor and a principle.

12. What is a program and why does a manager use it? Use an example to illustrate your answer.

13. "Method is the most important type of plan that a manager uses. Method is fundamental to all work accomplishment. Other plans expedite the effective use of methods." Do you agree with this statement? Substantiate your answer.

14. From your reading or experience, relate the content and use of a program which has or is being used. How might this program be improved? Justify your answer.

CASE 12–1. WITCO COMPANY

Operating in a highly competitive market, Witco Company managers have to achieve high efficiency to survive. For one of their products, ZD-7, consideration is now being focused on automating the assembly line. After several conferences with representatives of Acme Automation Company, it appears definite that an automated assembly line is entirely feasible and will provide higher quality, and a more accurate product than what is now being assembled manually. The proposed line would require 18 employees to operate it and would increase production by 40 percent over the present level. The equipment is offered at a price of $150,000 installed with ten months' delivery time required.

Currently the company operates two assembly lines, two shifts of eight hours per day, five days a week. Output is 20 units an hour per line which requires 24 employees. The average wage rate for the assembly line is $4.25 an hour for either the first or second shift. It is estimated that the automated line will require about 80 percent of the space the present lines require. The sequential steps are performed in an order best suited for automation.

The president of Witco Company favors the automation but feels he must have significant information to justify such a decision in order to gain his Board of Directors approval. He is somewhat disappointed that the work will not be completely automated—some assemblers will have to be retrained to bring and take away material and to hand feed material input into the automated line. He also feels the sooner the automation the better because present production cost must be reduced for the company to survive. In his opinion, cutting direct production labor is the best way to do this. The vice president of production disagrees, pointing out that skilled and experienced production help will be lost by the company and severance pay equal to one year's pay will have to be made. The personnel manager confirms the severance pay requirement, pointing out that the company is obligated by contract to make such payments. She also observes that training costs will be incurred in the amount, she estimates, of $1,000 per new assembler and perhaps $25,000 to cover training maintenance personnel. The president believes that training maintenance personnel is unnecessary. He claims the representative of the automated equipment told him that—based on his experience with installations in other companies—it is quite likely that no maintenance work will be required. The vice president of production counters that the company's present maintenance personnel should be trained to repair the automated equipment and keep it in proper running order.

Questions

1. What are some policies, budgets, and standards the company requires in order to draw up and decide on the master plan to be followed regarding the automated line? Discuss fully.
2. In your opinion, should the decision reached by the company be economically, socially, or politically based? Why?
3. What is your recommended action for the Witco Company? Give complete justification for your answer.

CASE 12–2. QUEENS FOUNDRY, INC.

Located in northern Indiana, Queens Foundry, Inc. produces cast-iron products primarily by two processes: (1) green sand, and (2) shell mold. The former lends itself to short-run jobs and to orders for a small quantity of castings. It is the older of the two processes. The shell mold is the more advanced and represents about 80 percent of the corporation's sales. About 65 percent of the corporation's total production is purchased by Advance, an electric motor manufacturer.

It is now the middle of January and Jo Ann Kirkdall, the major owner and president of the corporation, is reviewing fourth quarter reports for last year's operations. She notes that for the quarter they had about $1 million in sales and showed a reasonable profit. However, she also discovers that the corporation had almost $180,000 of unfinished castings in inventory. Immediately she asked Jacob Mintz, sales and shipping manager, and Conrad Bradford, production manager, to come to her office. The following discussion took place.

Kirkdall: Gentlemen, as you probably know, we had a fairly good quarter ending last December 31. I want to congratulate both of you for the fine job you have done in making this possible. However, I have noted we have nearly $180,000 in unifinished castings. This is fantastic. How in the world did this happen? Is it actually that high?

Bradford: Yes, it is high. We have unfinished castings all over the place. The storage areas both outside and in are filled to capacity.

Kirkdall: But why?

Mintz: Advance cut their delivery releases from 35,000 to 20,000 units a week. I talked with Murdock, the buyer there, in person at some length last October when the cutback began. I was told the smaller released quantity would be temporary—for one, maybe two months. This plus the fact that we need at least 12 tons of salable iron to be produced daily in order to keep from losing money, I decided to let our inventory build up for a short while.

Kirkdall: I think it is built up enough, especially when we don't have any releases for these castings.

Bradford: We can always go back to more green sand and less shell mold, but it costs more. Maybe Advance will pay more since the volume is smaller.

Mintz: No, I can tell you, they would not stand for that.

Kirkdall: Why not? It sounds fair to me.

Mintz: That could well be, but Advance doesn't see it that way. Besides, there is a specific selling price stated in the contract.

Kirkdall: Tell me, Jake, how do you determine what inventory is proper for us?

Mintz: It is mainly what the customer has ordered in the past— qualified, of course, by what the customer's projected needs will be in the future. At least that's been the way it's handled in the case of Advance.

Kirkdall: The determination of our inventory is mainly in the hands of the customer, is that right?

Mintz: Well, you might say that, but it really isn't that way. But the customer does influence it—and greatly, I'd say.

Questions

1. What is the problem faced by the corporation?
2. What major factors would you say permitted and contributed to this problem? Discuss.
3. What types of plans do you feel the corporation should follow regarding its inventory? Justify your answer.

PART IV
Organizing

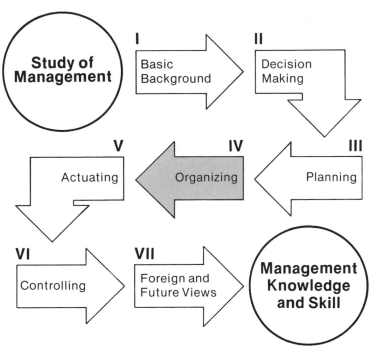

Chapter makeup for Part IV:

Our attention is now directed to organizing, the second fundamental function of management in the modified management process. This area of management is being researched and given much study especially from the behavioral viewpoint. The discussion in this part starts with what has been termed traditional organization. New developments and changes are then introduced showing how they are modifying the traditional concepts as well as putting into use entirely new organizational concepts. Specifically included are the meaning and use of organization, important changes taking place, authority and its current role in organization, and the influence of social and work environments. All these are giving new meaning as well as contributing more and more to the impetus of the dynamics of organization.

Without doubt, organizing is an exciting and challenging area of management study. The four chapters of this section give a concise picture of up-to-date organizational thinking:

Chapter 13

Organization structure and design

*The body travels more easily than the mind, and until we have limbered
up our imagination we continue to think as though we had stayed home.
We have not really budged a step until we take up residence in
someone else's point of view.*

John Erskine

Since the beginning of the human race, some persons have directed
efforts of others in a team effort toward various specific goals. The total
work to be done, as set forth by the plans, required the efforts of more
than one person. Hence, many hands and minds were brought together and coordinated so that not only the collective actions were effective, but also that the contribution of each individual was valuable
and hopefully satisfying and in keeping with the individual's respective knowledge and skill.

To discuss organizing in an orderly manner, we will start with some
traditional concepts, thus building a base and an awareness for organization. Following this, significant changes that have and are altering
our thinking about organization during the past decade or so will be
discussed.

MEANING OF ORGANIZING

Organizing brings together the basic resources in an orderly manner
and arranges people in an acceptable pattern so that they can perform
activities to accomplish stated goals. Organizing unites people in interrelated tasks. It is intended to help in getting people to work together effectively toward the accomplishment of specific goals.

The word "organizing" stems from the word "organism," which is
an entity with parts so integrated that their relation to each other is
governed by their relation to the whole. When a group of two or more
persons work together toward a common goal, the relationship and

interaction among them gives rise to problems such as who decides what issues, who does what work, and what action should be taken when certain conditions exist. Hence, persons working together effectively, each doing to the maximum what each can best do, and the persons achieving the total best possible results are basic in the concept of organizing. A satisfactory definition of organizing includes: *Organizing is the establishing of effective behavioral relationships among persons so that they may work together efficiently and gain personal satisfaction in doing selected tasks under given environmental conditions for the purpose of achieving some goal or objective.*

IMPORTANCE OF ORGANIZING

Organizing results in an organization structure which can be thought of as a framework which supplies the nucleus around which human beings can favorably unite their efforts. In other words, an important part of the task of organizing is to harmonize a group of different personalities, to fuse various interests, and to utilize abilities—all toward a given direction. And the hope is for *synergism* which is the simultaneous action of separate or individual units which together produce a total effect greater than the sum of the individual components. Organizing is a case where, contrary to basic mathematics, the sum is greater than the sum of its individual parts. We are interested more in the potency of the mixture than in the strength of its ingredients.

Organizing has always been important to us. Human collaboration—the dependency of people on each other—and protection against threats and antisocial behavior—have encouraged intense organization activity by all people over the centuries. Governments, armies, businesses, and institutions of all kinds have studied organizing with the intent to improve it or to utilize it better in their particular managerial endeavors. Furthermore, of all the basic management functions, organizing has been the most intensively studied, and contributions to this area are abundant.

Organizing can have a highly favorable effect upon managerial actuating and controlling. For example, actuating efforts are conditioned greatly by the quality of organizational efforts performed. Placing a person in the wrong job for that person, having the person report to a group leader whom the person doesn't get along with, or being with employees the person doesn't care to be associated with, can result in making motivational efforts extremely difficult.

FORMAL ORGANIZATION

A formal organization is one formed with official sanction and has four basic components: (1) the work which is divisionalized, (2) persons who are assigned to and perform this divisionalized work, (3) the environment under which the work is done, and (4) the interrelationships among the persons within a work group and also that among one work group with another work group.

Let us look closer at these four basic components. From the sought goals, the necessary work activities are derived. The work is divided into "packages of work" for these reasons: (1) the work is too big for performance by one person and must be divided to be performed by several people, (2) the distribution of work requires that the work be divided, and (3) the desire to achieve the advantages of work specialization necessitates that the assigned tasks require only the specialized skills of the personnel. However, as indicated in Chapter 4, work specialization cannot be applied to every situation without limit, for if it is extended too far, the employee's interest, work satisfaction, and "will to do" are impaired. Note, however, that in organizing, work combination is also included. This entails the regrouping of the divided activities into units believed more suited for effective performance from the viewpoint of the facilities and personnel available. Component No. 2 refers to persons who will perform the work, their experience, competency, behavior, and personal satisfaction, all of which must be taken into account in determining who should perform what specific work. Component No. 3, the environment under which the work is done, includes such things as the general climate of the work area, helpfulness of superiors, influence of competitive forces, activities of labor unions, location of the work performance, materials and machines, and government regulations and actions. The fourth and last component dealing with the interrelationships among employees is extremely important. These interrelationships set the stage for actuating efforts and give meaning to authority, which is discussed fully in Chapter 14.

The four basic components of organizing are included in the following steps of formal organizing:

1. Know the objectives of the organizing.
2. Break down the required work into component activities.
3. Group the activities into practical units based on similarity, importance, or who will do the work.
4. Determine the duties and provide the physical means for each activity or group of activities.
5. Assign qualified or potentially trainable personnel.
6. Inform each member what accomplishments are expected and what formal interrelationships exist.

FUNCTIONS AS ORGANIZATION NUCLEUS

Observe that in the above discussion, we started with the work and its division. This is the recommended procedure. To reverse this approach, i.e., start with persons to form organization units can in some instances prove highly productive, yet such units usually prove difficult to manage and extremely arduous to replace managers for them.

Principle of functions

Functions are the main entities around which a manager builds an effective organization structure.

COMMON BASIC ORGANIZATION UNITS

The overall pattern of many organization structures is built around three fundamental activities performed: producing, selling, and financing. The terminology may differ, but essentially these are the activities carried out. They are necessary for the operation and survival of the enterprise. In business enterprises these three activities are clearly visible, but in other types of undertakings one or more of the activities may be obscure. To illustrate, for a manufacturer of automobiles, the basic organizational units are production, sales, and finance; but for an airlines company, the use of operations (production), traffic (sales), and finance is common; and for an insurance company, the following is frequently found: underwriting and actuarian (production), general agencies (sales), and claims and investments (finance).

Why these three fundamental activities? Because most companies are concerned with the producing of a product or service for use by others. Since it is produced for use by others, it must be distributed or marketed; that is, people must be found who want the product or service and are willing to accept it at mutually agreeable terms to the seller (enterprise) and the buyer. Also to produce and to distribute the product or service necessitate the raising and the maintaining of sufficient capital; that is, the financing activities must be performed by some members of the enterprise.

ADDITIONAL ORGANIZATION UNITS

The scope of the three fundamental organization units and the complexity of the enterprise give rise to numerous types of additional organization units. These types will result mainly from such things as the nature and amount of the work to be done, the degree of specialization practiced, and the people and the work places available for the work.

To illustrate, under the fundamental unit of sales the scope of the work may be so broad that it is believed advantageous to divide the work into advertising, sales promoting, and selling. Hence, the manager in charge of sales splits off the advertising and sales promoting activities and for each places a subordinate in charge. A sales manager is appointed to manage the selling work in the field. These three additional units will appear in the organization structure at the level immediately below that of the fundamental organizational unit of sales. In a similar manner, assume the manager in charge of production established a unit of engineering and research, of factory work, and also of purchasing. These concepts are illustrated graphically by the chart shown in Figure 13–1.

FIGURE 13–1

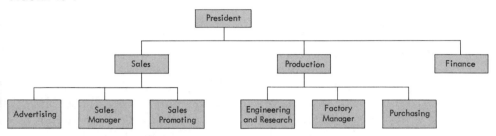

Now assume that the products and services of the enterprise continue to grow and conditions become such that further additional units are deemed necessary for efficient operation. Accordingly, from the advertising unit is spun off the two subordinate units of (1) television and radio and (2) magazines and newspapers, both of which are placed in the organization level below that in which advertising is located. This is illustrated by Figure 13–2. In addition, other units are established, as indicated by the figure. They include two sales units—one

FIGURE 13–2:   Showing the vertical growth of an enterprise from that illustrated in Figure 13–1

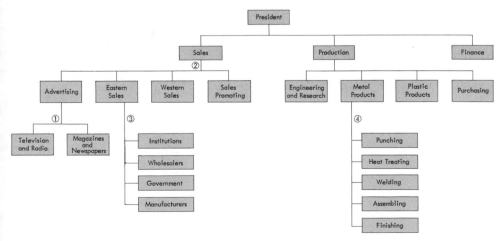

for the eastern and one for the western territory. Under the eastern sales unit are four units added to handle sales, respectively, to (1) institutions, including hotels, hospitals, and schools; (2) wholesalers; (3) government; and (4) manufacturers. Likewise under production, two units have been created. One is designated to include metal products, the other to encompass products made of plastics. Under the former, five units composed of punching, heat treating, welding, assembling, and finishing have been added as subordinate units. It can be readily seen that as the enterprise continues to expand, more units will probably be required.

ORGANIZATION STRUCTURE AND COORDINATION

At this point of our discussion it is well to inject the thought that in the divisionalization of work as well as in the regrouping of divided activities for organizing purposes, the resultant activities making up the structure should always be viewed as a totality or cohesive whole, never as separate functional units. To do otherwise destroys the organization as such, gives emphasis to the fundamental parts at the expense of the entire organization, and permits organizational islands to emerge, a condition bringing about much inefficiency. Figure 13–3

FIGURE 13–3

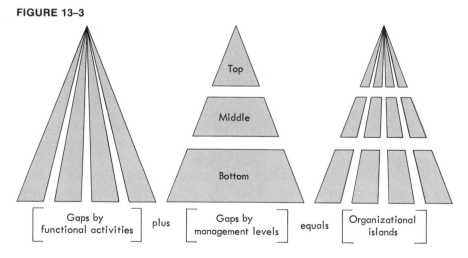

illustrates these separate functional activities plus gaps in the management levels giving rise to organizational islands. Thus the structure is not a unified whole, but is composed of separate organization islands. Each functional unit tends to consider its goals as primary, those of the total organization as secondary. Decision makers at a certain level make decisions that effect not only their function, but other functions as well and most of these other functions are for activities that concern relationships, primarily lateral and interfunctional. The result is the needs of other functions are not satisfied and the entire organization suffers.

What can be done to correct this condition? First, recognize that the gaps and islands do exist and that the functions are interdependent and subordinate to the entire organization. Second, implement a program to achieve understanding of this basic fact and enlist active support for the function goals to be totally integrated and supportive of the overall organization goals. Interfunctional committees, general management development programs, job rotation, and special task forces are helpful for this purpose. Third, avoid having a homogeneous group of specialists—a relatively self-contained work unit is superior. Contrary to popular belief, specialization works best when a manager has different types of work in his or her jurisdiction. Or expressed differently, design the work flow so that the least critical coordinations occur *between* groups and the most critical *within* a group. Fourth, try to factor new functions or new specializations into existing functions and specializations. Each time a key activity or management member is added, coordination has to be redeveloped.

MEANS OF DEPARTMENTATION

Departmentation results from the divisionalization of work, the desire to obtain organization units of manageable size, and to utilize managerial ability. An organization structure and design are shaped significantly by the departmentation followed. The chief means of departmentation include by (1) function, (2) product, (3) territory, (4) customer, (5) process, (6) task force, and (7) matrix. An organizer is free to use any means of departmentation in constructing an organization structure. In fact, in any given structure several means are typically used.

1. Departmentation by function. This common means is usually followed for the top and for the bottom organization levels. As implied by its name, the departmentation is by function or activity and it results in units, each one of which deals with a separate function or a group of similar activities. Referring again to Figure 13–1, departmentation by function has been followed for the top levels, i.e., sales, production, and finance, and also for the next level as indicated by advertising, sales manager, sales promotion, engineering and research, factory manager, and purchasing.

2. Departmentation by product. This arrangement is quite common for it is readily understood, stresses the utilization of specialized knowledge, and encourages a sensible degree of specialization. Examples include the departmentation of a department store which is segregated by products; loans of a commercial bank wherein commercial, personal, and industrial are common organizational units; and the organization of certain governmental executive departments, such as the Department of Interior. In Figure 13–2, departmentation by product is illustrated by the left portion marked with a "1" in which under advertising, the two units (1) television and radio, and (2) magazines and newspapers, are established.

3. *Departmentation by territory.* This is followed where nearness to local conditions appears to offer advantages, such as low cost of operation and opportunities to capitalize upon attractive local conditions as they arise. Territorial departmentation is especially popular for sales where the division according to some geographical market segregation appears feasible. It also provides a good arrangement for training and developing in that the executive can demonstrate ability in a certain territory and thus merit promotion to a more important area. In Figure 13–2 establishing the sales unit for eastern sales and one for western sales illustrates departmentation by territory, located by a "2" on the figure.

4. *Departmentation by customer.* When the major emphasis is upon being better able to serve buyers of the enterprise's products or services, a departmentation by customer is suggested. The teenage shop in the department store is illustrative, as is also a large bank's unit for loans to customers. A common breakdown is loans to retailers and wholesalers and loans to manufacturers. Under this latter unit are breakdowns such as (1) loans to manufacturers of primary metal, glass, and machinery; (2) loans to manufacturers of chemicals, petroleum products, paper, and transportation equipment; (3) loans to textile, apparel, and furniture manufacturers; and (4) loans to food processors and miscellaneous manufacturers. Departmentation by customer can usually be justified when a product or service of wide appeal is offered through numerous marketing channels and outlets. However, this organizational arrangement has a tendency to remain rigid, thus posing adjustment problems during widely fluctuating periods of enterprise activity. With reference again to Figure 13–2 the four organization units under eastern sales, marked by a "3" on the figure, depict departmentation by customer.

5. *Departmentation by process.* This means is logical and is used when the machines or equipment used require special skill for operating, or are of a large capacity which eliminates organizational dividing, or have technical facilities which strongly suggest a concentrated location. Economic and technologic considerations are the foremost reasons for adoption of process departmentation. It is most commonly found in production and frequently at the operative levels. Note the five units under the production unit for metal products in Figure 13–2, marked by a "4."

Using a process as a guide, there are three basic patterns available:

(1) serial, (2) parallel, and (3) unit assembly. The pattern followed will determine, in part, the organizational units adopted. In few instances will any of these patterns be used in its pure form. More commonly, part of the work will be processed under one pattern, part under another, and so forth.

Under the serial pattern, work moves through a single channel or assembly line and progresses step by step to completion as it passes the various work stations. This arrangement permits an employee to be highly specialized by individual work process and usually requires a brief breaking-in time for attainment of satisfactory output. However, the "cycle time," or total elapsed time from the beginning to the ending of a unit of work, may be small, and there is also the possibility of reduced employee work interest under the serial arrangement.

The parallel arrangement designates concurrent handling and provides for a number of different work steps to be performed within an organizational unit or by one employee. Actually the work divisions can be made on any of several bases, as long as the same work steps, or nearly so, remain in each segment. For example, operation Nos. 1, 2, 3, and 4 may be done by operator A on brass couplings while the same operation Nos. 1, 2, 3, and 4 may be done by operator B. Under the parallel arrangement, cycle time is reduced, movement of the work in process is minimized, and employee work interest is promoted. But training time for the employee may be increased since several work steps must be mastered.

Simultaneous handling is another way of expressing the unit-assembly arrangement. Here different employees perform different work steps upon a given amount of work at the same time. To illustrate, the work to be done is divided among employees A, B, and C. Simultaneously, employee A performs one particular operation on a batch of work, B operates on his batch, and likewise C on her batch of work. At appropriate times the different batches of work are shifted among the employees so that completion of the total work is accomplished. Under the unit-assembly pattern process, specialization is followed, yet the cycle time is minimized. Training is quite likely not to be excessive. The work, however, must be divided and routed to the various employees.

6. *Departmentation by task force.* This arrangement includes the assigning of a team or task force to a definite project or block of work which extends from the beginning to the completing of a wanted and definite type and quantity of work. A task force is usually relatively small, perhaps not over a dozen members. It exists for the life of the project and is then disbanded. It has a leader, is self-contained, and includes all the necessary knowledge and skill for performing the work. It is a preferred means whenever a well-defined project must be dealt with, or the task is bigger than anything the organization is accustomed to. Sometimes called project organization or project management, it is in keeping with the newer decision-making theories which are inclusive in their scope of operations, it encourages objective-mindedness, it gives the members somewhat of a free hand to accomplish the objective, and it emphasizes each member's developing and utilizing initiative and creativity in work efforts. Figure 13–4 illustrates departmentation by task force.

FIGURE 13–4:   Departmentation by task force

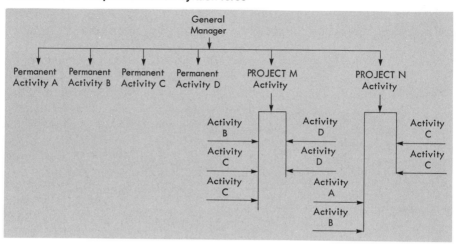

This has gained favor for many research projects outstanding of which are those of the missile or weapons system and outer space projects. It is widely used in public accounting firms, advertising agencies, management consultant organizations, and has proven effective for special projects concerning the factory or office.

Task-force departmentation does have shortcomings, however, such as some members feeling frustrated, having a sense of insecurity, and complaining of unstable organizations. These are brought about by the dismantling of the project organization at the completion of its mission and assigning the members to other project organizations. The determination of promotions and the building of identifiable careers also give rise to knotty problems.

7. Departmentation by matrix.   This is one of the important newer concepts of organization featuring not only departmentation on a highly technical basis, but also on a management basis as well. The supervision is dual, being technical from the technical chief and administrative from the administrative chief. This concept using a matrix form is shown by Figure 13–5. For example, in this figure five groups, A, B, C, D, and E represent five different technical skills. Each techni-

FIGURE 13–5:   Matrix departmentation concept

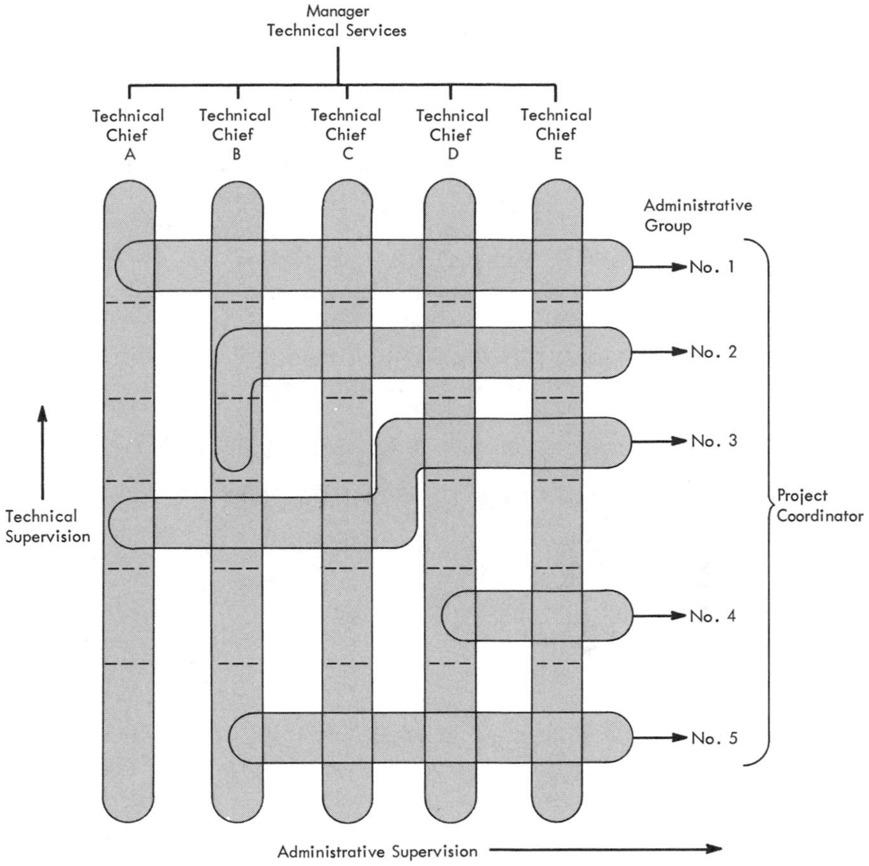

cal unit has a chief who reports to the manager of technical services. Simultaneously and cutting across these technical services are administrative groups made up of the technicians from the different technical groups. Administrative group No. 1, for example, consists of one technician from each of the five technical groups while administrative group No. 2 had none from technical group A, two from group B, and one each from C, D, and E.

The matrix departmentation, known also as grid or lattice work organization patterns, emerged as an answer to the growing complexity and size of enterprises which required an organization structure more flexible and technically oriented. By means of multiple reporting systems and interweaving communication lines for transmitting decisions made, a more balanced form of organization is achieved and one which tends to reconcile a company's breadth with its depth. If the task requires broad, problem-solving know-how, that can be supplied; on the other hand, if specialized advice in depth is needed, that can be offered. Among the well-known companies successfully using matrix departmentation are Caterpillar Tractor Company, American Cyanamid Company, and TRW.

Care should be exercised in adopting matrix departmentation. The traditional "one worker—one boss" management practice is severely modified. The matrix arrangement requires extensive communication and preferably it should meet internal company needs and not simply be grafted onto the existing organization in hope of demonstrating progressive management thinking. By following matrix departmentation, decision making may be slowed down and thus all managers must understand the rules of the game. Usually this necessitates an educational effort so that none feel their decision making is threatened and nonmanagement members learn how to function with two managers.

ADDITIONAL CONSIDERATIONS OF DEPARTMENTATION

In quite a few instances, the organizer is faced with the problem of where to place a specific activity in a specific organization structure. For such cases, the following considerations can prove helpful.

1. Place activity in unit having most use for it. Frequently, this proves effective even though the unit's activities and the newly assigned activity are quite dissimilar. Engineering, for example, in some business enterprises is under production; in others it is a part of sales. If the engineering activity is performed mainly to meet customers' requirements and requests, it might well be placed under sales. In contrast, if engineering concerns essentially problems of production and is used extensively by the production personnel, then engineering logically belongs under production.

2. Consider splitting an activity between two units. Most activities are best performed by one organizational unit; but for some the nature of activity may suggest dividing it between two organizational units. Checks or audits on the work done by other organizational units are illustrative. Inspection, for example, is commonly located within an organization so that its work will not be unduly influenced by operative production managers and nonmanagers.

3. Inject competition between units. In some instances the greatest opportunity for development occurs when certain activities are disassociated. The purpose is to provide a stimulus to greater achievements. Competition and the introduction of rivalry in an organization spurs managers to make the best possible showing in their respective efforts. The classical example in this respect is the organization of the General Motors Corporation, in which separate units are established and competition among them is consciously applied and encouraged.

4. Emphasize harmony and cooperation. Sometimes the departmentation has the prime purpose to achieve harmony and cooperation. Competitive effort within a segment of the organization structure is avoided. To illustrate, for a large retail distributor having branch stores and a strong mail-order division, one sales manager was placed in charge of all sales—both retail and mail order—for the purpose of preventing one type of selling to dominate at the expense of the other. However, the emphasizing of harmony in departmentation must be handled carefully and discreetly; otherwise the urge to create, excel, and accomplish are stifled and there is real danger ultimately of having spineless "yes-men" constituting the management members of the organization.

5. Follow manager's interest. Where to locate a particular activity is sometimes suggested by the interest of a manager. The assignment of a new activity or the transfer of an old one to an interested manager generally works out satisfactorily because having interest in the unit frequently but not always means that the manager will strive to see that it is performed well.

CENTRALIZATION AND DECENTRALIZATION

Additional concepts that affect the configuration of the organization structure are centralization and decentralization. Stated briefly, from the viewpoint of the total organization when decision making tends to be concentrated, centralization is present; when decision making tends to be dispersed, decentralization is present. The determining issue is how much decision making is performed by managers at the lower organization levels and by the nonmanagers.

To clarify the meaning of centralization and decentralization, Figures 13–6 and 13–7 have been included. The organization structure shown by Figure 13–6 features centralization. Assisting and reporting to the vice president in charge of production are six experts heading, respectively, units of purchasing, research, engineering, cost, standards, and public relations. The operative managers reporting to the vice president in charge of production are the plant managers of the four respective plants. In turn, department managers report to each plant manager. In this organization structure decisions pertaining to production are concentrated in the vice president production.

In contrast, under an arrangement stressing decentralization, the organization structure of the enterprise would appear like that shown in Figure 13–7. Each plant is now set up to operate more as a self-contained unit. For example, the manager of plant 1 has purchasing, engineering, costs, and standards departments reporting to her or him as well as departmental operating units. But note that the units decentralized are not the same for each plant manager. For example, plant 1 has a standards organization unit, whereas plant 2 does not have such a

FIGURE 13–6: An organization structure featuring centralization

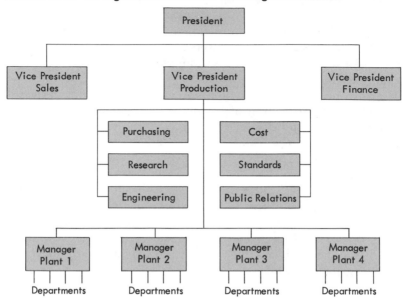

FIGURE 13–7: An organization structure featuring decentralization

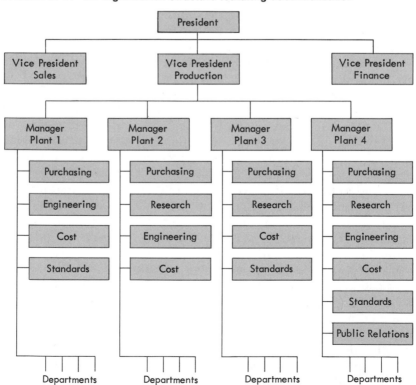

unit, but plant 2 has a research unit which 1 does not have. Plant 4 has both standards and research units. What is included and where depends in part upon the plant managers themselves and also how efficiently it is believed these activities can be performed at and for the particular plant. Also, taken into account will be the preferences of the top managers as well as the satisfactions gained from personal work efforts by managers under the respective individual circumstances and conditions.

Actually, centralization and decentralization are opposites and can be thought of as two theoretical extremes, neither of which are found in actual practice, but the degree or tendency to which either centralization or decentralization is practiced helps formulate the organization structure. We have assumed that the condition of centralization or of decentralization depends, respectively upon the concentration or the dispersion of decision making power. This is the management viewpoint. But the terms centralization and decentralization are also commonly used with reference to the concentration or dispersion of employees and physical facilities. From this point of view, the centralization of purchasing may mean the grouping of the employees performing purchasing and their desks, chairs, and files into one organizational unit. In contrast, decentralization may mean the dispersion of the employees and physical facilities of an enterprise.

It is entirely possible for centralization of employees and physical facilities to exist with decentralization of decision making and, vice versa, decentralization of employees and physical facilities with centralization of decision making. Generally speaking, when employees and physical facilities are centralized, decision making probably is likewise. However, when employees and facilities are decentralized, decision making can be either centralized or decentralized. For example, in a grocery chain with stores scattered over several states (decentralized employees and facilities), a store manager has no decision making over company advertising or purchasing decision making (centralized in main office). In another case, a manufacturer has employees and plants scattered throughout the United States (decentralized) with each plant doing its own purchasing advertising, cost, and product research work (decision making decentralized from home office and assigned to each plant).

EVALUATING CENTRALIZATION AND DECENTRALIZATION

As to be expected, most enterprises start out with a centralization of decision making arrangement because in the beginning managers feel that they are in better touch with activities and can apply their special abilities more forcefully under a centralized setup. With time, some decentralization takes place. Size of enterprise apparently plays a major role. As the scope and amount of managerial work increases the trend is toward decentralization. Also many advocates of decentralization point out that this arrangement encourages good human relations among employees and helps to give them status, freedom, and an opportunity to manage and earn promotions. The argument is that people are developed more under a decentralized than a centralized arrangement. In fact, a test of managerial decentralization is the extent to which one person or small group rule of the enterprise is eliminated and the enterprise management members of the lower organization levels are permitted to make and enforce decisions.

Just where between the two extremes of centralization and decentralization an enterprise should be organized depends upon the individual circumstances. Some experts claim that the use of automation, permitting large outputs in a concentrated area, favors centralized operations. Computers, for example, tend to centralize organizational authority over much paperwork processing. However, the greater availability of terminal units tied to the computer has emphasized a decentralized arrangement. Additional considerations could be cited, but the selection is managerial in that some managers with certain goals and available resources prefer the centralized arrangement, while others sincerely believe the decentralized is superior.[1]

To provide some evaluating basis, Figure 13–8 has been included. A listing of the major advantages from centralization and likewise those from decentralization are shown.

An interesting organization is that of the mammoth General Motors Corporation. Its guiding genius, the late Alfred P. Sloan, conceived in the formative days of GM "to divide it into as many parts as consistently can be done, place in charge of each part the most capable executive that can be found, and develop a system of coordination so that each part may strengthen and support each other." This has been termed "decentralized organization with centralized control." The units exercising major controls are centralized, and in the case of General Motors, financial controls play a prominent role. Buick competes with Oldsmobile, and likewise Frigidaire competes with Harrison Radiator; yet they are all coordinated by the central domestic office in Detroit. This organizational concept has contributed substantially to the growth of General Motors into a gigantic corporation.

---

[1] For literature on this subject, see M. Kochen and K. W. Deutsch, "Note on Hierarchy and Coordination: An Aspect of Decentralization," *Management Science*, September 1974, pp. 106–14; D. Clutterbuck, "Medicor Profits from Management Autonomy," *International Management*, September 1974, pp. 34–35; H. M. Carlisle, "Contingency Approach to Decentralization," *SAM Advanced Management Journal*, July 1974, pp. 9–18; and R. Manfield, "Bureaucracy and Centralization: An Examination of Organization and Structure," *Administrative Science Quarterly*, December 1973, pp. 477–88.

FIGURE 13–8

Important Advantages of Centralization

1. Power and prestige are provided the chief executives.
2. Uniformity of policies, practices, and decisions are fostered.
3. Full utilization of the main office and information specialists is promoted, due in large part to their proximity to the top-management level.
4. High qualified specialists can be utilized because the scope and volume of their work are sufficient to support and to challenge topnotch managers.
5. Duplication of functions is minimized.
6. The danger of actions drifting and getting off course is reduced.
7. Elaborate and extensive controlling procedures and practices are not required.
8. A strong coordinated top-management team is developed.

Important Advantages of Decentralization

1. A decentralized organization structure stresses delegation of decision making and lightens the load of top managers.
2. The development of "generalists" rather than specialists is encouraged, thereby facilitating succession into positions of general managers.
3. Intimate personal ties and relationships are promoted, resulting in greater employee enthusiasm and coordination.
4. Familiarity with important aspects of special work is readily acquired.
5. Efficiency is increased since the managers are near the activities for which they are held responsible and trouble spots can be located and remedied easily.
6. For multiunit enterprises keyed to geographical dispersion, full advantage of respective local conditions can be obtained.
7. Plans can be tried out on an experimental basis in one plant, modified, and proven before being supplied to similar plants of a company.
8. Risks involving possible losses of personnel, facilities, and plants are spread out.

MANAGERIAL JOB REQUIREMENTS

Most followers of formal organization have written (1) job requirements, and (2) manager specifications, and subsequently match these job and employee requirements to assign managerial personnel in the organization structure.[2] To assist in writing the job and employee re-

---

[2] The work of placing management members in an organization can be justified as within the work of organizing. These reasons are (1) organizing stresses human and social relations, (2) the true meaning of organizing must include consideration for the management members who are so organized, and (3) management personnel is acquired and assigned for an organization unit, usually a specific one—it is not done in a vacuum, or as an isolated act.

quirements, pertinent questions are asked, such as: What do we expect the manager to do? What are the exact requirements of the manager's job (the title or name is insufficient)? What important relationships must the occupant of this managerial job maintain and develop for the best operation both for the enterprise and for the individual manager? The format used can follow several designs. Figure 13–9 shows an

FIGURE 13–9: Location and concise statement of a particular position in an organization structure

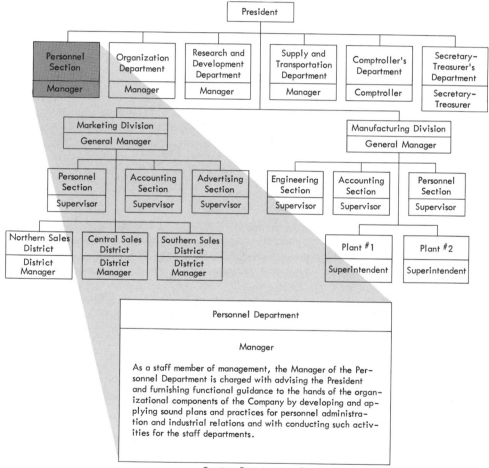

Courtesy Department on Organization, Standard Oil Company of California

arrangement especially effective. The figure illustrates a particular position on the formal chart and includes a concise statement of that position. Detailed and carefully outlined information concerning this same position is shown by Figure 13–10.

For a formal organization there are a series of job descriptions covering each job. But it should be noted that a few job descriptions include

FIGURE 13–10: A portion of the detailed information regarding a position in an organization structure (edited from original)

MANAGER, PERSONNEL DEPARTMENT

I. Function

As a staff member of management, the Manager of the Personnel Department is charged with advising the President and furnishing functional guidance to the heads of the organizational components of the Company by developing and applying sound plans and practices for personnel administration and industrial relations, and with conducting such activities for the staff departments.

II. Responsibilities and authority

Within the limits of an approved program and corporate policies and control procedures, the Manager of the Personnel Department is responsible for, and has commensurate authority to accomplish, the fulfillment of the duties set forth below. Manager may delegate to members of Department appropriate portions of responsibilities together with proportionate authority for their fulfillment, but may not delegate or relinquish overall responsibility for results nor any portion of accountability.

A. Activities
1. Formulate, or receive and recommend for approval, proposals for policies on personnel administration and industrial relations, administer such policies when approved, and conduct such activities for the staff departments.
2. Establish procedures for personnel administration and industrial relations, and establish and administer procedures for the initiation and maintenance of personnel records.
3. Negotiate, but not sign, agreements with employee groups and labor unions, and their representatives, affecting staff department employees or employees of both the Marketing and Manufacturing Divisions, and advise and assist in the negotiation of such agreements affecting employees of only one division, as requested.
4. Establish and conduct a company personnel office for the administration of personnel and industrial relations matters, and maintain therein personnel records of members of management and home office employees.
5. Participate in the selection of personnel for management positions, and conduct the initial interview of applicants for such positions and for employment in the home office.
6. Prepare, guide, and co-ordinate the personnel rating and personnel development programs, and formulate, or receive and recommend for approval, proposals for action based thereon.
7. Guide and co-ordinate the safety program and safety standards and practices, and disseminate applicable safety laws and orders.
8. Guide and co-ordinate employee benefit plans and programs, and conduct activities pertaining thereto for the personnel of the staff departments.

B. Organization of Department

1. Recommend changes in the basic structure and complement of department.

C. Personnel of Department

1. Having ascertained the availability of qualified talent from within the Company, hire personnel for, or appoint employees to, positions other than in management within the limits of approved basic organization.
2. Approve salary changes for personnel not subject to the provisions of the

all the duties and responsibilities that the job in reality entails. Writing job descriptions is a difficult and detailed task to be all-inclusive, and whatever is put into the written description is always subject to interpretation. Furthermore, over a period of time the typical executive alters the job content to some degree. An aggressive manager will move in and occupy areas not specifically defined as the work of another manager. It's another case of getting there "firstest with the mostest." Vacuums do not exist in most organizations for very long.

MANAGER SPECIFICATIONS

Turning now to manager specifications, we must answer, what kind of a person—what qualifications, background, ambitions, and beliefs—should we seek to fill each job? This is by no means an easy task. As pointed out in Chapter 1, the basic managerial skills sought are technical, human, and conceptual.[3] Competence for a managerial job is the product of a mix of both inherited and acquired qualities. In the main, those acquired are achieved in the course of a person's development and by influences to which the person has been subjected as well as the values of the culture to which one is a part. Usually of importance is the degree to which the job is structured, i.e., how much real autonomy will the individual have? Also, the performance expectations, general personality, willingness to accept responsibility, reaction to criticism, self-confidence, decisiveness, goals, ambitions, and remuneration expected are of significant importance. These qualities should be viewed as a composite. A deficiency may mean the candidate is unsuited for the job so specified, but at the same time favorable appraisals do not necessarily ensure success by the candidate. What the candidate *is* has usefulness, but of equal importance is what the candidate *does,* or the actions that must be performed to do the job successfully.

An interesting list of 15 managerial traits is shown by Figure 13–11. A manager cannot be selected by a scorecard, but lists of this sort serve as a general guide. To judge a human being is difficult especially when no attempt to measure against some standardized factors is made.[4]

From the written and specific job requirements and employee requirements for managerial jobs, the formal organizer has information upon which to construct an organization structure in keeping with one's wishes. As indicated above, the next step is to match as best possible the managerial job and the management member. This sounds quite simple, but it is seldom possible to find the wholly suited candidate who fulfills perfectly the specified total managerial job re-

---

[3] Page 9.

[4] See Chapter 16 for discussion of recruiting and selecting management members, and Chapter 21 for evaluating and developing management members.

FIGURE 13–11: Fifteen traits of fundamental significance in the success of a manager

A. Inborn Traits or Basic Equipment
   1. *Intelligence* as shown by IQ score, scholastic achievements, and honors.
   2. *Integrity* revealed by honesty and moral soundness.
   3. *Durability* or good physical fitness to withstand the rigors of managerial work.
   4. *Sensitivity* includes possession of both empathy and sympathy, consideration of others, both on and off the job.
   5. *Self-development drive* as identified by building up a record for solving tough assignments and seizing opportunities for self improvement.

B. Acquired Traits or Skills
   6. *Motivation* revealed by the demeanor of the people around a manager, the environment one creates, the will-to-do impressed upon others.
   7. *Communication* or the quality of expressing oneself clearly and succinctly and listening effectively.
   8. *Planning and organizing* as revealed by the group doing purposeful work, jobs clearly defined, and an energetic work force.
   9. *Teaching* or the ability to bring each individual up to each's highest potential.
   10. *Salesmanship* as demonstrated by success in getting others to accept one's ideas.

C. Inborn and Acquired Traits
   11. *Decisiveness* or being able to make up one's mind about what to do in a situation and selecting a choice of action.
   12. *Flexibility* encompasses the willingness to keep trying different means and approaches until the most satisfactory means is found.
   13. *Working with people* is the means by which a manager makes contributions.
   14. *Will to win* or an instinctive drive to excel others.
   15. *Picking other managers* or the ability to select people who will eventually move up and perhaps even beyond the selector.

Source: *Personnel*, May–June 1971. Used with permission of American Management Association, New York.

quirements. And even with time the "reasonably good" candidate may not match the stated job specifications.

COMMITTEES

Committees help shape and are a part of almost every organization structure and design. Existing at any organizational level, committees are common yet controversial, serve in various capacities, are known by many different names, and enjoy wide degrees of acceptance among managers. Extremely important work is accomplished via the committee route. Typically, educational enterprises are loaded with committees, and they are common in government, business, trade associations, and professional societies.

Literally the word "committee" means those to whom some matter or charge is committed. It can be defined as *a body of persons elected or appointed to meet on an organized basis for the discussion of and dealing with matters brought before it.* Usually a committee has a formally recognized and permanent place in the organization structure. Its makeup, duties, membership, and decision-making power may be carefully spelled out. For example, some business enterprises have at the top level, a planning and policy committee, or a general management committee made up of selected company executives. Likewise, in other types of enterprise, typical top committees are in the organization of the Atomic Energy Commission, the Tennessee Valley Authority, and state public utility commissions.

In addition, there are formal committees of a temporary nature. They are put together to discuss a particular problem and to determine either what action to take or suggest possible actions that might be taken. Further, what can be termed informal committees exist. They consist of an informal gathering of people, perhaps executives at luncheon, and discuss some aspect of company business. Such an informal committee has no formally designated purpose, authority, or organization, yet it does have influence and in some respects serves the equivalent function of a formal committee.

Committees are used for two reasons (1) the interaction of members serving as a group should produce superior results in contrast to those achieved by an individual, and (2) the complexity of organization with its large number of functions and various levels necessitate periodic exchange of information. A committee is an effective medium to meet these needs and serves not only as a communicative aid, but also as an effective coordinative medium. Figure 13–12 shows the main reasons for the widespread use of committees. In essence, these are advantages resulting from committee usage.

On the other hand, there are managers who honestly feel committees are the source of frustration and a big waste of time. They like to recite

> In all our towns and all our cities
> There are no statues to committees.

Further, they contend that the cost of committees greatly exceeds the benefits received from them. A committee provides the medium for people to assemble and talk over various matters. Admittedly, this is a time-consuming process, and of course while a committee is in session, its members cannot transact their important day-to-day duties, hence

FIGURE 13–12:   Reasons for the extensive use of committees

1. Expert and collective knowledge can be concentrated upon a specific problem. A wide range of experience can be tapped, exchange of ideas fostered,
   and effective give-and-take discussions encouraged. Employed is group
   judgment, which is believed superior for certain type problems and situations.

2. Coordination is assisted. Different views can be unified and integrated,
   agreed prescribed courses of action established, and maximum understanding among committee participants achieved. The receiving, relating, interpreting, and channeling of information makes this coordination feasible.

3. Too much authority of one person is prevented. By its very nature, a committee tends to distribute its authority among the committee members, who can
   watch and check each other's actions. This check on authority is most prominent in government, religious, and educational organizations. In the latter,
   for example, the president of a university is usually restrained by the committee, or board of regents, that appoints him or her, as well as by faculty
   committees and other university committees that, among other activities,
   determine operating policies, curriculum, salaries, and tenure.

4. Social values are provided. Committee membership provides prestige, permits recognition as an equal with other members who have status, and tends
   to satisfy the human desire to belong and to do something worthwhile.

5. Motivation is supplied. People like participation, and committee use encourages it. Cooperation is enhanced in the execution of a proposed action and
   is reasonably assured if the committee develops the plan. There is also
   knowledge acquired by the committee members and possibly pride of au-
   thorship gained by a member. Such characteristics have strong motivational
   value.

6. Education of members is promoted. Each participant's viewpoint is
   broadened; one gains an appreciation of the other unit's problems as well as
   those of the entire enterprise. Placing at least one manager on a committee
   and asking her to express herself first at each meeting can be practiced.

the possible loss of time is compounded. Also, a committee lacks accountability. All members of a committee are theoretically accountable for the committee's action, yet this is extremely difficult to assess,
especially if the committee's final position was reached by compromise. No one member, including the chairperson, can be held accountable for the committee's action. This lack of accountability
makes committees ineffective where the assignment calls for taking
action. Also, in some instances, committees are used by a manager as
an alibi or escape from responsibility. If the decision is likely to be
unpopular, escape from the consequences is possible by diffusing the
responsibility among the committee members. Furthermore, the
committee's decision frequently is one of compromise. Harmony is
sought and this is understandable, since the committee members are
also members within an enterprise who must work together in different capacities. Furthermore, they usually have some responsibility in

implementing their collective decision and a dissatisfied or recalcitrant committee member might sabotage the committee's action by not cooperating in the implementation efforts. In addition, certain issues may be avoided when all committee members know bringing them up for discussion and a decision will cause endless discussion and no decision.

ACQUIRING COMMITTEE EFFECTIVENESS

Like all practitioners of management, a member of a committee should have a clear idea of what is to be considered. The objective must be definite. It is relatively easy for the members to get off the beam and delve into areas not intended for their consideration. Helpful is the providing of written specifications giving the purpose, scope, responsibility, and decision making power of the committee as well as its relationships with the organization units of the enterprise.

Likewise, the decision making task of a committee should be defined and known to all concerned. This is a major prerequisite for successful committee work. Whether the committee is to decide and take action, or advise and counsel, or simply to serve as a sounding board for the chairperson must be known. In addition, the duties of each member should be pointed out.

The subject matter is another important consideration which affects a committee's effectiveness. Generally speaking, subjects pertaining to objective evaluations, broad means for achieving stated objectives, and evaluating past activities from an overall viewpoint are among those best suited for committee work. Basic issues, not masses of data, are best handled by committees. Experience shows that committees are not especially effective in collecting data for a particular project.

To expedite discussion and exchange of ideas the committee size should be from 3 to 17 members, with perhaps 3 to 7 as the preferred number. The committee members need to have a mutual respect for each other's interests, to understand the several possible viewpoints presented about an issue, to express themselves clearly and concisely, to think independently, and to integrate, as well as compromise, tentative conclusions presented for action. Many feel that for best results the members should be of about equal status.

The leadership provided by the chairperson is usually the key to successful committee work. Careful planning and preparing of an agenda, seeing that each member is supplied with appropriate data well in advance of the meeting, and keeping the discussions on the subjects at hand and moving along with each member given an opportunity for expression are among the "musts" for a good committee chairperson.

Finally, it is well to have adequate follow-up to the work of a committee. This is accomplished by a designated committee member taking the appropriate action—presenting the recommendation to an officer, distributing notes of the meeting to designated members, or instituting the action decided. Committees often become self-perpetuating; the task is to determine whether the purpose of the committee is still valid and if the committee is effective in terms of the purpose.

BOARD OF DIRECTORS

A board of directors is legally created by the papers of incorporation of a corporation, and by them it is given the authority to exercise the powers of the corporation, limited by any conditions set forth in the corporation's bylaws. It is by means of a charter, as stipulated in state statutes called incorporation laws, that the corporation comes into existence.

It must be remembered that board of directors' decisions are group decisions. The board is a group; its acts jointly as a board—never as an individual. Some boards determine decisions that virtually affect the life of the corporation while others serve basically as approval bodies for the actions of the top management group. Between these two extremes are a number of activities that can be considered typically performed by a board of directors. The feeling is growing, however, that a board should be the focal point for reaction to public, natural, and competitive forces. Where significant changes or pressures exist, some boards have added representatives of these new entities to their membership so that the viewpoints of these groups can be considered first-hand in the boards' decision making. There is also strong belief by some that community and public interests be represented on boards especially in the cases of quasi-public corporations. COMSAT (Communications Satellite Corporation) is a case in point. Further, the legal liability of a board member is being carefully reviewed and the trend is toward more and complete liability and responsibility for the decisions and acts taken.

In all, many items come to a board of directors for consideration and action. For convenience we will classify them under four headings: (1) objectives determination, (2) selection of top managers, (3) financial structure of the corporation, and (4) review and appraisal. A board of directors acts as a steward of the assets that belong to the corporate owners. Because of this stewardship, the board has the legal right and the obligation to determine the objectives of the corporation. These objectives are quite broad and are made primarily in the light of protecting and watching over the assets of the corporation for the benefit of its stockholders. Also, in a number of instances, the board plays an active role in formulating basic corporate policies.

The president of a corporation is almost always selected by the board of directors, but the selection of other top managers by a board varies widely. Commonly followed is the practice of the president nominating her or his top associates, subject to approval and confirmation of the board. In addition, compensation questions of base salary, bonuses, and expense allowances are answered by the board.

Financial matters such as approving or initiating changes in capital structure, the distribution of earnings, and the financial expansion or contraction by the corporation are decided by the board of directors. For example, almost without exception the board decides what portion of earnings should be paid to stockholders in the form of dividends, what portion used to decrease corporate indebtedness, and what portion to be plowed back into the corporate operations. Review and final approval of budgets dealing with overall corporate affairs are another common activity of a board.

The accomplishments of the management team is reviewed periodically by the board of directors. This is followed not only to find out if the objectives are being met, but also to motivate key managers by making suggestions helpful to them. This action commonly called "conscientious deliberation" involves asking pertinent questions designed to force the proponent of a particular action, commonly a corporate executive, to justify proposed or past action and to bring out possibilities perhaps not thought of previously. At the same time the board members can keep the corporation in tune with changing environment and conditions by their questioning and suggesting techniques.

It should also be noted that a board member performs many activities on an informal basis. One may, for example, talk informally with different executives of the corporation, or have lunch with managers not associated with the corporation to get their reactions to new ideas that the corporation contemplates using. Further, interviews with technological experts and attendance at special meetings may be in order to obtain information that may be of benefit to the board member's corporation.

What is the proper size of a board of directors? Opinions vary, but probably a minimum of five and not more than fifteen is most satisfactory for most corporations. The membership should be large enough to be representative, but not so large that it becomes unwieldly. If the board is merely a facade used basically for status and prestige, the question of size is not important.

How frequently do boards meet? Some meet once or twice a week. However, many meet about once a month, quarterly meetings are popular, and some meet only once or twice a year. The law requires one board meeting a year.

The composition of the membership will vary among boards.

Among the principal occupations of the members are top executives of the corporation, retired corporate executives, bankers, attorneys, prominent business leaders, investment and financial counselors, and educators.[5] The board makeup can be either from (1) inside members, i.e., employees of the corporation, resulting in an *inside board,* or (2) from inside and outside members (outside the corporation) resulting in an *outside board.* Inside boards bring satisfactory results when a sufficient number of qualified employees can be selected, the board's experience will help mature the members' thinking, and a relatively high technical knowledge is requisite for the decision-making process. Family-owned corporations commonly have inside boards, sometimes called *family boards,* because the owners believe outside help is not necessary or they fear having outsiders' participation. The chief advantage of using an outside board is to gain the benefits of members with diverse backgrounds, fulfill a sense of obligation to a community or to society, and promote good public relations. However, if an outside member lacks the time and interest to become thoroughly acquainted with the corporation's aims and operations, the corporation's advantages from having an outside board member may be greatly diminished.

PLURAL EXECUTIVE

The common meaning of plural executive is two or more executives usually with line authority at the top levels of organization. The specific area of operations may be a phase of the enterprise activities of one or more of the fundamental management functions. Plural executive is commonly found in planning, especially policymaking. Controlling in its broader phases may also be included to a somewhat limited extent. The plural executive also is especially effective for settling questions of jurisdictional dispute and for the formulation of objectives.

Use of the plural executive in organization structures is increasing. Not only is decision making being shared more and more, but too much is happening too fast in too many fields for one person to handle successfully all these diverse activities. Some companies such as General Electric, General Mills, Mead, and Chase Manhattan Bank use "offices of presidents." Armco Steel Corporation has a three-member "corporate executive office" to direct and operate jointly the corporation. By such means it is hoped that the needed broader scope of company operations at the top will be gained and top management in depth will be provided. Chemetron Corporation finds the plural executive especially helpful for product and profit improvement,

---

[5] Jeremy Bacon, "Corporate Directorship Practices," *Business Policy Study No. 125* (New York: National Industrial Conference Board, Inc., 1967), pp. 14–16.

better controls, and improved coordination. Theoretically, the plural executive has no person in charge and no one given ultimate decision making power. Decisions might be delayed, and considerable time may be spent in determining what action to take. To assist in making the arrangement feasible, the plural executive tasks usually are structured into major operating groups with an executive in charge of each group.

QUESTIONS

1. Enumerate and discuss the four basic components of formal organization.
2. What is the meaning of each of the following: (*a*) manager specifications, (*b*) departmentation by territory, (*c*) synergism of organizing, and (*d*) centralization.
3. How do you account for the widespread use of committees in organizing today?
4. Explain Figure 13–3 in your own words.
5. Discuss several social requirements of an organization, pointing out their major significance to a manager.
6. Have you ever worked in an organization where departmentation by task force was used? If so, describe the arrangement followed, and how successful it appeared to be. If not, do you believe the task-force arrangement would have improved the organization? Why?
7. As a manager, would you be inclined to favor decentralization? Why?
8. With reference to Figure 13–11, rate yourself on each of the 15 traits by scoring from 5 to 1 points for each trait (5 is maximum) depending on your judgment. What interpretation do you give your results? Elaborate on your answer.
9. What is the meaning of the term *centralization* as applied to a company's formal organization? What is meant by the term *decentralization?* Give an example of each.
10. You have been asked to give a 20-minute talk on "departmentation in organization." Outline the presentation that you would give.
11. With reference to a board of directors, discuss (1) the number and composition of its members, (2) the meaning of a family board, and (3) informal activities performed by its members.
12. What can be done to see to it that an organization remains an organization in the true sense of its totality, i.e., that the managers of the various functions do not tend to become independent and act on their own? Discuss.
13. Relate an experience wherein the use of a committee was not effective. In your opinion discuss what could have been done to make the committee's use satisfactory.
14. Define, point out probable future usage, and give advantages of having a plural executive in an organization.

CASE 13–1. BLUE BELL STORES, INC.

Fourteen stores of this corporation located in three different states specialize in essential food items, dairy products, and fresh meats. The central office is in Fort Wayne, Indiana. Wayne Pierce, president of Blue Bell Stores is a strong believer in decentralized operations. He feels the strength of the corporation lies in the competency of each store manager operating a sound retail store as the respective manager sees it. As a result, the local store manager decides what items will be carried in that store, prices charged, the number of employees, wages paid, hours the store is open, arrangement used for displayed products, and advertising.

The major activity of the central office is to (1) audit the records and reports sent in by each store manager; (2) consolidate this information into summary statements for the corporation; and (3) select examples of good store management from this information, and to describe and distribute such information in an inspirational newsletter each month to all store managers. About every six months a two-day store managers' conference is called by Mr. Pierce. At these meetings new ideas are discussed for improving the business, problems common to most of the stores are discussed, and tentative suggestions regarding what to do about them are developed. Mr. Pierce spends much of his time on the road calling on and discussing ways and means to improve the sales effectiveness of each store.

For the past seven to eight months, losses in the stores' operations have occurred. From his visits to the various store managers, each store appears to be busy, judged by the number of people visiting the store. Also the traffic count is high in each of the shopping centers where most of the stores are located. Some of the store managers complain to Mr. Pierce about the reports they are required to turn in to the central office saying they take too much time and they could better spend their time selling in the store.

Mr. Pierce is becoming quite concerned about the decline of the corporation's sales and profits. From available literature, Mr. Pierce knows that sales of all stores in the same category as Blue Bell Stores attained a 9.7 percent sales increase for the past six months just ended. The current financial position of five Blue Bell stores is critical and seven of the remaining nine stores of the corporation are just about realizing their total expenses.

What to do has been "bugging" Mr. Pierce for several months. When sales and profits first began to decline, Mr. Pierce along with many others attributed the change to a slackening in general business activity. Now he is not certain what the cause or causes are. He feels that perhaps special promotions and the revamping of the store items handled may be the answer, but in this regard, not one store manager agrees with Mr. Pierce. Several store managers flatly state they will quit if Mr. Pierce does not continue to let them manage the store as they feel it should be run. Mr. Pierce feels this is all bluff. His position has not wavered, however, from that of permitting the local store manager autonomy in the management of the store because, as Mr. Pierce states, it helps to take full advantage of local conditions, makes effective ties and relationships meaningful and effective, and facilitates greater store managerial enthusiasm and drive.

Questions

1. Is there a problem in this corporation? Explain.
2. Evaluate the corporation organizational arrangement as well as the managerial activity of Mr. Pierce.
3. As a store manager, what suggestions, if any, would you make? Why?
4. What action do you recommend Mr. Pierce take? Justify your answer.

CASE 13–2. FAIRMONT COMPANY

Vice President of Finance Walter Miles has three people reporting directly to him: the manager of general accounting, Harry Knapp; the manager of data processing, Charles Laferty; and Eleanor Pitts, the manager of cost accounting. Mr. Miles is known as a hard but fair manager. He listens to problems brought to him and assists his people in solving them. But he doesn't tolerate "back talk" and feels most meetings are a waste of time. He insists upon accuracy and completion of all reports and records on or before their due date. There are carefully stated job descriptions for each job and Mr. Miles follows them to the letter. His job as he sees it is to manage according to the wishes of his superior and the regulations and requirements contained in the several manuals available to all finance management personnel.

Harry Knapp follows the general mode of operations demonstrated by Mr. Miles. Although there is no official assistant to Mr. Miles, through seniority of ten years, Harry Knapp is considered next in line after Mr. Miles. Productivity is the key to success as Mr. Knapp sees it. He has work expectancies for each of his employees and evaluates each once a year to see if they need any help in attaining efficiency and to let them know they are doing all right, if such is the case. In Mr. Miles' opinion, general accounting is the best managed of his three units.

Charles Laferty has been with the company about 1½ years. He is a friend of Eleanor Pitts who used her influence to help Mr. Laferty get his present job. At that time, the then and still assistant of the department, James Harding, thought he should have had the job. He, along with others in the department, did not favor bringing in an outsider, but more important, he believed he was well qualified for the promotion as his work record was excellent. As the son-in-law of the works manager (with whom Mr. Miles does not get along too well), Mr. Harding feels this is at least part of the explanation why he was not promoted.

Since joining the company, Mr. Laferty has offered several suggestions for improving his department. Mr. Miles has listened intently but to date has not given him any "go-ahead" permission. Mr. Laferty pays a great deal of attention to the suggestions offered by Ms. Pitts. They eat lunch together and their families visit each other about every other week. James Harding knows this and feels Eleanor Pitts is interfering in data processing work. He recognizes that cost accounting is well managed and Ellie is doing acceptable work or she would not have been with the company for seven years.

About two months ago, Mr. Laferty injured himself in a skiing accident and was absent from work for five weeks, during which period Jim Harding took over. His work, however, was not satisfactory, in the opinion of Mr. Miles. "Jim simply doesn't follow orders" is the way Mr. Miles expressed it. Ms. Pitts made several attempts to help Jim Harding but was not warmly received. In fact, on the last occasion, Mr. Harding reported the incident to Mr. Miles who promptly told Ms. Pitts to stay in her own department. Mr. Miles was glad to see Mr. Laferty return to work.

During the next several weeks, Mr. Laferty was not physically up to par. He found it difficult to concentrate. Work in his department began to pile up and the inability to meet schedules caused inconvenience and difficulties in the other departments. Mr. Miles called Mr. Laferty to his office and told him things would have to improve quickly. James Harding, hearing of this, offered to work overtime and relieve Mr. Laferty of some of his duties. Mr. Miles did not reply to his offer.

Last Saturday morning, Eleanor Pitts was helping Mr. Laferty in his office. Several other data processing personnel were also working overtime. While Mr. Laferty was checking some old records in the storage room, James Harding walked in the department and saw Ellie Pitts working there. Mr. Harding became quite upset. After many verbal criticisms of past happenings in the office, James Harding asked Eleanor Pitts what she had against him. The reply was, "Nothing."

Questions

1. What is the problem?
2. Will formal organizing meet the company's needs satisfactorily? Why?
3. What would you do if you were James Harding? Mr. Miles?
4. What action do you recommend the company take? Justify your answer.

Chapter **14**

Authority and organizational relationships

Habits change into character.

Ovid

To complete our discussion of traditional organizational concepts, we now consider authority, its use and importance in organizing. Authority conditions the actions and behavior of every management member in an enterprise and represents the common cord tying together the various organization units, thus making possible the very existence of the organization and the effective working together of the total personnel.

CONCEPTS OF AUTHORITY

Authority is viewed by different people in a number of different ways. One popular viewpoint is that *authority is the official and legal right to command action by others and to enforce compliance.* Authority is exercised by making decisions and seeing that they are carried out. Compliance, however, is gained in a number of ways—through persuasion, sanctions, requests, coercion, constraint, or force. We can state that a person with authority influences the activity and/or the behavior of another individual or group than might otherwise take place. However, a person can have this influence without having authority, that is, no official or legal right to command and enforce action by others. We say such a person has *power.*

Power connotes a broader concept than authority and can be intentional or nonintentional. Power can be thought of as a strong influence of a controlling nature over the direction of an individual's behavior. Some prefer the concept of power as being the capacity of a person to secure dominance of his or her values over the values of another person. Power is a potential influence. In order for a social system to function, there must be some legitimate power. Like authority, power should not be permitted to concentrate in a single organizational unit; a delicate balance of power is vital for an organization to be most effective.

Unless there is an environment of legitimacy—meaning ethically and socially acceptable to all concerned—authority cannot be meaningful and operational. A moral right is involved. Persons in authority have the right to demand obedience and those subject to authority have the duty to obey. Without authority an organization cannot function. Effective group effort requires the existence of some authority.

Historically the concept of authority is from the government and the military. The reasoning goes like this. Authority comes into being from ownership, organization status, or legal decree. Ownership includes the right to put property to use and direct how it is used, an arrangement having both legal and social approval.

With the development of management, social change, and economic modification have come additional concepts of authority. For example, authority from "subordinate acceptance" identifies a type growing in importance. In this concept, authority is thought to come to the manager by the acceptance of the manager's power to make and enforce decisions by subordinates. In other words, according to this approach a manager has no authority until it is conferred upon that person by subordinates. Acceptance by the subordinates is the key in this line of explanation and reasoning. In addition, it stresses the social and ethical aspects of authority as well as leadership and communicative ability by the manager.

Why will a subordinate accept the authority exercised over him? The reasons are many. Among the most important are to gain approval and acceptance by other employees, to contribute to a cause or goal considered worthwhile, to avoid possible disciplinary action, to comply with moral standards considered proper, and to gain rewards. All of these are not exclusive with the acceptance approach, but they are emphasized in this approach.

The term "authority of the situation" is sometimes encountered in management literature. In nearly every enterprise, emergency and unusual events occur which are not provided for in the regular organizational setup. When such an event occurs, the person assuming authority to meet the particular circumstances is said to have derived authority from the "authority of the situation." Such authority exists during the extent of the emergency only or until the person regularly charged with the authority assumes command over the unusual event. It can exist in any type of organizing.

There is also "position authority," which is essentially the authority a person has by virtue of the superior position she occupies in the organization. Normally, subordinates recognize authority of those occupying higher hierarchical positions. And to a great extent the recognition is extended regardless of who occupies the position.

Since about 1950, the term "computer authority," or "technical authority," has come into use. The term is suggestive of its meaning. Computer authority stems from the decision-making power granted to processed data by a computer. But authority is a human possession, and hence, computer authority can be defined as that authority possessed by the person who either interprets computer-processed data or points out their significant managerial meanings for others.

PSYCHOLOGICAL AND SOCIAL INFLUENCES UPON AUTHORITY

From what has been stated it follows that there are important psychological and social attributes influencing the concept of authority. Without going into an exhaustive discussion here we can state that the following sources have influence upon authority and its usage: (1) control of sanctions, (2) personal liking, (3) expertise, (4) legitimacy, (5) coercion, and (6) status. Sanction can be defined as either a reward resulting from a willingness to respond favorably to a directive or a penalty exacted for failure to accept and follow a directive. In other words, a person's behavior within an organization is affected in part by the sanction utilized for or against that person. Personal liking is self-explanatory and is simply the human preference being followed for one individual over another. Expertise is recognition of excellence in a given area of endeavor to the degree that a willingness to follow orders issued by this learned source is practiced. A brilliant researcher in marketing, for example, may be frequently approached to give factual data concerning vital markets. From the viewpoint of the formal organization, he or she may have little or no authority; yet the researcher's answers are followed and so consistently that he or she appears to be one with extensive authority.[1] By legitimacy is meant formal authority existing within the formal organization and includes job titles, general decision-making rights, and accepted power granted to the holder of a formally defined position. Coercion is the use of force. The subordinate is compelled or restrained by force such as law and police enforcement to abide by orders. Status is a major consideration in authority. By status is meant the totality of attributes that rank and relate members in an organization. Compliance with directives is expedited because status rationalizes degrees of inequality and generally a person is inclined to take orders from one a person believes superior to oneself. Status tends to reinforce the authority relationship.

---

[1] As stated above, some consider such a person not to have authority but power, since the person cannot enforce personal answers or decisions.

Among the many factors affecting status, custom provides perhaps the best-known symbols of status. For example, persons occupying higher positions, or those of the top organization levels, usually but not always have a higher status than those in the lower positions. Common means to identify status include insignias, uniforms, titles, and special facilities. Insignias in a military organization, for example, are a common denominator of status throughout the organization. Vestments of church officiants, black robes of judges, as well as uniforms of certain hospital management personnel are formal symbols of status. Also, special facilities such as the ornate office, and the more luxurious carpeting, reveal status.

It is well to add that authority in organization is supported and sustained by society. The first years of a human's life are conditioned by one's parents. The child initially resents this intervention, but gradually begins to accept the imposed authority and obeys without too much question. Later this conditioning is duplicated and reinforced when the person enters school and by other subsequent group experiences. All these experiences tend to reinforce the authority relationships in an organization of business, a hospital, or the armed forces. Doing what the superior says tends to be habitual for many but not all people. In addition, social sanctions imposed become the accepted way of doing things in that if they are not followed, consequences beyond the penalties imposed within the organization take place. Of course, differences of opinion exist, but for purposes here, the point is simply that society does influence the authority functioning in an organization and in important ways.

LIMITS OF AUTHORITY

Traditionally we have viewed unlimited authority as an instrument of possible corruption. For centuries we have placed constraints on the acts of those in authority. In the modern business organization, for example, it is common to find that two or more management members must concur on certain issues before they are put into effect. The manager in charge of finance and the controller agree on the financing program before it is adopted, and a supervisor's recommendation for a pay increase for a subordinate must normally be approved by the personnel manager to become effective.

There are specific limits of authority. No one, not even a manager, can decide and enforce an activity which is beyond the capacity, either mentally or physically, of the subordinate to perform. A manager ordering a shop employee to manually lift an object weighing 1,800 pounds cannot enforce compliance with the order. Nor will the object be lifted even though the subordinate agrees with the request.

Likewise, a manager cannot expect compliance to a request for a stockroom helper to operate a gear-cutting machine.

Authority must also be in keeping with the accepted plans of an enterprise. In most cases, an objective cannot be ignored or a policy modified simply because a manager says to do so. Many management members have found that efforts to get certain changes made meet with seemingly endless difficulties. The articles of incorporation, established precedents, and long-standing implied agreements utilized in company affairs may place serious restrictions on the manager's exercise of authority. This is not to suggest that changes cannot be made. They can, but usually not at the caprice of a manager.

In addition there are many social limitations to the use of authority by a manager. The activities being ordered must be in keeping with the group's fundamental social beliefs, codes, creeds, and habits; otherwise the effective power of the exerciser of authority is limited. These social limitations upon authority are both within and without an enterprise.

In the case of labor unions and collective bargaining, for example, the right to collective bargaining is affirmed in the United States by several federal statutes which aim to protect the interests of employers, employees, and the general public. From the viewpoint of limitation of authority of a person having property, employers, under the present labor law, cannot interfere with the employees' right to bargain or not to bargain collectively as they choose. Employers cannot interfere with the establishing or the operating of labor unions, nor can an employer refuse to bargain collectively with employees. Further, constraints of governing laws and executive orders such as the Civil Rights Act—1964 Title VII, the Civil Rights Act—1966 Section 1981, the Age Discrimination Act, and Federal Executive Orders 11246 and 11375 place definite limitations on authority with the intent of eliminating discrimination and achieving equal employment opportunity for all citizens.

Last, there is the limitation of span of authority which is defined as follows: *Span of authority is the number of immediate subordinates that report to a manager.* Wide spans or a manager having a relatively large number of immediate subordinates usually results in few organization levels and a "flattening out" of the structure. A small number of organization levels expedites communication, but wide spans are challenging to a manager inasmuch as the scope of operation is broadened and the opportunity is present to grow and show what can be done. In contrast, narrow spans calling for a relatively small number of immediate subordinates expedite more personalized manager-subordinate relationships, perhaps more effective managing of the subordinates, and a "tall organization," i.e., one with relatively many levels.

The question arises: What is the proper number of persons to be subordinated to any executive? Proper span is basically a behavioral question and varies with such things as the ability of the manager, relative location of the managers in the structure, fear of possible rivals, faith in subordinates to perform satisfactorily, and the degree of teamwork that is present. However, the type of work is also important. For example, enterprises in which the work remains essentially the same and is repeated over and over again with slight, if any, change are usually successful in employing greater spans of authority than are those enterprises dealing with highly dynamic and volatile activities. Also, the necessity for frequent and involved communication usually requires a short span.[2]

Furthermore, the span of authority affects significantly the number of organizational relationships between the superior and the subordinates. Figure 14–1 gives pertinent data. Observe first that the number

FIGURE 14–1: The effect of the number of subordinates upon the number of organization relationships*

Number of subordinates	Number of relationships			
	Direct	Cross	Direct group	Total
1	1	—	—	1
2	2	2	2	6
3	3	6	9	18
4	4	12	28	44
5	5	20	75	100

* Source of these data are the mathematical findings of V. A. Graicunas, a French management consultant.

of these relationships is greater than the number of persons directly supervised because there are also relationships between the persons directly supervised. For example, a superior with two subordinates is concerned with direct relationship to No. 1 and No. 2, with cross relationships No. 1 to No. 2 and No. 2 to No. 1, with direct group relationships to No. 1 and No. 2 and No. 2 and No. 1 to the superior. All of this means, of course, that the tasks of supervision multiply rapidly as subordinates are added.

---

[2] Critical variables affecting the span of authority have been stated as (1) dependence of subordinates on their superior, (2) interdependence of subordinates' activities, and (3) interdependence of the work units with other units. See Robert G. Wright, "An Approach to Find Realistic Spans of Management," *Arizona Business Bulletin*, November 1970, pp. 20–28.

Principle of increasing organization relationships

As additional persons or units are added to an organization structure, the number of organization relationships increases at a much greater rate than the number of persons or units added.

RESPONSIBILITY DEFINED

At this point of our discussion on authority, we need to inject another important concept concerning organizing. This concept is responsibility. In the formal theory of organizing, *responsibility is the obligation of an individual to carry out assigned activities to the best of one's ability.* It is what one is expected to do in order to carry out one's prescribed job. Responsibility may be continuing or it may terminate with the accomplishment of a single action.

However, this concept of formal responsibility is being modified as, for example, when results management is used, the meaning of responsibility becomes: *Responsibility is the obligation of a person to achieve the results mutually determined by means of participation by one's superior and oneself.*

Some managers consider responsibility as having two parts or phases. The one is the obligation to carry out assigned activities to achieve results; the other is to account to a superior for the degree of success achieved in completing the prescribed work. The former is, of course, the formal organizational concept. The latter is also to a degree, but it, too, implies some of the modified organization thinking affecting organizing.

COEQUALITY OF AUTHORITY AND RESPONSIBILITY

The authority and responsibility of any manager should be coequal. In other words, responsibility is the inseparable twin of authority. Hence, a manager's authority gives a person the power to make and enforce decisions concerning his or her assigned or defined duties and that person's responsibility places the obligation upon the person to perform these duties by using this authority.

Authority without responsibility lacks an ultimate purpose or justification for existing, and likewise, responsibility without authority to carry out the assigned duties has a hollow ring. A manager cannot perform assigned duties if one lacks the necessary authority to see that the work is accomplished. On the other hand, one's failure to assume responsibility for the fulfillment of the assigned duties is an equally bad managerial situation.

Authority can be looked upon as the regulator. In other words, the amount and extent of authority tend to establish the amount and extent of responsibility. When a significant difference exists between the two, it may be advisable to encourage the manager to assume more responsibility compatiable with the authority being used or, in contrast, when authority is less than responsibility, to seek either more authority or less responsibility.

Principle of authority and responsibility

For sound organizational relationships the authority of a manager should be commensurate with responsibility and, vice versa, responsibility commensurate with authority.

It is important to point out that this coequality of authority and responsibility is achieved by means of modifying the process management approach by results management. When this is done, the member's participation in determining one's goals and being held to achieve them answers the problem of how to get authority to the one held responsible or vice versa, how to get responsibility to the one who has authority.

THE SOURCE OF RESPONSIBILITY

Responsibility comes into existence when a person with authority, or a manager, accepts the obligation to perform work and starts to utilize authority. The viewpoint taken here is that authority is the essential management entity to organizing. To achieve goals, the use of authority gives rise to the acceptance of the obligations for these goal attainments and it is these obligations that give rise to responsibility.

The acceptance of an obligation to perform work can take several forms. In a business enterprise it is the employee's agreement to accept employment and perform certain services. Generally, being given the job provides the authority to perform it. In a charitable or similar enterprise, it may be a simple written agreement or an oral statement or even an act that signifies the employee's or member's acceptance of the obligation to carry out certain work.

IMPORTANCE OF FIXED RESPONSIBILITY

Fixed responsibility means that acceptance of the obligation for the performance of a function places the obligation squarely upon the person making the acceptance. It is up to this person to carry out the function promptly and efficiently. The fixation of definite responsibility is important because it helps to develop the acceptor, assists in getting the work accomplished, points out areas needing remedial action, and minimizes buckpassing. It requires the individual so designated to perform the task.

Most persons like to measure up to the requirements of their jobs. When held completely responsible for a task, a person will execute his or her best efforts and demonstrate competency and ability to do the work. Fixed responsibility tends to develop initiative, resourcefulness, and reliability. Obstacles are overcome, problems are solved, and the immediate chief interest becomes one of successfully completing the task.

The managerial coordination of tasks within an organization structure is assisted by the fixation of definite responsibility. Knowing who is responsible for what work and when helps to locate the proper person for a specific task quickly and directly. Furthermore, areas where additional help or training appear necessary can be identified with a minimum of delay.

Principle of fixed responsibility

For any given period, an individual will accomplish most when responsibility for the completion of a definite task is fixed upon that individual.

TYPES OF AUTHORITY AND ORGANIZATIONAL RELATIONSHIPS

To make feasible the functioning of the formal organization a number of different types of authority are needed. The reasoning is logical: different managers need different decision making powers, both in type and amount, in order to make the formal groups' efforts meaningful and effective in attaining the specific goals. These various types, extending through the entire organizational structure, give rise to various formal relationships existing among the managers of the organization units and these relationships are required to make the organization function as designed.

It will be helpful to reiterate at this point that we are discussing and setting forth *formal organizing* as the basis for organization study. Later, we will find that modifications as well as entirely new approaches to organizing are present and followed. But to complete our formal organization presentation we need to discuss the different types of authority and subsequent organizational relationships required. For purposes here, the discussion will be confined to the following:

1. Line authority.
2. Staff authority.
    a. Specialist staff.
        1. Advisory staff.
        2. Service staff.
        3. Control staff.
        4. Functional staff.
    b. Personal staff.
        1. "Assistant to."
        2. General staff.

Line authority

The superior-subordinate authority relationship whereby a superior makes decisions and tells them to a subordinate who in turn makes decisions and tells them to a sub-subordinate and so on, forms a line from the very top to the very bottom level of the organization structure. The line of authority so formed gives rise to the name "line authority." This line of authority consists of an uninterrupted series of authority steps and forms a hierarchical arrangement present in all formal organization types.

Line authority is easily understood by members of an enterprise. A superior exercises direct command over a subordinate; this is the essence of line authority. Each member knows from whom one receives orders and to whom one reports. A person with line authority has charge of and is responsible for the work of a unit and its *direct contribution* toward the goals of the enterprise. Line authority is sometimes called direct operative authority. A manager with line authority is called a line manager or line officer.

Staff authority

The word *staff* literally means a stick carried in the hand for support. Hence, staff authority *originally* meant authority used to support line authority. This concept exists today and is valid. Staff means support and is intended to help the holder of line authority or the "doer." With the passing of time additional meanings of staff authority, or what this help consists of, have developed and are currently in use.

In most enterprises the use of staff in organization structures can be traced to the need for help in handling details, locating data required for decisions, and offering counsel on specific managerial problems. In the Armed Forces, for example, an officer commanding a large group does not have the time or perhaps the specialized knowledge to secure all the information necessary to arrive at decisions which are vital to a campaign being waged. Most staff authority relationships are characteristically a manager-to-manager authority relationship and exist among any managerial levels of an organization structure. The managerial recipient of staff authority is commonly called a staff executive or staff officer.

Line and staff organization

When both line and staff authorities are included in an organization it is known as a line and staff organization. Figure 14–2 shows an organization structure indicating what organizational relationships are line and what are staff. The line part of this structure, which represents the line of authority, extends from the president down through the three fundamental organizational units including (1) to the production

FIGURE 14–2: A line-and-staff organization structure

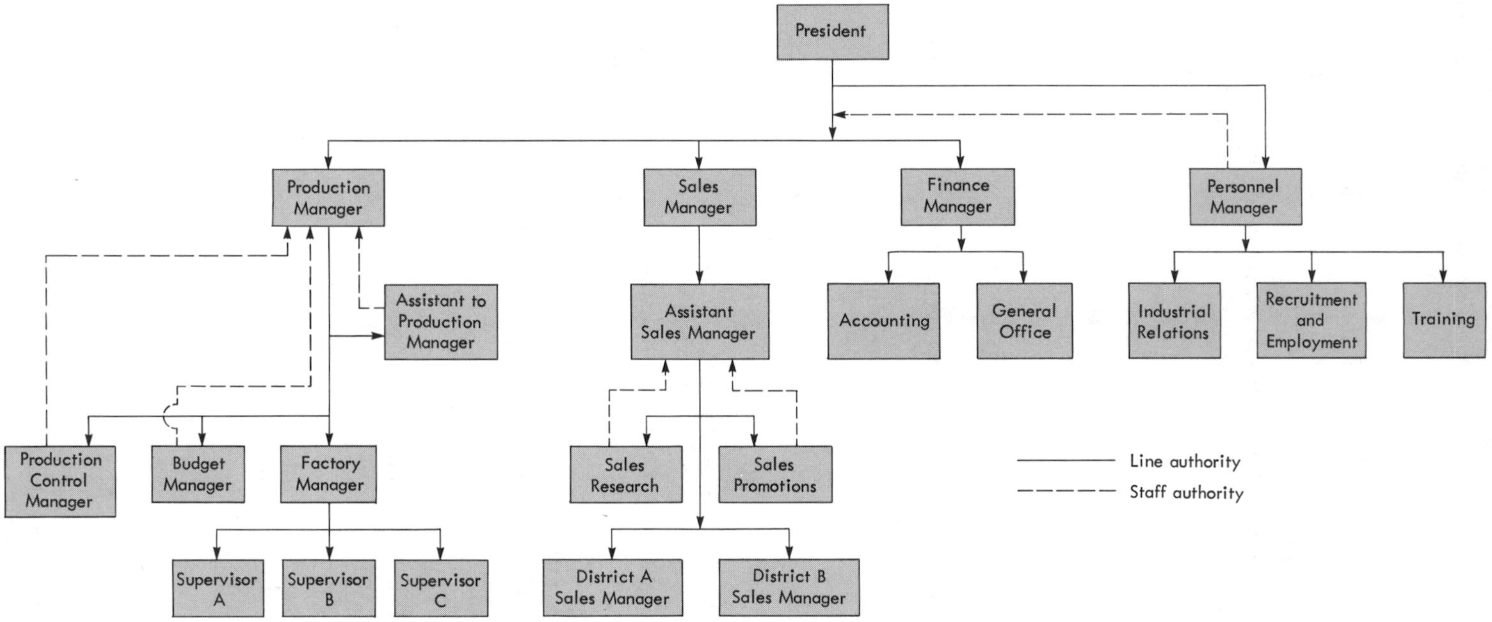

manager, factory manager, and three supervisors; (2) to the sales manager, assistant sales manager, and two district sales managers; and (3) to the finance manager, accounting, and general office. As drawn in the figure, the staff portion is represented by the production control manager and the budget manager under production, the sales research and sales promotions under the assistant sales manager, and the personnel manager reporting to the president. Observe that the line authority remains the avenue for direct performance of the work whereas the staff line exists to support the line. Also, generally speaking, most staff managers do *not* exercise their staff authority *along* the channels of line authority but rather *to* the line of authority. Also, it is helpful to remember that if the authority over the activities is *directly related* to the major objectives' accomplishment, the units are line. In contrast, if the authority over the activities is *indirectly related* to the major objectives' accomplishment, the units are staff.

Line–staff relations

In actual practice, the harmonious working together of line and staff management members encounters roadblocks; there are honest differences of opinion on who should decide what, which decision is best, and who takes what action when which decision is adopted. The difficulty is commonly a combination of the failure to (1) identify and utilize the staff authority, (2) recognize the true line-staff relationship, and (3) cope with a noncooperative behavior pattern by some management members.

Quite common is the line manager's complaint that staff people tend to grab credit for work that turns out successfully and lay the blame on line when the work does not. Staff managers tend to take advantage of the fact that they report and have frequent access to high line managers. It is easy for them to relate to the top line manager why a project is or is not successful. Another complaint is that staff assumes line authority. In their eagerness to inject their programs into what is done, they overstep their staff prerogatives and tend to "run the show." At one time most staff authority was advisory only; now a sizable portion of staff authority actually has mandatory power.[3] Furthermore, it is sometimes stated by line managers that staff assistance is impractical, unbalanced, and fails to take into account all the ramifications of the situation. What is offered stresses too much the staff's particular specialty. The big picture is ignored.

In contrast, those with staff authority do not always hold line managers in high esteem. From the staff viewpoint, difficulties in line-staff relationships commonly include that the line managers resist most new ideas and are too cautious and conservative. At times the line

---

[3] Discussion of different types of staff authority begins on p. 306.

manager is accused of ignoring the staff and wanting to run the department independent of staff support. Line has staff to help but doesn't make full use of it or calls it in too late to realize maximum benefits. Another common theme is that staff is not given proper and adequate authority. Staff authority managers are experts—they know more about their specialty than line, but they are not given the right kind and amount of authority to enforce their decisions.

What can be done to improve these relationships? A long list could be given, but suffice it to say: (1) acquire a better understanding of the basic authority relationships; (2) develop a clear concept of what the interrelationships of those with different type authority really are within the organization; and (3) stress interdependence, not separation of the various organization units and their respective managements. Better communication, clarifying the authority differentiation among various management members, emphasizing performance for the maximum benefits of the total enterprise, and holding members accountable for results are additional helpful means.

Organization is intended to achieve balanced teamwork. Consider a football team. Not every player can carry the ball, nor is every player a good lineman. You don't want a team made up all of fleet-footed halfbacks and pass receivers or all of good defensive tackles and guards. Playing good, hard, aggressive football requires a combination of different skilled players, each making decisions in a prescribed area of activity and performing certain individual actions which are well coordinated and executed. The mutual goal is well-known to all the players; and each contributes what that person can do best, when, where and in keeping with the overall plan and the group's or team's best joint efforts. Organizing in enterprises operates in a similar manner.

Advisory staff authority

The first type of specialist staff to be discussed is the advisory staff authority. Popularly associated with the term staff, it is of a specialized counseling nature to line managers. An advisory staff manager studies problems, offers suggestions, and prepares plans for the use and help of the line manager. The requirement is to recommend—to advise, not simply confirm and suggest only what the line person wants to hear. Usually the work of advisory staff can be accepted, modified, or rejected by the line manager. Advisory staff does not restrain line authority.

Advice is of little benefit unless it is utilized. To insure that the advisory staff will be used, the adoption of "compulsory staff service" is sometimes followed. This doctrine requires a line manager to listen to staff managers, but not necessarily to follow the advice they give.

The term "compulsory staff service" is unfortunate, since it is not compulsory in the sense of using the advice. Also, an advisory staff manager should talk with the line managers that will be affected by a proposed tentative recommendation before the staff manager submits it to their superior line manager. A recommendation that has cleared the managers who will be affected by it, and is so indicated by the staff manager, has an excellent chance of approval. The advisory staff person who is aloof, develops recommendations secretly, and refrains from listening to willing assistance of line managers may find suspicion and a prevailing negative attitude by others toward his or her work. The advisory staff manager's job is to sell, not tell, to advise, not to seek the advice of the superior on a problem. And the line manager should realize that she is receiving counsel, not command. What the line manager wants is help, not harassment.

The doctrine of "completed staff work" should be followed. This doctrine is outlined in Figure 14–3. All too frequently agreement to completed staff work is expressed but not put into practice.

FIGURE 14–3: Completed staff work doctrine of a company

1. As an advisory staff member, study your problem, prepare your answer, and present it in a *completed* form so that your superior need only approve or disapprove of your completed action.

2. Completed form means a finished, no-part-lacking presentation with all the necessary details included.

3. Refrain from piecemeal recommendations or asking your superior "what do you want done?" It is your job to supply what your superior should do with the problem being studied, to give answers, not ask questions.

4. The prescribed finished format need not necessarily be followed in your first presentation; one copy will suffice, but it should be neat and complete. The requirements covering the format, type of paper, and the number of copies can be met after your superior's decision is made on the recommendation.

5. Submit your completed form only after you can answer "yes" to this question: "As the superior would I be able to approve or disapprove this recommendation as it is presented in this report?"

Service staff authority

The manager with service staff authority has a service authority relationship, not an advisory relationship, to the line manager. Service units perform a service consisting of activities which have been separated from the line job. The formation and use of a service unit in organization is encouraged when the concentration of certain facilities to perform designated activities permit their more economical performance. The grouping of activities is made up usually but not always of the same or similar activities.

The formation of a service staff unit generally compels the line manager to use it because to continue to perform the work in the unit would be needless duplication. Hence line authority is restricted by the existence of service staff authority, and in this respect it differs from the relationship under advisory staff authority. In other words, the manager of a service unit typically makes decisions and enforces them concerning not only action within one's own unit but also action relating to one's unit facilitating the activities of other organizational units. One exercises line authority outside the unit, but has service staff authority from the overall viewpoint of the organization.

To illustrate, a factory manager (line authority) may request the product to be purchased (thus initiating the purchasing activity), but does not buy the product. The purchasing is performed by the purchasing department, a unit having service staff authority.

Control staff authority

Certain units have managers with staff authority who directly or indirectly exercise control over other units in an organization structure. Such managers are designated control staff authority managers and they realistically control directly by serving as an agent for a line manager or indirectly either through policy interpretation, procedural compliance, or reports and their interpretation supplied to line executives. The control staff authority manager does not simply advise; he or she controls. Control staff authority restrains line authority.

Examples of control staff include the extension of credit to customers, auditing, procedure for routing, expenditures, and inspection. The manager of inspection is an excellent illustration of control staff. The top illustration of Figure 14–4 shows the organization structure of a factory manager with three supervisors, A, B, and C. Each performs the inspection work of each's respective department. Assume there is sufficient inspection work to move it from each supervisor's unit and concentrate it in an inspection unit. This is illustrated by the bottom portion of Figure 14–4. The control unit is shown by the shaded area. The authority of the manager of the inspection unit is staff, yet that manager decides which products are acceptable and which are not and restrains the line authority of supervisors A, B, and C. Use of control staff authority (1) improves the caliber of inspection, (2) reduces the cost of inspection, and (3) permits specialization in inspection work.

Functional staff authority

For *specified activities* only, the authority of a manager may be exercised along lines other than the channels set up by the formal organization structure. This is done in the interest of convenience and

FIGURE 14–4

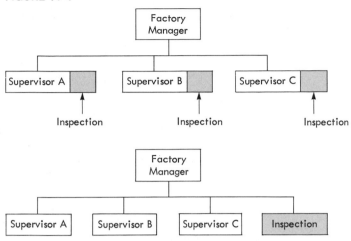

efficiency. Certain authority normally exercised by a line manager and concerning the restricted areas of activities will be delegated to another manager. Because such authority is specific or concerns certain functions only, it is called functional authority. It may be granted by either a line or a staff manager to another manager, who may be either line or staff. Where functional authority is authorized to operate, it restricts to a very large extent the normal authority in that area.

Figure 14–5 shows functional staff authority relationships in the production segment of an organization structure. For certain activities dealing with production and some dealing with production control,

FIGURE 14–5: Functional authority in organization structure

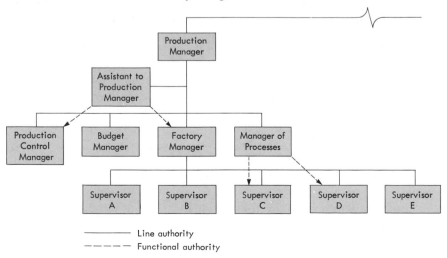

the production manager has authorized a staff person, the "assistant to" the production manager, to deal directly with the factory manager and the production control manager.[4] With functional staff authority the "assistant to" need not submit a recommendation to the production manager. Likewise, for specific activities, the manager of processes, a staff position, can work directly and with the authority of a line manager with supervisor's C and D. On activities outside the specified ones and in all matters concerning supervisors A, B, or E, the manager of processes counsels and gives recommendations to the factory manager, who is free to accept or to reject them.

If used indiscreetly, functional staff authority can damage line authority, destroy organizational departmentation, and bring chaos to organizing efforts. The extent to which functional staff authority should exist poses real difficulties. Some issues because of their specialized nature appear to require a competent staff person to interpret and presumably to administer in order to insure proper handling. Functional staff authority probably should be kept at a minimum so that the strength of line managers is maintained.

The "assistant to" manager

Turning our attention from the specialist to the personal staff authority type, the "assistant to" manager has no formal line authority but commonly has functional staff authority over a number of activities. A manager with this type authority can be viewed as a personal assistant with a limited set of duties and no major supervisory responsibilities. A major purpose for this type is to extend the superior line manager's capacity for handling a large volume of work which arises from a number of situations, such as (1) a large quantity of routine correspondence or documents must be processed, (2) understanding of technical material outside the experience of the superior is required, (3) many contacts, both outside and inside the organization are necessary, (4) time for the superior to exercise leadership and to visit and talk with subordinates is desired, (5) positions are needed for older, experienced executives requiring less strenuous managerial jobs, and (6) a training ground for the younger executives is desired.

However, some of these needs give rise to controversy. Many feel that the "assistant to" job become meaningless when the superior is away because people want to talk with the superior. This is true in some cases. The remedy is first, define by seniority and rank the status of the "assistant to" making certain that all understand and agree that communication and materials issued by the "assistant to" are those of the superior. Second, the superior must protect and back up his or her

---

[4] The status of the "assistant to" is that of a staff manager and is discussed in the immediate following pages of this chapter.

"assistant to." When the superior receives a complaint from a subordinate about a communication the "assistant to" issued, the superior should explain that he or she will inquire into it, check with the "assistant to," and if a reasonable explanation is received, explain the situation to the subordinate and show that the "assistant to" was acting reasonably and in line with the "assistant to's" authority. Another difference of opinion is that the "assistant to" position has limited value for training purposes for it does not include vital line experience. Another objection includes the distinct possibility of improper assignments of work within the scope of someone else being assigned to the "assistant to." Such a situation leads to misunderstanding and poor cooperation. No "assistant to" should be assigned work when he must rely on others for the fundamental execution of the assignment; the work should be assigned to the others. There are also some who fear that the "assistant to" may, in the name of the principal, or superior, take over the duties that rightfully belong to others. The person might even tend to create the impression that *he or she is the superior* rather than one who *is acting for the superior.* Furthermore, it is the belief of many that the title "assistant to" is inadequate. They suggest more appropriate terminology such as "special assistant," "executive assistant," "staff assistant," or "administrative assistant."

The assistant manager

Because the "assistant to" is frequently confused with the assistant, discussion of the latter at this time is appropriate. Unlike the "assistant to," the assistant manager is a line manager reporting directly to a line superior. When this line superior is the president of an enterprise, the title "executive vice president" may be given the assistant manager. In such cases the work might be divided, with the president handling overall planning, outside contacts, and public relations, and the executive vice president actually supervising the operations of the enterprise. Typically, the assistant manager does just what the title implies—assists the superior in fulfilling duties, directly supervises the subordinates, and acts for the superior. But frequently limitations are placed on the assistant manager's action, for example, to act for the superior only in the latter's absence, and to directly supervise subordinates in certain activities only.

Probably the best conditions under which the assistant manager can be used advantageously include those when the duties of the superior are heavy and the internal affairs to be handled are dynamic. Here the assistant can contribute effectively toward maintaining a fast output of heterogeneous work. Also a manager with direct line authority is available to keep the operations going during unavoidable absences of the superior. In addition, managerial work that necessitates much concentrated mental effort might best be handled by a manager with an assistant. The former can devote most of her energies to this type of work and avoid the interruptions caused by hour-to-hour affairs in her department—the assistant administering the normal operating affairs of the department. Finally, the assistant gains excellent training for the manager's job. He has line authority and is literally the one in charge.

On the other hand, some feel having an assistant manager is undesirable because it adds another organization level, thus hindering communication, and frequently it creates the situation of two rather than one doing a job without proper differentiation of activities. Also, by having an assistant, the principal may lose touch with the unit's activities, but it is possible for the assistant to keep up to date by means of spot checking and periodic reports concerning key activities. The question is also raised by critics that costs are increased. However, this depends upon the volume of work and individual circumstances.

The general staff

A second classification of the personal staff authority is the general staff. The military has used the general staff concept quite extensively, whereas in business the concept is relatively uncommon. General staff is a coordinated group which acts through its chief. Like other staff units, general staff may be advisory, service—usually in the sense of getting and supplying information—control, or functional, through supervisory activities. Action is taken and orders given in the name of the top executive or his office. In the general staff of the United States Army, for example, are G-1 Personnel, G-2 Intelligence, G-3 Operations, G-4 Supply, and G-5 Controller.

The general staff concept grew in response to a need to bolster a top manager's ability to handle large-scale operations. It has been employed with great success; yet in many instances it has proven very ineffective. A deciding factor apparently is the attitude and use the top manager makes of the general staff. Experience demonstrates that a practice of rotating general staff members to other areas and levels in the organization structure fosters their understanding for the line problems at lower levels. Staff members must keep aware of the ultimate results of their work. They should never be permitted to develop an immunity and sort of ivory-tower isolation to the realities of the situation.

ORGANIZATION CHARTS

As indicated on previous pages of this book, the customary arrangement of an organization chart is "top-down," that is, major functions at the top, successive subordinate functions in successively lower levels. But this is not the only way. Additional arrangements are (1) left-to-right, (2) circular, and (3) organizational chart and procedural flowchart. In the left-to-right chart, shown in Figure 14-6, the organization levels are represented by vertical columns, the flow of formal communication is from left to right. While not in common usage, the left-to-right chart offers advantages, including it (1) follows the normal reading habit of going from left to right, (2) visualizes the various organization levels clearly, (3) simplifies the understanding of how lines of command flow, (4) reveals quickly areas where organization levels are omitted by formal supervisory channels, (5) indicates relative length of lines of formal command, and (6) is compact and relatively simple to construct.

The circular chart, also shown in Figure 14-6, places the supreme position in the center of concentric circles. Functions making up the structure are clustered around this center in such a manner that the closer the position of the function to the center, the more important the function. Advantages of the circular chart include that it (1) portrays the actual condition of outward flow of formal command from the chief executive in many directions; (2) shows functions of equal importance clearly; (3) utilizes one dimension—from the center out—to indicate relative functional importance (the somewhat confusing "down from where" or "over from what" is eliminated); and (4) eliminates the undesirable concepts of bottom of the chart, top of chart, and the like, since a circular chart can be viewed from any direction.

The organization chart and procedural flowchart shown in Figure 14-7 (pp. 316-17) show the relationships among the various organization units with respect to a given actual work performance in the case of the illustration, for a purchasing procedure. The various functions and personnel involved in purchasing are highlighted on the organization chart at the upper portion of the figure. The purchases procedural flowchart at the bottom portion of the illustration depicts the various steps, in sequence, that take place in the purchasing procedure. To interpret the flowchart, follow the arrow lines and read each horizontal level, progressing downward on the chart. For example, beginning under stores, the requisition is made in duplicate, one copy going to accounts payable and the other to the purchasing agent.

Advantages in using an organization chart with a procedural flowchart include (1) an idea of the amount and the character of work performed in each organization unit is visualized, (2) the interrelation of activities within an organization are clearly revealed and unrelated activities are quickly spotted, and (3) procedural improvements and their relation to organization are shown—highly desirable information because improvements within the organization structure are commonly required in order to improve procedures.

FIGURE 14–6: Left-to-right (below) and circular (facing page) arrangements of organization charts

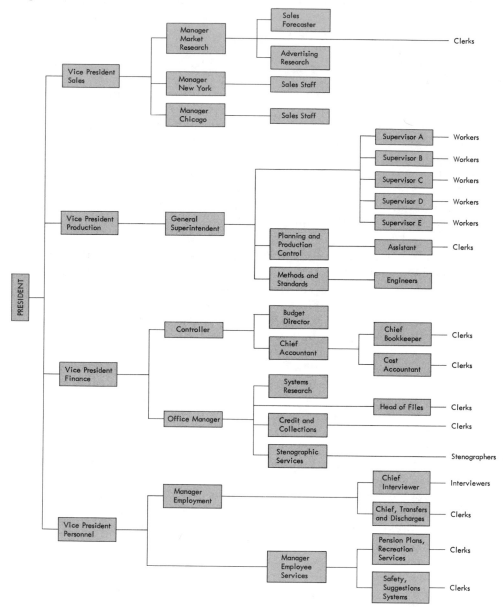

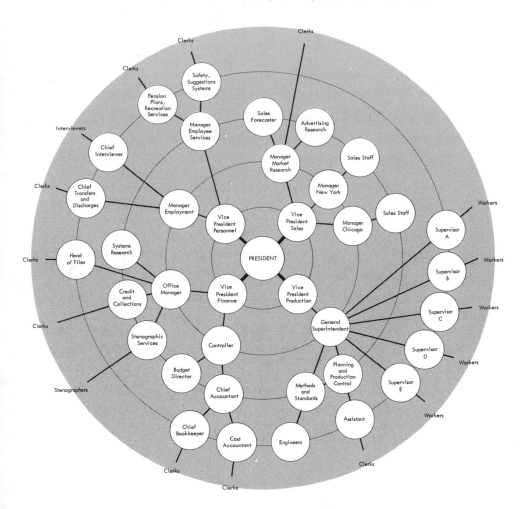

TITLES

A hierarchy of titles is expedited by use of an organization chart for it helps gain acceptance and gives meaning of the titles to all members of the enterprise. However, there are no standardized titles in relationship either to organization level or job content. The executive in charge of sales might be termed sales manager, general sales manager, director of distribution, or vice president in charge of sales. Furthermore that person can be at the top or intermediate organization level, and even though one is "sales manager," one may not perform precisely the same functions as other sales managers in other enterprises.

Preferably a title should serve two purposes: (1) help identify and define the nature of the work and its relative importance, and (2) indicate that the person possessing the title is competent and qualified to

FIGURE 14–7. Procedural flowchart for purchasing drawn in relation to organization chart to portray the interrelationship between the two

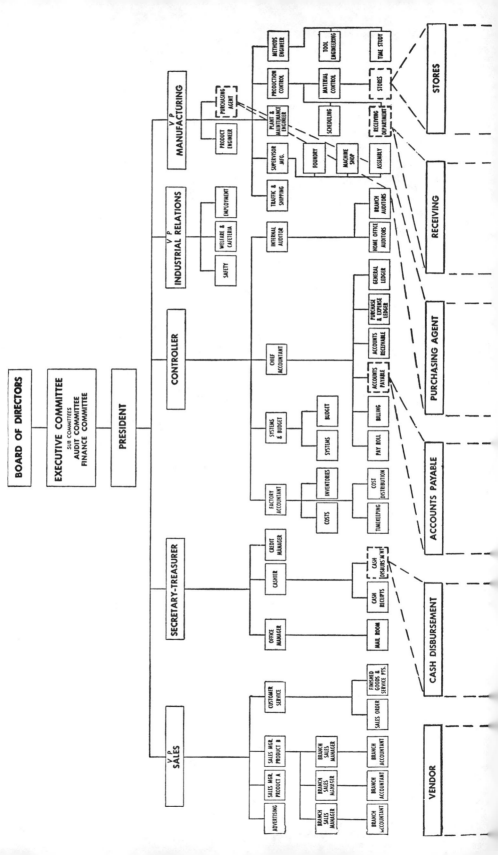

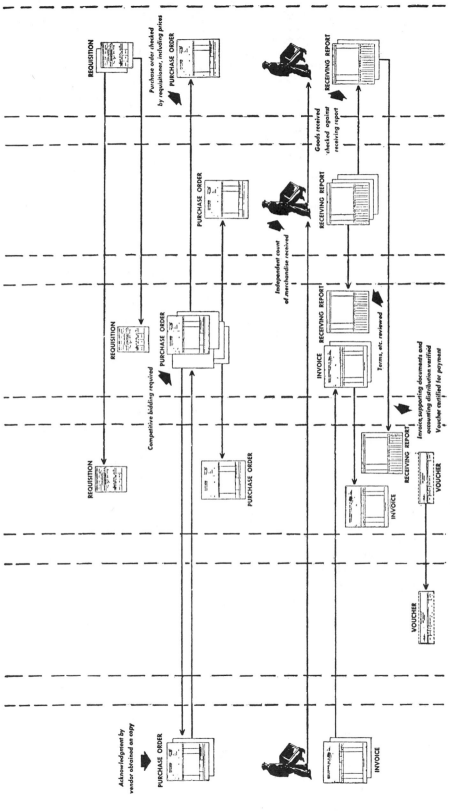

perform the tasks required in that position. A title is in the nature of a confidence; it signifies trust and faith in the individual and in that person's ability to see that the work is satisfactorily performed. It is not an embellishment, for to have worthwhile significance a title must be earned by the individual.

QUESTIONS

1. Does managerial authority have limitations? Justify your answer.
2. As you see it, what is authority and from whence does it come? Substantiate your answer.
3. Distinguish clearly between the two concepts in each of the following pairs: (*a*) completed staff work and compulsory staff service, (*b*) authority and power, and (*c*) tall organization and "flatten out" organization.
4. Does society influence the functioning of authority in an organization? Elaborate on your answer.
5. Define responsibility, and discuss the implications of your definition in the study of management.
6. Discuss the subject of line-staff relations in an organization.
7. Is the authority of a manager weakened by use of results management? Since authority and responsibility of a manager should be coequal, is your answer the same for the question, Is the responsibility of a manager weakened by use of results management? Justify your answers.
8. Discuss the meaning and the reasons for having fixed responsibility within an organization.
9. Give an example to show what is meant by one individual influencing the behavior of another by means of control of sanctions.
10. Discuss under what conditions you as a manager would be inclined to use a wide span of authority in your organization structure.
11. What are the advantages to a manager in using a left-to-right arrangement for an organization chart versus a top-down arrangement?
12. What actions may be taken to minimize the belief that the "assistant to" job is meaningless when the superior is absent? Discuss fully.
13. What is meant by each of the following: (*a*) authority of the situation, (*b*) computer authority, and (*c*) position authority. Use examples to illustrate your answers if you wish.
14. Explain Figure 14–7 in your own words.

CASE 14–1. CARR CORPORATION

Wally Zawacki (supervisor, Department 22, forming operations): You ask what my biggest problem is? I'll tell you. Too many bosses. That's it, too many bosses.

Tom Durkin (management trainee assigned to Clayton Wood, manager of manufacturing): Too many bosses, eh? Who, for example, is telling you what to do?

Wally: This smart guy from PIC (Production and Inventory Control) is always butting in with some change or asking silly questions. When I complain to Chet [Chester Jennings, general supervisor of metal work] he tells me, "I'm your boss. I'll tell you what do do."

Tom: Does he?

Wally: Yes, he keeps assigning me work, but he never gets this PIC guy off my back. I've told the guy from PIC to talk with Chet, not me, but he keeps coming to me and keeps me from getting my work finished on time.

Tom: Does the man from PIC talk with others out here in the factory?

Wally: I think he does. Barney [Barney LaSota, supervisor of Department 31] has complained to me about the same thing.

Tom: What does the PIC man say to you or what does he want to know?

Wally: Oh, all kinds of things. To speed up the work on an order, check on my inventory, if machine 172 is operating—just about everything.

The manager of production engineering is on par with the PIC manager. Both of them report directly to Mr. Wood. Tom Durkin was told by the manager of production engineering that he always gave information to either Mr. Wood or to one of the three general supervisors, handling respectively metal work, large machines, and small machines. These general supervisors, in turn relayed the information down the organization. The production engineering manager does not believe it is good organizational practice to either issue directives or secure information directly from the supervisors.

Subsequent study by Durkin revealed that the purchasing manager, reporting directly to Mr. Wood, buys all factory materials and supplies. Although reporting to Mr. Wood, the purchasing manager has complete authority over this function. About the only contact with Mr. Wood is when a request is made to try and speed up delivery of a lot of material that the factory needs.

Questions

1. Draw the organization chart based on the information provided.
2. Indicate authority type relationships that currently exist within this organization. Identify each type.
3. What recommendations to improve the organization can you offer? Discuss fully.

CASE 14–2. GORDON COMPANY

President Katherine F. Keith believes strongly that the company should establish an International Office in its present organizational structure to serve more adequately the increasing business being done with customers in Europe, South America, and the Middle East. She also would like to eliminate much of the present paperwork throughout the entire organization. She has discussed these objectives with her top management team including the five managers of materials, finance, production, sales, and personnel. All agree that the goals are desirable and further suggest that the entire present organization be reviewed to determine where desirable change might be made.

Reporting to the manager of materials is (1) the manager of procurement with two buyers and (2) the manager of inventory control with three senior clerks. A large portion of the company's business is wood products which are produced by four departments making up the Wood Products Division consisting of departments each headed by a management member of cutting, assemblying, finishing, and receiving and shipping. There is a manager in charge of the wood products division.

The legal counsel, a staff position, reports to the manager of finance. Also at one level reporting to the finance manager are the managers respectively of auditing, taxes, cost accounting, general accounting, credit and collections, and computer processing. At a lower level, but reporting directly to the finance manager are respectively the managers of payroll, billing, and leasing. The top production manager has an assistant to whom three managers report. They are in charge of engineering and research, metal products, and wood products. Below the assistant production manager is an advisory production cost reduction expert. Reporting to the metal products manager are the four department heads of spinners, welding, painting, and receiving and shipping. Above these management members and below the metal products manager is a quality control department consisting of a supervisor and two employees.

The company's distributive arrangement includes three sales regional offices: New York City from which five sales representatives travel; Atlanta which has three sales representatives; and Saint Louis with a like number. There is a very capable "assistant to" the sales manager. In addition, there is (1) a market research manager with three technicians and (2) an advertising manager with two helpers, both managers reporting to the sales manager. Reporting to the personnel manager are a manager of recruiting, selecting, and personnel maintenance; a wage administrator; and a manager of personnel records and services.

Questions

1. Draw the formal organization chart of the company.
2. Point out at least three areas for organizational improvement. Explain fully why you feel organizational improvement is possible in these areas.

3. What is your recommendation regarding the addition and location of an international organizational unit? Justify your views.

4. Can organizational improvement aid in reducing the amount of paperwork now performed by the company? Why?

5. What is your reaction to the company establishing a separate organization for the sale of metal and for wood products (the same as now exist for the production of these products)? Elaborate on your beliefs.

CASE 14–3.   KENYON-WERNER COMPANY

Helen Snelling is executive secretary to Mr. Evans, a cautious, retiring, and quiet man. She was transferred to his office about four months ago when the Louisville regional sales office of the company was closed. Top managers hoped to provide Mr. Evans with expert help by assigning Ms. Snelling, whose personnel record showed her to be capable, highly efficient, ambitious, somewhat impatient, and the possessor of a quick temper. She is 28 years old.

Reporting to Mr. Evans are James Root, head of accounting; Hortense Higgins, head of order writing; Francis Green, head of production scheduling; Beth Cooper, chief of switchboard operators and receptionists; and Henry Schwartz, chief of the mailroom. James Root, age 46, knows accounting very well, but he is not too good an administrator. He is inclined to let chores other than accounting work be unduly delayed and seems to have little perception of human relations problems within his unit. Well-liked and accommodating, he is accepted by his employees, but the top managers do not view him as a heavyweight to assume higher management responsibilities in the company.

In view of delay and uncertainty displayed by Mr. Evans, Helen Snelling is inclined to take action on those matters that, in her opinion, need attention. Usually her decisions have proven quite effective, but other members of the department object to her grabbing authority that doesn't belong to her. To illustrate, about two weeks ago, Ms. Higgins, age 50, and Ms. Snelling got into a verbal scuffle about priority in completion of the order writing for certain customers. The issue was settled by Mr. Evans, who decided it in favor of Ms. Higgins. Then he had a talk with Ms. Snelling about taking it easy and the folly of being too aggressive in business relationships. Only two days ago, during the lunch hour, Ms. Snelling answered Mr. Root's telephone, took a request for some records to be sent to the purchasing director, secured the wanted records from the file, and sent them to the purchasing director. Mr. Root found out about the request yesterday and spoke with Ms. Snelling about it. He stated that she was overstepping her prescribed duties and the least she could have done would have been to tell him about it or leave a note on his desk. Ms. Snelling said she did write him a note and was only trying to help. Mr. Root emphasized that he would not tolerate any interference by her and that he intends to report the incident to Mr. Evans. Later, in searching through papers on his desk, he found the note referred to by Ms. Snelling.

It is the opinion of Ms. Snelling that the people reporting directly to Mr. Evans are taking advantage of him and have been doing so for a long time. He is so buried in details that he delays many financial decisions. She is certain that the management personnel of the finance group are going in all different directions and that Mr. Evans doesn't realize this. In her own mind, Ms. Snelling is positive that her dealings with various heads within the finance group are for the best interests of the company. She also feels certain that the subordinates of Mr. Evans go ahead and decide issues, sometimes poorly, when the final decision should come from Mr. Evans, or at least with sanction by him and knowledge of what decision has been made.

Questions

1. What is the problem as you see it?
2. What important factors do you believe contributed to the present state of affairs? Elaborate on your answer.
3. What plan of action would you recommend to remedy the problem stated above? Discuss.

Chapter 15

Human behavior in the organizational environment

One never finds life worth living.
One always has to make it worth living.
Harry Emerson Fosdick

While the classical or traditional organization structure discussed in the two previous chapters is widely used, easily understood, and works reasonably well, it has been criticized by some management practitioners and students. In their opinion, this structure is too mechanistic, its goals are incompatible with those of its members, it encourages job defensive behavior, inhibits innovation, and hinders communication. More specifically, they contend that the specialization of work, the defining of spans of authority, the "one worker—one boss" concept, and management established objectives, standards, and work activities are inadequate and overlook human nature and the needs of people. Further, it is claimed that formal procedures and controls actually violate human rights and inhibit productivity. What is needed is loose organization not a tight hierarchy, human emphasis not technical emphasis, consultation not command, and multidirectional communication not vertical communication.

EMERGING CONCEPTS: THE ADAPTIVE ORGANIZATION

During the past several decades, the advance in information about human relations, the changing attitude of society to the individual and to the group, and technological innovations have brought a strong impact upon formal organization. In its pure form the formal organization is unable to accomodate the change that is required to meet current demands. For example, to adapt to the frequent changes caused by technological improvements, some advocate organizations should be of the temporary task force type. In addition, our judgment, understanding, and behavior, for example, performed in what we consider to be in the best interests of the company, may not coincide with what our superior or the formal organizer had in mind that we should do. We know that a manager brings attitudes and values to a job and these same characteristics influence one's work, perception, and beliefs utilized in applying the modified management process approach. Further, the organization environment permits the manager to develop good attributes or acquire bad ones, satisfy social needs or block them, and provide a sense of achievement and self-assertion or frustrate the manager in seeking these desires.

Therefore, for practical reasons, modification in the formal organization is taking place simply because all the details cannot be formally spelled out and we are dealing with human beings who interpret what they should do, are anxious to use their ideas, want recognition, and honestly feel they are improving and making the formal organization practical and workable under today's conditions. In the vernacular, "they want a piece of the organization action."

In fact, probably the major reason for modifying formal organization is the influence upon and the importance of people in organization. Regardless of the size or pattern, organization is always subject to the unpredictable initiative and responses of the individual members making up that organization. And these qualities remain human even when the humans are pressured for conformity and cohesion. Dictatorial managers learn this too late and usually to their sorrow.

But note this important fact: the formal organization commonly serves as a basis from which a modified, hybrid, or even a revolutionary form of organization is evolved. After all, organization is one of the activities that a manager uses to achieve both human and economic objectives and it is reasonable to expect modifications—even radical changes—in a structure in order to achieve the intended goals. And this is exactly what is happening. Participation, authority-acceptance by employees, and group effort to deal with modern complexities have become more common and an organization to accomodate them has won favor.

Some companies emphasize free-form organization which is characterized by a high degree of authority decentralization and few controls. Others retain strong planning and controlling—accurate projections, detailed plans, and proven methods. In all history of organizing, there appears the eternal question of proper balance between organizational efficiency and individual freedom. Scholars have never agreed precisely on what the proper balance is or how it should be accomplished. Some have envisioned individuals as selfish and aggressive and hence advocate groups organized to preserve peace, order, a desirable ethical conduct, and to achieve economical and social gains. But, in any organization that defends, protects, and makes possible the achievement of greater goals than otherwise possible, can the individual uniting with the group remain practically as free as before? The challenge is to obtain a balance of individual initiative and freedom of action with guidance and restraint. And to do this can all the members participate satisfactorily in the decision-making process concerning that organization?

The general nature of organization gives rise to the problem for we are concerned with imponderables dealing with the interactions among the characteristics of people and the task climates provided by organization. In the overall, do we gain more from permitting motivational situations within which we behave or from carefully defined relationships known to all and to which the individual, if necessary, must adopt? That is to say, all things considered, we live the best life, economically, psychologically, and socially, by working and behaving within a carefully prescribed and rational work situation, or we find more comfort in relatively unstructured situations in which people form and re-form into different work-oriented groups to perform present tasks and plan to overcome future work problems?

All this suggests that the best structure is probably adaptive to the required basic individual needs, and features a spirit of innovation and flexibility to meet changing demands. It includes the interaction of the key variables and balances them in keeping with the desired outputs of the organization. No one type of structure is universally appropriate. Questions such as these aid in developing thoughts about the suitability of the organization: Do we tend to cling to the present structure when confronted with new situations? Are the management members inclined to be intolerant of criticism? Is there a viable program for identifying the value of our human resources, encouraging and permitting them to utilize their full talents in contributing to the accomplishments of the organization?

NONFORMAL ORGANIZATION

Existing within formal organization is nonformal organization that permits and sometimes encourages behavior by members not intended or included in the formal organization. This nonformal behavior cannot only be desirable, which frequently it is, but it is also work oriented and contributes significantly to efficiency. Behavioral factors such as unnecessary socializing on the job, group values, and cultural likes and dislikes serve as bases for nonformal behavior in formal organization. These unintended conditions permit the examination of behavior in terms of *dysfunctions*, which are the characteristics or aspects of formal organization that cause unintended or unanticipated behavior.

In other words, nonformal organization results from the presence of formal organization dysfunctions. Whether it exists or not depends upon people—their behavior, reactions and beliefs about the particular dysfunctions. Strictly speaking, in pure formal organization thinking, the existence of dysfunctions is not recognized.

Dysfunctions are many, but probably structure, differentiation as to the type of decisions different members can make, and specifications of work processes are of greatest importance. Structure, for example, may give rise to communication blocks—by slighting prescribed channels or by the subordinate not revealing complete information to a superior because the subordinate believes it is to one's best interest not to report bad news or poor results to one's superior, especially if the superior evaluates performance of subordinates. In other words, the formal organization itself may tend to generate unanticipated behavior. Or consider the effect of formally spelled-out work processes. They can be dysfunctional in that they may not be applicable to all situations of the job, may cover the job only partially, or may conflict with orders given by a specialist. A person tends to condition any job that person occupies. One brings more than a physical body to perform prescribed work motions. Also present are impressions, interests, ambition, views, and feelings toward the person's job, compeers, superiors, subordinates, as well as all these toward that person.

Nonformal organization always exists along with formal organization. It serves as an adjunct, is intangible, and takes on different degrees of importance depending upon the activity and the person involved. A manager should be aware of the presence and influence of nonformal organization.

INFORMAL ORGANIZATION

There is also informal organization which is quite a different concept from either formal or nonformal organization. Whenever people work together there evolve informal groups bound together by common social, technological, work, or goal interests. Such a group constitutes an informal organization. It conditions many actions set forth by the formal and nonformal organizations and must be reckoned with in managerial organization. The leader of an informal organization is called an informal leader.

The specific determinants of informal groups are usually interests, similarity of work, and physical location. Employees having common interests tend to seek each other, discuss their common interests, and socialize. People like to be with people they know and, in turn, know them. Having mutual interests helps bring about this favorable condition. Performing the same type of work is a common determinant of informal groups. Here again there is a mutuality among such employees; they have job satisfactions that are common, confront similar problems, and talk about subjects high on each other's priority lists. Likewise, location is important. Frequent face-to-face meetings and being in close proximity while at work influence who is in an informal group and who is not. There are also other determinants including almost any common course which the person feels is personally important. Usually groups formed because of these "other determinants" are temporary and disintegrate after an objective or want has been satisfied or no longer exists. Many informal organizations are of this type. They can be viewed as spontaneous organizations. Usually such organizations do not emerge from following a rational plan. In contrast, groups formed because of interests, similarity of work, and physical location tend to be permanent.

Nothing destroys these informal groups for the very action of grouping people together to work toward common goals gives rise to these groups. It is in the nature of human behavior and of organization. Hence, a manager should utilize the informal organization because it is a part of the total organization facility. It is appropriate, for example, for the manager to point out his or her views to the informal leader and support them with the reasons, release accurate information, listen when the leader of the informal group speaks, and prior to making a decision, consult with the group on matters which are of deep concern to them.

To determine the structure of an informal group, analysis taking into account the measurement of social elements and interpersonal relationships is used. For example, an individual's expression of preference to associate with others who enhance one's feeling of satisfaction and personal worth is given high priority. For survival, the informal group requires continuing relationships among its members, and it has communication of its own variety, usually entirely apart from the formal communication prescribed by the formal organization. Further, it has what might be termed a scale of status values peculiar to itself. Also, the identifying and determining of the leader's characteristics have been subjected to much study, and a considerable amount of information on this subject is available.

Let us consider an example of the informal organization in action. This case deals with a distortion of an official procedure as set forth from the formal organization. At the main office of a restaurant chain the manager of planning and the manager of purchasing discussed the problem of inadequate stock of several items at many of the restaurants. Complaints from the local restaurant managers had been received for several months about stock-outs. The planning and purchasing managers decided the difficulty stemmed from the program being used by the computer to calculate the quantities to be purchased and delivered to the restaurants. Talking with the programming manager, they succeeded in getting a change made in the program. This change affected not only the stock-outs, but many other items as well. All three managers were aware that they were changing an official procedure without formal approval from the vice president of operations and the committee established to review all changes in computer programs. But they honestly believed that their action was in order because it solved a sticky and bothersome problem and offered an immediate solution whereas any formal review and consideration would require at least two months. Subsequently, it was found that the change did indeed take care of the stock-outs, but it also created a surplus in other items and, in total, an excess inventory at most of the restaurants.

THE BEHAVIOR VIEWPOINT

What we are saying is that the formal organization with its hierarchy of positions and tasks, is constantly being modified by the behavior of an individual member or of a group membership. Within the formal organization are inexorable forces which give rise to the nonformal organization and the informal organization. Back of the formal organization are the invisible nonformal and informal organizations through which much of the work is accomplished and no enterprise can exist without them. In some cases only these adjunct organizations will permit timely action. A vast number of contacts are made among people in the nonformal and informal organizations to solve problems, pass information along, and to achieve certain goals. Ideally, these adjunct organizations are compatible with the formal organization. However, with their ever-shifting and undefined structures, the nonformal and informal organizations are vulnerable to manipulation and opportunism. And it is commonly difficult to detect these perversions which can do considerable harm if not corrected.

Hence, it is paramount to understand why people behave as they do and especially within the organization environment. As pointed out in Chapter 2, the behavior and beliefs of people result in patterns called "cultures." All organizations have cultures which affect the conduct and the working of people together. A significant aspect of culture is the way it develops informally in an organization.

When writing about human behavior and organization, a key consideration is custom because much of our behavior is the result of custom. We get used to doing things in a certain manner, never really giving it much thought, let alone being rational or consciously determining a way of behavior. Customs become formulated mainly by means of experience. If we do a certain task a certain way and normally get certain acceptable results, we are inclined to do the same task in the same manner whenever it arises. In short, we develop a custom to be followed for this type of task. Customs become established with use. Simply to define duties and authority as done in formal organization does not make them customary behavior; they have to be accepted in actual use. Normally, if formal plans and instructions are not insisted upon by the manager, the subordinate will evolve the work pattern, and with usage this pattern will become the custom. When emphasis is placed on results and the results via custom are satisfactory, the importance of informal employee behavior in management is easily discernible.

In addition, most people have mental images of how an employee in a certain job should behave i.e., what that person's role is. We expect a production control manager to behave in a certain way and a sales manager to behave in a different way. These expected roles tend to influence the actions of their occupants. To fulfill expectancies, i.e., acquire acceptance socially by other members of the organization, most people strive to play the role expected of them. We dislike the director of research making light of basic research results obtained by members of that department or the company medical doctor not behaving as a true professional in his chosen line of work.

What can be done when there are honest differences in the desirability of an existent strong custom or in the formal concept of a job in comparison to the incumbent's views based on experience and preferences? With time, these differences will probably change, but it is unrealistic to expect them either to change rapidly or perhaps to move eventually in a direction exactly in keeping with the manager's wishes. The manager may find that one's best action is to get to know the members' behavior patterns better and figure out ways to utilize them. Or corrective change, as he or she sees it, may be preferred, but this may be unreasonably difficult, take too much time, and cost many dollars. However, if some modifications in behavior appear feasible, the manager may take any or all of the following actions: (1) explain what change is desired and give complete reasons for the change, (2) relate specifically how the change will benefit both the organization and the incumbent, (3) give examples and provide opportunities to demonstrate the suggested new behavior, and (4) encourage with rewards the incumbent who adopts the new for the old behavior.

Many believe that organization enhances favorably the behavior of a person, or at least the benefits outweigh the deficits. They argue that great personalities, leaders, and truths are made more effective by organization. The development, support, and accomplishment of worth-while goals are made possible by organization in which most members progress, the big people become bigger, and great people become greater. Without organization, they would descend rather than ascend. Organization supplies the needed facility for group study, cooperation, and mutual assistance, while at the same time it places the individual in a situation that challenges, stimulates, and develops that person's behavior so that it is favorable both to the person and to society.

SOCIAL INFLUENCES AND ORGANIZATION

The increasing attention being directed to behavioral aspects in organization has likewise brought emphasis to the societal factors of this function of management. Today an organization is a social entity as well as an economic arrangement. The justification for any organization is to provide goods or services required or desired by the society of which the organization is a part. And it must have the financial means to operate and survive. If organization is to serve and be a part of society, it needs to supply not only economic wants but also social and psychological needs of its members that should come from being a part of an organization.

Organizing can be viewed as representing a major part of environment from which stimuli emit that affect most people. In brief, from a person's environment, influences affect the individual who, in turn, responds to these influences. Hence, a person's behavior is conditioned by the organization of which that person is a part. Likewise, the person affects the organization. There is interaction between the individual and the organization; an individual becomes imbedded in the organization and features of the organization became embedded in the individual. One man, for example, may be stimulated by the organization to accomplish what he did not believe possible for him or, in contrast, suppressed by his organization stimuli to perform only what is required "to get by" and to say things he doesn't mean.

In management organizing, much of the interest in social influences upon the behavior or on group members cluster around either (*a*) conformity, or (*b*) change. Conformity to a group's standards is an outstanding example. Some of a group member's job satisfaction is received by means of group responses. To get too far removed from the group's standards can mean that the group's approval and acceptance of an individual may be lost. Furthermore, this conformity to a group's standards is illustrated by holding factory output to an accepted level informally set by the group. The individual member who exceeds it is promptly reminded of what the acceptable level of production is. This is a social group determinative. Interestingly the reverse situation is frequently found among a group of salespeople where higher and higher sales are sought and accepted by the group as approved behavior. In fact, the behavior of low sales producers may be viewed with disdain by the group members.

Changes tend to be accepted with a minimum of resistance when the change is initiated from within the group. People usually dislike change that destroys that to which they have become accustomed, primarily because the change is likely to break up established social relationships. In other words, we usually dislike giving up known present satisfactions for unknown future satisfactions. It should also be noted that typically the group supplies many beliefs and values to its individual members. In essence, the group influences attitudes toward many matters. For example, the prevailing belief of an individual frequently stems not from a personal knowledge or conviction about a matter, but from statements and "truths" provided by the group of which the person is, or wants to be, a part.

Ignoring social considerations is, in part, the answer to why a formal arrangement of functions according to a well-conceived, rational pattern does not assure automatically that sought results will be realized or that arrangement X will prove superior to arrangement Y purely because the activities in X are grouped more effectively. The simple truth is that the effect of the human beings and their social groups play a vital role in whether the results of organizing prove a success or a failure. What employees do to and for each other, their commonness of purpose, and their ability to make sound judgments and initiate proper action are fundamental considerations in the effectiveness of an organization.

INTERPERSONAL CONFLICTS IN ORGANIZATION

As pointed out in Chapter 4, conflict among members of an organization appears to be common. When confronted with conflict, a person quite likely adopts a form of behavior known as a defense mechanism. This is a person's way of enduring the conflict or living with the problem which commonly is exemplified by an insurmountable barrier preventing the accomplishing of a wanted satisfaction from the work efforts. The type of defense mechanism adopted depends upon the particular situation and especially upon the person. People differ as to what defense they take as well as to what limits of frustration they endure.

Among the more common types of defense mechanisms are (1) aggression, (2) regression, (3) resignation, and (4) compromise. *Aggression* identifies behavior that is attacking, assaulting, or taking the offensive against an offending person. It includes physical violence, but most examples in management are nonviolent such as spreading rumors about another whom is disliked, openingly accusing others of poor decision making, or speaking in a derogatory manner about a plan or program which is not favored.

Regression is characterized by retreating or retiring. Pouting and losing emotional control typify the person using a regressive defense mechanism. Likewise, emphasizing the past when it is assumed one's psychological wants were satisfied is a common type of regression and serves ideally as a defense against current realities.

Resignation, as implied by its name, is giving up. The belief is strong that there is no use trying. The job, fellow employees, and the total organization will not permit the gaining of job satisfaction. The best solution, at least for the time being, is to avoid the barrier by accepting the unsatisfactory work existence as best the person can.

Compromise includes changing the objectives, actually or symbolically, to relieve the frustration. For example, the person may claim that accomplishment of the initial satisfactions sought is really not wanted now, or a new goal along with new satisfactions are adopted. Commonly false reasons to explain present behavior are offered, believing such an approach will give protection and satisfaction.

It usually proves helpful to view conflict as an integral part of organizational life. As previously stated, it is not all bad; in fact, it can provide good qualities. For example, conflict can stimulate creativity and improve management. In many cases it prods the desire for self-defense and to increase the energy to do the tasks. Also, a greater diversity of viewpoints may help in revealing the best ideas. And it certainly makes each side more aware of their beliefs, their reasons why, and their own identities.[1]

To achieve these advantages, however, several essential conditions must be established. First, a mutual goal must exist. If the conflict stems from the participants seeking separate goals, attempts to alleviate the conflict is almost certain to be futile and frustrating. Second, the parties must have a common area of difference, known and agreed to by each side, that is, agreement on what they are disagreeing about is essential. No constructive help will emerge if the difference or problem itself is not clearly defined and mutually agreed to. Third, listening must be practiced by the contenders. "Hear the other person out" is an excellent slogan to follow. When each party sincerely strives to know and understand what the other party is saying, and can state the other's side not only objectively but also in a form acceptable to an opponent, a creative solution to the conflict is being formulated and probably is near at hand.

ORGANIZING AND THE CONTINGENCY APPROACH

To reiterate, the contingency approach in management stresses that the proper managerial actions to be taken in any case depend upon the particular variables of the total situation. The management function of organizing is strongly conditioned by the particular environment pres-

---

[1] See discussion of conflict in chapter 4, pp. 83–86.

ent or the one that is desired. In essence, the contingency theory (sometimes called the situational theory) points out that there is no single organization design that is superior for all conditions. The best one is the one that works best for the given total conditions and this is dependent upon the environment with which the organization must cope. That is to say the organization design according to the contingency theory is conditional in nature. When routine processes and differentiation predominate in the environment, a control-oriented behavior is acceptable. In contrast, when the processes are heuristic, the emphasis on integrated, change-oriented behavior seems more appropriate. Economic, social, and technological conditions plus human resources are among the important variables affecting the contingent organization design.

To illustrate, organization A in which the situation involves detailed, repetitive work performed in a mechanistic manner differs from organization B in which the work is nonrepetitive and requires much creativity. The structure, relationships, and interpersonal reactions of A compared with B will be significantly different. Another contingency factor pertinent to organization design is the stability of the business which is reflected in the environmental stability of the organization. A company trying to cope with highly cyclical sales and keeping abreast of fast moving technological changes normally will have a relatively unstable environment compared to a company with fairly constant sales throughout the year and little change in processing efforts. We might also note that with generous financing available, one company may resort to much automation with the resultant effect upon its organization whereas another company with limited funds uses much manual labor—a situation which influences the organization followed.

The important point here is that organization is contingent upon the important factors of its particular situation or environment. The contingency theory clearly emphasizes this principle.

ADDITIONAL THEORIES OF ORGANIZING

From studies to improve organization have emerged a number of theories on organization. In addition to what has already been discussed, the following theories merit consideration: (1) the fusion theory, (2) the systems theory, and (3) the quantitative theory.

The *fusion theory* of organization stresses the existence and action of a fusion process in organizing. Advocates state that an organization attempts to use the individual to further its goals, and vice versa, the individual hopes to achieve his or her goals by using the organization. Emphasis is upon behavior, dealing largely with role, not job, modification. The individual seeks, for example, possession of means, harmony, freedom of decision, and optimum performance by a "personalizing process." In turn, the organization provides a "socializing process," illustrated by work assignment and the practice of rewards and penalties. The "fusion process" brings about the fusion of the personalizing and the socializing processes.[2]

Under the *systems theory* organizing is viewed as a system of mutually dependent variables. It is similar in approach to the systems school of management thought discussed in Chapter 2. The basic parts of the organizing system are (1) the individual, (2) the formal organization or arrangement of functions, (3) the informal organization, (4) reciprocal patterns of behavior arising from role demands of the organization and role perception of the individual, and (5) the physical environment in which the work is performed.[3] The area of application of the theory can be extensive, both within and without the enterprise, or it can be intensive, applying to a specific and definite group. The terms *open system* and *closed system* identify these possibilities. Linking the basic parts are communication, balance or system parts maintained in harmonious relationship with each other, and decision making.

Another is the *quantitative theory* which provides an aura of objectivity to the study of organizing, even though it covers only a portion of the considerations that affect organizing work. For example, leadership, environment, and communication are excluded in the analysis. These pose difficulties in measuring, but of course, available arbitrary values can be either derived or assumed and utilized in the theory. Countable factors are employed for such factors as size of organization unit, number of decisions made by each manager, and the amount of work produced. No doubt mathematical models will be perfected for the study of organizing. In fact, some very interesting work is being done in this area, but as yet it does not constitute a complete theory.

TRADITION AND ORGANIZATION

Tradition has significant influence upon the effectiveness and survival of an organization. Tradition supplies that intangible thrust made up of an evolving system of assumptions, habits of mind, and customary behavior which gives an organization distinct characteristics. It can be viewed as what keeps an organization operating when membership or leadership change, even drastically. Tradition supplies the momen-

---

[2] E. Wright Bakke, *The Fusion Process* (New Haven: Yale University Labor and Management Center, 1953), pp. 7–34.

[3] Informal organization is discussed on pp. 326–28.

tum in human behavior to keep the efforts going so that many duties in complex operations are performed with minimum formal direction.

Tradition supplies the needed ingredient that permits pride by employees in their organization and in their work to exist. Whether being a member of ABC organization sets one apart or does not, depends more on the tradition in that organization than anything else. However, periodically tradition needs updating, but this is difficult to do because of the very nature of tradition. Briefly, when traditions get out of hand and require corrective measures, the needed action must be started at the top of the organization. This leads to the fundamental statement that tradition results from and is conditioned by the projection of past leadership.[4]

The influence of dedication, excellence, service, and loyalty are deep-seated and consciously respected to a reasonable extent in the church, university, and hospital organizations. The transmittal of these traditions from generation to generation with such a high degree of effectiveness is prime evidence of the heights to which human behavior can influence organization.

In addition, tradition is important in handling change. Most individuals abhor suddenness and it is helpful for the manager to remember that necessary change should be permitted to proceed in keeping with the active basic tradition present within the organization. Also, the change that has the most influence on basic tradition is that of human beings, not processes or machines.

THE PETER PRINCIPLE

When job demands, including knowledge, skill and role (how others expect the person to behave in the job), exceed the ability of the person, the condition is described as a demand overload. The person is performing to his or her maximum capacity yet cannot meet the job demands. According to the well-known Peter Principle everyone eventually faces this condition. Discussion of the principle, written in a humorous style, actually reflects much truth.[5] The principle states that every person in a hierarchy tends to rise to the level of his or her incompetence. That is, an employee starts off competent, then rises, through promotion, to a position where she or he is not competent to perform prescribed work.

The major weakness in this reasoning is, of course, the ignoring of the incumbent's ability to grow. Many persons do grow as they move

---

[4] Leadership is the subject of Chapter 25, p. 410.

[5] Lawrence J. Peter and Raymond Hull, *The Peter Principle: Why Things Always Go Wrong* (New York: William Morrow and Co., 1969), pp. 5 and 12.

upward. On the other hand, some do not or at best, very little. Somewhere for every person, there is a job bigger than that person, but the job may not be in the person's hierarchy and hence, the person probably never will be promoted to it.

Peter's Principle, however, is interesting from the viewpoint of human behavior and organization. Typically, a person uses the principle to explain the behavior of another—the boss or top staff person. Seldom does the person refer to the principle in reference to personal behavior. Also, human ambition and the urge to satisfy psychological needs make many people strive for promotion, competent or not. And they will likely continue to do so. It has ever been so and it is reasonable to expect it to continue.

DELEGATION OF AUTHORITY

Another and vital human behavior in organization is the delegation of authority by a management member. Organization units require the delegation of authority to their respective managers so that they can manage their respective units. Without delegation the chief executive, or president, would be the only management member of an enterprise. There would be only one department, and an organization structure would be absent. Delegation of authority is necessary wherever a manager must rely on another to help accomplish an objective.

In this discussion, delegation means conferring authority from one manager or organizational unit to another in order *to accomplish particular assignments. A manager does not just delegate authority.* The authority is delegated to get certain work accomplished. By this means, the area of operations is extended, for without delegation, a manager's actions are confined to what the manager alone can perform.

Delegation has a dual characteristic. As a result of delegation the subordinate receives authority from the superior, but at the same time the superior still retains all original authority. It is something like imparting knowledge. You share with others who then possess the knowledge, but you still retain the knowledge, too.

Customarily, delegation is considered as being from a higher to a lower level, but it can also be from a lower to a higher level or between levels on the same plane. In other words, *delegation can be downward, upward, or sidewise.* Downward delegation of authority is illustrated by a sales manager to the sales staff, upward delegation by state governments to the federal government, and sidewise delegation by certain churches in a federation of churches.

An outstanding disciple of delegation, Andrew Carnegie, made this pertinent statement: "When a man realizes he can call others in to help him do a job better than he can do it alone, he has taken a big step in his life." A manager must delegate primarily because of three reasons.

First, a manager is in charge of more work than one person personally can do. This brings up questions of the degree to which authority should be delegated. Second, delegating authority is the cardinal step in developing subordinates. All the benefits of executive training programs, seminars, and workshops go for naught if authority delegation is ignored. Third, organization depth is required by an enterprise. Managers are taken out of an organization through promotion, illness, resignation, and business trips. Others must be able to carry on if the need arises, and this suggests that they are participating in the work. A manager is one in a line of persons; he or she had a predecessor and sooner or later will have a successor.

THE MEANS OF DELEGATION

Figure 15–1 shows a portion of a format designed to show the authority delegated and to whom. This means, like all written delega-

FIGURE 15–1:   Form to indicate authority delegated to management members

DELEGATION OF AUTHORITY

Indicate the extent of authority for each of the following expenditures according to this code:

1 = complete authority; 2 = complete authority after consulting with superior; 3 = flexible —depends upon individual circumstances; 4 = no authority; and 5 = committee has authority.

Expenditures	President	Vice President	Divisional Head	Department Head	Supervisor
1. Purchase of machinery					
2. Purchase of materials or supplies					
3. Repair of machinery					
4. Settlement of claims against company					
5. Settlement of claims by company					
6. Extension of credit by company					
7. Adjustment of selling price by company					
8. Adjustment of salaries					

tion, makes the delegation specific and a matter of record. As such the authority relationship is clarified and uncertainty is removed. Such practice is advantageous both ways—to the delegator in thinking through the situation and deciding what specific assignments are being made, and to the delegatee who will know specifically in what areas and to what degrees she or he is to operate. In addition, specific written delegation helps inform anyone called upon to work with the delegatee in filling the assignments.

Criticism has been directed to the practice of written delegations in that it poses difficulties in stating written delegation for a new activity and reduces organization flexibility and emphasizes the parts rather than the whole of an organization structure. Unfortunately there is some justification for these views, but the underlying causes need not be permitted to exist. A tradition of organization flexibility can and should be established so that organizational changes are made when it is deemed in the best interests of achieving the work to be done.

Another very common means of delegation is trial and error which although somewhat deficient ultimately leads to some delineation of the specific assignments. This means provides flexibility which most delegators want, and makes it possible to adjust easily as conditions require.

WHY MANAGERS DON'T DELEGATE

If delegation is so important, the question might well be asked, Why don't managers delegate? They do delegate, of course, but neither sufficiently nor in certain areas. The reasons are many. Figure 15–2 shows the more common and important reasons.

GETTING MANAGERS TO DELEGATE

A number of measures can be followed to alleviate the problem of authority delegation. For convenience, the following ten points are listed and discussed.

1. Make the potential delegator feel secure. Typically the non-delegator is a hard worker, fully competent in a field, but feels insecure in his or her job. To promote security, point out clearly that the work being done and the contribution to the group are not being questioned. It may also help to grant the nondelegator an impressive title, an increase in pay, or provide special facilities such as an oversize office and services of a private secretary, as well as a private parking space.

2. Realize the need for and believe deeply in delegation. As long as a manager is limited to what personally can be accomplished, that manager will always be short of time and limited in achievements. A manager's need is to multiply output. It is nonsense to try to lead the

FIGURE 15–2: Major reasons why managers do not delegate

1. *The tendency of a human being to want to do things personally.* If charged with specific activities, the normal desire is to make certain the work is performed and the best way to ensure this is to do it yourself. Remember too that responsibility goes with authority. The nondelegator, in essence, retains the responsibility which one commonly feels is one's own possession and a mark of self-importance.

2. *Lack of assuming the managerial role when promoted to the managerial ranks.* In many cases, persons are promoted to managerial positions partly as a result of their willingness in the past to make decisions and when promoted, they continue to be decisive and make every decision in their unit.

3. *Fear of being exposed.* Delegation may reveal managerial shortcomings being practiced. Poor operating procedures, methods, and practices come to light. This fear is understandable, but exposure of the difficulties is the first step in correcting them.

4. *Unconscious acceptance of the indispensable person theory.* A manager may feel that he or she is really an indispensable person in the organization. Wanting to be missed and finding things not going so smoothly when absent is ego satisfying, but limits delegation.

5. *Desire to dominate.* For any number of reasons some managers have an intense desire to influence others, to make their presence felt in every company meeting, and "to run" their organization. They seem to enjoy working under pressure, to be busy with appointments, to have subordinates bring all matters to them for approval.

6. *Unwillingness to accept risks.* To delegate authority successfully, it is necessary to accept the risk that a subordinate may make wrong decisions. This risk must be taken if experienced managers are wanted. Most present-day managers are where they are today because somebody had faith in them and accepted the calculated risk inherent in delegating authority to subordinates.

7. *Attitude that subordinate is incapable of using authority properly.* As a matter of fact, the quality of performance may suffer, but a big part of a manager's job is to develop people and delegation of authority aids in this objective. Also, the delegator may fear that the delegatee, aided by delegation, will prove so capable that he or she either will threaten the delegator's job or qualify for promotion that results in the delegator losing competent help.

band and play all the instruments too. The only alternative is to acquire helpers, train them, and permit them to contribute in full measure. Commonly it is convincing to have the nondelegator take an inventory of the tasks personally done. Then have the nondelegator evaluate these tasks to determine whether it seems reasonable to do all these tasks personally, especially when heading up an organization unit. A manager must want to make delegation successful and strive to make it succeed. Delegation must be viewed as the way to develop subordinates, to liberate their energies purposively, and to build a real management team.

3. Establish a work climate free from fear and frustration.
Essentially psychological and social in character, the delegator
must have a feeling of confidence that delegation of authority will
reward, not penalize, her or him. Authority delegation should have the
blessing of the top managers, as evidenced in such things as a reasonable and satisfactory compensation, an impartial means for evaluating
a manager's work, and a significant part of the executive development
program.

4. Tie-in with intelligent planning.   Authority should not be delegated before the goals are clear. The extensiveness of the delegated
authority should be in keeping with the type of activities performed in
attaining the goals. Results management, recommended in Chapter 4,
permits management members to set their own goals with approval of
their superior. This very act of goal setting aids authority delegation for
it brings in close focus what authority will be required to achieve the
mutually agreed to goals.

5. Determine how the delegator keeps a hand in duties.   Since the
delegator retains overall authority for delegated duties, there is the
need to keep the delegator informed in order to protect his or her
accountability and to be fairly certain of the outcome. Few delegators
want to be merely the depository of the result. The delegating method
followed should provide the means for informing the delegator of the
status of the assignment in time to take corrective steps, if needed.
Among the many ways for the delegator to "keep a hand in it" are (a)
question subordinate periodically about the work progress, (b) require
written reports at prescribed times, and (c) schedule conferences for
reviewing what has been and what is intended to be accomplished.

6. Determine what to delegate and provide adequate authority.
To do this, the delegator can list all the various types of decisions and
tasks that must be performed and then rate each one in terms of (a) their
relative importance to the total enterprise and (b) the time required to
perform. These data serve to determine what type of decisions and
tasks should be delegated. The too common practice of delegating work
the delegator doesn't want to do personally should be avoided. Also,
give the delegatee a chance to participate in a *complete* undertaking.
Broad rather than narrow projects best serve to whet the imagination
and stimulate ingenuity.

7. Choose the delegatee wisely.   This might well be the person
with unused and the not so obvious abilities. A group's productivity
and satisfactions generally improve when the not so obviously qualified manager is given a chance to succeed. We tend to favor the
underdog. In addition, the assignment should be measured to the delegatee selected. It should be challenging but not too tough to finish.

8. Give assistance to delegatee.   The delegator does not assume
the role of a helpless onlooker. Typically, the delegatee is going to

require some assistance and commonly goes to the delegator for help. If the problem is clearly within the range of the delegated authority, the delegator should make the delegatee decide it. An effective question to ask the subordinate is "What do you thing ought to be done?" If the problem is complicated, assistance in helping the subordinate to identify and explore possible alternatives is recommended. But the delegator does not tell the subordinate the precise action to take.

QUESTIONS

1. Discuss the major reasons for wanting to change or to modify traditional or formal organizing. Do you feel formal organizing should be modified? Why?
2. Distinguish between nonformal organization and informal organization.
3. What is the Peter Principle and what is its contribution to the study of organization?
4. Discuss the behavioral viewpoint toward organizing and include in your answer in what ways this viewpoint influences an organizer's thoughts and actions.
5. What is the meaning of each of the following: (*a*) contingency theory of organizing, (*b*) nonformal organization, (*c*) free-form organizing, and (*d*) dysfunctions?
6. Enumerate some social considerations pertinent in the study of organizing.
7. Discuss the meaning, activity, and importance of informal organization.
8. Regarding interpersonal conflict—what is it? Is its existence in organization good or bad? What are some common defense mechanisms found where such conflict is present?
9. Discuss the fusion theory of organizing, pointing out its salient features.
10. What is delegation of authority and discuss two major reasons why managers don't delegate authority.
11. What are the common means of delegating authority? As a manager, which means would you follow? Why?
12. What is your understanding of an adaptive organization? How important do you feel it might be in the future? Discuss.
13. Discuss the importance and contribution of tradition in an organization.
14. Discuss (*a*) how a person can "keep a hand in" (avoid complete relinquishing of duties and responsibilities) while promoting delegation of authority to an assistant and (*b*) how to choose the delegatee wisely.

CASE 15–1. MERRYMAN SALES COMPANY

Cooney (sales representative): Mr. Korman, I've decided to leave the company.

Korman (sales manager): Leave the company? You can't do that!

Cooney: I find I'm not in business for myself like you said I would be. I work up a good sale, quote a price, and your people here in the office quote the customer a lower price and I lose the business. And I'm not consulted at all about what is going on. I'm leaving. I want no part of this.

Korman: Wait a minute. Give me the facts and I'll look into it right away and straighten it out.

Cooney: You've got a bunch of incompetents who have you buffaloed that they are helping you. It's a laugh. They have never sold anything. They don't know what it's all about. I don't want anything to do with them, especially your pet, Joe Fields [assistant sales manager]. He gives my customer a 3 percent reduction which cuts *my* commission, not his, by nearly $4,000.

Korman: He was probably trying to help.

Cooney: That kind of help I can do without.

Korman: I give you my promise, Cooney, I'll check over this whole deal and get back to you by the end of the week.

During the next day or so Cooney talked with several other company sales representatives and listened to their complaints of the company pressuring them to get more sales, of material not to the buyer's specifications being shipped, and of being repeatedly asked to make delinquent collections after somewhat questionable collection procedures have been tried. Cooney, now with the company seven months, began to believe more and more that his future was not with Merryman Sales Company.

Within three days Mr. Korman called Cooney to his office and explained the situation about the 3 percent price reduction on Cooney's order: "The customer had a better price from Spicer [a competitor]. Joe was convinced of this—the buyer was not bluffing. Several deals have occurred recently with Spicer coming in at a better price than Merryman. Joe was trying to help and make certain you got the order. That's all."

"Look," Korman continued, "the office is here to help you. We want you to succeed, not to lose any orders. Competition is tough and we have to meet price competition."

Cooney countered that he had worked closely with the customer and he was positive the customer did not want Spicer's product. Further, as a representative he was told that he alone has the authority to deal with the customer on all matters of developing sales, obtaining samples, negotiating prices, and determining delivery schedules.

Mr. Korman agreed but added, "It's a team effort, Cooney. You can't do it all alone. When the home office can help, we are going to do it."

Cooney decided that his job would not bring him the satisfaction he wants. The best action for him is to find another job, but meanwhile accept the conditions at Merryman as best he could. He has been following this course for the past two months. To date, he has been unsuccessful in finding a new job and his sales at Merryman are down.

Questions

1. What is the problem as you see it?
2. How do you explain the behavior of Mr. Cooney?
3. What would you do now if you were Mr. Korman? Mr. Cooney?

CASE 15–2. THE L.M.B. COMPANY

About 12 years ago, Mr. Bosworth started the L.M.B. Company in an alley garage with a few machines, two employees, one order, and plenty of nerve and enthusiasm. In these early days, he inspired the employees with keen understanding of their problems, active participation in all phases of the business, and in his ability to solve difficult problems confronting the small enterprise.

The company grew, and within ten years it was employing 230 people. Mr. Bosworth believed he had too much to do, but in his own words: "There is no one around here who has sufficient understanding and background to whom I can give some of my work." Mr. Bosworth found each day too short to finish his work. He worked till 10 or 11 P.M. every night and frequently took a briefcase of work home over the weekend.

Last year at the insistence of his associates, Mr. Bosworth hired an assistant, John Duff. He is kept extremely busy following up projects, "doing footwork," and assembling information. Although Mr. Bosworth asks his assistant's opinions on many issues, he does not permit the assistant to make any final decisions. While pleased with his performance to date, Mr. Bosworth has stated to his close friends that his assistant is satisfactory as an assistant; he has good ideas but is too young to command the respect of the others. Furthermore, in Mr. Bosworth's opinion, he cannot afford to take a chance with his assistant taking over important projects. Something might go wrong, and the company would suffer a severe setback.

Mr. Anthony Huss, works manager, entered Mr. Bosworth's office and the following conversation took place:

Huss: Mr. Bosworth, it looks like something is going to have to be done about this fellow Dan Reynolds, one of the assemblers. I wish we could get rid of him.
Bosworth: What's he done?
Huss: Those little parts we're running for Curtis—well, the assembly of them looked to me to be awful slow; so I asked Mike [Mike McCann, supervisor of Department 16 L, light assembly] what the

trouble was, and he told me some of the components were not absolutely correct and true like the blueprints call for, and as long as the parts making up the unit were off, he couldn't get out the production we want.

So I talked with the supervisor in punch press, welding, and automatic screw machine and warned them to look into it and get the parts "right on the button" before shootin' 'em over to light assembly.

Bosworth: Yes. And what did they say?

Huss: Oh, they said they would all right. No trouble with them. It's this guy, Dan Reynolds.

Bosworth: Yeah, what about him?

Huss: Well, apparently during lunch hour or one of the breaks or sometime, the workers got together—I mean some of them from punch press, some from welding, some from assembly—and got to talking about these Curtis parts. Reynolds had the nerve to tell them the parts were OK coming to his department. He said the trouble in putting them together is that the assemblers have no suitable fixtures and tools for this work. And the men agree with Reynolds. McCann is plenty sore and told me Reynolds should be put in his place. From his actions you'd think Reynolds believes he's the supervisor. In fact, McCann told me that Reynolds was out for his (McCann's) job. The workers go to Reynolds with many of their problems, shop as well as personal, and apparently listen to what he tells them. I told Mike not to worry about his job. Reynolds told me once that he never wanted a supervisor's job. Some action will have to be taken about this, Mr. Bosworth. Any suggestions on what you want me to do?

Bosworth: I'll come out in about 15 minutes. You go back to work, and I'll see you shortly.

Huss: Yes, sir. Thanks, Mr. Bosworth.

Questions

1. From the viewpoint of organizing, evaluate Mr. Bosworth as the chief executive of the company.
2. How do you explain the situation involving employee Dan Reynolds?
3. What action do you suggest Mr. Bosworth take? Substantiate your answer.

Chapter 16

Organization dynamics

Learning is a treasury whose keys are queries.
Arabian proverb

Organization is intimately associated with people who are living and changing. All living things change, none remains static. Hence, organizations change and wise managers recognize this fact and use organization dynamics to update and to improve the organization.

In contemplating any organization change, it is well to weigh the probable gains and losses before reaching a decision. In this respect a reaffirmation of the objective is helpful. Also, *preventive* organizational change should be stressed. This includes periodic efforts to detect areas where change is going to be needed to avoid serious organization trouble. It is erroneous to confine efforts solely to situations that currently exist, i.e., to concentrate upon *remedial* organization changes. Normally, what is called for is either an analysis in depth of the situation under question or a survey to uncover the broad contributing factors.

ORGANIZATION DYNAMICS

The reasons why organizations change are numerous but the four major reasons are as follows.

1. The handiwork that organizing creates makes for change. It emphasizes interdependence among various necessary units interacting upon one another. In addition, outside forces affect the organization, some units more than other units. All these interactions and forces create and maintain an organization but at the same time condition the activities of its various parts. In time, the organization becomes unbalanced, useless activities are performed, persons are improperly placed, inadequate communication exists, slowness in decision making is rampant, and misunderstanding of organization relationships is common.

2. Personnel change.   Employees retire, quit, die, are transferred, promoted, demoted, and fired. The human element in organization is a dynamic concept, and it must always be considered as such. Human beings change in their characteristics; for example, a job providing complete satisfaction for a young woman of 22 may not suffice 8 years later. To ignore organization dynamics as it affects the personnel of an organization is to court ultimate disaster. Further, a considerable amount of organization dynamics comes about due to a change in top management personnel. A new incoming top manager, for example, has the right and is expected to take some reorganization measures. Also, some personnel become obsolete primarily because the activity they perform becomes obsolete or the way of doing it changes drastically.

3. Product, service, and methods change.   Fluctuations in the demand of products or services provided by the organization is also important. This results not only in the buildup or reduction of the number of employees, but also of changes in the makeup and even of the existence of certain organization units. For example, "coordinators" and staff people change with the demands placed upon an organization. In addition, technological changes contribute to organization dynamics. New equipment or new materials in the office or shop may call for pronounced changes in work procedures and skill requirements. For example, changes in the production processes make for different organizational unit makeups and relationships.

4. Improvement sought.   Realizing the importance of organizing, the astute manager is always seeking to improve the organization being used. The developments in organization theory and the possible benefits to be gained from better organization help stimulate and keep alive organization dynamics. As stated in No. 1 above, organization in and of itself tends to become outmoded, develop shortcomings, and permit wasteful practices. In this respect Parkinson's Law can be cited, "Work expands so as to fill the time available for its completion."[1] Although written partly as a jest, elements of truth exist in the law for in reality, there frequently is no relationship between the work to be done and the number of employees assigned to it. The work tends to grow as there is time available to perform it. Further, as Parkinson points out, employees tend to make work for each other. Thus, wasteful organizational practices are increased and hamper efficient operations. On the other hand and in all fairness, it should be added that in a number of enterprises, some of the increase in personnel is justified due to the complexities of advancing technology and the governmental and social constraints within which the modern manager must operate.

---

[1] C. Northcote Parkinson, *Parkinson's Law* (Boston: Houghton Mifflin Co., 1957), p. 2.

An improvement of major importance is usually to better the organizational environment so that it is not only conducive, but encourages the free exchange of ideas, stimulation of creativity, and the resolution of difficulties promptly. It should be an environment in which uncomfortable questions can be asked. Also to be noted is that commonly the improvement sought is reduced expenses. This takes the form of getting along with fewer managers, eliminating organization units, or transferring the work to another unit. However, this is not to infer that the least expensive organization arrangement is the best and should always be adopted. Rather, the issue to be decided is whether the more expensive arrangement provides additional benefits in keeping with the sought objectives.

Another sought improvement making for organization dynamics is the tendency by some managers to "keep up with the Joneses." If a strong competitor reorganizes along certain lines, the urge to do likewise seems to prevail. A fad to establish a certain type department may spread rapidly among companies. At one time, the fashion was to adopt decentralization as a way of life. Some companies followed the trend without any assurance that decentralization was best for their individual circumstances. Finally, the best organization improvement deals with concentrating on what the organization can become, not what it is or has been. Looking ahead habitually with optimism is important in improving the organization and when this attitude exists, the opportunities for improvement, made feasible by organization change, will result in progress maximization.

Principle of dynamic organizing

Organizing is dynamic; it should take into account changes in the enterprise.

GROWTH PATTERNS OF ORGANIZATIONS

Since much but certainly not all organization dynamics concerns growth, let us sketch the normal growth patterns as a business enterprise expands. Basically the growth is (1) vertical, (2) horizontal, and (3) from a functional to a divisionalized type.

In most cases, the increase of an organization structure starts with vertical growth only. Assume Mr. Doe goes into business for himself. At the beginning Mr. Doe will perform all the fundamental activities himself. He will produce the product, sell it, supply and maintain his necessary finance. As his business increases, Mr. Doe finds the amount of work too great for him to handle; so he hires a person who can handle one of the three fundamental activities and retains the other two for himself. Assume this helper is Ms. Brown to handle production. Greatest efficiency is obtained by having the helper concentrate on one activity instead of spreading efforts over all three activities.

As the workload continues to increase, additional helpers are obtained. That is, Ms. Miller and a Mr. Smith may be secured to handle the fundamental activities of sales and finance, respectively. Mr. Doe, the owner, now concerns himself with the overall managing and the major issues only; he is assisted by three subordinates. Progress of the enterprise persists, and the amount of work becomes greater and greater, until a further segregation of the activities appears desirable. Accordingly, three helpers are obtained for each of production, sales, and finance. See Figure 16–1.

FIGURE 16–1

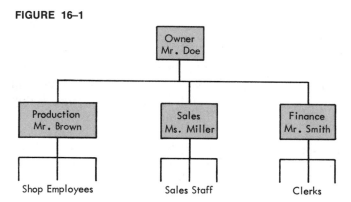

HORIZONTAL GROWTH OF ORGANIZATION STRUCTURE

As the amount of work increases, the complexities of the activities performed are quite likely to grow. This condition is brought about mainly by the nature of most work and the vertical growth of the organization. By way of illustration consider the production organizational unit only. Assume by vertical growth that there are several distinct production departments beneath the fundamental production unit and that there are seven or eight employees in each production department. In order to get out the work, each supervisor must perform many different types of activities, but among these activities some are more or less similar in their basic nature. For example, each supervisor is required to schedule work; to train, place, and promote production employees; and to see that the products manufactured are of acceptable quality and meet customers' specifications. In the interest of efficiency, it may be reasoned that the grouping of common activities and having them performed by a specialist in that particular work would be transferred to a unit such as shop scheduling with an expert scheduler in charge. Likewise, a unit of personnel to handle training, placing, and promoting of all shop employees and another unit to handle the inspection work of all products manufactured by the company may be established. This arrangement is shown in Figure 16–2.

As a result of this arrangement, the organization structure has been expanded horizontally. A continuation of vertical growth has been checked, in part, by avoiding duplication, wasteful competition, and overlapping of work among organizational units.

FIGURE 16–2: Showing the horizontal growth of the production department from that shown in Figure 16–1

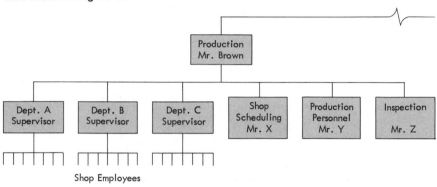

Shop Employees

FUNCTIONAL TO DIVISIONALIZED GROWTH

Most companies grow *from a functional type;* that is, the beginning organizational structure is departmentized by major functions, *to a divisionalized type* of organization which is usually *on either a product or a territory basis.*[2] At the same time, centralization of authority tends to become decentralized. The functional organizational structure is used at the start because it is direct, economical, and a simple way to organize. Eventually, with growth, the divisionalized organization structure is adopted because it better meets the basic organizational needs of the enlarged, diversified company. A graphic portrayal of the common pattern for organizational growth is shown by Figure 16–3.

The divisionalized type of organizational structure breaks the functional organization into relatively small, self-contained organizational units. Each such unit is set up so that it can compete in the open market against outside enterprises as well as other divisions inside the same enterprise. The various units are tied together at the top by a central headquarters and staff. Thus, an organization is formed that can compete with dynamic smaller companies and is flexible. Growth and diversification, either in the form of new products or new territories, can be accomplished without distorting the basic structure.

---

[2] Reference is made here to the departmentation at the top levels of organization. As explained in Chapter 13, other means of departmentation are usually not employed at the top levels.

FIGURE 16–3:   The common pattern for organizational growth

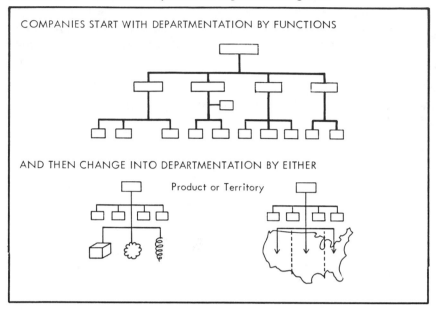

COMMON WEAKNESSES OF ORGANIZATION

As inferred in comments above, unless sufficient managerial efforts are continuously applied to organizing, defects will appear and develop in an organization. The severity, type, and location of the difficulty will vary somewhat with the individual case, but one common mistake is to spend little or no effort toward improving the structure in light of what is currently to be accomplished. That is, the objectives are changed, but the organization structure remains status quo. Another common weakness—the newer concepts about organization are not considered. The old traditional authoritarian hierarchy is used in all cases. Insufficient attention is paid to giving the employee more participation and freedom in deciding issues that concern him or her, in utilizing the employees' knowledge, skills, and ideas about work performance, and in making available the satisfaction of needs derived from the work experience and effort. Also, changes in organization are erroneously considered to consist exclusively of personnel replacements. New persons are placed on a faulty structure. And it is not uncommon to find management members devoting their full time to assignments not requiring their special training and experience. Furthermore, the work specialization may be carried too far. As a result the organization units are too small and the employee's interest and enthusiasm for the job are low. Along with this excessive activities breakdown is usually found a complicated pattern of authority relationships among the many organization units. Simplicity of the organization structure is ignored. Finally, authority may not be properly delegated and may be greatly unbalanced among the various organization levels. Any one of these organization defects offers tremendous challenge for improvement to the alert manager.

WHO GUIDES ORGANIZATION CHANGES FOR IMPROVEMENT

With both organization dynamics and organization weaknesses present, the question can be asked, who guides the organization changes for improvement, when, and how are these efforts done? Let's answer the who part first. Four sources are most common: (1) the manager, (2) a committee, (3) a department of organization within the organization itself, and (4) an outside management consulting firm.

A great many companies follow the belief that organizing is the manager's job and that person should perform this function for the specific unit in order to fulfill the managerial requirements satisfactorily. The separate organization plans thus developed are coordinated by the president or another top manager. Counsel and discussion with the manager submitting the organization work is usually followed. In other companies a committee is appointed to recommend and help adopt reorganization plans. The managers affected by the changes are active in participating and in implementing the revised organization. Commonly they are members of the committee. A department of organization within the organization itself exists in some companies. It is a specialized staff group whose purpose is to keep the organization vibrant and up to date by suggesting improvements and helping the managers in their organizing efforts. Usually such a department has from three to ten members headed by a manager who reports to the president. Excellent results are reported from the use of a department of organization. A modification of this arrangement is to rely rather heavily upon the existent personnel department for aiding managers in improving the organization. There is merit in this practice because proper placement, motivation, and employee work-satisfaction are enhanced. An outside consulting firm provides expertise with a fresh outside viewpoint, helps in getting any change implemented, and completing the work within the time constraints. Very satisfactory results are reported from the use of the consulting firm source.

When to change

From the viewpoint of timing the organizational change, either of two extremes or some compromise between them can be adopted. The two extremes are (1) to make the changes within a relatively short period—the so-called earthquake approach—or (2) to make the changes on a continuing basis spread out over a relatively long period.

The earthquake approach is quite common. It may coincide, but not necessarily, with the appointment of a new manager who wishes to make a fresh start or "to do things his or her way." It is decisive, and emphasizes the do-it-and-get-it-over-with viewpoint. Yet it may destroy harmonious and productive relationships, curtail employee participation, and damage morale. However, it minimizes the suspense of employees wondering what is going to happen next and affecting their work output adversely as a result of their suspicions and fears.

In contrast, organizational changes can be brought about over extended periods of time. For example, a manager may take 3, 6, or 12 months to accomplish an organizational change. This extended period of time has its favorable aspects in that it permits ample consultation with managers about the changes and their suggestions regarding them. Then too it provides time for thorough indoctrination about contemplated changes. It represents the conservative, let's-be-sure-before-we-go-ahead attitude and is in keeping with the current practice of giving serious consideration to employees' viewpoints. It is essential to recognize that usually too much organization change too soon is disturbing to those affected by it. While organization dynamics is a reality, there is also a need for organization stability. Most of us accept a certain amount of change as inevitable, but when the amount becomes what we consider excessive we are disturbed, may become frustrated, and our work attitudes change in ways that are not helpful to our work efforts.

FIGURE 16–4:   Four major factors suggesting change in an organization

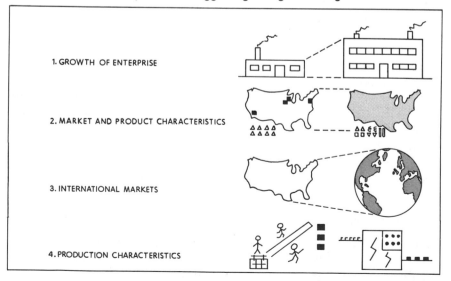

1. GROWTH OF ENTERPRISE

2. MARKET AND PRODUCT CHARACTERISTICS

3. INTERNATIONAL MARKETS

4. PRODUCTION CHARACTERISTICS

Certain concrete considerations will assist in deciding when a change is indicated and should be made. The precise timing, however, is still a matter of the manager's judgment. Figure 16–4 shows four factors to be considered.

HOW ARE ORGANIZATION CHANGES FOR IMPROVEMENT MADE

Depending upon the discretion of the evaluator, any one of several general overall approaches can be followed. The first approach in evolving desirable organization changes is what might be termed the *packaged* approach. Here the organization is analyzed for violation of pragmatic beliefs concerning what an effective organization should be. For example, areas having too great a span of authority, an uncommon mixture of activities, or persons doing work not in keeping with their individual skills and desires, would be noted.

The *means and resources* approach concerns how the organization sustains itself and attains objectives. Of special interest is that undue strain is not placed on its members and that material resources are not dissipated. Adaption to environmental and internal problems, minimization of tension among organizational subgroups, the degree to which individual wants and needs are fulfilled, and the satisfying of its social requirements by an organization are the focus of attention under this approach.

Commonly the *informal* approach is used. To uncover possible areas for improvement, short, pertinent questions are asked such as those illustrated in Figure 16–5. Answers to such questions reveal areas requiring remedial action. To utilize the informal approach effectively may require considerable firsthand knowledge of the structure and the various relationships existing therein.

Or the approach of *comparison* can be utilized. In it, the organization is compared with those of competitors and others of somewhat similar enterprises. Care must be taken to obtain sufficient information about the others so that comparisons are valid. Diagrams of competitors' structures are insufficient because the actual content of many organizational units may not be revealed by the diagrams, and the influence of the respective personnel upon the work being accomplished with the respective structures is unknown.

Another approach is the *ideal* approach. In this case the ideal organization is visualized and conditions for its existence assumed. Questions like the following might be asked: What is new in organization thinking that we might use advantageously? What structure would be best? What should each manager do? What authority is necessary? What responsibility should exist? The ideal is then compared to that being evaluated, and areas for improvement noted.

FIGURE 16–5: Typical questions for use in evaluating an organization

1. Are the stated objectives the proper ones to be sought by the enterprise?
2. Are the main efforts being directed toward obtaining the stated objectives?
3. Are the management members completely qualified by training and experience to achieve these major goals? If so, are these members in proper organizational positions?
4. Is the overall organization pattern adequate? Are the various activities logically related and grouped for maximum effectiveness?
5. Are all necessary activities specifically assigned to individuals in the proper organization units?
6. Does every management member fully understand his or her work, authority, and relationships to other management members?
7. Is authority adequately delegated?
8. Would results management or job enrichment improve the working together of the people in the organization?
9. Do any departments appear to operate too independently?
10. Can project organization be used advantageously? Matrix organization?
11. Are there any management members who direct too many subordinates?
12. Are there probable replacements for management members at different levels for the next five years? 10 years?
13. Are present management members being developed for greater efficiency and effectiveness?
14. Are periodic evaluations used to measure management members' progress and potential?
15. Is there an organization chart and manual, and if so, are they updated?

There is also the *quantitative* approach. This employs the use of measurements, especially those obtained by calculating various ratios. For example, the ratio of managerial to operative employees, the amount of staff to line people, the number of organizational units for the number of employees, enterprise and industry comparisons of each ratio data, as well as industry and national comparisons, are among the types of quantitative data that may be used. The quantitative approach is effective where it can be used. Reliable data for its use, however, are not always available.

AN ORGANIZATION ANALYSIS

An organization analysis is more precise, individualized, and detailed than the general approaches just discussed. It consists of the following actions and usually gives excellent results.

First, bring together all available written materials dealing with the organization. This includes the statement of purpose and scope of the organization and each unit of it, job descriptions, performance appraisals of management members, and qualifications needed as well as those not needed or used by each of these members in their present positions. Next, review these materials, carefully noting whether they are consistent, non-overlapping, and directed to the major goals of the organization. Following this, develop job requirements to accompany the position description of each management member's job. Likewise, analyze each manager's apparent qualifications and relate each manager's education, experience, knowledge, and skill to job requirements. Fifth, for each management member compare job requirements and individual qualifications. Underscore in pencil any job requirement not possessed adequately by the manager; underscore in ink any qualification that apparently is not needed by the manager on her or his current job. Segregate those pencil underscored areas that normally can be acquired through development work from those that cannot be acquired to assure acceptable performance within reasonable time limits. Analyze the ink underscored areas, showing unused abilities, and relate them to other requirements of other jobs. Last, design various possible organization patterns and positions breakdowns, using existing managerial personnel, but noting the type of personnel needed if not presently within the organization. The proposed alternatives are subsequently evaluated against criteria selected by the top manager or group performing the analysis.

As an alternative to this procedure and especially helpful in analyzing a department and emphasizing simplicity and participation is the approach of first, choosing a task force made up of department head, assistants, immediate staff, and nonmanagers of the department. Strive to get a group that will have team effectiveness. Next, have the department head list the department's functions ranked in subjective order of importance. Step 3, have each employee fill out an activity survey sheet each day for several weeks or the length of the work cycle. The survey sheet shows for a given employee the type and amount of work performed. Concurrent with the collection of these data, the task force defines the purpose or main thrust of the department. Next, an analysis chart is prepared summarizing the data obtained from the sheets, the functions, the purpose definition, the costs and the hours spent on each activity. Normally, activities will be reported that do not relate to the functions list. Modifications must be made. Sometimes additional functions must be included. The next step is to have the team study the activity-function information and follow up with a series of wide open discussions with the intent of deciding what the organization problems are of the department and what should be done about them. Subsequently possible organization changes emerge, are analyzed and modified. Those agreed to are listed in order of priority, along with their respective justification, and are recommended to top management for approval.

Regardless of the approach followed, it is advisable after the revised organization is decided upon, to provide revised operational procedures to expedite changes within the organization. These revised operational procedures (ROP) outline what specific activities are to take place in the performance of specific work. In writing and using ROP, concentrate on the changes that are required. This is the information the employee really needs to know to carry out the change. Also, the precise timing of putting ROP into effect should be carefully planned so that a coordinated change is secured. Extreme care should be taken to see that the ROP is inclusive and shows all details. It should not be considered a temporary stopgap but a carefully thought out change. Flexibility and adjustments, in keeping with how it works out and with the suggestions of the employees, should be honored. Further, the flow of the work must be maintained. Proper standards of work output should be established and adequate records kept to insure that this flow is not impeded. Usually this necessitates special activities during the transition period.

ORGANIZATIONAL DEVELOPMENT

Closely akin to organization analysis for improved effectiveness is organizational development (OD). The latter stresses the concept of improving or developing the existing personnel to their full potential. It can be viewed as more personnel-oriented than structure-oriented. Formally defined, *organizational development includes efforts to improve results by getting the best from employees, individually and as members of working groups.*

Two types of criteria are used to measure the improvements, (1) soft, and (2) hard. Soft criteria includes leadership style, enthusiasm of manager, employee satisfaction, harmonious relationships, and team spirit. To measure soft criteria, observations, personal interviews, and prepared formats are used. The latter are printed forms which when filled out supply data to reveal the characteristics of the organization.

In contrast, hard criteria include things dealing with the achievement of objectives. In the case of a business enterprise, representative examples are the amount of sales, net profit, and productivity. Actually, these hard criteria are extremely difficult to evaluate. Net profit, for example, results from a number of forces and while the amount is important, it certainly is not the sole measurement that should be used. Yet, if an organization is profit-oriented, profit should be reckoned with.

Actually, in OD evaluations the use of soft criteria is dominant. Work group problems normally can be identified and expressed by soft criteria. Change can be evidenced. Further, considerable research, particularly that of the Institute for Social Research at the University of

Michigan, supports the idea that soft criteria changes are followed by similar changes in hard criteria.[3]

CHANGE PERSONNEL OF ORGANIZATION

Organization dynamics along with improvement in the organization effectiveness result in personnel change. An individual manager changes with time. The person may have grown tremendously and now possesses much managerial knowledge and skill. On the other hand, the person may have become overconservative, inflexible, negative in viewpoints, or emotionally unstable. Also, job requirements change. During the past, the present incumbent could perform competently, but with the addition of new or complex duties, the person seems unable to perform the work effectively. "Executive obsolescence" is becoming increasingly common with the wide, sweeping changes taking place in our economy. In other instances the individual apparently has been moved up too fast, such a move being dictated by an emergency, inadequate management development, or excessive pushing by a sponsor. The person simply doesn't have the necessary qualifications to do the work adequately.

What should be done? Answers range from quiet means of assistance to the extreme of terminating employment. The action followed should be tailored to suit the particular circumstances. The decision followed should include not only consideration for the effect of the action upon the individual concerned, but also for the effect upon the group of which the individual is a member.

Specifically the following alternatives can be used:

1. Hire new managerial members.   Such members usually bring new ideas, new ways of carrying out the managerial functions, and a fresh viewpoint on problems. A recent managerial addition is usually nonbiased, does not belong to a special clique, has no vested interests, and brings objectivity and enthusiasm to the job.

2. Give counseling.   For the superior to talk things over with the incompetent subordinate and suggest possible actions to improve performance is especially effective for temporary periods of incompetency brought about by additional duties, a crisis, or adjustments either of a social or economic nature. As a result of counseling, better understanding between the two parties is promoted, areas in which help is needed can be spotted and the assistance given, and needed encouragement can be provided.

---

[3] Jerome L. Franklin, *Organization Development: An Annotated Bibliography* (Ann Arbor: Institute for Social Research, 1973). This gives many sources for further study. Also helpful are Harold J. Leavitt, L. Pinfield, and E. Webb (eds.), *Organizations of the Future: Interaction with the External Environment* (New York: Praeger, 1974), and H. F. Rush, *Organization Development: A Reconnaissance* (New York: The Conference Board, 1973).

3. Transfer the incompetent executive. For this approach to be followed there must be flexibility in the organization and "open" managerial positions at various levels. Certain transfers designate changes to insure technical training and the development of managerial skill, while other transfers take place essentially to find out where the particular individual fits into the organization. The distinction is not always clear, but generally speaking, transfers for incompetency are characterized by an excess of transfers within the same organizational level or a failure to move vertically within reasonable time periods.

4. Use staff positions. To provide for required manager changes in an organization, a person can be moved from a position of line authority into one of staff authority, usually that of advisory staff. To make the change attractive, the staff job is commonly at a higher organizational level than the present line job. Commonly the transferee is told that there is a difficult problem in the new area and that the manager is wanted to help straighten it out. The change can be accomplished quite painlessly, especially if the staff position carries prestige and no reduction in salary. This method successfully removes incompetents from important line authority decisions where great damage might be done; yet it retains the benefits of the manager's experience and knowledge for special problems. However, the method may degrade the reputation of the true worth of a staff manager by developing the erroneous viewpoint that staff is a graveyard for line managers who do not make good.

5. Terminate the employment. This is the most extreme way to handle incompetency. The manager resigns under force or from pressure applied in subtle ways. The simple statements that "your work is not up to expectations" or "things haven't worked out," can be used with the expectation that the person will quit. In contrast, a number of indirect means can be followed including giving the manager very little, if anything, to do so that, in time, the manager will voluntarily resign. Another technique is withholding important facts from the manager, omitting his or her name on important memoranda, and excluding the person from conferences. Also, there is always the method whereby the top manager becomes "unavailable" for consultation to a management member.

RECRUITING AND SELECTING MANAGEMENT MEMBERS

Organization dynamics and changes in organization personnel bring up the subject of recruiting and selecting managerial members. Recruiting is the fountain feeding the potential managerial pool; without adequate recruitment the management personnel dries up and the survival of an enterprise is threatened. Today, the best persons no longer hunt jobs; the jobs hunt them. To get desirable candidates an enterprise must aggressively let its interests and wants be known to likely candidates. The watchful and enthusiastic cooperation of present managers, alumni, and nonmanagement members in locating such talent should be tapped. It should also be noted that under the federal equal employment opportunity legal regulations, efforts must be made to inform likely candidates of vacancies. Five effective sources for candidates are:

1. Other companies. Commonly used for managers, this source gets candidates with new ideas and different approaches. Managerial inbreeding of poor decision making is thus minimized. However, outsiders may not bring special results to the company. Reliable standards in judging applicants' qualifications are required.

2. Promotions from within company. This source is popular with employees, emphasizes opportunity in line with service to an enterprise, frequently serves as a strong incentive, and offers a pool of potential managers to the enterprise. However, for this source to be productive, aggressive efforts to ferret out likely candidates are necessary. In addition, an unbiased means for evaluating candidates in line for advancement should be established. Viewed quite realistically, many employees are neither hired for possible future managerial work nor are they interested in assuming the task of making the decisions and having the obligations inherent in managerial work. Yet they are competent, faithful, satisfied employees and essential to the company's success, even though their managerial potential may be low.

3. Graduates from universities and special schools. Such graduates by virtue of their specialized training are believed to possess a satisfactory background upon which further training and experience pertinent to the future management of the enterprise can be based. Many young men and women are now receiving higher formal education emphasizing managerial subjects, but college graduation alone does not ensure a candidate of management caliber. When this source is used, the skill of the recruiter and the reputation of the company are important. The recruiter's knowledge of the company, of the university, and especially of the job are highly significant. Recruiting from many schools is superior to that of dealing with one school.

4. Advertisements. This source reaches candidates who otherwise probably would not know of the vacancies; it is a democratic process. A number of candidates are usually found by this means, but many probably will be unqualified; hence, effective selection devices must be employed for these candidates. Also the media employed influences the results obtained.

5. Employment agencies. Many of these perform creditable work and give entirely satisfactory results. However, most agencies are not equipped to screen applicants to the individual criteria of the hiring company, and hence careful selection of such candidates by the enterprise is usually in order. On the other hand, some agencies offer quite extensive personnel services.

Selection of the executive candidate can follow several approaches, but the format visualized in Figure 16–6 is recommended. Beginning at the top of the figure, the candidates recruited are subsequently

FIGURE 16–6

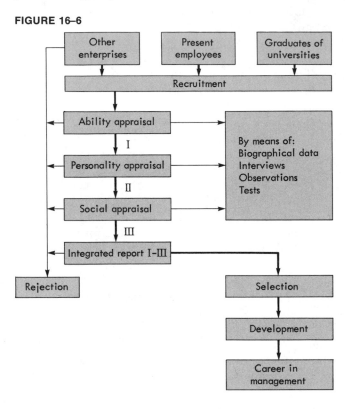

appraised for ability, personality, and social factors by means of biographical data, interviews, observations, and tests. The appraisals need not necessarily be in this order, since they are integrated, and from the results the candidate is either rejected or selected. Observe that at any of the appraisals or at the integrated report, the candidate may be rejected.

The ability appraisal takes into account the candidate's education, training, experience, technical skill, and achievement as well as mental ability, imagination, and similar basic abilities necessary to perform the job. Personality factors are those attributes of the candidate required to get along with people, to stimulate them to work willingly toward a definite goal, to operate under pressure or adverse conditions, to take criticism, and to maintain emotional stability. Social factors include the applicant's manners, general appearance, grooming, willingness to travel, and willingness to geographically relocate. Few, if any candidates, are tops in all desirable qualities. The composite score is what is important.

As shown in Figure 16–6, the first means for appraisal is biographical data which reveal the candidates past accomplishments, personal background, employment record, and outstanding past successes. Certain of these data are most helpful for selection work. From considerable research, the Life Insurance Agency Management Association, for example, believes the following items most significant.

1. Specific work done in recent years.
2. Whether presently employed.
3. Length of present or last employment.
4. Organizations of which applicant is an active member.
5. Offices held in the above organizations during the last five years.
6. Approximate net worth of applicant.
7. Minimum monthly living expenses.
8. Amount of life insurance carried.

Interviews, observations, and tests are also used. By means of the interview, the applicant's background, training, and education can be thoroughly explored and pertinent questions asked relative to the person's aims, interests, and activities. In contrast, the candidates may be brought together as a group along with the interviewers. An extended informal social meeting lasting through a day and an evening might be arranged, during which time detailed observation of the candidates takes place in order to judge reactions to situations, ideas advanced, willingness to use knowledge and skills, and the ability to communicate effectively. Psychological tests are available to measure a number of traits, such as interest, personality, mechanical aptitude, emotional maturity, and leadership. The chief difficulty in using tests for management personnel is the lack of agreement on what qualities are necessary for competency. Furthermore, the requirements may differ from one enterprise to another. Commonly used is a battery of tests covering various attributes. Present tests are helpful, but not as significant as the recruiter might like them to be. If the score is sufficiently low, they suffice to disqualify a candidate, but success in the present tests does not predict success in the management job.

QUESTIONS

1. What are some common weaknesses found in organization? Select one weakness and relate how you would go about correcting it.
2. Is it possible for a manager to make organization dynamics work to personal advantage? Discuss.

3. Tell what is meant by each of the following: (*a*) earthquake approach, (*b*) executive obsolescence, and (*c*) revised operational procedure (ROP)?

4. Discuss Parkinson's Law and its relationship to organization dynamics.

5. Discuss the consideration for international sales and production as a factor bringing about change in an organization.

6. Figure 16–5 lists 15 questions on the subject of organization evaluation. Select any three and relate how the answers to these questions would help you improve an organization.

7. Gloria Brady's answer to each question given in Figure 16–5 is "Yes." Is it probable that Ms. Brady will lose her department manager job? Why? Discuss.

8. Distinguish between the two concepts in each of the following pairs: (*a*) vertical organization growth and divisionalized growth, (*b*) the comparison approach to organization evaluation and organization analysis, and (*c*) the means and resources approach and the ideal approach.

9. Describe in some detail what approach you believe you would follow for determining whether an existent organization is relatively good or bad.

10. Discuss the subject of who plans and implements organization change.

11. What is your understanding of the statement "the handiwork that organizing creates makes for change"? Discuss.

12. This chapter offers several alternatives for handling change of personnel believed not measuring up to the job requirements. Name three of these alternatives. Select one of these and describe under what general conditions you would use this particular alternative.

13. Discuss Figure 16–6 in your own words.

14. What is organizational development? Discuss the use of soft criteria to measure improvements in OD studies.

CASE 16–1. HAWTHORNE CORPORATION

Bob Welsh (informal group leader): Don't worry, Ned. We'll select a group from the department and talk with Horace Holgren ourselves.

Ned: Gee, thanks, but it won't do any good.

Ned Stevens, a college student, has been hired for temporary work during the summer. He proved to be extremely capable as a computer programmer and when September arrived indicated that he wanted to retain his job as he needed the dollars and planned to finish college by taking evening classes. The supervisor of the data processing department was delighted to know that Ned wanted to stay, but Horace Holgren, the personnel manager, refused to approve Ned as a permanent employee. Ned, he emphasized, was hired as a temporary employee primarily to fill in for those away on vacation. Further, the hiring agreement specified "temporary employee," the personnel budget does not permit putting Ned on the regular payroll, and retaining any summer-employed college student would violate a corporation precedent of some 11 years—college students hired for the summer were always terminated in September.

Bob Welsh along with four other regular employees from the general office made an appointment with Mr. Holgren to discuss the situation. During the conference it was pointed out that Ned worked well with his group and was a good producer. He wanted to stay and data processing can well utilize his services. Besides, his wages are relatively nominal and Ned is the type upon whom the company can build in the future.

Mr. Holgren agreed that Ned's record with the company was good, but he was adamant against giving consideration to breaking the longstanding policy of no permanent status for summer college students. He pointed out that this policy has proven very effective. It provided excellent practical experience to the college student, permitted the corporation to look over a group of likely future candidates, and financially aided "the temporary" so that he or she could finish college. All these considerations, pointed out Mr. Holgren, are to the student's best interest over the long run.

The group expressed its disappointment at Mr. Holgren's comments and stand. Welsh called Holgren's answer "a biased, archaic viewpoint" and one that certainly will lead to difficulties and a loss in the employees' cooperation—a situation certainly not in the corporation's best interest. He said, "I am reflecting the consensus of the great majority of all employees out there in the office when I state that Ned Stevens should be hired permanently. We intend to do everything possible to see that such action is taken."

Questions

1. What actions could the office work force take? Discuss.
2. What action do you believe it will take? Elaborate on your answer.
3. As a counselor to Mr. Holgren, what would you indirectly suggest that he do? Why?
4. If you were Mr. Holgren, would you have handled the situation from the beginning in a different manner than he did? Justify your viewpoint.

CASE 16–2. SEBO CORPORATION

As a large supplier of automobile accessories, lighting equipment and plastic parts, this company enjoyed favorable growth on its reputation to supply superior products at competitive prices and in keeping with buyers' schedules. Each year tooling for new models of automobiles requires millions of dollars and rearrangement of the factory floor plan. This work necessitates a large force, the management of which is given very close attention.

Until two years ago, a portion of the formal organization of the production plant was as shown by the accompanying Exhibit 1. Definite functionalization was believed necessary. For example, if a problem arose in die casting, one person or a group of persons in die casting was responsible and stayed with the problem until a satisfactory answer

EXHIBIT 1

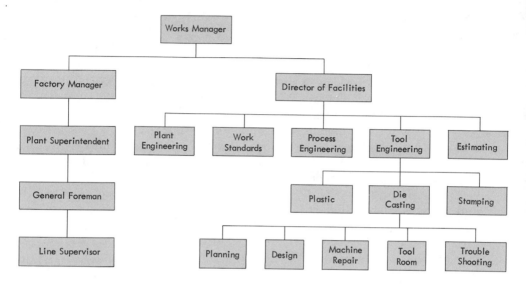

was found. Experience showed, however, that too much time was spent in the shop by nonproductive personnel, who as a consequence did not have sufficient time for designing and developing work. Further, it proved extremely difficult to estimate time and cost for following up on tooling and trouble shooting.

As a result the organization structure was changed to that shown by Exhibit 2. This took place two years ago. The change was triggered by the new works manager who joined the company at that time. Of course, the unsatisfactory results from the then existent organization made the suggested move to improve it highly acceptable. The new works manager believed emphasis upon specialization and industrial engineering were what was needed. A comparison of Exhibit 2 with Exhibit 1 reveals that immediately below the works manager a department of industrial engineering was established with units of work standards and plant layout. In addition, production engineering was established with four engineering departments—process, tool, plant, and development. This represented some shuffling around of activities that had been under the director of facilities (see Exhibit 2). However,

EXHIBIT 2

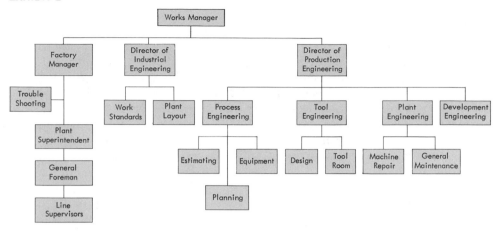

to date, this arrangement has not resulted in solving the problem that existed before its adoption.

Personnel from industrial engineering gave extra effort to locate and analyze the various production problems being encountered, but in general their efforts were late and, in a number of cases, duplicated the efforts of specialists from tool engineering design and also process engineering. Further, the specialist approaches a problem from a relatively narrow viewpoint. Feedback and communication are poor. Estimators and planners were not aware of production or design problems. In several instances the designers were putting this year's mistakes into next year's tools. Further, the production person's problems were not being reflected in the new cost estimates being prepared.

The works manager is very much concerned about the present situation. For the first two months of this current model year just concluded, the company, in order to maintain its reputation for meeting buyers' schedules, has spent over $165,000 in air shipments and nearly $900,000 in overtime.

Questions

1. What is the problem faced by Sebo Corporation?
2. Other than those of organizing, what factor would you feel might have influence upon the problem faced by this company? Discuss.
3. Point out the major changes made in the company going from the organization structure shown in Exhibit 1 to that in Exhibit 2.
4. What action do you recommend the works manager take? Why?

CASE 16–3. DILLMAN COMPANY

Dillman Company was recently acquired by Kamack Corporation, whose executives are well aware of the inept management team of their new subsidiary. Mr. Paul Wood, the principal owner and president of the acquired company, had been the real genius and spark plug back of Dillman's remarkable record. Now 69 years of age, Mr. Wood is happy to retire and let somebody else take over. Associates of Mr. Wood had let him run the show since he was very successful and wanted to do it. They answered his beck and call, always agreed with him, made few decisions, and kept themselves busily occupied on minor activities and of little consequence in the total viewpoint of the company.

Kamack's executive committee decided that the best way to clean house and get an aggressive, hard hitting management group for the new Dillman division was to hire an outsider for one year to trim and revitalize the management personnel. Neither the limited appointment nor the objective of this new general manager was to be publicized. Accordingly, Mark Yost was appointed to the general manager's post of Dillman, an act which came as a total surprise to all employees, customers, and the public.

Mr. Yost immediately sought to evaluate the management team with whom he was now associated. He requested various progress reports, one-year plans, cost estimates, and the like. He held meetings and voiced approval of some activities and disapproval of many other activities. He requested programs be drawn up to achieve goals which he spelled out in some detail. After two months, the consensus was that the pressure was on, Mr. Yost was a very demanding person, was difficult to please, and was trying to make a name for himself with the top brass of Kamack. Two managers had quit, one was asked to leave, and it was rumored that five more were to be terminated. Over half of the 21 top and middle managers indicated they would leave if successful in finding another job. One department was eliminated and three other small organizational units were consolidated into one large unit.

At the end of eight months under Mr. Yost, Dillman's operations were beginning to show definite signs of increased efficiency and lower unit costs on many of its products. The executive committee members of Kamack were well pleased. Profits, in fact, were increasing. They realized Mr. Yost was not well liked by most of the management members of the old Dillman Company, but he was getting a job done and had very successfully incorporated four new managers Kamark had recommended that he hire. They offered Mr. Yost an extension of his one-year contract, but he turned it down, explaining it did not give him adequate compensation for what he was accomplishing. At the end of the year, announcement was made that Mr. Yost was resigning and a new general manager would be named in the near future.

Questions

1. As you see it what was the problem of Dillman Company and what factors contributed to it? Discuss.

2. What major alternatives were available to Kamack Corporation after acquiring Dillman Company?

3. Do you believe a results management approach by Kamack Corporation would have proven successful in this case? Discuss.

4. What recommendations are in order to the executive committee members of Kamack Corporation? Why?

PART V
Actuating

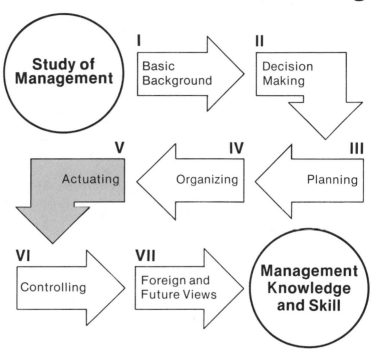

Chapter makeup for Part V:

17. Human behavior and management.
18. Managerial motivation.
19. Leading.
20. Communication.
21. Appraising, developing, and compensating.

The third fundamental function of management to be discussed is actuating. It deals intimately with the human resource which in the ultimate is the center about which all management activities revolve. Actuating offers tremendous challenge and appeal. A person's values, attitudes, hopes, needs, ambitions, expectations, satisfactions, and interactions with other persons and with the physical environment are all involved in the actuating effort.

In the opinion of many, actuating is the most important fundamental function of management. Vital and pervasive, it conditions and is a part of every managerial action taken. And it exists at every level, location, and operation throughout an enterprise. To achieve and maintain success in management, proficiency in actuating is absolutely necessary.

Chapter 17

Human behavior and management

*Though as individuals we are different and separate, each of us is moved
by the same enduring principles, the same urges, the same needs. Hence,
in facing the problems of human relations, let us view them in terms
of that paradox—an infinite variety of individuals bound together
by great common needs.*

Thomas N. Terry

Actuating is the third fundamental function of management to be
discussed in some detail. Our planning and organizing efforts are vital,
but no tangible output is achieved until we implement the proposed
and organized activities. This requires actuating, or the putting or
moving into action. Actuating emphasizes working with people to win
their enthusiasm, desire, and energy toward achievement of mutual
objectives. The following definition is helpful. *Actuating is getting all
the members of the group to want and to strive to achieve objectives
of the enterprise and of the members because the members want to
achieve these objectives.*

CHALLENGE OF ACTUATING IN MANAGEMENT

Getting members of a company to work together more efficiently, to
enjoy their work, to develop their skills and abilities, and to be good
representatives of the company, presents a major challenge to the
managers of that company. Basic to effective actuating is enlightened
management—managers must demonstrate by their behavior and decisions a deep concern for members of their organization. Fundamental to management success is having members perform work that they
like and want to do, belief and trust in each employee, development
and maintenance of a mutually satisfactory work environment, and
acceptance of the fact that the willingness and capacity for each person
to perform enthusiastically conditions the success of most endeavors.

Basically, actuating starts within one's self and not with actuating others. A manager should be personally motivated to progress and to work harmoniously and purposefully with others, otherwise it is almost impossible to actuate others. However, it is difficult to become self-actuated. It comes from within a person, from a strong desire, an intense feeling, and an enthusiastic willingness to pursue a goal regardless of any hurdles which must be overcome.

To obtain greatest success in actuating, one should always be objective in its determination and use. To do this it helps to focus on the behavior, not on the person behaving. Concentrate on what one does, how one acts, and one's responses and reactions to certain events. Observations, not inferences, reporting, not judging, and interpreting behavior in terms of more or less, not either/or, are further requirements for valid objective insight so important in actuating.

Actuating efforts are highly personalized and herein lies much of the challenge. We should not try to stimulate efforts in an attempt to increase equally everyone's satisfaction or try to make everyone equally happy. There are always differences. People differ like fingerprints. Performance will not be equal; neither will their rewards and satisfactions from their work.

IMPORTANCE OF THE HUMAN RESOURCE

The true importance of the human resource of any enterprise lies in its ability to respond favorably and willingly to performance objectives and opportunities and in these efforts gain satisfaction both from accomplishing the work and being in the given work environment. This requires that the right people, with the right mix of knowledge and skills, be in the right place, at the right time to perform the necessary work. An enterprise is made up of humans banding together for mutual benefits and the enterprise is made or destroyed by the quality and behavior of its people. What distinguishes an enterprise is its human resource having the ability to use knowledge of all kinds. It is solely through the human resource that all other resources can be effectively utilized.

The value of a company's managers and nonmanagers is gaining greater and greater recognition. One of the newer frontiers is the work being done by the accountants in developing a means for quantifying the human resource and including it in a company's assets. As a part of a standard financial and accounting reporting system, the importance of the human resource will be highlighted as well as better use of it being advocated and promoted.

Modern views toward the human resource are that the human being is (1) a whole person with needs and a future, (2) a marginal renewable resource making its conservative and effective use desirable, and (3) is not only a present but also a long-range contributor to the goal attainment and well-being of the enterprise and the community. Figure 17–1 shows important attributes of managerial practices featuring the importance of the human resource.

FIGURE 17–1:   Managerial practices in line with recognizing the importance of the human resource

1. Selection of candidates is based on developing a qualified person. Techniques followed place emphasis upon future performance guided not only by the past, but by the present and potential possibilities.

2. Orientation of the human resource members includes the broad view of the total enterprise's activities, the work environment, and the community involved.

3. Job structure is viewed as changeable and can be adjusted in keeping with the characteristics of the labor supply. Jobs are adjusted to fit the human being, as well as the human being changed and developed to fit the job.

4. Motivational efforts are not focused solely on financial gains, but also on fulfillment of self-wants and job satisfaction.

5. Minimal supervision is practiced, group members know what is to be achieved and are to a great extent self-directing, like their work, and have pride in their accomplishment of it.

The truth is that every enterprise depends upon human beings and further, every problem and every decision involves the human element. The potential for improving human resources is terrific because most people are lucky if they use 25 percent of their potential. Managerial planning is successful because *people* put together the right combinations of activities; organizing proves effective because *people* adopt it in order to work together effectively; and controlling is effective because it helps *people* to reach their goals competently.

It is also well to keep in mind that all enterprises are built to serve people—both within and without the enterprise. We in our dignity and sanctity are the center about which all material things revolve. This human-element-centered approach further emphasizes the importance of the human resource and its foci of attention in all actuating efforts.

ACTUATING PREMISES

Human behavior is conditioned by the cultures in a society. As pointed out in Chapter 3, culture refers to learned behavior. It influences what is desirable and conditions what is possible.[1] Cultures include past achievements and provide a practical means for a person to cope with the present environment; that is, a person stores and

---

[1] See page 51.

carries over knowledge and accepted behavior patterns from one generation to another. Different societies have different cultures. For example, either beef or pork is used in some cultures to satisfy hunger, but in other cultures, fish or seafood is the only accepted means.

Cultural variations give rise to differences in human motives. What will arouse greater effort and interest in one culture may fail completely in another. Some will encourage individual effort while others place emphasis upon group effort; some bless certain kinds of economic endeavor while others condemn it or at least make the endeavor very difficult to attain. In the United States, for example, our cultural heritage causes us to question authoritarianism more than is the case in a number of other countries. Likewise, the democratic approach in economic affairs further illustrates this state of affairs. Hence, the cultures of a society can be said to condition human behavior and provide a part of the background against which actuating must take place.

Another and highly important premise of actuating is the fundamental viewpoint that top managers have toward their human resources. A popular and effective statement illustrating opposite views is that provided by Theory X and Theory Y.[2] The chief characteristics of Theory X are:

1. Most employees of a firm work as little as possible and are by nature resistant to change.   Basically the employee will do only what has to be done; work is disliked and hence, trouble is common in trying to achieve goals.

2. Most employees must be persuaded, rewarded, punished, and controlled to modify their behavior to fit the needs of the organization.   They are self-centered, and indifferent, passive, and even resistant to the needs of the organization.

3. Most employees want direction supplied by a formal manager and they want to avoid job responsibilities whenever possible.   Employees therefore must be led and directed by a recognized manager in authority within the company.

In contrast, Theory Y includes:

1. Most employees of the firm do not inherently dislike work. They expect to expend physical and mental efforts in performing their jobs.

2. Most employees have the capacity for assuming responsibility and the potential for development, but management by its action must make them aware of these characteristics.   When committed to specific objectives, an employee will exercise self-control in trying to attain that objective.

---

[2] Douglas McGregor, *Leadership and Motivation* (Cambridge, Mass.: M.I.T. Press, 1966).

3. Most employees want to satisfy social, esteem, and self-actualization needs. The employee wants to use intellectual potential, imagination, and judgment in performing the work in the best way. Management should achieve an environment in which employees can achieve their objectives best by directing their efforts toward objectives of the company.

It is easy to see that a manager predominantly of a Theory X type presents a climate and an attitude which is the direct opposite of a manager following Theory Y. In this day and age and for practically all cases, Theory Y should be adopted and aggressively followed, for it will give the better actuating results.

The ramifications of Theory X and Theory Y and their influence upon management raise some interesting questions. First, what influence does the manager, in recruiting and selecting, have upon the corporation in selecting an X-follower? A Y-follower? Will a manager who is an X-follower tend to select followers of X? It seems likely that inbreeding takes place. The X-manager will probably select an X-follower because such a person represents what the selecter believes, understands, and follows. Another interesting question, in view of government hiring and promoting requirements, is there much choice in the selection work? The answer—there is choice, but it has been narrowed. Making equal opportunity viable assures neither a preponderance of X-followers or Y-followers. It is conceivable that the mix of applicants from the recruiting pool is quite similar to the mix of the human resource of the hiring enterprise.

Theories X and Y have spawned Theory Z, A, B, C, AA, BB and so forth. Taking an overall perspective, it would seem that some people do not want responsibility, they do not object to being led; in contrast, others are ambitious, have ideas, and want to be leaders. The majority probably fall somewhere in between. For example, a person may want to lead in some activities, but is reluctant to lead in other activities. In general, a human being is concerned primarily with personal needs and may cooperate with others in order to satisfy them. A manager is a human being the same as a subordinate. Both manager and nonmanager need understanding, compassion, and the capability for trusting and giving. The key to progress in good human relations lies in both the manager and the nonmanager trying to grasp the meaning of the needs of the other and to work together to find new and better ways of achieving mutual goals.

EMPLOYEE LOYALTY REPORT

Let us review the highlights of a study giving employees a chance to communicate about something important to them—their relationship with employers.[3] The results of this study will lend reality and importance to actuating, reveal the beliefs and views of employees regarding their work and work relationships, and suggest possible actions managers might take regarding their actuating efforts. The sample includes over 2,500 design engineers and kindred occupations from over 400 different companies. The average respondent is 38 years old, in the $15–25,000 income bracket, and has been with the present employer for over five years, and over 72 percent indicated they might change jobs within the next two years.

In all, 65 percent of the respondents were definitely satisfied or somewhat satisfied with their jobs and work. This is a majority, but on the other hand nearly 25 percent of the respondents stated they were somewhat dissatisfied, with an additional 10 percent stating they were definitely dissatisfied. These dissatisfied employees represent the opportunity for improvement. What reasons did they give for their dissatisfaction? Included are (1) the amount of communication they receive about what is going on in their company, (2) unknown career paths and promotional opportunities, (3) challenges they receive, (4) opportunities to influence decisions, (5) recognition for work accomplished, (6) knowledge of what is expected, and (7) a sense of accomplishment.

Those in the higher salary ranges tend to have a relatively higher satisfaction and a less chance for changing jobs. Their answers, however, in this survey showed little correlation with the number of years worked. Analysis of the total results of the survey showed that the years of service did not relate directly to the level of satisfaction. Hence, it was concluded that the money-makers were most satisfied—whether young or old did not matter. Yet those receiving higher salaries did not indicate higher salaries as the reason for their satisfaction. They indicated greater responsibility, more authority, and more status symbols. Salaries are important especially to design engineers whose initial salary often is favorable, but does not rise rapidly with years of experience. Inflation and technical obsolescence must also be reckoned with. Additional selected data from the survey results are shown in Figure 17–2.

The results of this particular study are typical of research in this area. For the sake of brevity, these can be stated as follows: (1) the erroneous belief persists that supervisors can keep top managers appraised and updated on employee morale, (2) employee dissatisfaction exists and is greater than commonly expected, (3) compensation and fringe benefits are important but are not the sole cure for much dissatisfaction, and (4) commonly management members do not have knowledge of what is troubling employees.

---

[3] This discussion is based on an excellent article by T. F. Gautschi, "Survey Report on Employee Loyalty," *Design News*, April 7, 1975, pp. 225–32.

FIGURE 17–2:   Selected data from employee loyalty report

Factors believed important in considering whether to leave present employer:

1. More socially relevant job.
2. Opportunity for early retirement.
3. More opportunity to work with people rather than material things.
4. More highly regarded job.
5. Better physical working conditions.

Factors believed important in staying with present employer:

1. Recently changed jobs and reluctant to change again.
2. Opportunity for early retirement.
3. Investment in company pension or retirement plan.
4. Age of respondent.
5. Spouse's unwillingness to move.

Improvements are clearly possible. The areas of dissatisfaction such as inadequate communication, unknown promotional possibilities, challenge of work, and opportunity to influence decisions, are all under the province of management. An enlightened management by means of some positive action and effort can reduce these shortcomings. These are representative of the area to which managerial actuating is committed.

THE HUMAN BEING

This wanting and striving to achieve mutual objectives are conditioned by the behavior of a person in an organization. We can understand better a person's behavior when we have knowledge of individual characteristics. A human being's heredity and learning experience combine to produce a personality which means the total person—the sum of what he or she is and hopes to be or not to be. A manager works with this total person. The future personality of a person is influenced by that person by means of the decisions made among alternative life experiences. Because each person's heredity and experiences are different, every individual is different. And being different, each person will behave differently from everyone else.

A sequence of stimulus and response make it possible for a human being to learn. A stimulus is an event that a human being can sense; a response is the mental or physical action taken by the human being because of the stimulus received. A reflex is a stimulus-response pattern. A given stimulus can bring about one or several responses and, in contrast, several stimuli can produce the same response. To illustrate, giving A an increase in salary can result in (1) working harder, (2) reducing absenteeism, and (3) improving quality of work. Giving an increase in salary to A and a different job to B can result in reducing absenteeism by both A and B. Basic factors influence reflexes. Some of the more basic, but useful of these factors appropriate to management are given in Figure 17–3.

FIGURE 17–3: Some basic factors applicable to stimulus and response

1. If a person considers a response is rewarding, continuation of response is likely. Contrarily, if considered nonrewarding, the response is discontinued; that is, the unrewarding behavior is stopped.

2. If the reward from the response is considered great, it will command attention.

3. An immediate reward produces faster action and learning than a delayed reward.

4. Frequent, repeated stimuli have a tendency to develop stable patterns of responses.

5. Responses differ in their difficulty among people. If several paths are available to what a human being wants, the tendency is to select the easier one.

Complexes are acquired by human beings early in life and continue throughout life as new situations are experienced. A complex consists of interrelated feelings, memories, and emotionally charged ideas. It is quite an important influence upon a person's behavior and is revealed when confronted with a situation that sparks the individual's complex. Typically a person has a whole range of emotional beliefs and feelings on each of many different subjects—school, busing, foreign powers, politics, and law enforcement. Depending upon the subject as well as the individual, the reaction of a person may be quite rational, but in many cases a nonrational and emotional behavior is found. In these instances, the logic of rational thinking gives way to expressions conditioned by complexes. And it is entirely possible for several persons to hold identical emotionally tinted ideas and argue vehemently regarding the basic truth of their stand on a particular issue. Further, unrelated subjects are easily tied together by a complex. Thus, a successful ecologist relates everything to a perceived concept of the importance of attaining clean rivers, lakes, and air. These feelings dominate thinking and the ecologist makes associations that no one else is able to make.

Complexes do not lie dormant. They constantly influence a person's perception, thinking, decisions, and actions. Immediate reaction to a situation is the rule. Rationale and analysis are absent; what stand to take on a given subject is determined by expressing an emotional complex derived from past experience or hearsay information. Even though repressed, complexes are expressed. They are disguised by expressing them in acceptable terms. Normally a person justifies complex-determined behavior to herself or himself, but to others it may be intolerable. Many times when a complex is justifiable, one unconsciously hides one's individual complex from oneself and from others, apparently feeling that it is not to be generally known. In essence, the person's actions are based on deep-rooted feelings and memories that even one neither fully understands nor recognizes.

NATURE OF HUMAN BEHAVIOR

People are people whether they are in Palatka, Florida or Clear Creek, Indiana, in an office or in a factory. They bring to their place of work all their physical and mental differences, their individual values, their personal problems. Every person has a personality and complexes determined mainly by that person's heredity, social conditioning, and experience.

Being born to and for action, people take action and whatever is capable of suggesting and directing action has power over people. Having energy, the mind must work to some degree and in some direction. And this working normally requires direction. A person takes action to seek satisfaction, but the meaning of satisfaction, both in content and degree, is not the same for everyone. In fact, the action may be contradictory because one does not always understand what one wants and may take actions which are not in keeping with personal goals. This condition exists usually as a result of inner conflicts, deep-seated complexes, or avoidances by means of some defense mechanisms.

"Things are not always what they seem." The astute manager knows that people differ, the challenge is to know how they differ. By observing, studying, and talking face-to-face with a person, a great deal can be found out about that person. The manager must learn to seek and to listen for what the individual cannot or is unable to reveal or to say in expressing one's true point of view. Asking only such questions as will help one to express oneself fully is an effective practice. And the manager who listens in a patient and friendly manner is usually rewarded.

While people differ, there are common factors or general observations that are pertinent in helping a manager to understand human behavior and to utilize such knowledge in improving the management practiced. These common factors applicable to the individual, not the group are given in Figure 17–4. Group behavior is discussed later in this chapter.

FIGURE 17–4:   General observations pertinent to satisfying employee wants

1. Habit and emotion are of major importance in explaining people's behavior; reason is of secondary importance.
2. A sense of belonging to an acceptable group and of feeling important are strong motivating forces to most people.
3. People want credit for work accomplished when they deserve it.
4. Employees want to use their highest abilities and enjoy a sense of accomplishment on their jobs.
5. Employees want to achieve things of which they can be proud.
6. Employees prefer supervisors whom they respect and trust.
7. Criticism or unfavorable comparison of an employee's work in public is resented by most employees; they dislike "losing face."
8. The acceptance of new ideas and changes is more likely to take place if people are prepared for them; normally the instituting of sudden changes should be avoided.
9. When doing their work incorrectly, employees want to be told about it along with the correct way.
10. Reprimands and remedial actions are expected by most employees when they violate established and known means of operations; most employees prefer not to have the soft, "good Joe" type of superior.

ASSUMPTIONS OF HUMAN BEHAVIOR THEORIES

If one examines what the behavioral theorists say, it can be observed that a common set of assumptions underlie most of their ideas and suggestions. And these suggestions can be coordinated in order to obtain the best possible effect. The first assumption is that human skills and knowledge are not utilized to the maximum with the result that most persons enjoy from their work a less than satisfying experience that they might otherwise enjoy. As a result, work is an uninteresting, unsatisfying experience to many. However, work constitutes a major potential source of satisfaction. This state of affairs results in a psychologically damaging effect upon the person. The second assumption is that the underutilization of human resources damages the economic effectiveness of the organization. Human talents are valuable; to underutilize them is inefficient. Further, it is contended that when the work doesn't meet their desires for self-worth and satisfaction, the person may withhold efforts and energies. The third assumption includes that the challenge is to structure the work experience and to process or accomplish it in such a manner that both the needs of the individual and of the organization are economically met. In other words, the integration stimulates the individual to meet personal needs and at the same time contributes to the maximum in accomplishing the organization's needs.

We just stated above—"the challenge is to structure . . . and to process or accomplish. . . ." Let's take a closer look at these terms. To the behaviorist, structure means a structurally-oriented approach such as (1) *job enrichment,* which is a redesign of the job content, (2) *participation* or the involvement of people in decisions affecting them, and (3) *project organization* or project orientation for selected groups to achieve a specific project. In other words, structure-oriented means the work is structured in such a way that the most favorable behavior is practiced and the maximum mutual satisfactions are enjoyed. In contrast, process or accomplished oriented approaches include (1) *results management* or the mutual goal-setting and planning process to achieve the goals with review of progress regularly, (2) *transactional analysis* designed to improve communication and intra-company relations (discussed in Chapter 20), and (3) *team building* consisting of efforts to improve problem solving ability, cooperation, and the sharing of information. The process-oriented approach deals with the ways in which people relate to each other within an organization.

MINI-STATEMENTS OF HUMAN BEHAVIOR THEORIES

What are the major contents of several popular human behavior theories? We include these to give some acquaintance of the behavioral contributions being made to management knowledge. The discussion here is indicative only; it certainly is not conclusive and is not intended to be.

Maslow pointed out that human motivation is related to the satisfaction of five important needs making up a hierarchy. The needs include psychological, safety, affection, esteem, and self-actualization (see also Chapter 18). Also the development of an awareness for growth within a human being was emphasized. McGregor contended that a manager's way of working with people is based upon one's beliefs about people. From this he evolved the concept of Theory X and Theory Y discussed earlier in this chapter. Herzberg conceived a human being as having two fundamental needs (1) for psychological growth, and (2) for avoiding pain and discomfort (see Chapter 18). The former is satisfied through work or other activities, the latter through the conditions that surround what a person does. Well-designed work can be motivating in and of itself.

Argyris advances the belief that poor employee behavior—low productivity, poor work quality, high absenteeism—results from the lack of the organization to meet individuals' growth needs. Further, interpersonal incompetence, not technical difficulties, is the cause of most problems in organizations. Likert advances the idea of four systems of management extending from the least desirable which features tight work standards, personnel limitations, and high work pressure, to the most desirable where strong work groups, with participative and supportive management are linked by overlapping membership. To illustrate, such things as group decision making in a multiple overlapping group structure and supportive management will usually involve high confidence and trust, a favorable attitude toward managers, and excellent communication which results in high productivity, low absence, and low cost. In contrast, the least desirable system of management leads to little confidence and trust, low levels of cooperation, and poor communication. The organization should be such that all interactions and all relationships of each member with the organization should be supportive and build the person's sense of importance and worth in light of that person's values and expectations. Also, Likert emphasizes that the human resource is also valuable in the accounting or economic sense. Any lessening of this human asset diminishes the economic value of the organization.

IMPORTANCE OF GROUPS

Considering the individual only as an individual does not give the true behavioral picture of an individual. The reason: A person is not only an individual but commonly a member of a group. We know that group behavior differs significantly from individual behavior. That is, in expressing desires and gaining satisfactions, the individual as an individual behaves differently than when behaving as a member of a group. The satisfying of group demands also satisfy in various degrees the wants of the individuals making up the group. Each individual does not set out alone to satisfy needs irrespective of others in the group. Rather one seeks to satisfy one's wants by working together with others as a group. Every member contributes something toward the accomplishment of the common group goal. Each depends on the other, and the entire group is united in this mutual interest in order to achieve the predetermined objective.

Figure 17–5 is an attempt to show these concepts graphically. At the top of the drawing are spaces indicating five individuals, A, B, C, D, and E. Each works toward the Goal shown at the bottom of the drawing the return for which it is hoped will bring satisfaction of personal individual wants, as indicated by the arrows and their identifications. The contribution of individual A to the goal is indicated by the area marked A_1. Likewise that of B, C, D, and E is marked B_1, C_1, D_1, and E_1, respectively. These contributions are not necessarily equal, but they are vital to the entire goal achievement and are interrelated. A_1,

FIGURE 17–5

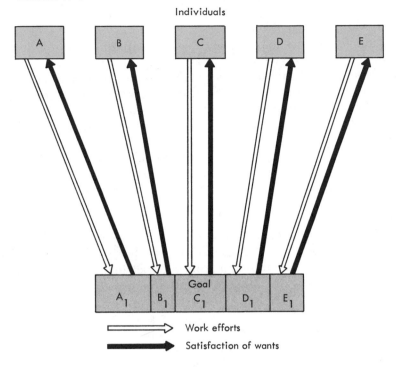

for example, depends somewhat on the success of B_1, and the achievement of E_1 contributes to the entire goal which affects A_1, etc. More and more we are witnessing the group taking precedence over the individual. Although the desire for individuality is strong, a normal human being possesses a gregarious instinct and is most content when part of a group.

Frequently in the integration of individuals' efforts into a smooth working group, the individual loses some individual personality and changes behavior. When this transition occurs, the individual's behavior becomes mainly that demanded by the group. Common goals, beliefs, and actions of the group predominate. This welding of individuals into an operating unit makes for teamwork characterized by the mutual dependence of the members upon one another.

GROUP BEHAVIOR

Group behavior is an entity of its own; it is not simply a summation of the behaviors of the individuals making up the group. A group has characteristics exclusively its own. For example, a group tends to be more emotional than most individuals.[4]

The values and behavior of an individual are related and usually subordinated to the member group. An individual who is affiliated with a definite group will not normally change personal behavior from that of the group if such a change sets him or her apart or deviates from the group's accepted behavior. A group has values of its own. They normally are expressed as standards of group behavior. A goodly amount of behavior conformity by members is necessary for a group to survive. This takes place by a process called socialization which is the assimilation by the individual of required values and behavior to be a group member. In essence, a member concedes to group pressure. Yet some nonconformity is usually tolerated and is desirable. Such a practice makes for progress and gives spice and human interest to the group.

As a group member, the work output and efficiency of a person commonly surpasses that achieved when that person works alone. Selecting one individual from a group, indoctrinating him or her with specialized training, and then returning that person to the group may result in trouble rather than in hoped-for progress. The trained individual has the problem of remaining in or perhaps reinstating self as a part of the group and yet retaining and applying the training given. The better application of group human relations to bring about the change would be to establish the need for the change among certain members and have them suggest and promote the change for the group. A member of a group is more likely to listen and believe what a co-member says in comparison to what an outsider says. In fact, anyone working with a group soon realizes that one must share the group's values and beliefs, perhaps feel like a member of the group, in order to accomplish aims by means of the group's efforts.

Groups form to bring together individuals having a common interest and to gain strength in acting as a unit. The unity theme is well expressed in this Aesop Fable:

> To quarrelsome sons who fell out
> Their father had these words to shout:
> "A single stick soon snaps.

---

[4] For information on group behavior see the following: T. O. Jacobs, *Leadership and Exchange in Formal Organizations* (Alexandria, Va.: Human Resources Research Organization, 1971); Alan C. Filley and Robert J. House, *Managerial Process and Organization Behavior* (Glenview, Ill.: Scott, Foresman and Company, 1969); A. Paul Hare, *Handbook of Small Group Research* (New Yjork: The Free Press of Glencoe, 1962); G. C. Homans, *The Human Group* (New York: Harcourt, Brace & World, 1950); H. T. Leavitt, *Managerial Psychology*, (Chicago: University of Chicago Press, 1964); J. G. March and H. A. Simon, *Organizations* (New York: John Wiley and Sons, Inc. 1958); R. M. Stogdill, *Individual Behavior and Group Achievement* (New York: Oxford Press, 1959).

A bundle takes all raps.
Unity—that's what strength's about."

Once formed, a group tends to strengthen itself and as stated above brings pressure on its members to conform to the group's beliefs and behavior. It is not uncommon for an individual to belong to several groups, each with a different interest. Sometimes these interests conflict and make for difficult decisions by the individual member. However, it should be noted that constantly changing group relationships are the rule, and these provide opportunities for resolving many conflicts.

A group's cohesiveness and productivity is higher when the members are permitted to form or select their own work groups. Under such conditions the job satisfaction of each member tends to increase. The members of the group fit together, adjustment in behavior is a minimum, and each individual works with fellow employees that are liked and with whom there is a preference to work. Also of interest is the influence of the group leader. For example, the group leader's statements made in introducing a new member to a group considerably influence the group's acceptance of the newcomer. Not all barriers, however, can be dissolved by introductory remarks. Favorable introductory comments elicit favorable group acceptance while opposite clues given in the introduction evoke relatively low group acceptance.

Figure 17–6 lists general observations helpful to a manager in un-

FIGURE 17–6: Group behavior observations

1. The purpose that causes the group to form influences the actions of the group.
2. Group behavior tends to be more irrational, more emotional than individual behavior. The action of a group is commonly that of oneness or of opposition.
3. Some groups have low cohesiveness; their members drift in and out. Other groups have high cohesiveness and receive strong and continuous support of most members.
4. Pressure to conform to the group's views is made greater and more effective in the high cohesive group that in the low cohesive group.
5. Typically when differences arise within a group, some members will be strongly for and some against, but the large majority will hold a compromise view, i.e., they are "middle-of-the-roaders."
6. Extremists refusing to conform in a high cohesive group are eventually cut off from the group. Initially, strong efforts are made to change the extremists, but failure to do so is followed by rejecting the dissenters.
7. In general, those group members trying hardest to influence other members are the most willing to accept the opinions of others.

derstanding group behavior. There are exceptions to these generalizations depending on the particular circumstance, but in the main they represent the normal group behavior to expect.

In general, a group can be influenced more effectively by dealing with the group as a unit rather than with the components of the group or the individuals singly. That is, it is frequently less difficult to sway a group than an individual. This is true for several reasons. First, when members of the group change their attitude, the individual can see that a personal change will not reduce one's relative ego-involvement. Second, changes or acceptance of persuasive efforts are often more effective on a group than on an individual, the influence of mob psychology and group motivations being exercised. Third, the attainment of an atmosphere of high enthusiasm, helpful for inducing changes, can best be reached with a group.

QUESTIONS

1. What are the three basic assumptions behavioral theorists make regarding human behavior? Select one of these assumptions and discuss in some depth.
2. Discuss the challenge of actuating in management.
3. State a clear definition for each of the following: (a) stimulus and response, (b) Theory Y, (c) group cohesiveness, and (d) complex.
4. Enumerate five general observations pertinent to satisfying human wants.
5. Relate to the extent you care to, the complexes that you have. Do you feel they influence your behavior? Discuss.
6. Discuss fully an actuating premise that you feel is important for a manager to keep in mind.
7. In your opinion, does the operation of Theory X influence the selection of new employees in any given company? Why?
8. Name and briefly discuss three managerial practices that are in keeping with recognition of the human resource importance.
9. Distinguish between structure-oriented and process-oriented approaches to human behavior study and give examples to illustrate your answer.
10. Discuss the importance of group behavior in managerial actuating work.
11. Distinguish between the two concepts given in each of the following: (a) McGregor's basic beliefs about human behavior and Likert's views about human behavior; (b) the human resource as a marginal renewable resource and as an infinitely renewable resource; (c) work as a potential source of satisfaction and the "good Joe" type of supervisor.
12. Is it easier to persuade an individual or a group? Justify your answer.
13. Name and briefly discuss three observations about group behavior.
14. Explain Figure 17–5 in your own words.

CASE 17–1.   UNGER PRODUCTS, INC.

You are the manager of a nonferrous castings department employing 24 production people. Although the total work force of the corporation is made up of different nationality groups, the employees in your department are of the same ethnic origin and represent a close-knit group. There is an informal leader who appears to interpret all communications from management members and who maintains a satisfactory work output. Another informal leader is active in handling grievances or complaints about the work or working conditions. When a job opening occurs in the department, this informal leader takes it upon himself to find a replacement—always from the same ethnic group. Neither you or any formal management member has objected since dependable help seems to be acquired this way and your department members appear to want it this way.

During the last three months, several problems have come up that have caused you to do some serious thinking about your group and your management of it. For example, several months ago, the demand for nonferrous castings took a sharp spurt upward. After considerable planning and reviewing, top management decided working overtime for several weeks was the only answer. Accordingly, you announced that overtime of 4 hours on Monday, Wednesday, and Thursday for the next three weeks would be followed. Time and one-half would be paid, time allowance for supper granted, and every member was expected to work overtime. However, your workers told you that they were not going to work overtime. You pointed out the need for it and asked for their cooperation. Still they refused and without giving any specific reason.

Another occasion concerns a new assistant production engineer fresh out of college, hired to improve the quality of the corporation's products and to lower production costs. He was friendly, and a quite serious young man of a different ethnic type than the members of your department. This new engineer requested from your department some sample castings of a somewhat unprecedented design for test purposes. Several of your experienced workers told you the design of the requested castings will not work. Reluctantly they made the castings requested. Shortly thereafter you were informed that the test castings were a failure. When your workers heard the news several remarked, "I knew it. That kid doesn't know what it is all about," and "I told you so. But I do what I'm told. That way I keep out of trouble."

Two weeks ago, your department received a new piece of equipment to try out. After the manufacturer's representative explained to your workers how to operate this equipment, it was used to run several orders. The rate of production for the new equipment was nearly twice that of the process now followed in the department. After several days of operating, the equipment became inoperative. Inspection by the manufacturer's representative showed sabotage. You suspect some members of your department of committing foul play, but you don't know who they are or if, in fact, sabotage is the cause.

This morning the monthly production report shows your department is No. 2 of the 11 departments in the factory. The works manager just finished a telephone call to you congratulating you on your excellent record.

Questions

1. What group actions or forces appear to be present in your department? Discuss.
2. Do you feel any change by you is in order? Elaborate on your answer.
3. What actions do you believe you should take? Why?

CASE 17–2. JAVES COMPANY

Leonard Hart, director of engineering design and research, joined Javes Company right after receiving his M.E. degree. He started as a trainee. Winning promotions from time to time, he has now been with the company 27 years. For the past four years, he has been in his present capacity as a major officer of the company. Leonard Hart likes his job and he likes the Javes Company. Ambitious and a very hard worker, he is well thought of by his compeers in management and has the reputation of running a good department. Now 50 years of age, he well realizes that he has reached the top of his bracket, that there are no future promotions for him at Javes, and that no further financial incentive is available to him. By staying with the company for the next 15 years, he will retire with an attractive pension.

His wife, Lenora, is active in church and several community associations. She likes the small town where the company is located and enjoys her large number of friends. Their younger of two daughters is getting married next month and Lenora is looking forward to increasing her social activities in the future and expects to continue residency at their present address.

Elsworth Rieter, president of Javes Company, has observed that Mr. Hart is losing some of his enthusiasm and willingness to take on extra company assignments that he used to request. Arranging for the company's annual picnic and handling contributions for United Charities are illustrative. It's not that Mr. Hart is not as energetic as he once was. He jogs a mile every morning, plays golf twice a week, and spends considerable time in his workshop at home making all sorts of gadgets. He is in excellent physical condition. Mr. Reiter has informally discussed Mr. Hart's behavior on special occasions with the vice president of finance, who says, "Leonard has changed somewhat. He realizes he has reached his peak and is starting to level off." What neither Mr. Reiter nor the vice president of finance know is that for the last year, Mr. Hart has attempted to find a better job, but to date has been unsuccessful in locating one. He is beginning to accept the idea that there probably isn't a better job for him than the one he has and he should remain where he is.

Questions

1. What is the problem?
2. Assuming Leonard Hart spends the rest of his work life with Javes Company, do you feel problems will arise relative to the behavior of Mr. Hart? Discuss.
3. What actions do you recommend the company take? Why?

Chapter 18

Managerial motivation

We come into this world crying while all around us are smiling.
May we so live that we go out of this world smiling while
everybody around us is weeping.

Persian proverb

How can I get my members to care more about their work?

What kinds of conditions bring out the best in them?

What motivates employees to do their best and derive satisfactions from their work?

Questions such as these are foremost in most managers' minds. In the opinion of many, the key to work performance is motivation. It can be defined as follows: *Motivation is the desire within an individual that stimulates him or her to action.* The degree or extent of stimulation depends upon the person's expectations of the level of satisfaction one feels can be achieved. Studies regarding the relationship between motivation and an individual's or a group's productivity, effectiveness, and satisfactions derived have shed considerable light upon this fascinating subject area. According to these investigations, the most important factors affecting motivation can be summarized as (1) personal wants and needs, (2) goals and perceptions of the person or the group, and (3) the manner in which these needs and goals will be realized.

When employees enjoy their jobs, find the work challenging, and like the general work environment, they will usually put forth their best efforts and perform their tasks enthusiastically. On the other hand, if employees cannot wait for the end of the work day, are alienated from the results that are obtained from their efforts, and feel their work is terribly boring, they will not do their best. What they will do is the minimum required to keep their jobs.

NEEDS, WANTS, AND GOAL ORIENTATION

Why does a human being desire to achieve anything? Basically to fulfill an unsatisfied need. We all have needs—physical, economic,

390

political, and so forth—and we consciously or unconsciously, by our behavior, seek to satisfy them in order that we live the life we believe we want to live, or the life that somebody we believe in tells us we should live. From the viewpoint of management, the satisfaction of these needs is related to the individual and one's work, superiors, associates, and work environment.

To comprehend motivation, it is necessary to gain an understanding of why people behave as they do in given situations and to realize the many different forces that human behavior takes. A basic premise is that the great majority of behavior with which a manager deals is goal oriented. The patterns of the normal motivation behavior concept can be illustrated as shown in Figure 18–1. Beginning at the left, an un-

FIGURE 18–1:   Patterns of normal motivational behavior

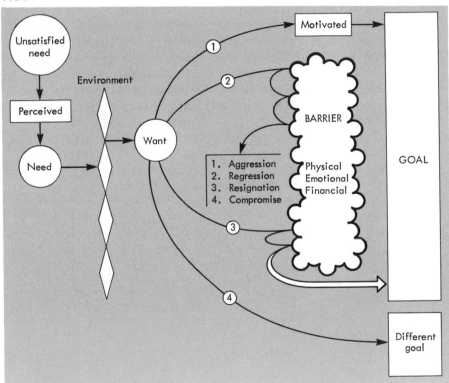

satisfied need is perceived by the individual. Tension is created as the awareness for this need increases. This tension gives rise to a motive for the person to satisfy the need. Reviewing his or her environment and being guided by past experience and knowledge, the person interprets the need in terms of a want. That is, the want can be viewed as an environmental conditioned specific way the need will be satisfied. For example, both A and B may perceive a need for esteem. A expresses this as a want for a successful legal career, B as a professional football player. These different wants result from the environmental conditioning which has taken place for each individual. With the want identified, the person then engages in behavior directed toward the achievement of a specific goal (line 1 on the figure). This effect will continue until the tension created by the need deficiency is reduced or another need deficiency is perceived as more important and the motivational process continues.

However, not all behavior follows the normal motivational pattern. The person may encounter a barrier in the path of reaching the goal (see lines 2, 3, and 4 in the figure). As a result, adjustments must be made. Several alternatives exist. One is shown by line 2 which is the case where the person cannot reduce the tension and becomes frustrated. Resort to defense mechanisms such as aggression, regression, resignation, and compromise takes place.[1] A second alternative, line 3, is a change in behavior by the individual in order to reach the goal. The third alternative, line 4, is a change in the goal itself.

The preference–expectation theory advanced by Victor Vroom in 1964 offers additional assistance worthy of inclusion here.[2] This theory is based on two premises:

1.   A person subjectively assigns values to the expected outcomes of various courses of action and therefore has preferences among the expected outcomes.

2.   Any explanation of motivated behavior must take into account not only the ends that people hope to accomplish but the extent to which they believe that their own actions are instrumental in producing the outcomes they prefer.

A person may place a high value on bringing about a certain outcome, but if one does not believe that any personal act will affect what happens, one will not act. On the other hand, if a person anticipates to a great degree that a highly valued act depends on her or his actions, that person will become highly motivated to act.

HUMAN NEEDS

The task of motivating is not easy. Typically, the employees of a company have different backgrounds, experiences, hopes, desires, ambitions, and psychological makeups. They see events in different terms, and their reactions to their work, to each other, and to their surroundings are subject to considerable variations. Psychologists

---

[1] These defense mechanisms are discussed in Chapter 15, pp. 331–32.

[2] Victor Vroom, *Work and Motivation*, (New York: John Wiley and Sons, Inc., 1964), pp. 17–33, 121–47.

have developed different classifications of human needs ranging from one basic need to some 25 needs. The sex drive, power, and desire for individuality are examples of well known single motives.

The importance of the various needs or wants which motivate humans was expertly expressed by the late Prof. Douglas McGregor in these words:

> Man is a wanting animal—as soon as one of his needs is satisfied, another appears in its place. This process is unending. It continues from birth to death. Man continuously puts forth effort—works, if you please—to satisfy his needs. . . . A satisfied need is not a motivator. This is a fact which is . . . ignored in the conventional approach to management people.[3]

A very useful classification of needs developed by psychologist A. H. Maslow recognizes five basic human needs which make up a hierarchy of needs.[4] A graphic representation of this hierarchy is shown in Figure 18–2. An elaboration of the needs include:

1. *Physiological needs,* exemplified by hunger and thirst; these needs are the basic or starting point for most needs. Their satisfaction is necessary for the

FIGURE 18–2:   **Hierarchy of five basic human needs**

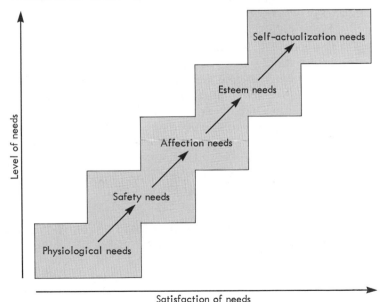

_____

[3] Paul R. Lawrence, et al., *Organizational Behavior and Administration* (Homewood, Ill.: Richard D. Irwin, Inc., 1961), p. 224.

[4] A. H. Maslow, "A Theory of Human Motivation," *Psychological Review,* July 1943, pp. 370–96.

preservation of life. Once satisfied they cease to operate as a prime motivator of behavior.

2. *Safety needs* constitute the second level of needs. They consist of the need for clothing, shelter, and having an environment of a predictable pattern such as job security, pension, and insurance.

3. *Affection needs* include the need to belong, to be a wanted member of a group, not only of a family, but a work group as well.

4. *Esteem needs* are represented by needs for self-respect, achievement, and for recognition by others. The desire for prestige and status is an important aspect of the drive for achievement. Esteem needs represent the fourth level of basic human needs.

5. *Self-actualization needs*, the capstone of the hierarchy of needs is represented by self-fulfillment, one doing what one can do—one's ultimate in one's contribution to one's society. It represents the complete realization of one's full potential.

In contemporary society the needs lower in the hierarchy are more completely satisfied than the higher needs. Many, for example, have the great majority of their physiological and safety needs fulfilled. It is the affection needs and the esteem needs that require satisfying and, for the top, or self-actualization needs, relatively still fewer people gain satisfaction for them. However, this hierarchy of needs is not always followed in a rigid pattern. There are reversals and substitutions. A research chemist, for example, may neglect to eat and sleep (physiological needs) in the midst of creativity. Likewise, some persons center on esteem needs—the acquisition of wealth, for example, almost to the exclusion of affection needs—the need to belong to a group. In many cases such a situation may have developed due to a suppression of affection needs early in life with a resultant emphasis on esteem needs as a substitute. Needs are relative in their strength and are individualistic. A "lower" need does not necessarily have to be fulfilled before a "higher" need emerges.

WORK AND MOTIVATION

Work itself is an extremely important consideration in motivation. Historically, work has been viewed as a provider of opportunity to share in the task of developing and sustaining the universe and its inhabitants. It influences cultural values and determines the circumstances under which we live. Concern about work and its role in our lives continues to be an important issue.

Work is regarded differently by different persons. Some revere it for its own sake, but the vast majority perform it essentially for what they believe they are getting from it; that is, doing the work is, in the ultimate, related to the personal goals which the person is trying to achieve. A person tends to work with zeal if the satisfaction from the work is high and in keeping with what the person wants. In essence, the reason one gives much of oneself to one's work is that the work gives to that person much of what is sought.

Does a person work because he or she has wants that cannot be satisfied without money? Some do, some don't. A number of people who are well fixed financially continue to work hard and maintain a punishing schedule of activities. Others work hard, but not for material gains. Missionaries, teachers, clergy, and some scientists are examples. Probably they could make more money in some other field of endeavor but they are passing this up, at least for the present, for nonmonetary returns or rewards. What is motivating these hard workers? Is it desire for power, is it pride, is it a set behavior pattern, or is it love of action? It could be any one or all of these—or any of a number of other considerations.

It appears that work must provide a psychic income to a person. Over the long term, work cannot be simply an instrumental act in order to acquire a material possession such as a car, a new chair, or a house. In the ultimate, a person wants work that is personally meaningful and when this is lacking, motivational efforts are extremely difficult to attain. As evaluated by the employee, the four major aspects of work that are important include

1. The general nature of the work—its challenge and the use it requires of one's talents.
2. Freedom to perform the work, to employ personal ideas, to feel vital in the efforts bringing about work accomplishment, and to make decisions about the work.
3. Opportunity to grow and to develop through training, feedback on performance, and to receive a reasonable variety of assignments.
4. Recognition of work achievement in a forthright, sincere, and timely manner.

HERZBERG DUAL-FACTOR THEORY

According to Frederick Herzberg, a well-known behavioral scientist, two distinctly different types of influence tend to determine employee satisfaction. They are maintenance factors and motivational factors. The maintenance factors include such things as salary, physical working conditions, job security, pleasant supervision, and fringe benefits. The absence of some of these factors may lead to dissatisfaction and absenteeism by the employee. Maintenance factors are commonly called "satisfiers" because their presence helps make an employee satisfied, while their absence causes an employee to be dissatisfied. Note, however, that the presence of satisfiers *will not* motivate an employee beyond what is necessary to maintain the job. Rather, meeting the maintenance factors serves to prevent job dissatisfaction. Once the employee's expectations have been met, additions to the maintenance factors have little, if any, effect on performance.

To motivate requires the opportunity to meet the needs for employee autonomy, competence, and achievement. And this is where the motivational factors come into play. These factors are aspects of the task or work itself. They include challenge, chance for personal growth, and performance feedback. In other words, as viewed by the employee, the work having these characteristics means motivational factors are present. These factors contribute heavily to the satisfaction of the employee and have a positive effect on his or her performance.

Sometimes the theory is referred to by the concept of *job content* and *job context*. Job content refers to the job or work itself. Since the motivational factors emerge from the work-worker relationship, they are included under job content. Commonly the term *intrinsic* is employed because the motivational factors belong or emerge from the work itself and the employee. On the other hand, *job context* includes the maintenance factors. It is referred to as being *extrinsic* because job context factors or maintenance factors are outside the main thing that is being considered, namely the work itself and the employee.

From what has been stated, it follows that—according to this motivational theory—the motivational factors, or the job content, is of relatively more importance. It is most desirable to have motivating factors, but motivating factors are never entirely satisfactory unless maintenance factors are reasonably satisfactory and effective. The two are obviously closely related in most work situations. But observe that motivational factors, or job content, are always timely and act to reinforce behavior as it occurs. They must be present and correct if motivation efforts are to reach their zenith. In contrast, maintenance factors tend to be of relatively short duration; they lose some of their impact and importance with time.

The conclusion to be drawn here is that the work itself should be designed so as to stimulate and challenge the employee and provide the opportunity for that person to grow to the peak of her or his potential. When the work offers the employee no more satisfaction than a paycheck, a comfortable place to work, and an agreeable boss, apathy and the amount of effort to get by are quite likely to be present. In addition, it is helpful to keep in mind that job satisfaction is most likely to result from accomplishment coming from performance behavior. That is, satisfaction comes from and is the result of performance. Herzberg observed that the belief in achievement feasibility and making achievement leads to motivation, it is not the reverse, i.e., motivation leading to achievement.[5]

---

[5] Herzberg, Mausner, and Snyderman, *The Motivation to Work* (New York: John Wiley and Sons, Inc., 1959), pp. 5–22.

Criticism has been leveled against the Herzberg Theory. The main thrust is that where employee satisfaction resides depends upon the expectation of the person involved. Satisfaction, it is contended, can reside in either or both job content and job context. Further, the same classifications of job conditions can lead to satisfying or dissatisfying incidents because different carrying agents are responsible. To illustrate, credit for good or satisfying events is usually taken by the person, and the blame for bad events is placed on others.[6]

THE MOTIVATING JOB

It will be helpful to discuss briefly and in keeping with current thinking, what constitutes a motivating job. By providing such jobs, motivating will be encouraged and enhanced. First, the job should consist of an adequate series of tasks to permit the employee to know the start and the finish of what has been accomplished. The popular concept of 25–30 years ago that the fewer tasks a person learns and performs result in lower training time and costs is going by the board. In most cases, what such a practice does to today's employees is to overwhelm them with inherent repetitiveness and resultant boredom. The result: Employees are not motivated. Consider the job of a young clerk in a retailer's office. His job was to pull invoices from envelopes, sort the invoices into seven stacks, and deliver them to another clerk. His work was changed. Now he processes, for each of 25 vendors, all transactions including adjusting shortages to crediting payments. His reaction: "I like being responsible for my vendors. When 5 o'clock comes around I feel I've accomplished something that is worthwhile."

Second, the job should permit the employee to decide and run one's own work as much as possible. The motivating manager might ask herself, "How can the employee be made more autonomous—more on her own? Is reporting to me first always necessary?" Freedom to use creativity, to suggest and to adopt better ways and solutions to problems, all within the mutually understood constraints between oneself and one's superior, makes for a highly motivating job for most people.

Next, frequent, objective, and adequate feedback should be supplied the employee. It is important especially in motivating for an employee to know the ways in which performance improvements can be made. If a feedback is given every six months, it is quite likely to be the frequency at which the employee will seek to improve performance. Letting one know monthly or even weekly is far more motivational. Adequate communication and a redesign of the work so that the

---

[6] Schwab and Cummings, "Theories of Performance and Satisfaction: A Review," *Industrial Relations,* no. 4, 1970, pp. 408–30, and Schneider and Locke, "A Critique of Herzberg's Incident Classification System and a Suggested Revision," *Organizational Behavior and Human Performance,* vol. 6, 1971, pp. 441–55.

job itself provides adequate feedback are additional and effective means to follow.

Last, the manager can help in making the job of a motivating type by following certain definite practices. Among these are to set an example and demonstrate that showing enthusiasm for a task—no matter how large or small—conditions job satisfaction. Also, raising personal goals and demonstrating most goals can be accomplished if one is willing to pay the price in devotion to a cause, and plain hard work can also influence in a positive way the employee's attitude toward work. In addition, the manager can reflect by actions a belief in his or her group members and of their abilities to contribute, to grow, and to find personal fulfillment from their work efforts.

MOTIVATION AND CHANGE

From what has been stated it follows that in many cases success in motivation requires change—especially change in behavior on the part of the person being motivated. Too many times the actuating effort is just words—complete agreement exists regarding the end results, but nothing really takes place to move in the direction of the desired change.

To induce change we need to remember that the behavior of a given individual adds up or represents a sort of equilibrium. Further, a person is not likely to change; a person tends to stay with what that person now possesses; in fact, one may resent any attempt to change him or her because it will require new personal adjustments. Then too, in some cases, there is also the question of how much change is possible and still be ethical. What is right may be interpreted in light of law, economic interests, and moral beliefs. In management, the influence of superiors, lack of company policy, and general practices within a given industry may regulate to what extent behavioral change can be made within generally acceptable ethical limits. Actually the behavior of others, ethical or not, is commonly used as a criterion by a manager to justify decisions.

A major difficulty in getting behavior changed is the general belief that such a change is an admission by the people changing that what they had been thinking and doing they now admit to be erroneous. And they reason, they should have been more intelligent and discovered their own errors. So there is a very strong face-saving element present in most major behavior changes.

Help can be given a person in changing behavior. Persons are influenced favorably or unfavorably by examples provided, experiences permitted, frames of reference supplied, encouragement of certain motives, and the discountenance of other forces. An existing behavior represents the outcome of motives supporting that behavior. Some motives exert a stronger influence than others. To change the behavior it is frequently helpful to weaken the supporting influences to certain motives. To use a frontal attack in an effort to substitute a new motive for an old one is usually ineffective. Removal of accustomed influences meet resistance and arouses defenses.

The weakening of supporting influences can be attempted in various ways. Among the more common is to provide facts and knowledge which can be evaluated. The attempt here is to stress greater rational consideration than emotional. Supplying expert or authoritative explanations or viewpoints along with the reasons for such viewpoints can also be employed. In some instances it is effective to get the individual to review personal experience, to become more aware of what it means, and to try to reevaluate it. Frequently it is effective to alter the relationship of the individual with the reference group, that is, to reduce the ego-involvement by lowering the favorable respondence of the group to the behavior. An effective way is to talk with the group, point out major reasons for the change with emphasis given to possible gains to be realized by the group's members, request their cooperation and support, and appeal for a favorable decision.

VALUES, ATTITUDES, AND MOTIVATION

For an individual the basic value system held ultimately determines who and what that individual is, how one relates to oneself, to others, and to one's job. Hence, values are important in motivation because of their influence upon a person's behavior. Any dissonance between organizational values and individual values can certainly create problems of motivation.

This suggests finding out and understanding just what the values of people in an organization are and how they relate to goals trying to be achieved by the organization. With such knowledge, adjustments and programs can be devised to clarify both personal and company objectives, develop better understanding, and heighten commitment to a cause or causes deemed vital. In addition, a reduction can be won in the far too prevalent tendency of designing motivational programs in keeping with a manager's perception rather than taking into account the perceptions of all involved in the program.

An attitude is a way a person tends to feel, see, or interpret a particular situation. It focuses on a specific physical, social, or abstract object predisposing its holder to respond in some preferential manner. An attitude is intangible; it is determined by another from the way a person acts or responds to a situation, person, group, event, or institution. An attitude is not the same as a value. The latter has more to do with modes of conduct and final states of existence, plus a value is a more lasting criteria for guiding action. Typically a person has many, many attitudes, but perhaps not more than 15 basic values.

Attitudes merit attention in motivation, but it is well to point out that an attitude is neither (1) a motive nor (2) a response. Attitude refers to probable direction, not the behavior itself. Attitude is not a drive or force, as a motive is, but simply a state of readiness to respond. It follows that attitudes do not necessarily lead to expression or action. A person can have an attitude concerning an enterprise or another person without taking any action with respect to either of them. In fact, most people have experienced this particular state of affairs.

A common classification of attitudes is (1) positive or constructive and (2) negative or destructive. A positive attitude emphasizes success and encouragement. In contrast, a negative attitude stresses possible hurdles or the viewpoint that in a given case the objective cannot be attained. Most objectives are accomplished far more effectively when positive attitudes prevail. Optimism is a matter of attitude. Managers must first think they can before they can. Success and victory thrive under the influence of positive attitudes. The kind of atmosphere in which managers are going to work and live is determined more by their attitudes than anything else. Figure 18–3 gives an excellent creed to follow for developing favorable attitudes.

Attitudes are learned or acquired during daily life experiences. They are founded perhaps more on an emotional than on a rational basis. People are not born with attitudes. From infancy on, a person acquires traditions, beliefs, opinions, and knowledge, all of which help to formulate attitudes. Attitudes are acquired in one or a combination of three ways (1) past experience, (2) acceptance of the attitude of the group of which a person is a member, and (3) a statement of an authoritative source. While all three of these sources are important, that of experience is probably most common. To a significant degree, a person feels and thinks toward an object as one has personally witnessed that particular object. An arbitrator's attitude toward settling collective bargaining disputes will probably differ from that of a retired business leader in Florida.

The influence of experience upon attitude is brought out by a popular Mother Goose rhyme which goes—

> Pussy-cat, pussy-cat, where have you been?
> I've been to London to look at the Queen.
> Pussy-cat, pussy-cat, what did you there?
> I frightened a little mouse under the chair.

What would you expect a cat to do? To perform those actions which a cat does from experience. Likewise, an employee sees only what one's mind has been trained to observe and does what one's firsthand

FIGURE 18–3:   An excellent creed for developing favorable attitudes

The optimist creed

Promise yourself—

To be so strong that nothing can disturb your peace of mind.

To talk health, happiness, and prosperity to every person you meet.

To make all your friends feel that there is something in them.

To look at the sunny side of everything and make your optimism come true.

To think only of the best, to work only for the best, and to expect only the best.

To be just as enthusiastic about the success of others as you are about your own.

To forget the mistakes of the past and press on to the greater achievements of the future.

To wear a cheerful countenance at all times and give every living creature you meet a smile.

To give so much time to the improvement of yourself that you have no time to criticize others.

To be too large for worry, too noble for anger, too strong for fear, and too happy to permit the presence of trouble.

Christian D. Larson

Courtesy Optimist International, St. Louis, Mo.

experience suggests should be done—this experience sets the stage for many of one's attitudes.

SUGGESTED MOTIVATORS

The following ten motivators usually give excellent results. For any given case, the choice should be guided by the individual circumstances and followed by careful and diligent application of the motivator. Included are:

1. Job enrichment and rotation.   To a great extent the approach of simplifying jobs, hiring people to do these very simple jobs, and permitting each employee to perform only one of several of these very simple tasks is going by the board. We know with reasonable certainty that this is the road to smother any interest or challenge in the job and to generate apathy, boredom, and fatigue. The degree to which these undesirable concepts are reached depends upon the individual. Also with the average employee having a higher education than years ago, with the unions and their demands, and with the changing attitude toward authority, we know that slicing the work into very thin strips just doesn't fit modern job requirements.

Job rotation is also winning favor. Under this arrangement an employee is rotated from one job assignment to another. Periodically job switches take place, thus hopefully minimizing boredom and disinterest. The jobs included in the program should represent a composite designed to develop the employee and expose him or her to a variety of work to satisfy individual needs.

2. Participation.   Participation encourages and permits contributions to decisions, goals, and plans along with suggestions as to how these can be implemented. It can be formally defined as *both mental and emotional involvement of a person to make contributions to the decision-making process, especially on matters in which personal involvement of the person exists, and to assume one's share of the responsibility for them.* The motivational basis is that people like to be asked their opinion and know that their ideas and beliefs have some weight in the ultimate management action taken. The underlying assumptions are: People derive satisfaction from being a part of the management action, from doing as effective a job as practical, and having self-control rather than organization control utilized. By using participation greater acceptance· to change is accomplished. Most people more readily accept what they in part helped create than something entirely foreign to them. Also, participation supplies the feeling of belonging and being wanted. It inflates or at least recognizes a person's ego and provides a needed sense of importance. In addition, it encourages better decision making, gets people to accept responsibility, promotes teamwork, and emphasizes the use of creativity.

Participation cannot be applied universally to all people. Best results follow when (1) employees are interested in and ready to assume responsibility; (2) objectives of the enterprise are well stated and known to all employees; (3) adequate knowledge about the subject exists among participants to deal with the subject at hand; (4) time to participate is available; (5) participants are familiar with the constraints to be observed (legal requirements, company policies, etc.); (6) effective communication exists; and (7) each participant knows personal position and status will not be adversely affected by one's participation.

3. Results management.   As initially discussed in Chapter 4 and mentioned throughout this book, results management properly handled is highly motivational. Each employee actively engages in determining one's own objectives and how that person intends achieving them, with final approval given by the superior, and the evaluation of the subordinate's efforts based on results using the employee's objectives as the standard, have tremendous built-in motivational qualities. The subordinate becomes results-minded, as well as practical with respect to how and when certain tasks can be completed. Further, the required self-appraisal of the person's abilities helps that person to realize where one's strength or weakness lie and to behave accordingly.

We say a great deal in management about a manager knowing precisely what the objectives are, exercising authority and responsibility to do the work properly, and receiving a feedback on "how am I doing." Results management provides all these things. They are built right into the approach. In essence, each employee is made the manager over his or her own work affairs. The results are up to the person who takes over, manages, and is judged on the results achieved. This appears to be an ideal managerial arrangement, the zenith of true and effective motivating efforts.

4. *Multiplier manager.* A manager seeing himself primarily as a multiplier of others aids in promoting motivation. A multiplier manager acts in the context of how one's behavior assists others in the work group to do a better and more effective job. Asking each subordinate, "How good have I made you look?" encourages and helps build that subordinate's self-confidence.

An advantage of being a multiplier manager is that individuals are led to develop fully and completely their own talents. Also, there is a very close relationship formulated between the interests and skills of each subordinate and the requirements of the enterprise. Further, evaluation of management personnel is enhanced. Questions answered include: Are the plans and ideas suggested up to date? Is the person letting obsolescence overtake him or her? What work or training is being done to improve the person's management knowledge and skills?

5. *Power of mind.* It was Emerson who wrote, "What you are speaks so loudly that nothing you say can be heard." We become what we think. This implies an enormous challenge and is vital in management motivating. A manager should know what one's subordinates really think, if one hopes to motivate them. Further, the manager should know what is needed to improve the value of the mind that each of one's subordinates brings to work each day. Having information of this sort will help in getting answers to what changes and improvements in the thinking of a group should take place. Progress along this line will assist significantly in improving motivation.

Trying to motivate employees who spend too little time in environments where they are exposed to the sort of people, information, and actions that will help them, is part of the problem of motivation. What a person's mind attends to continually, that person believes. Employees come to believe that their work environment, the caliber of their top management, and so forth, mediocre though it be, is par for the course—it is what work environment and top management are in their minds and they accept it for what it is. And the same holds true for employees working under good environment and effective top management in that this type of work life becomes the accepted condition.

6. Realistic human relations. These are essential because normally organizational objectives are not primarily to provide for the needs of members. Further, the granting to the typical employee extreme permissiveness and encouraging him or her to do anything the person feels like doing does not contribute to want satisfaction or to desired development. Following a "hands-off," no direction, universal agreement, harmony-at-any-price managerial role is an unrealistic approach and usually does not result in effective motivating.

Many a manager has found that following a program of "make the employees happy and try to be liked, then they'll produce more" just isn't always effective. This does not mean that a manager should be dictatorial, operate as a lone wolf, be unfriendly, and make oneself difficult to get along with. One need not be a "hard-boiled" boss; neither does one have to be a "soft-boiled" boss. The latter is as bad as the former. "Soft-boiled" managers stress the belief that no one should be asked to do anything that he or she does not want to do. They operate on a "management by consent" basis—the manager waits long enough for employees to arrive at the idea themselves. Trouble arises if they do not want to do what must be done. If it is imperative that it be done, the manager had better get it done. "Soft-boiled" managers usually indicate to the employees that management has abdicated, the enterprise is wishy-washy, there is no firm direction, and inefficient performance will be tolerated.

The great majority of employees want to contribue and accomplish work that to them is satisfying. Inherently they want to please their superior and at the same time gain satisfaction from their work efforts and relationships. They respond to a sense of fairness, duty, and work. They resent being manipulated by any means, direct or indirect, and prefer a forthright answer to a forthright question.

7. Work accomplishment environment. This includes a work climate which has the presence of a pressure to get things done. When this exists to a high degree, the success of motivating is usually high. The need to achieve, getting projects finished, and the value of time are prominent attributes that make for a high work accomplishment environment.

Variations in the work accomplishment environment exist not only by type of company, but also by department. In other words, some departments in an organization, for example, might have a high environmental factor, while in others it may be low. But there is no question that the degree of environment work accomplishment factor influences the organization's way of life, characterizes its management team, and mode of performing work.

8. Flexible working hours. There is considerable interest in altering the work week to suit better the employee's convenience. Various work weeks are being used, all with the aim of lengthening the leisure between work periods. Most common are the four-day, 40-hour week with three days off (4/3); the three-day, 36-hour week with four days off (3/4); and the seven-day, 70-hour week with seven days off (7/7). Of these the 4/3 arrangement is most popular. There are also "gliding time" arrangements whereby the employee is permitted to change working hours from day to day, usually with the provision that "core" times be observed, i.e., times when everybody works due to the nature of the operation. If core time is 9 A.M.–noon and gliding time applies, a person may work 7 A.M.–noon and 1–4 P.M., leaving early to attend to personal business or leisure pursuits. Having less trips to make to and from work as is the case with the 4/3 arrangement over the five-day week (5/2), time available to take care of personal matters, and the opportunity to avoid peak traffic jams, are viewed by many as advantages and it is believed improves the work environment and attitude of the employee toward one's job.

9. Effective criticism. This can be a springboard for improving an employee's behavior and performance. Adopting a positive approach makes criticism less difficult as well as more effective. The superior should examine one's own motives before one criticizes. He or she should be sure to plan what is going to be said in order to make the content and presentation the best possible. It is also helpful to know whether a consistent behavior pattern or merely a one-time occurrence is being dealt with.

It is well to point out that mistakes are a part of growth, and progress is more likely if mistakes are brought out in the open. Further, that although there are faults in the present behavior and performance, there are also good points about what is being done. Keep the criticism on use of personal efforts for improvement now, not next week or next month. Resolve mutual immediate and realistic goals. Try to set up specific time schedules for improvements.

An effective plan to follow is: First establish the basic problem. Then say the negative things you have to say. Be specific in examples of unsatisfactory behavior. Next, ask the subordinate for specific ways in which he believes he can improve the unsatisfactory behavior. Help by suggesting ways yourself and work them out with the subordinate. Following this, point out the subordinate's outstanding good points and how they demonstrate potential for improvement. Last, close the conversation, but do not do this until you believe the problem and its solution has been fairly discussed.

10. Zero defects. Designed to motivate employees to adhere consistently to high standards of work excellence, zero defects (ZD) programs have been extremely effective. The goal is to make the defects zero by avoiding mistakes, oversights, unreliable products, and delivery delays. ZD programs rely upon recognition of the importance of the human element and the self-will of personnel to want to give outstanding quality work performance. It emphasizes self-motivation to acquire pride and workmanship and to manufacture acceptable quality parts and products.

In establishing a ZD program it is best to give it positive identification from the top to the bottom of the entire organization. A manager of the program should be appointed, comprehensive training about it provided, and a dramatic kickoff date established. Promotional efforts, such as the display of ZD posters, awarding of ZD pins, and distributing ZD stickers for car windows, assist greatly in motivating a high rate of interest in the program. Some use the term PRIDE (Production of Reliable Items Demand Excellence), but by whatever name it is known, favorable results predominate. To illustrate, in a sheet metal shop, weekly data revealed that of a total of 13,800 production work-hours expended, 82 work-hours were spent on correcting production errors. After the ZD program was in effect, these 82 work-hours for correction were reduced to only 16 work-hours, a reduction of over 80 percent.

QUESTIONS

1. What are the most important factors affecting motivation? Discuss.
2. Define each of the following: (*a*) zero defects, (*b*) job enrichment, (*c*) hierarchy of needs, and (*d*) flexible working hours.
3. From the viewpoint of the employee, what are the four aspects of work that are important?
4. What are maintenance factors and of what importance are they in the Herzberg Dual-Factor Theory?
5. Relate a personal experience in which you were motivated by striving to achieve recognition by others.
6. Explain Figure 18–1 in your own words.
7. In what ways do the contributions to motivation by Maslow differ from those of Herzberg? Discuss.
8. What is the preference-expectation theory and of what importance is it in motivation?
9. Discuss the influence of values and attitudes upon motivation.
10. A recent motivational study shows that "feeling one's work is worth doing" is very important. Primarily this means that (1) the job fits the person, (2) reward is given for competence, (3) opinions are asked for, (4) learning is a part of the job, and (5) agreeable relationships with peers exist. Suggest how each of these may be developed and utilized.
11. Relate the help and the relative benefits a manager's motivating efforts can gain by giving careful consideration to job content and job context.
12. What is the meaning of and what are some useful suggestions for using participation as a motivator?

13. Why does the typical member of an organization tend to resist changing behavior? Of what importance is this in motivation?

14. What are some considerations that tend to make a job motivating? Discuss in some detail.

CASE 18–1. BRANDIS COMPANY

Archie Fitzgerald has worked for the Brandis Company, a manufacturer of data processing equipment, for the past seven years. He joined Brandis from a competitor because he believed he could "get ahead" with Brandis whereas he didn't see his future clearly with his former employer. Archie appears to be happily married, and has two sons, ages 13 and 11. His wife, who is liked by everyone, is socially minded and the Fitzgeralds have many friends and entertain frequently at their home. Mrs. Fitzgerald is a member of several prominent local organizations. Archie likes baseball, is a stalwart supporter of the local Little League Baseball activities, and makes a hobby of umpiring local amateur baseball games.

As assistant sales manager of an eight-state district, Archie must travel quite a bit. He is out of town perhaps an average of two nights a week. He enjoys this field sales work and likes the challenge of helping prospective customers, closing sales, and working with his sales representatives. Yet this travel interferes with his home life which he feels is important to himself, his wife, and their sons. In talking a number of times with his superior about reducing this travel time, Archie was told quite emphatically that travel is a part of the job and that he understood and accepted this when he came with the company. Archie recently has found out that within six months or so he probably could get transferred to an inside job with Brandis. But this job pays only two thirds of his present earnings and will necessitate moving to another city. Since being with Brandis, Archie has lived in three different cities, moving each time for a promotion. He hesitates to suggest moving again to his wife as he is certain she will view it with disfavor, but on the other hand would probably go along with the change if Archie wants to move.

Archie feels he has made progress, and his pay is about the same as that of others in similar positions with the company. He reasons that although the company keeps telling him his sales record is outstanding, he doesn't get pay that is outstanding. The sales manager for the sales territory Archie is in is, in Archie's opinion, very difficult to get along with. There are days when Archie feels frustrated and dreams of forgetting about his career at Brandis and starting all over again. For the past three months, business has been slow and Archie's work accomplishments have declined. Last week, for example, Archie was unable to close a big order from the only large prospect he has worked on during the past seven weeks.

Questions

1. Is there a problem? If so, what is it and what factors have contributed to its presence? Discuss.
2. What considerations or possible alternatives should Archie consider?
3. What action should Archie take? Why?

CASE 18–2. REDRIDGE COMPANY

Melvin Foster is a big enigma to the production manager of Redridge Company. Now in his second year as assistant production manager, Mr. Foster hasn't measured up to expectancies and the production manager now feels something must be done to correct the situation. Production is suffering and problems in this area have become commonplace.

At the request of the president, an outside firm was engaged to study and offer improvements in current procedures for handling material throughout the factory and also to control inventory better than the present arrangement. Subsequently, recommendations offering estimated savings of $90,000 annually were given. Mr. Foster has personally discussed this recommendation with the purchasing agent and each of the several supervisors involved. It has also been a major topic of discussion at each of three monthly production department meetings. The tone of these meetings has been one of approval to proceed with the suggested changes. When the president asked the production manager where the project stood, he (the president) was told, "Mr. Foster is handling this and has gone over the recommendation a number of times. Possible alternatives have been created and then destroyed. Mel is trying to reach the best possible solution, I suppose, but I will check with him at once and get the project moving. Mel realizes he has to live with whatever he approves so, as of now, I haven't gotten on him about it."

The personnel manager had some difficulty with Melvin Foster in determining a vacation schedule for the workers in his department. Mr. Foster asked each of the supervisors, and they, in turn, asked each of their employees for preferences for their vacation time. The result was overlaps in periods requested. Following this, much time was spent in efforts to eliminate the overlaps and conflicts. Several employees complained informally to the personnel manager that "the company asks you when you want your vacation; you tell them; then they say you can't have the time for which you have put in."

It is known that Melvin Foster is, above everything else, keenly interested in getting production out. This is his common theme and he keeps repeating it to members of the production department. He insists that work schedules be achieved. Quite commonly, Foster makes repairs on equipment and machines to avoid any delay or interruption in production. He started this practice as a supervisor and the maintenance staff have never objected to him doing this repair work. His ability to do this has, in many instances, lessened the emergency nature in connection with much of the maintenance work on production machines.

Questions

1. What is the problem as you see it? Justify your viewpoint.
2. Evaluate the work of Melvin Foster pointing out his strong and his weak points.
3. What action do you recommend be taken? By whom? Discuss.

Chapter 19

Leading

Whatever fortune brings
Don't be afraid of doing things.
A. A. Milne

Most effective leaders are highly motivated persons. They strive willingly for high objectives and set high standards of performance for themselves. They are curious, energetic, and challenged by the unsolved problems surrounding them. They eagerly assemble all their energies to overcome any barrier blocking their successful achievement of the goal being sought.

The leader's actions and the way his or her followers perform tasks significantly affect not only the material results achieved, but also the satisfaction of the followers in performing the work. A leader triggers a person's "will to do," shows the way, and guides the group members toward group accomplishment. Leading is a necessary ingredient of management.

MEANING OF LEADERSHIP

Changes in organizations, history, and society result from efforts of a relatively few superior individuals. These individuals may dedicate their lives to a certain mission; they may desire power and influence over others; or they may possess boundless energy and willpower to accomplish certain values which to them have supreme significance.

Leadership has been defined in various ways. It has, for example, been referred to as a process of influencing the actions of an organized group in goal setting and accomplishment; also as an influence under which followers accept willingly the direction and control by another person or the leader. For purposes here, we can state that *leadership is the relationship in which one person, the leader, influences others to work together willingly on related tasks to attain that which the*
410

leader desires. Observe that leading has to do with one person *influencing* others in the group. Further, this influence comes about from the relationship between the leader and a group member or members, i.e., there is *interaction* or reciprocal reactions of people in a group to each other. These two words, influence and interaction, are basic in any discussion of leadership.

The influence of a leader is of two different types. First, there is the leader's own performance that directly affects the group level of work. An important part of this is the handling of authority and the subsequent authority relationships that the leader establishes.[1] Second, there is the behavior the leader takes to affect the group's viability and members' satisfaction.

What are the bases upon which a leader influences a subordinate or a group of subordinates. Helpful is the five-fold framework of power, defined in terms of influence as offered by John French and Bertram Raven.[2] They identity: (1) *coercive power*, which relies on fear and is based on the expectation of the subordinate that punishment is given for not agreeing with superior's actions and beliefs; (2) *reward power* sees that rewards are granted for compliance with superior's actions and wishes; (3) *legitimate power* is derived from the supervisor's position in the organization; (4) *expert power* stems from an individual's possessing some special skill, knowledge, or expertise; and (5) *referent power* which is based on identification of a follower with a leader who is admired and held in high esteem by the follower.

This framework supplies distinction among the possible power bases and is helpful in knowing from whence the power arises and something of its nature. Actually the first three powers—coercive, reward, and legitimate—are primarily of organizational factors, while the last two—expert and referent—are of individual factors.

Interaction between a leader and members of the group or among group members relates the leader to the group members in some way and likewise the group members are related to the leader. Overall these relationships are conditioned by the active forces present in the environment within which the leader and group operate. These relationships vary and are frequently quite dynamic. These changes are brought about in part by the reactions of the people (the leader and his group) to one another.

How much interaction should take place for good leadership to exist. It depends upon what is to be achieved, the behavior of the people involved, the knowledge and ideas that each one can contribute toward solving a problem, and the permissiveness of the general

---

[1] See Chapter 14.

[2] John R. P. French and Bertram Raven, "The Bases of Social Power," in *Group Dynamics*, D. Cartwright and A. F. Zander, eds. (Evanston, Ill.: Row, Peterson, and Co., 1960), pp. 607–21.

environment. If the whole affair is somewhat routine and takes place with some degree of regularity, little interaction is required. On the other hand, if the issue calls for new ideas, is constantly changing, and affects seriously the leader and many members of the group, the need for interaction is great, if not critical.

THE LEADER

Above all else, a leader has a mission or goal to accomplish. A leader may write off his or her whole life as a sunk cost to achieve this cause that person feels is worthy and vital. In other words, a leader is "for something" and commonly the objective is ahead of that of contemporaries. The importance of a cause is also borne out in the literal meaning of leader as "one who goes." Where does he go? To seek a worthwhile goal. And in doing this, the leader explains the objective clearly and forcefully in terms that show it is to the follower's best interest for this goal to be achieved.

A leader leads, but does not push. The leader pulls followers to heights of accomplishment they may not have believed were possible. A leader knows the individual characteristics of key followers, knows what qualities will elicit their best efforts, and serves at the same time he or she leads. The leader has an ability to awaken emotional as well as rational powers of the follower. In fact, leadership appears to be more emotional than intellectual or rational. The leader realizes this and seeks to cultivate the emotional nature of the followers realizing that power comes from dedication, not knowledge alone. An interesting comparison between leadership and nonleadership practices is clearly illustrated by the following.

A leader	*A nonleader*
1. Inspires a follower.	1. Drives the follower.
2. Accomplishes work and develops the follower.	2. Accomplishes work at expense of the follower.
3. Shows the follower how to do the job.	3. Instills fear in the follower by threats and coercion.
4. Assumes obligations.	4. Passes the buck.
5. Fixes the breakdown for failure in attaining the goal.	5. Fixes the blame on others for failure in attaining the goal.

A LEADERSHIP MODEL

Leadership is a product of many forces acting and interacting simultaneously. Every manager is required to achieve some degree of integration of these varying and complex forces, otherwise there is a void in the manager's leadership necessary to perform the managerial job effectively. The leadership model presented here is based on this statement: *Leadership comes from a complex relationship existing between (1) the leader, (2) the led, (3) the organization, and (4) social values and economic and political conditions.* This concept is diagrammed in Figure 19–1. Shown at the top by the letter "L" is the

FIGURE 19–1: Leadership is a complex relationship

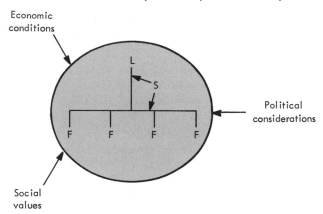

leader and one's characteristics. Followers (the led) are represented by the four Fs while the S points out the organization structure. Encircling the entire structure and affecting each part of it are social values, economic, and political considerations.

The model consisting of these four variables can be depicted graphically as shown in Figure 19–2. Leadership, shown in the center, is made up of the four variables surrounding leadership. The first is the leader and includes such things as that person's values, i.e., the deep beliefs and convictions that condition one's perceptions and behaviors, confidence of the leader in the group members, extent of sharing in decision making by group members, and general circumstances the leader prefers, i.e., what circumstances provide the leader the most comfort. Proceeding clockwise to the second variable, followers, the forces within those being led include identification with the management's objectives, interest and involvement in solving a problem, and other factors as shown in the figure. Likewise, variable No. 3, organization, and No. 4., social values, economic and political conditions are indicated on the illustration along with representative forces of each.

Under 3b, degree of interdependent specialization followed, when this amount is high, effective coordination between the specialized

FIGURE 19–2:   A leadership model

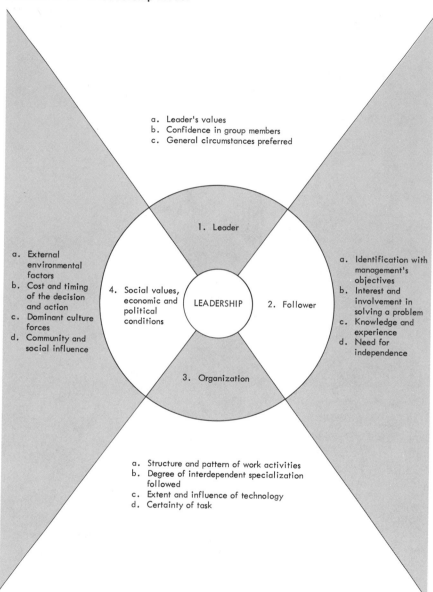

a. Leader's values
b. Confidence in group members
c. General circumstances preferred

1. Leader

a. External
    environmental
    factors
b. Cost and timing
    of the decision
    and action
c. Dominant culture
    forces
d. Community and
    social influence

4. Social values,
    economic and
    political
    conditions

LEADERSHIP

2. Follower

a. Identification with
    management's
    objectives
b. Interest and
    involvement in
    solving a problem
c. Knowledge and
    experience
d. Need for
    independence

3. Organization

a. Structure and pattern of work activities
b. Degree of interdependent specialization
    followed
c. Extent and influence of technology
d. Certainty of task

groups necessitates more lateral relationships. Also the followers tend
to center their interests upon their own work and do not see the impact
of their actions on others. Likewise, the extent and influence of
technology, 3c, has a strong influence upon leadership. Technology
frequently governs to what degree the task is structured and hence, to

what extent the employee's work behavior is specified and major decisions centralized. The leader has more influence when one can tell a follower what to do and how to do it as is the case where the work is highly structured; commonly standard operating instructions and detailed manuals are provided. The work is programmed in detail; little is left for the group member to decide. In contrast, work dealing with research projects, committee assignments, new product development, and managerial policies do not lend themselves to predetermined detailed tasks for their successful accomplishment. As such, the influence and the type of leadership given employees doing such work differs from that when the tasks are highly structured. Certainty of task, 3d, is also important. When the exact and specific work make-up is known, an active and controlling leader is usually effective. In contrast, when the task is uncertain a permissive and passive type of leadership appears effective.[3]

Variable No. 4, social values, economic and political conditions, takes into account that the leadership practiced is influenced by the external environmental factors to which the leadership should be in harmony. In addition, social values from the outside, such as social legislation and education of followers, economic and political conditions, including standards of living, change in markets, and modifications in taxes, bring about changes that subsequently lead to a redefinition of acceptable and effective leadership.

BASIC CONSIDERATIONS OF LEADERSHIP

The leader has the ability to determine what actions will best help accomplish the group's goals. This necessitates an understanding of how the actions as a leader will affect the work of the group as well as the members of the group. It involves effective decision making and its implementation. The decision, no matter how derived, is usually closely related to the leader's perception and analysis of the group's problems within the framework or background of the entire organization. This is more than the ability to make an effective decision in the ordinary meaning of that wording, because commonly the leader must stress unique situational and interactional factors so that the best action is initiated and unfavorable results are minimized.

The leader's role and the degree of acceptance by the group conditions the leadership. Shared information and close emotional and knowledge ties between the leader and the group contribute to both the leader's and the group's effectiveness. The leader should give high priority to gaining the understanding and confidence of group members. Likewise, followers must believe in their leaders. The means by

---

[3] F. E. Fiedler, "Engineer the job to fit the manager," *Harvard Business Review*, September–October 1965, pp. 115–22.

which one becomes a leader include both formal and informal means and consist of (1) inheritance, (2) personal power, (3) appointment by a superior, (4) elected by peers, or (5) recognized by subordinates. The leader should take the leadership role defined by the formal organization or if from an informal organization, assume the expected leader's role. Over a period, the leader's formal role may become diluted, and one may have to rely upon the informal situation to maintain adequate leadership. It should also be noted that some irritations are almost always present in leader-follower relationships. It is simply in the nature of people's behavior. Many elect, accept, or recognize others to get them to do what they know they should, but will not do unless leadership is present. The leader can be liked or disliked, but must have the respect of the followers. Those being led expect practical help from their leaders. Hence, the successful leader seeks the identity of being known as one who can and does satisfy the needs of the group, assists in having desirable working conditions, and helps set realistic goals. In return, followers normally support such a leader and make it easier for that person to be a leader.

Leadership requires followers. To be effective the leader must retain and develop the continued acceptance and the confidence of the group members. They remain willing followers primarily because the leader satisfies their needs, stands for a cause they believe in, or is probably the best leader they can hope to get under the prevailing circumstances. To get followers, the leader seeks to give the impression of being a person capable of complete understanding of the followers' difficulties, a person of action, and an achiever of mutual aims.

The style of leadership and the situation affect the results obtained. As pointed out by the contingency approach to management, the same leadership behavior will not be equally effective in all situations. The interactions of the variables affecting leadership make this so. Few individuals excel as leaders in every situation. More correctly we need to state, for example, that leader A is effective in situation A and ineffective in situation B. Commonly, a leader becomes involved in different work environments calling for different types of leadership behaviors. Some leaders are flexible and do adjust to each situation, but many others apparently cannot. Yet, we cannot afford to discard a leader who is a specialist simply because one does not perform effectively in a particular leadership job. Hence, we try, through training, to get flexibility in the leader or to change one's leadership behavior. Typically, this is not too successful. More hopeful are adjustments of the followers or of the environmental variables. Suggestions as to how such changes might be realized include the following. Variations in authority may be tried such as giving the leader final and complete authority over the department or limiting it. Another possibility is to have all decisions approved by the leader's superior before they are put into action. Also, modifications of the task structures can be considered. Some can be spelled out while others are defined in broad outlines with assignments left to the initiative and imagination of the leader. Further, the homogeneity of the group the manager works with can be altered, thus changing one's work efforts and one's relationships to the new group.

Time influences leadership. For example, most leaders are influenced somewhat by the time in which they live, as revealed by the opportunities which either exist or can be created during their active work life. We are all conditioned to a greater or less degree by the general modus operandi of the time in which we live. Furthermore, a time of emergency seems to bring about a greater emphasis upon leadership. In an emergency, people look for a leader to lead them out of their difficulties. An awareness of leadership tends to get lost in the orderly, methodical achievement of the group's aims. Few ships' captains prove their worth in a calm sea, and it is the same with enterprises. To the leader, emergencies are opportunities to serve. On the other hand, it is also true that in emergencies people tend to blame the leader for their troubles, pointing that that person led them into difficulties. Hence, leadership has its penalty, or price to be paid.

Finally, a leader operates in the light of publicity; people know one's achievements or failures. When successful, many will emulate the achievements, but a few will envy those accomplishments. The more outstanding a leader is, the more one becomes a target for the envious few. A leader who is mediocre is let alone. The reasons for this appear to lie in the interaction of human relations and in the operations of groups. No leader is perfect in the eyes of all. A leader is probably assailed because of being a leader, and concerted efforts to equal or excel the leader are added proof of that leadership. There are always a few who delight in clamoring denial of a leader's achievements. However, the successful leader is not deterred from an appointed goal by these minority cries. He or she continues to lead and remains a leader.

LEADERSHIP STYLES AND THE MANAGERIAL GRID

The Managerial Grid developed by industrial psychologists Blake and Mouton offers interesting and helpful insights into leadership styles.[4] Plotting concern for production horizontally on a chart, and concern for people vertically, leadership styles as expressed by these two variables can be shown. Figure 19–3 shows such a chart with 1 on the horizontal axis representing the lowest and 9 the highest concern for production. On the vertical axis, 1 represents the lowest and 9 the highest concern for people. A location on the chart of 9,1 indicates a leadership type featuring the highest concern for production and the

---

[4] The material for this section is based on the excellent book by Robert R. Blake and Jane Srygley Mouton, *The Managerial Grid* (Houston: Gulf Publishing, 1964).

lowest concern for people. Likewise, 1,9 shows the lowest concern for production and the highest concern for people. In the identification scheme the first digit stands for concern for production, the second digit for concern for people. Blake and Mouton plotted five major leadership styles. These plus the identification of each include:

		Type of leader	*Style*
1,1	Little concern for either production or people.	The deserter type.	Worst leadership style.
1,9	Lowest concern for production, highest for people.	The missionary type.	People-oriented style.
9,1	Highest concern for production, lowest for people.	The autocrat type.	Production-oriented style.
5,5	Comfortable concern for both production and people.	The compromiser type.	Maintain present balance style.
9,9	Highest concern for both production and people.	The executive type.	Peak of leadership styles.

It is possible by means of the grid and selected management areas to identify the leadership style in any given circumstance. To illustrate, for the area of managerial philosophy, the incumbent may check as most representative of personal behavior one of several descriptive paragraphs on a test. If the paragraph stating

It is best to set high standards, reward those who meet them, and deal firmly with those who do not.

is checked as most applicable, the leadership style of 9,1, concern for production, but not for people, is indicated. In contrast, if the paragraph

I have found that in general people work for self satisfaction and security at all organizational levels. In the long run, maintaining production at a comfortable level is the best bet.

is most applicable, the leadership style is 1,9, concern for production is low, but for people is high. Interestingly, compromisers, or 5,5 identity, are common in the area of management philosophy, but not in other areas such as planning and executing plans and orders, where a definite inclination either to the production or to the people concept is found.[5]

---

[5] Klos, L. A. "Measure Your Leadership with the Managerial Grid," *Supervisory Management*, April 1974, pp. 10–17.

FIGURE 19–3: Managerial Grid

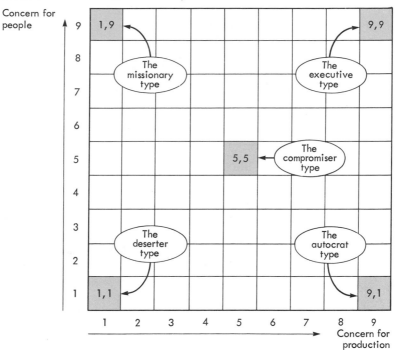

Representative of a paragraph indicating a compromiser in management philosophy is

The use of positive and negative incentives to obtain desired performance is superior. The executive must be firm, but fair. Machines are important, but so is morale of your people.

TO BECOME A LEADER

The question is frequently asked, what can I do to become a leader? The answers are numerous and various. As already stated, leadership is a complex phenomenon and does not lend itself to simple answers. Long lists of leadership essentials exist. Nevertheless for purposes here and while not conclusive, we will discuss only three factors—involvement, high motivation, and positive human traits.

Involvement includes the ability to immerse yourself in not only your work, but with people too. Interest, dedication, stick-to-it-iveness might be substituted for the word "involvement." Leaders work with material things and with people to get the work accomplished, to achieve the goal. Leadership being a four-faceted concept —the leader, the led, the organization, and the social, economic and political environment—as stated earlier in this chapter, means that almost everyone can at times show leadership behavior.

Almost without exception, a leader possesses a highly developed desire for achievement. One's needs are intense with terrific drives from within to achieve self-set goals. Unfinished work and unsolved problems intrigue and challenge the leader. Also the accomplishment of what the leader believes is good for either country, community, company, or self, or all of these, drives one to achievement in keeping with carefully made and detailed plans, time tables, persuasion, endless energy, and steadfastness of purpose.

Traits have long been used to distinguish successful leaders from those less outstanding. Realistic, resourceful, self-starting, emotionally stable, skillful communicator, self-assurance, and socially participative are among the common qualities usually included. Developing these traits *and practicing them* help to qualify a person as a leader. In essence, traits as such help to describe the type of personality having the potential for leadership. A person may possess self-starting and self-assurance capabilities, for example, but the question in leadership is, are they used and if so, for what purposes. The relative strength and importance of a desirable trait shifts and changes depending upon the individual situation. The personality, existing in a given leadership circumstance, tends to serve as an integrator of the various potential traits.

THEORIES OF LEADERSHIP

Leadership has been subjected to considerable research and study and, as a result, there are today numerous theories of leadership being expounded. They include differences in opinions, methodologies, explanations, and conclusions. Each has its group of advocates who profess their particular theory as the right and proper one. Interpretations from the various theories have given rise to controversies; by no means is there complete harmony among the concepts advanced by the various leadership theorists. Although more is known today about leadership than ever before, we still do not have complete and integrated theories about it that represent the totality of leadership. There is no known one best way of leading people. Leadership practice and style constitute a complex web of factors.

For convenience, we will discuss six leadership theories which represent collectively a large portion of the thinking being done in this area and also illustrate diverse and valid approaches to the study of leadership. Included are (1) the situational theory, (2) the personal-behavior theory, (3) the supportive theory, (4) the sociologic theory, (5) the psychologic theory, and (6) the autocratic theory.

SITUATIONAL THEORY

This approach to the explanation of leadership suggests that there must be enough flexibility in the leadership to adjust to different situations. Leadership is multidimensional. In this theory, leadership is made up of four variables: the leader, the followers, the organization, and the social, economic and political influences. While all are importance, much attention is directed to the organization and the social, economic, and political environment. However, adjustments to the leader and to the followers also are subject to much analysis. A common problem for which this theory can be helpful is determining whether applicants for a leadership job are competent. Are they, for example, available because the particular situation of their former position did not permit them to lead even though they tried to adjust to it? In contrast do their former positions indicate an inability to lead, as such?

Research on adaptive leadership suggests that there is a type of leadership that is most appropriate in different situations. In studies by Fiedler, three dimensions were used to measure the leader's effectiveness, including (1) the degree of confidence the followers have for their leader, (2) the degree to which the followers' jobs either are routine or are ill-structured, and (3) the degree of power inherent in the leadership position. The interaction of these three dimensions determine whether "controlling, active, and structuring" (CAS) leadership, or "permissive, passive, and considerate" (PPC) leadership will probably be the most effective. It appears that CAS leadership is best in settings that are either very favorable or very unfavorable in terms of the leader's power, structured task, and group support. In contrast, for intermediate settings, PPC leadership appears preferable. That is, the permissive leader obtains optimum group performance in situations where the tasks are reasonably structured and the leader must be diplomatic—the leader's power and the group's support are of an average amount, neither highly favorable nor highly unfavorable. Further, Fiedler recommends that situations be made more congruent with the leader's mode of operation, since leadership style of the leader is quite difficult to change.[6]

PERSONAL-BEHAVIOR THEORY

Leadership can also be studied on the bases of the personal qualities or behavioral patterns of leaders. This approach emphasizes what

---

[6] Fred E. Fiedler, A *Theory of Leadership Effectiveness* (New York: McGraw-Hill Book Co., Inc., 1967); and Fiedler, "The Effects of Leadership Training and Experience: A Contingency Model Interpretation," *Administrative Science Quarterly*, December 1972, pp. 453–70.

the leader does in leading. An important contribution of this theory is that a leader neither behaves the same nor takes identical actions for every situation faced. One is flexible, to a degree, because one feels one must be to take the most appropriate action for handling a particular problem. This suggests a leadership continuum whereby the leader's actions and amount of authority used are related to the decision making freedom or participation available to the subordinates.[7]

Figure 19–4 illustrates the leadership continuum concept. The top

FIGURE 19–4:   Continuum of leadership behavior

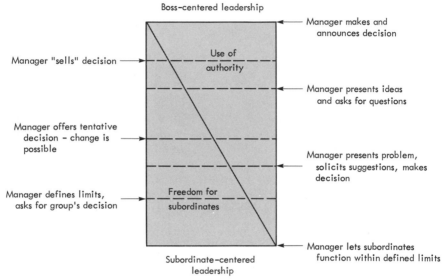

Source: Adapted from Robert Tannenbaum and Warren H. Schmidt, "How to Choose a Leadership Pattern," *Harvard Business Review,* March–April 1958, pp. 95–101.

of the figure represents boss-centered leadership, the bottom, subordinate-centered leadership. In going from top to bottom, less and less authority is used, and more and more freedom for subordinates. For each of the seven levels of leadership shown is included a short statement of the manager's action at that level. For example, at the third level from the top of the figure, the manager presents ideas and asks for questions. In reality, this means that different styles of leadership can be employed depending upon the leader's evaluation of the situation, capabilities, desire to decide the issue, and the amount of control one wishes to exercise.

Several pages back we discussed leadership with reference to the managerial grid with the concern for production and the concern for

---

[7] Robert Tannenbaum and Warren H. Schmidt, "How to Choose a Leadership Pattern," *Harvard Business Review,* March–April 1958, pp. 95–101.

people. Referring again to Figure 19–3, managerial leadership emphasizing concern for people is subordinate-centered shown at the top of the figure. Results obtained by use of subordinate-centered leadership tend to show high productivity, low absenteeism, low labor turnover, and low quality rejects when compared to results from the use of work-centered leadership.[8] Hence, it appears that the wise manager for most situations will use and develop subordinate-centered leadership wherever possible.

However, one must not conclude that work-centered leadership should be avoided. It depends on the variables of the situation—the leader's preferences and judgment, the followers, the organization, and the environment. Here again the contingency approach is helpful. Under certain conditions, the work-centered approach provides satisfactory results. To illustrate, in some business companies the founder or founder's relatives have worked extremely hard to attain their enterprise's current position and they feel strongly about continuing to emphasize work accomplishment and to control the destiny of their enterprise.

SUPPORTIVE THEORY

Here the leader takes the position that followers want to do their best and that one can lead best by supporting their efforts. To this end, the leader creates a work environment which promotes the desire by each follower to perform to the best of one's ability, cooperate with others, and develop one's own skills and abilities. Suggestions about how better to do the work, what improvements in working conditions can be made, and what new ideas should be tried out are encouraged. The leader gives general managerial overseeing and encourages subordinates to use their creativity and initiative in handling the details of their jobs. Decision making by the leader includes consideration for the followers' opinions and recommendations which they aggressively seek.

The supportive theory is termed "participative theory" by some. This follows due to the leader encouraging followers to participate concerning decisions to be made. Others call it "democratic theory of leadership" and while it does have democratic aspects, it neither implies rule by the majority or by vote. On the other hand, in the supportive theory the leader considers subordinates as social equals and has respect for their knowledge and ideas.

On the plus side, proponents of the supportive theory claim the practice of helping the follower and treating each as an individual with human dignity and rights makes for a cooperative, productive,

---

[8] Rensis Likert, *New Patterns of Management* (New York: McGraw-Hill Book Co., Inc., 1961).

and satisfied employee. The leader wins acceptance and the enlightened mode of operation prevails. Further, unilateral authority is rejected, and unwarranted special privileges are minimized. In contrast, there are opponents to the supportive theory. They object on the grounds that group influence on decision making leads to confusion, a great waste of time, and "watered-down" decisions. Further, they state that individual rights and dignity are entirely possible without sharing in what amounts to managerial activities by nonmanagement members. Also, it is claimed the theory violates traditional tenets of private enterprise where the owner or an authorized agent is endowed solely with the decision making process.

SOCIOLOGIC THEORY

In this theory leadership is viewed as made up of work efforts that (1) facilitate the activities of followers and (2) strive to reconcile any organizational conflicts between followers. The leader establishes goals with participation by the followers in the final decision making. Goal identification gives direction that followers often require. They know what performances, beliefs, and behaviors are expected of them. But the efforts to accomplish the goal influence the interactions among the followers, sometimes to the degree that disruptive conflict within or between groups exists. Under such a condition, the leader is expected to take corrective measures, exercise leadership influence and reinstate harmony and co-operative effort among the followers.

From the practical viewpoint, a leader does attempt to facilitate the activities of followers, but in some cases goals are set by others and, further, one may find conflict resolution almost beyond one's power to influence. Again, the particular situation, the individual differences of group members, and the competency of the leader are the underlying causes.

PSYCHOLOGIC THEORY

Perhaps better identified as the psychological overview, this approach to leadership advocates that the major function of a leader is to develop the best motivation system. The leader stimulates subordinates to contribute to organizational objectives as well as to satisfy their own personal goals. Leadership that motivates gives considerable attention to the subordinate's attributes such as recognition, emotional security, and opportunity in keeping with one's desires and needs. The satisfaction of these needs in a manner that aids organization to be more successful represents what the psychologic theory leader must perform.

The needs of human beings were discussed in the previous chapter.

Programs to satisfy these needs are the challenge of the psychologic leader. This theory of leadership is quite broad and general. The techniques for motivating are many and success is usually associated with applying the correct technique for the particular individual circumstances. There is no one best consistent motivational plan that a leader can follow.

AUTOCRATIC THEORY

Leadership as envisioned under this theory features commands, enforcements, and somewhat arbitrary actions in the leader's relationships with subordinates. The leader tends to be work-centered; closely supervises to ensure that designated work is performed and utilizes measurements of production to help in this effort. The formal organization structure is respected at all times for which economic security as steady employment, promotions along prescribed paths, and status symbols to denote relative formal rank are granted. Orders and directives are employed, but frequently an explanation or reason for them is not given. However under the autocratic theory, the leader is not viewed as an inflexible autocrat always making decisions without regard to human values, but the preponderance of one's leadership behavior tends to have these characteristics.

The autocratic leader uses commands generally supported by sanctions of which discipline is among the most important. Discipline may either bring about the giving of rewards or the establishing of a system of penalties, as, for example, giving a pay increase for high productivity or penalizing for excessive defects in the quality of the product. Enforcement by the autocratic leader depends on power to reward or punish. The belief prevails that most humans work better in a climate where the acceptance of a prescribed habit of obedience exists. Accordingly, both the contentment and the productivity of an employee are aided when the employee knows where one stands and what is expected—a modus operandi helped by the sanction of discipline.

QUESTIONS

1. What are the four components, the characteristics of which make leadership a complex relationship?
2. What is meant by each of the following: (a) leadership continuum, (b) referent power, (c) democratic theory of leadership, and (d) leadership?
3. Explain Figure 19–2 in your own words.
4. State your reaction to the following: The tremendous amount of attention and study devoted to leadership during the past decade points to the one best way of leading people. It is known as supportive leadership and every manager would profit by using it.

5. Enumerate five theories of leadership and discuss one of these fully.

6. What is the managerial grid? How might it be used to identify leadership style in any given circumstance?

7. Discuss Figure 19–4 in your own words.

8. What are the significant differences, if any between the personal-behavior theory and the supportive theory of leadership?

9. Discuss the influence of time upon leadership.

10. Enumerate some important characteristics of a leader.

11. As a member of an organization, give an example you have experienced of a leader's behavior and action that affected the members' satisfactions.

12. Discuss autocratic leadership, pointing out its meaning, characteristics, and means of enforcement.

13. Discuss several basic considerations of leadership.

14. As you see yourself and as a manager, what type of leadership would you probably use most of the time? Why?

CASE 19–1. GRANVILLE PARTS CORPORATION

Glen Wheeler, owner and president of Granville Parts Corporation, is displeased with the service being given to customers. He feels it has eroded to the level where corrections must be made immediately including possibly some changes in personnel. Accordingly, he informed his general manager, Clark Jenkins, that measures were to be taken to gain factual evidence that the corporation's customers were not being handled as they must be for an auto, tractor, and farm implements parts supplier to be successful. Wheeler indicated he personally was going to start next Monday morning to make observations about what employees are doing, and to review and study correspondence to determine the caliber of these materials and to determine how long it required to fill and ship an order. Most important, however, was a monitoring system affecting all company telephones covering all incoming and outgoing telephone calls. In talking about the study, Jenkins was told by Wheeler that he (Wheeler) would personally supervise the program and he knew the employees (15 total, including office and storeroom employees) would welcome the opportunity to prove their worth to him. Wheeler told Jenkins to notify the employees of the study project.

Jenkins did as directed. The announcement was followed by surprise and a general feeling of "What was old man Wheeler trying to find out? Is he going to sell the business? Or is somebody going to get laid off?"

After a week of the program Wheeler stated to Jenkins, "Herb Dykes is absolutely rude to customers. If I were a customer, I would have nothing to do with him. Also that new woman Cynthia Zimmer, is far worse than not answering the telephone at all. I doubt if she can answer a single question a customer asks her. The corporation is wasting money having her around. I also have calculated that from the time an order is received until it is shipped takes an average of 3½ days. This is terrible, Clark. Absolutely terrible. House of Parts (a competitor) claims 1-day shipment. I believe these are some valid reasons why our business is slipping. Clark, I want you to think about it and be in my office next Wednesday morning . . . no, I mean Thursday morning to outline what you recommend be done about correcting this bad condition we have."

Questions

1. As Clark Jenkins, what action would you take? Why?
2. What are your general impressions about Mr. Wheeler? Mr. Jenkins? Discuss.
3. What action do you feel the management of this company should take? Justify your answer.

CASE 19–2.   McGRATH FURNITURE CORPORATION

Eve Raymond accepted the presidency of McGrath Furniture Corporation last week. Formerly she was executive vice president of a large magazine publishing firm in the New York City area. When this corporation was purchased about six months ago by another corporation, Ms. Raymond was informed that there was no suitable place for her in the merged setup, but she could remain for three months with pay and seek to relocate. Accordingly she talked with friends and also Executive Placements, a firm specializing in locating employment for top executives. Without solicitation, she received an attractive offer from a publishing house competing with her former employer, but she turned it down. She did not feel it was the thing to do; she could not work enthusiastically for a former competitor. From Executive Placements the offer of the presidency of McGrath Furniture came about. The challenge of being in a different industry, in the top spot, and making new friends appealed to her. Her husband urged her to accept. He wanted to get out of New York City and pointed out that the small town in South Carolina where McGrath is located would be ideal for raising their children, ages 9, 12, and 14.

McGrath Furniture Corporation was owned by the Burleigh McGrath family. When Burleigh McGrath, the president, died, the survivors decided there was no one in the employ of the corporation able to assume the presidency. They believed the corporation had an excellent sales manager and also a splendid factory manager, but neither had the broad vision of the total corporation's operations to assume the presidency. Mrs. Burleigh McGrath, an accountant, supervised the finance, accounting, and tax activities of the corporation.

Eve Raymond's personal history showed her to be an outstanding graduate student in college. She earned majors in both business administration and marketing, believing that with two specialties she could always use one or the other to gain advancement. She made a good appearance and projected the image of one who knows where she is going and how she is going to get there. She always engaged in administrative work, never in that requiring technical specialist ability and knowledge. One of her top qualities is her persuasiveness—an uncanny ability to win others to her way of thinking. But some think she acts too much as an independent, overwhelms others, decides too quickly, even giving the impression of being impulsive. It was generally agreed, however, that Eve Raymond was fearless; she'd tackle a complicated problem and stay with it to a conclusion. She also has a sense of humor and typically, after giving an order involving some knotty situation, would add some humor to make the order more palatable.

Things appeared to go quite well at McGrath for Ms. Raymond but a certain environment perturbed her. Work was performed on time, costs were in line, and sales orders were received in a satisfactory volume. Her management compeers were friendly and cooperative, yet distant. She learned a great deal from them about the furniture business and they seemed most willing to help. But after four months, Ms. Raymond felt she was not getting full and enthusiastic cooperation. She did not feel that she or her family were fully accepted by the management team. There was a tendency for them to go to Mrs. McGrath with problems that she thought should be handled by her. She wasn't quite certain where she stood, but during visits with Mrs. McGrath certain statements were made by her indicating everyone seemed pleased that Ms. Raymond was with them.

Ms. Raymond involved herself in the project of acquiring some factory machines and rearranging a portion of the factory layout, but she quickly sensed that this activity caused resentment by the factory superintendent. Several attempts by Ms. Raymond to change the superintendent's attitude about this were futile, so she withdrew. Sales were being maintained and since she realized she knew very little about the marketing of furniture she decided to stay out of this area. Besides it entailed considerable traveling and her family wanted her to stay home.

Seven months after Ms. Raymond was hired, installation of a computer system began. This had been ordered prior to Ms. Raymond's employment with the company. There were a great many problems to be worked out. Mrs. McGrath was overwhelmed with the tasks to be completed so that the records and reports would be computerized. She informed Ms. Raymond of her problem and suggested that perhaps she might like to assume direction of the computer installation and it would give her first-hand insight into the operations of the company.

Questions

1. Evaluate Ms. Raymond's decision to join McGrath Furniture Corporation as president. Discuss fully.
2. What is the problem faced by Ms. Raymond?
3. What recommended action do you suggest Ms. Raymond take? Justify your answer.

Chapter **20**

Communicating

*No point of view, once expressed, ever seems wholly to die
our ears are full of the whisperings of dead men.*
Alexander Gray

Unless people understand the meaning or significance of what we are trying to say, they are not in a position to offer effective cooperation. A manager's success depends in great measure upon ability to work with people, to get ideas across, to receive suggestions, and to attain an informed and an informative group. In brief, we can say that communicating deals with the art of developing and attaining understanding.

COMMUNICATING AND MANAGEMENT

Communicating is one of the most important facilitators of managerial activities. Without it facts, ideas, and experiences cannot be exchanged. A manager moves ideas and information from his or her mind to other minds. The effectiveness of this transition of what the manager knows, thinks, and feels, determines and conditions managerial accomplishments. The fact is that in everyday living the mere presence of another person encourages communication. It is a universal human propensity and as some aptly state, "You cannot not communicate."

Understanding is the target in communicating and this emphasizes the need for knowing the subject, being aware or finding out what the recipient knows about it, and anticipating questions and answers. A good check upon yourself when communicating is to ask: Have I left anything out that will contribute to a better mutual understanding? Help in answering this question is provided by remembering that communication is highly affected by the human element. The astute manager knows that many factors influence people and takes these factors into account when interacting with them. Communication is

430

essentially a human transaction and the influence and importance of human behavior confront any person who wants to communicate with another. Being sensitive to the other person's needs and feelings represents an important part of the communication effort. The simple truth is that communication is difficult between two persons who do not respect or like one another.

The need is ever present to communicate effectively; each such opportunity represents a chance to improve managerial competency. Specifically, communication enables the manager to obtain data for decision making, to assist in identifying problems, to know what actions are needed. Others know the manager primarily by what the manager is able to communicate to them. Actually nothing happens in any organization until somebody communicates.

Communication is a means, not an end. It makes possible the management process and serves as the lubricant for its smooth operation. Communication helps managerial planning to be performed effectively, managerial organizing to be carried out effectively, managerial actuating to be followed effectively, and managerial controlling to be applied effectively. Management is inclusive of communication, not communication of management.

Successful communication is the result of and not the cause of competent management. Conceivably one might be an excellent communicator but a poor manager. However, a competent manager is nearly always a good communicator. Actually, communication should never be thought of as an independent activity. It is an essential ingredient of almost everything a manager does.

From time to time what is assumed to be a problem in poor communication is actually a case of inept management. Excellent communicative efforts and the use of various devices and gimmicks will fall short of expectancy and may result in total failure if the management is ineffective. Communicating poor plans or utilizing a badly conceived organization structure, for example, are not corrected solely by astute and sophisticated communicating.

CLASSIFICATION OF MANAGERIAL COMMUNICATION

There are five types of managerial communication that warrant discussion here. First is the *formal communication* which follows the chain of command of the formal organization. For any such communication the path of transmission is prescribed, the format designated, and official sanction is provided. Second is the *informal communication*, commonly referred to as the grapevine. Most managers use it to supplement formal communication. They do this by finding out how the informal operates within their particular organization, identifying its major connections, and providing constructive information for it to handle. The grapevine can be very effective. Third is *nonformal communication*. It exists due to unintended conditions of the formal organization that cause unanticipated behavior to take place. That is, the formal organization itself tends to generate unanticipated behavior.[1] Nonformal communication is effective, nearly always exists in a large group working together, and tends to be continuous and permanent. Fourth is the *technical communication* which is employed by people⁴ working in the same area. Representative is the communication among people working with the computer. This type of communication is specialized, effective, and somewhat limited. Fifth, and last, is *procedural and rules communication*. Such communication is commonly set forth as a manual of the particular organization. It informs about specific policies and rules and when they are applicable. Formal communication channels are not utilized. While somewhat rigid, such communication does contribute to efficiency. Rules, for example, are specific and authoritative guides for action, making it unnecessary for a manager to decide each issue each time it happens. Rules require little or no interpretation and cover numerous situations.

THE PROCESS OF COMMUNICATING

The first consideration in managerial communication is the determination of its exact purpose in terms of receiver response. This requires some thinking. For example, is the response intended to be used to help reach a decision, persuade the recipient to a new point of view, or build a favorable attitude toward a given concept? Next, the communication should be planned with stated purpose in mind and in a format believed effective to get understanding and an honest response from the receiver. To illustrate, if the communication is to inform about a forthcoming meeting, certain data should be included and the message put in a given format. However, if the purpose is to build goodwill, the communication must be planned with this purpose in mind and certain data included. In this case the format may be far different. Last, preparation of the communication should include provision to receive an effective expression by the receiver. The better the understanding of the receiver's thoughts and behavior by the sender of the communication, the more effective the presentation can be. A communication is adapted to the needs and interests of the receiver in order to reach one and to cause one to react in a manner that accomplishes the purpose of the sender.

In communicating there is always a giver, a message, and a receiver. A condition or event stimulates the giver and one becomes aware of its existence. Out of this, comes the need to transmit an idea or feeling about this event to someone. Wanting to share an idea provides the

---

[1] See also the discussion on nonformal organization, Chapter 15, pp. 325–26.

need for communicating. To do so one must decide what to communicate that will accomplish the purpose. Accordingly one arranges words and symbols in some meaningful sequence keeping in mind that one seeks a favorable response from the receiver. The message is then transmitted to the receiver who perceives the words or symbols and translates them into accustomed patterns. The meaning of the message is thus obtained and hopefully the receiver responds. To do so, the receiver selects a reply message to satisfy his or her desire, arranges it in what one believes is an effective format and transmits it to the giver. In return this reply stimulates the initial giver and others to have responses. Thus, the process of communicating continues, each time a giver sends a message the receiver or another person may respond by further communicating ideas and facts.

This leads to the observation that in much communicating the process followed is two-way, meaning that to obtain the thought or idea being conveyed, when one speaks, another listens, or when one writes, another reads. However, communication itself may be multiway depending upon the type of communication being used.

To reiterate, a manager tells, informs, and requests, but for communication to be effective, one must also listen, ask, read, reply, and interpret. When communication moves freely in both directions, greater exchange of ideas and concepts is won and the way is open for greater understanding. Mutual acceptance and a willingness to receive or transmit must be present. In fact this back-and-forth exchange of ideas is implied by the "com" (meaning "with") at the start of the word communication. It is an error for a manager to assume that the job of communicating is to hand it out; the other person is supposed to do all the listening and reading.

This interaction of communication has been called the communication equation. Using verbal communication for illustrative purposes, this equation is shown below.

$$
\left.\begin{array}{l}
\textit{Giver} \\
(1)\ \text{Stimulus} \\
\qquad plus \\
(2)\ \text{Interpretation} \\
\qquad plus \\
(3)\ \text{Behavior}
\end{array}\right\} equals \left\{\begin{array}{l}
\textit{Receiver} \\
(4)\ \text{Perception} \\
\qquad plus \\
(5)\ \text{Interpretation} \\
\qquad plus \\
(6)\ \text{Behavior}
\end{array}\right.
$$

The giver has a stimulus that brings pressure on that person to try to influence the receiver. Next, the giver must interpret this fact, and third, when the interpretation is completed, the giver expresses the interpretation by talking. As a result, the receiver perceives the communication. This is step No. 4 and includes the receiver hearing or receiving the message. It covers that person's apprehension of the information being transmitted. Fifth is the receiver's interpretation of the message. This is influenced by many different factors. Sixth and last is the reaction of the receiver. Here we are interested in what behavior is shown such as the expressions made—shaking of head, nodding approval, or stating that agreement or disagreement is the reply.

HUMAN BEHAVIOR AND COMMUNICATION

Of all the variables affecting communication, human behavior is probably the most important. Communication is between persons and is subjected to all the influences that condition human behavior. If somebody doesn't trust or respect you or your viewpoint, it's easy for that person to be distracted by the dislike or distrust. As a result, that person tends not to hear, read, or believe anything you communicate. Although we will include a number of considerations in this discussion, they are suggestive only and should not be considered as complete. Foremost is the openness existing in the relationship between the persons communicating. Is the environment one of dictation or that of a participative means? Simple, basic honesty is vital in any communication situation, but beyond this, candid disclosure of personal feelings, willingness to express contrary opinions, and frankness in evaluating the efforts of fellow employees are likewise significant. When openness does not exist, a person may filter a communication if one feels it will harm one's chances for promotion or—in the case of bad news—upset one's superior. As a result information is commonly distorted as it ascends from the bottom to the top of an organization. Employees tend to shape their behavior to need-satisfying rewards. It is not uncommon for subordinates to refrain from communicating information that is potentially threatening to them or their superiors.[2] Likewise, a communication issued at the top management level may be considerably altered by the time it reaches the bottom level. Limited study shows that some 75 percent of a communication can be lost in its downward flow from top to bottom of an organization through five levels.

Another consideration is the degree of motivation by either the giver or the receiver. When communicating, people have various motives— to persuade, to tell, to entertain, and to reinforce ideas. The enthusiasm displayed and the interest shown definitely condition the communication. When it is planned to appeal to the assumed motives of the participant, it usually is more effective. There is also the consideration of a person behaving based on "either-or" thinking. Early in life we learn to use so-called polar terms as near/far, objective/

---

[2] D. Katz and R. L. Kahn, *The Social Psychology of Organizations* (New York: John Wiley and Sons, 1966), pp. 245–46.

subjective, black/white, and we think and speak in this way. Actually most things don't conform to these convenient extremes. And by taking the position of either-or, a person commits oneself to a position where compromising or viewing a situation correctly is not feasible and places rigidities in communication.

"Allness" orientation is another human behavior consideration. It is the conveyance of an impression of totality. Example: *All* car dealers are dishonest. You *never* listen to me. Such all-inclusive statements are not only seldom correct, but they block the thought processes that are needed to make communication successful. It is better to use relative values when you use evaluation terms, i.e., "As I see it . . ." or "It appears that. . . ." Such action aids communication. A fifth consideration is making and acting on unjustified assumptions. Everyone makes assumptions about a working environment and the people in it. But when a high- or a low-level assumption is made without checking the facts, trouble and communication breakdown can take place. It is well to be alert to the assumptions made and the reader should not assume that the receiver understands what one has been told. That assumption is one of the biggest causes of communication failure. Mutual understanding must not be taken for granted.

Snap reactions are another consideration. When the receiver's behavior is such that one feels little will be gained by listening or reading carefully, the communication is almost certain to be ineffective. The possibility that the giver has a new idea, fact, or point of view doesn't occur to the receiver. Frequently this condition exists in communication between two persons in conflict or when one person is short tempered. Sometimes this type behavior is called "signal reaction" since the person acts as though triggered by a signal from someone else. Fear is another consideration and plays an important part in communication when emotionally loaded words like *failure, death, strike, liar,* and *defeat* are used. Fear can affect the translation of information. When communication is expressed under tension or nervousness, its effectiveness can be changed considerably—usually disadvantageously, yet in some instances, advantageously, by increasing mental and physical energy and alertness.

Last, but by no means least, is the behavior exemplified by an unwillingness to listen or to read. One must listen or read so one knows what is transmitted. Many management members spend one half of their time listening and reading. One may learn a great deal by these means. The problem is that we retain only a small portion of what we hear or read, and that for but a brief time. For example, estimates are that immediately after listening, a person remembers only one half of what was heard, and two weeks later remembers only one fourth of it. This is explained, in part, by the fact that the brain functions much faster than the average of 100 words per minute of a speaker. As a result the mind wanders, and gets off the subject of the communication. Many try to guess what is going to be said next, evaluate what has been said, or direct their attention to some physical attribute of the giver and pay no attention to what is said. In addition, too many communications contain too many words. The reciever loses interest because of the mere quantity. And likewise, too many messages harass a person; the listenership and readership pace becomes irksome. Figure 20–1 shows several practices to follow in order to achieve good listening habits.

Figure 20–1

---

1. Makes it clear that what is being said to him or her is *the* important subject of the moment.
2. Does not interrupt.
3. Avoids arguing—permits the speaker to say his/her piece.
4. Keeps an open mind by hearing what ideas are being expounded and holds off any criticism until digesting all that has been stated.
5. Holds personal ego in check and does not appear overly knowledgeable about the subject.
6. Screens out the facts and eliminates the irrelevant material.

LANGUAGE AND COMMUNICATING

Language can be thought of as a set of symbols for conveying ideas from one person to another. It results from human beings living together. As the need to communicate arose, language was developed. A variety of symbols are used including color, signs, emblems, characters, noise, numbers, and alphabetical letters. Normally in the selection of symbols the user tries to follow the predominant custom for communicating within the given field, and keeps in mind what the selected symbols will mean to the receiver.

Figure 20–2 shows some of the symbols in common use today. If you were a proofreader, the top line would show different symbols which convey definite meanings to you. The second line is meaningful to a musician. To the musician, these marks stand for concepts just as much as alphabetic letters do in a written word. Going down the lines in the illustration, the third line is that of the telegraphic operator, and following in sequence the symbols are in mathematics, electronic tape, shorthand, electrical networks, and stock exchange ticker tape.

Alphabetical letters arranged into words are among the most common symbols used. A word is simply a symbol of an idea or object. The word "pencil" symbolizes a particular object, and to English-speaking people it means that particular object alone. That is, a word is not a

FIGURE 20–2: Communication utilizes a wide variety of symbols

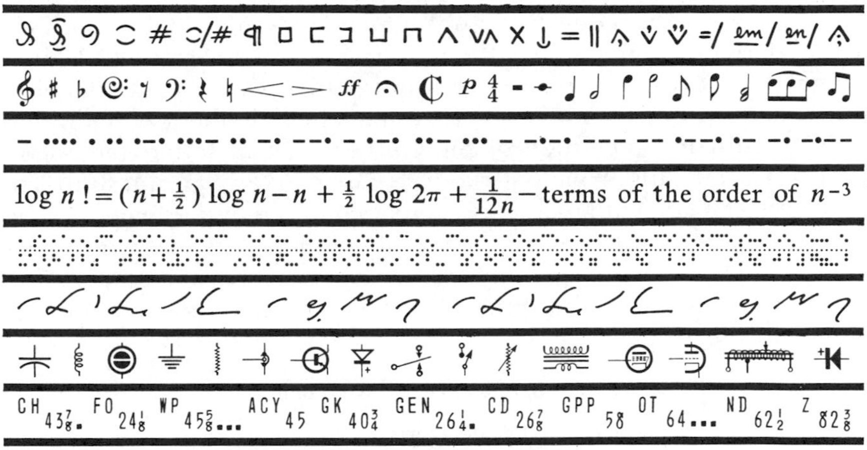

$$\log n\,! = (n+\tfrac{1}{2})\log n - n + \tfrac{1}{2}\log 2\pi + \frac{1}{12n} - \text{terms of the order of } n^{-3}$$

person or thing but a *label which represents* a person or thing that can be distinguished. Broadly speaking, there are two classifications of words: (1) extensional and (2) intensional. The former includes words for persons, places, objects, materials, and fixed-label concepts, such as units of measurement. "Girl," "Ohio," "watch," "copper," and "centimeter" are examples. Extensional words are definite and refer to standards which are widely accepted. There is little misunderstanding about the meaning of extensional words. In contrast, intensional neither always connote an identical meaning to different persons nor the same meaning to the same person at all times, and this is where difficulty arises in communication. To illustrate, the word "easy" is subject to different meanings. "The examination is easy" can connote different meanings to different students, and "he is an easy boss" implies a different meaning to the word "easy" than that of the previous example. The word "round" for example, has over 70 different meanings.

The meaning of words is influenced by association. For example, the word "pay" brings to mind different words to different persons. To the executive it might suggest "bonus," "checking account," "dollars," "twice a month," or "bills." To clerks of the personnel department, "starting," "promotion," "job evaluation," or "increase" may be thought of; while to another employee it may be associated with "food," "clothes," "car," "family," "date," or "blonde."

Word differences and choice constitute a serious obstacle to mutual understanding. Barriers exist simply because different evaluations and meanings are given the words and symbols used, and this condition tends to remain even when both sides are trying hard to communicate effectively. The meaning ascribed to a word or symbol is influenced by the amount of education the participant possess. In the case of words, as more and more education is obtained, not only does a person's vocabulary increase, but also the variety of word associations. Called language devices, they help attract and hold a person's attention and enrich the message or the reply. Examples include the use of alliteration, or utilizing repetition of the initial constant letter; metaphor, which is a comparison made without the use of *like* or *as;* and simile, or comparison made with *like* or *as.* Selection of the proper word can be difficult. Failure to recognize the variety of meanings that words convey, use of trite expressions, and inclusion of negative and unfavorable words weaken a communication. Figure 20–3 shows some guides to follow in this respect.

FIGURE 20–3: Suggestions for word choice

1. Use specific, definite words

Specific	*General*
refrigerator	product
table	thing
private office	your place
mail	send

2. Avoid trite expressions, such as:

I beg to advise
We are happy to inform you
As per statement attached herewith
We have your kind favor of

3. Use a single word for a group of words

Use	*Do not use*
like	in the nature of
before	prior to
now	at the present time
because	in view of the fact that

Word choice and use can be carried to extremes so that the communication is completely lost. A. P. Herbert, a member of the British Parliament, being disgusted with government ineffective jargon, translated Lord Nelson's immortal phase:

"England expects every man to do his duty"

into the clumsy, meaningless:

"England anticipates that, as regards the current emergency, personnel will face up to the issues and exercise appropriately the functions allocated to their respective occupational groups."

There is also "body language" which includes the facial expressions, the twinkle in the eye, the gestures made, and the tone of the voice. For example, a word spoken in a context of anger can have an entirely different meaning from the same word spoken in friendliness. The statement "All right, I'll show you how to do the work" can be said with various points of voice inflection, emphasis, and gestures so that different meanings are imparted to the listener—for instance, a feeling of encouragement or, in contrast, a feeling of impatience.

Some include dress under body language, claiming a person has opportunity for self-expression through dress. The worth of an employee is not measured by a particular clothing style and there is no one right way to dress, but dress does help project the image of a person.

BLUEPRINT DRAWINGS

Figure 20–4 shows an example of a blueprint drawing which employs special symbols for communicative purposes. Blueprints communicate accurately information that is difficult to convey by most other communi-

FIGURE 20–4: Blueprint of a slider block

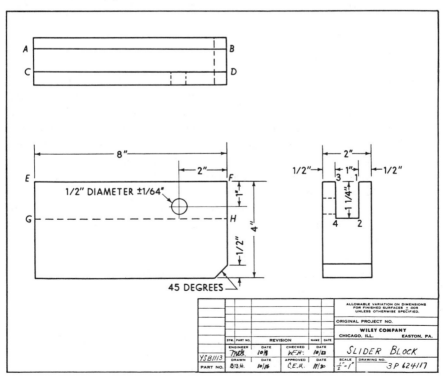

cation media. Furthermore, blueprint drawings are in common use not only by factory employees but also by industrial salespeople, purchasing agents, estimators, product designers, and research people.

The standard arrangement of a blueprint drawing shows (1) top, (2) front, and (3) end view, with the top immediately above the front view and the end view immediately to the right of the front view. This is the arrangement shown in Figure 20–4. The dimensions of the object such as length, height, and width are shown, as well as a "title block" to indicate pertinent information, such as name, part number, drawing number, drawn by, checked by, approved by, type of material used, tolerances, and the type and date of changes made on the print. See lower portion of the illustration.

Visible edges are shown by solid lines, invisible edges by dotted or broken lines. The dimensions of circular locations are shown from a center line; for example, in Figure 20–4, front view, the center of the half-inch-diameter hole is located two inches from the right edge of the slider block and one inch down from the top edge, *E-F*. Degrees are used to indicate the dimensions of angles as indicated in the illustration. The permissible deviations or variations from the stated dimensions are shown either (1) in the title block or (2) on the drawing itself. To show details of the interior, a sectional view is used. This represents what would be seen if a section or a part of the object were cut away.

IMPROVING COMMUNICATING

The first step in improving communicating is to believe in its essentiality in management. By means of communication a manager finds out about problems, draws up plans, assists employees to satisfy their basic wants, gives instructions, and checks on results. Each manager is obligated to state every communication clearly, to listen sympathetically, to respond considerately, and to act promptly.

Once its importance is fully accepted, the next step is to recognize communication as a means of improving human relations, not solely as a means of getting things done. The most effective communication takes place among people with common points of view. The manager who fosters good relationships with group members will have less difficulty in communicating with them. Human behavior must be taken into account. Honest, factual, and complete information must be distributed. Help in how to communicate should be provided all management members.

Third, take time to plan effective communication. This boils down to (1) expressing the communication clearly, and (2) achieving good listenership and readership. What to communicate is vital, but consideration for how and when to communicate are also essential.

Also, seek to establish a work environment that encourages upward communication. The results-management approach to the management process is a modern way to achieve this condition. As stated in Chapter 4, results management encourages each management member to manage one's own unit of operations with full authority and responsibility, emphasis being on the results achieved. With such an arrangement, communicating from the bottom up is encouraged and is closely tied to efforts taking place to accomplish the sought-for results. Upward communication is also encouraged by the manager expressing an interest in the problems and views of the subordinates, and by not discriminating against anyone because of the information given.

Cultivation and use of the corporate grapevine is one of the best ways to improve communication. The grapevine is extremely effective, rapid, elusive, and filters every nook of every organization. No corporate security is too rigid for its penetration. Because it is unaccountable for its errors and shows little respect for persons or perogatives, many managers wish the grapevine would wither and die. But it never will. It is a normal part of any organization and nothing a manager can do will sound its death knell. Far better to realize it is here to stay and has strong influence on communication. The smart approach is to get to know it, cultivate it, and use it wherever advantageous and possible to do so. This means a manager should listen to the grapevine, know who its leaders are, how it operates, what it is doing, and the information it is carrying. Actually, employees are going to engage in office talk, shop talk, and sales talk, no matter what. An active grapevine reflects their need to discuss their work and its environment with people they know, trust, and with whom they have a common interest. It is really a sign of the workforce's vitality and genuine interest in their work. It is a fact of organization life.

Consider using a task force. This approach has proven quite successful especially in financial institutions. Line and staff members of the company along with an outside communication specialist are selected by the top manager to form the task force. This group's goal is to improve communication. It meets weekly to discuss communication issues and problems and to evaluate alternatives and solutions to follow. The first task is to put aside assumptions about what is wrong and get basic information on what the real communication needs are by interviewing employees at all levels. Questionnaires can also be used. Also, qualified members of the task force review current communication literature and study existing practices in other like enterprises to ascertain what others are doing. Findings from both the survey and the research are carefully analyzed from which data recommendations as well as supporting information are compiled by the task force. A report is then presented to top management, spotlighting the major findings and recommendations which are acted upon in a series of joint sessions of top managers and the task force. This total approach usually proves successful because the credibility of the task force is high, employee participation is featured, the task force develops its members, and after the work is over the task force tends to contribute its support of its recommendations.

Furthermore, know intimately the needs of the receiver. When the information being communicated is vital to the participants' needs, the communication will tend to be more effective. Therefore, try to include "what's in it for me" in every communication. This requires creativity and effort, but pays big dividends in improving communication. Among the list of items which usually rank high in employees' interest are company and industry outlook, expansion plans, labor policies, personnel changes, organization changes, company finances, research activities, company ethics, and taxation.

It is also well to remember, "One picture is worth one thousand words." Hence, use appropriate illustrations and charts to get your idea across. Be sure the visual is relevant to the idea being communicated. If possible add glamour to the communication. Simply to state, "The government is spending $1 billion for this project," is dull and it doesn't evince real understanding by the receiver. In contrast, the following is exciting and penetrating: "The government is spending $1 billion—the equivalent amount for a person working 40 hours a week, 50 weeks a year, at $5 an hour for 100,000 years. If one started with the year 1, less than 2 percent of the job would be completed today."

Utilize communication feedback. By observing incoming feedback a manager can adapt a response to this latest information. To become rooted in a position or viewpoint because, "It is the way I see it," or "I've always handled it this way," can lead to serious difficulties. The feedback can reveal whether the communication is effective or not, and why. It enables a manager to improve personal communication.

Finally, avoid overcommunicating. Too much communication is equally as bad as too little communication. If people are deluged with company communication, many of its aims are probably lost or defeated. There is always the danger of talking and writing too much on a subject that holds only casual interest or need for the recipient.

TRANSACTIONAL ANALYSIS

In addition to exchanging information, people communicate to reinforce their feeling about themselves. As such they make transactions with each other. These transactions can make participants comfortable and free to work or they can make people uncomfortable and be entrapped in emotional conflicts. The identification and analysis of these transactions from communication is what transactional analysis (TA) is about. It assists in understanding human behavior and is helpful in motivation, counseling, interviewing—in fact, anywhere where communication plays an important role. The transaction is shaped by the particular ego state of each person. There are three basic patterns used (1) parent, (2) adult, and (3) child. The parent ego stage is acquired from external feelings and experiences imposed upon a person as a young child when the only alternative was to accept without question. It admonishes, criticizes, and is prejudicial. The adult ego is factual, logical, and objective, has no predetermined feelings and evaluates a situation by investigation and analysis of facts. The child ego features the characteristics of a child—curosity, imagination, and rebelliousness.

Likewise, there are three basic types of transactions, (1) complimentary, (2) crossed, and (3) ulterior. Complimentary transaction is one in which the originator gets the kind of response expected. Crossed is when quite a different response from the one expected is received. And ulterior involves messages between ego states that are different from the apparent or spoken ones.

Examples of several will clarify their meanings. A complimentary transaction child-parent includes:

A (child): I need help. Can't get through to Mr. Yeats. Can you give me a lift?

B (parent): Sure, glad to do so. Don't worry. I'll handle him.

A crossed transaction parent-child:

C (parent): I need help. Can't get through to Mr. Yeats. Can you give me a lift?

D (child): No way. I've got more than I can do now. Why come to me with your problem?

An ulterior transaction parent-child:

E (parent): That's the second time you have made that part. It doesn't have to be perfect you know.

F (child): Right. I'll be finished in a couple of minutes.

On the surface, this appears to be an adult-adult transaction. However, the true hidden meaning is parent-child since the following is meant:

E (parent): I'll settle for the second attempt. I can't wait any longer.

F (child): Here's your part. Why do I get these jobs when they are not in my line of work and I don't have the tools for them?

TA can assist in improving communication and also influence the behavior of another. *Stroking* is one such technique whereby recognition or praise for performance is stated to the other person. If negative, the stroke is called a *discount*. Knowing the ego being addressed, it is possible to communicate the most appropriate statement. A child ego statment, for example, is commonly best countered with an adult comment. The way we feel about others and ourselves determine in great measure the kind of transactions we make with others and the strokes or discounts we give and seek. And it also determines the effectiveness of our communication.

There are basically two ways we can feel about others and ourselves—OK and not OK. This makes for four *life positions:*

1. I'm OK—you're OK.   Both giver and sender are a pleasure to everyone concerned. They feel worthwhile as persons and view others in the same acceptance.

2. I'm OK—you're not OK.   The person feels good about self but distrusts others. Frequently one is pushy, not accepted by others, and may even be offensive to them. The parent ego is common and the child ego in others may be offended.

3. I'm not OK—you're OK.   A sort of self-demeaning relation to others is present. The holder feels inferior and does not think well of self. Approval of others may be paramount and even when achieved does not bring lasting satisfaction. If the not OK has a child ego, defenses are commonly put up for fear of failure or rejection.

4. I'm not OK—you're not OK.   This totally negative situation toward self and others poses difficulties. Seeing little worth in life or work makes for a communicator requiring extra patience and understanding by a manager. Some so-called hard-core unemployables may be in this classification. Fortunately, the extreme in this category or totally negative to self and others is rare and when existent, may require professional help.

POPULAR FORMAL COMMUNICATION MEDIA

For communicative purposes a manager has a number of formal media available. Formal media are those officially recognized and approved. Illustrative are:

1. Interviews—regular and special.
2. Departmental meetings.
3. Mass meetings.
4. Conferences.
5. Telephone calls.
6. Company newspapers.
7. Company magazines.
8. Company handbooks.
9. Information booklets on products, selling, and display materials.
10. Employee-benefit publications—pension plans, insurance, and savings.

11. Special-purpose publications—executives' messages and company policies.
12. Payroll inserts.
13. Plant bulletin boards.
14. Posters.
15. Annual report to employees.
16. Supervisory publications.
17. Direct-mail letters.
18. Film strips, slides, and motion pictures.

Studies conducted to find out the relative effectiveness of various media reveal some interesting data. Memos, letters, and bulletin boards are relatively the least effective for most communication. In general, face-to-face communication carries the message much better than printed media. Also, the fewer the organizational restraints, the faster the communication. For example, having to clear information with higher authorities tends to slow up the communication process. The impact of communication is greatly increased when the release is from as close to the top management level as possible, thus giving the communication official flavor.

COMMUNICATION—MEETINGS, DIRECTIVES, AND DESIGNS

Group meetings have grown to occupy a major role in communication. Some have described them as a way of managerial life and facetiously state that a manager who isn't at a meeting is likely to either be coming from or going to one. Meetings provide participation, give members a sense of belonging and of importance, and are excellent distributors of information. They do, however, have some drawbacks. Commonly, only a few members make any real contributions, many come to the meetings without any real preparation and are content to rely on the others. Also, meetings take considerable time and even though a strong person is at the helm, discussions tend to get off the subject. Further, meetings give excessive advantage to the quick, glib, politic, convincing speaker who may neither offer the best idea nor supply the best comments. Suggestions for making meetings effective are listed in Figure 20–5.

Directives include orders, instructions, and reports. Essential to execution are orders. They tell *what* is to be done, *who* is to do it, and *when, where, how,* and *why.* However, in certain cases, some of these components may be implied or may be omitted; for example, the order, "Effective November 27, Charles E. Hunter will become supervisor of Department 17," answers the *what, who, when,* and *where,* but the *how* and the *why* are omitted. An order should be subjected

FIGURE 20–5:   Fourteen ways for a chairperson to build helpful meetings

1. Don't call a meeting to decide something you can and should decide your-self, or when a series of telephone calls to individuals will adequately serve the purpose.

2. About three days in advance of the meeting, send out notices giving the time and place of the meeting, appropriate material or research data, the agenda to be covered, and the approximate time the meeting will require, establishing a definite starting time.

3. Indicate clearly the purpose of the meeting to all members; that is, whether to supply advice, arrive at a decision, or accept or reject a certain proposal to be presented.

4. The day before the meeting review your notes for completeness. Give thought to possible questions that might be raised.

5. Make certain all members are informed of the meeting.

6. Encourage each member to participate.

7. Ask questions that cannot be answered with a "Yes" or "No."

8. Employ generous amounts of visual material but don't usurp all the time with a show.

9. Get all members to express themselves; do not permit one member to monopolize the discussion.

10. Be specific; make the discussions apply to the particular issues.

11. Keep to the agenda; let each member have a chance to express herself or himself, but get them back to the subject at hand if they wander, and sum up succinctly immediately following what they have stated.

12. Do not permit telephone calls to be transferred to the meeting room while committee is in session.

13. Present facts first, then proposals for solutions.

14. Write up all proceedings of the meeting and distribute copies to all group members and to the superior to whom the group reports.

only to the interpretation intended by the giver. In many companies a verbal order is confirmed in writing so that its issuance can be verified and a record maintained. The obligation for the order's execution should be definite and mutually known. Belief by the recipient in the meaning and intent of the order is paramount and to gain such belief an explanation or the "reason why" for the order is effective. People usually are willing to follow an order when they clearly see the gains from such action, especially if the gain is to them or for a purpose in which they believe. In contrast, fear of consequences if the order is not followed is likewise a powerful force. The power to enforce should be behind every order; but in many instances, potential enforcement is most effective as a threat rather than actual execution.

Instructions stress the how-to-do-it aspect, and their use helps to insure correct and orderly execution of the work. An instruction can be defined as *oral or written information on a recommended manner in which a particular kind of task is to be performed.* With reference to written instructions, all elements of the work performance are included. Written instructions are not easy to compose. Required are detailed data and a skill in seeing the task from the recipient's or other person's viewpoint. Clarity of expression and a sequence of steps to follow are of major consideration. Written instructions are especially helpful in the case of tasks which repeat from job to job, the work can be performed without separate and individual managerial action. In addition, the availability of how-to-do-it information is increased, thus making the indoctrination and training of employees less difficult. On the other hand, written instructions are costly to prepare, inject rigidity into the handling of the work, and stifle creativity.

Defined as *a factual presentation of information directed to a particular audience for a specific purpose,* a report is oral or written and used mainly for subjects of a technical or operational nature. Most serve either as (1) informational reports or (2) investigational reports. The former stress data on developments, trends, and favorable-attitude growth. The latter are concerned with analysis and interpretation of data, presenting recommendations, and suggested solutions to stated problems. The various stages from investigation to presentation of a report should be followed and use of a detailed outline to prepare a report is recommended. Subject headings should be indicated. Flexibility in the format of the report is helpful, yet some standardization in format makes for consistency and ease of comprehending the communication. Reports can be very costly and control over their number and content should be followed.

Designs include efforts by managers to improve their image with the public. Included are name, plant signs, name plates, advertising insignias and slogans, and stationery headings. These designs affect corporate image, reputation, or impressions of a corporation—verbal and visual—which exist in the mind of the public. They are the end product of a broad spectrum of communication. Some claim the public's image cannot be changed stating it is not appearance but what is done that determines the image. This is true, but it is likewise important to remember that basically people judge other things, including an enterprise, from what they see and hear. Designs are an important part of a company's communication. While frequently not discussed in managerial communication discussions, they concern a vital and delicate external influence of any enterprise—public opinion.

QUESTIONS

1. Justify this statement: Communicating is important in management.
2. What are some ways that improved listenership and readership can be obtained? Discuss one of these ways in some detail.
3. What is the meaning of each of the following: (*a*) life positions, (*b*) communication barrier, (*c*) symbols of communication, and (*d*) intensional words?

4. Have each one of a small group of friends write down five words that come to mind as you read off the following words: (a) dollar, (b) football, (c) oil, (d) president, and (e) music. Analyze the results. What do they mean from the viewpoint of language and communicating?

5. What significance do you attach to the statement "Communication is a necessary adjunct to management, not management itself"? Discuss.

6. In your opinion does the use of results management aid or hinder communication? Justify your answer, using an example to illustrate your views.

7. Discuss the grapevine as a means of improving communication.

8. Distinguish between each of the following pairs: (a) allness-orientation and openness in communication, (b) body language and alliteration, (c) crossed transaction in communication and stroking.

9. With reference to Figure 20–5, select six ways you feel are most important. Justify your selections.

10. Recall a situation in which you have been a participant and in which communication was ineffective, resulting in some embarrassing or dire consequence. Suggest effective communicating for this situation that would have avoided the dire consequence.

11. What is transactional analysis, how is it used, and for what purposes is it helpful?

12. What is included under communication designs and what is their significance in management?

13. Write concise but complete instructions for one of the following: (a) putting a cassette in a tape recorder; (b) checking and correcting the air pressure in an auto tire; (c) tying a bow tie; (d) starting and driving an automobile; (e) installing the film in a movie projector; and (f) washing the inside and outside of a house window.

14. Indicate what medium of communication would you use for each of the following and give reasons for your choice: (a) you are a department head and have decided to accept a new position with a different company and feel you should now tell the members of your department about the change; (b) as a typist in a large department store you feel you are underpaid and intend to let your boss know about this; (c) as personnel manager in your firm, you need to inform the employees of a new fringe benefit program your company is providing beginning in about six weeks; (d) you are a senior partner in a public accounting firm and want to squelch rumors that your company is merging with a competitive accounting firm; and (e) by a telephone call you have been informed that your immediate superior will be hospitalized for three weeks and you are to take charge.

CASE 20–1.   SEELEY CORPORATION

It is a long-standing policy of Seeley Corporation to transfer its middle management members and management trainees from store to store in order for them to gain needed experience and to become better acquainted with the personnel of the corporation and its mode of operation. Seeley Corporation is a national chain of retail stores. Typically, management personnel is transferred every two years on the average.

Yesterday Albert Pershing, manager of the hardware department at the Minneapolis store, requested his assistant and recent transferee, Elbert Alderson, to improve the merchandise arrangements and displays of popular items generally sold during the spring months. The way Pershing put it to Alderson was, "Get a good arrangement. I want to improve our sales at least 50 percent on these spring house repair items. So get with it, El, and let's come up with a winner." Also today when Pershing was informed that one of his management trainees, Jerry Mann, was being transferred to Dallas, he told Christine Sikes, a retail clerk in his department, to take up a collection from the department members and select a suitable gift for Jerry.

Several days later, Pershing observed the merchandise arrangements and displays that Alderson had put up. They were nothing like what he (Pershing) had in mind. He became furious, sought Alderson and told him quite emphatically of his disappointment in such a display of hardware items. "They won't sell one extra dollar's worth of business. In fact, they are terrible. We want to improve impulse buying—put some creativity into it. Get what you have over there out of here as quickly as you can" were Pershing's statements.

Christine Sikes told employees she was taking up a collection to get Jerry a two-suiter luggage piece. All but one member of the department contributed. Her comment, "I don't believe Jerry wants a two-suiter. He certainly doesn't need it. Really, he has everything and shouldn't expect us to give him a gift. Christine doubled her contribution and said nothing to Pershing about the incident.

Questions

1. Is Albert Pershing using communication effectively? Why?
2. What significance do you put on Christine Sikes' action of covering for the noncontributing member and saying nothing to Pershing about it?
3. What suggestions do you believe are in order to improve communication among employees of the hardware department? Discuss.
4. What considerations other than communication do you feel should be considered in improving the interrelationships and work environment of the department? Why?

CASE 20–2. OXFORD COMPANY

Mr. Melvin Snyder, factory superintendent, takes trips through the factory at different hours and on different days. He likes to talk with the operative employees and ask them questions about their work, their families, the material they are using, and the machine being operated. He believes such conversation makes for better morale and also lets him know what is taking place in the shop.

Every Monday morning at the weekly production meeting he will bring up some aspect of information picked up from the previous week's shop visits and ask for an explanation of it. Usually his production management personnel will answer him, but Mr. Snyder will continue, asking about other bits of information he received until his associates are unable to answer or inform him that he has erroneous information. Mr. Snyder, however, insists that the operative employees are telling him the truth and sometimes he points out that the same information is given him by different employees in different departments. Some of his associates have suggested that they accompany Mr. Snyder during his shop tours, but he will have no part of this, stating that the operators will not talk when their immediate superior or more than one management member is with him. He claims the friendly, sincere atmosphere he has achieved with many of the workers in the shop is a definite advantage and helps communication, and he doesn't want to jeopardize it in any way.

Mr. Snyder is not entirely satisfied with his production management associates. In his judgment his production control manager, Benjamin Lake, just doesn't seem to comprehend what he is told. Mr. Snyder admits the manufacturing work is getting quite complicated, but it irks him when Benny just stands there and replies "Yes," "Yes," "Yes." Mr. Snyder has noticed that Benny says he understands a request or a suggestion or a change given to him, but then proceeds to go about his work as if nothing had been said to him. Mr. Snyder would like to promote the assistant production control manager, Tom Roth, to the production control manager's job, but he doesn't know as yet what to do with Benny.

This morning while on a plant tour he talked with a production control clerk who told him Tom was leaving the company for a better-paying job. In reply to Mr. Snyder's question, "Where's he going?" he was told, "He's going to work for his father-in-law who owns a trucking business."

That afternoon, Mr. Snyder summoned Benny Lake to his office.

Snyder: Benny, I understand Tom is leaving the company. Is that true?
Lake: Yes, sir. That is what he told me a couple days ago.
Snyder: How come you did not tell me?
Lake: Well, sir, I thought he might change his mind. It's not certain yet as I understand it.
Snyder: It doesn't sound good to me.
Lake: If he does leave, we will just have to do the best we can without him. And we have some capable people in production control. I didn't want to bother you with problems of my department, Mr. Snyder.

Snyder: Bother? That's no bother. I want to know about matters like this.

Lake: Yes, sir.

Questions

1. What is the problem the company faces? Discuss
2. Are Mr. Snyder's actions generally good or generally bad for the company? Why?
3. What action do you recommend the company take? Be sure to include how you would implement your proposed action.

Chapter 21

Appraising, developing, and compensating

Where a man does his best with only moderate powers,
he will have the advantage over negligent superiority.

Jane Austen

Managerial appraising, developing, and compensating are top activities of actuating. Demonstrating a genuine interest in a person's performance, improving how one is doing, helping to develop needed skills, and compensating on a mutually fair basis are always of significance. Typical managers want to know how they are doing, where they can improve, and what pay they will be receiving. The emphasis throughout this chapter is on the manager. However, these actuating activities of appraising, developing, and compensating apply also to nonmanagers, and we shall refer to them from time to time.

APPRAISING MANAGERS

Appraisal of personnel is performed by means of a tool called performance appraisal. The more perceptibly this tool is applied, the more valid the judgment and the development of employees can be. Stated formally, *performance appraisal is the official and periodic evaluation of an employee's job performance measured against the job's requirements.*

In and of itself, appraisal has its beneficial attributes. When a manager appraises the performance and potential of those reporting to one, a new and helpful understanding about them is acquired. The evaluator becomes more aware of what they are doing, in what possible ways they can be helped, and what can be done to speed their growth and develop a greater interest in self-improvement.

There are two major reasons for evaluating performance (1) to appraise the manager in one's present job, and (2) to determine the manager's developmental needs, if any. Under the first reason, we are inventorying the managerial power to know what we have. This is the starting basis. The second reason is to determine the difference between required and present performance, a gap which represents the developmental need to be fulfilled. We want to pinpoint present developmental requirements accurately, to catch poor management practices before they snowball into costly errors, and to find out in what areas help can be given to spur the manager to do a better job.

Is justification for salary increases another purpose of evaluating performance? Yes, this is a usage. However, modern thinking is that discussions concerning salary and promotions should be made at a separate time from appraisals dealing with current performance and developmental needs. This viewpoint is justified by noting that performance is only one factor among many considered in increasing compensation, for example, salary ranges, relative position within a given range, and available funds are also usually taken into account. Probably more important is that if during an appraisal, salary enters the process, it tends to take over as the interest and the goal, with the result that appraisal and developmental needs become secondary and commonly are distorted in order to justify an increase or promotion.

Criteria used

Usually one person does the performance appraisal, although in some instances a group of three may appraise separately, and combine their ratings into a composite value of the group. The appraiser should have first-hand information and knowledge of the manager being rated and of the work or results being accomplished. Frequently this means the immediate supervisor should do the appraising. However, in some cases, a person trained in appraisal work performs the task.

Appraising accurately is difficult. Having to state capabilities and accomplishments in writing necessitates keen observation, good judgment, and objectivity. To some degree what is stated as the person's performance reflects the appraiser's concept of performance adequacy and the person's most outstanding personality characteristics. The evaluator tends to describe the appraisal in terms of personal values and understanding. Top management members, for example, are commonly appraised in terms of profits realized, selected personal virtues, and subjective job-related factors. For middle and lower level managers and also nonmanagers, selected traits for rating performance are common. Included, for example, are job knowledge, judgment, creativity, initiative, drive, and self-expression. The assumption is that estimated measurements of these traits make for a certain behavior which is indicative of the ratee's accomplishments at work. Some question the use of traits in performance appraisal. The relationship between capabilities and performance, while probably related, is not fully known. Also the appraisal is judgment-based; it is influenced to some degree by the rater's thoughts about the ratee and may not be wholly objective. On the other hand, this influence may be very minor and not nearly as important as some critics suggest.

The trend in appraising is toward "measured appraisals." Under this arrangement performance is evaluated in realistic and quantitative terms, such as reduce scrap loss by 5 percent, raise quality production runs to 98 percent "acceptable," and sell 125 percent of quota. Performance is measured in terms of the ratee's accomplishment of these goals. Measured appraisals minimize subjective judgment and express performance in universally understandable terms. However, they may tend to stress certain goals excessively and introduce too much rigidity into the individual's efforts as a team member of the organization. Further, the goals and work must be measurable. Also, when a person's performance is a part of a total effort the individual appraisal may give rise to controversial issues.

Observe that the measured appraisal approach is in keeping with the concept of results management which places emphasis upon the results. Quantitative work should be evaluated first followed by qualitative tasks. Quantitative tasks can be *measured;* qualitative tasks can be *judged.*

There is some practice of blending the trait and measurable approaches, thus certain attributes of an employee's performance must be judged, while others can be evaluated in terms of specific measurements. In addition, all are related to a definite period and to the overall goals of an enterprise.

Interviews are helpful in ascertaining specific information and obtaining answers to questions, all of which combined with observations and consultation of records of achievement assist in formulating the performance appraisal. Usually printed forms are used to assist and guide the evaluators.

In analyzing the person's performance the rater focuses on discovering *why* the person achieves what one does, *how* much is it, and *how* well it is done. In this work, asking questions such as these are helpful: Were the objectives reasonable—not too difficult, not too easy? Were they in keeping with the person's qualifications? Was concentration upon the objectives possible or were there extenuating circumstances and distractions?

THE APPRAISAL CONFERENCE

The person being rated has a right to know what is one's own appraisal. This is a key consideration in performance appraisal and is the purpose served in having the appraisal conference. Preparation for this conference makes it much easier for both the rater and the ratee. The latter should be advised several days before the appointed time so that one can be prepared and able to make a contribution. The ratee usually knows fairly well what the appraisal will be. Nevertheless, differences usually arise and careful handling by the rater is mandatory.

In preparing for the conference, it is recommended that the rater observe these suggestions:

1. Outline the points you wish to cover.
2. Emphasize that the purpose is to help the person to improve job performance.
3. Concentrate on strengths.
4. Ask the person to give suggestions for improvement to get into the discussion of weaknesses.
5. Give specific examples and means for improvement.
6. Encourage the person to talk, to express beliefs and feelings—you listen.
7. Do not make reference to other management members.

During the conference refrain from making any criticism, for to do so may put the ratee on the defensive with attempts to discredit parts of the appraisal or to sit silently through the interview and thus prevent good communication. Point out that the conference is confidential and its purpose is to review the job and work so that each has a better understanding of it.

Seldom is complete agreement reached, and differences may be scattered over several points. But with time at least part of the differences may diminish. Hence, the appraisal interview may be looked upon as a period to get the appraisal to the ratee along with some explanations. Then terminate it and let the ratee "think it over." Later, get together again and discuss it more openly.

Sometimes the initial reaction of the ratee is that the evaluation is unfair in parts—too much is expected, or the fault is really with someone else. With time it frequently happens that the ratee begins to see and admits to self that the rating is fairly accurate. With this comes the realization that to get ahead the wise course is to correct the deficiencies enumerated by the appraiser. The ideal solution is for the rater and the ratee to agree on a self-development plan initiated by the ratee to bring about improvement in performance. The rater assists in this effort, but refrains from telling the ratee exactly what to do. Schedule follow-ups. Have the ratee sign the appraisal form to avoid any future misunderstanding.

PERFORMANCE APPRAISAL IN PERSPECTIVE

Above all else, performance appraisal must be fair. Outstanding and par performance should be recognized. Likewise, substandard performances should not be glossed over. Rigid impartiality is the key.

Remember that performance appraisal is continuous. Never think of it as a chore to be done every six months or every year. Observe a member's performance as frequently as convenient. Give help, instructions, encouragement, ask for ratee's opinions, and review the work accomplished as required. Always try to compare the performance with the specific job objectives and requirements mutually agreed upon. Recognize that there are problems in running an effective performance appraisal program. But it need not be ineffective if proper training in its implementation is supplied, complete understanding of it is maintained, and feedback on its actions is utilized. Finally, move in and take action, if required, and at the same time inform the ratee the reasons for the action and the effect of the action upon him or her.

DEVELOPING MANAGERS

Most modern managers are developed; few are "born managers." Present-day qualifications are far more than matters of natural endowment. And dependence solely upon informal association with immediate superiors for meeting the developmental needs is slow, incomplete, and frequently ineffective. It pays to have the very best managers and formal developmental efforts to this end are an investment that pays excellent returns. As employed in this discussion, the development of managers is thought of as *the application of planned efforts to assist in maintaining and improving managers in order that they can more effectively attain the objectives of the enterprise.*

Managerial developmental efforts are established for a number of reasons. They include: to improve sales, lower production cost, acquire better teamwork, instill greater enthusiasm, and add confidence. More precisely, however, the types of benefits commonly cited by managers as expected and received are:

1. Improved communication among management members and better use of informal discussions about their work.
2. Identification of broad, inclusive problems which affect several operating departments and which require managerial attention.
3. Evaluation of adequacy and suitability of company policies.
4. Keeping up to date on current managerial developments.
5. Revealing certain weaknesses of superiors hindering subordinate efforts, and suggest possible remedial actions to be taken.
6. Securing better cooperation and teamwork among management members.
7. Stimulating managers to appraise and develop their subordinates.

8. Encouraging the promotion of qualified managers.
9. Uncovering poorly placed management members, and bringing about needed transfers for mutual advantage.
10. Assisting in college recruitment efforts.

Current concepts on management development

Programs designed to help develop managers are so varied and difficult to define that any significant trends in their makeup and application defy expression in a few simple terms. Management development programs are changing. To a great extent the rigid, highly systematized developing procedures have been abandoned. In their place, management members are performing more informal training or development work. The program is sustained by top managers and line managers. Management courses dealing with technological advances, the behavior of people, social responsibility, and changes in the business environment have expanded.

The true objective is to see that the learner leaves the group able to do certain specific things or to mull over concepts and formulate ideas and thoughts helpful to one in performing one's job. The objectives have changed from that of developing *learned* managers to *learning* managers. The latter is the real need of today and of the future. With all the evolutionary change and growth around us, the modern manager must cope with this highly dynamic state of affairs and relate personal knowledge and skill to the projected tomorrows. Problems are viewed more as opportunities than threats of failure, and the manager is becoming more of a finder of answers than a giver of answers. In brief, she or he is learning along with the group; the manager is finding out with them how best to meet certain situations and what decisions should be made. The learning manager stresses participative learning, interacting with other people, and working with problems that are meaningful.

There is, of course, need for knowledge transfer, and programs for this purpose are and should be utilized. These are the familiar "how-to" courses. But usage of these, namely straightforward lecture presentations of explicit and prescribed policies and practices has revealed the need for an awareness of others and a recognition of the setting into which the knowledge must be placed. In essence, this helps move management development efforts into an unstructured laboratory situation. The highly structured classroom situation is not typical of the condition faced by the manager.

There is belief by many that managers of today acquire and improve their managerial skill primarily from experience, self-study, and on-the-job experiences. These practical sources are effective because they pinpoint the training to the specific and contemporary needs of the manager. Specifically, in-house training courses and much present-day formal management education are short on skill development although they provide management knowledge in an acceptable format. The more popular reasons for this state of affairs are believed to include that authoritarian top level managers want technically competent people to carry out their directives—the need is not for skillful subordinates, manager conformity is required by the large bureaucratic organization—you supply what the organization wants, and human resource development efforts are viewed by many as mobile and as such a modest investment in them appears prudent.[1]

While as yet not an accepted practice, there is more and more thought being given to providing time for needed management development from the manager's work period. No longer is a weekend or a night a week sufficient to keep abreast of the lengthy and special knowledge that the manager of today requires. Sometime in the future a leave of absence with pay may be an accepted custom so that a manager can go to the proper source for developing and refueling.

Basic developmental considerations

Management development should produce changed behavior which is more in keeping with the requirements for attaining both the organization's and the personal goals than the previous behavior. This change frequently consists of a number of small steps resulting from the training, but the cumulative effect is considerable and is the end result sought. It is also basic that a terminal behavior is identified before the development efforts start.

Essential to a developmental program is genuine top-management support in the form of leadership and the providing of required resources willingly and enthusiastically. Requirements, potentials, and limitations of the development work must be recognized by the top managers and realistic goals approved. Benefits are usually slow in being realized; hence, top managers should not expect quick favorable gains.

Performance problems are commonly viewed as developmental problems. The manager below standard is assumed to need simply "the right kind of training." Unfortunately, most of these casual observations neglect to identify the real problems which no amount of training will correct; namely, basic poor management as exemplified by a poor organization structure, inept leadership, or unrealistic expectations. It is helpful to ask whether performance can possibly be im-

---

[1] Robert F. Pearse, "Manager to Manager: What Managers Think of Management Development" (American Management Association, 1974).

proved without training, by providing the necessary resources and means supplied by competent managerial actions.

No program develops a manager; one develops oneself. The program simply makes a person aware of the growth possibilities and encourages self-help. The urge to acquire knowledge and skill must be strong *within* the individual. No amount of organized managerial training will succeed unless the individual's desire, ambition, and will to achieve are present. The self-directed approach should guide the development efforts with high value being placed on personal initiative and self-sufficiency. The program should emphasize improving work on the *present job*. Normally this is the beginning of a manager increasing efficiency and of preparing for greater responsibility.

Seldom does real learning take place until the learner sees and understands the value to oneself of learning and applying. Developmental efforts are usually most effective when (1) the learner perceives a reward from doing so, (2) practice in applying the new knowledge (skill) is available, and (3) support and feedback are supplied by a person respected and recognized by the learner as competent and fair.

Management development programs are pervasive and represent a continuing process. No one individual or one department is completely responsible for management development. The ultimate responsibility is shared, and it requires constructive action and thought by all the management members at all levels. Furthermore, management development flourishes only when it is given a property of continuity. A seminar one year, nothing the next, and several meetings the next contribute little toward genuine management development.

Upon completion of a course, a manager may have to wait some time before trying out the new knowledge and skill. This "delay gap" can cause frustration and sometimes even loss of the manager, who may find employment with another enterprise. All promises of promotion should be withheld until the job opening is known to be definite and the manager has completed the program successfully. The reward should come not before, but after performance is demonstrated. The developmental program should be viewed as an opportunity and a privilege to attend and to participate.

Major sources for identifying development needs

The needs to be fulfilled by developmental efforts are commonly not identified adequately. Especially is this the case with managers. To supply this information a number of sources can be used. Surveys and interviews give useful information. Upper managers can be asked what developmental needs their subordinate managers should have. An alternative is to ask the manager at any level to indicate the kind and amount of developmental work one requires to perform the present job satisfactorily.

Assessment centers are another source. Here the managers as a group are subjected to a series of management exercises and conditions for several days and their behaviors are noted by trained assessors. Each manager is confronted with typical management problems such as planning, determining how to motivate others, counseling, making decisions, and recommending the way decisions should be implemented. Impressions of the assessors are recorded on special forms, analyzed, and made into a report which reveals the manager's behavior under the test conditions and possible areas for developmental efforts.

Data from performance appraisals are an excellent source as is also job descriptions that provide information such as the duties, responsibilities, to whom the manager reports, who reports to the manager, and the organization authority held.

Short- and long-range plans are still another source for from them what future activities requiring what managers, when, and where are revealed. In addition, position analysis can be used. This is a review and analysis of each managerial position and its incumbent in view of present and future needs of the company. To illustrate, Figure 21–1

FIGURE 21–1:   Pertinent data on management personnel of an enterprise

Organization level	Number of management positions	Cumulative number of management positions	Average age (years)
Top...............	4	4	65 for retirement
Middle............	16	20	55 for hiring
Lower	80	100	45 for hiring

shows the number of management positions, the cumulative number, and the average age of retirement or hiring at the various organizational levels. Since the *average* length of service between top and lower levels is 20 years (65 – 45) and the cumulative number of management positions for all levels is 100, an *average* of 1/20 of 100, or 5 managers must be promoted to the lower level each year to maintain the status quo of the organization.[2]

---

[2] This technique for analyzing promotional possibilities has been taken from H. A. Simon, D. W. Smithburg, and V. A. Thompson, *Public Administration* (New York: Alfred A. Knopf, Inc., 1950), pp. 344–52.

Participative media for management development

The major participative means, arranged alphabetically, include:

1. Committees. Serving on an active committee has training value. By this means the member gains a wider perspective, experiences situations involving the resolution of conflicting ideas, learns to adjust to others' viewpoints, and gains practice in reaching decisions and getting work done by and through the efforts of others. Preferably a major committee with line authority should be selected.[3]

2. Problem solving. The trainee is given a written description of a situation or "case" that necessitates managerial action. Either as an individual or a member of a group, the trainee is required to (1) identify the problem, (2) analyze the facts and conditions leading to the problem, (3) state a recommended plan of action to solve the problem, and (4) justify that particular plan of action. The cases should be carefully selected and pertinent so that their use meets the developmental requirement of the trainee.

3. Conferences, seminars, and special meetings. The exchange of ideas, discussions bringing out the many facets of a problem, and practice in analyzing situations and determining what should be done are typical of the advantages from conferences and seminars. A good leader of the discussion is paramount. Special meetings are formal and administered by company officers. Basic information covered includes company policies, services, and problems encountered.

4. Decentralized organization structure. The more decentralized the organization structure, the greater the need and the opportunity to learn by managing. Basically this means opens up the opportunities to learn by doing. Decentralization, viewed as a means of management development, assumes that qualified people are given managerial duties and that they will receive help from their superiors.

5. Games. Participants are divided into teams which make business decisions dealing with a given set of conditions of an enterprise, commonly expressed by an initial operating statement. Each team starts with exactly the same financial position and with identical choices available. In a typical game each team makes decisions for quarter-to-quarter operations, covering such areas as pricing, make-or-buy decisions, purchasing new equipment and borrowing from the bank. Each team competes with the other teams. The greatest improvement in the company's financial position within a given number of quarters is the goal. The results are quantitative, not qualitative. Games permit trainees to broaden their viewpoints, to visualize interrelated activities, to gain experience in decision making, and to comprehend the results of their decisions.

---

[3] See also Chapter 11 for discussion of committees and their use.

6. In-basket exercises. This is a type of business simulation in which the trainee playing the role of a manager receives a packet of background information and several items of correspondence and memos that are placed in his or her "in basket" and necessitate managerial action. Within a prescribed period, the participant reads the papers, determines the problems, establishes priorities, and decides what actions to take. After the time period, a general discussion is held among the group on how the various situations were handled, and a consensus is usually reached on the most effective ways of dealing with the situations presented.

7. Job rotation and use of strategic jobs. Service with carefully selected successive jobs, or job rotation, throughout the major portions of an enterprise provide broadening, balancing, and enriching experience. A general idea of what the trainee is to acquire from each job should be established, and the trainee should be made aware of the respective goal before each job. Job rotation is probably most effective for managerial jobs of the lower and middle levels. About four to six months should be spent on each job.

A special variation of job rotation is the use of strategic jobs which hold unusual opportunities for self-development. Factors identifying strategic jobs are (1) key decisions are made and carried out, (2) opportunities to solve difficult problems are present, (3) contacts with top managers and personnel outside the company are required, and (4) effective leadership is needed to fill the job.

8. Learning on the job. This is a common and effective means for training managers. Nothing can replace the actual experience of meeting problems and situations as they really are, coping with various personalities, and witnessing the outcome of various personal efforts. Observation *and participation* are necessary for learning on the job. Suggestions, assistance in difficulties, the sharing of facts, and explanations of reasons for certain decisions by a senior manager are usually helpful to the trainee.

9. Role playing. Realistic face-to-face conflict encounters between two persons, such as between a superior and a subordinate or a management member and a customer, are simulated by use of this medium. The trainee learns how to cope with a variety of situations and to develop skill in dealing with people. Participants gain valuable insights not only from their actions but also from a feedback session where they can listen to a tape recording of what they said, note the outcome of their actions, and profit from comments of observers.

10. Task force. This group is set up to meet a specific and usually nonrecurring problem. Trainees analyze the actual problem and participate in decision making to solve it. Practice in acting constructively in a group situation is demonstrated, and a chance to evaluate the trainee's ability to think is provided.

In addition to these ten major types, there are a number of effective but less common means. They include:

1. *Farm system*—a person is developed at a branch or subsidiary for future employment at the main or parent company.
2. *Junior board of directors*—primarily for a group of trainees who operate similarly to a regular board of directors.
3. *Problem-solving*—in which a "case" or situation is given the person to identify the problem, recommend action to follow, and justify the recommendation made.
4. *Second team*—a reserve management team which takes over at regular intervals relieving the first team of managers.
5. *Sensitivity training*—groups of trainees are subjected to controlled conditions designed to increase each member's awareness of her or his effect on others as well as that member's own subconscious motivations.
6. *Special assignments*—the trainee is given complete freedom to handle a special assignment, such as supervising the development of a new product or representing the company in a local civic association, in order to gain practical experience in achieving goals and observing how and what is accomplished.

Nonparticipative media for management development

In contrast, the nonparticipative means, arranged alphabetically, include:

1. Coaching. Use of the best methods for the given managerial work, familiarity with the makeup of the job assignment, policies and procedures to follow, are supplied by coaching. For greatest effectiveness, coaching should be provided by the trainee's superior and conducted on a continuous or regularly scheduled basis. Long periods of no coaching is a common error and nullifies many of the training benefits. Coaching is essentially helpful when applied during the early training period of an individual.

2. Counseling. Support to the trainee in a temporary period of difficulty can be supplied through counseling. An emotional crisis, adjustment to the work, or some hurdle in filling the job successfully can frequently be overcome by talking over the problem with one skilled in listening, questioning, and observing, and capable of offering pertinent suggestions to alleviate the difficulty. The objective is to help the counselee gain a better understanding of self. Followed is either (*a*) directive counseling in which the counselor finds that one can and should apply the answer to the trainee, or (*b*) nondirective counseling in which the counselor facilitates the trainee's adjustment to understand the difficulties and has the trainee solve the problem personally.

3. Lectures.   One of the oldest means for developing managers, lectures permit concise presentations of knowledge by a recognized expert and qualified speaker. This medium is personal and can be highly effective. Visual aids make a lecture more effective, and the inclusion of models and demonstrations helps provide a forceful presentation.

4. Observation posts.   This means stresses learning by observation. "Assistant to" positions make good observation posts in the development of managers.[4] Candidates holding assistant-to positions are close enough to their superiors to observe managerial activities which can be employed for future use by them.

5. Planned special readings.   If the need is primarily to extend the cultural background of the manager, it is usually effective to use special reading assignments. Selected topics, articles, and books dealing with management techniques, current affairs, or present-day problems can be used. In some instances the trainee is requested to report to the trainer and discuss the particular assignment, or written answers to specific questions relative to the reading may be required.

6. Programmed instructions.   This approach focuses the trainee's attention on the significant points while one learns. Questions are asked in a sequence that advances from the simple to the difficult and complex. A response by the trainee is required at each step in the sequence. The programmed sequence is presented in a series of "frames," or separate views on the screen of a machine. Each frame requires response by the trainee. Any knowledge or skill that can be specified can be programmed. Advocates of programmed instruction claim learning time can be reduced from 30 to 50 percent, retention is greatly improved, self-pacing by the trainee is emphasized, and a high level of achievement is attained.

7. University management development programs.   Many universities offer or sponsor conferences, institutes, workshops, special courses, and "programs" especially designed to help in the development of managers. The scope of these offerings differs widely. Some include a concentrated and specialized course extending for several weeks; others offer more extensive work in the form of 8-, 10-, and 13-week courses. Some are full time, some are part-time. The approach and material content differ among sponsors.

In addition, there are developmental efforts by means of (1) *special courses*—when the need is for specific knowledge or specific information for a trainee is required, and (2) *professional association membership*—whereby attendance at meetings, special seminars, workshops, informal discussion with members, and reading the associ-

---

[4] The "assistant to" is discussed in Chapter 14, Authority and organizational relationships.

ation's journal contribute to and promote the important "develop yourself" philosophy.

COMPENSATING

When the individual wants money or what money can do or buy for him or her, the subject of compensating becomes quite important. Compensating is an intriguing, interesting, yet highly complicated subject. Its contribution is a sort of an "all-purpose" type that has different values to different people. For example, the purchasing power of money received may be critical to one manager, while to another money acquisition is not wealth but a symbol of achieving recognition and status, while to another it means gaining individual economic freedom.

Fundamentally, a manager's compensation is based upon (1) time only, (2) performance only, or (3) a combination of time and performance. The first is illustrated by a straight salary per year to a director of research. This means is common and is usually followed when it is difficult or costly to measure performance. The second, paying for performance only, is represented by the sales manager who is paid a percentage of total net sales. The third, a combination of time and performance, can be thought of as the base compensation for time only and incentive pay for how well the job is done, that is, job performance. There are numerous combinations of these three bases used.

The specific amounts paid are the result of many different forces. Foremost are three basic considerations: (1) the size of the company, (2) the industry, and (3) the contribution of decisions made.[5] These are interrelated. Also there are important qualifications to each such as age, geographical location, experience, and scarcity of knowledge and skill. We will say more about these in a moment. The influence of company size upon compensation has been studied quite thoroughly. As to be expected, the large company has more highly paid managers than does the small company. This follows because the large company has relatively greater assets and usually greater profits, and decisions put into action have more scope and greater impact than do those in a small company. Secondly, the industry appears to be significant. Certain industries appear to be high-paying, while others are low-paying enterprises. The mode of operation, facilities, growth, degree of competition, whether currently propelled or running on past momentum, and policies followed are among the most influential factors accounting for differences. The third consideration, the contribution of decisions made, reaffirms the truism that a manager is paid for managing.

---

[5] Arch Patton, *Men, Money, and Motivation* (New York: McGraw-Hill Book Co., Inc., 1961), p. 43.

More enlightening is the fact that higher managerial compensation seems to be associated with enterprises that deal in products and services that change rapidly, where a high degree of creativity is required, where the effect of decisions is quickly translated to statement of profit and loss, where there is no sheltered competitive life, and where there is an individual- not group-centered environment.

Age appears to have some bearing on compensation. With time a manager's wants change. While no two managers are alike even in the same age group, it is possible to generalize on the basis of age. Figure 21–2 shows possible relationships in this respect. There is also the

FIGURE 21–2: Possible relationships between manager's age and characteristics of compensation

Age in years	Characteristics affecting compensation
20–30	Is ambitious and aggressive, needs self-esteem, seeks opportunity, wants chance to make good.
31–45	Has demonstrated definite accomplishments, seeks more current, not deferred, compensation, wants challenging compensation arrangement.
46–55	Current compensation still important, but deferred and fringe benefits are attractive.
56–65	Visualizes forthcoming end of career, deferred compensation and fringe benefits wanted, longs to "do something" nonfinancial for others that employs mature experience and judgment.

condition of geographical location. Managerial compensation is relatively high in certain areas and low in others. Highest managerial salaries tend to be paid for jobs located in the larger cities, but there are notable exceptions.

Opinions differ as to whether compensation is motivational. Those who feel it is point out that certain necessary conditions must exist. These include: (1) the goal of high compensation should be mutual and rank high with both the company and the individual, (2) the manager must be convinced that the application of one's energy and skill will lead to achievement of the goal, that performance improvement is rewarded with greater compensation, and (3) the manager believes he or she is able to and will improve present results achieved, that improvement is attainable and within his or her capability.

Relativity of the amounts being paid also influences the motivational effect. For example, $35,000 a year paid to a manager in Company A may be highly motivational because it is well above that being paid to most managers in Company A. In contrast, $35,000 a year in

Company B may not be motivational because it is not above that paid most managers in Company B.

This relativity factor has given rise to compensation plans termed (1) shallow or (2) steep. In the former the differentials of base compensation among the managers are relatively small and commonly indicate the condition where managers tend to be conservative and make major decisions very slowly. For the latter, or steep arrangement, a great differential between the top managers and the middle and lower manager groups exists. Usually this reflects great emphasis on aggressive and dominant leadership and decision making at the top.

Base pay

Total compensation is made up of base pay plus a variety, if any, of extra payments including bonus, profit sharing, financial incentives, and fringe benefits. The base pay is normally adjusted periodically in keeping with the results achieved by the manager, the length of service, inflation, and the cost of living. The foundation upon which total compensation is built is base pay. It also determines, in effect, the amount of (1) the cash bonus, (2) company-paid life insurance coverage, (3) the pension the employee will receive, and (4) the deferred compensation. Furthermore, it is base pay that is publicly known if compensation is revealed; and it provides the status symbol and the measure of approval for an individual among associates.

Base pay represents the stable long-term value of a position. Different job requirements are reflected by different base pays. This is one reason why the ambitious manager seeks a better job, that is, one of a higher compensation and therefore one that requires more and pays more. Base pays differ primarily because of tradition and the knowledge, skill, and responsibility requirements of the work.

Bonus, commission, and profit sharing

As a general rule, both bonus and commission are payments over and above base pay. They are based on performance as evaluated on one or a number of factors. In some cases, bonus and commission are related to profits, but this is not mandatory. Also, a graduated scale, not a fixed percentage, is sometimes used to determine the amount of bonus. From the managerial viewpoint, a bonus payment is a onetime action with little future pay commitment. This should be clearly understood by the recipient.

A common formula is to put 6 or 7 percent of profits in excess of a determined amount into a bonus fund and to divide this fund among bonus recipients. Many feel a figure of about 10 percent of base pay is a minimum for annual base pays up to $20,000. Above this amount something like a 15–20 percent bonus appears to be in line. But there is no widely accepted range. And payment of a bonus has disadvantages. Usually its payment is fairly far removed from the time of actual accomplishment, and associating the bonus with excellent work may be difficult for the person receiving it. Also, giving the recipient a large sum of money at one time may result in it being spent unwisely. In addition, the recipient may be inclined to always agree with the superior who has the power to give or deny a sizeable bonus.

Commissions are actually a type of bonus. They are directly related to the recipient's performance and are influenced by what one alone is directly responsible for doing. Commissions are usually effective.

Profit sharing is one of the oldest types of compensation used by business enterprises. Profit sharing is a broad subject and has many ramifications. The basic compensation should be sound before profit sharing is used. Different patterns can be followed; however most include payment of a portion of net profits into a fund that is credited to the account of each participant, commonly in proportion to base salary or in keeping with performance. Most profit sharing features retaining or investing the funds for payment to participants at some future date. Thus a future "nest egg" is built up. There are usually certain tax advantages too.

Profit sharing emphasizes a single and meaningful objective and results in a company paying when it can best afford to pay. Managers receive a valuable compensation supplement. On the other hand, opponents claim that many managers cannot directly influence profits very much by their own performance, that the pay and performance are widely separated, and that morale may suffer when profits sink or investments of profit sharing funds decline.[6]

Deferred compensation

Pensions, contractual payments, and stock options feature deferred compensation. These means are used because it is believed that they can do for the individual employee what one cannot or will not do for oneself because of lack of fortitude, determination, knowledge of finance, or knowledge of tax laws.

Pension plans are popular. Over 90 percent of the larger companies have pension programs, but there are significant differences in their makeup. The trend is very definitely toward the noncontributing type, meaning all payments to the pension fund are made by the employer, but in many plans the employee pays into the pension fund. Retirement at age 65 is a common provision, but earlier retirement on a

---

[6] The Profit Sharing Council of America, 20 N. Wacker Dr., Chicago, Ill. 60606, has many informative booklets on profit sharing available to the public.

selective basis is possible. However, the cost of the pension program is nearly 50 percent higher for retirement at age 60 in comparison with that at age 65. Many of the pension funds are what is known as a trusteed pension plan, meaning that the dollars set aside for pensions are invested in a trusteed plan. Also many pension funds are insured pension plans meaning the funds for the pensions are provided by means of insurance.

Pension plans have these advantages: (1) employees are provided economic security at retirement, (2) older employees are retired on an orderly basis, thus giving younger employees an opportunity to advance in the organization, and (3) the employee receives more deferred compensation because the employer can get more benefits at a lower cost due to a larger purchase and income tax structure, and (4) the employee feels the company is a good place to work.

ERISA, the popular acronym, for the Employee Retirement Insurance Security Act of 1974, provides broad federal protection for employees who are members of benefit and pension plans. The Act goes a long way toward securing the benefits to members of private pension plans. The law also covers on-the-job benefits such as plans for hospitalization, major medical, and unemployment. Actually the legal provisions provide a protective umbrella over participants in covered plans for their working life and retirement. Basically, the two objectives of ERISA are (1) assure that pension plan participants know what they are entitled to, and (2) guarantee that they get it. These goals are achieved by requiring employers to communicate rights about the plan to participants, reforming the practices and rules covering vested amounts (the payments by or for an employee in a given plan), establishing rules governing the conduct of pension managers, ensuring the funds set aside for pensions will be there when participant become entitled to it, and monitoring for compliance with ERISA requirements.

Another interesting development in pensions is ESOP, Employee Stock Ownership Plan, a deferred compensation arrangement by which a company bestows its stock on its employees. In the opinion of many the expanded ownership of the employer's stock by employees is not only desirable but essential. Under ESOP with gifts of stock the company has the right to deduct as a cost an amount equivalent to the market value of the stock given the employees. Thus, the company's income tax is reduced. The stock contributed is put in a trust which administers individual accounts for each member. ESOP operates under regulations provided by ERISA and the Tax Reduction Act of 1975. For the unwary, legal pitfalls exist in ESOP, hence, the help of expertise in the area is strongly suggested.

A contractual payment is an agreement between employee and employer whereby the employee, after retirement or term of employment, is paid a stated amount of money periodically over a stated period. The method of deferred compensation can be mutually beneficial. It enables the sales manager, for example, with fluctuating earnings to level and spread them out, thereby reducing taxes on current earnings. To the employer, contract payments represent a known expense over a definite period. It is possible to renegotiate contract payments from time to time. However, all such agreements must be in keeping with government regulations concerning such matters.

A stock option grants the right to buy common stock of a corporation at a stipulated price within a stated future period. Stock options are highly motivating. With them, a manager, by achieving good results, can increase the price of a company's stock by increasing its earnings, exercise his or her stock option to purchase shares at a relatively low price, and then sell them at the current high price, thus realizing a handsome profit.

Financial incentives

Financial incentives normally provide extra compensation in return for accomplishment over a mutually agreed base or standard. Earnings are related with accomplishment according to a specific plan or formula. Financial incentives offer recognition in the form of extra compensation for extra effort. The total incentive arrangement should be carefully defined and closely tied in with the financial goals of the enterprise. The amount paid to a manager should be related to what that person accomplished or contributed during a given period (usually a year for managers), and be in keeping with a distribution formula known to all participants. Finally, alternatives of payment should be provided, that is, a choice between current or deferred income, cash or stock. The opportunity to choose increases the incentive value.

No incentive is self-operating. Proper guidance and attention must be provided so that the program is modern and vibrant. An incentive program is only as effective as its administration. General observations of help in this respect are shown in Figure 21–3.

Principle of financial incentive

The urge to do more work output for more pay is influenced mainly by the relative importance of more money to the recipient and that person's evaluation of the fairness of the plan under which the extra pay is received.

A famous and highly successful financial incentive plan has been followed for several decades by the Lincoln Electric Company of Cleveland. This plan covers all employees, managers as well as non-managers. During the past decade, the company has paid annually a cash bonus of about $16 million to its nearly 2,000 employees, or an average of over $8,000 per employee. In addition, over $1 million was

FIGURE 21–3:   Important observations of managerial financial incentives

1.   The participants must have a strong desire for extra earnings.

2.   A measurable output, mutually understood, should be utilized.

3.   Temporary bases as standards of reference should be held to a minimum and be clearly designated as such.

4.   The standard of reference must be current and in keeping with present levels being followed.

5.   A known and identifiable relationship must exist between the effective effort of the manager and the measured accomplishment.

6.   Effective effort of the manager must be proportional to the monetary reward paid.

7.   Extra pay rewards should go to those making extra performance.

8.   Quality contributions over the work output must be established.

9.   Accuracy and fairness should take precedence over simplicity—difficult calculations can be reduced to convenient formulas or tables of data.

10.   A three-, six-, or twelve-month period is usually an effective length for which incentive pay is calculated.

paid for employee retirement annuities. The plan operates as follows: Each year a target is set for cost reduction. Then all employees help to achieve it and to give highly efficient performances. Annual turnover of employees is less than 1 percent, and annual absenteeism averages 1.5 percent. Incentive pay is calculated by multiplying the base wage rate by the merit rating of performance by the incentive factor. This factor is the value of total incentive paid divided by the total number on payroll. Each recipient is constantly reminded that the incentive pay is not a gift, but a result of his or her outstanding results achievement. Due in part to the high effectiveness of its incentive plan, the company has been able to maintain competitive selling prices for its products, which are welding equipment and electric motors.

Nonfinancial incentives

In a discussion of compensation, nonfinancial incentives should be included. These are symbols of achievement and are important at all levels, but especially so for managers. As already pointed out in previous chapters, people strive for recognition, prestige, and pride of accomplishment. Basically, every employee expects recognition and respect for work well done. If these are received when earned, a person's energies are almost limitless.

Titles are an excellent example of nonfinancial incentives. Many, if not all, managers will work harder and more objectively for a wanted title than they will for monetary reward. Why is this? Because the title gives them prestige, the sense of having arrived, of being somebody among their compeers. The student of management should never underestimate these qualities. Of course, in times of rapid inflation, the amount of money in the pocket takes on additional significance. Nevertheless, these nonfinancial rewards are sought. Special furnishings in a manager's office, a special conference table, carpeting on the floor, as well as having a secretary and being given awards and certificates are additional examples.

Principle of nonfinancial incentive

Nonmonetary rewards for extra achievements have strong incentive value.

Mostly for lower level managers and nonmanagers, incentive merchandise is one of the most effective means ever devised to stimulate work efforts. It consists of giving, free of cost, standard brand merchandise selected from a catalog to those whose job performance equaled or exceeded a stated goal. Sometimes an all-paid vacation trip is offered. Frequently the array of offered merchandise is publicized to the participant's spouse and family, who supply additional motivating stimuli for the employee to accomplish the goal and receive the merchandise. Incentive merchandise is popular with sales people.

Fringe benefits

These have become the miscellany catch-all of compensation. They include various and sundry types of payments—some current, some deferred, some small, some large, some individual, some group, some financial, some nonfinancial. Figure 21–4 shows a listing of some of the more common fringe benefits extended managers.

The great majority of fringe benefits are socially desirable, but any

FIGURE 21–4:   Types of fringe benefits to managers

1. Contribution to group insurance plans.	9. Paid sick leave.
2. Counseling, financial advice, legal aid.	10. Reserve military duty.
	11. Scholarships.
3. Discounts on purchases.	12. Time spent at seminars and conferences.
4. Termination pay.	
5. Use of company library.	13. Travel and moving expenses.
6. Medical and dental care.	14. Vacation pay.
7. Military service allowance.	15. Sponsorship of company athletic teams and summer camps.
8. Paid club memberships, magazine subscriptions.	16. University courses.

actuating impact seems to be lost in many instances. There is a lack of personalizing the benefits and for the most part they are viewed as expected assistance. Little or no weight is given job performance. Then too, there is no competitive edge, the manager can obtain the same benefits with any of several employers, and acquires them automatically. It appears that fringe benefits are in the nature of socially desirable upward adjustments in base pay and ensure that certain benefits are provided.

QUESTIONS

1. What is the meaning of each of the following: (*a*) programmed instructions, (*b*) development of managers, (*c*) fringe benefits, and (*d*) performance appraisal?

2. As a director of management training, would you favor the use of in-basket exercises? Why? The use of lectures? Why? The use of games? Why?

3. As you see it, should problems concerning performance be viewed as appraisal difficulties or development difficulties or what? Justify your answer.

4. Discuss the major sources for identifying developmental needs.

5. Discuss the appraisal conference, giving what it is, preparing for it as a manager, and actually conducting it.

6. Relate your understanding of an understanding manager. Is this type important today? Discuss.

7. In your opinion, do fringe benefits have incentive value? Discuss.

8. What are the objectives of ERISA and how are they to be achieved?

9. As a manager would you favor the use of nonfinancial incentives? Why?

10. Of the ten participative means for developing managers offered in this chapter, select three that appeal most to you. Give reasons for each of your selections.

11. What are the differences between coaching and counseling? Between bonus and stock option? Between measured appraisal and financial incentive?

12. What type of future form of compensation would you like to see adopted? Discuss your suggested plan pointing out its advantages as you see them.

13. Do you feel performance appraisal is essential to effective modern management? Justify your answer.

14. Discuss the subject of base pay as a part of the total compensation picture.

CASE 21–1. OLAFSON MANUFACTURING COMPANY

Joseph Durland, vice president of manufacturing, has three persons reporting directly to him, the manager of manufacturing A, the manager of manufacturing B, and the manager of manufacturing services. Other top management members include Roscoe Scott, president; William Godfrey, vice president marketing; and Harry Rittenhouse, director of personnel. Early Tuesday morning January 9, Mr. Durland finds these "in-basket" items:

No. 1   January 8, 197–

Memo

TO: Joseph Durland
FROM: William Godfrey

   While having lunch yesterday with Charlotte Bright of Hathaway Products, she mentioned that her people are getting quite concerned about delays in shipments of special products from our plant. I'm certain you agree that Hathaway is a good account and we want to do everything to keep them satisfied.

No. 2   January 6, 197–

Mr. Joseph Durland
V.P. Production
Olafson Manufacturing Company
Muncie, Indiana

Dear Joe:

   Just to remind you and your gang at Olafson that we are depending upon you to provide us with a stimulating and worthwhile program for our January meeting on Monday January 15, 197–.
We are all looking forward to seeing you then.

                                        Cordially,

                                        Clyde Ridler
                                        Director of Manufacturing
                                        Acorn Company

No. 3   Jan. 8, 197–

MEMO

To: Joe Durland
From: Roscoe Scott

   During our monthly meeting on Friday January 26, 197–, I would like to give appropriate time to discuss thoroughly the action we might take to increase the efficiency in our welding department. This appears to be a trouble spot, and to date little progress in correcting the situation has been attained.

Also at your convenience, please give me your thoughts on the suggested revision in fringe benefit payments covering hourly personnel. If you have any agenda suggestions for this upcoming meeting, please forward them as soon as possible.

No. 4   Jan. 5, 197–

To: Joseph Durland
From: Sidney Schlagel
        Manufacturing B
Subject: Accident Claim—Kenneth Kahn

Supervisor Kenneth Kahn, who was injured three weeks ago making an emergency machine repair, is now claiming that he did not receive his full entitlements. I am told he has engaged the services of Kevin Whitcomb, a lawyer, who plans to sue the corporation and several of our people.
What should I do about this?

No. 5   January 5, 197–

Personal—Confidential

To: Joseph Durland
From: Harry Rittenhouse
Subject: Alexis Kovak

From the grapevine and a usually reliable source, I have learned that Alexis Kovak in R&D has been looking around and now has a firm job offer on which she is to reply by the middle of next week. Knowing that you feel Kovak is an excellent employee and a valuable person in our organization, I thought I'd let you know about this for whatever action you want to take.

Questions

1. What action should Mr. Durland take on each of the "in-basket" items?

2. Record your answers on a spread sheet with listings of (*a*) the item number, (*b*) for each item what action you recommend and with whom, and (*c*) for each item what your reasons are for your recommended actions—and if you do not take action at this time, when you would, with whom, and why.

3. Do you suggest any priorities be followed by Mr. Durland? Discuss.

CASE 21–2. SHERWIN CORPORATION

In the main office of Sherwin Corporation, Alice Cunningham has worked her way up from Clerk C to Clerk B to Clerk A where she now is. The gross pay per month for these three job classifications are

Clerk A $525
Clerk B 475
Clerk C 425

Alice believes that the extra effort and required work of a Clerk A job compared with a Clerk C job is too great for the differential of $100 per month. Hence, she has requested a Clerk C job and claims she is entitled to a job C because of her seniority with the company.

The office manager, Richard Champion, reacted that it wasn't proper for an employee to downgrade herself. He argued that the corporation helped develop and train Alice and the corporation was not going to throw away these training efforts. Further, he contended that there weren't any Clerk C job openings and that the corporation was under no obligation and had made no commitment that employees could downgrade themselves if they so requested.

Alice Cunningham claimed her request was valid and cited the corporation's policy on seniority which reads, "Promotion, demotion, addition or subtraction in the working force will be based on length of continuous service and ability to perform the work." Alice contends she qualifies under this written directive. She has the continuous service and she has the ability to perform Clerk C work.

Questions

1. Do you feel an employee should be permitted to downgrade oneself? Why?
2. What actions do you recommend be taken by Richard Champion? Why?
3. How should this case be settled? Justify your answer.

CASE 21–3. UPPER STATE UNIVERSITY

Professor Ziegler: It certainly is a pleasure to see you again, Dean Bolnick. And you are looking great!

Dean Bolnick: Thank you. It's nice to see you, Dr. Ziegler.

Ziegler: I hear you are making some changes in your Graduate School of Business. Will you tell me about them?

Bolnick: Certainly. Glad to. Let's talk about curriculum first. Business schools generally are of one of two categories—those developing students as general managers and, at the other extreme, those developing specialists. Like most others, we at Upper State have found that the product turns out either as a generalist who lacks depth of knowledge in any area or a specialist with insufficient overall vision. On a first job the generalist is usually given a specialized task to do, special company training is given, and the chances of ever getting the more general management role is jeopardized. Meantime, the specialist gets off to a better start, but is less able to see the whole picture. Each discipline looks at its own problems. There is not enough interplay. It's business, not a portion of business that we must be interested in.

Ziegler: Yes, I agree. What are you going to do about it?

Bolnick: We are going to turn out only one type of graduate—the general manager armed with a specialty. That's what they do over in the Med. School—a great body of general understanding is required usually before the person can begin to become a specialist. I believe right now we have too many pat devices for decision making. Solving a problem should be measured in progress rather than finality.

Ziegler: Yes. I understand you are also developing a performance appraisal plan for professors.

Bolnick: Right. At present we do not know how competent each professor is in instructing. If we don't receive any complaints, we assume one is OK. But there *is* a difference among professors. At the end of five years' service, a faculty member can be promoted to the next higher rank—from associate to full professor, for example. A committee consisting of the dean, department heads, and three full professors at large recommend who should be promoted. These recommendations are then submitted to the university's administrative council who consider and make the promotions.

Ziegler: On what basis does your School of Business committee make its decisions?

Bolnick: That's a good question. Really, that's the problem. Some feel the candidate should have completed some writing and have it published. Others stress activity in local community affairs. Others give weight to the candidate's contacts and business executives one personally knows. Some insist that the candidate have a Ph.D. or D.B.A. Now, all of these considerations have validity and are important. I look upon them favorably. But I think we should remember that usually the person was originally hired to teach.

Ziegler: You have faculty members who are nonteaching?

Bolnick: Yes, such as our director of business relations and our director of the research bureau.

Ziegler: I see what you mean. To me, it is unrealistic to assume that a professor can be proficient in all these areas.

Bolnick: I couldn't agree with you more.

Ziegler: Sounds like there are politics in your present practices.

Bolnick: Yes, I guess I would have to say there is. Surprisingly, they come up with a fairly good selection. And it gives some of our faculty participation, which is what they want. I think there will be politics in any approach we devise, but I feel we can make improvements over what we're doing now.

Ziegler: How do you handle pay increases while a professor remains within a given rank?

Bolnick: Each year one is given an increase of $500 up to a maximum of five years. This is automatic. Also, we have a cost of living adjustment that varies from year to year. In addition we have ranges of compensation for each rank from instructor to full professor.

Questions

1. What are your reactions to the curriculum changes stated by Dean Bolnick? Discuss.

2. From the viewpoint of management study, what interpretation do you give Dean Bolnick's statement, "Solving a problem should be measured in progress rather than finality"? Discuss.

3. Present a plan you recommend for handling the promotion of faculty members. Justify your answer.

PART VI
Controlling

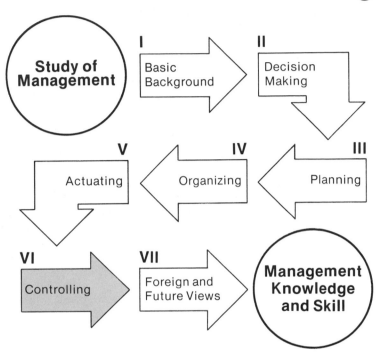

Chapter makeup for Part VI:

The fourth and last fundamental function of management to be discussed is controlling. It is undergoing change, but not to as great a degree as that of the other fundamental functions. Most noteworthy are the efforts to make controlling more acceptable and the new and interesting techniques followed in applying controlling.

The meaning and benefits derived from controlling start our discussion of this important function. Subsequently the need to develop self-controlling, the importance of updating controlling techniques followed, and the application of controlling techniques followed, and the application of controlling to the total enterprise as a unit and to quantity, quality, time use, cost and budgetary action are presented.

Chapter 22

Management controlling

It takes less time to do a thing right
than to explain why you did it wrong.

Henry Wadsworth Longfellow

Are the managerial efforts resulting in the desired goal achievement? To answer this question necessitates evaluation of results. If the results are not within reasonable expectancy, corrective measures are applied. This evaluating, and correcting if necessary, constitute the work of management controlling.

CONTROLLING DEFINED

Controlling is *determining what is being accomplished, that is, evaluating the performance and, if necessary, applying corrective measures so that the performance takes place according to plans.* Controlling can be viewed as the activity for detecting and correcting significant variations in the results obtained from planned activities. It is in the nature of things that some errors, loss of efforts, and ineffective directives take place and make for unwanted deviation from the intended goal. So the function of controlling is necessary. But it is important to keep in mind that the purpose of controlling is positive—it is to make things happen, i.e., to achieve the goal within stated constraints, or by means of the planned activities. Controlling should never be viewed as being negative in character—as a hurdle in getting objectives won. Controlling is a managerial necessity and a help not an impediment or a hindrance.

Controlling exists at every management level. For example, the president of a company commonly has expectancies for various overall corporate items such as those illustrated by the top portion of Figure 22–1. Likewise, data for members at other levels are shown in the figure. When the actual achievements are determined and compared to the respective expectancies, we have controlling taking place.

FIGURE 22–1:   Controlling takes place at all management levels

	Expectancy	Actual accom- plishment
For the president (annually)		
Net sales	$50,000,000	$47,671,280
Net return on investment	19 percent	17 percent
Net profit.............................	$ 7,500,000	$ 6,481,668
For the department manager (monthly)		
Tons of M–35 produced	2,240	2,232
Direct labor hours	1,520	1,670
Indirect labor hours	200	187
Downtime hours	30	72
For the individual employee (weekly)		
Units produced	750	681
Quality ratio	99	98
Scrap	56	67

CONTROLLING AND THE MANAGEMENT PROCESS

If the other fundamental functions of management, that is, planning, organizing, and actuating, were performed perfectly, there would be little need for controlling. However, very rarely, if ever, is there planning that is perfect, organizing above any possible reproach, and actuating 100 percent effective. Controlling, in the formalized management meaning of the term, does not exist without previous planning, organizing, and actuating. Controlling cannot take place in a vacuum. It is related to and a part of the outputs of the other three fundamental functions of management. The closer the linkage the more effective the controlling.

How Emerson Electric Company controls its costs in good and in bad times is illustrative. To meet competitive pressures the management trimmed manufacturing cost by redesigning the company's electric motors and using material substitutions (planning), centralized purchasing for its diverse manufacturing operations (organizing), and emphasized employee participation in decision making and adopted job enrichment programs (actuating). The result: controlling to these new management standards, annual savings of millions of dollars in production are gained. The motor is built at less cost, but the product quality is not cheapened.[1]

Planning bears special close relationship to controlling. As already discussed, planning identifies commitments to actions intended for future accomplishments. Controlling is performed to help in seeing to it that the commitments are carried out. Failure of controlling means sooner or later failure of planning, and success of planning means success of controlling. When controlling clearly demonstrates that the

---

[1] David P. Garino, "Frugality, Inc.," *Wall Street Journal*, June 4, 1975, p. 1.

planning cannot be implemented, a modified or new plan must be developed. When unacceptable performance under a plan becomes common, the controlling tends to trigger thinking of how best to alter the plan or even to abandon it. Also, to reiterate it is well to note that a plan should identify and specify the controls needed, otherwise it is not a viable plan.

Principle of controlling

Effective controlling assists in the effort to regulate the planned performance to assure that performance takes place as planned.

This close dovetailing of planning and controlling is illustrated in a number of management devices and techniques. Budgetary control is an excellent example and is discussed in Chapter 25.

THE CONTROL PROCESS

Figure 22–2 shows graphically the control process. Beginning at the upper left, the sequential steps are depicted.

Controlling consists of a process made up of three definite steps which are universal:

1. Measuring the performance.
2. Comparing performance with the standard, and ascertaining the difference, if any.

FIGURE 22–2:   The control process

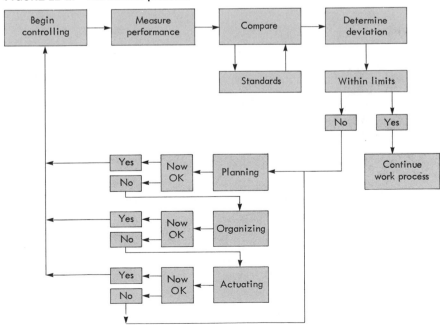

3.   Correcting unfavorable deviation by means of remedial action.

Stated in a slightly different manner, controlling consists of (1) finding out what's being done, (2) comparing results with expectancies, which leads to (3) approving the results or disapproving the results, in which latter case applying the necessary remedial measures should be added.

Of special importance in controlling is the feedback. It can be considered a system made up of the elements shown in Figure 22–3. The goal setter or manager defining the expectancy (upper left) gives requirements to an information processor which is either a person with the needed information to control or a computer with proper information. In turn, the information processor relays the required information to the control sensor, also a person or a computer, where the control process is carried out, i.e., expectancies of the goal setter are compared with what is being actually achieved by the fundamental management functions. In addition, what goals are set or their modification as well as the information used and the operation of the control sensor are affected by external forces as indicated at the top of the figure.

FIGURE 22–3:   The feedback-controlling operation viewed as a system

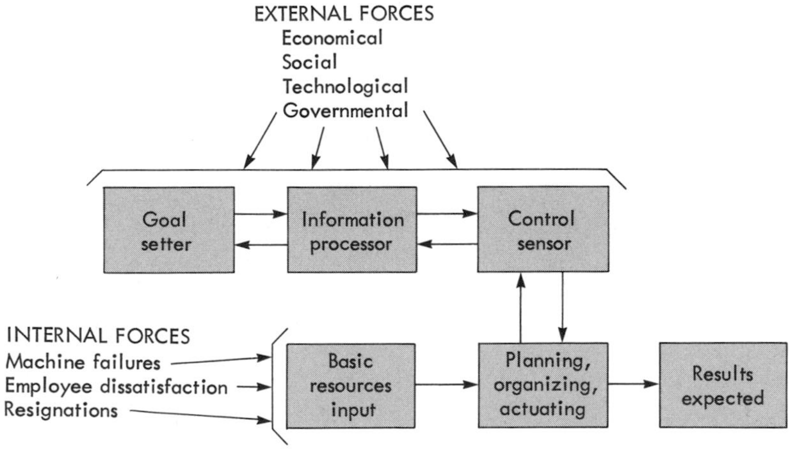

INFLUENCE OF POLICIES, PROCEDURES, AND STATISTICAL TECHNIQUES UPON CONTROLLING

Rather than wait for results and compare them with expectancy, it is possible to exert a controlling influence by limiting activities in advance. Representative is the effect of applying policies and procedures which in the case of the former limit the scope within which decisions are to be made, and in the case of the latter, define what specific actions and in the prescribed sequence are to be followed. The degree to which they are or are not followed is best evaluated by applying the control process.

Actually, the control influence of policies and procedures (a part of the planning efforts) reflects the closeness of planning with controlling. And it should be observed that controlling helps unify understanding of policies and procedures. Consistency in the use of policies and procedures is aided by the controlling efforts followed. To illustrate, a sales manager may have a policy that any change in price from the published prices must be authorized in writing by the manager; no field salesperson is permitted to change any price. In effect, this gives clarification of the existent policy and provides control to the sales manager and permits one to know what is going on and exercise regulation and restraint over it.

Certain statistical techniques can also be employed in controlling efforts. For example, the normal curve and probability theories are used in controlling quality. In essence this approach defines mathematically what deviations can be considered normal or "in the nature of things" for a given situation and are acceptable and also what deviations are not normal and hence unacceptable and call for corrective action. Statistical quality control is discussed in Chapter 24. Like policy and procedure influence, statistical quality control indicates, in advance, probable results. Hence, the requirement of waiting for results, controlling typical of the feedback, is eliminated.

MEASURING THE PERFORMANCE

Returning to the control process, the first step of measuring the performance, starts with a consideration for the problems of measuring. Succinctly stated, measurement is the ascertainment of the quantity or capacity of a well-defined entity. Without measurement, a manager is forced to guess or employ rule-of-thumb methods which may or may not be reliable. Measurement requires a measuring unit and a count of how many times the unit is contained by the quantity of the entity under consideration. In Chapter 12, we discussed the major considerations in measurement under the heading of standards—their establishment and feasibility.[2]

In measuring an entity there is always the question of what characteristics to consider. This challenges the best imagination. Generally, the entities being measured can be classified into two groups: (1) those concerned with the achievement of a complete program or total accomplishment and (2) those concerned with output per unit of applied direct labor. The former is broad in scope, deals in terms of overall

---

[2] See pp. 249–50.

progress, and is normally of most concern to members of the higher organization levels. For such cases the measurement is commonly by objectives. Also profit centers and cost centers can be used.

In the second group or those concerned with output per unit of applied direct labor, a more detailed and precise measurement is normally applied. Why is this? Because it is easier to measure such output than the performance embodying a complete program. For direct-operative employees the performance is confined within a relatively small area and covers direct productivity in its own right. Work which is highly repetitious, requires little judgment, flows at a fairly steady rate, and is entirely objective can usually be measured quite accurately. In contrast, work of a creative nature, irregular in occurrence, and varying considerably in its makeup is difficult to measure. Hence, due to the relative difficulty of measurement, some work is more difficult to control than is other work.

Sometimes it is helpful when confronted with measurement problems for control purposes to think in terms of tangible and intangible achievements. Units produced, cards filed, and samples distributed are tangible measurements. They indicate the count of a number of like units whose total gives a value of relative standing to a known entity. On the other hand, there are many intangible results in the typical enterprise. Data on them cannot be gathered directly, hence dependence upon such means as judgment and indirect clues are used. The development of executives, the building of employee morale, the effectiveness of communication, and the efficiency of purchasing may be cited as a few of the more important intangibles.

The actual carrying out of measurement of performance is achieved in many different ways. Discussion of some of the more common ways will be deferred until several pages later. At the moment we will proceed to the second step in the controlling process.

COMPARING PERFORMANCE WITH THE STANDARD

Step No. 2 of the control process is comparing performance with the standard. In effect this evaluates the performance. When there is a difference between the performance and the standard, judgment is frequently required to resolve the significance of the differential. To establish a rigid absolute variation or even a range for what is satisfactory is inadequate. Relatively small deviations from the standard merit approval for the performance of some activities, while in other cases a slight deviation may be serious. The manager performing the controlling work must therefore analyze, evaluate, and judge the results to the best of one's ability.

In this respect, the spotting of feedbacks is especially helpful. Also, seeking suggestions from those performing the work or those close to it indicating what control efforts might be taken, are pertinent. Also, any trend data for the subject are helpful. In addition, the indicating of controllable, as differentiated from noncontrollable, items should be included. In most cases, this controlling step of comparing performance with the standard should be done as close to the point of performance as possible. This expedites controlling efforts and assists in locating areas to be corrected and usually results in minimum losses.

In comparing performance with the basis of control, it is *the exception* to which managerial attention should be directed. The manager does not need to concern oneself with situations where performance equals or closely approximates the expected results. Furthermore, concentration on the exceptions necessitates less work, for normally the number of items having significant variances is small compared to the total. This brings up the subject of the managerial principle of exception.

Principle of exception

Controlling is expedited by concentrating on the exceptions, or outstanding variations, from the expected result or standard.

This principle is important in controlling. It means that much of the controlling effort is directed to the exceptional cases, or those that do not conform adequately with the standard or basis of control. It is only the exceptional cases that require remedial action. To illustrate, controlling the prices at which 100 items are purchased will probably reveal but five prices out of line; that is, these five are the exceptions and can be investigated further. Much time and effort are saved in controlling by applying the principle of exception.

Closely akin to controlling by the exception principle is to control by concentrating on the use of key points only. The innumerable activities of an enterprise preclude the control of every activity. Any attempt to include all facets of an enterprise into a control system results in many details, and too much time spent on attempting to control relatively minor activities. The key points selected will vary with the type of enterprise but are normally those areas or activities about which other activities tend to cluster. In some instances, so-called bottleneck operations provide adequate key control points. Examples include one person signing all checks (also providing excellent control over expenditures), designating an individual to handle all purchasing, and compiling a daily record in dollars of total orders received and total shipments made. In a medium sized toy manufacturing company, the president concentrates controlling efforts on five key points: (1) shipments, (2) customers' orders, (3) inventories, (4) production efficiency, and (5) forecasts. Simple ratios can be worked out among selected key points to provide a quick, meaningful review.

CORRECTING DEVIATION BY MEANS OF REMEDIAL ACTION

This is the third and last step of the control process. It can be viewed as enforcing the seeing-to-it that operations are adjusted or efforts are made to achieve results in keeping with expectancies. Wherever significant variances are uncovered, vigorous and immediate action is not only called for but imperative. Effective control cannot tolerate needless delays, excuses, endless compromises, or excessive exceptions.

The corrective action is put into effect by those having authority over the actual performance. As indicated above, it may involve modification of the planning as, for example a change in a procedure or method or a new way to check the dimensional accuracy of parts being manufactured. In some instances, an organizational modification may be in order, while in other cases a change in motivation might suffice. Reestablishment of the objective in the employee's mind or a review of a policy and its application may be all that is necessary.

For maximum effectiveness, the correcting of the deviation should be accompanied by fixed and individual responsibility. Holding a particular individual responsible for this work is one of the best means of achieving expectancy. Fixed, individual responsibility tends to personalize the work. It becomes one's job, one's responsibility to take the necessary action to reach satisfactory performance—one's responsibility to make any correction which might be necessary. In short, somebody does something about it and that somebody is definite and known.

Remedial action is preferable to corrective action. That is, this last step of the control process implies more than ferreting out trouble and correcting it. The real cause of the difficulty should be uncovered and efforts taken to eliminate the source of the discrepancy. In this way, genuine assistance and cooperation are obtained. In addition, a favorable attitude toward control is achieved, and this is especially important.

OBTAINING DATA ON ACTUAL PERFORMANCE

Let us return to step No. 1, measuring the performance, and review the means commonly followed in obtaining data for this step. The discussion will be confined to three sources: (1) personal observations, (2) oral reports, and (3) written reports.

The first, or personal observations means going to the area of activities and taking notice of what is being done. It represents one of the oldest means of finding out what is being accomplished. The methods being followed, the quality and quantity of work, attitude of employees, and the general operation of the area are among the types of things which might be observed. There are many who feel that there is no adequate substitute for firsthand direct observation. Advocates of this method believe that the use of direct contacts gives an intimate picture of what is going on and a certain feeling or sense of satisfaction in seeing the work being done and in talking with those doing it.

Many sales executives visit their various sales offices periodically in order to get firsthand information on how sales performance is going and what lines of products are not selling as well as expected. On-the-spot checks can be made with the sales staff, and their reasons for sales surplus or deficiency from the established goal can be obtained. In many instances, calls are made with the local sales supervisor and individual salespeople to check market reactions, advertising effectiveness, and the approach and selling techniques of the salespeople, and to keep in touch with customers.

Personal observation is especially helpful for checking and reporting intangibles. There is probably no satisfactory substitute for observing firsthand the morale of a work group, for watching training efforts being directed upon new recruits, for listening to a prospective customer's reactions to a recently developed product, or for talking over the problems confronted by the junior executives of the enterprise. The personal contact makes for a realistic appraisal and for greater understanding and appreciation of what's behind the data used to measure the particular entity.

On the other hand, use of the personal observation approach has its disadvantages. Foremost is that it does not provide accurate quantitative values, and the information acquired is in broad and general terms. Precision is not obtained. Also, personal observations are time-consuming and take the executive away from his other tasks. Situations requiring immediate attention and decision might be delayed because the executive is somewhere in the shop or in the sales territory. Also, there is the possibility that the good intentions of the executive might be misunderstood by the employees. The practice of having to see for oneself might be interpreted as mistrust or lack of confidence in the employees. The practice might even be viewed as unnecessary snooping. Last, direct contact at best is limited in many instances to a few employees and happenings; it is neither possible to talk with all employees nor to see all that is going on.

Oral reports

Another means of measuring performance is oral reports. This may take the form of either a series of interviews or one large group meeting in which informal discussions are held. One common example of oral reports is the practice of salespeople reporting personally to their

immediate manager at the close of each business day on the accomplishments, problems, or customers' reactions encountered during
the day. The manager not only learns what is going on but also is able
to give suggestions and other help to the sales personnel. Frequently,
oral reports are supplemented with direct observations and personal
calls upon customers.

Oral reports maintain certain elements of the personal observation
method in that information is transmitted orally and personal contact is
included. The facial expressions, tone of voice, and general evaluation
of the performance by the reporter can be observed, and questions can
be asked at the most opportune time in order to clear any misunderstandings or to gain additional information. Tentative answers to
conditions needing remedial action can also be worked out at the time
of discussion. Furthermore, oral reports can provide wide and complete coverage, a condition not always possible under the personal
observation method.

Written reports

In all enterprises, but especially the larger ones, written reports are
used to provide information on performance. These reports lend themselves to comprehensive data and are adaptable for statistics which are
somewhat involved and detailed. Written reports also supply a permanent record, should comparison or study at a future date be desirable.
Frequently, written reports are supplemented by oral reports and direct observation.

There are numerous types of written reports; some are primarily
descriptive, others are statistical; some cover limited areas of operations, others deal with the entire enterprise. Figure 22–4 gives some
ideas as to the type of control reports used. The well-known balance
sheets and profit and loss statements are not included here. They are
discussed in the following chapter dealing with overall controls.

A written report used for controlling factory work is shown by Figure 22–5. Information is shown by departments on the amount of work,
the rate of accomplishment, and the number of employees and work-
hours. For example, reading across the top line, in the cutting department there were 7,621 units of work on hand at the beginning of the
week. During the week 6,280 units were received and 6,550 units
were completed, leaving the amount of work on hand at the end of the
week of 7,351 units. More units were completed than received, and so
the backlog of units was reduced. To accomplish this, six full-time
employees working 240 regular hours and 18 overtime hours were
employed. If desired, these data might be reduced to units produced
per work-hour and compared with the standard for this type of work.
The output and personnel data for the other departments listed are

FIGURE 22–4: Various types of control reports are used by a typical company

Report Type	Information Shown
Daily machine	Idle machine time, its cause, and cost per hour of operation.
Production control	Factory work ahead of schedule, factory work behind schedule with brief explanations of each. Data are shown by days for four-week period. Possible corrective actions for each lot of work are included.
Area sales	Planned and accomplished sales by territories, products, and sales people are issued monthly with comparable figures for six months, and for one year ago.
Delivery performance	Actual and planned quantities of undelivered units at end of each day are prepared daily and also in a cumulative weekly and monthly report.
Daily quality	Includes for each inspector the quantity of units inspected, hours worked, units inspected per hour, and quantity of rejected units along with brief comments on reasons for rejection.
Daily accounts receivable	Shows number of sales invoices held for needed additional information, number of nonposted remittances, and number of credit sales not yet posted to customers' accounts.

FIGURE 22–5

OUTPUT AND PERSONNEL REPORT

Week ending: Feb. 7, 197–

Department (listed in production sequence)	Work units at beginning of this week	Work received	Work output	Work units on hand at end of week	Number of full-time employees	Total hours worked Regular time	Over-time
Cutting	7,621	6,280	6,550	7,351	6	240	18
Coiling.	845	784	500	1,129	4	152	27
Soldering and assembly	1,012	815	712	1,115	12	474	..
Testing	427	712	805	334	2	80	..
Finishing	714	800	760	754	6	220	8
Shipping	305	700	818	187	4	157	..

read in the same manner as those of the cutting department. Observe that the work output of one department is not necessarily the work received by the next department in the list; that is, the cutting department completed 6,550 work units, but the coiling department received only 784 units. Why is this? Because the measurement or meaning of a work unit is not necessarily the same for both departments and also the units were not transported to the coiling department during the week. This illustrates the fact mentioned above that the measurement factor used is determined by the characteristics of the particular work. It usually is not the same for each factory department. After the product is completely assembled, the measurement is usually a unit of the finished product.

Reports should be reviewed periodically as to their need. Too frequently the preparation of useless controlling reports is permitted to continue. Also, it is a good practice to include the preferences of the receiver and to keep in mind the use to which the report is put. In addition, requiring a short interpretation or summary about the performance data is effective. Only pertinent data should be included; too many data can cause confusion. Some advocate the use of whole numbers and the omission of the cents figure in dollar data in order to simplify the report.

ANTICIPATORY CONTROLLING

Ideally, what we would like in controlling is a warning or signal to indicate we are about to get into trouble without reducing or stopping our productive efforts. The "after-the-fact" checkup is helpful, but much time and effort can be saved if we can utilize a red flag warning of impending excessive deviations. We have already alluded to this desirable advantage in the discussion above mentioning statistical quality control.

Any activity can be controlled with respect to any or all of the following factors (1) quantity, (2) quality, (3) time use, and (4) cost. In fact, these are the controlling factors included in any functional type. To illustrate, sales control deals with controlling sales and this is accomplished by controlling with reference to quantity of sales and to cost of sales. Figure 22–6 shows the interrelatedness between controlling by function and by factor.

Relating these control factors to key questions in a matrix form is shown in Figure 22–7. Anything likely to go wrong and require controlling will fall under one or more of these categories. By asking, "What is likely to go wrong?" we are looking for probabilities and are guided by judgment and experience in dealing with the particular activity. We seek the critical areas or happenings upon which we can focus before we get into trouble. Significant variations result from

FIGURE 22–6: Controlling by factors or by functions is interrelated

	Functions			
Factors	Production	Sales	Finance	Personnel
Quantity	Is factory output satisfactory?	Is sales volume up to expectancy?	Is the working capital sufficient for the needs of the enterprise?	Is the work force adequate?
Quality	Are specifications for raw materials, dimensions, and test runs being met?	Do the products being sold represent a satisfactory balance among the company's total line of products?	Should bonds, preferred stock, or common stock be utilized?	Are the proper skills available within enterprise and are they utilized?
Time use	Are the finished products completed within proper periods and shipped on time?	Are salespeople making a sufficient number of calls per day?	Should short-term or long-term borrowing be utilized?	Are individual tasks adequately and fairly measured?
Cost	Are the dollar expenditures for raw materials and direct labor satisfactory?	Is the cost of advertising, sales promotion, and the sales force satisfactory for the sales being obtained?	Are the interest payments for use of borrowed funds in line with current market?	Does the enterprise's wage structure meet "going levels" of the community?

FIGURE 22–7

Basic control factor	What is likely to go wrong?	When and how will you know?	What action should be taken and by whom?
Quantity			
Quality			
Time-use			
Cost			

numerous conditions but most common are (1) human error—effort falling short of expectation and incompetency, (2) unexpected results—strikes, critical material shortages, and new processes, (3) failures—machines and shipments, and (4) uncertainties—managerial decisions, income, and sales or those activities about which we have made projection but the actual outcome of which we are not certain.

The question "When and how will you know?" is intended to reveal the feedback information that probably will signal the impending danger or difficulty. Normally, this is some type of information in a ratio form, line graph, or computer printout.

The last question, "What action should be taken and by whom?" is intended to cause a "thinking through" of who is going to do what when certain difficulties arise. Emphasis should be given to placing the decision making of the action to be taken upon the individual responsible for the particular program. To do this, all control information must be given the person held responsible for handling the control issue. However, by looking ahead and deciding the best answer to what action should be taken and by whom, it will be seen that certain issues had probably best be handled by a group or by management members of a high level. Issues involving policy adjustment, technical questions, design variations, and emergency situations, are illustrative. The point here is that thought has been given and a plan devised for handling the situation where it is believed significant deviations will take place. Such anticipatory efforts in controlling are worthwhile and make for a satisfactory arrangement in achieving needed control.

RESULTS MANAGEMENT AND CONTROLLING

As pointed out in Chapter 4, under results management the employee participates in establishing personal objectives and determining how one intends to achieve these objectives. All this is done with knowledge and participation by one's superior so that the objectives are mutually agreed upon. Further, the expected results serve as the standard against which the performance is evaluated.

This approach gives a new concept to controlling. It is not simply an authoritarian follow-up, but becomes viewed as a tool to assist in guiding efforts and an aid to help in achieving the objectives one has set for oneself. Controlling becomes more meaningful and acceptable to the employee under results management. It is something one can use to one's advantage as well as to the advantage of the company.

Results management includes appraisal by results. This is a strong motivator. Results are tangible, easily understood, and self-informing—the employee knows "how am I doing." And one can find this out easily on one's own and be self-directed. Further, one can self-modify one's efforts in a manner that one believes in and will strive to make successful.

Appraisal by results is preferred and used by the true professional. Consider a star big league baseball player. This player is big league because of the results achieved, not the activities performed. Getting the home run when it is needed, striking out the heavy hitter, or completing a sensational fielding play are illustrative of results and appraisal on that basis is what makes such a player valuable and motivates one to do one's best at all times.

CONTROLLING AND THE HUMAN ELEMENT

The human response to controlling is vital. The best controlling is a positive activity enthusiastically demanded by the employee. As stated above, the use of results management makes this condition possible. But if not using the results approach, the enlightened manager should recognize and promote the idea that controlling helps employees to do their work better, to win respect, to contribute to the progress of their work unit. Admittedly checking and reviewing work can bring grim news, but this can serve as a challenge and an opportunity to improve what is being accomplished. Most people gain much satisfaction from doing a good job, and one of the best ways of motivating employees is to expect them to do a good job. This positive element of controlling should always be emphasized.

Specifically what can a manager do? For one thing, one can be aware of the employee's need to know what is expected. This is fundamental in any motivational effort. Also, the astute manager will explain the controls in terms of the need and importance of the activity, its consistency, effect upon co-workers, and so forth. True, such logical agruments may not change the employee's attitude, but a basis for self-rationalization by the employee is provided.

Another suggestion is that the manager should explain the control measurement used. Better yet is to allow the operative employee to participate in setting the controls followed. Usually excellent suggestions are obtained. And be sure to make adjustments when the particular situation appears to warrant it. Also, strive to understand the employee's point of view of the controls, what one likes and dislikes about present controlling and what one feels would be an improvement. Further, it is usually helpful to assume the attitude "Let's find out working together what the problem really is and then put our heads together and find the means for correcting the difficulty."

The "bottom-of-the-pyramid" approach should be followed. This means that the feedback data are given first to the manager and non-managers of the bottom units so that they have a chance to take action on how the results are being achieved before those in the higher levels get into the act. Actually this makes for enriching jobs and gives employees some degree of control over their own situation. In some instances reports on a day's work (quantity and quality) are given to nonmanagement members only, who decide and implement the corrective actions, if needed. If the same problem is reported the following day, the information is relayed to the manager of the group and together they (manager and nonmanagers) decide what's to be done about it.

A number of firms have used relatively unsophisticated arrangements to bring the operative employees into the controlling efforts. In one instance, free coffee and doughnuts for a week are supplied to employees of a department producing 98 percent or more of its total operations in accordance with the established controls. Contests have also proven successful and can be significant in motivating the use of controls positively.

MAJOR GUIDES TO EFFECTIVE CONTROLLING

It is helpful to recognize the basic characteristics of controlling so that this fundamental function of management can be used advantageously. Controlling results from derivative action and must be continued to provide current valid data. The orientation is of the future, control reports, for example, are not merely reports of the past. The question to be asked is not only "What did they do in cutting and shaping today?" but also "What are they going to do differently tomorrow?" Furthermore, controlling is concentrated at points or interfaces where change occurs. The control process does not cover an operation in total. This suggests that the location of control points should be selected carefully with especial attention given to avoid strain among organizational relationships. In addition, the mere creating of certain controlling does not guarantee its working successfully. The inception and adoption of the controlling must contain reasonable certainty that it will work. It must be practical and it must give fulfillment of a known and stated objective. Another characteristic is that controls must be enforceable. If the controlling effort is directed toward what is really a fantasy, it is likely to produce much resentment by the people involved in it.

It is well to keep in mind that the standard is the key in controlling. This is the basis for the evaluation and the standard should employ some form of measurement—quantitative if possible. Controlling diminishes in effectiveness as standards become inexact. Furthermore, controlling is needed and should continue as long as a plan is being implemented and causing action. When the plan is achieved or discarded, the controlling can be stopped. The consensus of most managers is that multiple controls, not a single one, should be utilized. While the controlling followed should be simple, the use of one type only is commonly inadequate. Economic, financial, social, and technical controls appear necessary. Among the more common controls are inventory control, production control, maintenance control, quality control, salary control, sales control, advertising control, and cost control.

Controlling should be subjected to controlling. Actually controlling differs widely in effectiveness and cost. It is entirely possible to have good controlling at low cost and also poor controlling at high cost. If the controlling effort costs more then the loss it is designed to avoid, the controlling cure is worse than the disease. In this case, the controlling should be improved so that it is economically sound. Probably a check by means of a random sample would suffice.

Adequate authority for the person doing the controlling is also important. Taking the proper corrective action necessitates sufficient authority to accomplish this task. A person controlling must be free to control; and this means freedom from being buried in details, yet keeping in close touch with what is going on. Usually the person with line authority should handle any corrective measures taken, the staff authority manager being involved only in the control steps of measurement and comparison of performance.

Another consideration is to provide predetermined control data, commonly expressed in dollars to operate a unit, to the individual in charge of the work being done. To illustrate, if the expenditures of a department are not to exceed $25,000 for the next quarter, the manager of that department would be informed of this fact and given complete control information to help maintain costs within the predetermined amount. Predetermined amounts of expenditures are usually arrived at by means of a budget which is discussed in Chapter 25.

QUESTIONS

1. What is meant by the control process?
2. Explain Figure 22–3 in your own words.
3. Relate from your experience or reading how a company's controlling efforts involve its managerial planning, organizing, and actuating.
4. For what types of work do you favor the use of personal observations by a manager in order to find out what is being accomplished? Defend your viewpoint.
5. Discuss the close relationship between planning and controlling.
6. What is meant by feedback and of what importance is it in controlling?
7. Distinguish carefully between the concepts in each of the following pairs: (a) bottom-of-pyramid approach and time-use as a factor of controlling, (b) controlling and managing, and (c) profit centers and measuring intangible achievements.
8. Referring to Figure 22–5, as a manager what control activities would you take based on these data? Assume the following standards: cutting, 35.4 units per hour; coiling, 2.5 units per hour; soldering and assembly, 1.9

units per hour; testing, no standard; finishing, 3.5 units per hour; and shipping, no standard. Based on these additional data, what control action do you feel is in order? Why?

9. Discuss means the manager might use to obtain a favorable human response to controlling.

10. Discuss the subject of anticipatory controlling, pointing out its purpose, questions asked, and probable helpfulness to a manager.

11. From your experience give an illustration where the principle of exception either should be or is being applied in the controlling of work.

12. Does the use of results management eliminate the use of managerial controlling? Why?

13. Elaborate on the statement "Managerial control has no single type."

14. Discuss four guides which you believe are helpful in making controlling effective.

CASE 22–1.   ARNOLD-WEBBER, INC.

Valerie Davis was promoted to head of the accounts payable unit. She was formerly in charge of customer relations and did a very respectable job—good enough to win the promotion. She gets along well with people, learns fast, and is extremely loyal to the corporation. Some were surprised when told of the promotion, but most realized that Ms. Davis was ambitious and played the game of "office politics" very well.

Some weeks after Valerie Davis took over her new job, her supervisor, Mr. Mark Shidler, began receiving complaints from the cost accounting unit about billing errors originating from Ms. Davis' unit. Mr. Shidler asked Ms. Davis to look into the matter of improving her unit's work. The immediate reaction of Ms. Davis was that the complaint must have originated from Tom Boggs, a senior member of cost accounting, and a contender for the accounts payable job that she received. It was no secret that Tom felt he should have been given the promotion based on background and training, service with the company, and knowledge of the work.

Valerie reviewed available information and found the volume of work in her unit had decreased about 11 percent during the past six weeks. However, she observed that all the billing clerks seemed to be busy during work hours. She talked with the former head of accounts payable and was told Hattie Zurk, one of the five billing clerks, was found to be the source of much inaccurate and sloppy work when complaints were received some six months ago. Valerie talked individually with each of the billing clerks and asked them to cooperate in eliminating errors in their work. Each assured her of their complete cooperation. But the errors persisted.

Several days later, Valerie decided to have Hattie and Janice (another billing clerk) submit their work to her for double checking. Accordingly, the next morning she informed Janice of that procedure and received an answer, "OK, if that's what you want." But when Hattie was informed, she looked surprised and lost her temper, yelling, "You're picking on me! My work is accurate—I check it carefully! You are trying to get rid of me and get a friend in! All of us have been waiting for you to change things!" Valerie explained she was not blaming anyone and she had no plans to recommend letting any of the billing clerks go. But Hattie was unconvinced.

Next day Hattie telephoned saying she had been delayed and would not report for work until 2 P.M. During lunch with a friend from sales, Valerie learned that a close girlfriend of Hattie's was formerly engaged to Preston Wilson, an engineer in research and development. He is now dating Valerie.

Questions

1. In your opinion what is the problem?
2. Comment on Ms. Davis handling of the billing errors in her unit.
3. What key considerations in management controlling does this case bring to light? Discuss.
4. What is your recommended action for Ms. Davis? Why?

CASE 22–2. KAVANAUGH SALES CORPORATION

Last year sales of this corporation were $4.3 million, on which $283,000 profits before taxes were realized. Mr. Kavanaugh, president of the corporation, decided to take measures to improve both sales and profits. After talking with several close business friends at the Oruro Country Club and with his corporation counsel, for whom he had considerable respect, Mr. Kavanaugh formulated his plans to put the corporation in better financial condition. He called a special sales strategy meeting for all of the 42 salespeople.

In several sessions at this meeting, Mr. Kavanaugh made these announcements:

1. The company needs more sales, and more aggressive efforts by the salespeople are imperative.

2. To assist in sales growth, the company has established a market research department headed by Dr. Don Kamura, an experienced researcher in the sales areas in which the corporation now operates.

3. The present schedule of costs of products to salespeople will be adjusted. This is necessary because certain charges now being made for products of the company do not cover their costs. However, in other cases, some reductions in charges by the company may be put into effect.

4. The present sales contract under which each salesperson works will remain intact. The company will continue to recognize each salesperson as an independent business person—independent in all actions and considered an individual, not an employee. Specifically, salespeople will continue to negotiate the price paid by the customer. Whether the margin received by the salesperson will remain within the present range of 23 to 25 percent of the selling price to the customer will depend on what price the salesperson gets for the product. As mentioned above, the salesperson will be billed at a higher price for certain products.

5. A new line of products will be added to those now handled by the company. This new line may be considered by some salespeople as too sophisticated for them to handle. It will require new product knowledge and good, hard selling. This new product line will represent entry by the company into a market which is huge and unit sales for which are much larger than any of the company's present products.

The last two hours of the meeting were given to answering questions by the sales staff. After this, the meeting adjourned.

Six months later the records showed that both sales and profits have seriously declined. The situation is especially critical as the company is operating at higher overhead costs due primarily to the expenditures for market research and promotional efforts for the new product line. Recently Mr. Kavanaugh talked with several key salespeople about making a pro rata charge on each sales order to cover the expenses for market research which is, in the final analysis, being conducted to assist the salespeople make more sales. The salespeople voiced vigorous opposition to such an arrangement. Also, two months ago, in order to compile a manual, the company requested each salesperson to describe in writing an experience showing how a new customer was gained, a sales objection overcome, or an old customer reinstated. To date, only one reply has been received by the company.

Dr. Kamura expressed the opinion that the salespeople did not seem interested in improving their compensation and was at a loss to know what to do. Mr. Kavanaugh indicated that if improvements were not soon shown, he would be forced to make some drastic changes.

Questions

1. What is the problem faced by the company?
2. What are your reactions to Mr. Kavanaugh? Discuss.
3. Relate your recommendation to the company managers.

Chapter 23

Overall managerial controls and audits

*Not merely what we do but what we try to do and why
are the true interpreters of what we are.*
C. H. Woodward

An important and popular type of managerial controlling is that of overall controlling, in which the entire enterprise, or a relatively large portion of it, is considered as a unit. Overall controls provide simple, yet effective bench marks for measuring and evaluating performance. Akin to overall controlling is the management audit. It includes a review and evaluation of management either overall or of areas selected for analysis. Usually certain selected attributes are employed as guides.

The work of overall managerial controls and audits goes beyond rendering an opinion on financial statements. More effectiveness throughout the organization is the modern goal. Recommendations for managers and their use of basic resources are wanted. Also the degree to which projects and programs achieve their objectives with what expenditure of time, effort, and money has gained favor. We will discuss overall controlling first and follow this with comments pertaining to audits.

CONTROLLING OVERALL PERFORMANCE

A manager can easily get deeply engrossed in a certain specific type of controlling and concentrate control efforts on activities having the greatest personal interest. However, keeping a watchful eye upon the overall performance helps a manager to maintain the needed broad viewpoint of management, to see the interrelation of the various activities, and to foster a desired balance among goals and efforts. Further, it helps the manager to see "the forest, not simply the trees."

In the case of a national and international enterprise having many plants and sales offices in different locations, the need for overall performance controlling is apparent. Accepting control over each separate unit as being sufficient can lead to autonomy of the enterprise so that it eventually will consist of a series of small units rather than a completely integrated large unit. Furthermore, viewing the entire enterprise as a unit and controlling its action from a single vantage point usually results in maximum coordinated work. Certain activities, like the raising of necessary capital funds, frequently can best be handled and controlled from an overall viewpoint of the entire enterprise. At the same time, it is possible for the overall performance to be satisfactory while some of the elements of the performance may require remedial action. That is to say, controlling overall performance is helpful but not necessarily conclusive. Controls over limited areas are also needed in order to keep the respective elements of performance within the desired limits.

OVERALL CONTROL REPORTS

Most helpful for controlling overall performance are (1) the balance sheet, (2) the profit and loss statement, and (3) special reports designed to show selected pertinent data. For each type report, showing the information for several consecutive years reveals important trends and is a common practice. Such reports are called *comparative*, i.e., a comparative balance sheet shows data in balance sheet format for several consecutive years.

1. Comparative balance sheet.   This is an important accounting document showing the financial picture of a company at a given moment. It itemizes in an accounting statement three elements: (1) assets, (2) liabilities, and (3) shareholders' equity. Assets are the value of the various items owned by the corporation, liabilities are the amounts owed to various creditors by the corporation, and stockholders' equity is the amount accuring to the corporation's owners. The relationship among these three elements is: Assets equal liabilities plus stockholders' equity. This is called the balance sheet equation.

Figure 23–1 shows a comparative balance sheet. In this figure it can be observed that during the year the company has grown as a result of enlarging its building and acquiring more machinery and equipment by means of long-term debt in the form of a first mortgage. Additional stock was sold to help finance this expansion. At the same time accounts receivable were increased and work in process reduced. Observe that total assets ($3,053,367) equals total liabilities ($677,204 plus $618,000) plus stockholders' equity ($700,000 plus $981,943 plus $75,620).

A summary of balance sheet items over a relatively long period

FIGURE 23–1

Comparative Balance Sheet for the Years Ending December 31

Assets	This year	Last year
Current Assets:		
Cash	$ 161,870	$ 119,200
U.S. Treasury bills	250,400	30,760
Accounts receivable	825,595	458,762
Inventories:		
Work in process and finished products	429,250	770,800
Raw materials and supplies	251,340	231,010
Total Current Assets	$1,918,455	$1,610,532
Other Assets:		
Land	157,570	155,250
Building	740,135	91,784
Machinery and equipment	172,688	63,673
Furniture and fixtures	132,494	57,110
Total Other Assets	$1,202,887	$ 367,817
Less accumulated depreciation and amortization	67,975	63,786
	$1,134,912	$ 304,031
Total Assets	$3,053,367	$1,914,563

Liabilities		
Current Liabilities:		
Accounts payable	$ 287,564	$ 441,685
Payrolls and withholdings from employees	44,055	49,580
Commissions and sundry accruals	83,260	41,362
Federal taxes on income	176,340	50,770
Current installment on long-time debt	85,985	38,624
Total Current Liabilities	$ 677,204	$ 622,021
Long-Term Liabilities:		
Fifteen-year, 5 percent loan, payable in each of the years 1958 to 1971	210,000	225,000
Five percent first mortgage	408,600	
Registered 5 percent notes payable		275,000
Total Long-Term Liabilities	$ 618,600	$ 500,000
Stockholders' Equity:		
Common stock: authorized 1,000,000 shares, outstanding last year 492,000 shares, outstanding this year 700,000 shares at $1 par value	700,000	492,000
Capital surplus	981,943	248,836
Earned surplus	75,620	51,706
Total Liabilities and Stockholders' Equity	$3,053,367	$1,914,563

uncovers important trends and gives a manager further insight into overall performance and areas over which adjustments should probably be made. For example, Figure 23–2 shows a 10-year summary of the consolidated financial condition of an enterprise. Data arranged in this manner increase their managerial value.

FIGURE 23–2:   Ten-year summary of consolidated financial condition (in thousands of dollars)

	Cash and government securities	Accounts receivable	Inventories	Plant and equipment (net)	Current liabilities	Long-term liabilities	Total stockholders' equity
This year	8,421	9,970	10,500	6,411	5,120	4,800	23,900
Last year	6,491	6,022	9,440	5.820	5,375	5,100	17,130
2 years ago	4,904	4,010	7,780	3,075	3,845	4,200	14,600
3 years ago	3,570	5,320	7,940	3,995	2,427	5,500	12,160
4 years ago	2,322	5,455	7,026	3,112	3,822	2,900	11,740
5 years ago	2,961	4,485	4,951	3,180	2,704	1,750	10,250
6 years ago	2,943	5,148	4,093	2,965	3,193	3,600	8,900
7 years ago	2,153	4,160	5,130	2,687	4,440	3,555	6,775
8 years ago	2,411	2,472	4,190	2,251	4,800	2,270	4,450
9 years ago	2,945	1,540	2,707	1,040	2,272	2,430	3,600

2. Profit and loss statement.   This is an itemized financial statement of the income and expenses resulting from the company's operations during a stated or accounting period of time. Basically it shows income less expenditure. Figure 23–3 illustrates a comparative statement of profit and loss arranged to expedite data comparison for two consecutive years. In this illustration the operating revenue of the

FIGURE 23–3

Comparative Statement of Profit and Loss for the Year Ending June 30			
	This year	Last year	Increase or decrease
Income:			
Net sales	$253,218	$257,636	$ 4,418*
Dividends from investments	480	430	50
Other	1,741	1,773	32*
Total	$255,439	$259,839	$ 4,400*
Deductions:			
Cost of goods sold	$180,481	$178,866	$ 1,615
Selling and administrative expenses	39,218	34,019	5,199
Interest expense	2,483	2,604	121*
Other	1,941	1,139	802
Total	$224,123	$216,628	$ 7,495
Income before taxes	$ 31,316	$ 43,211	$11,895*
Provision for taxes	3,300	9,500	6,200*
Net Income	$ 28,016	$ 33,711	$ 5,695*

* Decrease.

enterprise has increased while expense likewise has increased but at a smaller rate resulting in a higher net income. From comparative statements of this type, a manager can locate troubled areas and set out to correct them. Some managers draw up tentative profit and loss statements as plans and use such statements as goals toward which to strive. Performance is measured against these goals which amount to standards for control purposes.

Controlling by profit and loss is applied most commonly to an entire enterprise or, in the case of a consolidated corporation, to its sub-sidiaries. However, if controlling by departments is followed, a profit and loss statement is drawn up for each department. Thus, the con-tribution of each department to net income of the entire enterprise is ascertained. In essence, this approach amounts to each department's output being measured along with charging so much cost, including overhead, to each department's operation. The department's achieve-ment of showing a net income of an expected amount is considered a standard for measuring its performance. To illustrate, suppose a manu-facturer has three departments: punching, welding, and assembling. The punching department produces and sells its products and services to the welding department, which in turn sells its products and ser-vices to the assembling department. Each department is thought of as a separate enterprise with its own applicable profit and loss statement. This approach works out satisfactorily for departments that produce tangible or physical results. However, where a department's output is predominantly intangible, as for example with certain staff and service units, control by profit and loss statements is unsatisfactory and other media should be used.

3. *Special reports.* There are a variety of special reports de-signed to expedite overall controlling. Illustrative is Figure 23–4 which shows pertinent data on production and shipments, factory op-erations, and finances. By studying the data and comparing them with other like control sheets in this series, a manager can know what is going on. On items warranting further investigation, other written re-ports showing the source and more detailed information would be consulted. For example, under material scrapped, it might be helpful to find out what departments are responsible for the loss and the rea-sons for the spoilage.

KEY RATIOS OF TOTAL ACTIVITIES

An effective approach used by managers for checking on the overall performance of an enterprise is the use of key ratios. The ratios are determined from selected items in the balance sheet and the profit and loss statement. A ratio is the numerical relationship between two numbers. Analysis by ratio is the process of determining the relations

FIGURE 23–4:   An effective form of periodic report used for control purposes

No._____ Year _____	CONTROL SHEET THE MARK MERRIMAN MANUFACTURING CO. Week ending:_____					
PRODUCTION AND SHIPMENTS:						
	This Week		Cumulative This Month		Same Period Last Year	
	Amount (dollars)	Percentage of Expectancy	Amount (dollars)	Percentage of Expectancy	Amount (dollars)	Percentage of Expectancy
Orders. . . . . Production. . . . . . Shipments . . . . . . Orders unfilled . . .						

FACTORY OPERATIONS:			
	This Week	Cumulative This Month	Same Period Last Year
Total direct worker–hours . . . . Total indirect worker–hours . . . . Percentage of plant capacity . . . . . . Material scrapped (dollar value). . . . . Number of employees added to payroll. . Number of employees subtracted from payroll			

FINANCE:	
Cash on hand . . . . Balance in bank . . . . Deposited in bank . . . . Accounts receivable . . . . Accounts past due	Accounts payable . . . . Bank loans. . . . . Other payments or loans. . . . . _____ . . . . _____ . . . .

of selected items in accounting statements. Some ratios have wide recognition and acceptance. Many are helpful in indicating possible strengths and weaknesses in the company's operations.

For purposes here, we will show how eight different ratios are calculated and discuss each briefly. Ratio analysis is too vast a subject to treat here in any detail. Figure 23–5 shows the balance sheet of the Peggy Lynn Products Company and the following ratios are calculated from data given in this figure. The ratios are shown in Figure 23–6.

1. Current assets to current liabilities. This ratio is sometimes called the "net working capital ratio." It provides an indication of the extent to which current assets may decline and still be adequate to pay current liabilities. In the illustration, the ratio is 2.11, which is generally considered satisfactory. Some analysts place a ratio of 2 to 1, or 2.00, as the desirable minimum.

2. Sales to inventory. This ratio does not reflect true inventory turnover because sales are at selling price and inventory is at cost.

FIGURE 23–5: Balance sheet and other pertinent data

PEGGY LYNN PRODUCTS COMPANY
Balance Sheet
December 31, 197–

Current assets:				Current liabilities:		
Cash:				Notes payable:		
Cash in bank	$ 32,846.85			Bank	$50,000.00	
Petty cash fund	300.00	$ 33,146.85		Trade	13,925.00	$63,925.00
Accounts receivable	$173,465.30			Accounts payable		87,058.77
Less: Reserve for doubtful accounts	6,118.25	167,347.05		Accruals		11,571.25
				Federal income tax		87,000.00
Inventories:				Other taxes		16,948.00	$266,503.02
Raw materials	$123,655.40					
Work in process	60,521.62			Funded debt:		
Finished goods	177,831.70	362,008.72	$562,502.62	First mortgage 4½% bonds		100,000.00
Fixed assets:				Capital stock:		
Land	$ 28,500.00			Common stock—par value $1.00 per share; author-		
Building	$156,620.00			ized 500,000 shares, issued and outstanding		
Less: Reserve for depreciation	22,050.00	134,570.00		400,000 shares		400,000.00
Machinery and equipment	$248,300.00					
Less: Reserve for depreciation	40,500.00	207,800.00	370,870.00	Surplus		176,000.00
Deferred charges:		$ 2,380.00				
Unexpired insurance		6,750.40	9,130.40			
			$942,503.02			$942,503.02

Tangible net worth .... $ 576,000.00
Net working capital 295,999.60

Total sales 2,100,000.00
Earnings 175,000.00
Average number of employees 100

$562,502.62
266,503.02

FIGURE 23–6:   Ratios determined from data in Figure 23–5

1.   Current assets to current liabilities:

$$\frac{562,502.62}{266,503.02} = 2.11$$

2.   Sales to inventory:

$$\frac{2,100,000.00}{362,008.72} = 5.80 \text{ times}$$

3.   Revenue created per employee:

$$\frac{\dfrac{2,100,000}{12}}{100} = \$1,750$$

4.   Transaction time:

$$\frac{362,008.72 \times 365}{2,100,000} = 62.8 \text{ days}$$

5.   Fixed assets to tangible net worth:

$$\frac{370,870.00}{576,000.00} = 64.4\%$$

6.   Current liabilities to tangible net worth:

$$\frac{266,503.02}{576,000.00} = 46.3\%$$

7.   Funded debt to net working capital:

$$\frac{100,000.00}{295,999.60} = 33.8\%$$

8.   Return on investment:

$$\frac{175,000}{942,503.02} = 18.6\%$$

Furthermore, the data are for the year end; they are not average figures for the year. A value of 5.80 times, as found in the illustration, is probably lower than it should be. Either sales should be increased or inventory reduced. This latter course merits further analysis. For example, current assets exclusive of inventories are only about 75 per-cent of current liabilities, a situation which might prove serious if inventories become difficult to dispose.

3.   *Revenue created per employee.*   This is for a definite period, usually one month, and is calculated by dividing the dollar shipments by the average number of employees. To illustrate, monthly shipments can be considered as total sales, $2,100,000 divided by 12, or $175,000, which amount divided by the average number of employees, 100, gives $1,750 per employee per month. What constitutes a satisfactory

ratio depends upon the type of enterprise, but most analysts believe that the range is between $1,500 and $2,000 per employee per month. If the revenue per employee is too low, it usually signals that there is idle production time, methods are poor, sales are being missed, or incorrect sellings prices are being used.

4. Transaction time. This is the time required to carry out the entire operation of providing form and place utility to the products and services by the enterprise. Transaction time is found by dividing the average inventory by the net shipments. Frequently a time period of one year is used to avoid wide fluctuation in this value. In our illustration we will use the inventory amount at the end of the year, which is the only inventory figure available and consider sales equal to shipments. The transaction time is then equal to inventory, $362,008.72, multiplied by 365 (number of days in one year), divided by net shipments, $2,100,000, or 62.8 days. Transaction time varies considerably with the type of enterprise. For meat packers and foundries, the value may be around 20 to 25, whereas for canneries it may be as high as 100. When transaction time of an enterprise is excessively high for its particular industry, it frequently means inadequate control over the amounts produced, too much paper work, excessive delays, or incomplete inventory control.

5. Fixed assets to tangible net worth. If this ratio is too high, it indicates that too much of the firm's net worth is tied up in fixed assets, that is, land, building, and machines. Comparisons with past experience of the enterprise and with others in the same general business are desirable. When this ratio is too high, it means probably that the firm is short of capital for current assets and wil be obliged to borrow. In this illustration, the ratio figures 64.4 percent, which seems higher than it should be. Based on this ratio alone, either the fixed assets should be reduced or the tangible net worth increased.

6. Current liabilities to tangible net worth. For the business illustrated, this ratio is 46.3 percent, an amount which appears reasonable and satisfactory. With the information from ratio No. 5 above, that fixed assets are probably out of line with tangible net worth, either current liabilities or funded long-term debt may be out of line, since both current liabilities and funded debt plus tangible net worth constitute the entire right side of the balance sheet and equal total assets on the left side. Ratio No. 6 shows current debt is satisfactory so that the funded or long-term debt probably is the one needing adjustment and could be increased in the case illustrated.

7. Funded debt to net working capital. When this ratio is excessive, the working capital might be depleted to amortize the funded debt. In this illustration a value of 33.8 percent is obtained. There is no apparent danger in this case; as a matter of fact, the funded debt could be a little higher without hindering the company's operations.

8. *Return on investment.* Many managers have adopted the use of this ratio in their overall controlling. It is a rate of return from capital, not an amount or rate of profits. It can be viewed as a ratio of profit to capital employed. The ratio can be calculated for any base, be it a group of machines, an organizational unit, or the entire company. However, it is most satisfactory for a large organization unit and preferably for the entire company. It is difficult, for example, to determine the earnings derived from sales, and their cost, from the output of one machine.

The return on investment, R, is equal to E, the earnings, divided by I, the total investment. Expressed algebraically:

$$R = \frac{E}{I}$$

An alternative and popular means of calculating the ratio is to multiply the turnover of sales, or sales divided by investment, by the earnings divided by sales. Expressed as a formula:

$$R = \frac{S}{I} \times \frac{E}{S}$$

This is shown graphically by Figure 23–7.

For our illustrative company, the return on investment is found by dividing earnings ($175,000) by investment ($942,503.02) giving 18.6

FIGURE 23–7: Calculating the return on investment shown graphically

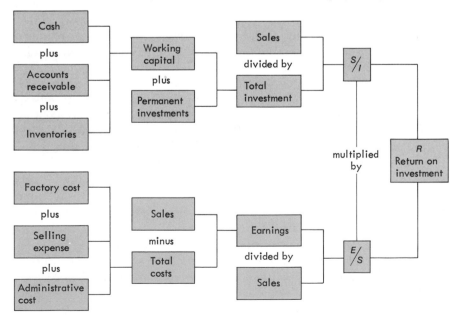

percent. This appears reasonably satisfactory. Some companies attain 25–28 percent, while many are in the 10–12 percent bracket.

Based on these various ratios as a group and reviewing Figure 23–6 it can be stated that the Peggy Lynn Products Company is in a reasonably satisfactory condition. The net working capital appears adequate, current liabilities are not excessive, and the company is not in need of funds. The funded debt could be increased without harm to the company. The fixed assets may be slightly larger than desirable; but with time and due to depreciation, they will decrease. In contrast, the tangible net worth should increase as continued favorable operations are maintained and surplus is increased. The present level of sales appears reasonably good but if possible should be increased through price adjustments or greater output with existent facilities.

EVALUATION OF RATIO USAGE

As seen in the above discussion any ratio must be interpreted to give it meaning and this must take into account its source, the accuracy of the factors from which the ratio is calculated, and its probable relative value and meaningfulness to the operations of the managers of the company. Comparison of ratios within a company or among comparable companies is sensible for such comparisons are pertinent and valid. On the other hand, when a company's ratios are compared to those of a dissimilar company or to those of an unknown and arbitrary industry classification of companies, the analyses are meaningless because the samples are neither representative nor comparable.

It is well to keep in mind that ratios are not ends in themselves but possible indicators of what has taken place. There is danger in calculating too many ratios—for to interpret too large a number for a given company may pose extreme difficulty and a complicated maze of probabilities that almost defy application. Some managers feel that ratios give too much emphasis to certain concepts and place excessive rigidity into a manager's work. Too much emphasis upon the ratio of sales to inventory, for example, may relegate other considerations, quite important, to a secondary position. That is, such things as research, product development, managerial development, and progressive personnel practices may not be given sufficient attention. Such viewpoints appear to have merit, and the manager may wish to temper use of ratios with other control media.

The ratio, return on investment, has been subjected to a great deal of discussion by managers. It does focus attention upon how successful the results are in making the best use of capital employed and it provides a single comprehensive figure that is easy to observe and to note trends. However, the measurements used in return on investment are not always reflective of the true worth of the values being used. In addition, it is contended by some that the investment decisions should be made by the same manager against whose efforts the return on investment is being used. If he or she does not have control over investments the validity of the ratio is open to question. Furthermore, return on investment is valid at the planning stage, but not in the short-range responsive control process. When it is decided to keep an operation active, it makes little difference whether 1 percent or 30 percent is earned. The commitment has been made. What does matter is this: Are the results better or worse than the plan anticipated?

COMPARABLE COMPANIES RATIOS

Another type of overall controlling is a method employing comparable companies ratio analysis. This is feasible only if data from comparable companies in the same industry are legal and available. Actually this approach is little used in the United States, but it is not uncommon in several European countries. By this approach, similar companies exchange key ratio figures—not actual amounts of dollars, francs, or marks—for mutual enlightenment. For example, information on profit to sales, return on capital, and overhead cost to total cost might be used. Figure 23–8 gives a simplified example.

FIGURE 23–8: Comparable companies ratios are helpful in locating sources of difficulties

	Company A	Company B	Our company	Comments
Profit margin	5.8%	6.3%	3.2%	Profit margin is off
Return on capital	16.6	17.4	9.1	Return on capital is too low
Production costs	71.5	69.9	76.7	Our production costs are out of line
Production overhead costs	16.8	16.6	16.1	Production overhead is OK
Labor costs	9.5	6.5	13.3	Labor costs are the big problem
Cost of materials	45.2	46.8	47.3	We are paying too much for materials

For best results, comparison should be on a continuing basis, say from year to year. Deviations indicate departure from the practices of others, but this is not necessarily a danger signal. Conformity need not exist. The deviations point out areas that might warrant close scrutiny and possible alterations.

FIXED AND VARIABLE COSTS ANALYSIS

An additional important means of overall managerial control is the use of fixed and variable costs and their subsequent analysis in so-called break-even charts. Costs for the enterprise are segregated into (1) fixed and (2) variable with respect to the volume of work output. Fixed costs are expenditures which *tend to remain fixed* or relatively constant regardless of the volume of work output for a period. There is no absolutely fixed cost for all times. Items such as executives' salaries, depreciation, and interest on borrowed money are examples of fixed costs. On the other hand, variable costs are expenditures which are related to and *tend to change directly* with the volume of work output. Direct material costs and salespeople's commissions are examples of variable costs.[1] See Figure 23–9.

FIGURE 23–9: **Examples of fixed and of variable cost**

Cost	Fixed	Variable	Semivariable	Varies with
Building	x			
Depreciation	x			
Maintenance			x	Units manufactured
Packaging material		x		Units packaged
Raw material		x		Units manufactured
Wages	x	(if not directly related to volume of work output)		

Fixed and variable costs analysis provides a picture of how the enterprise is set up costwise for operations, what volume of work is necessary to break even, that is, where total income equals total expenditures and there is no profit, and what the profit possibilities are at various levels of sales.

Four fundamental constraining factors should be kept in mind:

1. Sales equal fixed cost plus variable cost plus or minus profit, or

$$S = FC + VC \pm P$$

2. At break-even point: sales equals fixed cost plus variable cost, or

$$S_{BEP} = FC + VC$$

3. Variable costs and profits vary with sales.
4. Fixed costs remain fixed within the range of the sales being considered.

---

[1] A third classification, semivariable costs, is also sometimes used in cost behavior analyses. Semivariable costs vary with the volume of work output but not in direct proportion to it. When the volume is zero, some semivariable costs exist—they are never completely eliminated.

Algebraic solution

Assume a company has sales of $3 million, variable costs are 40 percent of sales, and fixed costs are estimated at $1.5 million. The problem is to find the profits, if any, at this level of sales and the break-even point. Also, the profits, if any, at sales of $4 million and at $2 million are to be calculated.

Solving this problem by algebra, we first substitute values in formula 1 given above.

$$S = FC + VC + \text{Profit}$$
$$\$3,000,000 = \$1,500,000 + 40\% \text{ of } \$3,000,000 + \text{Profit}$$
$$\$3,000,000 = \$1,500,000 + \$1,200,000 + \text{Profit}$$
$$\$300,000 = \text{Profit}$$

To determine the break-even point, use formula 2 given above.

$$S_{BEP} = FC + VC$$
$$100\% \, S_{BEP} = (100\% - 40\%) \, S_{BEP} + 40\% \, S_{BEP}$$

Fixed cost remains fixed, so

$$100\% \, S_{BEP} = \$1,500,000 + 40\% \, S_{BEP}$$
$$60\% \, S_{BEP} = \$1,500,000$$
$$S_{BEP} = \$2,500,000$$

For profit at sales of $4 million using formula 1:

$$\$4,000,000 = \$1,500,000 + 40\% \text{ of } \$4,000,000 + \text{Profit}$$
$$\$900,000 = \text{Profit}$$

For profit at sales of $2,000,000 using formula 1:

$$\$2,000,000 = \$1,500,000 + 40\% \text{ of } \$2,000,000 + \text{Profit}$$
$$-\$300,000 = \text{Profit (loss)}$$

GRAPHIC SOLUTION

Figure 23–10 shows the graphic solution to the same problem. The horizontal axis of the chart represents volume or output; the vertical axis is used to show dollars representing sales cost and profit. To construct the chart, we first draw the fixed cost line which is the horizontal line, AF, on the chart. It is $1.5 million above the base line and has this same value regardless of the amount of output, since fixed costs are fixed. Using the line, AF, as a base, line AV is drawn representing variable cost between lines AF and AV. This line will pass through point A and since variable cost equals 40 percent of sales dollars, the line will slope upward to the right at a rate of 40 to every 100 increase in sales. At sales of $3 million, fixed cost is equal to $1.5 million,

FIGURE 23–10:   Break-even chart

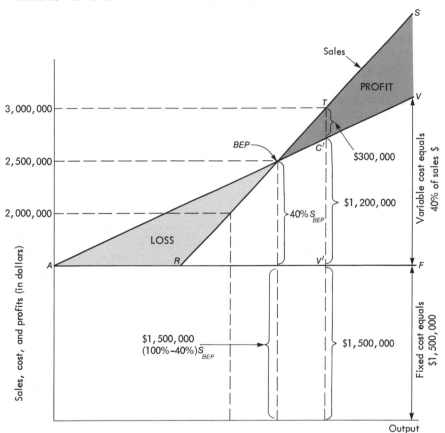

variable cost $1.2 million, and profit $300,000. These values locate point *T* which in on the sales line, *RS*. Another point on this sales line is the break-even point which we will determine and then draw in line *RS*. The break-even point dollar value is determined by recognizing that the fixed cost, or $1.5 million, is equal to 100 percent minus 40 percent of the sales at the break-even point. Hence, if 60 percent is equal to $1.5 million, then 100 percent is equal to $2.5 million, which equals sales at the break-even point, or the total dollar value of the dotted vertical line on the chart through the break-even point. As indicated above, by joining points *T* and the break-even point, the sales line *RS* is determined. Subsequently, cost and profit value patterns can be read directly from the chart. At $2 million sales, for example, fixed cost is $1.5 million, variable cost is $800,000, with profit showing a deficit or loss of $300,000.

UTILIZING BREAK-EVEN POINT ANALYSIS

It behooves managers to arrange the setup of an enterprise in keeping with a reasonable range of sales expectancy. In the above example, if the sales were likely to be between $2 million and $2.5 million, it is apparent that this company will be profitless. It is geared to handle a larger sales volume. On the other hand, if there were reasonable certainty that sales will maintain a fairly high-volume range, say from $6 million to $10 million, it can be shown that greater profits will be realized if some of the present variable costs are converted into fixed costs through mechanization or some other means.

Consider the data in Figure 23–11. In this illustration the level of

FIGURE 23–11

Original setup

Sales	Fixed costs	Variable costs (40 percent)	Total costs	Profits
$ 4,000,000	$1,500,000	$1,600,000	$3,100,000	$ 900,000
6,000,000	—	2,400,000	3,900,000	2,100,000
8,000,000	—	3,200,000	4,700,000	3,300,000
10,000,000	—	4,000,000	5,500,000	4,500,000

Break-even point $2,500,000

Revised setup

Sales	Fixed costs	Variable costs (15 percent)	Total costs	Profits
$ 4,000,000	$3,000,000	$ 600,000	$3,600,000	$ 400,000
6,000,000	—	900,000	3,900,000	2,100,000
8,000,000	—	1,200,000	4,200,000	3,800,000
10,000,000	—	1,500,000	4,500,000	5,500,000

Break-even point $3,529,412

sales has been assumed equal to $6 million; that is, profits are identical at this sales level in either the original or revised setup. Comparing the revised with the original, fixed costs have doubled and variable costs reduced from 40 to 15 percent of sales. As a result, profits change also. The results are typical and lead to an important principle:

Principle of variable-cost and fixed-cost relationships to profit potential

For a given enterprise, the lowest variable and highest fixed costs consistent with a break-even point which is less than the smallest probable total sales result in the maximum profit potential.

Over the past several decades, many companies have increased their break-even point by increasing fixed costs, primarily due to au-tomation, so that relatively, fixed costs represent a greater proportion of total costs. A high break-even point means high sales volumes must be secured in order for the company to survive. Various means of easing this pressure or of operating more effectively with present facilities are listed in Figure 23–12.

FIGURE 23–12

To ease demands of high break-even point, an enterprise can—

1. Increase the number of units sold.
2. Add new products or services which indicate reasonable sales volumes. Give particular attention to items smoothing out seasonal fluctuations.
3. Redesign present products to provide a wider margin.
4. Increase selling price to acquire a larger dollar sales volume, if demand is constant.
5. Lower selling price to attract a broader market, if demand is elastic.
6. Eliminate slow-moving, nonprofitable items when research and sales efforts clearly show little improvement is likely.
7. Consolidate departments or functions to reduce costs.
8. Modernize methods used in production and selling processes.
9. Install more efficient machines and equipment in factory and in office, the capacities of which are within the economic limits of reasonable sales expectancy.
10. Watch carefully the costs of sales promotion and advertising efforts to help insure maximum effectiveness in these fields.

From the viewpoint of fixed- and variable-cost relationships, many companies are presently in a position that if their respective sales decline 20–25 percent, they are in serious difficulty to match total income to total costs. The relative flexibility of the operations provided by variable costs has been lessened. At the same time, rigidities in the form of fixed costs have become more dominant, and fixed costs must be paid regardless of the sales amount. In other words, as fixed-cost items increase, it takes more dollars obtained from sales to cover these fixed costs.

RETURN ON MACHINE INVESTMENTS

Another type of control usually considered in the overall category is the return on machine investment. A major consideration in machine selection is labor cost reduction, but translating the estimated savings into a return on machine investment poses a real problem. However, the arrangement shown by Figure 23–13 offers an effective approach. In the illustration the cost of the new machine is $9,000, with direct

FIGURE 23–13:   Computing return on machine investment

Work Sheet
The cost of the new machine is $9,000

	Old Machine	New Machine
Direct labor costs per hour	$1.50	$1.70
Extra direct labor costs per hour	0.27	0.20
Total	$1.77	$1.90
Divided by number of parts produced per hour	110	200
Total direct labor cost per piece	$0.0161	$0.0095

The new machine produced *1,500* pieces per day (7½ hours running time per day)

At *0.0161* per piece on old machine, they would cost	$24.15
At *0.0095* per piece on new machine, they would cost	14.25
Labor savings per day	$ 9.90
Annual savings, labor (5-day week, 50 weeks per year)	$2,475.00

Desirable annual rate of recovery of capital invested in the new machine, assuming it has a 10-year* profitable life ($1/10$ of cost)	$ 900.00
Amount recovered annually tax-free by 20-year* depreciation schedule (½ of above)	$ 450.00
Additional amount to be recovered annually out of excess of income over cost	$ 450.00
Earnings required annually before taxes (at 43%) to recover above amount (above figure divided by 0.57)	$ 789.47
Annual capital recovery required over the 10-year period; *$450.00* from depreciation plus *$789.47* from profit before taxes	$1,239.47

Total annual savings	$2,475.00
Required annually for recovery of capital	$1,239.47
Annual net return on investment	$1,235.53
Rate of annual return on capital invested; annual net return *$1,235.53* divided by *$9,000.00*, the cost of the new machine	13.73%

* These periods vary, of course, depending on the nature of the machine and the product.

Source: Format of work sheet through courtesy of National Machine Tool builders' Association.

labor cost per hour of $1.70, extra direct labor costs per hour estimated at $0.20, and a machine capacity of 200 parts per hour. Comparable data for the old machine are direct labor, $1.50; extra direct labor, $0.27; and capacity, 110 pieces. This information is shown at the top of the illustration; and by simple arithmetic, the value of the total direct labor cost per piece for the old machine and for the new machine are shown. Next the direct labor savings in using the new machine are calculated. In this case the amount is $9.90 per day, or $2,475 per year.

Consideration for depreciation allowance and federal income taxes is now made. Experience shows that, owing to design changes and improvement, many machines have relatively short lives; hence the investment should be entirely recovered from earnings before a later model or new type of equipment brings obsolescence to existent machines. In the illustration, a 10-year straight line period is used. At the same time, the U.S. government may not allow this rate of recovery, and for tax purposes the period defined by the government must be used. For depreciation, the figure of 20 years is arbitrary and is used in the illustration. Should the company elect to use the now permitted "fast write-off," the period is shortened considerably from the 20 years. Referring again to Figure 23–13, the desirable annual rate of recovery of capital invested is one tenth of the original machine cost, or $900. The amount recovered tax free, based on a 20-year depreciation, is one half of $900, or $450. Assuming the company is in the 43 percent income bracket, the earnings required annually to recover $450 or $789.47, which added to the depreciation cost of $450 equals $1,239.47, the total amount required for recovery of capital. The difference between this figure, $1,239.47, and the total annual savings to be realized from the machine, $2,475, represents the annual net return on investment. In the illustration this amount is $1,235.53, which based on the machine cost of $9,000 represents a 13.73 percent return on machine investment. Or stated another way, over a 10-year period, the investment in the machine will be fully recovered and at the same time $1,235.53 will be earned annually, representing a return of 13.73 percent per year.

In some instances it may appear advisable to rebuild the present machine rather than to replace it with a new one. To determine whether such a course should be followed, an analysis similar to that just discussed can be utilized. Usually significant gains in the output per hour are not realized from a rebuilt machine.

It is suggested that the work sheet illustrated in Figure 23–13 be used in cases where (1) obsolete machines are not fully depreciated and (2) fully depreciated machines are still operating. In the former case, the amount of unrecovered investment can be charged to the company's profit and loss account. If the used machine is sold, the amount received can be used to reduce the loss. To charge unrecovered investment to the price of a new machine tends to decrease the rate of return on the new machine investment. Likewise, in the second case, that of a fully depreciated but still operating machine, the amount realized by its sale should not be deducted from the price of a new machine because such a practice tends to increase the rate of return on the new machine investment. An alternate practice is to consider the difference in investment required. Under this practice the unrecovered cost of the old machine is not added to the cost of the new machine but net receipt from the old machine when sold is deducted from the cost of the new machine.

LIMITED AREAS FOR OVERALL CONTROLLING

While the term, overall controlling, usually connotes control efforts over the entire enterprise, popular usage of the term has made it apply to control efforts over large major areas. Usually, such controlling is relatively intensive and in considerable depth. Representative of such controlling is that which deals with any of the following: (1) market standing of the enterprise, (2) profitability, (3) materials acquisition and usage, (4) employee performance (both managerial and nonmanagerial), development, and attitude, (5) capital or financial resources, (6) productivity, (7) physical resources, and (8) public responsibility. Applying controlling to these broad areas helps to minimize unexplained losses in sales, material, time, profit, manpower, capital, and facilities.

By way of explanation, let us elaborate upon one of the major areas just stated—for example, No. 3, materials acquisition and usage. In what activities of this area is it probably most important to set up and implement controls? First, in purchasing, to insure that competitive bids are sought and accurately recorded, that material specifications, promised delivery dates, and quality are maintained. Second, in receiving, to check authorization to accept materials, identity of materials, quantity by count or weight, damage to materials, packaging, units of shipment, and grade or quality of materials received. Third, in the factory, to determine when to replenish supply of a given material, to prevent distortion of production records leading to faulty material needs, to clear batches of finished production or parts in machine areas when work shift changes, to prevent and discourage waste of materials, and to provide safe, temporary storage for materials on the factory floor and to provide a place where such material is free from pilferage and damage.

ACCOUNTING AUDITS

Verification of the various reports and statements such as those discussed above is accomplished by accounting audits. The periodic inspection of accounting records, to see that they have been properly prepared and are correct, assists in overall controlling. Checks are made of the accuracy of records, and at the same time review and appraisal of projects, activities, and procedures can be made. Comparisons between what was expected to be accomplished and what actually is being accomplished can be made, any deviations revealed, and suggestions offered for remedial action. Unfortunately, suggestions by accounting auditors are not always given sufficient attention by the operating manager, usually because one doesn't fully understand the reasons for the particular recommendations or the auditor fails sufficiently to impress the manager that remedial action is needed. The auditing of accounting records and reports is performed by members of an outside firm of public accountants. To know that the records are accurate, true, and in keeping with approval accounting practices forms a reliable base for sound overall controlling purposes.

THE MANAGEMENT AUDIT

The periodic assessment of a company's managerial planning, organizing, actuating, and controlling compared to what might be called the norm of successful operation is the essential meaning of management audit. It reviews the company's past, present, and future. The areas the company covers are examined with a view to determine whether the company is achieving maximum results out of its endeavors, identifying areas where improvements are needed, and keeping expenditures to a minimum while carrying out required operations. A management audit cannot be conducted until the company has been operating a sufficient time to establish its behavior pattern. The benefits derived from a management audit are many, including:

1. A check on new policies and practices for both their suitability and compliance.
2. Identification of major areas needing shoring up.
3. Promotion of better use of company staff organizational units, especially when audit is conducted by company personnel.
4. Improved communication that informs all employees on the "state of the company."
5. Measurement of extent to which current managerial controls are effective.
6. Determination of the reliability of the management data developed within the organization.

The management audit is concerned with the broad scope and deals with the interrelatedness of all the activities being performed. It does not appraise individual performance. Results discovered are given in an audit report which is written from a viewpoint and style designed to set forth clear statements of results and recommendations and to make them as impersonal as possible. The job of the auditor is to audit; implementation of his or her recommendations is the prerogative of the manager having the particular authority for the activity under question. The custom is to provide one inclusive audit report from each audit. In addition, however, it is an excellent practice to provide an audit report covering a specific area direct to the manager who can make the change recommended. In other words, if a manager can make a desired change, an audit report should go to that manager.

Any attempt to audit an activity as pervasive, important, and dynamic as management is certain to be fraught with great difficulty. Imponderables must be overcome, concepts created, and new management trails blazed. Among the management needs is knowledge of value formulation, what relative importance do we and should we attach to people, new products, opinions of customers, attitudes, and so forth.

IDENTIFYING AREAS FOR AUDIT

Among the more common undesirable practices it is hoped a management audit will uncover are the performance of unnecessary work; duplication of work; poor inventory control; use of an improper number of employees for a specific quantity, quality, or type of work; uneconomical use of equipment and machines; wasteful use of resources; and following procedures that are more costly than necessary. If social goals are included in a company's objectives, the audit should determine whether the efforts and expenditures being made are achieving reasonable accomplishments in the social objectives sought.

A number of techniques can be followed by the management auditor to identify areas warranting a penetrating examination. We will briefly consider here some of the more common means. First is the reviewing of internal reports that managers utilize to obtain data on progress, accomplishment, and present status of work. Of special interest are disclosures of projects upon which management has not acted. Inquiries about such inaction and its justification may point out weaknesses that need correction.

Second is to select key systems or procedures used by the company and follow them from start to finish. This approach provides an insight into the present efficiency and the way the work is being done. For example, by noting the capabilities of the personnel involved, the usefulness of the prescribed systems and procedures, and the degree of participation by employees in what areas and in what manner, the audit can uncover possible inadequacies and suggest possible areas or improvement.

Also, interviews with managers and nonmanagers are an important source of valuable information. Discussion with responsible personnel must be handled carefully. Prior to any formal interview, the interviewer should have some background and knowledge of the company so that constructive and pertinent questions can be asked. Also, the atmosphere should be conducive to response. Whom to talk with is significant and the selection should be made only after appropriate thought has been given to this consideration.

ATTRIBUTES USED IN AUDITING

To perform a management audit it is helpful to set up a list of qualifications desired with the credit valuation attached to each. The selection and respective weights given these qualifying factors are highly flavored with judgment and in many cases, quite controversial. The audit itself assesses (1) what the company has done for itself and (2) what it has done for its customers or recipients of the products or services provided. To reach these assessments, evaluations on a number of factors may be deemed necessary and include attributes dealing with financial stability, production efficiency, sales effectiveness, economic and social affluence, personnel development, earnings' growth, public relations, and civic responsibility.

Figure 23–14 shows a list of 12 qualifications for use in the man-

FIGURE 23–14:   Attributes and relative weights for use in a management audit of an advertising agency

```
                           Management Audit

                                                    Maximum points

  1.  Overall
      a.  General reputation ......................................      50
      b.  Financial stability ......................................      60
      c.  Increase in billings of 15 percent per year ..............      65
      d.  Retention of clients ....................................      75
  2.  Work within agency
      a.  Objectives stated and sought .........................     100
      b.  Policies and practices pursued .........................      60
      c.  Employee relations ...................................      90
      d.  Vendor relations .......................................      50
  3.  Outside work with clients
      a.  Creative services ....................................     215
      b.  Contact work with client .............................      90
      c.  Contact work with trade ..............................      70
      d.  Advertising budget and media recommendations ........      75
                                                                   ------
            Total .............................................    1,000
```

agement audit of an advertising agency. The attributes are divided into three main groups and under each one are listed specific qualifications. The maximum points assigned to each attribute are indicated. For example, the highest value is accorded creative services with a maximum of 215 points.

When a buyer of a manufacturing company seeks to evaluate a possible purchase, one normally looks into a number of factors concerning the prospective company. Although one's purpose and proposed action differ from that of the management auditor, it is of interest to note some of the considerations which a buyer investigates for whatever help and suggestions they may provide in planning a management audit. Among the common factors are a summary of the financial statements for the past ten years; the trend in the total number of employees by skills; appraisal of working conditions; compensation methods followed; list of machines including their age and condition; production work load for the past year; principal materials and purchasing methods used; inventory by type of product and by dollars; trend in sales performance; ten-year forecast for industry of which company is a member; research activities and facilities; credit report from bank; and review of competitive practices. These items would be modified depending upon the individual case and conditions.

QUESTIONS

1. As a manager, do you feel you could do a reasonably good job of controlling without the use of overall controls? Justify your answer.

2. Enumerate some advantages and some disadvantages in using ratios for overall controlling purposes. Do you favor the use of ratios for such purposes? Justify your answer.

3. Discuss the ratio "return on investment," pointing out the favorable as well as the unfavorable viewpoints commonly commented upon in discussing this ratio.

4. Justify the identifying of Figure 23–4 as a "control report."

5. Distinguish between the two terms in each of the following pairs: (a) profit and loss statement and current liabilities to tangible net worth, (b) an overall control and the validity of a control ratio, (c) accounting audit and management audit.

6. With reference to Figure 23–10, (a) why is line AF a straight horizontal line? (b) what does the break-even point represent? (c) if sales increased to $5 million, would the value of the break-even point change from that of $2.5 million? Why?

7. With reference to Figure 23–11, under the revised setup show the calculations to determine the data given on the break-even point and on profits when sales are $10 million.

8. For the ratios of total activities included in this chapter, would you say that they are related or unrelated? Explain your answer.

9. What is meant by a manager using comparable companies ratios and do you favor such usage? Why?

10. Enumerate six major areas for which overall controlling is usually desirable.

11. In what ways does a management auditor identify areas probably warranting close examination?

12. What is indicative to the manager of the ratio "fixed assets to tangible net worth"? Of the ratio "return on investment"?

13. Discuss some common benefits derived from a management audit.

14. Enumerate six considerations normally considered important by a prospective buyer of a company in having a management audit made of that company.

CASE 23–1. TEAGUE PRODUCTS, INC.

The manufacturing executive committee is discussing whether an investment in a new machine costing $16,000 installed should be made. The new machine would replace an old machine that has only a small salvage value. The works manager, Mr. James Rosen, favors letting an outside party have the old machine at no cost in return for moving it out of the shop. Mr. Rosen favors getting the new machine. He reasons that since the output of the new machine will be double that of the present old one, or from 50–100 pieces per hour, the operator's pay will increase slightly—from $3.75 an hour to $4.25 an hour, and a 7 percent annual cost of $16,000 could be used, substantial manufacturing savings will result to the corporation. He also points out that the new machine will make greater production possible and the factory space occupied will be less than what the present old machine requires.

Gregg Spruce, chief of maintenance, claims that the amount of time his crew must spend in order to keep the old machine producing acceptable parts is excessive and must make utilizing the old machine very costly. "My guess is we'd be money ahead if we told our customers not to consider us as a source for these parts anymore."

To this statement, Robin Pietra, an accountant, quickly responded that such a move would be against Teague Products' long-standing policy. Further, it would set a bad precedent and could endanger possible loss of other customers. She pointed out that the present costing system does include maintenance cost which, she admits, is high and if possible should be reduced or eliminated. She argued that the best way to decide the machine purchasing issue was to determine the net return on capital investment. In Pietra's opinion this should be a minimum of 15 percent. And she emphasized that net means after depreciation and federal income taxes have been given proper consideration and taken into account in calculating this rate of return.

Questions

1. Using the suggestion of Mr. Rosen, calculate, for one day the cost per unit by including the cost of direct labor and of capital. Evaluate this cost figure.
2. Calculate the annual net return on machine or capital investment in keeping with Ms. Pietra's suggestions.
3. Other than cost and return on investment, what are important considerations in deciding whether to buy a factory machine?
4. What is your recommendation to the corporation? Why?

CASE 23–2. DOUGLAS CORPORATION

The balance sheet for the year just ending is:

Balance Sheet
December 31, 197—

Assets

Current Assets:

Cash in banks or on hand		$ 5,462,377.24
Accounts receivable, less reserves		1,812,390.65

Inventories—at cost or market, whichever lower:

Raw materials, parts, and supplies	$1,833,345.12	
Work in process	747,772.50	
Finished goods	381,600.31	2,962,717.93
Total Current Assets		$10,237,485.82

Fixed Assets:

Machinery and equipment	$ 606,370.05	
Furniture and fixtures	284,917.80	
Improvements to leased property	177,650.00	
Tools, dies, jigs, fixtures	42,606.64	
	$1,111,544.49	
Less: Reserves for depreciation	270,271.84	
Total		841,272.65
Total		$11,078,758.47

Liabilities

Current Liabilities:

Accounts payable		$ 1,533,776.35
Accrued items:		
Payroll, commissions, etc.	$ 151,463.36	
Interest	18,925.16	
Federal and state taxes	457,593.60	$ 627,982.12
Total Current Liabilities		$ 2,161,758.47
Long-Term Notes Payable		2,800,000.00

Capital Stock and Surplus:

Common stock—par value $1 per share; authorized, 5,000,000 shares; issued and outstanding, 4,000,000 shares	$4,000,000.00	
Paid-in surplus	2,117,000.00	
Total Capital Stock and Surplus		6,117,000.00
Total		$11,078,758.47

For the same year, a net earnings of $1,320,714.35 on net sales of $23,164,357.60 was shown by the company. This is more clearly indicated by the following:

Statement of Earnings
For Year Ending December 31, 197–

Net sales	$23,164,357.60
Less: Cost of goods sold	14,007,861.19
Gross Profit on Sales	$ 9,156,496.41
Selling, general administrative expenses	6,355,782.06
Profit from operations	$ 2,800,714.35
Provisions for federal and state taxes	1,480,000.00
Net earnings	$ 1,320,714.35

The executive committee of the corporation believes that the net earnings figure is relatively low for the amount of the company's net sales and is of the opinion that some overall controls should be instituted. The average number of employees for the year is 1,427.

Questions

1. Calculate each of the following ratios: (*a*) current assets to current liabilities, (*b*) fixed assets to tangible net worth, (*c*) funded debt to net working capital, and (*d*) return before taxes on investment.

2. Evaluate each of the above ratios in terms of what it means to the Douglas Corporation.

3. As a member of the executive committee, what are your specific recommendations for improving the operations of the corporation?

CASE 23–3. HEMPY CORPORATION

This corporation's fixed costs are $5 million with sales equal to $20 million. Serious thought is being given to increasing fixed cost. Mr. Farley, president of the company, states that such action will mean more profit to the company over the next five years. He would double the present fixed costs, change the format of the corporation's fixed, variable, and profit by keeping the profits at their present level and adjusting variable costs to make this new format of the corporation possible. Estimate of sales for the next five years follows:

Year	Sales (in millions)
Next year	$25
2 years ahead	18
3 years ahead	15
4 years ahead	22
5 years ahead	26

Present variable costs equal 60 percent of sales.

Questions

1. Call the format of the corporation as it is now, pattern No. 1. For this pattern calculate the following (a) variable costs, (b) profit, and (c) break-even point.

2. Call the proposed format, pattern No. 2. At sales of $20 million, calculate (a) variable costs, and (b) the break-even point.

3. Calculate the profits for each of the next five years at the respective estimated sales for pattern No. 1, and also for pattern No. 2. Is Mr. Farley's statement correct?

4. What general statements or inferences do you derive from the study of your calculated data? Discuss.

Chapter 24

Quantity and quality controlling

Many receive advice;
only the wise profit by it.
Publilus Syrus

Two important and common areas of controlling are for quantity and for quality. With reference to the former, the ideal situation is to have materials, projects, and papers move in an orderly fashion in accordance with a desirable plan. For the latter, or quality controlling, the aim is to have sufficient control to insure that a specific quality of the product or service is supplied. In this chapter, we deal first with quantity controlling, followed by quality controlling.

CONTROLLING QUANTITY

In the typical enterprise, materials, products, and papers from various and widely dispersed sources are procured, processed, and redistributed to various geographical areas. We would like to have the flow moving in a manner that gets the right things at the right places and at the right times. With a host of different items handled, a variety of machines employed, various skills utilized, and the general activity fluctuating, the complexity of quantity controlling is quickly perceived.

Figure 24–1 shows the typical flow. For simplicity, only three raw materials and one finished product are depicted. Beginning at the left, the securing of materials from various suppliers can be termed *input*. Where required, flow of these materials is physically regulated by means of utilizing storage facility S as shown in the figure. The materials are processed, that is, subjected to manufacturing operations transforming them into a desired product. This can be termed *process*. Last, the finished products are distributed to customers, either by sending direct to customer or by utilizing warehouse facility W from whence shipment is made to the customer. This phase of business can

FIGURE 24–1:   Quantity flow of materials in a manufacturing enterprise

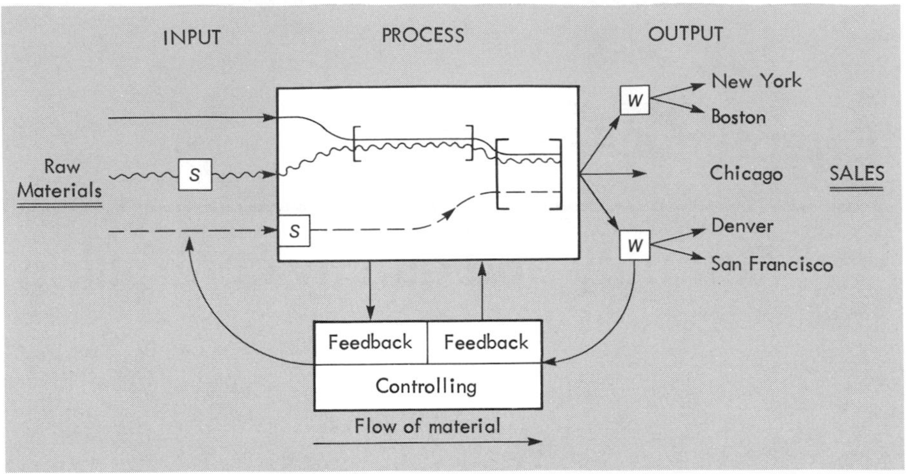

be termed *output*. Hence, the physical quantity flow of material is regulated when needed by means of a storage facility and a warehouse facility. In addition, there is a controlling unit which determines what materials, when, and where will be permitted. In other words, this unit controls the quantity of material for the entire system, *input–process–output*, by measuring the performance or flow, comparing it with prescribed standards, and determining the amount of correction or feedback, if any. It is performing the control process dealing with quantity. Its action plus usage of storage and warehouse facilities implements the quantity controlling work.

SALES AND QUANTITY CONTROLLING

The ultimate regulator of the flow of materials through the manufacturing cycle is effective consumer demand. In the final analysis, this is the real reason for the existence of the entire system. Usually over a period, there are inevitably variations in consumer demand. To a great degree, both the flow of *input* and *process* can be controlled to harmonize with these demand variations of *output*. For any given case, the scope of quantity controlling depends upon the individual situation. Some include relatively small areas, while others are quite extensive in scope. In the interest of clarity, it is desirable to select an area which is important, basic, and about which there is usually some knowledge. Hence, for purposes here the subject of quantity controlling as applied to sales has been selected.

QUANTITY CONTROLLING OF SALES

Effective quantity controlling of products and services is conditioned by good control over the sales efforts. Without adequate sales control unbalanced sales exist, i.e., those products are being sold that are easiest to sell. It is also common to find that only certain customers are being sold. Some buyers are called on regularly, while others are called on infrequently or not at all. Without sales control there is also the tendency for some sales areas to be much stronger than other areas, and the gap between the good and the bad areas will tend to increase unless managerial efforts are made to correct the situation. In addition, some areas are quite likely to have a deficit, while others will have a surplus of sales personnel. To be sure, quantity controlling can be applied to products and services moving to markets no matter where these markets are, but the most effective quantity controlling is possible when effective sales control exists. Hence, we will point our discussion to sales control realizing this, in turn, is intimately connected with quantity controlling.

BASIS OF SALES CONTROL

While the measuring and the evaluating of sales performance are not especially difficult, the determination of the basis of control for sales is fraught with problems. In fact, *for sales, determination of the basis of control poses the real difficulties.* Hence, over the next several pages, we will discuss in the necessary detail how this basis of control is determined. Involved are three factors, (1) the sales control unit, (2) the sales potential for this unit, and (3) the characteristics of the sales outlet being employed for the distribution of the product or service.

Sales control unit

A sales control unit is normally a geographical area to which sales can be identified. Its use expedites such things as ascertaining the trend of sales, new accounts acquired, size of orders, and comparisons between sales and costs.

Common sales control units include (1) political units, such as states, counties, and cities; (2) marketing areas, such as consumer trading areas, wholesale trading areas, and sales territories; and (3) areas in which certain industries or technical processes are concentrated, that is, textiles, chemical, aircraft, and electric motor manufacturing. In many instances, a state is too large a unit for effective control. If Ohio sales increased, it would be difficult to tell whether Dayton, Cincinnati, Cleveland, or another area or areas were mainly responsible for the change. However, states may prove useful control units for products where state regulations or taxation are involved, for example, in the sale of gasoline, and cigarettes. Counties and cities as control units provide a smaller and more self-contained unit; they are easily understood and especially helpful for companies selling in a limited territory.

For consumer goods, the consumer trading area as a control unit is common and offers many distinct advantages. A consumer trading area is a region about an important trading center from which buyers normally perform the major portion of their purchasing. The boundaries of a trading area are predicted upon the flow of trade, purchasing habits of consumers, size of trading center, nearness of other trading centers, and transportation facilities.

In the case of industrial product sales, the best control unit might constitute selected areas in which buyers of the product are located. The market for industrial products tends to be concentrated; hence, logical areas for control purposes must be selected accordingly. For example, bearings are not sold in all markets, as is the case with candy and chewing gum. The areas in which bearings are marketed make up the logical control units for that product.

From what has been stated it can be seen that a number of factors enter into the task of selecting the control unit. Generally speaking, the control unit should not include too many products or too great a geographical area. It should reflect self-contained areas of normal sales operation or of a usual line of products so that the results by control units are meaningful to the particular company using them. Comparisons betweeen costs and sales accomplishments should be expedited by the control unit selected. Abnormal conditions influencing sales either in one area or of one product should be minimized by the proper selection of the control unit.

Sales potential

Sales control requires an acceptable sales level or par which sets up the objective of the selling activities. Decisions whether to promote more vigorously in one area than another, to accept sales obtained for a product as satisfactory, or to hire more salespeople can best be reached when there is a sales potential—an established sales goal covering a definite period.

To establish these potentials equitably necessitates considerable data, judgment, and experience. The work can commence by dividing the entire market to be served into the greatest number of sales areas that the available funds for selling will provide. Next, estimate the total company sales for the next period. This involves evaluation of the general market conditions, the ability of the company to produce, and its requirements. The subsequent step is to pro rate the total sales figure among the individual sales areas. This is based on the inherent characteristics which are known or believed to influence sales areas. Some areas are capable of buying more than others, for example, the Chicago area compared to the Rockford, Illinois, area. How much more the potential in Chicago is over that of Rockford depends upon the factors considered and the weights attributed to each one. The factors used must have a causal relationship to the product being sold. Past sales, number of persons employed, buying power, and age are factors commonly used.

Characteristics of sales outlets

The third consideration in the establishing of a basis for sales control is the characteristics of sales outlets. Not all outlets are identical in makeup; they differ in regard to size, type of ownership, management, methods of purchasing, and, in the case of industrial goods, for what type of industrial product or service the goods are being bought. Any program of sales control is affected by these outlet characteristics, and their influence should be taken into account whenever possible.

Figure 24–2 shows an interesting breakdown of sales data of retail

FIGURE 24–2: Boston sales district breakdown

Sales District Code	Broker- age Area Code	All Retail Outlets		Total Grocery		Total Independents		Total Chains		Popula- tion 1970
		Stores	Sales ($000)	Stores	Sales ($000)	Stores	Sales ($000)	Stores	Sales ($000)	
2	203	220	$14,918	31	$4,918	27	$2,393	4	$2,525	21,614

Independent Split—By Volume Group							
Under 50 M		50–100 M		100–300 M		Over 300 M	
Stores	Sales ($000)	Stores	Sales ($000)	Stores	Sales ($000)	Stores	Sales ($000)
10	$350	13	$972	3	$731	1	$340

Courtesy A. C. Nielsen Company, Chicago

outlets in a Boston sales district. In this area, there are a total of 220 retail outlets with total sales of $14,918,000. Of these outlets, a total of 31 are grocery retail outlets, accounting for $4,918,000 of sales. In turn, these 31 grocery outlets shows that 27 are independents (independently owned) and 4 are chain stores. Furthermore, the independents vary considerably by sales volume: 10 independents do less than $50,000 annual sales, 13 stores from $50,000 to $100,000, 3 stores from

$100,000 to $300,000, and 1 store over $300,000. These data are included in the lower half of the illustration. If a company found that it paid to concentrate its sales efforts on outlets doing a sales volume of over $100,000 per year, only four independents and four chains would be visited by the company in the particular sales area discussed.

In addition, the somewhat intangible yet powerful considerations such as the buyer's attitude toward the company, extent of cooperation in use of display material, care taken in informing salespeople of the product's superior features, and interest in promoting sales are significant. Many companies make up route sheets for their salespeople so that important outlets are not overlooked, calls are not wasted on outlets that are too small, and a proper mix of independent and chain stores are called upon.

MEASURING SALES PERFORMANCE

With the basis of control established, the common control process of (1) measure performance, (2) compare performance with standard, and (3) correct deviation can be followed. We prefaced this with a discussion of establishing the standard because the measuring of performance must be in the same units as those of the standard, thus making valid the comparison between performance and the standard.

In the case of sales, the unit is commonly dollar sales, although product units, number of calls, number of prospects interviewed, number of displays set up, cities covered, or miles traveled may prove satisfactory and are easy-to-measure units. The choice depends upon the individual circumstances. Most sales activities are highly personalized—the human element is of great significance. Hence, the measuring of sales performance may stress information concerning the sales personnel activities. Figure 24–3 shows a weekly report which provides for summary information of salespeople's activities and important analysis and ratios. This type of information is helpful in knowing what sales work is going on in the field and, when compared with the basis of control, whether sufficient calls are being made, orders being secured, and promotional work in the form of displays being carried out.

Data for such a weekly summary report are obtained from salespeople's reports which are mailed daily to the sales office. The makeup of these reports varies considerably among different enterprises. Some require quite elaborate and detailed information, while others are simple statements of who was called on and the results of the interview. It is advisable to confine the sales reports to pertinent data only. Too much detail tends to dampen the salesperson's enthusiasm for such a program and the sales control efforts fall short of what they might be. On the other hand, sufficient data should be re-

FIGURE 24–3: Form for securing data used in sales control work

```
                    SUMMARY OF SALES STAFF'S ACTIVITIES
                                          Week ending: _____
  1.  Total days reported:
  2.  Total calls on wholesalers:
  3.  Total orders from wholesalers:  _____    $ _____
  4.  Total calls on retailers:          (number)        (dollars [approx.])
  5.  Total orders from retailers:    _____    $ _____
  6.  Displays set up:                    (number)        (dollars [approx.])
      Window:
      Island:
      Other . . . . . . . . . . . :
        _____ :
        _____ :            _____
      Total
- - - - - - - - - - - - - - - - - - - - - - - - - - - - - - - - - - - - - - - - -
      Analysis                  Wholesalers           Retailers
  1.  Average calls daily  . . . . . . . . . . . . . . .
  2.  Order-to-calls ratio  . . . . . . . . . . . . . . .
  3.  Average-size order in dollars  . . . . . . .  $                    $
  4.  Displays-to-calls ratio  . . . . . . . . . . . . .
```

quested to gain all the information deemed essential to the control work. To illustrate, this might require from each salesperson a daily report including the name and address of each prospect called upon; what, if any, sales orders were secured; the conditions of the dealer's stock; whether a display was installed; general comments about the sales interview, and an evaluation of future business prospects with each buyer.

Activities of competitors

The measuring of sales performance, as well as comparing it with the standard, must take into account how and what competitors are doing. Special promotional deals by competitors might call for a change in sales strategy by a company, with corresponding adjustments in its control pattern. The nearness of a competitor to a particular market might require special efforts by a company—efforts arranged and implemented through a sound sales control program. Although a competitor's efforts might be uniform throughout a large region, it is seldom that the effects of these efforts are uniform. What the effects are, segregated by small well-defined areas, furnishes the most useful information.

Some companies have their salespeople write informal reports every week or month outlining information on such subjects as the activities of competitors including the apparent results of their (competitors) special promotional efforts, including exhibits, samples, trade shows, and advertising campaigns. The content of such reports vary considerably.

Comparing sales performance with standard

By comparing the sales being accomplished with the standard or basis of control, the degree of market penetration is determined. This penetration is an indication of how successful a sales job is being done within the area considered. It is entirely possible to believe that area A with sales of $100,000 for the past year is doing a better job than area B with sales of $60,000. However, the true measurement of effectiveness takes into account the respective sales potentials of the two areas. Should the sales potential in area A be $200,000 and in B, $75,000, the degree of market penetration in A is 50 percent ($100,000/$200,000), while in area B, the penetration is 80 percent ($60,000/$75,000). In this illustration, area B is actually doing a better sales job, based on sales potentialities, than is area A. Information of this sort for all territories of a company is extremely valuable in controlling the sales efforts.

Correcting the sales deviation

When the sales performance is significantly less than its respective standard, the correcting of the deviation may take many different forms. The product or service may need revamping, price may require adjustment, or the use of different marketing outlets may be suggested. In many cases, however, improvements in the sales staff's effectiveness is sought. The better selection of personnel, more thorough sales training, improved motivation through sales contests, sales meetings, and incentive pay may be followed. Sometimes the sales standard or basis of control is adjusted. In any event, if sales are below expectancies, the proper quantity of goods or services moving through the normal channels of business is lacking and merits managerial attention.

CONTROLLING QUALITY

Another major type of controlling is that exercised to achieve a specific quality. Due primarily to the closer tolerances required for high-precision products, the demand for higher speeds of production, and the increasing demand for "trouble free" products, quality control has become a major consideration in today's industry. To most people the word quality means high quality and a consistent quality. But the more accurate and practical use of the term is that the quality is satisfactory for the intended purpose, is the best in terms of what price is acceptable for the product or service to which it applies, and is of a level that gives dependable results; i.e., the product or service always satisfies the need about quality. To help assure the proper quality, either or both (1) inspection and (2) statistical quality control are employed.

Inspection control

By inspection a manager seeks to determine the acceptability of the parts, products, or services. The basis for inspection control is usually a specification commonly referred to as an inspection standard. Inspection is made by comparing the quality of the product to the standard by means of a visual or a testing examination. Sometimes inspection reverts to a sorting procedure that classifies acceptable from unacceptable parts. Ingenious devices and machines have greatly simplified what formerly were difficult inspection tasks. The heaviest responsibility for inspection lies with manufacturing personnel—they make the product. Whether a product is acceptable or not is influenced chiefly by the operative personnel, whether they are concerned and want to make certain that proper quality is achieved. The inspector checks what has been made. But he or she should also serve as a helper in suggesting ways to improve or maintain the quality. The role is not all passive.

The question arises regarding how often inspection should be made. Usually the answer resolves to a consideration of what it costs to inspect versus what it costs not to. The challenge is to keep inspection costs minimum, yet insure desired quality. In some cases every part is inspected. This is called 100 percent inspection. When the inspection is less than 100 percent, it is termed partial or sampling inspection. Parts having high value or those showing from experience to have a tendency to run to a large number of rejects, are commonly subjected to 100 percent inspection.

In general, it is desirable to inspect (1) raw material to ensure manufacturing efforts are starting with proper materials, (2) finished parts and products to know that correct parts are to be assembled or products are right when shipped, (3) before a costly operation to make sure you're adding this operation on a proper base, (4) the output of automatic machines periodically so that possible errors are confined to small quantities, (5) before an item is covered as in an assembly so you know parts to be covered are right, and (6) before an operation that cannot be undone, for example, in mixing paint.

Statistical quality control

Statistical quality control (SQC) seeks to assist in controlling the process that produces the parts. In other words, it is preventive as well as remedial. It is based on the statistical theories and methods of probability to sample testing. Many of the efforts to insure proper quality have always been done on a sampling basis; that is, a relatively few of the entirety are inspected. However, with statistical quality control the risk involved in assuming the sample has the same characteristics as a lot is known, and better quality control with minimum inspection costs can be achieved. The risk is not eliminated, but the probability of the reliability of the samples is expressed in numerical terms.

Why use statistical quality control? First, it helps prevent defects from being made. In operation, accurate measurements of the parts at the machines are taken, compared to predetermined standards, and the decision reached whether the operation should continue or not. When and where to look for sources of trouble are revealed. Costly errors can be located and corrected before large scrap and rework losses due to quality deficiency occur. Another important reason for using statistical quality control is to supply an audit of quality regarding the producer's products. A universally understood measurement is supplied. In addition, the reasonableness of the quality standards established are checked. Frequently this is a "free extra" but in some cases quite important information to have.

The basis of statistical quality control

When a person makes many identical parts, some are a little large and some a little small, but most will be approximately the same. The middle or average will be the most frequent, with smaller and larger sizes as extremes from the average. When the frequency or count of the items by size is plotted with size on the horizontal scale and count on the vertical scale, what the statistician calls a normal, or bell-shaped, curve is obtained. A measure of the dispersion or spread of the sizes from the average or central tendency size is indicated by the standard deviation, which is a statistical concept calculated by (1) finding the difference between the arithmetic means of all sizes and the value of each size, (2) square each difference, (3) add the squared numbers and divide the sum by the number of items, and (4) take the square root of the quotient. For a normal distribution of sizes illustrated by a normal curve, 68.27 percent of the sizes will be between one standard deviation on either side of the arithmetic mean size, 95.45 percent between two standard deviations, and 99.73 percent between three standard deviations. Figure 24–4 illustrates these concepts.

The variations in size between 0.995 and 1.005, with most of the sizes at 1.000, can be considered due to chance. It is in the nature of things resulting from the process employed—the machine used and the part made—that this variation will take place within the pattern

FIGURE 24–4

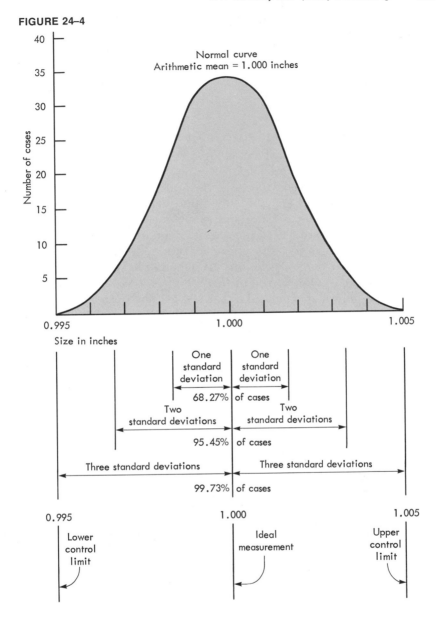

indicated. However, when from this same process a size is manufactured outside the limits indicated, it is not due to chance or expected variation but to an assignable cause. Stated differently, it is not normal, referring to Figure 24–4, for a size 1.007 to be made from this particular process. If a size 1.007 occurs, something has gone wrong in the process because this size out of normal limits is due to an assignable cause. Such a cause may be traced to such things as internal temperatures and friction changes of the machine parts, a dull tool, improper dimensions of raw material, or the setting of machine being changed unintentionally. Knowing when an improper size is made as a result of an assignable cause makes it feasible to stop the machine and find and rectify the cause.

CONTROL CHARTS

In actual practice, control charts are constructed so that an operator can tell whether the process is performing in a consistent, satisfactory manner. To construct a control chart, on-the-job data are collected from which an average and standard deviation values can be calculated. These values are then compared to the specifications or desired limits. If the actual values are within the specification limits, the process is all right or the limits can be narrowed since production already is concentrated in a narrow range. In contrast, if outside the specification limits, the process must be improved or the specifications loosened.

The general format of control charts shows time horizontally and the quality variations vertically. Samples of production are inspected periodically, perhaps hourly, every two hours, or daily, and the results plotted on the chart. If within the control limits, all is well; if without, corrective action is taken. Figure 24–5 shows a control chart with pro-

FIGURE 24–5:   Control chart for statistical quality control

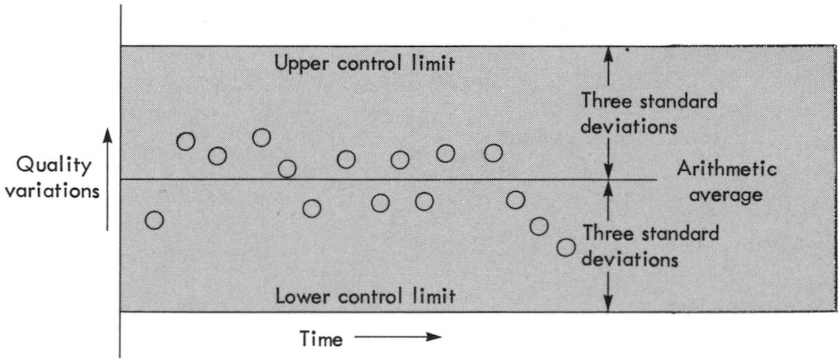

duction values plotted on it. Based on this illustration, the work being done is of a satisfactory quality since all the plotted values are within plus or minus three standard deviations of the arithmetic average. Each plotted value is obtained by averaging several specimens taken at the time indicated. (Frequently for each value the spread of these specimens is plotted on a range or bar chart which is not illustrated here.)

Some SQC people would state that a possible danger is indicated by the trend of the plotted values at the right of the chart in Figure 24–5. If successive readings continue this downward trend, a future reading could be below the lower control limit, thus signaling the quality is unsatisfactory and due to an assignable cause. In such an event, the process would be stopped; the assignable cause determined and corrected. The value of the limits establishing the width of the acceptance band can be calculated by several different statistical formulas, but in each case the fundamental basis is predicated upon the theories of probability and sampling. It is common practice to post the control chart near the site of the operation, not only for convenience but also to promote interest in quality work.

The above discussion is based on what is termed "variable inspection"; that is, the *measurement* of a characteristic is included. The average of measurements and deviations from this average are vital. In contrast, "attribute inspection" is concerned with whether a product is acceptable or not. An inspection of a finish on a product illustrates attribute inspection. The vital consideration in attribute inspection is the percentage of products rejected or as commonly expressed with ratios as the number of defects per 100 items. The average defective percentage or ratio along with the upper and lower limits are determined, similar to the method described above. Likewise, the interpretation of the chart is the same.

SUGGESTIONS FOR MAKING QUALITY CONTROLLING EFFECTIVE

Quality control is demanding work. The following commonsense guides for quality control management are highly recommended.

1. Define quality control being sought in terms of company's objectives. Be results-minded. View quality controlling in terms of its contributions and cost to the end objectives.

2. Keep manufacturing sharing responsibility for quality. Develop a congenial cooperative relationship with manufacturing personnel. Help them to be quality-minded and to realize they are an important part of whether required quality levels are attained.

3. Use cost-of-quality reporting. Know how well quality control is in comparison with the quality plan. Through proper reports and data be able to talk in managerial terms of quality costs, return on investment, and specific causes of quality difficulties.

4. Investigate every detail in seeking the answer to "What can go wrong?" and "What has gone wrong?" Although sometimes unpleasant, it is quality control's responsibility to lead the way in finding potential sources of difficulties.

5. For a new product, insist on a trial production run under regular manufacturing conditions.   Only in this way can you be reasonably certain the quality of the product is satisfactory and compatiable with the process used. Accepting a product development process of a pilot or experimental run is not reliable and can give rise to problems involving quality control.

QUESTIONS

1. Discuss the importance and implications of the sales control unit in sales controlling.
2. Enumerate the more important considerations entering into the task of selecting the control unit for quantity sales controlling.
3. Discuss the influence of competitors' activities upon sales controlling efforts of company A and relate what the sales manager of company A can do about such activities.
4. Distinguish carefully between the two concepts in each of the following: (*a*) control chart of statistical quality control and a standard deviation, (*b*) sales control unit and *input*, and (*c*) *output* and a bell-shaped curve.
5. What differences, if any, are there between standards and sales potentials? Explain.
6. A friend asks you, "Why isn't simply comparing actual sales with expectancy of sales a good way to control sales quantity?" What is your answer?
7. Describe the meaning of Figure 24–1 in your own words.
8. Suggest ways in which deviation from a sales standard may be remedied. Discuss one of these ways in some detail.
9. What is the widely accepted meaning of quality? Is it in keeping with practical quality control? Why?
10. Enumerate five recommendations as to where and when inspection is desirable.
11. Suggest several ways in which quality controlling can be made more effective.
12. Explain the significant differences between inspection and statistical quality control.
13. Do you agree with this statement: Controlling, no matter how carefully devised, will not ensure that satisfactory quality products are being manufactured. Justify your answer.
14. Interpret the meaning of a statistical control chart where all the recorded values taken every half hour for the past 24 hours have been between one and two standard deviations below the arithmetic average.

CASE 24–1.   SETTLE MANUFACTURING COMPANY

A special unit made of plastic and wood has been supplied to Everett Electronics Corporation for the past 17 months. To date, six different orders, each for 5,000 units, have been supplied at a selling price of $10 each. Material cost for each unit is $1.10; labor cost for each unit is $2.85.

The sales representative of Settle Manufacturing Company has tried to get the purchasing agent at Everett Electronics to place a contract for these units with her company and has offered a selling price of $8.90 each for a contract specifying a minimum of 15,000 units to be delivered over a six-months' period. However, the purchasing agent claims he doesn't know how many of these units, if any, of this design he will need in the future. The sales representative says the purchasing agent has been telling her this since the second order was placed some 15 months ago. In the opinion of the sales representative, it is probably a 50–50 chance that Everett Electronics Corporation will continue to buy the unit for at least the next nine to ten months.

Another purchase order for 5,000 of the units was received today. The vice president of production favors making 15,000 of these units in the production run. To justify this view, the vice president points out that the setup cost for the machines to make the units is $12,500, the reduction in material cost would amount to 10 percent, and the past usage by Everett of about 5,000 units every three months appears reasonable. However, more importantly, he sees greater profitability in manufacturing the unit, if Settle Manufacturing Company produces them in larger quantities.

The accounting department estimates that it will cost 8¢ per month per unit for storage and that the salvage value is $1.00 per unit.

Questions

1. Calculate the following: (a) for 5,000 unit manufacturing lot, the difference between the total revenue and total manufacturing cost; (b) for 15,000 unit manufacturing lot, the difference between the total revenue and total manufacturing cost assuming buyer purchases 5,000 units now, 5,000 units in three months, and 5,000 units in six months; (c) same as (b) except buyer purchases only 5,000 units now; (d) same as (b) except buyer purchases only 5,000 units now and 5,000 units in three months.

2. What alternatives are available to Settle Manufacturing Company? Elaborate on your answer.

3. What decision do you believe the management of Settle Manufacturing Company should reach? Why?

CASE 24–2. BLAKE CORPORATION

For some time the manufacturing of a small shaft used in a typewriter has presented a quality problem for the Blake Corporation. The shaft must be held to tolerances of plus or minus .0015 from the critical 0.5000 dimension. Due to the volume required, three similar machines are used to produce these shafts. Quality control manager John Ludlow believes a process capability or machine accuracy study should be made so that the abilities of the production machines can be determined and catalogued. In this way, Mr. Ludlow contends, information will be known whether the machines being used are satisfactory in view of the tolerances needed.

Accordingly, for each of the three machines, he made measurements of 30 consecutive shafts in the exact order in which they were made. Readings by machines are shown in Exhibit 1.

EXHIBIT 1

Machine 1	Machine 2	Machine 3
.5008	.5006	.4988
.5012	.5003	.4986
.5013	.5001	.4990
.5009	.4996	.4990
.5011	.5001	.4989
.5007	.5000	.4995
.5007	.4995	.5001
.5005	.4998	.5007
.5000	.5000	.5012
.5001	.4999	.5018
.4998	.4996	.5005
.4990	.4998	.5000
.4989	.5001	.4990
.4993	.5000	.4980
.4991	.5000	.4980
.4988	.4999	.4977
.4994	.4998	.4985
.4997	.5001	.4995
.5000	.4999	.5003
.5010	.5000	.5010
.5005	.5003	.5016
.5006	.4998	.5020
.5010	.4998	.5021
.5003	.5000	.5015
.5000	.5001	.5008
.5010	.4997	.5013
.5005	.4996	.5019
.5008	.5000	.5014
.5000	.5001	.5020
.4994	.5003	.5017

Mr. Ludlow indicated that 30 for the number of readings was arbitrary, that 250–300 would be better, but that the readings made would be indicative, if not conclusive.

The supervisor, Marty Hogan, said he believed the operator and the material have a lot to do with the quality. "They can't be ignored," he claims. "I've seen it many times—an inadequately skilled operator can impair the output of the best machine made. Even if you know or think you know the machine is OK, it doesn't ensure proper quality."

"You have a point there Marty, but on this work, the work of loading the material into the machine is quite simple," replied Kevin Kennedy, factory superintendent. "You know the material is from Super Products, a most reliable source. Plus our tests show the material to be homogeneous and right on the button with respect to specifications."

Questions

1. What significance are you inclined to give the viewpoints expressed by Mr. Kennedy? By Mr. Ludlow? By Mr. Hogan? Discuss.

2. Draw the control chart for each machine. The upper limits will be 0.5015 (0.5000 + .0015), and the lower limit 0.4985 (0.5000 − .0015).

3. Are the three machines satisfactory for manufacturing the small shafts? Justify your answer.

4. What is your recommendation to the Blake Corporation? Why?

Chapter 25

Time use, cost, and budgetary controlling

Take time to work—it is the price of success;
Take time to think—it is the source of power;
Take time to play—it is the secret of perpetual youth;
Take time to read—it is the fountain of wisdom;
Take time to be friendly—it is the road to happiness;
Take time to laugh—it is the music of the soul.

Old English prayer

Time is our most unique resource. It is scarce, it is totally inealstic, and it is totally perishable. Time cannot be stored and it cannot be regained. All persons have the same amount of time at their disposal. It is how a person uses one's time that counts. The allotment of time can't be increased, but the return from the use of time can be increased by effective management. Hence, time use is a cardinal factor of much controlling and is a challenge faced by most management members.

PERSONAL TIME USE BY MANAGER

Controlling time use starts with a manager's efficient use of time. In fact, one of the first criteria for success in management is to learn to manage your time. The issue to be resolved is: Do you make effective use of time or do others decide how you use time? In other words, is time managing you or are you managing time? Minutes and hours should be used purposefully. Low achievers lose primarily because they fail to put time to work for them.

A good starting point is to gain information of your present time expenditure pattern. For this purpose, keep a daily log by 15-minute intervals as to what activity is performed. A form like that shown in Figure 25–1 is helpful. For the appropriate period, the activity is written in, a checkmark made in the proper column whether managerial or

546

FIGURE 25–1: Daily log sheet

TIME	ACTIVITY	IS ACTIVITY		COMMENTS
		MANAGERIAL	NONMANAGERIAL	
8:30				
8:45				
9:00				
9:15				
9:30				
9:45				
		%	%	
TOTALS				

nonmanagerial, and comments added. At the end of the day, the totals and respective percentages are calculated. Similar log sheets are made out for each working day for a period of 12 weeks, which is sufficiently long to supply a representative picture of the various activities. A manager should make one's own activity audit. He or she is the one involved and is the one to benefit.

These fundamental data are then analyzed with a view to gain understanding of how time is being used and deciding how time can be put to better use. That is, improvements are sought; time robbers are eliminated. Interruptions, trivia, and nonessential activities are reduced. The manager may have to say "no" more frequently to nonessentials seeking one's attention. The really essential activities are identified, but in this work it is best not to be too ambitious. Reasonable goals achieved are more satisfying.

Having determined what to do, the next step is to schedule the events by proposed time expenditures. If possible, assignments should lead into one another. Varying the types of work helps maintain interest in it. Expect interruptions and allow for them in the schedule, but don't let them get out of hand. A manager should know when he or she works best—at the beginning of the day, at the end, first of week, or whatever it is. Then schedule the toughest jobs for this period. It is helpful to take the 15 minutes at the end of each day to firm up the schedule for the following day.

When a person performs work in a manner and sequence planned, the probability is that the best use of time is being followed. Unforeseen occurrences or emergencies will arise but these can be minimized by anticipating situations that result in emergencies and avoiding them. Urgency is not the same as productivity. However, the planning should allow accessibility to a manager. Being inaccessible frequently prevents a manager from knowing what is going on. The ability to discriminate between what is important and what is not is paramount.

TIME USE AND PRODUCTION CONTROL

An excellent example of time-use controlling is that included under the common term of production control. With respect to a given production order, this control is performed to assist in utilizing designated materials, machines, and workers for the proper amount of time and at the right time. Production control, as the term is commonly used, is not restricted to time use controlling only.

Production control data normally includes the amount, type, and kind of materials required for each manufacturing order released to the factory. The necessary material must be on hand or be delivered by a definite date in order that production can be started and continued. To expedite material requirements, notices or requisitions to purchase showing complete data on required material and when needed are sent to the purchasing department. Commonly such data are called bills of materials.

The manufacturing process, made up of various sequential production operations, is determined by production planning. But the meshing together of all production orders so that the best total pattern of activities is followed is the contribution of production control. By best pattern is meant that dovetailing of various requested production efforts which supply the finished products when desired at a minimum of time and cost. This usually entails maximum machine utilization, full use of operators' skills, adequate material available and ready for use, and efficient intraplant materials handling. For purposes of this discussion and also in the interest of clarity, we can consider the essential production data utilized in production control as consisting of (1) routing, (2) scheduling, and (3) dispatching. The first two, routing and scheduling, are basically planning efforts. They supply production expectancies and are included here to provide the needed background for the third activity, or dispatching, which is essentially a controlling function.

Routing

Routing concerns the establishment of the path which the production will take in its travel through the plant. The route sets forth the operations to be performed and the sequence to be followed. The machines, attachments, and work areas to be utilized at each production step are indicated. In some cases, the specific machine to be used is designated, while in other cases only the machine division is named, in which case the supervisor determines which particular machine will be used. Routing also provides data on the time allowed to complete each respective operation. These values are usually obtained from the use of time standards. Frequently, the route sheet is supplemented by drawings, blueprints, instruction sheets, or any information helpful in the handling of the order.

Scheduling

Scheduling is the assigning of time values (clock or calendar) for carrying out the various operations in an orderly and synchronized manner. Figure 25–2 shows a popular type of chart used for this purpose. Its general appearance is that of a large visible file with overlapping pockets hanging vertically. At the extreme left, cards similar to those used in regular visible files are inserted in the visible margins, a separate card being used for each order. Pertinent data covering the order are written on the card. In the extension of the visible margin to the right, a "loader card" is inserted for each operation indicating the scheduled starting and total time to complete the operation. Time is shown horizontally. The length of the card represents the scheduled time for an operation. For example, on the top line, order No. 17542, the first operation is shear and is scheduled to start at period 5; the time scheduled is 40 periods, so the card extends from 5 to 45.[1] The next operation is blank, requiring 30 periods. It is scheduled to follow the previous operation immediately, or from 45 to 75. The next operation, form, begins at 85. Nothing is scheduled between periods 75 and 85 on this order, and so a blank or white space appears in the visible margin. Different color stripes on the bottom of the loader cards are used to indicate different operations. In Figure 25–2 these are shown by different designs and crosshatching.

The controlling aspects of the chart are the indications of the production progress of each operation. This is accomplished by means of a color signal, moved across the margin of the card as the work progresses (vertical mottled spaces on chart). For order No. 17542 the signal is approximately at period 68, and it is the same for order No. 17543. The vertical line transcribing all margins at period 85 is the "Today" or present time. Comparing the signals on each order with the "Today" line shows whether the order is behind, on, or ahead of schedule. In the illustration, order Nos. 17542, 17543, and 17546 are

---

[1] On the scale of periods of the chart the segment identified by number 1 means 0 to 10 units, so that unit 5 is midway of this segment. Likewise, unit 45 is midway of segment identified with a 5 on the chart.

FIGURE 25-2: A chart illustrating scheduling of orders by operations

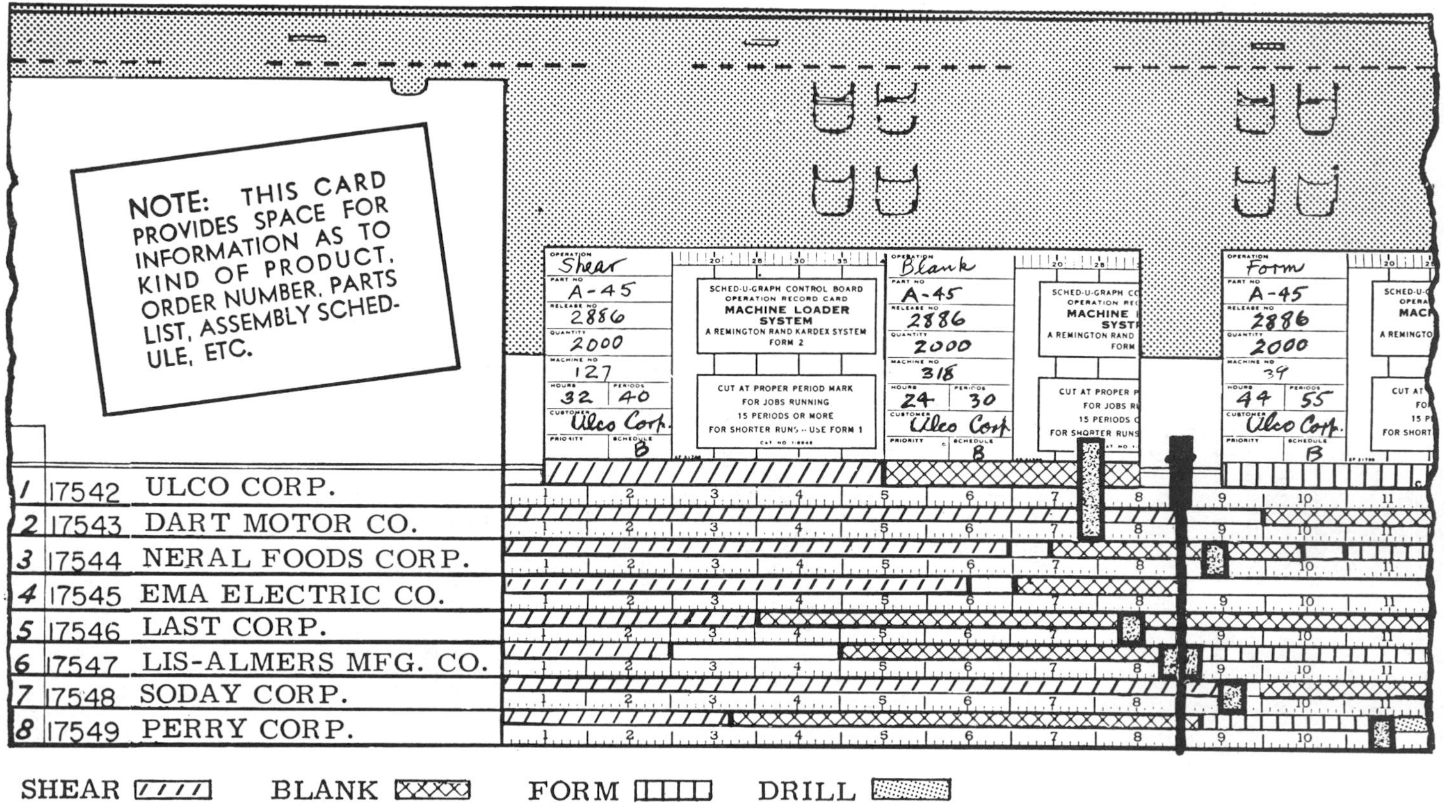

SHEAR ⬚⬚⬚   BLANK ⬚⬚⬚   FORM ⬚⬚⬚   DRILL ⬚⬚⬚

behind schedule, order No. 17547 is on schedule, and order Nos. 17544, 17548, and 17549 are ahead of schedule.

Orders should not be completed too far in advance of the time scheduled, otherwise extra handling and storing are required. In contrast, orders completed after the scheduled time may cause costly delays and possible disruption of the smooth flow of subsequent operations.

Dispatching

This last part of production control emphasizes conformity with plans and correction of the deviation, if any. Dispatching provides the authority to move what materials where and when. It maintains the scheduled movement of materials through the plant. Dispatching includes securing reports on work progress, informing on the progress at each key production step, and handling of emergency situations, such as machine breakdown, shortage of help, and excess waste of material. These reports might take the form of cards upon which operators report their time, a trucker's card that material has been moved to another area, or a message telephoned by the supervisor to the dis-

FIGURE 25–3: **A move ticket**

Mfg. Order No. S29735	Quantity 1,500	Part No. ZV22R8	Class 2

Style Regular	Spec. No. 383S54	Design R-13	Special Notes
Specifications of Material XXND-59 Plastic Sheet 0.320" x 9/32' wide 1/4" Blank			None

Deliver to _____ Dept. No. __44__ Machine No. __12__ Area No. __—__	Delivery time _____ Date __1-/5/7-__ Clock time __11:05 A.M.__ Delivered by _____ (Signed)	Receiving time _____ Date _____ Clock time _____ Received by _____ (Signed)

patching unit. Figure 25–3 illustrates a dispatching move ticket which serves as written authority to convey a specific lot of material to the next department and machine at which the immediately successive operation will be performed.

CONTROLLING OF COST

Cost as a factor for controlling is generally recognized as an indication of managerial efficiency. The capability and quality of managers to get out the work is important, be it selling or producing, but this achievement *at what cost* is a further consideration of managerial effectiveness. In the case of most enterprises, over the long period of time, total costs must be covered by total income; otherwise the enterprise will cease to exist.

Cost, represented by dollar expenditures, must apply to a known physical unit which determines the quantity and the identity of the part, and operations. Trade practices, experience, and desires of management members are among the important factors affecting the choice of the cost unit.

The first step of cost controlling is to measure performance in terms of cost. We start with specifying the particular type of cost being used. Four common types of cost are (1) material, (2) labor, (3) selling, and (4) overhead. With the exception of overhead, costs are commonly segregated under the headings of (1) direct and (2) indirect. Figure 25–4 shows the common cost types.

These four common costs are interrelated and give rise to other types of cost. These are illustrated in Figure 25–5. For example, direct material cost plus direct labor cost equals *prime* cost which added to *factory overhead* cost equals *manufacturing cost.*

How are cost data on current activities collected? There are several sources. For example, direct material cost is ascertained by means of adequate records maintained as a part of normal purchasing practices. The invoice price, less discounts, transportation, and special charges are known for every item purchased. In many cases, these net purchase prices are reduced to cost per selected unit and posted on the records of the storeroom. Normally, material is issued by the storeroom or stores department only upon receipt of a properly signed requisition, and this practice provides an allocations record so that the proper amount and kind of material can be charged to the proper cost unit.

The direct labor cost data are obtained by having the employee keep a record of the job order number worked on, the operation performed, and the time spent on each operation. These data are written on labor time cards which are simply an accounting by the employee of how time was spent. The validity of the data depend upon the employee's understanding of the purpose and use of such information, the desire to cooperate, the importance attached to such information by managers, and the effectiveness of supervision.

Factory overhead cost is calculated in a number of ways, but taking a certain percentage of either material or labor, or both, is a common

FIGURE 25–4: Common types of cost segregated as direct or indirect

	Expenditures	
	Direct	*Indirect*
Material	Expenditures for materials which are or become a part of the product or service. *Examples:* Sheet metal, cloth, wire, and wood which are allocable to the specific product or service.	Expenditures for materials not a part of the product or service but required in executing the work. *Examples:* Cleaning compound and sandpaper.
Labor	Expenditures for labor which has a bearing straight upon the product or service. *Examples:* Machine operator, assembler, and packer.	Expenditures for labor which does not have an immediate or a straight connection to the product or service. *Examples:* Trucker, cost clerk, and methods person.
Selling	Expenditures for sales activities which are immediate and without an intervening influence upon the sales of the product or service. *Examples:* Commission payments to sales staff and salespeople's salaries.	Expenditures for sales activities which are not of an immediate or straight influence upon the sales of the product or service. *Examples:* Advertising, market research, sales offices, and cost of training sales personnel.
Overhead	Expenditures for all activities which are not allocable exclusively to material, labor, or selling. Overhead costs are in addition to material, labor, and selling costs and considered as one group, i.e., not segregated into direct and indirect. *Examples:* General managerial costs, legal expenditures, depreciation, insurance, rent, light, power, and telephone.	

practice. However, the allocated estimates of factory overhead made to separate cost units must add up to the actual total factory overhead costs; otherwise some of the cost units are not supporting their proper burden. To meet this requirement, adjustments in overhead sometimes must be made. Selling expense is obtained from records maintained by the sales department. Likewise, general administrative cost is determined from information maintained by the accounting department.

FIGURE 25-5

Total cost is commonly considered as made up of several component costs.

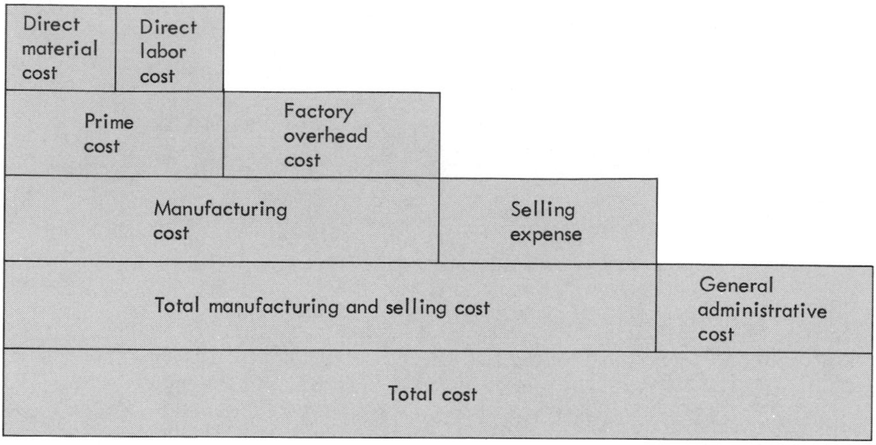

Direct material cost	Direct labor cost			
Prime cost		Factory overhead cost		
Manufacturing cost			Selling expense	
Total manufacturing and selling cost				General administrative cost
Total cost				

OVERHEAD COST

Overhead cost, from the viewpoint of expenditures for all activities not allocable exclusively to material, labor or selling, significantly affects cost information and merits further discussion. These costs are determined by numerous influences, including the circumstances surrounding a given enterprise, the product or service manufactured or sold, and the manner of managerial operations. Overhead costs are an individual consideration and must be evaluated for each enterprise. For example, some units probably require more of the activities going to make up overhead costs than do other units. The majority of an executive's time might have been devoted to solving the problems in producing and selling product X, and little, if any, attention was given to products Y and Z. Also important is the extent and action of competition. Most enterprises have the problem of keeping their prices competitive but at the same time of securing their overhead costs as required for survival. To allocate too much overhead on a product might result in "pricing themselves out of the market." Competition might permit more overhead on certain items and less overhead on others.

Generally speaking, rates dealing with time are preferable to those dealing with dollars. This follows from the fact that most elements making up overhead costs are functions of time, that is, depreciation, insurance, salaries, and rent; hence, time rates are likely to move in step with overhead charges.

Overhead costs are rarely uniform throughout an entire organization; they will be greater in some areas than in others. This suggests the desirability of establishing various overhead costs for different areas in keeping with their respective overhead requirements. With this in mind, overhead cost rates can be based on any of three major bases: (1) on the plant as a whole, (2) on each department, and (3) on each cost center.

Methods of distributing overhead costs

How are overhead costs distributed? Figure 25–6 gives six different ways. No one basis is ideal for all products of an enterprise; selection

FIGURE 25–6

Method of distributing overhead costs	Formula	Expressed in terms of
1. Direct labor hours	Total overhead costs ÷ Total direct labor hours	Dollars per direct labor hour
2. Direct labor costs	Total overhead costs ÷ Total direct labor dollars	Percentage of overhead per direct labor costs
3. Direct material costs	Total overhead costs ÷ Direct material costs	Percentage of overhead per direct material dollar
4. Product unit	Total overhead costs ÷ Total number of product units	Dollars per product unit
5. Machine rate	Overhead for machine ÷ Machine-hours	Dollars per machine-hour
6. Cost center	Overhead for selected group of machines ÷ Machine-hours	Dollars per selected group of machine-hours

should be made on what is believed will result in the most accurate and useful cost control.

The first, or *direct labor hours,* is popular and simple to apply. It is useful where labor is the main productive element or represents a large portion of the total cost. However, this method ignores variations in size and type of equipment. An hour of direct labor might mean a worker operating a simple lathe in one case; while in another instance it might include a huge and complicated punch and forming machine. The second, *direct labor costs,* or hours times rate per hour, is similar to direct hours, except the hours are weighted according to the wage rate structure. Where the variances in wage rates are small, the results from direct labor costs and direct labor hours are nearly identical. The use of *direct material costs* assumes that variations in direct material are in direct proportion to variations in overhead costs. This is true for some continuous manufacturing processes. The fourth, *product unit,* is easy to use, and it provides satisfactory results for large-volume manufacturing of a single product or of a few that are quite uniform and similar. Fifth, *machine rate,* is most helpful where machines are an important productive element and overhead costs are influenced far more by machines than labor time or cost. Last, *cost center* is the machine rate method extended to include several machines which are normally used as a unit or center in the production process. This method simplifies the distribution of overhead costs but like the machine rate requires extensive records and competent clerical personnel.

COMPARING COST PERFORMANCE WITH STANDARD

Comparing cost results with cost expectancies, or the second step of the familiar control process, reveals whether any cost variances exist. In most cases, the expectancy, or the standard, for cost control is the standard cost which is expressed in dollars and is a predetermined cost computed by an analyst. Standard cost is supposed to represent the normal amount of total expenditures, including material, labor, and overhead, for the accomplishment of the work. Strictly speaking, a standard employee using standard materials and methods should represent an expenditure equal to the standard cost.

From the practical viewpoint, another type of standard cost, called *basic standard cost,* is used. It is in the nature of a predetermined standard from which actual costs can be expressed as relative percentages with the basic standard cost as the base. For example, a basic standard cost might be $1; but under conditions of high material cost and labor rates, the actual cost might be $1.50. Knowing the variance and evaluating its amount, the basic standard cost is a perfectly valid basis of control, although it does not represent the standard cost, that is, the one under what is considered normal prevailing circumstances.

CORRECTING COST DEVIATIONS

Spotting the cause of a cost variance and taking steps to correct it are, of course, helpful. However, one of the most effective means for keeping costs in line is to acquire a cost consciousness among the entire work force. This is exemplified by helping every employee to think in terms of cost expenditures, to plan for keeping costs minimum, and for each employee to regulate one's work action so that the costs incurred are acceptable. That is, every employee should have the responsibility to control costs on all activities over which one has charge or has intimate influence in the normal sequence of the work.

From the practical viewpoint, implied in the meaning of cost controlling is usually cost reduction, even though current performance costs are well within the limits of cost expectancies. The constant challenge facing most managers is to reduce costs. For the most part, cost reduction is achieved by (1) preventing waste in materials and time, (2) improving the operational processes and methods, and (3) encouraging new ideas for more effective operations.

Cost reduction, however, is not too salable. The typical employee is not enthusiastic about lowering costs. It is usually necessary to explain why reductions are in order and how they will probably affect the employee. In many instances employee job security is improved through the lowering of costs. An employee should be informed regarding whether one's costs are satisfactory or not. In addition an employee needs to be informed about the effect of cost reduction upon one's job and that of co-workers. If loss of job is probable there is reasonable certainty that an employee cost reduction program will not be entered into heartily. If loss of job is involved, explanations of how necessary adjustments will be handled and the disposition of such things as layoffs, transfers, process changes, and the like should be covered in detail. It should also be pointed out that normally it is easier to find many small cost reductions than a few big ones, but the aggregate of the former make up sizable savings.

COST-EFFECTIVENESS METHOD AND VALUE ANALYSIS

Two additional concepts in cost reduction merit discussion. They are (1) cost-effectiveness method and (2) value analysis. The costing of a firm's resources cannot always be measured entirely in monetary terms nor do relative costs always reveal which of several activities is the most desirable or efficient. Consider the proposed cost or the allocation of funds for research facilities. The cost of a research and development endeavor is difficult to assess. Likewise, institutions such as hospitals and colleges face similar cost control questions because the value of their "product" is only partially economic.

An interesting form of cost effectiveness is planning-programming-budgeting-system (PPBS). It is an effort or a means to promote greater efficiency and economy by developing more rational approaches to decision making. Initiated by the U.S. Department of Defense, PPBS consists of identifying objectives and alternative methods of meeting the objectives being subjected to systematic analysis comparing projected costs with benefits. Focus is made on the output of a program and its judged values in relation to its projected cost. It is helpful in trying to arrive at a rate of return for a planned action. In addition, it helps identify what may have to be foregone when one action is selected over another. To illustrate, is it better for the federal government to expend $5 million for aid to public education or to assist in efforts to get rid of pollution by cleaning up the air and rivers?

Value analysis is a technique utilizing an organized creative approach to identify unnecessary costs in a product or service and subsequently substituting different materials and methods to obtain equal performance at lower cost. This technique, sometimes referred to as value engineering, can be used to reduce the cost of existent products or to assist in designing products before they are manufactured. The meaning of "value" as used in value analysis is established by comparison. It can be of two different types (1) *use* value or the properties and qualities that accomplish an activity and (2) *esteem* value which is the attractiveness and features that stimulate a buyer to own or to prefer the given product. Hence, by means of value analysis the objective is to achieve the lowest cost of providing acceptable performance and features the buyer's or user's wants.

The three basic steps of value analysis are: (1) identify the function, (2) evaluate the function by comparison, and (3) develop value alternatives. For each part of a product, these key questions are asked in order to identify unnecessary costs: What is the item? What does it cost? What does it do? What else will do the job? What will that cost? The answers obtained show what costs are unnecessary, what alternatives are available, and what the costs are of these alternatives. With this information the alternative giving the best value can be selected and utilized.

BUDGETARY CONTROLLING

Budgetary controlling is one of the most widely recognized and used means of managerial controlling. It encompasses the planning-controlling combination approach referred to in Chapter 22. Precisely it can be stated that *budgetary controlling is a process of finding out what's being done and comparing these results with the corresponding budget data in order to approve accomplishments or to remedy differences.* Budgetary controlling is commonly termed budgeting.

Fundamental budgetary considerations

In private industry, budgetary control begins logically with an estimate of sales and the income therefrom. This follows, since the ultimate controller is sales. However, in the case of governmental enterprises, the amount appropriated serves the same purpose as sales in private enterprises. In determining the sales estimates, the forecasting should be based on sound research to as great an extent as possible. Guesses should be confined to those areas in which no factual information is available. To expedite the forecasting work, at least in the initial stages, it is advisable to concentrate on the key items. Trying to do a complete study on every single item can result in doing a haphazard job on all items. Final estimates are a result of judgment plus careful analysis and interpretation of available factual informa-tion. Likewise, the probable selling expenses in attaining the esti-mated levels pose another problem of forecasting and require firsthand information and knowledge of the particular marketing activities.

Figure 25–7 shows a budget with estimates for sales and expenses for the first three months of the year, January, February, and March.

FIGURE 25–7:   A sales-expense budget

	January		February		March	
	Expec-tancy	Actual	Expec-tancy	Actual	Expec-tancy	Actual
Sales	$1,200,000		$1,350,000		$1,400,000	
Expenses:						
General overhead ...	310,000		310,000		310,000	
Selling	242,000		275,000		288,000	
Production	327,000		430,500		456,800	
Research	118,400		118,400		115,000	
Office	90,000		91,200		91,500	
Advertising	32,500		27,000		25,800	
Estimated Gross						
Profit	80,100		97,900		112,900	

Space is provided for entry of the actual accomplishments so that com-parison by each item between expectancy and actual is expedited. Note that the total expenses plus estimated gross profit equals the total sales expectancy.

Budgeting is based on data which are either of (1) a constant or (2) a variable classification. Constant means the budget standards are for a fixed or constant level; that is, the targets remain constant, and the estimates are believed to be based on a high degree of accuracy. In contrast, variable includes budgeted estimates at several levels so that variations in sales, production, cash, or other key data can be recog-nized.

Budgeting can be supplied to the total or any segment of an enter-prise. It is not confined to matters of finance. Units other than dollars are commonly used. For example, budgeting of production in physical units and of labor by different skills is extensively employed by indus-try.

Another consideration of budgeting is the budget period. All budgets are prepared for a definite time period. Many are for periods of one, three, and six months. One year is a common period. The length of time selected depends upon the main purpose of the budget-ing. The period chosen should include the complete normal cycle of activity for the enterprise. For example, seasonal variations should be included both for production and for sales. Commonly, the budget period coincides with other control devices, i.e., managerial reports, balance sheets, and statements of profit and loss. In addition, the extent to which reasonable forecasts can be made should be considered in selecting the budget period.

Budget estimates are adjusted as developments take place and more information becomes available. One common approach involves a periodic review tied in with a progressive moving average. To illustrate, an enterprise might forecast for the next 12-month period in March, June, September, and December. In March, 1978, the estimate would cover March 1978–March 1979; in June, 1978, for June 1978–June 1979; etc. Progressive adjustments are possible in connection with each forecast. An alternate is to make a yearly forecast in January with revised forecasts in March, June, and September for the remaining months of the year. Some companies follow what can be termed "moving budgeting" which features a yearly forecast, then as each month is completed, another month is added to the period. For example, at the completion of November 1978, a forecast for November 1979 is added so that a moving 12-month forecast is maintained. Regardless of the practice adopted, revisions are made at any time when believed necessary.

It requires time to achieve a level of effective budgetary control. Too much should not be expected of budgetary control within too short periods of time. It requires time-consuming experience, judgment, and a desire to make budgeting effective before tangible and good results are attained. Habits are not changed overnight. Experienced managers neither expect to correct deep-seated difficulties instantly nor to witness sudden miracles as a result of budgetary control.

Applying budgetary control

Variances are almost certain to appear and should be expected within reasonable limits. Any operation which is clearly out of line should be noted and possible reasons for the difference ascertained. It is the duty of the budget director to review the results with the responsible operating heads or department heads concerning matters relating to their particular activities. Assistance should be given the person in charge of the activity to discover and to curb unfavorable departures or trends. Suggestions are in order as to what remedial actions might be taken; information and assistance in seeking improvements should be stressed.

In most cases, utilizing participation of the people involved in the work that has proven below par will prove effective. The budgetary process should serve everyone concerned; it should not be viewed as the exclusive controlling mechanism of top management members.

And in turn, let the person responsible for the particular work under question inform those who performed the work of the results and enlist their suggestions and cooperation in what can be done to correct the undesired variances.

Budgeting, like any activity, requires the support of top management. For the most part, employees will view the importance of budgeting in the same light that top management members do. Hence from time to time and as the occasion requires, meetings, special drives, contests, and the like can be utilized effectively to improve and maintain budgeting efforts. Budgetary meetings, for example, are of great assistance in ironing out differences of opinion and in reaching mutual agreements on what should be done.

Usually the budget director sends copies of all budget reports issued to various department heads and to one's superior or the top-ranking executive over all budgeting activities. This not only keeps the chief executive informed but also helps assure proper backing on corrective actions recommended by the director. Simple, yet concise, timely, and complete reports should be issued.

It is recommended that specific approval be required for non-budgeted items. From time to time, unforeseen items are included in the budget. They should be specifically approved by the person in charge of the work. This fixes responsibility and makes the manager aware of these nonbudgeted items.

Like many practices in management, budgetary control has its proponents as well as it opponents. Commonly cited advantages as well as disadvantages are listed in Figure 25–8.

Human behavior and budgeting

When it is all said and done, the ultimate purpose of budgeting is to direct and control human behavior of managers and of nonmanagers. Unfortunately, the belief is common that budgeting is employed to utilize best a company's dollars and direct the actions of its management members. In too many cases it has become a tool emphasizing ends within itself. The fault lies mainly in the failure to recognize the human behavior inherent in controlling. Employees want budgeting to do something *for* them, not something *to* them.

The question is not whether budgetary controls are necessary, but are they being administered in a manner that makes them really effective. To those requested to abide by them, the requests or directives may not carry the importance or make the same sense as they do to the issuing party. Under such conditions the recipient cannot be enthusiastic about budgeting and may adopt an acquiescence, a grudging acceptance of it, or quiet subversion. The result is that subconsciously persons absolve themselves from responsibility for the budgeting re-

FIGURE 25–8. Commonly cited advantages and disadvantages of budgetary controlling

> Advantages:
> 1. Budgetary controlling is subject to human judgment and shortcomings. fostered.
> 2. Efforts are directed in the achievement of common goals.
> 3. Use of the principle of exception is emphasized.
> 4. Fixed responsibility is expedited.
> 5. Actions are likely to be prescribed only after study and careful consideration of the facts.
> 6. Weaknesses in the organization, managerial ability, and personnel are revealed.
> 7. Waste reduction is promoted; needless spending is minimized.
> 8. Labor and equipment utilization is stabilized and improved.
>
> Disadvantages:
> 1. 1. Budgetary controlling is subject to human judgment and shortcomings.
> 2. Budgetary controlling neither ensures satisfactory results nor controls automatically.
> 3. Adequate standards are mandatory and not always used.
> 4. Forecasting is required and it is fraught with uncertainties.
> 5. The data must be interpreted and proper evaluation given them.
> 6. The communication required with budgetary controlling is frequently lacking.
> 7. Success in budgetary controlling requires a long learning period.
> 8. Budgetary control requires much time, money, and effort for its successful use and to "keep it in line."

sults and make it appear that they are abiding by the controls when in reality they are busy minimizing them. The outcome is the loss of budgeting effectiveness.

Budgetary controlling handled in light of today's management knowledge does not lead to conflict. But certain beliefs about employees are necessary to achieve the most from budgetary controlling. Most managers and nonmanagers can relate their activities to company goals if they are told what the company goals are. Both top and lower level managers can be satisfied if both participate in formulating the controlling whereby they will be managed. Budgetary controlling is not a one-person operation, with a manager issuing orders and insisting that certain steps be followed. Effective budgetary controlling helps all members of a company do their jobs better. Everyone in the enterprise should participate and feel that the budgeting practices are assisting him or her and making the enterprise a better place in which to work.

FIGURE 25–9.   The drawing up of budgets

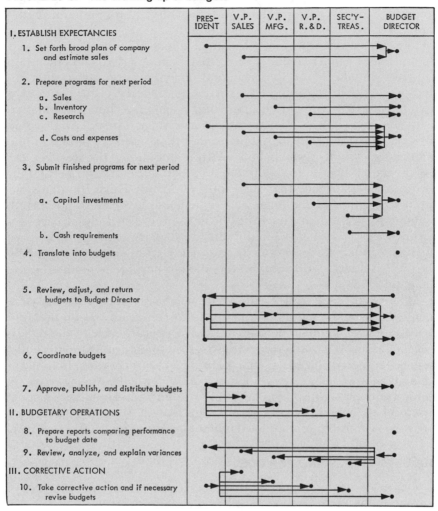

	PRES-IDENT	V.P. SALES	V.P. MFG.	V.P. R.&D.	SEC'Y-TREAS.	BUDGET DIRECTOR
I. ESTABLISH EXPECTANCIES						
1. Set forth broad plan of company and estimate sales						
2. Prepare programs for next period						
a. Sales						
b. Inventory						
c. Research						
d. Costs and expenses						
3. Submit finished programs for next period						
a. Capital investments						
b. Cash requirements						
4. Translate into budgets						
5. Review, adjust, and return budgets to Budget Director						
6. Coordinate budgets						
7. Approve, publish, and distribute budgets						
II. BUDGETARY OPERATIONS						
8. Prepare reports comparing performance to budget date						
9. Review, analyze, and explain variances						
III. CORRECTIVE ACTION						
10. Take corrective action and if necessary revise budgets						

Formulating the budget

A graphic presentation of this budget preparation is shown by Figure 25–9. Under the first heading of "Established Expectancies," there are seven steps, starting with the estimate of sales and ending with the approval of the budget and its publication. In addition, the chart indicates the efforts for budgetary controlling. The second heading of "Budgetary Operations," consisting of two steps, encompasses those portions of the control process dealing with finding out what is being accomplished and comparing it with the expectancy. The last heading, "Corrective Action," made up of one step, is the familiar, correcting deviation, if this is necessary. In most instances, a budget committee exists to formulate and to assist in implementing the budgetary work. Meetings of the committee, at which the budget director serves as chairperson, offer an excellent medium for coordinating the various functions, securing greater cooperation, and encouraging participation. Major departmental objectives and constraints are determined and this information is disseminated by the committee members to their respective interested members. Then the tentative estimates of each respective organization unit is prepared. All possible information is supplied so that plans are prepared in keeping with the general constraints established. Within due time, the various departmental estimates are completed and submitted to the budget director. A series of meetings then follows during which the plans are discussed, adjustments suggested, and possible changes indicated. Sometimes preliminary meetings between the director and each department head are held. Finally, all the departmental estimates are evolved in their final approved form. They are then consolidated by the budget director and submitted to the top-management member for final approval.

Although practices differ widely, normally a member of top management serves as the chief coordinator for drawing up the budget and using it. He or she need not necessarily be concerned with the details but should resolve conflicting interests, recommend adjustments when needed, and give official sanction to budgetary procedures. In the case of large enterprises, the development of the budget estimates may be guided and carried out by a specially designated executive. In some instances the job of budget controller is created. More commonly, the treasurer, controller, or chief accountant is charged with these duties.

BUDGETS—TYPES AND PERIODS

There are many types of budgets available. In the interest of simplicity the more common are listed as follows:

1. Sales budget.   Usually the data are given by months, sales areas, and product.

2. Production budget.   This is commonly expressed in physical units. Required information to prepare this budget includes: types and capacities of machines, economic quantities to produce, and availability of materials.

3. Cost production budget.   Sometimes this is included in production budget. Comparing production cost with sales price shows whether adequate margins are being obtained.

4. Step budget.   Shows the production estimate for various assumed levels of production or capacities of present production facilities.

5. Purchasing budget. Designed and used to minimize excessive material inventories and yet have a balanced and adequate inventory on hand at all times to satisfy projected production and sales.

6. Labor budget. Assists in determining the number and type of skills or people required. Demands are forecast from production and sales estimates.

7. Cash budget. This is a very important and really essential budget to every enterprise. It is best to prepare it after all other budget estimates are completed. The cash budget shows the anticipated receipts and expenditures, the amount of working capital available, the extent to which outside financing may be required, and the periods and amounts of cash availability.

Figure 25–10 shows a cash budget. Estimated sales for January are $130,000, with total receipts forecast at $180,500, some receipts being received from sales of former months. Disbursements during

FIGURE 25–10:   Work of cash budgeting

	Jan.	Feb.	March	April	May
Estimated sales	$130,000	$120,000	$170,000	$175,000	$160,000
Receipts:					
Accounts receivable	$ 8,000	$ 5,000	$ 12,000	$ 10,000	$ 8,000
Accounts receivale	132,500	100,000	85,000	108,000	117,000
Notes receivable	40,000	40,000	35,000	40,000	40,000
Total	$180,500	$145,000	$132,000	$158,000	$165,000
Disbursements:					
Direct labor	$ 45,000	$ 49,000	$ 49,000	$ 49,000	$ 51,000
Indirect labor	18,500	18,500	18,500	18,500	20,000
Purchases	24,000	57,000	72,000	55,000	50,000
Overhead salaries	9,000	9,000	9,000	9,000	9,000
Taxes	10,000	10,000	63,000	10,000	12,000
Insurance	—	—	—	2,800	—
Dividends	22,000	—	—	22,000	—
Total	$128,500	$143,500	$211,500	$166,300	$142,000
Excess or deficiency (*)	$ 52,000	$ 1,500*	$ 79,500*	$ 8,300*	$ 23,000
Cash balance at start of month	27,500	79,500	81,000	49,750	41,450
Borrow	—	—	48,250	—	—
Repay	—	—	—	—	—
Cash balance at end of month	$ 79,500	$ 81,000	$ 49,750	$ 41,450	$ 64,450

January are figured at $128,500, leaving an excess of $52,000 ($180,500 − $128,500). Since the cash balance at the start of the month is $27,500, the cash balance at the end of January will be $52,000 plus $27,500, or $79,500. During March the company will borrow $50,000 from the bank at 7 percent interest for six months. Interest charges will therefore amount to $1,750 for this period; the amount advanced to the company will be $48,250 ($50,000 − $1,750), which will be repaid in six months (during September) in the full amount of $50,000.

8. Master budget. The principal or supreme budget includes all major activities of an enterprise. It brings together and coordinates all the activities of the other budgets and can be thought of as a "budget of budgets." Customarily it does not show sufficient details from which operating departments can guide their respective activities. For working purposes, one or several of the above-mentioned types is employed.

QUESTIONS

1. Explain how each of the following costs are calculated: (a) factory overhead cost, (b) direct labor cost, (c) direct material cost, and (d) selling expense.
2. Do you feel that cost is an indication of managerial efficiency or to put it another way that cost controlling is probably the preferred type of controlling to be performed by a manager. Justify your viewpoint.
3. You have been asked to give a five-minute talk on "The manager and use of a manager's personal time." Outline the major topics you would cover in this task.
4. Discuss the meaning and function of dispatching in production control.
5. With reference to Figure 25–2, answer the following: (a) What was the scheduled time for shearing on order No. 17544? (b) Has the forming operation started on order No. 17549? (c) Is the order for the Ulco Corporation ahead or behind schedule? (d) Is the time period from 2 to 4 of Lis-Almers Manufacturing Company available for work? Why?
6. List and explain three methods for distributing overhead costs. Explain their validity and importance in establishing a basis of control.
7. Distinguish between the concepts in each of the following pairs: (a) basic standard cost and time use control, (b) a constant and a variable type of budget, and (c) prime cost and cash budgeting.
8. Discuss the subject "correcting cost deviations."
9. What is value analysis and how is it performed?
10. Enumerate five prominent advantages of budgetary control. Five disadvantages.
11. In your own words describe the meaning of Figure 25–9.
12. Discuss the subject "human behavior and budgeting" carefully, pointing out the salient features in this area as you see them.
13. Referring to Figure 25–10, explain how the cash balance, $64,450, at the end of May is calculated.
14. Suggest several ways in which budget estimates can be revised and brought up to date. Which method do you prefer? Why?

CASE 25–1. WORSHAM COMPANY

Ed Wisner (manager, special research and development, a unit of special services): To me, the whole thing is petty and I don't intend to do anything about it.

Bruce Donahue (vice president of special services): I see your point, Ed, but that's the wrong attitude to take. These people see your gang leaving for lunch before 12 and returning at 2:30 or maybe 3:00 P.M. And your people come walking in for work in the morning at 8:45, 9:05, 9:20—whenever they feel like it. How do you think this looks to others?

Ed: I guess they are jealous. To me, if they want to feel that way, let them. It's results that count. And we are getting excellent results. Take the new plan and organization for maintenance. The floor plan for the new plant addition—all the innovative ideas put into it. The cost reduction plan in Department 71 . . . the . .

Bruce (interrupting): Yes, I agree. The results of your unit are outstanding and I am indeed well pleased. You have achieved far more than I thought you would for a unit that has existed for only 18 months.

Ed: Sixteen months.

Bruce: Sixteen months. But the unusual hours kept by your people is causing trouble with some of the other departments. All other staffs and special units keep regular hours. It seems to me that an equitable solution is to have all department heads insist on keeping the same hours for everybody throughout the plant.

Ed: Well, if you want my people to punch a clock, OK. But you know they work late many a night. Nobody sees them working past 5:00 P.M. It's giving them their freedom, to do it their way, that is so important in getting the results my unit is achieving.

Bruce: You've been a good manager, too, and that helps.

Ed: Thanks.

Bruce: Ed, think about it some more, will you? And let's get together again, say, day after tomorrow at 4:00 P.M., OK?

Ed: OK, at 4:00 P.M. day after tomorrow.

Questions

1. Evaluate the viewpoints taken by Ed Wisner. By Bruce Donahue.
2. What is the problem? Could it have been avoided? Explain.
3. What is your recommended action for Mr. Donahue to take? Justify your answer.

CASE 25–2. UNITED UNIVERSITY

Vera P. Fitzmaurice, assistant business manager of United University, claims that a major need of the university is not more classrooms but better utilization of classrooms it now has. She estimates that the current utilization is somewhat less than 50 percent and that the distribution over the available school day hours is particularly bad. For example, Saturday morning utilization is extremely low, and on Tuesdays and Thursdays there is a relatively small amount of classroom space utilization. She feels efforts should be made to improve this general situation. To bring this about, she admits many adjustments will be necessary, especially in schedules of classes, room preferences, and the like. But awareness of the problem is the first step toward its solution.

To justify her viewpoints, Ms. Fitzmaurice compiled data on current classroom usage in one building of the university. See Exhibit 1. In

EXHIBIT 1

Room number	Capacity	Hours used					
		M	T	W	Th	F	Sat
First floor:							
100	20	3	—	3	—	3	—
101	20	2	4	2	4	2	—
102	35	5	3	5	3	5	—
103	35	5	3	5	3	5	1
104	25	6	5	6	5	6	—
105	110	2	—	2	—	2	1
106	45	7	4	7	4	7	—
107	45	5	4	5	4	5	—
108	40	6	2	6	2	6	2
Second floor:							
201	12	4	1	4	1	4	1
202	12	2	—	1	1	—	1
203	35	6	2	6	2	6	3
204	25	5	1	5	1	5	—
205	65	6	5	6	5	6	2
206	65	7	3	7	3	7	—
207	45	6	2	3	2	6	—
208	40	7	2	4	2	7	—
Third floor:							
303	35	4	6	2	6	2	—
304	25	1	2	1	2	1	—
307	45	6	3	3	3	3	—
308	40	7	4	3	4	3	—

other words, room 100 has a student capacity of 20 and is currently being used for 3 hours each Monday, Wednesday, and Friday. No other classes are officially scheduled in it for the current school period. University classes are held hourly from 8 A.M. to 5 P.M. (with no classes between 12 noon and 1 P.M.) and on Saturday from 8 A.M. to 12 noon. A 10-minute break between classes is permitted to enable students to get from one room to another.

Questions

1. Classify the data into four arbitrary groups including (*a*) rooms up to and including 25-student capacity, (*b*) from 26- to 45-student capacity, (*c*) from 46- to 65-student capacity, and (*d*) over 66-student capacity. For each group, determine the percentage of utilization.
2. Do you agree with the general statements made by Ms. Fitzmaurice? Substantiate your answer.
3. What do you recommend Ms. Fitzmaurice tell the university's governing board or top management group? Discuss.

CASE 25–3. STEVENS COMPANY

"I can't put my budget together until the sales department tells me what they expect to sell this forthcoming year by units and by weeks," says Howard Barton, works manager. "There has been talk about dropping some of the slow movers from the line, but that decision is not up to me. If it were, I'd drop several whole lines we are making— they simply give rise to too many problems."

"The sales budget, as usual, will be ready by the deadline date of December 5," comments Earl Matthews, sales manager. "We have not as yet come to a conclusion about how much we'll spend for advertising. That decision will depend upon what new products, if any, we market next year. The executive committee is now grappling with the new products verdict. With the economy like it is, I would not be surprised to find the committee making a very conservative decision."

Sam Brendesi, traffic manager, has done nothing about drawing up a budget for the next fiscal year because Mr. Barton told him several months ago that beginning next year the transportation unit was to be transferred from production to sales. Mr. Brendesi indicated he would be very happy to get rid of the budget preparation. During the past he has figured on rail freight for many shipments, only to have them changed to air freight upon special request by the sales department. Likewise, in several instances shipments were made by special expedited truck when in Mr. Brendesi's opinion it wasn't necessary. The customer often complains of excess transportation costs and, adjustments are made with the excess being charged to his department. Mr. Brendesi points out that transportation costs average about 18 percent of the total selling price and thus transportation really warrants a separate organizational unit to assist in keeping transportation costs in line.

Questions

1. Discuss what general problems in budgetary controlling this case illustrates.
2. What are your reactions to views expressed by Mr. Brendesi? Discuss.
3. What action should be taken by the Stevens Company? Why?

PART VII

Foreign and future views of management

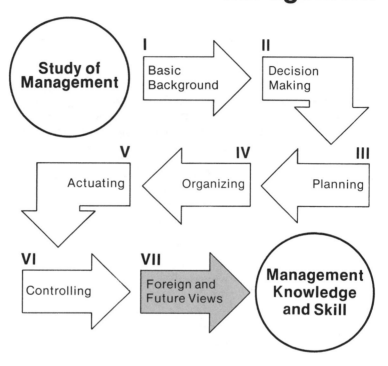

In this closing Part are given some insights into managements of foreign countries and ideas pertaining to the future of management. Regarding the first, foreign managements, the material is written to aid understanding of management in an international context. A career in management in this day and age may well involve some aspect of how management is conducted in a foreign country. For example, how important are the customs of the people, social forces, and unions? What type of organization is followed? Do employees in foreign enterprises participate in decision making? Answers to questions such as these are given.

With respect to future views of management, it appears that significant differences will exist. The role of the future manager, the influence of future technological and social environments, and the change in management members' needs and requirements, especially the handling of manager obsolescence, are among the topics presented. In all, it is believed future management will win new peaks of accomplishment beyond our present most optimistic predictions. Achieved will be a greatly improved quality of life for all and the opportunity for each human being to rise to his or her highest destiny.

Chapter **26**

Comparative management

To be conscious that you are ignorant
is a great step to knowledge.

Benjamin Disraeli

When a company crosses national boundaries it probably will encounter some difficulties arising from the different environments, beliefs, governmental influences, social customs, and forces found in the foreign country. It is easy to comprehend, for example, the problems likely to be faced in marketing a new cosmetic in a foreign country. First of all, can the foreigner be persuaded to use such a product in view of prevailing social customs and forces? What is the right selling price? How is the best way to get the product to the buyer, i.e., what channel of distribution should be used? What are the government restrictions?

The examination of such types of problems is giving rise to a relatively new management field known as comparative management. Succinctly stated, *comparative management is the identifying, measuring, and interpreting of similarities and differences among managers' behavior, techniques followed, and practices applied as found in various countries.* The emphasis is upon a comparison of existent managements in foreign countries with U.S. management and also among the various foreign types. Some prefer a definition that includes all the management problems of operating in a foreign environment and others feel the foreign environment is the critical area upon which to focus. Both these views have merit. Certainly problem solving is essential in the practical application of any management. An important influence in the conduct of management is the total environment in which it operates.

THE MANAGEMENT PROCESS IN FOREIGN COUNTRIES

All through this book we have stressed the fundamental functions of management: planning, organizing, actuating, and controlling. This is

573

basically what a manager does whether in the United States or in a foreign country. However, what is trying to be achieved and the means being followed for achievement can and do differ among countries. Why do they differ? Primarily because of managers' beliefs, attitudes, experiences, customs, and values. These, in turn, are needed and shaped by the general environment within which the manager operates. Comparative management therefore includes analyzing and comparing each fundamental managerial function with each environmental determinant of the foreign country. In organizing, for example, the structure evolved, the work division used, the work groups formed, and the status of authority and responsibility will be conditioned by the environmental factors present in the foreign country. The interaction between the environment and the management process conditions the behavior and the relationship of the manager to one's work and to one's subordinates.

Both management knowledge and skill will make for similarities and differences. Having the knowledge to manage is always important and this can vary both in scope and depth among various countries. Likewise for management skill, or the applying of the knowledge, but it seems likely that in most cases management skill or lack of it may account for a significant portion of the findings of comparative management.

Figure 26–1 shows specific environmental factors classified by economic, social, technologic, and law, related to several managerial activities. For example, objective setting is conditioned economically by basic needs and fiscal requirements, and legally, by governmental regulations. The relative influence of each environmental factor varies in significance in each country. The chart is suggestive only.

COMPARATIVE MANAGEMENT QUESTIONS

1. Why study comparative management?   There are several reasons why an understanding of management in an international context is desirable. First, comparative management helps the realization that there are managerial differences across nations. Knowing these can be valuable to a manager going overseas, to the researcher, and to the student of management. Second, ideas helpful for improving management can be obtained. For example, knowledge of how Sweden handles labor relations may prove helpful to the U.S. manager and vice versa, our knowledge of information processing may answer a difficult problem for the Peruvian manager. The transfer and utilization of the managerial idea is likewise expedited. Third, facilitation is given world understanding and trade. Simply getting to know how managers in foreign countries do their tasks makes not only for better understanding, but also expedites trade and cooperation. Fourth, de-

FIGURE 26–1: Selected environmental factors relationship and effect upon several managerial activities.

Selected environmental factor	Objective setting	Planning	Organizing	Actuating	Controlling
Economic	Basic needs. Fiscal requirements.	Inflation problems. Resource availability. Basic policies.	Individual or group-oriented. Labor specialization.	Participation. Fringe benefits. Wages.	Monetary regulations. Quotas.
Social	Religious influence. View toward contributions to culture.	Population size and growth. Importance of time.	View toward cooperation. Attitude toward authority. Interpersonal cohesion.	Work ethic. Strength of family ties. Mobility of individual.	Importance of achievement. Extent of belief in efficiency.
Technologic	Literacy level.	Selection of means. Attitude toward unemployment. Size of demand.	Availability of technicians.	Willingness to change. Scientific orientation. Technical training available.	Attitude toward machines and research.
Law	Regulation by government.	Choice of means. Centralized by government? Political stability.	Political influence. Legal actions toward organizations	Bribe tolerance. Taxes.	Reports required by government. Import-export restrictions.

velopment of skills necessary to understand their and our ways of management are encouraged. Mutual gain is thus experienced. Last, the effectiveness of management is increased because (1) a willingness to accept change in management is encouraged and (2) the opportunity to see how similar problems are solved in different manners is offered. In other words, the ability to perceive worthwhile differences and to observe how to act in varying situations are made available.

2. Is the trend toward convergence of management practices a result of comparative management? To date, there is no concensus. Some feel that the increasing interactions of cultures, economic interdependence of nations, and the quest for world peace are bringing about a oneness of management actions. A common set of managerial beliefs is becoming more relevant. In part the proponents argue this is coming about due to the strong influence of multinational companies.[1] Also the claim is made that "one-worldness" is becoming a reality. Similar products are found all over the world—Pepsi-Cola, hamburgers, Japanese radios, and Swiss watches. Likewise, cultural differences, although still existing, are eroding with time.

On the other hand, there are those who strongly believe the predominant management of a given foreign country will continue to differ to a greater or lesser degree from the managements of other countries. To holders of this view, the environmental factors, especially those of a social and legal nature will dominate. Management will adjust to the environment and not the environment to management. However, it is of interest to note that most of the Japanese companies establishing plants within the United States are basically employing Japanese management practices and United States plants in Taiwan are almost in total following practices prevalent in Taiwan. While certainly not conclusive, it does point to the lack of any trend as of now whether management is going to be the independent or the dependent variable.

3. Are there semantic difficulties in analyzing and researching comparative management? The answer is a strong "Yes." Certain words connote certain concepts in one country, but different concepts in another even though the same language is spoken in each. To illustrate, the word *leader* has a different meaning in Australia than in the United States. Even the word *manager* does not have anything near a uniform meaning throughout the world. And words like *status, security,* and *esteem* mean different things in different countries. In some countries the meaning and the measurement of what it means are both in the single word. Further, a number of managerial terms originated

---

[1] A multinational company is a large company having branches, divisions, or subsidiaries in countries foreign to that of its home office and operations. Multinational companies are discussed near the end of this chapter.

in the United States and have been adopted unchanged in foreign languages, but the common meaning of the word in the foreign country has grown to mean something quite different than the original U.S. term. And any manager from the U.S. speaking to a group of foreign managers quickly learns that the idiomatic expressions "That's what makes Sammy run" or "You're on the spot" conveys either an erroneous meaning or nothing to the listener.

GENERALIZATIONS ABOUT FOREIGN MANAGEMENTS

To generalize about foreign managements is not easy because of the managerial diversity found among countries and even within a country. The whole subject of what management prevails in each country is well beyond the scope of this book. For our purpose, eight popular management topics have been selected and a discussion of each will be made from the viewpoint of comparative management. We start with customs.

1. Customs

The words of Schiller, "There is deep meaning in an old custom," are especially appropriate in writing of the importance of customs in comparative management. Through the centuries in many foreign countries it has been a custom to take considerable time before a decision is made on a business proposal. A seemingly endless number of people and committees must approve and there are cases where several years elapsed before the final word was forthcoming. Friendships rank high and doing business with relatives and close family friends has priority. This is why at an initial meeting considerable time is spend on completely irrelevant business subjects. They wish to develop the required state of friendship. In South America and the Far East haggling over a price is expected. Sellers ask for more than they expect and buyers will be pleased if they can haggle the price down. The time required is considered unimportant, it is exchanging pleasantries and being friendly that counts. In the manner of making payments, a 90-day promissory note may be viewed the same as a cash payment. Customarily a known rich person considered a friend is not asked for money with an order and, in contrast, there is reluctance to grant credit to a stranger, even one who presents good credit credentials. Interest rates are usually higher in Latin America and Asia compared to those in the United States. It is always best to agree in advance on the price of any small service, as once the service is performed it is too late to negotiate.

In most foreign countries it is not customary to invite business acquaintances for dinner at one's home. Such entertainment is done at clubs or restaurants. Usually to receive an invitation to a private home is an honor and to use it for furthering business aims is considered a violation of a sacred hospitality custom. Coat-and-tie dress is preferred for men for all meetings. Handshaking is accepted in most countries, but it is best to leave the initiative in this respect to those of the host country. In the Middle East Moslem countries it is considered bad manners to link arms in public or to put your arms around your spouse. Such gestures are considered private manners and should be confined to private quarters. Actually, privacy is preserved in most foreign countries. Family matters are discussed much less in the office or plant than is the custom in the United States. The preferred feeling about family, weekends, and evenings is that they are to be considered private and kept separate from business. Use of first names are frowned upon during business meetings. The formal, "Señor Bodone" is used, not "Fernando" or "Ferdie." Status symbols may or may not exist. Diction and language may indicate status as does the name or title. As a general rule, however, family, connections, or friendships represent the most important status symbols.

2. Social values

In discussing comparative management, social values are of extreme importance. They greatly influence how the management task is carried out. In Japan, personal qualifications are given much weight in recruiting. A person initially hired as an operative worker probably never will become a management member and one hired as a manager assumes managerial status at the start of employment. A lifelong commitment by both the individual and the firm is the viewpoint taken toward employment. A person with regular employee status has a job for one's working lifetime or till age 55. Retirement at this age is believed desirable since it brings fresh talent into the managerial ranks and widens the opportunity for younger employees, and provides a reasonable "retiree period" to be enjoyed by the loyal and faithful employee. There is some job hopping, but in Japan minimal job mobility is the general rule. Most Japanese feel deep loyalty to the company employing them. Women are employed in great number, but most are considered temporary workers. It is anticipated they will drop employment, marry, and raise a family. However, the status of women is slowly changing. Many qualified recent college women graduates as well as older women seeking employment find difficulty in locating jobs and their plight is bringing about some modification in the employment practices. Family ties are viewed as sacred and family members help each other in every way possible. Competition between families is intense. Age is respected and usually possesses authority.

A multilingual, multinational people is represented by Yugoslavia which as a federal state contains four languages and five nationalities. While still highly agricultural, there has been within the last several decades a large migration to the urban areas. Social values have helped condition the management style followed, especially those dealing with general personnel practices and co-determination which is discussed later in this chapter. In India, social values are very important in the management styles followed within that country. The varied racial origins and languages have their effect, but the family system has great influence and is the foundation on which many companies are based. Nepotism is widespread and formal authoritarianism is the usual practice. Typically both the manager and the nonmanager like to assert their individual opinions, but strong leadership is wanted and expected. In general, the status of the business leader is not as high as that of the professions and of civil service.

3. Education

In most countries of Western Europe, future managers are selected and groomed young with special training beginning at age 15 or 16. There are extensive educational systems in the industrial countries. Attendance at U.S. schools is not uncommon. The Grande Écoles in France is one of the outstanding schools for managers. A graduate of this school is probably in the managerial class for life. Some details on the German system gives enlightment on the makeup of European management education. The student starts with four years of elementary followed by nine years of high school. Upon entering the university a student must select a field of specialization; should one change later to another discipline one must start anew. The fields of study include the sciences, philosophy, medicine, law, and theology. The first degree is the "Diplom," after which the "Dr." can be pursued requiring at least two years and more often three to four years. For management, there are two schools: (1) *Hohere Technische Lehranstalt* (HTL) and (2) *Hohere Wirtschaftsfachschule* (HWF). The former is strongly technical with its graduates enjoying a good reputation in business and filling many middle-management technical positions. Admission requirements are 10 years of elementary and high school and one year of directed practical experience. The latter, or HWF, emphasizes subjects in the commercial and somewhat technical areas. The admission requirements are similar to those of the HTL. Again the graduates are successful in finding positions in middle management. In 1971, the HWF and the HTL acquired the status of an advanced institute for vocational studies. The eventual goal is their integration into *Gesamthochschule* or a comprehensive university system. There is also what in the United States would be referred to as a college of commerce. Called *Wirtschaftshochschule*, business subjects at the university level are offered. The graduate receives a *Diplom Kaufmann* (business diploma). In addition, the universities offer a variety of business courses extending from several days to 10–12 weeks in both day and evening sessions. Typical topics include leadership, information systems, marketing, and industrial engineering.

The Japanese stress formal education. The literacy rate in Japan is one of the highest in the world. Since about 1950 education in management at universities has developed and is designed to meet the requirements for modern industry. Entrance requirements are high and are based on formal educational criteria. In contrast, in India, only in selected areas is the literacy rate high and even there the multiplicity of languages retards communication. Many universities exist but the subjects offered are mainly pure sciences, mathematics, law, and humanities. There are numerous special business schools where the emphasis is upon certain skills such as computer operation, typing, and recordkeeping. The education for management at a professional level is low relative to the size of the population.

4. Selection and promotion of personnel

European managers have more restrictions in the area of employment than do U.S. managers and this has made the European manager more careful in dealing with and in utilizing the human resource. Who is hired and fired is handled in a much more constrained area of operation. Ingenuity is required to utilize the limited skills available in some areas and to achieve high human resource utilization. In most foreign countries, college graduates are considered a reasonably good group from which to select future managers. However, by no means does this group represent the only and in some cases the best source. There is no single selection procedure followed.

In Japan, candidates are sought who not only have the required skill or potential for the work, but also conform to the viewpoints of the members of the company. By quite thorough referrals, interviews, and tests, potential employees with ideas and desires at variance with those of the company are excluded from selection. Normally a recruit is on probation for the first two years during which period one may leave and be replaced by another. During the probationary period one is considered a temporary, not a permanent employee. It is tremendously advantageous to have a degree from the "right" school, because many of the large and prestigious Japanese corporations recruit primarily from these schools. And it should be noted that although the entrance examinations are rigorous and include comprehensive and difficult questions, any person can apply regardless of family background. Thus, the opportunity for upward economic and social mobility is available.

Further, occupational specialty is not of major concern. The collegiate managerial recruit joins the company as a management trainee and some day may have a top management job in the company. The viewpoint taken is that the new member is becoming a member of the organization and the expectancy is that one will be given a wide variety of assignments over one's total working career. Incompetence in one assignment or changing needs of the company are not justifiable grounds for terminating employment. And keep in mind, as stated above, that at the time of hiring both the company and the individual make a permanent and irrovocable commitment to each other.

It has been said that in Europe when a person retires everyone knows who the successor will be. Promotion reaches down the line for the one who is advanced. The general practice is to wait for your superior to retire, then promotion comes. But there are so many exceptions to this mundane approach that it certainly is limited. The younger generation, reacting rapidly to it, are insisting that ability should be considered. Seniority alone is inadequate and inequitable. In Germany, there is a tendency for managers to specialize in certain selected areas, but advancement is gained either from within the company or from without, i.e., inter- as well as intra-company mobility is followed, but the focus is upon one type of industry. Yet company loyalty is highly thought of in Germany. Substantial bonuses and pensions, for example, are given to long-time employees in addition to public social security payments. Actually studies show that many German managers come from the lower social class. The reason most often cited: the devastation and disruption suffered during World War II.

In Japan, promotion is handled informally with attention and judgment given mainly to the person's family and contributions made to the company. Few Japanese companies use a performance rating system as is followed in many U.S. firms. Yet a pure seniority system has not been used for several decades. For managers, a ranking system has been adopted. Rank reveals personal status rather than the actual work being done. The manager's education, ability, accomplishments, and length of service are taken into account by rank. The connection between rank and the job held is loose. Hence, it is possible for a competent manager to move up but without the rank or a manager with little current competence can have high rank but be on a less responsible job. This dual system makes it possible to deal effectively with "deadenders." However, seniority still is considered vital by the Japanese. But in Japan as in Europe, seniority has come under attack. The major reasons for this in Japan are (1) the increase in some companies for requiring retirement at age 57 rather than 55 has meant higher labor cost due to older and higher paid employees, and (2) younger workers are getting impatient with the system. The extension of the retirement age to 57 is by no means universal or for that matter even common. The old practice of 55 years has been subjected to criticism and change to the 57 years was adopted primarily due to efforts of unions, the growing life expectance, and labor shortages in certain industries. In contrast, due to sluggish economic conditions, some Japanese companies, mainly the smaller ones, are following policies which nullify lifetime employment by such means as requesting early voluntary retirements and laying off all employees for a stated period.

5. Participative decision making

In almost all foreign countries we are seeing more participation by the employee in decision making. No longer is the employee accepting a passive role which simply permits one to react to management decisions. What is now wanted is to know what is being considered, and for one's views to be taken into account. In some way, the employee wants to feel associated with the decision making process of the enterprise for which she or he works. What traditionally has been reserved for unilateral decisions by management members is now being opened to some degree for participation by all employees or their representatives. No longer accepted as a matter of course is for the manager alone to decide the working hours, to determine how the work is organized, and to handle work distribution. In short, a recasting of the employer-employee work relationship is taking place in most foreign countries.

Work councils, work committees or similar bodies are a main means through which the foreign employee participates and the trend is toward widening and strengthening one's activity. Typically in many European countries the role trend of these bodies appears to be toward sharing, not merely advising or suggesting in the decision making process on matters of economic and financial operations. We will discuss this development in some detail under the following heading, co-determination.

Around the world there now exists a variety of degrees and ways in which employees participate in managerial decisions that affect them. Similarities and dissimilarities exist even within a given country. The most different and probably the most interesting in comparison to that in the United States is the arrangement followed in Japan. There decision making is by consensus or *ringisei* which means "reverential inquiry about a superior's intentions." By nature, the Japanese spend much time on finding out what others are thinking and how they feel about issues. The prevailing belief is that the Japanese manager must know how subordinate's feel about a certain issue, otherwise one cannot maintain the peace and harmony of the group. Further, ringisei is well suited because the manager in Japan sees one's task as improving the initiative of members and creating an atmosphere in which the members are actuated to seek better solutions.

A decision is always started by an employee at a low level in the organization. This is justified by realizing change within a company should come from those closest to the thing being changed, hence, change is elicited from below. For example, an employee who has an idea or a problem prepares an outline of that idea or problem, called the "ringisho," and explains how it should be used or will help in solving a problem. This contribution is circulated to the various superiors in succession. The intent is to reach a consensus by coordinating very closely the activities of each area affected by the issue. The decision reached, usually after considerable discussion and exchange of thoughts, in essence creates a commitment of all parties to the chosen solution. To the Japanese this quality of commitment is vital—perhaps even more important than the quality of the decision itself. Keep in mind the Japanese manager's status is well defined, but the manager's role in decision making is not one of being burdened with decision making in the Western World sense. Each manager plays a key role in shaping decisions by encouraging the subordinate to develop the proposal until it has merit and is worthy of referring to the next higher manager in the organization.

Decisions of considerable importance are analyzed with extreme care and the effort is taken to ascertain the viewpoints of all who may be affected by it as well as everyone in the company who may influence its outcome. The result is a minimum of disagreement over decisions implemented. The superior does not alter the ringisho but motivates and assists the writer of it to change and improve it in order that consensus about it can be reached. The initiator of a ringisho always carefully checks it to make certain nothing in its contents will offend the superior or evoke outright disapproval. Thus conflict is avoided.

The Japanese decision making procedure is centuries old, yet it features modern management techniques from the U.S. viewpoint and is giving excellent results to Japanese industries. The approach stresses asking the right questions and logically from this the right answers emerge. It is also claimed that formulating the decision at the end after all have had their say is superior to making the decision at the beginning and then striving to sell it to others. Naming the advantages of the Japanese decision making process include: (1) emphasizes initiative from the bottom up, (2) makes a manager a facilitator of decision making, not an issuer of edicts, (3) uses the manager's experience and judgment in decision making, and (4) gives close attention to the personal welfare of the employee. On the other hand, it does have disadvantages. For one, it takes a lot of time. The process is slow. Second, those at the lower levels of the organization frequently lack the understanding of issues involving an overall comprehension of the total organization. Third, fixed responsibility from the individual point of view is lacking. The contribution of any one member is lost in the composite of the group's decision adopted. Fourth, it may prove inadequate in deciding critical issues such as those affecting the very existence of the company or of a crisis nature.

6. Co-determination

The concept of co-determination, or joint management, whereby employees have representation on boards of companies is gaining favor in a number of foreign countries. In Europe, Austria, Belgium, Denmark, West Germany, Norway, and Sweden have laws requiring labor representatives on the company's board. A law setting up a legal framework for the election of workers on corporate boards was being considered in France as of late 1976. Only companies of more than 2,000 employees would be affected and the conditions of their joining would be decided on a case-by-case basis. In 1975, the management of Chrysler's United Kingdom plant in Great Britain agreed to the workers having a seat on the board. Elsewhere more and more new issues are being subjected to bargaining with the unions. Fiat in Italy, for example, now holds consultative meetings with the union and bargains over production quotas, cutbacks, days of operation, and shifting jobs of employees. Also, it is becoming common for European workers to have a wide range of veto powers over management decisions through work councils and board membership. The demarcation is becoming increasingly blurred as to whether consultation, negotiation, or joint dealing is the practice to be followed.

To gain an insight into co-determination let us look more closely at its history in Germany where it is called *Mitbestimmung*. In a German company the executive committee (*Verstand*) is the legal decision making body. As a body it is earmarked for the direct and active management of the company. A supervisory board (*Aufsichtsrat*) nominates members for the executive committee. Membership by a person in both the executive committee and the supervisory board is forbidden. Back in 1951 a law was passed providing for one-third of the supervisory board members to be elected by employees in the mining and iron and steel industries. The law provides for employees to have one half of the representatives on supervisory boards of companies with 2,000 employees or more. Interestingly, at least one of the employee representatives must be a white-collar employee. In effect the German arrangement is two-tiered; the supervisory board acts on proposals by the executive committee and also serves as a judge of the management performance of the executive committee. Perhaps, multi-tiered would be more appropriate since usually at least four levels exist in a typical German enterprise (1) the top managers or what we would term, enterpreneurs, (2) higher managers or the senior executives, (3) middle managers, and (4) lower managers.

There are also workers' councils which are exclusively employee bodies. Members are elected for three years, the number of members depends upon the number of employees in the company. For 9000 employees the council would have about 30 members. Meetings are held during working hours at employer's expense, and the chairperson is commonly free from all regular company work. A council has the right to co-decide in social matters—change of payment procedure, overtime, accident prevention, vacation plans, and must give approval to management before it can act on personal matters—hiring, promoting, and transferring. The council is entitled to see company financial information only on "business matters." German companies which have over 100 employees also have an economic committee commonly of six members, half of whom are elected by the workers' council, half by the employer. The committee seeks and is informed about the economic situation, production programs, and other matters that affect the employees' interests. Both the workers' council and the economic committee meet monthly with the employer.

Overall the results from the German arrangement have been very favorable. Within the past several years, the relatively few strikes have been settled amicably and with modest wage increases. Controversial issues have been settled to the satisfaction of both parties. The records show that in some German companies the executive committee has never had a vote cast against what it proposed.

During the mid-1975 meeting of the International Labor Organization (ILO) a proposal was made to promote worker participation around the world.[2] It was opposed by employers' delegates and was lost in committee.

Not all unions favor co-determination. In Italy the preference is to preserve their arm's length relationship with management. The feeling is that fundamental changes in job design and improvement of the work environment at the worker level are superior to the illusory power of sitting on the board. In Japan several companies are seriously considering some degree of co-determination but to date the idea has not gained much headway. In the United States it is not well received. The attitude of the unions is that they are strong at the worker level where it counts. Further, having board representation reduces the

---

[2] "Co-Determination: When Workers Help Manage," *Business Week*, July 14, 1975, pp. 133–34.

union's effectiveness. A conflict of interest is created and compromise and weakness by the union results. In addition, playing the role of an evaluator and adversary—accepting the good, rejecting the bad— makes for more effective participation.

The whole arrangement in Yugoslavia is different and merits review. Its features are economic decentralization with workers decreed by government to participate actively in management. The Yugoslavian enterprise has a Workers' Council (*radnicki savet*) made of workers and also a Managing Board (*upravni odbor*) made up sometimes but not necessarily of selected members from the Workers' Council. Members serve for not more than two years. A rotating basis is followed so continuity is maintained. In addition, the "Executive" consisting of the manager, vice manager, heads of staff and departments are selected. However, in the case of the manager the appointment must be made by the Workers' Council. Every member of the Executive competes for a job with other applicants every four years and it is common for appointments to be for one term only. Every member of the Executive must be aware that at all times one is "working for the workers" who have a right to challenge and question any Executive directive. There are also various commissions and committees.

Within the enterprise, the Workers' Council has the top authority and its list of duties corresponds somewhat to a board of directors of a U.S. corporation. The Managing Board is concerned with the direction of the enterprise in keeping with the annual economic plan which is prepared and implemented within the enterprise. The Executive is in charge of direct work actions. Disagreements within the enterprise are settled by the Workers' Council. Furthermore, the commune (*opstine*) has much authority over enterprises within its area. A commune is a small division of the country and represents a local governmental unit. There are approximately 800 communes in Yugoslavia. Each has high autonomy and possesses political and economic jurisdiction over enterprises. A commune can, for example, directly intervene in the activities of the Workers' Council or the Managing Board, dissolve either or both of them as well as the enterprise itself.

There are problems, however, in the Yugoslavian workers' system. Since the employee receives two forms of income—wages and bonuses—one is inclined to choose the bonus more frequently than deciding to forego it in order to build up the financial assets or surplus of the enterprise. After payment of obligations to government, the local community, and the suppliers, the workers are entitled to all residual earnings of their enterprise. How much of these residual earnings to use as workers' bonuses and how much for production purposes, i.e., retain as investment in the enterprise is a decision they make. In probably too many cases too little is retained in the enterprise so that it can be operated at top efficiency. Such actions are taken even though there are personal income taxes, no tax on enterprise earnings, and a very small tax on retained earnings. Secondly, some evidence shows that participation in the Workers' Council is dominated by top managers and staff employees. Especially is this the case when the subject is of a technical nature. In contrast, on questions of placement, welfare, and human relations, the workers become more active.[3] A third difficulty is the lack of adequate management experience and expertise by some members of the bodies charged with managerial duties. This dearth is multiplied when it is realized that council members rely to a great extent upon analysis and interpretation of financial statements and various reports. Further, these written documents are prepared by the Executive members and those under their supervision. It would seem that some irregularities in these reports might be possible, but perhaps they are small, if any. With time it is reasonable to expect an increase in the degree of competency.[4]

7. Job enrichment

For the past several decades job enrichment has been used in foreign countries. Sweden, for example, is perhaps the outstanding example. In this country many examples show that the work organization has been changed toward more independently functioning units and the work role has been altered to provide the employee with more varied tasks to make the work more challenging. The arrangements are designed to provide self-managed work teams. The traditional assembly line is eliminated being replaced by the assembly work teams. By being a member of a small work team the individual becomes closely involved in a bigger work effort and yet is closer to the end result being sought by performing the work. To achieve enrichment via job content, several approaches are followed. One is job rotation whereby an employee works several different jobs during a day or five or six during a week for physical and psychological change. Employees are encouraged to learn several jobs and to become versatile within reasonable limits. Another approach is job enlargement whereby expanded duties are performed in order to make the work more challenging and interesting. It is common to find quality control and machine maintenance being the responsibility of the operator. The intent is to have the job more challenging and of greater interest to the operator, not simply one consisting of a larger mix of boring tasks. Furthermore, in a number of instances the work environment is also changed in order to

---

[3] Josip Obradovic, "Workers' Participation: Who Participates?" *Industrial Relations,* February 1975, pp. 17–22.

[4] For a scholarly discussion and evaluation see George A. Wing, "A Worker-Managed Economy," *Business Horizons,* February 1971, pp. 19–28.

add to the job's attractiveness. Examples include more open space between factory buildings, more daylight, separate entrances and relaxation areas for each group and buffer zones between groups, giving desired privacy.

Considerable interest and experimentation in job restructuring is taking place in Japan. Problems dealing with the assembly line have been given priority apparently because of their monotonous characteristics and difficulty in getting employees to accept or remain on such jobs. Permitting more time to complete the work, adding new work assignments, and increasing the responsibility have been tried, resulting in various degrees of success. The plan-do-see approach of giving autonomous groups weekly production goals and letting them plan, carry out, and check the work, has proven most effective— increasing employee satisfaction, production, and quality.

8. Unions

Activities of unions in foreign countries appear to be going through a period of change. The key issues as well as the principles and procedures followed by the union vary considerably among the countries so that the initial impression in studying them is one of bewilderment. The system followed in each country has grown out of the traditions and requirements representative of that respective country. However, there are some basic features and trends which appear similar among Western European countries. There all unions are under government pressure to show moderation in wage demands and also member pressure to improve members' standard of living by not permitting any reduction in their economic purchasing power.

Of significant importance are these two points. First, collective bargaining agreements in Western Europe are closely tied in with the law. Second, agreements are reached primarily at the industry, not the enterprise level. To illustrate, with the exception of Great Britain and Ireland, an agreement is enforceable by law in that it is automatically incorporated into the employment contract of the employee. In some cases it is viewed as sort of a delegation of state's rule making power to the union or employees' organization. Once the agreement is reached it becomes embodied in the law of the country and remains so for the period specified in the agreement, independently of the will of the parties. A new claim by a union is first reacted to by the employer not so much on economic grounds, but on whether the law permits such a claim to be made and allows bargaining on this issue. Under the second point, bargaining at industry not enterprise level, makes for far-reaching effects upon an entire industry, uniformity of agreement, and concentration of bargaining power. An industry bargaining unit is more prone to get into politics and many Western European unions have strong political beliefs. In a number of foreign countries a union is closely affiliated with a certain political or a religious belief. Since about 1975, there has been some development toward enterprise level bargaining. Joint union-management commissions, for example, have been set up in Italy to study production line techniques.

Common issues include pensions, hours of work, and job security. There is wide diversity, however, among the scope of interests by unions. For example, Danish unions are active in increasing the workers' share of ownership, in France preference is given early retirement and high minimum wage, and in Italy a concentration on a range of social improvements is present. Likewise, the extent of union membership varies widely. In France, some 25 percent of the work force are union members while in Belgium and Sweden the figure is approximately 70 percent.

German unions have interesting aspects for the U.S. management student. They are organized by industries not by professions. A toolmaker, a clerk, and an engineer working in the metal trades industry all belong to the IG-Metall Union. There are 16 Industrial Trade Unions (IG) (*Industriegewerkschaften*) who support the parent organization, German Federation of Trade Unions (DGB) (*Deutche Gewerkshaftsbund*). Frequently mentioned IG members are (1) Public Service, Transport, and Traffic Trade Union, and (2) Art Trade Union. Some 35 percent of German employees are union members. Autonomy of the employers' associations and of the union is adhered to. An employer's bargaining is done by the regional employers' association who, as mentioned above, bargains with only the one union. A number of collective bargainings are conducted at the company level, but they affect a minority of employees. Arbitration provisions are included in most agreements. At least 75 percent of the union members must consent to a strike before it can be called.

In Japan, unions are relatively less active than in Western European countries. There are examples, however, where the Japanese union has initiated and proposed measures to improve the working relationships and environment. Issues include elimination of benefits differentiation among employees, decentralizing authority more, and increasing union participation in promotions and training activities. Since 1974 *Domei*, a large Japanese union, has focused more of its efforts on work improvement and workplace activities. Another Japanese union, *Automobile Workers Union*, in seeking to find means for improving job satisfaction, concluded it should be accomplished individually not institutionally. In its report, the union made an interesting suggestion that every job should have (1) rewards and promotions for its holder, (2) opportunity for social contacts, and (3) long range goals.[5]

---

[5] Joseph Mire, "Workers' Morale In Japan," U.S. Department of Labor *Monthly Labor Review*, June 1975, p. 51.

FRAMEWORK OF COMPARATIVE MANAGEMENT

Hope is expressed from time to time that some day professional codes for the practice of management will be written and used throughout the world. It is frequently suggested that the start is to write such a code for adoption by international bodies. However, from what has been stated in this chapter, it appears at least for the present that any uniformity or standardizing of world management practices is not in the realm of reality. True, some degree of integration might well be highly desirable. But consider the fact that managers achieve given objectives through various managerial means; there is no one way of doing things. Universal applicability of either the authoritarian activities-oriented or the participative results-oriented management style does not exist. The similarities and differences found in management around the world result from a number of factors. We have in this chapter pointed out some of them. Important are prevailing customs, social factors, values, and beliefs. These constitute important variables and are likely to remain during the foreseeable future.

If we view information of comparative management as positive and contributive in that it represents practices and developments from a variety of approaches, and find the means to verify comparative management information, some synthesis of the comparative area around a common framework may be developed. This would certainly add to our knowledge and skill of managing. Suggested is a type of inventory or stock-taking that would classify and present in a comprehensive format existent empirical knowledge. Background information classified as to the predominant managerial values used; managerial attitudes prevailing; type of decisions made, how and by whom; and the basic interaction within and without the enterprise, would serve as a starter. Specific elements under each major classification would be added, such as under attitudes the elements might include the manager's dominance in the use of staff personel and of incentives, the importance accorded the human resource, and the employment of control mechanisms. Further, the framework would make factual comparisons among key areas such as the relative managerial effectiveness using the criteria of both economic and social considerations. For convenience, functional classifications might be followed, i.e., the effectiveness in the personnel and in the financial activities using appropriate evaluation means in each area.

MULTINATIONAL COMPANIES

One reason for interest in comparative management is the growth of international operations which involve foreign managements and a need to know and understand them. At one time the management of overseas operations was handled by a subsidiary of a parent company and served for the most part in the capacity of an export agency. Headquarters of the subsidiary were usually in the home country and major decisions were made there. Foreigners viewed them as giving employment to few people and minimal contribution to their (the foreign) economy. Recognizing the unique problems of international operations there subsequently evolved a truly world company with a single organizational structure that included production, sales, finance, and personnel activities. From this emerged the multinational company. It can be thought of as a normal development of a genuine world economy.

The multinational company came into being essentially because of the existence of large world markets some of which developed quite rapidly. The existence of political trade agreements also helped to promote world trade. The big world market was made accessible and efforts to serve these markets were expedited. Also, especially in the developed countries, organized capital markets with available capital were available and their managers were willing to provide the needed capital to develop the world trade and make possible the multinational company. In addition, improved world communication and transportation facilities were available and made it feasible and relatively easy to carry out many of the required efforts.

As might be expected, serious problems have arisen in the management of multinational companies. Following consistent policies in keeping with its world operations commonly result in conflict with the different legal systems, customs, and values of the different societies and countries in which the company is doing business. Labor practices and collection procedures, for example, may differ widely between two countries. Commonly these differences are difficult to settle because the differences are deeply rooted and beliefs change slowly. Corrective action includes the practice of decentralization of authority, but the results are anything but uniformly successful. Another consideration is that close relationships with several nations seemed required and in cases of economic or political conflict between such nations, the multinational company is put on the spot. Embargoes, employment regulations, and taxes are representative of such problems. In some instances it appears that no matter what action the multinational company takes, it will suffer some loss. Finally, there is the difficulty of retaining management members. Typically, the British manager accepts and stays with a management position in a foreign country. The U.S. manager is willing to go to the foreign country for awhile, but eventually hopes to return home. In contrast, there is a tendency for neither the French or the German manager to consider a management job in a foreign country as desirable.

QUESTIONS

1. What is comparative management and of what importance is it to a manager?

2. Discuss some customs in foreign countries that are of interest (to the United States) and helpful to the manager engaged in international operations.

3. Define each of the following (a) ringisei, (b) Diplom Kaufmann, (c) multinational company, (d) rank as used in Japanese management.

4. Relate the procedure followed in Japan by which employees participate in management decisions.

5. Distinguish clearly between the makeup and the functions of a workers' council in a German company and of one in a Yugoslavian enterprise.

6. With reference to multinational companies (a) why did they come into existence and (b) what are some serious problems their managers must solve?

7. Explain Figure 26–1 in your own words.

8. The book points two fundamental points of great significance in understanding Western Europe unions and their activities. What are these points and why are they important?

9. Discuss co-determination as it applies in the management of some foreign managements.

10. Discuss several important contributions of Swedish management to job enrichment.

11. Give the highlights of co-determination as followed in Yugoslavia. How do you feel this arrangement could be improved? Justify your answer.

12. What are the advantages and also the disadvantages of the Japanese employee participation system? Do you favor it? Why?

13. With all the differences existing among foreign managements do you feel it feasible to develop a meaningful framework of comparative management? Why?

14. Discuss the personnel selection process as conducted in Japan. Do you feel it is effective? Discuss.

CASE 26–1.   CARSON COMPANY

Inquiring for his mail at a hotel in Florence, Italy, Mark Carson, age 23, was handed a telegram informing him of the death of his father, Mr. Carl Carson, age 51. The news came as a terrible shock to Mark because in a letter of two weeks ago, his father stated he was enjoying good health. Since college graduation last year, with a major in sociology and a minor in economics, Mark has traveled abroad; he had always wanted to see the world. His travels took him to the northern countries of South America, the Far East, the Middle East, and all over Western Europe. He was about to return to his hometown, Bisband, Ohio, when the sad news of his father's death arrived.

The Carson Company, founded and developed by Carl Carson, made a variety of molded plastic products. Sales are around $30 million a year, profits after taxes $1.65 million, and employees total 2,300. Carl Carson dominated the management and was characterized by some as being firm. He believed a product well designed and engineered was the key to a successful company. He worked hard, expected others to do likewise, paid above going wages, "ran the show," believed strongly that it was management's job to make decisions, listened to but did not seek ideas and suggestions from others, and was considered absolutely honest in all his business and private activities. There is no union at Carson Company. Many of the employees have been with the company for 10–15 years; 83 percent have been Carson employees for over four years.

Mark Carson knew that he was the sole heir to his father's estate, which among other possessions included a 63 percent stock ownership in Carson Company. This was the result of a deathbed pledge made by Carl to his wife (Mark's mother) when she died. At that time, Mark, their only child, was a freshman in college. Mark has been told from time to time by his father that he (the father) didn't think much of Mark's ideas concerning life and how to run a business. In fact, Carl never approved of Mark working for the company in any capacity during summer vacations. Rumor has it that Carl hoped Mark would mature, drop his crazy ideas about so-called social improvements, decide to groom himself to manage the business, and start to take hold and become an active part of Carson's management. Carl Carson approved and paid for Mark's travels saying, "OK, young man. You see how the rest of the world lives and then you'll appreciate what you have here and—I hope—get some commonsense in your head."

At the end of seven months, the estate was settled—Mark was in the "driver's seat." During this period Mark observed and talked with various members of the company at all levels and at different types of jobs. He believed strongly that there were many things the company should be doing but wasn't. And he was deeply convinced that some changes should be made not only for the benefit of the employees, but also for management's own good. The company's legal counsel on several occasions made strong appeals for Mark to sell his ownership in the company.

Shortly thereafter, at a specially called Board of Directors meeting, Mark asserted that he intended to take an active role in the company's management. He was not going to sell out. Also, he planned to institute practices successful in the managements of foreign countries especially with reference to employee participation and employees' councils. From his travels he had observed such practices were helpful to the employees and in his opinion this is what they need. Furthermore, he was going to see to it that several departments were reorganized on a task force basis so that the employee would be better able to satisfy more of his or her needs. In addition, he was requesting the resignations of Mr. Clark Blake, controller, age 59, and Mr. Henry Mott, the works manager, age 62, on the grounds of "incompatability with the new Carson leadership." In this connection the company would negotiate proper termination pays and pension payments.

Questions

1. What is the problem?
2. In general, do you feel the company can benefit by adopting practices of foreign managements? Why?
3. As best you can from the limited information, evaluate the actions of Mark Carson. How do you explain his behavior?
4. As an outsider asked to offer advise, what actions would you recommend and by whom? Justify your answer.

CASE 26–2.   ORSON PRODUCTS COMPANY

Jim Whiting (assistant production manager of Orson Products Company): Uncle Fred, it looks like me, Martha, and the kids will be living in a foreign city, Rozzumi, How about that?"

Fred Zroc (production manager of Buena Terra Company): Rozzumi? How come? Going to quit Orson?

Jim: No, it's a promotion by Orson. They've offered me the plant managership of our plant there. It's a real opportunity. Just think, I'll run the whole plant. I'll be the one in charge. More money, more responsibility, more experience. You know, I can't believe it.

Fred: Yes, I see. Have you given them your final decision?

Jim: No. not yet. I wanted to talk it over first with you, Uncle Fred. You've given me pretty good advice during the past and I feel your comments are always good to have, especially on something like this.

Fred: Well thanks. I never have gone for any of those foreign jobs because I think you can do better staying with a good native company and working your way up. You take my situation here at Buena Terra. My superior, Bob Claggett, will retire in two years and I am in line for the very top production job. By playing it right, I'll get that job and be on top right here where I know the people and the people know me. Among friends, you know. The big consideration though is that I like it right here.

Jim: Yeah, I know you do. But you understand I'd like to see some of the world. Seems to me it will be fun, excellent experience, and look good on my record.

Fred: If you want to see the world, Jim, start saving some money regularly for an extensive trip. Go leisurely and as a gentleman, not as a person with a lot of work responsibilities and problems.

Jim: You are saying I should turn down this offer?

Fred: No. It's a decision you'll have to make, Jim. I am only trying to help you decide.

Jim: Yeah.

Fred: What about Martha? How does she feel about moving? How about the kids and school?

Jim: She's never been out of Missouri and she's all for going somewhere. And the kids—well I've missed my guess if they are not simply thrilled to go.

Fred: How large is Orson's plant in Roselumi—or whatever its name is?

Jim: Rozzumi. Our plant there is about one fourth the size here.

Fred: It's quite a bit smaller, then. Frankly, I think I know you well enough, Jim, to say that I'll give you three to four years until you'll be itching to come back.

Jim: That's possible. But I will certainly have a broadening experience and opportunities to solve problems I might never get here.

Fred: Yes, and you'll also lose touch with the main office of Orson and while you're gone somebody else will slip into the better spot here. They haven't promised where you will go from Rozzumi have they?

Jim: No, and I don't see how they can. On the other hand, Uncle Fred, Orson is doing more and more international business. It's our growth segment. And making good in it would be a feather in my cap.

Questions

1. Draw up a listing of reasons for and also against Jim Whiting accepting the foreign assignment.

2. What decision should Jim Whiting make? Why?

3. Assuming Jim accepts the Rozzumi offer, what preparations do you suggest he make before going? Discuss.

Chapter 27

Management in the future

*Press on. Nothing in the world can take
the place of persistence.*

Ray A. Kroc

To predict the future development of management requires bold-
ness, much judgment, and the acceptance of considerable risk. The
future begins with the present; it is not an immense and sudden jump
to a distant destination. Study of where we are today in management
thought, and how we got there, gives clues to what concepts and practices may be terminated, continued, or initiated during the years
ahead. This, however, is only a part of the prognostication. It is reasonably certain that the future of management will be more than a mere
projection of its past.

Powerful forces operating within a changing environment will
bring about significant changes. Many of our current managerial concepts and beliefs will fall by the wayside and, in addition, a number
will be significantly altered. New ideas, new techniques, and new
frames of reference will evolve to develop a way of management
thinking that both serves and survives the new society that calls for
symbiotic relationships among all kinds of organizations—economic,
political, educational, governmental, and philanthropic. Important
questions demanding answers will be numerous. Representative are:
Can the managers cope with the forces that are changing the environment in which they operate? Can the effectiveness of management be
continued? On what basis should managers of the future be judged?
Can management education keep pace with the demands placed upon
it?

MANAGEMENT THOUGHT

Management thought has always been and probably will continue
to be highly dynamic. New theories will emerge and old ones will be

discarded. Some consolidation among the many present management theories is to be expected. The future may well bring a viable integration of presently separate schools of management. Dynamic management thought will continue because a discipline as vital as management—with its involvement in fundamental issues affecting human wants, values, and technology—is certain to attract scholars and practitioners to contribute to a modern and meaningful theory.

The environment under which management thought will evolve will probably continue to be disorderly. It is doubtful that the future manager will be blessed with a placid environment. This means the future manager must have skill in attaining dynamic flexibility and a responsiveness to change in all managerial efforts. One will learn to manage in what amounts to almost a constant confusion, a state of affairs that is ever dynamic.

At the present level of management thought, too much managerial knowledge is available to manage arbitrarily. On the other hand, insufficient knowledge is available to manage with certainty. In some managerial areas we can predict results from selected actions with an acceptable degree of certainty, but in other areas we are still in what can be termed the descriptive stage. That is, we can apply certain managerial knowledge, but we are not positive that specific results will ensue from such action. In the future, the ultimate status of management thought will be for a manager in a given case to be able to prescribe accurately and consistently what should take place to attain stated objectives. In other words, once the manager has the symptoms identified he or she can then prescribe exactly what to do, with assurance that the desired results will be forthcoming.

CHANGES IN PRIORITIES AND VALUES

The first priority for the future manager will be survival of the company that he or she manages. There exists considerable indications to foretell that the prevailing managerial style and emphasis of today will probably not remain so. Changing priorities and values in our economy and society will necessitate modification. To illustrate, until a few years ago it was the prevailing belief that managers contributed to our prosperity by generating much wealth and income for employees and citizens. Economic accomplishments never before won became commonplace. Yet despite such gains, much dissatisfaction arose caused mainly by values, managerial styles, and leadership practiced.

Questioned was the basic assumption that economic growth provides most of the things that most of the people want. Asked were questions such as: Should irreplaceable resources be used at a rate that cannot be sustained? Is our value of possessing material wealth more desirable than that of developing good relationships with other human beings? Does wealth impede the development of satisfying relationships? Additional signals of change can be mentioned. They include the embracing of a present-minded, we-want-it-now attitude, living for pleasure and rejecting the work ethic, openly expressing dissatisfaction with work agreements, criticizing traditional institutions, and disregarding authority.

Let us examine more closely a representative group of changes in priorities and values. For purposes here, we include the areas of (1) education, (2) individualism, (3) land and capital, (4) influence of government, and (5) quality of life.

1. Education

As pointed out in Chapter 2, formal education in the United States has increased on a broad front so that more people have more formal education than ever before. In 1900 some 200,000 were enrolled in our colleges; today the figure is nearly 10 million, an increase of 5,000 percent. The proportion of students graduating from high school today is equivalent to those who went only as far as the eighth grade three decades ago. With more formal education, people normally develop a desire to use their knowledge, read more, and are aware of external events and developments that may affect them. In brief, the human resource today wants to perform work that is challenging and meaningful. This means that some changes in management style are in order.

2. Individualism

The belief is being pushed aside that if each individual follow self-interests the result will be what is in the best interest for society. The independence of the individual, one's right and duty to be oneself was once a cornerstone of all efforts. But with the complexity of organizations today, the mode of living, and the growing role of government as the protector, independence of the individual has lessened and interdependence of individuals and of the individual and the corporation have increased. Individual fulfillment today depends on a person's place in an office, a factory, a neighborhood, or a community. Each of these has special needs and the survival of a person in any of these groups depends upon the recognition of these needs. Pluralism, not individualism, is the trend today. This different state of affairs makes for changes within which management is performed. The social ethic rather than the individual ethic is becoming the manager's guide.

3. Land and capital

The long standing concept of an owner of land having authority over its use is no longer the view of many who favor usership rather than ownership, i.e., they feel the land should be enjoyed by the community of which they are a part. It is not in society's best interest for each landowner to do what each pleases with the land each owns. Some predict we shall soon have a land-use law by the federal government to assist the states in developing long-range planning for land use which would include not only economic but also environmental and ecological needs. The question is should the owner, government, or the public have the primary rights to land? Stated differently, as an owner of a piece of land can I cut down a tree on my land or can the government or the public forbid and restrain me legally from doing so?

Capital's role and influence pose some interesting possibilities. All estimates are that during the next several decades we shall require an enormous amount of new capital. What will be its source? Will the normal sources of savings from income and taxes be adequate to meet the capital needs and if so, what will their effect be upon the economy? Further, consider the anticipated growth in pensions. Nearly one half of our workforce is covered by pension funds. By 1980 it is estimated the total pension fund assets will approximate $250 billion, an amount which if invested in private corporations would represent a sizeable portion of their total assets. More startling is the fact that in the making is more and more withdrawals from the productivity role (pensioners) to live from the productivity of a much slower growing number of workers. To keep this program viable will challenge managerial innovation.

4. Influence of government

The trend has been toward government expansion. As of the mid-1970s some 20 percent of our total workforce, or one out of every five employees, is employed by a governmental agency. It is reasonably certain that government influence will not be diminished in the future, at least not to any appreciable degree. Many feel it will increase. Government is moving into more and more economic activities, such as regulation of employment, safety, product standardization, and wage payments. There is little doubt that government will continue to be important in both its service and its regulatory functions. As a result it will condition the environment in which every enterprise must be managed.

5. Quality of life

Another change in priorities and values concerns the quality of life. Included here is enjoyment of pleasant interactions with one's family and friends, freedom and time to pursue a hobby, a satisfactory level of material living, and opportunities to participate in creative efforts that are believed to be worth while. The way a person lives and under what conditions are being given more attention. The trend is toward satisfying the desire to be recognized by others and to be affiliated as a good member of a known social organization. Less emphasis is being directed toward the quality of life where seeking wealth and income has top priority.

FADING INDUSTRIAL ERA

Some feel that the current economic, social, and political turbulence marks the fading of the American industrial era leaving behind such traditional values as the work ethic and limitless growth. Certainly a number of citizens are questioning the continuing viability of some of the major institutions. A study released by 100 insurance executives points out that many Americans no longer find work "necessary for physical survival, no longer satisfying for some who know they could be replaced by machines."[1] The lower productivity, loafing on the job, and looking to government and employers for financial security are cited as evidence of an eroding work ethic. Technology will continue to eliminate menial jobs making it more difficult for the less educated person to find a job. Eventually a reassessment of the welfare system, transportation, and public housing programs will take place in order to improve their contribution in solving the economic and social problems they are intended to mitigate and soften.

MORE INVOLVEMENT AND INTERRELATIONSHIPS

The fundamental issues of participation, self-actualization, and a democratic work environment are not theoretical abstractions. They are basic in one's day-to-day work experience and relationships of human beings. The employee wants more involvement in management affairs and we shall see more of this in the future.

Participation will increase and take on many different forms. More nonstructured, informal group activities will appear and be utilized because they are in keeping with the desire for more involvement and at the same time more freedom. For people to have a part of the action will become the standard and accepted practice.

More widely used will be results management, some modification of it, or a development emerging from it that emphasizes participation. The format will be an approach which gives the participant the satisfactions he or she needs and wants. Results are what count, getting them is what management is all about. Activities as the indirect way for achieving specified goals will decline in usage.

---

[1] "Trend Analysis Program Report" (New York: The Institute of Life Insurance, 1975), p. 4.

All of this means, of course, that the working environment will become more democratic. The ideas of a subordinate will be listened to more carefully and one will be "more on one's own." The superior will be less authoritarian in his dealings with subordinates, but authority—being essential to group accomplishment—will exist. It will be respected and obeyed because it satisfies those being ordered or led. Its form will stress acceptance and willingness of subordinates.

This desire on the part of participants to have greater influence has been with us for the last several decades. Witness the growth of labor unions, demands of teachers and government employees, and requests of students of universities. Taking place is a narrowing of the gap of power differentiation between the manager and the nonmanager.

Interrelationships will become increasingly more important. The manager of the future will depend a great deal on the ideas and feedback received from the group members. Group action, arriving at concensus from group discussion, give and take, will be the order of the day. As the results sought or the problems encountered become greater, the future manager will bring a larger number of capable people to focus on the issues and to bring them to a mutually satisfactory solution. The "loner" as a manager will become a rarity. Actually the role of the future manager will be more of a counselor, more of one who suggests and advises, one who is a member of the group and not a superior separate from the group and telling the members what to do. A hallmark of the future manager will be the informal, fluid workways of her or his work behavior.

SOCIAL CONSIDERATIONS

We are committed to improving social conditions and there is nothing on the horizon to indicate that continued efforts in this direction will slow down or cease. The trend is strong and will continue toward viewing enterprises not solely as economic entities, but also as entities of the broad sociocultural environment. Society affects organizations through a host of influences—custom, law, institution, and so forth—and in turn, organizations affect society.

Society is a dynamic and demanding master. Changes in values, new attitudes toward the human resource, and re-valuation of how management affects a human life are causing managers to consider social as well as economic goals in their managerial pursuits. In this respect two alternatives appear feasible (1) view social objectives as legitimate for the enterprise they manage, or (2) abdicate social responsibilities to the government and pay taxes to support the public efforts. Social reform is the heart and the instigator of many changes that are and will take place in management.

The challenge of the social demands and the suggested goals are well expressed in this statement:

> There is now a pervasive feeling in the country that the social order somehow has gotten out of balance, and that greater affluence amid a deteriorating environment and community life does not make much sense.
>
> The discontinuity between what we have accomplished as producers and consumers and what we want in the way of a good society has engendered strong social pressures to close the gap—to improve the way the overall . . . system is working so that a better quality of life can be achieved by the entire citizenry within a well functioning community.[2]

The goals include:

1. Elimination of poverty and provision of good health care.
2. Equal opportunity for each person to realize his or her full potential regardless of race, sex, or creed.
3. Education and training for a fully productive and rewarding participation in modern society.
4. Ample job and career opportunities in all parts of society.
5. Liveable communities with decent housing, safe streets, a clean and pleasant environment, efficient transportation, good cultural and educational opportunities, and a prevailing mood of civility among people.[3]

In essence, managers are being asked to contribute more to the human needs and the quality of life. Achievements in providing material products and service are inadequate in view of present and future requirements. The challenge is to merge economic objectives with social objectives so that multiple objectives will be achieved to satisfy multiple claimants. Satisfaction of both the economic and the social needs are desirable. The former not only for their own contributions in and of themselves, but also to aid in making feasible the meeting of the latter, or social needs, which are wanted to restore the dignity of the human being and a proper balance among human values. At present, it seems we are making progress in this transition, but we are certain neither of what precisely we are trying to achieve nor how specifically we are trying to achieve it. In the future, management will successfully mold these different orientations and foster a new style of leadership that satisfies long sought for economic and social needs.

THE HUMAN RESOURCE

To answer the question, "What will management of the future be like?" depends upon what the future attitudes, wants, behavior, and

---

[2] "Social Responsibilities of Business Corporations" (New York: Committee for Economic Development, Research and Policy Committee, 1974), p. 5.

[3] Ibid.

potential of people will be like. The human resource will remain the critical center about which all changes will revolve.

During the period 1975–85 the majority of the U.S. population will be persons less than 25 years old. Statisticians tell us that the increase in 18-year-olds will be well over one million every year during this period. This heavy youth segment will have to be reckoned with simply by virtue of its number. But more importantly, these young people are socially aware and they are eager to achieve. Industry and government will have to find jobs for them—jobs which challenge their intellect. Future managers will be heavily involved in these efforts.

Also, managers of the future must find ways to provide suitable jobs for minority members, the nonskilled, and the disadvantaged. Further equitable arrangements for the upgrading and promoting must be made available and practiced. As yet the ideal solution to this vexing problem has not been found, but future managers hopefully will find a reasonable answer.

High turnover is likely to continue to be a problem in the future. The reasons are many, including the fact that the better educated employee is more restless. He or she not only changes jobs, but also careers. One way for a person to improve one's lot in life is job shopping. A person does not hesitate to change jobs because there is little fear of failure. In addition, people today are more mobile. Having the same address for more than four years is becoming the exception, not the rule.

Future effective leadership will help supply the answers to the difficult personnel problems. As our knowledge of management grows we should, in the years ahead, have many leaders with the sensitivity, as well as the toughness and the skill, to assist in finding answers to the additional human-value and human relationship problems that then will arise. Employees expect more from employment than money and both their breadth of interest and of experience are expanding and will continue to do so. Television, the automobile, travel abroad, and higher education are all contributing to greater expectations of life.

MANAGER OBSOLESCENCE

A major difficulty with us now and destined to increase is manager obsolescence. The major cause is a manager's failure to recognize that preemployment education and skills will not serve through one's work life without periodic updating learning effort. Management changes, and the one practicing it must change in order to maintain the status of a manager. How best to handle manager obsolescence will plague the future manager. Some have the illusion that if they just work hard now, the future will take care of itself. The truth is that it does not. To minimize manager obsolescence, these suggestions are offered:

1. Acquire maximum flexibility.   Normally this suggests acquiring a broad education, maintaining interest in many different areas, and keeping up not only with a specialty, but also with general fields of contemporary leading activities. For example, an accounting executive should have in addition to one's own expertise, some basic, up-to-date knowledge of business law, economics, and computer data processing, if one is to share a common perspective with associates.

2. Continue education for life.   Refresher courses, in-service programs, and evening university courses assist a manager to avoid obsolescence. Likewise, the scanning of pertinent periodicals will help in knowing what is going on, what subjects are mentioned most frequently, and toward what forces research is being directed. In effect, the objective is to have not only a major, but also a minor, field of interest and in this way be in position advantageous both to oneself and to one's employer.

3. Realize own feelings are vital.   Fear and passivity are the two outstanding factors conducive to creating obsolescence. A person must believe that he or she is doing useful work and is contributing to a worthwhile activity. This includes not only the proper personal attitude, but also the ability to maintain consistent interaction with helpful superiors. It is for this reason that many employers practice systematic reassignment of managers, i.e., a planned change of moving managers from job to job with the specific intent of increasing the person's breadth of knowledge and understanding as well as improving one's confidence in oneself. In the future we shall probably see more companies in which managers work at specific jobs for only a few years and then are shifted to other jobs or leave the organization. Such a program has certain advantages. First, it recognizes the limits of a job in the context of a person's increasing age and experience. Second, it limits the incumbent to the period in which the job remains challenging. Third, the program provides a needed stimulus to prevent a person suffering from one's own procrastination, which is an ally of obsolescence.

EMPHASIS UPON PLANNING

The manager of the future will spend more time on and make greater use of planning. This follows because the future manager will be required to anticipate change, not just react to it. Further, with all the changes taking place, it will quickly be realized that thorough and intensive planning is the best way to cope with this dynamicism. A reasonable corporate fluidity will have to be maintained at all times. High on the priority list will be the ability to anticipate the consequences of current actions and current plans. Included will be the capability to restructure the enterprise, to develop management radar techniques to spot changes in both the economic and social systems, and to operate successfully under increasing governmental regulatory measures.

Future managers will plan in quite a sophisticated manner. The ever changing bundles of opportunities and strong appeals for progress will place a high premium on efficient planning efforts. New approaches and techniques of planning will be developed to meet these needs. Innovation in planning will be mandatory. To illustrate, assume the energy crunch becomes very serious so that transportation methods would have to be changed. With the redistribution in private and public carriers, necessary conferences might be planned via telephone or closed-circuit television with documents transmitted via facsimile. Fewer personal calls would be made by salespeople. Better grouping of calls and adjustments in the frequency of seeing a given customer would be made. Physical distribution of products would also become more difficult and probably bring about modifications in buyers' requirements and an overall flexibility in the distribution system fully comprehended by but a few at the present time.

MANAGEMENT AS A RESOURCE

Gaining increasing acceptance during the years ahead will be the concept that management is the important resource which is basic to most achievement. This is the normal outgrowth of (1) management maturing, and (2) management knowledge and skill being practiced by more and more people, whether officially designated as management or nonmanagement members. With the development of management it has become evident that management is purposive, is concerned with obtaining results, and is the effective applicator of knowledge including that of many sciences and disciplines. In its broadest meaning, it is a means toward achievement and is fundamental in our efforts to progress. The current problems of blighted cities, polluted rivers, and bankrupt business enterprises, will be solved only by management. By its use, the required actions to eradicate these problems will be evolved and implemented. Likewise we will continue our leadership as a nation and as a people as long as our managerial efforts are effective. Management knowledge and skill are now recognized as one of the important resources of any nation. There are no nations that are undeveloped, there are only nations that have a dearth of competent management.

With every member of an enterprise performing more or less managerial activities to accomplish stated goals, realization will spread rapidly that management indeed is the important resource basic to accomplishment. Management to more and more people will be the means to gain their goals and to satisfy their needs. Hence, the trend toward more involvement by members of an organizatiɔn in its management plus experience in utilizing management will accelerate the concept of management as a basic resource.

Emphasis on management as a resource will in time sharɔen our means to solve just about any problem we set our minds to solving. Some, in fact, feel that we already have a surplus of management means. But this ability to use the management resource effectively will stimulate thinking on the purposes toward which this means should be used. In this light, the future could bring much more on the determination and evaluation of goals deemed worthwhile. What objectives should we be seeking as a person, as a company, as a nation, as a society? In turn, this emphasis on end-results will stimulate thought on values, philosophy, and more consideration for the cultures in which we operate. More attention will be given these areas by the manager of the future.

TECHNOLOGY

One area that is certain to have a tremendous impact upon future management is technology. It will continue to offer discoveries and developments that the human mind will find difficult to believe. New material resources far ahead of anything available today will become commonplace and challenge the new manager's innovation to utilize effectively. Automation will increase and big improvements in task performance in all fields—production, sales, and various services— will be widespread. Computerized operations, affecting both information processing, decision-making and the operating of manufacturing processes will dominate the work in many enterprises especially those in service areas such as universities, libraries, and hospitals where, for instance, electronic equipment will eventually alter the entire enterprise as we know it today.

With these technological changes, the manager of the future will have to be able to judge their value and benefit to the enterprise and make the needed changes to acquire the advantages they offer. One may find that due to technology the nature of the enterprise's activities change rather rapidly, greater investments in machines and equipment are required, greater standardization is promoted, and mass markets must be acquired. But in a larger sense, they are simply considerations in the intelligent application of technology which can lead to our progress. Technology makes it possible for us to tailor and control work and its environment. But there is a price to be paid. It is the dependency upon the technology. And for every technical advance there is no practical retreat, for such an abandonment would mean a reduction in our range of comfort and possibly numbers—a condition spelling catastrophy and one which we will not accept voluntarily. It is also true that every technical advance has its undesirable side effects. The machine tied workers to the factory, the agricultural technical improvements multiplied production of certain plants, but also gave rise to all kinds of vermin who fed on those plants now available in greater quantities.

The challenge is to find an enlightened way in the use of technology. It can be used to aid in accomplishing both economic and social goals. It can be kept in balance with other means and in keeping with the needs of humans. This is one of the important tasks facing the future manager. It is the old question of being smart enough to use technical knowledge advantageously and of our being master of science rather than science being master of us.

ORGANIZATION CHANGES

The organizational structure of the future will place less emphasis on its hierarchical structure and more on equalitarian efforts. This does not mean that everyone deferring to the member with the best idea or greatest knowledge will be followed. Some direction appears essential and the superior-subordinate relationship will remain although in quite a different context than is prevalent today. Humans have always demanded structure in our life. We depends on human relationships, some routine, and some of habit to survive. Complete human autonomy is a romantic ideal. But the increasing emphasis on human resources and the quest to maximize their contributions will bring about significant changes in the working relationships of people. An adaptive rather than a mechanistic structure seems to be the order of the future. Its format will vary depending upon the preferences of the manager, the members of the workforce, and the type of work to be done.

Many feel that a considerable number of current large organizations are nearing the size of being unmanageable. The question to be decided is whether the gains accruing from size—economies of volume and financial resources—outweigh the losses—low productivity and poor morale. However, management is changing and this, in part, is due to the need to manage large, complex organizations. With management know-how as it was in 1950, many of the present very large organizations are unmanageable. But the modern manager of today uses different techniques and the manager of the future will improve and add to these approaches.

Small organizations will continue to occupy key positions and will be viewed with respect. Their managers will have many of the problems of their compeers of large organizations. In many cases, the techniques followed may be similar but the means of application may differ. Small organizations fulfill a definite role in that they supply a needed balance to the economy, provide a choice to the prospective employee and the purchasing agent, and take care of the inevitable interstices resulting from operations of the very large organizations.

There appears to be growth in the company that purchases some of its parts for its products from the outside. In other words, it is not a self-sufficient, fully integrated enterprise. This trend will probably continue and can even spread to the elimination of certain major functions. For example, more and more companies are having their accounting and data processing work done by an outside organization. Research and development work is another function that might be farmed out. Others are plant maintenance, plant security service, and janitorial service. In general, the better candidates to farm out are services which the company's top managers feel are extraneous to their major activities or that they do not want to or cannot afford to provide the necessary manpower and facilities to perform themselves. All of which simplifies the management of the company. Bothersome specialized activities are removed and costs of these discarded activities can be better controlled since the work by the outsider is handled on a contract basis.

MASS NONROUTINE TASKS

One of the significant challenges to the future manager will be the efficient accomplishment of mass nonroutine tasks. For convenience, work can be divided into two large categories, routine tasks and nonroutine tasks. Routine tasks, familiar to most of us, are repetitive, relatively simple, identifiable tasks. Amenable to machine operation, automation has been employed extensively to perform much of this work and new peaks of accomplishment have been won.

In contrast, nonroutine tasks require a new order of solution. Typical are problems dealing with environmental control, crime, transportation, and space exploration. Characteristically nonroutine tasks have few end products in contrast to mass routine tasks where the output is large in volume. Also, nonroutine tasks are individual; their solutions are not applicable in total to other problems. To illustrate, the water pollution problem in Cleveland is unique to Cleveland and the solution cannot be applied in total to another city. The solution is tailored for Cleveland only. In addition, nonroutine tasks frequently are broad in scope and may involve not only private industry, but the community, government, and university efforts. Another characteristic is that nonroutine tasks are complex and commonly have no widely accepted solution. Often considerable individual creativity and judgment must be used to supplement current managerial tools and techniques. Further the management of these tasks requires the use of large amounts of information covering many subjects and necessitating the services of social scientists, engineers, technicians, and professional aids. It appears that more and more time of future managers will be devoted to the solving of nonroutine tasks.

MANAGER OF THE FUTURE

What sort of manager will be needed to guide our corporations and institutions of the future? In order to coordinate the multiplicity of disciplines and functional efforts, the manager of the future will be a generalist, secure in his or her own background and area or competency, but intelligently committed to broader areas and goals. In brief, the future manager will not be confined to any managerial parochialism. He or she will maintain a balance among economic, social, and technological goals.

A common career pattern will be that of a manager who functions equally at ease heading a private corporation, a major foundation, a university, or a governmental agency. Operating effectively at the critical juncture between private and public interest, the future manager will have empathy with specialists; a grasp—with some sophistication—of technical methodologies, and a workable knowledge of most functional tools. Managerial skill will be transferable and experience will be relevant across most organizational lines.

The ability to cope with problems of pressure will be an outstanding characteristic. The future manager will be capable of absorbing quickly enormous amounts of knowledge and data, classifying them, and deriving and implementing good decisions from them. At the same time, knowledge will be more widely distributed throughout the organization. It will not be concentrated within a relatively few management members. Information will be available to decision centers via a network of information flow that is inclusive and sophisticated.

The future manager will be exceptionally skillful in

1. Motivating employees.
2. Merging economic and social objectives.
3. Achieving good relationships with peers and subordinates.
4. Designing effective organizational structures.
5. Utilizing self control and commitment of employee.
6. Evaluating the feasibility of technology advances.
7. Establishing rapport with governmental agencies.

Although there are many managerial difficulties ahead, the future for management not only looks bright, but also essential for society. The makeup of management and its implementation will change considerably, but constant improvements directed toward the best life to be lived in terms of quality of living will prevail. Difficult management problems will be mastered, achievements beyond our fondest expectations will be won, and fundamental questions will be resolved. At long last, managerial techniques and abilities will be available so that human beings have the opportunity to fulfill their highest destinies.

QUESTIONS

1. Has management reached its peak so that decline in its importance can be looked to, or, in contrast, will management become more important and be more widely applied? Justify your answer.

2. In this chapter, five changes in priorities and values are discussed. Select two from this discussion you feel are probably most important and discuss each at some length.

3. What is meant by the statement that "In the future, management interrelationships will become increasingly more important"?

4. As you see it, will the day ever come when a manager will be able to prescribe accurately and consistently? Why?

5. Give your reaction to this statement: "Technological and social forces are destined to clash even more in the future than we have witnessed during the past. This basic confict has given rise and will continue to increase in intensity and thwart many efforts of the future manager." Why?

6. Do you agree with those who claim the American industrial era is fading? Justify your viewpoint.

7. As you see it, discuss what might be some of the foremost social demands faced by the manager during the next several decades.

8. Assuming you have attained a position of considerable power in shaping national affairs, would you advocate placing constraints upon the development of technology? Upon the use of technology? Discuss fully giving reasons for you answers.

9. Justify the viewpoint that managerial planning will increase in importance in the years ahead.

10. Elaborate on this statement: "Too much managerial knowledge is available to manage arbitrarily."

11. Will the environment in which the future manager operates probably be more orderly than that of the past ten years? How will your answer affect the manager of the future?

12. Enumerate several ways to minimize the effect of manager obsolescence. Discuss thoroughly one of these ways.

13. List five actions in which the future manager will be exceptionally skillful. Discuss one of these in detail.

14. From your own experience give an example showing the narrowing of the gap of power differentiation between the manager and the nonmanager.

CASE 27–1. NEFF CORPORATION

The managers of Neff Corporation are highly respected in various trade circles for their competency, fairness, and progress. Specialists in metal and plastic fabricated parts, their output serves primarily the home building, automobile, and home portable appliances industries. The corporation is in a very strong financial position. Over the years it has accumulated quite a large surplus.

The president and his chief associates believe it desirable to appraise the corporation's future possible developments with respect to direction, speed, and future goals. Currently, its long-range planning efforts cover a ten-year period, but the proposed efforts would be for the period beyond. For example, what changes might exist 25 years from now in the trades now served and which changes probably will require alterations in the corporation's present mode of management? Also, should the corporation get into any different trades from those it now serves? What new developments on the market should the corporation be considering? What changes in management should they be preparing for now?

"Perhaps we should commence by defining what needs we are now meeting and go on from there," was suggested by the president in a recent address. "Maybe it is to our best interests to develop diligently the trades we are now in. On the other hand, perhaps we should be getting into others which offer good promise. Maybe we ought to use a part of our surplus to purchase other companies. Or possibly we ought to be starting new divisions. I just don't know."

Questions

1. What alternatives are open to the corporation? Discuss.
2. What important managerial changes do you envision the corporation will face within the next 25 years? Elaborate on your answer.
3. Outline in general form what actions you recommend the Neff Corporation top management take. Justify your answer.

Annotated bibliography

Annotated bibliography

The sources are listed alphabetically by author's name. Each source is coded by a bold-face number shown in parenthesis indicating for what management area the source is especially helpful. The code numbers correspond to the main sections of this book, *Principles of Management, 7th edition,* and are as follows:

Code no.	*Especially helpful for*
I	Basic background for management
II	Decision making
III	Planning
IV	Organizing
V	Actuating
VI	Controlling
VII	Foreign and future views of management

Academy of Management Journal. Mississippi State; Miss.: Academy of Management. Features excellent articles on current management theory written by well qualified authors. The Journal publishes original research of an empirical nature. (**I**)

Academy of Management Review. Mississippi State, Miss.: Academy of Management. Contains timely and interesting articles that move forward managerial theoretical conceptualization and indicate possible linkage candidates for theory and research in management. Articles of an original research nature are not published in the Review. (**I**)

Ackoff, Russell Lincoln. *A Concept of Corporate Planning.* New York: Wiley-Interscience, Inc., 1970. A basic book on planning, dealing with the nature and content of planning, policies, design, organizing the planning, and controlling the planning efforts. (**III**)

————, and Emery, Fred E. *On Purposeful Systems.* Chicago: Aldine-Atherton, 1972. Emphasis upon useful methodology in social sciences with respect to social systems. (**I**)

Administrative Management. New York: Geyer-Macallister Publications. (Monthly.) Practical, down-to-earth articles along with new findings in administrative efforts make this publication worthy of the reader's time and effort. (**I**)

Albers, Henry H. *Principles of Management: A Modern Approach,* 4th ed., New York: John Wiley & Sons, (Wiley-Hamilton) 1974. Concerned with the basic elements of executive action, this book is interdisciplinary in approach drawing from many fields of learning. The psychological and social foundation of authority is discussed at length. (**I**)

American Foundation for Management Research, Inc. *Management 2000.* New York, 1968. Speeches given at the dedication of the AFMR Management Learning Center, Hamilton, N.Y. Many contain ideas and forecasts of what management at the beginning of the 21st century will be like. (**VII**)

American Management Association. *Control Through Information.* New York. A series of pertinent articles emphasizing practical examples to show the importance and need of information for controlling to be effective. (**VI**)

———. *General Management Series.* New York. (Periodic.) Management information consisting of papers presented at conferences and ensuing floor discussions of the General Management Division of the Association. (**I**)

———. *Managers' Forum.* (Monthly.) A six-page pamphlet giving timely information on management activities. Featured in each issue are a message from the president of the association and a discussion of trends and perspectives for the manager. (**I**)

———. *Management Review.* New York. (Monthly.) A digest of articles selected from several hundred different publications. The articles are of special interest to managers. (**I**)

———. *Personnel.* New York. (Bimonthly.) An excellent source of articles by leaders in the field of personnel.

———. *Personnel Series.* New York. (Periodic.) (**V**)

———. Special research reports. New York. (Irregular.) Special studies on various management subjects which are of interest to practitioners and students of management. (**I**)

American Standards Association. *American Standards Yearbook.* New York. (Yearly.) The official annual publication of the association, which serves as a clearinghouse for the coordination and development of standards. Informative literature on the subject and a listing of the standards developed are included in the publication. (**VI**)

Anthony, Robert N.; Dearden, John; and **Vancil, Richard E.** *Managerial Control Systems.* Homewood, Ill.: Richard D. Irwin, Inc., 1965. Excellent text and cases on subject of management control. Emphasizes cost control areas with control profit centers and capital acquisition. (**VI**)

Argyris, Chris. *On Organization of the Future.* Beverly Hills, Calif.: Sage Publications, 1973. Interesting speculations regarding the future of management with logical reasons given to justify such developments. (**VII**)

———. *Interpersonal Competence and Organizational Effectiveness.* Homewood, Ill.: Richard D. Irwin, Inc., and the Dorsey Press, Inc., 1962. Describes a successful change of top executive behavior and integrates the interpersonal relations theory with laboratory education. (**V**)

Arizona Business. Tempe: Arizona State University (Monthly except bimonthly during the summer). An excellent puolication giving the latest developments in management, especially in the areas of organization and actuating. (**I**)

Barnard, Chester I. *Organization and Management.* Cambridge, Mass.: Harvard University Press, 1948. The essentials of how groups function together, principally from the viewpoint of intuition, not logic, are expressed in this informative book. (**IV**)

Bellman, Richard E., and **Kalaba, Robert.** *Dynamic Programming and Modern Control Theory.* New York: Academic Press, 1965. Presents an introduction to the mathematical theory of the planning-controlling process. Demonstrates the bewildering array of special factors frequently present and shows how dynamic programming takes them into account. (**VI**)

Belcaso, James A.; Hampton, David R.; and **Price, Karl F.** *Management Today.* Santa Barbara, Calif.: John Wiley & Sons, Inc. (Wiley-Hamilton), 1975. This integrated package of experience, text, readings, and cases expedite use of the experiential approach in the study of management. The student gets involved with management concepts and problems—an effective teaching approach. (**I**)

Bennis, Warren G., and **Schein, Edgar H.** *Leadership and Motivation* 2d ed. Cambridge, Mass.: M.I.T. Press, 1966. A collection of essays, addresses, and lectures on the importance, practice, and challenge of the human resource working within an organization. (**V**)

Bierman, Harold, et al. *Quantitative Analysis for Business Decisions.* 4th ed. Homewood, Ill.: Richard D. Irwin, Inc., 1973. Describes and explains quantitative techniques and models used in solving business problems. (**II**)

———, and **Smidt, Seymour.** *The Capital Budgeting Decision.* New York: Macmillan, 1971. Explains the use of the budget in financing projects and also supplies pertinent guides to economic analysis. (**VI**)

Bonini, Charles P. *Simulation of Information and Decision Systems in the Firm.* Englewood Cliffs, N.J.: Prentice-Hall, Inc., 1964. An award winner of the Ford Foundation Doctoral Dissertation Series, this volume describes a simulation model of a hypothetical firm which is subjected to informational, organizational, and environmental factors affecting the decision making of the firm. The book reflects excellence in research and competency in writing. (**II**)

Bowen, Earl K. *Mathematics: With Applications in Management and Economics.* Rev. ed. Homewood, Ill.: Richard D. Irwin, Inc., 1967. Well written and incisive, this book presents the mathematical approach to management and economics decision making in an admirable manner. (**II**)

Branch, Melville. *Planning: Aspects and Applications.* New York: John Wiley & Sons, Inc., 1966. A well-prepared book on this important area of management. Illustrations included are especially effective. (**III**)

Brown, Ray E. *Judgment in Administration.* New York: McGraw-Hill Book Co., Inc., 1966. Informative book pointing out causes of failure in administration along with suggestions for eliminating them. Based on practical experience, the material is helpful for the decision maker. (**II**)

Buffa, Elwood S. *Operations Management: The Management of Productive Systems.* Santa Barbara, Calif.: John Wiley & Sons, Inc. (Wiley-Hamilton) 1976. Features the application of systems analysis to the operations aspects of productive activity. Both humanism and socio-technical methods of job design are explored and woven into the discussions. (**I**)

Business Horizons. Bloomington, Ind.: School of Business, Indiana University. (Quarterly.) Helpful articles, timely and well written, on subjects of interest to the management member or trainee are featured by this excellent publication. (**I**)

Business Week. New York: McGraw-Hill, Inc. (Weekly.) A popular and widely read business magazine that features special articles on timely subjects of interest to both the practitioner and the student of management. (**I**)

California Management Review. Berkeley, Calif.: Graduate School of Business Administration, University of California. (Quarterly.) Features articles bridging creative thinking and management thought. It is an excellent source of ideas and information. (**I**)

Carlisle, Howard M. *Situational Management: A Contingency Approach to Leadership.* New York: AMACOM, 1973. Designed to give the reader a better understanding of the importance of environment in leadership and management, this book is informative and explains the contingency managerial approach. (**I**)

Carzo, Rocco, Jr., and **Yanouzas, John.** *Formal Organization: A Systems Approach.* Homewood, Ill.: The Dorsey Press, 1967. New thinking applied to organizing is effectively presented in this book. (**IV**)

Christensen, C. Roland; Berg, Norman A.; and **Salter, Malcom S.** *Policy Formulation and Administration.* 7th ed. Homewood, Ill.: Richard D. Irwin, Inc., 1976. One of the best books available on the subject of policies and their use by managers. (**III**)

Cohen, Allan R.; Fink, Stephen L.; Gradon, Herman; and **Willits, Robin D.** *Effective Behavior in Organizations.* Homewood, Ill.: Richard D. Irwin, Inc. 1976. An informal personal style of writing and using illustrations from the students' world impress the reader as material is presented on individual behavior, interpersonal relations, change, and leadership. The cases are excellent. The book is designed to apply the material to realistic problems observed or encountered by the student. (**V**)

Collier, James R. *Effective Long-Range Business Planning.* Englewood Cliffs, N.J.: Prentice-Hall, Inc., 1968. An excellent book on planning including both the practical considerations for planning and the process of planning. The book is well written and the coverage is adequate. (**III**)

Conference Board. *Studies in Personnel Policy.* New York. (Irregular.) Nearly 100 separate studies dealing with the identification, establishment, and adjustment of policies pertaining to the field of personnel. (**III**)

————. *Perspectives for the '70's and '80's.* Report of distinguished experts who identify the major trends now emerging and likely to create major public problems in the 1970's and 1980's. Also included are research results of how aware the public is of these trends and possible problems. (**VII**)

Dale, Ernest. *Management: Theory and Practice.* 3d ed. New York: McGraw-Hill Book Co., Inc., 1973. Describes current management skills and techniques in a well-written book. Has interesting anecdotes and gives attention to social responsibility, job enrichment, and managerial creativity. **(I)**

————. *Organization.* New York: American Management Association, 1967. New concepts in organization are discussed based mainly on in-depth study of organization practices in 166 companies. **(IV)**

————. *Readings in Management.* 3d ed. New York: McGraw-Hill Book Co., Inc., 1975. Selected articles in management are provided by this volume. **(I)**

Dalton, Gene W., and **Lawrence, Paul R.** *Organizational Change and Development.* Homewood, Ill.: Richard D. Irwin, Inc., 1970. Case studies regarding organizational change plus addresses, essays, and lectures dealing with organization change. Well selected collection and helpful in the study of this management area. **(IV)**

Dalton, Gene W.; Lawrence, Paul R.; and **Lorsch, Jay W.** *Organizational Structure and Design.* Homewood, Ill.: Richard D. Irwin, Inc., 1970. Deals with corporate divisional relationships in highly diversified firms, use of product and function in organization, and environmental and technological determinants in organization design. **(IV)**

Davis, Keith. *Human Relations at Work: The Dynamics of Organizational Behavior.* New York: McGraw-Hill Book Co., Inc. 1967. The basics of human motivation and the influence of both leadership and of formal organization are included in this presentation of an integrative theory of organizational behavior. Well written, this book includes examples of ways to improve managerial relationships among compeers, superiors, and subordinates. **(IV)**

————, and **Bloomstrom, Robert C.** *Environment and Society.* 3d ed. New York: McGraw-Hill Book Co., Inc., 1975. The responsibilities that business has toward society and its total environment are expertly handled in this excellent book. A systems framework is used for the organization of the material. **(II)**

Davis, Stanley M. *Comparative Management: Organizational and Cultural Perspectives.* Englewood Cliffs, N.J.: Prentice-Hall, Inc. 1973. Informative and interesting with excellent material on differences in organization and values among managements of countries in Africa, Latin America, Asia, Europe, and North America. **(VII)**

Decision Sciences. Atlanta: American Institute for Decisional Sciences. (Quarterly.) Selected articles dealing mainly with the decisional sciences are offered by this highly accepted publication. **(I)**

Dessler, Gary. *Organization and Management: A Contingency Approach.* Englewood Cliffs, N.J.: Prentice-Hall, Inc., 1976. In essence a survey of what is known about organization today. The contingency view is followed—no single view of management universally applicable. Research findings are included to support the main points. **(I)**

Donnelly, James H., Jr.; Gibson, James L.; and **Ivancevich, John M.** *Fundamentals of Management: Functions, Behavior, Models.* 2d ed. Dallas,

Texas: Business Publications, Inc., 1975. Different theories of management as applied to various institutions—business, government and schools are discussed to show that the contemporary manager can benefit by blending the various approaches. (I)

Drucker, Peter F. *Management: Tasks, Responsibilities, Practices.* New York: Harper and Row, 1974. An excellent book that offers thought provoking material about where management is going, where it should be going, and what present managers should be doing about it. (I)

———. *The Age of Discontinuity.* New York: Harper and Row, 1969. Interesting reading directing attention to the new forces that are creating the society of tomorrow and their possible implications upon management. The book provides guidelines to our changing society. (I)

Duncan, W. Jack. *Essentials of Management.* New York: Holt, Rinehart, and Winston, 1975. The broad orientation including nonbusiness applications of management and the emphasis on research makes this book comprehensive and outstanding. Excellent sketches of persons prominent during the emerging era of management as a definite discipline, are features. The newer behavioral and management science materials are included. (I)

Dyckman, Thomas R. *Management Decision Making under Uncertainty.* New York: Macmillan Co., 1969. A complete and thorough writing directed to an introduction to probability and statistical decision theory in the solution of managerial problems. (II)

Dun's Review. New York. Dun & Bradstreet Publications Corp. (Monthly.) Informative articles on important current management subjects are featured by this outstanding magazine. (I)

Emory, William, and **Niland, Powell.** *Making Management Decisions.* Boston: Houghton Mifflin, Inc., 1968. The basic concepts and techniques enabling one to make better decisions and to do this more effectively is the core idea of this well-written book. The newer concepts of managerial decision making along with the older and widely used techniques are included in this volume. (II)

Ewing, David W. ed. *Long-Range Planning for Management.* 3d ed. New York: Harper and Row, Inc., 1972. A book of readings which are helpful in assisting the reader to think through planning problems and to understand better their basic function of management. (III)

Fayol, Henri. *General and Industrial Management.* London: Sir Isaac Pitman & Sons, Ltd., 1949. A pioneer treatise in management literature brought forth in a new English printing from the original appearance in French in 1916. An important volume which reemphasizes the background against which managerial developments have taken place. (I)

Ferguson, Charles R. *Measuring Corporate Strategy.* Homewood, Ill.: Dow Jones-Irwin, 1974. A concise and complete treatment of management auditing as it applies to organization structure, compensation, resource allocation, and the total corporation. Emphasis is centered around the possible contributions of auditing to implement the corporate strategy. (VI)

Fiedler, Fred E., and **Chemers, Martin H.** *Leadership and Effective Management.* Glenview, Ill.: Scott, Foresman, 1974. An effective book dealing with how to get people to cooperate on a common task in order to achieve a shared goal. How one becomes a leader, how leaders behave, and what makes a leader effective are the areas covered. (**V**)

————. *A Theory of Leadership Effectiveness*. New York: McGraw-Hill Book Co., Inc., 1967. A good book on leadership containing the highlights of some 15 years research of this area. A theory of leadership effectiveness is propounded. (**V**)

Flippo, Edwin B. *Management: A Behavioral Approach*. 2d ed. Boston: Allyn and Bacon, 1970. The traditional and behavioral managerial approaches are presented by discussing one, then the other, covering the methods and philosophies of each, and following the general plan of the major management functions. (**I**)

French, Wendell L., and **Bell, Cecil B. Jr.** *Organization Development: Behavioral Science Interventions for Organization Improvement*. Englewood Cliffs, N.J.: Prentice-Hall, Inc. 1973. Scholarly treatment of an important managerial area. The book is inclusive and contains helpful examples and illustrations. (**IV**)

Gabriel, H. W. *Techniques of Creative Thinking for Management*. Englewood Cliffs, N.J.: Prentice-Hall, Inc., 1961. Explains how to become creative by means of a mental process consisting of simple, orderly steps. (**V**)

Gantt, H. L. *Industrial Leadership*. New York: Association Press, 1921. This volume is a classic in the management field. The book constitutes addresses delivered in 1915 before the senior class of the Sheffield Scientific School, Yale University, and includes chapters on leadership, training, principles of task work, results of task work, and production and sales. (**V**)

George, Claude S. *The History of Management Thought*. Englewood Cliffs, N.J., Prentice-Hall, Inc., 1968. An outstanding and scholarly work on a most interesting subject—the history of management thought. Certain to be enjoyed by all who are interested in how management started, developed, and expanded into what it is today. (**I**)

Gilbreth, F. B., and **Gilbreth, L. M.** *Applied Motion Study*. New York: Macmillan Co., 1919. A pioneer book in the field of motion study and one which still offers valuable information to the present-day reader. (**III**)

Greenwood, W. E. *Issues in Business and Society*. 2d ed. Boston: Houghton-Mifflin Co., 1971. A book of readings organized to make a comparative analysis between traditional management theory and that of the behavioral scientists. Well-organized and pertinent articles are a feature of the book. (**I**)

————. *Decision Theory and Information Systems*. Cincinnati: South-Western Publishing Company, 1969. A book of readings selected to answer questions regarding which methods and processes are vital to the preparation of all future managers. A full panorama of decision theory is covered. (**II**)

Gregory, Carl E. *The Management of Intelligence*. New York: McGraw-Hill Book Co., Inc., 1967. Scientific problem solving and creativity are exceptionally well handled in this excellent text. (**V**)

Gulick, Luther, and **Urwick, Lyndall.** *Papers on the Science of Administration*. New York: Institute of Public Administration, Columbia University,

1937. A classic in management literature pointing out sound and fundamental concepts along with their application in the field of administration. (**I**)

Haney, W. V. *Communication and Organizational Behavior.* 3d ed. Homewood, Ill.: Richard D. Irwin, Inc., 1973. Well-written and thorough, this book focuses on what happens inside the communicator before and as he or she writes or talks. Valuable suggestions are offered for improving communication. (**V**)

Harvard Business Review. Cambridge, Mass.: Graduate School of Business Administration. (Bimonthly.) Outstanding articles on business subjects of unusual interest for the management practitioner or student are offered by this publication. (**I**)

Haynes, W. Warren; Massie, Joseph L.; and Wallace, Mare J., Jr. *Management: Analysis, Concepts, and Cases.* 3d. ed. Englewood Cliffs, N.J.: Prentice-Hall, Inc., 1975. Thought-provoking and effectively written, this book supplies basic concepts and sound philosophy about management. (**I**)

Hellriegel, Don, and **Slocum, John W., Jr.** *Management: A Contingency Approach.* Reading, Mass.: Addison-Wesley Publishing Co. 1974. An integration of various managerial approaches is presented within present concepts of management. The view is taken that an organization integrates with and shapes the environment in which it operates. (**I**)

Henderson, Richard. *Compensation Management: Rewarding Performance in the Modern Organization.* Englewood Cliffs, N.J.: Prentice-Hall, Inc. 1975. Develops effectively the relationships between work and rewards and the essentials of a reward system fundamental to any organization. (**V**)

Herzberg, Frederick. *Work and the Nature of Man.* New York: The World Publishing Co., 1966. Thought-provoking book on the general theory of work and man's behavior gives new considerations and possibilities to managerial action and to the psychological contributions that are feasible. (**V**)

Hicks, Herbert G., and **Gullett, C. Ray.** *The Management of Organizations.* 3d. ed. New York: McGraw-Hill Book Co., Inc. 1976. A text on management theory unifying different viewpoints and providing a concept of management that is current. Discussions on what organizations are, why they exist, and how to make them more efficient are well done. (**IV**)

Hilton, Peter. *Planning Corporate Growth and Diversification.* New York: McGraw-Hill Book Co., Inc., 1970. Spells out the fact that corporate growth can be effectively planned. Draws from case histories and makes planning a live subject. Well written and coverage is quite satisfactory. (**III**)

Holden, Paul E.; Pederson, Carlton A.; and Germane Gayton E. *Top Management.* New York: McGraw-Hill Book Co., Inc., 1968. Reveals the management policies and practices of 15 leading industrial corporations. It is well written and informative. (**I**)

Horowitz, Ira. *An Introduction to Quantitative Business Analysis.* New York: McGraw-Hill Book Co., Inc., 1965. Covers decision-making theory, mathematical programming, game theory, and inventory controlling in simple, easy-to-understand language. (**II**)

―――. *Decision Making and the Theory of the Firm.* New York: Holt, Rinehart, and Winston., 1970. Decision making tools that operations research and economics can offer management are provided by this text. The scope, limitations, and level of sophistication of these tools are also pointed out. **(II)**

International Management. New York: McGraw-Hill Book Co., Inc. (Monthly.) For the person interested in what's going on in foreign management, this publication is a must. **(VII)**

Jennings, Eugene E. *Executive Success: Stresses, Problems, and Adjustments.* New York: Appleton-Century-Croft, 1967. An interesting and well-written book on the meaning and importance of leadership; the thesis is presented that ours is a society without leaders. **(V)**

Johnson, R.; Kast, F.; and **Rosensweig, J.** *The Theory and Management of Systems.* Rev. ed. New York: McGraw-Hill Book Co., In., 1967. A provocative and thorough presentation of the systems concept and its use in management. **(I)**

Journals of Business. Chicago: University of Chicago Press. (Quarterly.) One of the better journals dealing with business, economics, and trade subjects. **(I)**

Jucius, Michael J. *Personnel Management.* 8th ed. Homewood, Ill.: Richard D. Irwin, Inc., 1975. A well-known and comprehensive text in the area of personnel management. All facets of the subject are covered, and the book is well organized. **(V)**

Kast, Fremont E., and **Rosensweig, James E.** *Organization and Management: A Systems Approach.* New York: McGraw-Hill Book Co., Inc., 1974. An excellent book, providing a better understanding of the managerial role in a complex and dynamic organizational society. Organization is viewed as a sociotechnical system made up of subsystems: goals and values, technology structure, psychological, and managerial. A chapter on comparative analysis and contingency views is included. **(I)**

Kelly, Joe. *Organizational Behaviour* 2d ed. Homewood, Ill.: Richard D. Irwin, Inc. 1974. A modern treatment of an important subject area, this volume deals with the existential-systems approach to organizational behavior and strives to integrate micro- and macro-behavior. Well organized and complete, it offers helpful models build around the dimensions of structure, process, and values. **(V)**

Kolasa, Blair John. *Introduction to Behavior Science for Business.* N.Y., N.Y.: John Wiley and Sons, Inc., 1969. An informative and complete presentation of the behavioral field, concepts followed, and some results of research in this area. Profitable reading for the manager and the nonmanager. **(V)**

Koontz, Harold, and **O'Donnell, Cyril.** *Management: A Systems and Contingency Analysis of Managerial Functions.* 6th ed. N.Y., N.Y.: McGraw-Hill Book Co., Inc., 1976. A modification of the former *Principles of Management*, this new volume presents the concepts, theory, and techniques from an operational and practical managerial viewpoint. Ideas and findings from the classical, behavioral, and quantitative schools of management are included. **(I)**

————. *Management: A Book of Readings.* 4th ed. New York: McGraw-Hill Book Co., Inc., 1976. A well-selected group of 79 readings pertinent to management are offered by this book. The articles are presented in keeping with a logical outline and are easy to locate and to read. (**I**)

Lawrence, Paul R., and **Lorsch, Jay W.** *Organization and Environment.* Cambridge: Harvard University Graduate School of Business Administration, 1967. The ways in which the internal structure and processes of an organization relate to its different external environmental conditions are included in this book. Also found in this volume is helpful information concerning response to changing technology and organizing for innovations. (**IV**)

Leavitt, Harold J. *Managerial Psychology: An Introduction to Individuals, Pairs, and Groups in Organizations.* 3d ed. Chicago: University of Chicago Press, 1972. An interesting and helpful revision of a highly successful book. Topics such as perception, cognitive dissonance, behavior change, needs, power approaches, group behavior, competition, cooperation, and so forth are all included in this volume. (**V**)

LeBreton, P. P., and **Henning, D. A.** *Planning Theory.* Englewood Cliffs, N.J.: Prentice-Hall, Inc., 1961. An integrated approach to the work of planning, providing complete treatment for each step in this important managerial area. (**III**)

Leonard, W. P. *The Management Audit.* Rev. ed. Englewood Cliffs, N.J.: Prentice-Hall, Inc., 1962. Points out the means and the performance of an audit of management in a given enterprise. (**VI**)

Levinson, Harry. *Executive Stress.* New York: Harper and Row, Inc., 1970. Mental health and the meaning of work are the two basic concepts about which this book is written. Sound advice to aid the manager—emotions or stresses to cope with—and how to function at his or her best on the job are discussed thoroughly. (**V**)

Likert, Rensis. *The Human Organization: Its Management and Value.* New York: McGraw-Hill Book Co., 1967. This popular book is a stimulating volume to those wishing to improve the management of human resources of an organization by using the results of quantitative research. The effect of management upon productivity, labor relations, and human asset accounting, for example, are given much attention and many ideas to insure better human resources utilization are contained in the book. (**V**)

Lincoln, James F. *Incentive Management.* Cleveland: Lincoln Electric Co., 1951. The use of incentives as a main core in managerial work is advanced and substantiated in this detailed and well-organized book. (**V**)

Lindgren, Henry C., and **Byrne, Donn.** *Psychology: An Introduction to a Behavioral Science.* 3d ed. New York: John Wiley and Sons, 1971. An accurate understanding of human behavior and an overall view of psychology as behavioral science is made feasible by this well-organized and well-written book. (**V**)

Lippitt, Gordon L. *Organizational Renewal.* New York: Appleton-Century-Crofts, 1969. An interesting and well-written book in which are presented the ways for initiating and maintaining constructive, flexible response to contemporary attitudes regarding an organization's social and economic responsibilities. (**IV**)

Litterer, Joseph. *The Analysis of Organizations.* Rev. ed. New York: John Wiley & Sons, Inc., 1965. An interesting treatment of organization, pointing out the technical, economic, and social factors both within and without the organization, is supplied by this book. **(IV)**

———— (ed). *Organizations: Structure and Behavior (Vol. I.)* and *Organizations: Systems, Control and Adaptation (Vol. II.).* New York: John Wiley and Sons, 1969. Selected readings provide an array of thinking about organization. The coverage is quite extensive and the book is helpful to the management student. **(IV)**

Luthans, Fred. *Introduction to Management: A Contingency Approach.* McGraw-Hill Book Co., 1976. Gives emphasis to the contingency management approach and the need for the manager to integrate conceptually the environment with management theory. Discussions of the important management variables are included and suggestions for bridging the gap between management theory and practice are offered. **(I)**

McDonough, A. M., and **Garrett, L. J.** *Management Systems: Working Concepts and Practices.* Homewood, Ill.: Richard D. Irwin, Inc., 1965. A basic and helpful book on systems and their use in managerial work. **(II)**

McGregor, Douglas. *The Human Side of Enterprise.* New York: McGraw-Hill Book Co., Inc., 1960. A strong, convincing presentation of the importance of people in an enterprise. **(V)**

McMillan, Claude, and **Gonzalez, Richard.** *Systems Analysis.* 2d ed. Homewood, Ill.: Richard D. Irwin, Inc., 1968. Excellent coverage of systems and their contribution in management study and application. **(II)**

McNichols, Thomas J. *Policy Making and Executive Action.* 4th ed. New York: McGraw-Hill Book Co., Inc., 1972. Although a casebook on business policy, the introductory pages, as well as the cases, highlight the importance of policy making in carrying out management work. **(III)**

Maier, Norman R. F., and **Hayes, John J.** *Creative Management.* New York: John Wiley & Sons, Inc., 1962. The interaction btween man and the organization and the compartmentalizing of value systems through unilateral judgments are among the many facets discussed in this book. Suggested actions by the manager are included. **(III)**

Management Science. Providence, R.I.: The Institute of Management Sciences. (Monthly.) Excellent articles on the theory and practice of quantitative measurements in management. **(II)**

Managerial Planning. Oxford, Ohio: Planning Executive Institute. Excellent and helpful material in the area of planning assists the reader to keep abreast of this fascinating area of management. **(III)**

March, J. G., and **Simon, H. A.** *Organizations.* New York: John Wiley & Sons, Inc., 1958. A classic in the area of behavioral study—motivation, conflict, and rationality upon managerial organizing. **(IV)**

Maslow, Abraham H. *Motivation and Personality.* New York: Harper and Row, Inc. 1954. A classic on motivation and the make-up of a person's behavior commonly referred to as personality. In this volume the often referred to theory of human motivation—the hierarchy of human needs and their satisfaction—is included. **(V)**

Massie, Joseph L.   *Essentials of Management.* 2d ed. Englewood Cliffs, N.J.: Prentice-Hall, Inc., 1971. The elements of management are summarized in this compact book. Management is viewed as an interdisciplinary study and contributions to management by the behavioral and quantitative science are included in the text. **(I)**

Mee, John F.   *Management Thought in a Dynamic Economy.* New York: New York University Press, 1963. A concise, thought-provoking presentation of management thought development and probable future trends in management study. **(I)**

Megginson, Leon C.   *Personnel: A Behavior Approach to Administration.* Rev. ed. Homewood, Ill.: Richard D. Irwin, Inc., 1972. The importance of the human factor and of interpersonal relations in administration are stressed in this well-organized text. **(V)**

Miller, David W., and **Starr, Martin K.**   *Executive Decisions and Operations Research.* 2d ed. Englewood Cliffs, N.J.: Prentice-Hall, Inc., 1970. Excellent treatment of role mathematical approach can play in determining decisions. **(II)**

Miner, John B.   *The Management Process: Theory, Research, and Practice.* New York: Macmillan Publishing Co., Inc., 1973. A basic management text designed to integrate the various major approaches of management and to put emphasis on scientific research findings. Management is dealt with as a distinct entity dealing primarily with problems related to human resources. **(I)**

Moore, Franklin G.   *Production Management.* 6th ed. Homewood, Ill.: Richard D. Irwin, Inc., 1973. A complete, concise volume on management as applied to production. Gives reasons why as well as the practices in this important field. **(I)**

MSU Business Topics.   East Lansing: Michigan State University Bureau of Business and Economic Research (Quarterly.) Timely topics, well written, and covering a multitude of business management and economic subjects are made available by this well known publication. **(I)**

Nation's Business.   Washington D.C.: Chamber of Commerce of the United States. (Weekly.) Widely distributed and read, this publication is basic and contains many excellent articles on management particularly from the viewpoint of developments and changes of interest to the practitioner. **(I)**

Newman, William H.; Summer, Charles E., Jr.; and **Warren, E. Kirby.**   *Concepts, Behavior, and Practice. The Process of Management.* 3d ed. Englewood Cliffs, N.J.: Prentice-Hall, Inc., 1972. A well-presented integration of viewpoints from the behavioral science and decision-making theories with fundamental ideas presented regarding the scope, meaning, and operations of management. **(I)**

O'Connell, Jeremiah J.   *Managing Organizational Innovation.* Homewood, Ill.: Richard D. Irwin, Inc., 1968. A helpful volume on the important subject of organization design and change. The planning and controlling required for organization innovation are given special in-depth attention. **(IV)**

Odiorne, George S.   *Management by Objectives.* Rev. ed. New York: Pitman Publishing Corp., 1970. The thesis that effective management aided by precise definition of both corporate and personal goals is developed. The material is well presented. (**I**)

————. *Personnel Management by Objectives*. Homewood, Ill.: Richard D. Irwin, Inc., 1971. An effective book on personnel management, stressing the management by objective viewpoint. (**I**)

Operations Research. Baltimore, Md.: Operations Research Society of America. (Bimonthly.) Articles detailing methods, as well as results by operations research, are stressed by this publication. Stimulating and thought provoking characterize most of the papers included. (**II**)

Peach, Paul. *Quality Control for Management*. Englewood Cliffs, N.J.: Prentice-Hall, Inc., 1965. Describes probability theories, statistical methods, and sampling techniques and places emphasis upon statistical quality control. (**VI**)

Personnel Journal. Santa Monica, Calif. (Monthly.) Special articles of interest to those in personnel, Résumés of personnel research projects, and notes on activities in this field are featured. This is an outstanding publication. (**V**)

Pollock, Theodore M. *Managing Creativity*. Boston: Cahners Books, 1971. This practical guide in two volumes (1) managing others creativity, and (2) managing yourself creativity, gives numerous suggestions for improving one's potential and accomplishing more satisfaction from work by the common sense application of creativity. (**III**)

Porter, Lyman W.; Lawler, Edward E. III; and Hackman, Richard. *Behavior in Organizations*. New York: McGraw-Hill Book Co., 1975. Well written and inclusive, this book focuses on the individual and the organization with emphasis on their interactions. Important topical areas are treated in an integrated fashion with work situations being used. An important section of the book deals with the influences of different organizational practices and social actions on the members' feelings and on the interpersonal actions that take place. (**V**)

Porter, Lyman, and Lawler, Edward E. *Managerial Attitudes and Performance*. Homewood, Ill.: Richard D. Irwin, Inc., 1968. The job attitudes of managers and their performance are the center of attention. The material is approached by developing a conceptual model and presenting relevant empirical data. Well written and presented. (**V**)

Prince, Thomas R. *Information Systems for Management Planning and Control*. 3d ed. Homewood, Ill.: Richard D. Irwin, Inc., 1975. Basic treatment of information approach presented in understandable language. The book contains excellent cases for discussion. (**II**)

Quick, Thomas L. *Your Role in Task Force Management: The Dynamics of Corporate Change*. Garden City, N.Y.: Doubleday & Co., Inc., 1972. An easy to read style is used in setting forth the points to follow in order to obtain organizational improvement, and group effectiveness from the use of task forces. Suggestions also include how to formulate and evaluate task forces. (**IV**)

Ross, Joel E., and Murdick, Robert G. *Management Update: The Answer to Obsolescence*. New York: AMACOM, 1973. Thought provoking and well written, this book is intended to get the reader to realize that change in management, marketing, engineering, social responsibility, MIS, and so forth is taking place. With all this change many managers are becoming obsolete. What to do? They must develop a general understanding of business and keep themselves updated in their specialized area of activity. Some timely suggestions are offered. (**IV**)

Reeves, Elton T.   *The Dynamics of Group Behavior.* New York: American Management Association, 1970. Offered is very readable and easy-to-comprehend material on the importance of group dynamics and its use by a manager. (**V**)

Rowland, Virgil K.   *Evaluating and Improving Managerial Performance.* New York: McGraw-Hill Book Co., Inc., 1970. One of the better books proving practices of managers from many different companies. The practices have been assembled, classified, explained, and evaluated. There is a good group of chapters on evaluation of management performance. (**V**)

Rubenstein, A. H., and **Haberstroh, C. J.**   *Some Theories of Organization.* 2d ed. Homewood, Ill.: Richard D. Irwin, Inc., 1966. Supplies a selection of papers dealing with organization theory classified by structure, leadership, change, communication, control, and decision making. (**IV**)

Sales Management.   New York: Sales Management, Inc. (Monthly.) Excellent articles dealing with management problems in the field of distribution are offered by this well-respected periodical. (**I**)

Schein, Edgar H.   *Organizational Psychology.* Englewood Cliffs, N.J.: Prentice-Hall, Inc., 1965. Stresses a system analysis of psychological problems which arise within organizational structures. Both individual and group functioning are included. (**IV**)

Schleh, Edward.   *Management by Results.* New York: McGraw-Hill Book Co., Inc., 1962. A stimulating presentation on the theme that management will make its important contribution to society when the objectives of the enterprise are harmonized and meet the needs of its employees. This theme is expanded to show that it is the effective means for tying all management levels together. (**I**)

Schlender, William E.; Scott, William G.; and **Filley, Alan C.**   *Management in Perspective: Selected Readings.* Boston: Houghton Mifflin, 1965. A very good selection of readings that are helpful to the management student. Readings provide good cross-section of current management thinking. (**I**)

Schoderbek, Peter P.   *Management Systems.* Rev. ed. New York: John Wiley and Sons, 1971. A book of well-selected articles covering such major topics as systems, measurement, management information systems, computers, systems design, PERT, and real-time systems. (**II**)

Scott, W. G.   *Organization Theory: A Structural and Behavioral Analysis.* 3d ed. Homewood, Ill.: Richard D. Irwin, Inc., 1976. An excellent presentation of the use of behavioral sciences as the formulation for explaining organization and management processes. (**IV**)

Shrode, William A. and **Voich, Dan Jr.**   *Organization and Management: Basic System Concepts.* Homewood, Ill.: Richard D. Irwin, Inc. 1974. Offering basic managerial concepts essential for the manager of the future, this text is organized within the general systems approach and supplies a philosophy of management and organization helpful in today's changing environment. (**I**)

Sisk, Henry L. *Management and Organization* 2d ed. Cincinnati: South-Western Publishing Co., 1973. An offering of basic management organized essentially around the systems, behavioral, and functional approaches. **(I)**

Sloan Management Review. Cambridge, Mass.: M.I.T. Press. (3 times during the academic year.) Scholarly articles on important current subjects makes this magazine outstanding. **(I)**

Social Research. New York: New School of Social Research. (Monthly.) Interesting articles offering the social aspects of some current-day problems, many of which affect the work of the manager. **(I)**

Spurr, W. A., and **Bonini, C. P.** *Statistical Analysis for Business Decisions.* Homewood, Ill.: Richard D. Irwin, Inc., 1967. Statistical methods as scientific tools in the analysis of business problems is the core of this book. From simple analysis to simulation and Bayesian decision theory are included. **(II)**

Steers, Richard M., and **Porter, Lyman W.** *Motivation and Work Behavior.* New York: McGraw-Hill Book Co., 1975. One of the better books on motivation, the reader gains knowledge of (1) what motivation is and its historical development, (2) the major contemporary theories of motivation, and (3) how these theories are related to other organization variables. Text material is integrated with selected and pertinent articles from various expertise sources. **(V)**

Steiner, George A. *Business and Society.* New York: Random House, 1971. A comprehensive book giving wide coverage to important interrelationships and issues dealing with business and society. The subjects of changing values, corporate powers, pollution, ethics, technological issues—to name a few—are included in the discussions. The role of government, education, unions, and consumers in these societal subjects is also included. **(I)**

————. *Top Management Planning.* New York: Macmillan Publishing Co., Inc., 1969. Extensive coverage of planning by top managers including in-depth discussion of major problems encountered in planning efforts are clearly set forth in this well-written and well-organized book. **(III)**

————. (ed) *Managerial Long-Range Planning.* New York: McGraw-Hill Book Co., Inc., 1963. Describes in detail how successful long-range planning is performed by some major companies and government agencies. **(III)**

Stockton, R. Stanbury. *Introduction to Linear Programming.* Rev. ed. Boston: Allyn and Bacon, Inc., 1963. A complete, yet concise, presentation of linear programming and its uses in business. The book is well organized and the concepts presented in an effective manner. **(II)**

Stokes, Paul M. *A Total Systems Approach to Management Control.* New York: American Management Association, 1968. A practical and helpful presentation of controlling which offers much material of value to the operating manager. **(VI)**

Sutermeister, Robert A. *People and Productivity.* 2d ed. New York: McGraw-Hill Book Co., 1969. Selected readings integrating the findings of current behavioral research studies dealing with employee productivity and job performance are featured by this book. **(V)**

Taylor, Frederick W. *Scientific Management.* New York: Harper & Bros., 1947. This book combines the important managerial literature of Frederick

W. Taylor, including *Shop Management, The Principles of Scientific Management, and The Testimony before the Special House Committee.* (**I**)

Timms, Howard L. *Introduction to Operations Management.* Homewood, Ill.: Richard D. Irwin, Inc., 1967. Competent treatment of a subject frequently not handled with the clarity and logic displayed in this book. Book explains mathematical approaches in a style understandable to the layman. (**II**)

Tipper, Harry, Jr. *Controlling Overhead.* New York: American Management Association, 1966. Emphasizing practical controlling overhead cost, this book is for the person who wants to do something about the cost of overhead. Suggests a program and explains why and how to implement it. (**VI**)

Torgersen, Paul E., and **Weinstock, Irwin T.** *Management: An Integrated Approach.* Englewood Cliffs, N.J.: Prentice-Hall, Inc., 1972. A behavioral, decisional, and systems theory presentation of management. Coherence and clarity feature this book. The summaries and questions at the end of chapters are especially well done. (**I**)

Towle, J. W. *Ethics and Standards in American Business.* Boston: Houghton-Mifflin, Inc., 1964. Papers from a symposium on ethics and business make up this helpful volume. (**III**)

University of Michigan Business Review. Ann Arbor: The University of Michigan Graduate School of Business Administration. (Bimonthly.) One of the best resources by collegiate business and management schools, it has long enjoyed a reputation for excellence and articles with contemporary viewpoints. (**I**)

U.S. Department of Commerce, Bureau of Standards. *The Standards Yearbook.* Washington, D.C. (Irregular.) This volume gives a picture of the activities and accomplishments of the federal government and of national technical societies and trade associations in standardization. (**VI**)

U.S. Department of Labor, Bureau of Labor Statistics. *Monthly Labor Review.* Washington, D.C. (Monthly.) Official governmental publication containing pertinent data on labor and economic subjects along with timely articles in these fields. (**V**)

Uyterhoeven, Hugo E. R.; Ackerman, Robert W.; and **Rosenblum, John W.** *Strategy and Organization: Text and Cases in General Management.* Homewood, Ill.: Richard D. Irwin, Inc., 1973. Strategy formulation and implementation are emphasized with orientation pointed to the practitioner. A conceptual framework is developed to assist in the application of strategy. (**IV**)

Vernon, Raymond, and **Wells, Louis T. Jr.** *Manager in the International Economy.* 2d ed. Englewood Cliffs, N.J.: Prentice-Hall, Inc., 1972. The basic considerations and problems encountered in foreign trade are discussed in this book. International trade, payments, and investments are highlighted. The managerial considerations in the establishment of new foreign subsidiaries are discussed as is also the solving of organization problems and joint venture difficulties. Part II includes selected cases dealing with international business problems. Well written and organized, this book is quite rewarding to the reader. (**VII**)

Webber, Ross A. *Management: Basic Elements of Managing Organizations.* Homewood, Ill.: Richard D. Irwin, Inc., 1975. This book is a well written management text. It is designed for students to think about and to develop their own theories about management. The material is presented from the viewpoint that people, tasks, technology, and environment are the major components influencing management action. The book is relevant and well organized. (**I**)

Whyte, William Foote. *Men at Work.* Homewood, Ill.: Richard D. Irwin, Inc., and the Dorsey Press, Inc., 1961. Discusses the problems of men and women adjusting to their work from the behavioral scientist viewpoint. The book is well written, provocative, and informative. (**V**)

————. *Organizational Behavior: Theory and Application.* Homewood, Ill.: Richard D. Irwin, Inc., 1969. A comprehensive coverage of organization behavior employing an interdisciplinary approach, but strongly flavored of sociology. Excellent coverage is given of individuals and groups in the organization context and the introducing of change. (**IV**)

Wolf, W. B. *The Management of Personnel.* San Francisco: Wadsworth Publishing Co., 1961. A highly readable text covering the major topics of personnel management in an interesting and effective manner.

————. *The Basic Barnard.* Ithaca, N.Y.: Cornell University Press, 1974. Introduction to Chester I. Barnard's theories of organizaton and management with insight to his managerial philosophy, articles, and lectures.

Indexes

Index to cases

Index